I0481449

NATIONAL EDITION

The 2018 U.S. Product & Retail Outlook report
is the leading annual publication that describes over 200
product lines and their sales through 20 retail industries.
Published each year in April, the Outlook report provides the
most current and accurate estimates of the size of the
product lines and their distribution channels.

With over 700 pages, the 2018 U.S. Product & Retail
Outlook features:

2018 product line sales totals for each retail industry
2019 forecast product line sales totals for each retail industry
5-year trend product line sales totals for each retail industry
Product line sales by 7 company size categories (by employee size of company)
Summary tables showing matrix of product line sales by retail industry
Industry definitions and descriptions

The Outlook report is available for purchase in
either PDF, spreadsheet (Excel) or print format edition.

The 2018 U.S. Product & Retail Outlook report is an
essential reference tool for industry researchers, market
analysts, CEOs and leading industry executives.

Copyright © 2017 By C. Barnes & Co.

Printed in USA

TABLE OF CONTENTS

TABLE OF CONTENTS

TABLE OF CONTENTS

TABLE OF CONTENTS

TABLE OF CONTENTS

USERS' GUIDE

The Barnes Reports are the leading publications on U.S. industries and estimates and forecasts on sales and employment demographics. As a way of making the most of this information, we have included a few suggestions and tips to aid you in processing and using this information.

Managers, planners, and market researchers use this information for a variety of activities:
- Sizing markets and segments – You can estimate the size of the regional markets you sell in and your company's market penetration into that market. You can do the same with the market segments in which you participate.
- Sales territory potential – You can estimate your market penetration and also the market potential in any regional area or market segment.
- Sales forecasting – With the estimates on the size of the industry, market researchers supporting a sales force can then estimate and forecast the future size of the industry.
- Advertising strategies – You can use this information for forecasting and estimating sales potential and target advertising campaigns.
- Competitive analysis – You will use the information to locate your possible competitors (if it is not already known), to estimate their size, growth and strengths and weaknesses and to see what market segments in which they participate.

We recognize that many managers today are asked to provide detailed analysis of their markets, sales territories, distribution channels, and product placements. We have organized these reports in a logical format making your market analysis and research tasks easy to accomplish.

SUMMARY OF PRODUCT LINES SALES BY INDUSTRY

SALES (MILLIONS OF U.S. DOLLARS)

Main Category	Sub Category	U.S. Industry	Year			
			2016	2017	2018	2019
Grocery Foods	--	Home centers	0	0	0	0
Grocery Foods	--	Hardware stores	69	71	72	74
Grocery Foods	--	Supermarkets & grocery stores	56,849	57,652	58,683	60,096
Grocery Foods	--	Beer, wine, & liquor stores	1,667	1,706	1,752	1,810
Grocery Foods	--	Pharmacies & drug stores	1,355	1,382	1,411	1,448
Grocery Foods	--	Gas stations w/ conven. stores	11,853	12,047	12,265	12,563
Grocery Foods	--	Men's clothing stores	0	0	0	0
Grocery Foods	--	Women's clothing stores	1	1	1	1
Grocery Foods	--	Family clothing stores	2	2	2	2
Grocery Foods	--	CD, tape & record stores	0	0	0	0
Grocery Foods	--	Department stores	408	397	392	389
Grocery Foods	--	Warehouse clubs & supercntrs	2,600	2,727	2,837	2,898
Grocery Foods	--	Office supply/stationery stores	1	1	1	1
Grocery Foods	--	Electronic shopping & mail-order	1,051	1,115	1,180	1,238
Grocery Foods	--	Book stores	41	40	39	39
	Meat, Fish & Poultry	Supermarkets & grocery stores	9,925	10,066	10,246	10,492
	Meat, Fish & Poultry	Beer, wine, & liquor stores	95	97	100	103
	Meat, Fish & Poultry	Warehouse clubs & supercntrs	336	352	366	374
	Produce	Supermarkets & grocery stores	7,832	7,942	8,084	8,279
	Produce	Beer, wine, & liquor stores	10	10	10	11
	Produce	Warehouse clubs & supercntrs	245	257	267	273
	Frozen Foods	Supermarkets & grocery stores	4,430	4,493	4,573	4,683
	Frozen Foods	Beer, wine, & liquor stores	29	29	30	31
	Frozen Foods	Warehouse clubs & supercntrs	271	284	296	302
	Dairy Products	Supermarkets & grocery stores	6,765	6,860	6,983	7,151
	Dairy Products	Beer, wine, & liquor stores	120	122	126	130
	Dairy Products	Gas stations w/ conven. stores	1,361	1,383	1,408	1,442
	Dairy Products	Warehouse clubs & supercntrs	211	221	230	235

SUMMARY OF PRODUCT LINES SALES BY INDUSTRY

SALES (MILLIONS OF U.S. DOLLARS)

Main Category	Sub Category	U.S. Industry	Year			
			2016	2017	2018	2019
	In-Store Bakery Prod.	Supermarkets & grocery stores	1,268	1,286	1,309	1,341
	In-Store Bakery Prod.	Beer, wine, & liquor stores	18	18	18	19
	In-Store Bakery Prod.	Warehouse clubs & supercntrs	63	66	68	70
	Bakery-Off Premises	Supermarkets & grocery stores	2,125	2,155	2,193	2,246
	Bakery-Off Premises	Beer, wine, & liquor stores	66	67	69	72
	Bakery-Off Premises	Gas stations w/ conven. stores	491	499	508	521
	Bakery-Off Premises	Warehouse clubs & supercntrs	82	86	89	91
	Delicatessen Items	Supermarkets & grocery stores	2,838	2,878	2,930	3,000
	Delicatessen Items	Beer, wine, & liquor stores	65	67	69	71
	Delicatessen Items	Warehouse clubs & supercntrs	85	89	92	94
	Soft Drinks	Supermarkets & grocery stores	2,260	2,292	2,333	2,389
	Soft Drinks	Beer, wine, & liquor stores	673	689	707	731
	Soft Drinks	Pharmacies & drug stores	406	414	423	434
	Soft Drinks	Gas stations w/ conven. stores	3,679	3,739	3,807	3,899
	Soft Drinks	Warehouse clubs & supercntrs	190	199	207	212
	Soft Drinks	Electronic shopping & mail-order	108	115	122	128
	Soft Drinks	Book stores	4	4	4	4
	Candy	Supermarkets & grocery stores	749	760	774	792
	Candy	Beer, wine, & liquor stores	173	177	182	188
	Candy	Gas stations w/ conven. stores	1,490	1,515	1,542	1,580
	Candy	Warehouse clubs & supercntrs	186	196	203	208
	All Other Foods	Supermarkets & grocery stores	18,657	18,920	19,259	19,722
	All Other Foods	Beer, wine, & liquor stores	419	428	440	455
	All Other Foods	Warehouse clubs & supercntrs	932	978	1,018	1,040
	All Other Foods	Gas stations w/ conven. stores	4,832	4,911	5,000	5,121
	All Other Foods	Pharmacies & drug stores	949	968	988	1,014
	All Other Foods	Electronic shopping & mail-order	943	1,000	1,058	1,110
	All Other Foods	Book stores	36	35	35	35

SUMMARY OF PRODUCT LINES SALES BY INDUSTRY

SALES (MILLIONS OF U.S. DOLLARS)

Main Category	Sub Category	U.S. Industry	Year			
			2016	2017	2018	2019
Beer, Wine, Liquor	--	Supermarkets & grocery stores	2,665	2,703	2,751	2,817
Beer, Wine, Liquor	--	Beer, wine, & liquor stores	32,335	33,085	33,980	35,111
Beer, Wine, Liquor	--	Pharmacies & drug stores	464	474	483	496
Beer, Wine, Liquor	--	Gas stations w/ conven. stores	3,791	3,853	3,922	4,018
Beer, Wine, Liquor	--	Department stores	1	1	1	1
Beer, Wine, Liquor	--	Warehouse clubs & supercntrs	118	124	129	131
Beer, Wine, Liquor	--	Electronic shopping & mail-order	157	166	176	185
Beer, Wine, Liquor	--	Book stores	1	1	1	1
	Liquor	Supermarkets & grocery stores	520	527	537	550
	Liquor	Beer, wine, & liquor stores	13,680	13,997	14,376	14,855
	Liquor	Gas stations w/ conven. stores	127	129	132	135
	Liquor	Warehouse clubs & supercntrs	12	13	13	14
	Wine	Supermarkets & grocery stores	879	891	907	929
	Wine	Beer, wine, & liquor stores	9,399	9,617	9,877	10,206
	Wine	Gas stations w/ conven. stores	195	198	202	207
	Wine	Warehouse clubs & supercntrs	51	54	56	57
	Beer	Supermarkets & grocery stores	1,267	1,284	1,307	1,339
	Beer	Beer, wine, & liquor stores	9,256	9,471	9,727	10,051
	Beer	Gas stations w/ conven. stores	3,468	3,525	3,589	3,676
	Beer	Warehouse clubs & supercntrs	54	57	59	61

SUMMARY OF PRODUCT LINES SALES BY INDUSTRY

SALES (MILLIONS OF U.S. DOLLARS)

Main Category	Sub Category	U.S. Industry	Year			
			2016	2017	2018	2019
Drugs, Health/Beauty	--	Home centers	1	1	1	1
Drugs, Health/Beauty	--	Hardware stores	1	1	1	2
Drugs, Health/Beauty	--	Supermarkets & grocery stores	6,994	7,093	7,220	7,393
Drugs, Health/Beauty	--	Beer, wine, & liquor stores	117	119	123	127
Drugs, Health/Beauty	--	Pharmacies & drug stores	38,696	39,464	40,277	41,357
Drugs, Health/Beauty	--	Gas stations w/ conven. stores	435	443	451	461
Drugs, Health/Beauty	--	Men's clothing stores	1	1	1	1
Drugs, Health/Beauty	--	Women's clothing stores	835	861	877	898
Drugs, Health/Beauty	--	Family clothing stores	222	223	227	233
Drugs, Health/Beauty	--	Department stores	1,277	1,240	1,225	1,217
Drugs, Health/Beauty	--	Warehouse clubs & supercntrs	827	867	902	922
Drugs, Health/Beauty	--	Office supply/stationery stores	0	0	0	0
Drugs, Health/Beauty	--	Electronic shopping & mail-order	21,912	23,244	24,587	25,800
Drugs, Health/Beauty	--	Book stores	5	5	5	5
	Prescriptions	Supermarkets & grocery stores	3,574	3,624	3,689	3,778
	Prescriptions	Beer, wine, & liquor stores	6	6	6	6
	Prescriptions	Pharmacies & drug stores	32,523	33,169	33,853	34,760
	Prescriptions	Department stores	367	357	352	350
	Prescriptions	Warehouse clubs & supercntrs	257	270	281	287
	Prescriptions	Electronic shopping & mail-order	16,970	18,001	19,041	19,981
	Nonprescriptn. Meds	Supermarkets & grocery stores	524	531	541	554
	Nonprescriptn. Meds	Beer, wine, & liquor stores	25	26	27	27
	Nonprescriptn. Meds	Pharmacies & drug stores	2,564	2,615	2,669	2,740
	Nonprescriptn. Meds	Department stores	63	61	61	60
	Nonprescriptn. Meds	Warehouse clubs & supercntrs	89	94	98	100
	Nonprescriptn. Meds	Electronic shopping & mail-order	417	443	468	492

SUMMARY OF PRODUCT LINES SALES BY INDUSTRY

SALES (MILLIONS OF U.S. DOLLARS)

Main Category	Sub Category	U.S. Industry	Year			
			2016	2017	2018	2019
	Vitamins Supplemts.	Supermarkets & grocery stores	420	426	434	444
	Vitamins Supplemts.	Beer, wine, & liquor stores	8	8	9	9
	Vitamins Supplemts.	Pharmacies & drug stores	487	497	507	521
	Vitamins Supplemts.	Department stores	49	47	47	46
	Vitamins Supplemts.	Warehouse clubs & supercntrs	59	62	64	66
	Vitamins Supplemts.	Electronic shopping & mail-order	2,495	2,646	2,799	2,937
	Health Aids	Supermarkets & grocery stores	398	403	410	420
	Health Aids	Beer, wine, & liquor stores	14	14	14	15
	Health Aids	Pharmacies & drug stores	829	845	863	886
	Health Aids	Department Stores	41	40	39	39
	Health Aids	Warehouse clubs & supercntrs	68	72	75	76
	Health Aids	Electronic shopping & mail-order	878	931	985	1,033
	Cosmetics	Supermarkets & grocery stores	353	358	365	373
	Cosmetics	Beer, wine, & liquor stores	41	42	43	44
	Cosmetics	Pharmacies & drug stores	959	978	998	1,025
	Cosmetics	Department Stores	426	414	409	407
	Cosmetics	Warehouse clubs & supercntrs	75	79	82	84
	Cosmetics	Electronic shopping & mail-order	939	996	1,054	1,106
	Other Hygiene Needs	Supermarkets & grocery stores	1,725	1,750	1,781	1,824
	Other Hygiene Needs	Beer, wine, & liquor stores	23	24	24	25
	Other Hygiene Needs	Pharmacies & drug stores	1,316	1,342	1,370	1,407
	Other Hygiene Needs	Department Stores	330	321	317	315
	Other Hygiene Needs	Warehouse clubs & supercntrs	277	291	303	309
	Other Hygiene Needs	Electronic shopping & mail-order	165	176	186	195
	Hearing Aids	Pharmacies & drug stores	18	18	18	19
	Hearing Aids	Electronic shopping & mail-order	48	51	54	57

SUMMARY OF PRODUCT LINES SALES BY INDUSTRY

SALES (MILLIONS OF U.S. DOLLARS)

Main Category	Sub Category	U.S. Industry	Year			
			2016	2017	2018	2019
Soaps & Cleaners	--	Home centers	70	71	71	72
Soaps & Cleaners	--	Hardware stores	163	167	171	175
Soaps & Cleaners	--	Supermarkets & grocery stores	1,939	1,966	2,001	2,049
Soaps & Cleaners	--	Beer, wine, & liquor stores	62	64	65	68
Soaps & Cleaners	--	Pharmacies & drug stores	217	221	226	232
Soaps & Cleaners	--	Gas stations w/ conven. stores	137	140	142	146
Soaps & Cleaners	--	Women's clothing stores	0	0	0	0
Soaps & Cleaners	--	Department stores	175	170	168	167
Soaps & Cleaners	--	Warehouse Clubs & Superctrs.	212	222	231	236
Soaps & Cleaners	--	Office Supplies & Stationery	1	1	1	1
Soaps & Cleaners	--	Electronic Shopping/Mail-Order	62	66	70	73
Paper Products	--	Hardware stores	1	1	1	1
Paper Products	--	Supermarkets & grocery stores	1,991	2,019	2,055	2,104
Paper Products	--	Beer, wine, & liquor stores	38	39	40	41
Paper Products	--	Pharmacies & drug stores	174	177	181	186
Paper Products	--	Gas stations w/ conven. stores	168	171	174	178
Paper Products	--	Family clothing stores	0	0	0	0
Paper Products	--	Prerecorded Tapes/CDs Stores	0	0	0	0
Paper Products	--	Department stores	136	132	131	130
Paper Products	--	Warehouse clubs & supercntrs	190	200	208	212
Paper Products	--	Office Supplies & Stationery	12	11	11	11
Paper Products	--	Electronic Shopping/Mail-Order	384	407	431	452
Paper Products	--	Book Stores	1	1	1	1

SUMMARY OF PRODUCT LINES SALES BY INDUSTRY

SALES (MILLIONS OF U.S. DOLLARS)

Main Category	Sub Category	U.S. Industry	Year			
			2016	2017	2018	2019
Men's Wear	--	Home centers	4	4	4	4
Men's Wear	--	Hardware stores	35	36	36	37
Men's Wear	--	Men's clothing stores	7,513	7,353	7,273	7,238
Men's Wear	--	Women's clothing stores	1,337	1,377	1,403	1,437
Men's Wear	--	Family clothing stores	9,297	9,333	9,516	9,761
Men's Wear	--	CD, tape & record stores	0	0	0	0
Men's Wear	--	Department stores	857	833	823	817
Men's Wear	--	Warehouse clubs & supercntrs	171	179	187	191
Men's Wear	--	Electronic shopping & mail-order	1,716	1,821	1,926	2,021
Men's Wear	--	Book stores	120	116	115	114
	Coats/Jackets	Men's clothing stores	342	335	332	330
	Coats/Jackets	Women's clothing stores	96	99	101	104
	Coats/Jackets	Family clothing stores	590	592	603	619
	Coats/Jackets	Department stores	40	38	38	38
	Coats/Jackets	Warehouse clubs & supercntrs	10	11	11	12
	Suits/Formal Wear	Men's clothing stores	1,622	1,588	1,570	1,563
	Suits/Formal Wear	Women's clothing stores	41	43	43	45
	Suits/Formal Wear	Family clothing stores	342	343	350	359
	Suits/Formal Wear	Department stores	38	37	36	36
	Sport Coats/Blazers	Men's clothing stores	620	607	600	597
	Sport Coats/Blazers	Women's clothing stores	34	35	35	36
	Sport Coats/Blazers	Family clothing stores	203	204	208	213
	Sport Coats/Blazers	Department stores	13	13	13	12
	Dress Slacks	Men's clothing stores	601	588	581	579
	Dress Slacks	Women's clothing stores	61	63	64	65
	Dress Slacks	Family clothing stores	549	551	562	576
	Dress Slacks	Department stores	20	19	19	19
	Casual Slacks/Jeans	Men's clothing stores	983	962	951	947
	Casual Slacks/Jeans	Women's clothing stores	295	304	309	317
	Casual Slacks/Jeans	Family clothing stores	1,947	1,955	1,993	2,044
	Casual Slacks/Jeans	Department stores	221	214	212	210
	Casual Slacks/Jeans	Warehouse clubs & supercntrs	45	47	49	50
	Work Uniforms	Men's clothing stores	102	100	99	98
	Work Uniforms	Family clothing stores	269	270	275	282
	Work Uniforms	Department stores	8	8	8	8

SUMMARY OF PRODUCT LINES SALES BY INDUSTRY

SALES (MILLIONS OF U.S. DOLLARS)

Main Category	Sub Category	U.S. Industry	Year			
			2016	2017	2018	2019
	Dress Shirts	Men's clothing stores	564	552	546	544
	Dress Shirts	Women's clothing stores	84	87	88	91
	Dress Shirts	Family clothing stores	665	668	681	698
	Dress Shirts	Department stores	38	37	36	36
	Sport Shirts/T-Shirts	Men's clothing stores	1,101	1,077	1,066	1,060
	Sport Shirts/T-Shirts	Women's clothing stores	431	444	452	463
	Sport Shirts/T-Shirts	Family clothing stores	2,194	2,202	2,245	2,303
	Sport Shirts/T-Shirts	Department stores	195	189	187	185
	Sport Shirts/T-Shirts	Warehouse clubs & supercntrs	30	32	33	34
	Sweaters	Men's clothing stores	256	251	248	247
	Sweaters	Women's clothing stores	90	93	95	97
	Sweaters	Family clothing stores	647	650	662	679
	Sweaters	Department stores	28	27	27	27
	Sweaters	Warehouse clubs & supercntrs	7	7	7	7
	Socks/Underwear	Men's clothing stores	168	164	162	162
	Socks/Underwear	Women's clothing stores	51	53	54	55
	Socks/Underwear	Family clothing stores	453	454	463	475
	Socks/Underwear	Department stores	107	104	102	102
	Socks/Underwear	Warehouse clubs & supercntrs	32	34	35	36
	Sports Apparel	Men's clothing stores	336	329	326	324
	Sports Apparel	Women's clothing stores	31	32	33	34
	Sports Apparel	Family clothing stores	317	318	325	333
	Sports Apparel	Department stores	50	48	48	47
	Sports Apparel	Warehouse clubs & supercntrs	17	18	19	19
	Accessories	Men's clothing stores	646	632	625	622
	Accessories	Women's clothing stores	109	112	114	117
	Accessories	Family clothing stores	617	620	632	648
	Accessories	Department stores	50	49	48	48
	Accessories	Warehouse clubs & supercntrs	7	8	8	8
	Custom-made	Men's clothing stores	85	83	82	81
	Sweats/Warm-ups	Men's clothing stores	87	85	84	84
	Sweats/Warm-ups	Family clothing stores	496	498	507	520
	Sweats/Warm-ups	Department stores	52	50	50	49
	Sweats/Warm-ups	Warehouse clubs & supercntrs	14	15	15	16

SUMMARY OF PRODUCT LINES SALES BY INDUSTRY

SALES (MILLIONS OF U.S. DOLLARS)

Main Category	Sub Category	U.S. Industry	Year			
			2016	2017	2018	2019
Women's Wear	--	Home centers	3	3	3	3
Women's Wear	--	Supermarkets & grocery stores	20	20	20	21
Women's Wear	--	Pharmacies & drug stores	41	41	42	43
Women's Wear	--	Men's clothing stores	186	182	180	179
Women's Wear	--	Women's clothing stores	38,755	39,935	40,662	41,653
Women's Wear	--	Family clothing stores	15,254	15,314	15,613	16,015
Women's Wear	--	Department stores	1,731	1,682	1,661	1,650
Women's Wear	--	Warehouse clubs & supercntrs	227	238	247	253
Women's Wear	--	Electronic shopping & mail-order	5,902	6,261	6,623	6,949
Women's Wear	--	Book stores	61	59	59	58
	Fur Garments	Women's clothing stores	53	55	56	57
	Fur Garments	Family clothing stores	20	20	21	21
	Dresses	Women's clothing stores	4,699	4,842	4,930	5,051
	Dresses	Family clothing stores	998	1,002	1,022	1,048
	Dresses	Department stores	132	128	127	126
	Dresses	Warehouse clubs & supercntrs	8	9	9	9
	Coats/Outerwear	Women's clothing stores	1,781	1,835	1,868	1,914
	Coats/Outerwear	Family clothing stores	751	754	769	789
	Coats/Outerwear	Department stores	69	67	66	66
	Coats/Outerwear	Warehouse clubs & supercntrs	6	6	7	7
	Suits/Blazers	Men's clothing stores	29	28	28	28
	Suits/Blazers	Women's clothing stores	2,717	2,799	2,850	2,920
	Suits/Blazers	Family clothing stores	1,353	1,358	1,384	1,420
	Suits/Blazers	Department stores	261	253	250	249
	Suits/Blazers	Warehouse clubs & supercntrs	3	3	3	3
	Slacks/Jeans	Men's clothing stores	43	42	42	42
	Slacks/Jeans	Women's clothing stores	10,427	10,744	10,940	11,206
	Slacks/Jeans	Family clothing stores	2,985	2,996	3,055	3,134
	Slacks/Jeans	Department stores	260	253	250	248
	Slacks/Jeans	Warehouse clubs & supercntrs	59	62	64	66
	Shirts/Sweaters	Men's clothing stores	49	48	47	47
	Shirts/Sweaters	Women's clothing stores	13,664	14,080	14,336	14,686
	Shirts/Sweaters	Family clothing stores	4,901	4,920	5,016	5,145
	Shirts/Sweaters	Department stores	253	246	243	242
	Shirts/Sweaters	Warehouse clubs & supercntrs	47	49	51	52

SUMMARY OF PRODUCT LINES SALES BY INDUSTRY

SALES (MILLIONS OF U.S. DOLLARS)

Main Category	Sub Category	U.S. Industry	Year			
			2016	2017	2018	2019
	Sports Apparel	Women's clothing stores	522	538	548	561
	Sports Apparel	Family clothing stores	441	442	451	463
	Sports Apparel	Department stores	199	194	191	190
	Sports Apparel	Warehouse clubs & supercntrs	16	16	17	17
	Hosiery/Socks	Women's clothing stores	358	369	376	385
	Hosiery/Socks	Family clothing stores	350	351	358	367
	Hosiery/Socks	Department stores	53	52	51	51
	Hosiery/Socks	Warehouse clubs & supercntrs	17	18	19	19
	Bras/Panties	Women's clothing stores	607	626	637	653
	Bras/Panties	Family clothing stores	534	537	547	561
	Bras/Panties	Department stores	219	213	210	209
	Bras/Panties	Warehouse clubs & supercntrs	29	31	32	33
	Lingerie/Sleepwear	Women's clothing stores	960	989	1,007	1,032
	Lingerie/Sleepwear	Family clothing stores	450	451	460	472
	Lingerie/Sleepwear	Department stores	119	116	115	114
	Lingerie/Sleepwear	Warehouse clubs & supercntrs	22	23	24	25
	Hats/Wigs	Women's clothing stores	78	80	82	84
	Hats/Wigs	Family clothing stores	252	253	258	265
	Accessories/Bags	Women's clothing stores	2,058	2,121	2,159	2,212
	Accessories/Bags	Family clothing stores	1,392	1,397	1,425	1,461
	Accessories/Bags	Department stores	143	139	137	136
	Accessories/Bags	Warehouse clubs & supercntrs	15	15	16	16
	Custom-made	Women's clothing stores	14	14	14	15
	Custom-made	Family clothing stores	96	97	98	101
	Sweat Tops/Pants	Women's clothing stores	558	575	586	600
	Sweat Tops/Pants	Family clothing stores	678	680	693	711
	Sweat Tops/Pants	Department stores	6	6	6	6
	Uniforms/Misc.	Men's clothing stores	18	17	17	17
	Uniforms/Misc.	Women's clothing stores	259	267	272	279
	Uniforms/Misc.	Family clothing stores	53	54	55	56
	Uniforms/Misc.	Department stores	13	13	13	13
	Uniforms/Misc.	Warehouse clubs & supercntrs	4	4	4	4

SUMMARY OF PRODUCT LINES SALES BY INDUSTRY

SALES (MILLIONS OF U.S. DOLLARS)

Main Category	Sub Category	U.S. Industry	Year			
			2016	2017	2018	2019
Children's Wear	--	Supermarkets & grocery stores	8	8	8	8
Children's Wear	--	Pharmacies & drug stores	6	7	7	7
Children's Wear	--	Men's clothing stores	108	105	104	104
Children's Wear	--	Women's clothing stores	244	251	256	262
Children's Wear	--	Family clothing stores	3,779	3,794	3,868	3,968
Children's Wear	--	Department stores	627	609	602	598
Children's Wear	--	Warehouse clubs & supercntrs	163	171	177	181
Children's Wear	--	Electronic shopping & mail-order	741	786	831	872
Children's Wear	--	Book stores	8	8	8	8
	Boys' Clothing	Men's clothing stores	78	76	75	75
	Boys' Clothing	Women's clothing stores	50	52	53	54
	Boys' Clothing	Family clothing stores	1,369	1,375	1,402	1,438
	Boys' Clothing	Department stores	194	189	187	185
	Boys' Clothing	Warehouse clubs & supercntrs	40	42	43	44
	Girls' Clothing	Men's clothing stores	25	25	25	24
	Girls' Clothing	Women's clothing stores	114	117	119	122
	Girls' Clothing	Family clothing stores	1,469	1,475	1,504	1,542
	Girls' Clothing	Department stores	187	181	179	178
	Girls' Clothing	Warehouse clubs & supercntrs	37	39	41	41
	Infants' & Toddlers'	Men's clothing stores	4	4	4	4
	Infants' & Toddlers'	Women's clothing stores	80	82	84	86
	Infants' & Toddlers'	Family clothing stores	941	944	963	988
	Infants' & Toddlers'	Department stores	246	239	236	234
	Infants' & Toddlers'	Warehouse clubs & supercntrs	86	90	93	95

SUMMARY OF PRODUCT LINES SALES BY INDUSTRY

SALES (MILLIONS OF U.S. DOLLARS)

Main Category	Sub Category	U.S. Industry	Year			
			2016	2017	2018	2019
Footwear Products	--	Hardware stores	23	23	24	24
Footwear Products	--	Supermarkets & grocery stores	5	5	5	5
Footwear Products	--	Pharmacies & drug stores	47	48	49	51
Footwear Products	--	Men's clothing stores	369	361	357	355
Footwear Products	--	Women's clothing stores	1,348	1,389	1,415	1,449
Footwear Products	--	Family clothing stores	1,899	1,906	1,944	1,994
Footwear Products	--	Department stores	365	354	350	347
Footwear Products	--	Warehouse clubs & supercntrs	58	61	64	65
Footwear Products	--	Electronic shopping & mail-order	1,280	1,357	1,436	1,507
	Men's Footwear	Men's clothing stores	288	282	279	277
	Men's Footwear	Women's clothing stores	27	28	29	29
	Men's Footwear	Family clothing stores	369	371	378	388
	Men's Footwear	Department stores	66	64	63	63
	Women's Footwear	Men's clothing stores	13	13	13	13
	Women's Footwear	Women's clothing stores	1,288	1,328	1,352	1,385
	Women's Footwear	Family clothing stores	830	833	849	871
	Women's Footwear	Department stores	185	179	177	176
	Children's Footwear	Family clothing stores	149	150	153	157
	Children's Footwear	Department stores	33	33	32	32
	Men's Sneakers	Men's clothing stores	60	59	58	58
	Men's Sneakers	Family clothing stores	275	276	281	288
	Men's Sneakers	Department stores	36	35	35	35
	Women's Sneakers	Women's clothing stores	20	21	21	22
	Women's Sneakers	Family clothing stores	211	212	216	222
	Women's Sneakers	Department stores	36	35	35	34
	Children's Sneakers	Family clothing stores	59	59	60	62
	Children's Sneakers	Department stores	7	7	7	7
	Footwear Access.	Family clothing stores	6	6	6	6
	Footwear Access.	Department stores	1	1	1	1

SUMMARY OF PRODUCT LINES SALES BY INDUSTRY

SALES (MILLIONS OF U.S. DOLLARS)

Main Category	Sub Category	U.S. Industry	Year			
			2016	2017	2018	2019
Household Appliances	--	Home centers	329	330	332	336
Household Appliances	--	Hardware stores	315	324	330	339
Household Appliances	--	Supermarkets & grocery stores	1	1	1	1
Household Appliances	--	Department stores	367	357	352	350
Household Appliances	--	Warehouse clubs & supercntrs	78	82	85	87
Household Appliances	--	Electronic shopping & mail-order	472	501	530	556
	Kitchen Appliances	Department stores	249	242	239	237
	Kitchen Appliances	Warehouse clubs & supercntrs	25	27	28	28
	Laundry Appliances	Warehouse clubs & supercntrs	2	2	2	2
	Other Appliances	Department stores	118	115	114	113
	Other Appliances	Warehouse clubs & supercntrs	51	53	56	57
Small Appliances	--	Home centers	26	26	27	27
Small Appliances	--	Hardware stores	242	249	254	261
Small Appliances	--	Supermarkets & grocery stores	27	27	28	28
Small Appliances	--	Beer, Wine & Liquor Stores	0	0	0	0
Small Appliances	--	Pharmacies & Drug Stores	212	216	221	227
Small Appliances	--	Women's Clothing Stores	2	2	2	2
Small Appliances	--	Family Clothing Stores	0	0	0	0
Small Appliances	--	Department Stores	138	134	132	131
Small Appliances	--	Warehouse clubs & supercntrs	81	85	88	90
Small Appliances	--	Electronic Shopping/Mail-Order	286	304	321	337

SUMMARY OF PRODUCT LINES SALES BY INDUSTRY

SALES (MILLIONS OF U.S. DOLLARS)

Main Category	Sub Category	U.S. Industry	Year			
			2016	2017	2018	2019
TVs & Video Equip	--	Home centers	0	0	0	0
TVs & Video Equip	--	Hardware stores	24	25	25	26
TVs & Video Equip	--	Supermarkets & grocery stores	1	1	1	1
TVs & Video Equip	--	Pharmacies & drug stores	47	48	49	50
TVs & Video Equip	--	Women's clothing stores	1	1	1	1
TVs & Video Equip	--	Family clothing stores	4	4	4	5
TVs & Video Equip	--	Prerecorded Tape/CD Stores	0	0	0	0
TVs & Video Equip	--	Department stores	281	273	270	268
TVs & Video Equip	--	Warehouse clubs & supercntrs	181	190	198	202
TVs & Video Equip	--	Office supply/stationery stores	1	1	1	1
TVs & Video Equip	--	Electronic shopping & mail-order	1,880	1,994	2,109	2,213
TVs & Video Equip	--	Book stores	329	319	316	314
	Televisions	Prerecorded Tape/CD Stores	0	0	0	0
	Televisions	Department stores	108	105	103	103
	Televisions	Warehouse clubs & supercntrs	82	86	89	91
	Televisions	Electronic shopping & mail-order	217	230	243	255
	Video Recorders	Prerecorded Tape/CD Stores	0	0	0	0
	Video Tapes/Discs	Prerecorded Tape/CD Stores	0	0	0	0
	Other Video Equip	Department stores	173	168	166	165
	Other Video Equip	Warehouse clubs & supercntrs	100	104	109	111
	Other Video Equip	Electronic shopping & mail-order	1,663	1,764	1,866	1,958

SUMMARY OF PRODUCT LINES SALES BY INDUSTRY

SALES (MILLIONS OF U.S. DOLLARS)

Main Category	Sub Category	U.S. Industry	Year			
			2016	2017	2018	2019
Audio Equipment	--	Home centers	1	1	1	1
Audio Equipment	--	Hardware stores	16	16	16	17
Audio Equipment	--	Supermarkets & grocery stores	51	51	52	53
Audio Equipment	--	Beer, wine, & liquor stores	0	0	0	0
Audio Equipment	--	Pharmacies & drug stores	157	160	163	167
Audio Equipment	--	Gas stations w/ conven. stores	1	1	1	1
Audio Equipment	--	Prerecorded Tape/CD Stores	0	0	0	0
Audio Equipment	--	Department stores	235	228	225	224
Audio Equipment	--	Warehouse clubs & supercntrs	160	168	175	179
Audio Equipment	--	Office supply/stationery stores	2	2	2	2
Audio Equipment	--	Electronic shopping & mail-order	2,718	2,883	3,050	3,200
Audio Equipment	--	Book stores	597	580	574	571
	Stereos & Compon.	Prerecorded Tape/CD Stores	0	0	0	0
	Stereos & Compon.	Department stores	118	115	113	113
	Stereos & Compon.	Warehouse clubs & supercntrs	71	75	78	79
	Stereos & Compon.	Electronic shopping & mail-order	749	794	840	881
	Pianos	Prerecorded Tape/CD Stores	0	0	0	0
	Musical Instruments	Prerecorded Tape/CD Stores	0	0	0	0
	Tapes & CDs	Prerecorded Tape/CD Stores	0	0	0	0
	Tapes & CDs	Department stores	116	113	112	111
	Tapes & CDs	Warehouse clubs & supercntrs	88	92	96	98
	Tapes & CDs	Electronic shopping & mail-order	967	1,026	1,086	1,139
	Sheet Music	Prerecorded Tape/CD Stores	0	0	0	0
	Other Musical Items	Department stores	0	0	0	0
	Other Musical Items	Warehouse clubs & supercntrs	1	1	1	1
	Other Musical Items	Electronic shopping & mail-order	1,002	1,063	1,125	1,180

SALES (MILLIONS OF U.S. DOLLARS)

Main Category	Sub Category	U.S. Industry	Year			
			2016	2017	2018	2019
Furniture	--	Home centers	131	132	132	134
Furniture	--	Hardware stores	259	267	272	280
Furniture	--	Supermarkets & grocery stores	1	1	1	1
Furniture	--	Men's clothing stores	0	0	0	0
Furniture	--	Women's clothing stores	30	31	31	32
Furniture	--	Family clothing stores	8	8	9	9
Furniture	--	Department stores	193	188	185	184
Furniture	--	Warehouse clubs & supercntrs	91	96	100	102
Furniture	--	Office supply/stationery stores	724	700	677	659
Furniture	--	Electronic shopping & mail-order	1,324	1,404	1,486	1,559
	Upholstered Furn.	Department stores	27	26	26	26
	Upholstered Furn.	Warehouse clubs & supercntrs	3	3	4	4
	Sleep Sofas/Futons	Department stores	3	3	3	3
	Sleep Sofas/Futons	Warehouse clubs & supercntrs	3	3	3	3
	Mattresses	Department stores	24	23	23	22
	Mattresses	Warehouse clubs & supercntrs	22	23	24	25
	Home Furniture	Department stores	45	43	43	43
	Home Furniture	Warehouse clubs & supercntrs	8	8	8	8
	Office Furniture	Department stores	95	93	91	91
	Office Furniture	Warehouse clubs & supercntrs	56	59	61	63

SUMMARY OF PRODUCT LINES SALES BY INDUSTRY

SALES (MILLIONS OF U.S. DOLLARS)

Main Category	Sub Category	U.S. Industry	Year			
			2016	2017	2018	2019
Flooring & Coverings	--	Home centers	426	427	429	435
Flooring & Coverings	--	Hardware stores	59	60	62	63
Flooring & Coverings	--	Supermarkets & grocery stores	0	0	0	0
Flooring & Coverings	--	Women's clothing stores	0	0	0	0
Flooring & Coverings	--	Department stores	31	30	29	29
Flooring & Coverings	--	Warehouse clubs & supercntrs	1	1	1	1
Flooring & Coverings	--	Electronic shopping & mail-order	229	243	257	269
	Soft Floor Coverings	Home centers	151	152	153	154
	Soft Floor Coverings	Hardware stores	22	23	23	24
	Soft Floor Coverings	Department stores	30	29	28	28
	Soft Floor Coverings	Warehouse clubs & supercntrs	1	1	1	1
	Hardwood Flooring	Home centers	24	24	24	24
	Hardwood Flooring	Hardware stores	7	7	7	7
	Hardwood Flooring	Department stores	1	0	0	0
	Other Hard Flooring	Home centers	251	251	253	256
	Other Hard Flooring	Hardware stores	30	31	32	33
	Other Hard Flooring	Department stores	0	0	0	0
	Other Hard Flooring	Warehouse clubs & supercntrs	0	0	0	0

SUMMARY OF PRODUCT LINES SALES BY INDUSTRY

SALES (MILLIONS OF U.S. DOLLARS)

Main Category	Sub Category	U.S. Industry	Year			
			2016	2017	2018	2019
Hardware & Software	--	Home centers	28	28	28	29
Hardware & Software	--	Hardware stores	3	3	3	4
Hardware & Software	--	Supermarkets & grocery stores	0	0	0	0
Hardware & Software	--	Prerecorded Tapes/CDs Stores	0	0	0	0
Hardware & Software	--	Department stores	42	40	40	40
Hardware & Software	--	Warehouse clubs & supercntrs	113	119	124	126
Hardware & Software	--	Office supply/stationery stores	1,034	1,001	968	941
Hardware & Software	--	Electronic shopping & mail-order	14,449	15,327	16,213	17,013
Hardware & Software	--	Book stores	82	79	79	78
	Computers & Equip.	Department stores	31	30	29	29
	Computers & Equip.	Warehouse clubs & supercntrs	77	81	84	86
	Computers & Equip.	Electronic shopping & mail-order	13,332	14,143	14,960	15,698
	Computers & Equip.	Book stores	40	39	38	38
	Software	Department stores	11	11	11	10
	Software	Warehouse clubs & supercntrs	36	38	40	40
	Software	Electronic shopping & mail-order	1,117	1,184	1,253	1,315
	Software	Book stores	42	41	40	40

SUMMARY OF PRODUCT LINES SALES BY INDUSTRY

SALES (MILLIONS OF U.S. DOLLARS)

Main Category	Sub Category	U.S. Industry	Year			
			2016	2017	2018	2019
Kitchenware/Furnishing	--	Home centers	183	183	184	186
Kitchenware/Furnishing	--	Hardware stores	343	353	360	370
Kitchenware/Furnishing	--	Supermarkets & grocery stores	254	257	262	268
Kitchenware/Furnishing	--	Beer, wine, & liquor stores	31	32	32	34
Kitchenware/Furnishing	--	Pharmacies & drug stores	132	135	138	141
Kitchenware/Furnishing	--	Gas stations w/ conven. stores	1	1	1	1
Kitchenware/Furnishing	--	Men's clothing stores	15	14	14	14
Kitchenware/Furnishing	--	Women's clothing stores	122	125	128	131
Kitchenware/Furnishing	--	Family clothing stores	1,376	1,381	1,408	1,444
Kitchenware/Furnishing	--	Prerecorded Tapes/CDs Stores	0	0	0	0
Kitchenware/Furnishing	--	Department stores	384	373	368	366
Kitchenware/Furnishing	--	Warehouse clubs & supercntrs	133	139	145	148
Kitchenware/Furnishing	--	Office supply/stationery stores	5	5	5	5
Kitchenware/Furnishing	--	Electronic shopping & mail-order	3,964	4,205	4,448	4,667
Kitchenware/Furnishing	--	Book stores	58	56	56	56
	Cookware	Department stores	105	102	101	100
	Cookware	Warehouse clubs & supercntrs	56	58	61	62
	Dinnerware	Department stores	96	94	92	92
	Dinnerware	Warehouse clubs & supercntrs	13	14	15	15
	Decorative Access.	Department stores	99	96	95	94
	Decorative Access.	Warehouse clubs & supercntrs	39	41	43	44
	Other Kitchenware	Department stores	84	81	80	80
	Other Kitchenware	Warehouse clubs & supercntrs	24	25	26	27
	Giftware	Office supply/stationery stores	4	4	4	4
	Giftware	Book stores	41	39	39	39
	Other Furnishings	Office supply/stationery stores	1	1	1	1
	Other Furnishings	Book stores	17	17	17	17

SUMMARY OF PRODUCT LINES SALES BY INDUSTRY

SALES (MILLIONS OF U.S. DOLLARS)

Main Category	Sub Category	U.S. Industry	Year			
			2016	2017	2018	2019
Jewelry & Watches	--	Hardware stores	1	1	1	1
Jewelry & Watches	--	Supermarkets & grocery stores	26	27	27	28
Jewelry & Watches	--	Beer, wine, & liquor stores	9	9	9	10
Jewelry & Watches	--	Pharmacies & drug stores	57	58	59	61
Jewelry & Watches	--	Gas stations w/ conven. stores	1	1	1	1
Jewelry & Watches	--	Men's clothing stores	10	10	10	10
Jewelry & Watches	--	Women's clothing stores	1,143	1,178	1,199	1,228
Jewelry & Watches	--	Family clothing stores	457	459	468	480
Jewelry & Watches	--	Prerecorded Tapes/CDs Stores	0	0	0	0
Jewelry & Watches	--	Department stores	243	236	233	232
Jewelry & Watches	--	Warehouse clubs & supercntrs	75	79	82	84
Jewelry & Watches	--	Office supply/stationery stores	1	1	1	1
Jewelry & Watches	--	Electronic shopping & mail-order	3,334	3,537	3,741	3,926
Jewelry & Watches	--	Book stores	17	17	17	17
	Gold Jewelry	Department stores	39	38	37	37
	Gold Jewelry	Warehouse clubs & supercntrs	21	22	23	23
	Diamond Jewelry	Department stores	70	68	67	67
	Diamond Jewelry	Warehouse clubs & supercntrs	19	20	20	21
	Other Fine Jewelry	Department stores	134	130	128	128
	Other Fine Jewelry	Warehouse clubs & supercntrs	36	38	39	40
	Costume Jewelry	Men's clothing stores	5	5	5	5
	Costume Jewelry	Women's clothing stores	985	1,015	1,033	1,059
	Costume Jewelry	Family clothing stores	171	172	175	179
	Other Jewelry	Men's clothing stores	5	5	5	5
	Other Jewelry	Women's clothing stores	158	163	165	170
	Other Jewelry	Family clothing stores	286	288	293	301

SUMMARY OF PRODUCT LINES SALES BY INDUSTRY

SALES (MILLIONS OF U.S. DOLLARS)

Main Category	Sub Category	U.S. Industry	Year			
			2016	2017	2018	2019
Books	--	Hardware stores	0	0	0	0
Books	--	Supermarkets & grocery stores	126	127	130	133
Books	--	Beer, wine, & liquor stores	3	3	3	3
Books	--	Pharmacies & drug stores	50	51	52	54
Books	--	Gas stations w/ conven. stores	22	23	23	23
Books	--	Women's clothing stores	1	1	1	1
Books	--	Prerecorded Tapes/CDs Stores	0	0	0	0
Books	--	Department stores	28	27	27	26
Books	--	Warehouse clubs & supercntrs	73	77	80	82
Books	--	Office supply/stationery stores	17	16	16	15
Books	--	Electronic shopping & mail-order	3,000	3,183	3,366	3,533
Books	--	Book stores	7,501	7,290	7,211	7,176
	Trade Books	Book stores	3,991	3,879	3,837	3,818
	Paperbacks	Book stores	242	236	233	232
	Religious	Book stores	464	451	446	444
	General Reference	Book stores	62	60	60	59
	Textbooks	Book stores	2,480	2,410	2,384	2,372
	Professional Books	Book stores	75	72	72	71
	Other Books	Book stores	188	182	180	180

SUMMARY OF PRODUCT LINES SALES BY INDUSTRY

SALES (MILLIONS OF U.S. DOLLARS)

Main Category	Sub Category	U.S. Industry	Year			
			2016	2017	2018	2019
Toys & Games	--	Home centers	0	0	0	0
Toys & Games	--	Hardware stores	57	59	60	62
Toys & Games	--	Supermarkets & grocery stores	66	67	68	69
Toys & Games	--	Beer, wine, & liquor stores	4	4	4	4
Toys & Games	--	Pharmacies & drug stores	159	162	166	170
Toys & Games	--	Gas stations w/ conven. stores	3	3	3	3
Toys & Games	--	Men's clothing stores	1	1	1	1
Toys & Games	--	Women's clothing stores	5	5	5	6
Toys & Games	--	Family clothing stores	731	734	748	767
Toys & Games	--	CD, tape & record stores	0	0	0	0
Toys & Games	--	Department stores	329	320	316	314
Toys & Games	--	Warehouse clubs & supercntrs	203	213	222	226
Toys & Games	--	Office supply/stationery stores	9	8	8	8
Toys & Games	--	Electronic shopping & mail-order	1,877	1,991	2,106	2,210
Toys & Games	--	Book stores	23	23	23	22
	Toys	Pharmacies & drug stores	140	143	146	150
	Toys	Department stores	221	215	212	211
	Toys	Electronic shopping & mail-order	975	1,034	1,094	1,148
	Games	Pharmacies & drug stores	6	6	6	6
	Games	Department stores	107	104	103	102
	Games	Electronic shopping & mail-order	242	257	272	285
	Hobby Goods	Pharmacies & drug stores	13	13	13	14
	Hobby Goods	Department stores	0	0	0	0
	Hobby Goods	Electronic shopping & mail-order	660	700	741	777

SUMMARY OF PRODUCT LINES SALES BY INDUSTRY

SALES (MILLIONS OF U.S. DOLLARS)

Main Category	Sub Category	U.S. Industry	Year			
			2016	2017	2018	2019
Sporting Goods	--	Home centers	7	7	7	7
Sporting Goods	--	Hardware stores	155	159	163	167
Sporting Goods	--	Supermarkets & grocery stores	13	13	13	13
Sporting Goods	--	Beer, wine, & liquor stores	9	9	9	10
Sporting Goods	--	Pharmacies & drug stores	7	7	7	7
Sporting Goods	--	Gas stations w/ conven. stores	50	51	52	53
Sporting Goods	--	Men's clothing stores	12	12	12	12
Sporting Goods	--	Women's clothing stores	3	3	3	3
Sporting Goods	--	Family clothing stores	51	51	52	54
Sporting Goods	--	Department stores	210	204	202	200
Sporting Goods	--	Warehouse clubs & supercntrs	151	158	164	168
Sporting Goods	--	Office supply/stationery stores	1	1	1	1
Sporting Goods	--	Electronic shopping & mail-order	3,235	3,432	3,630	3,809
	Exercise Equip.	Department stores	43	42	42	41
	Exercise Equip.	Warehouse clubs & supercntrs	30	31	32	33
	Firearms	Department stores	33	32	32	31
	Firearms	Warehouse clubs & supercntrs	34	35	37	38
	Fishing Equip.	Department stores	18	18	17	17
	Fishing Equip.	Warehouse clubs & supercntrs	19	20	21	21
	Camping Equip.	Department stores	45	44	43	43
	Camping Equip.	Warehouse clubs & supercntrs	22	23	24	25
	Bicycles	Department stores	28	28	27	27
	Bicycles	Warehouse clubs & supercntrs	20	21	22	22
	Boats	Department stores	5	5	5	5
	Boats	Warehouse clubs & supercntrs	8	8	8	9
	Boats	Electronic shopping & mail-order	254	270	285	299
	Other Sporting Equip.	Electronic shopping & mail-order	2,981	3,162	3,345	3,510
	Other Sporting Equip.	Department stores	37	36	36	36
	Other Sporting Equip.	Warehouse clubs & supercntrs	18	19	20	20

SUMMARY OF PRODUCT LINES SALES BY INDUSTRY

SALES (MILLIONS OF U.S. DOLLARS)

Main Category	Sub Category	U.S. Industry	Year			
			2016	2017	2018	2019
Hardware	--	Home centers	2,035	2,039	2,051	2,075
Hardware	--	Hardware stores	8,813	9,062	9,252	9,504
Hardware	--	Supermarkets & grocery stores	79	80	82	84
Hardware	--	Beer, wine, & liquor stores	0	0	0	0
Hardware	--	Pharmacies & drug stores	66	67	68	70
Hardware	--	Gas stations w/ conven. stores	100	101	103	106
Hardware	--	Men's clothing stores	0	0	0	0
Hardware	--	Department stores	206	200	198	197
Hardware	--	Warehouse clubs & supercntrs	117	123	128	131
Hardware	--	Office supply/stationery stores	0	0	0	0
Hardware	--	Electronic shopping & mail-order	719	762	806	846
	General Hardware	Home centers	324	325	327	331
	General Hardware	Hardware stores	2,771	2,849	2,909	2,988
	Tools & Equip.	Home centers	545	546	549	556
	Tools & Equip.	Hardware stores	3,081	3,168	3,235	3,323
	Plumbing Supplies	Home centers	568	569	573	579
	Plumbing Supplies	Hardware stores	1,526	1,569	1,602	1,645
	Wiring Supplies	Home centers	98	98	98	99
	Wiring Supplies	Hardware stores	392	403	411	423
	Welding Supplies	Home centers	1	1	1	1
	Welding Supplies	Hardware stores	57	59	60	62
	Electrical Supplies	Home centers	499	500	503	509
	Electrical Supplies	Hardware stores	985	1,013	1,034	1,062

SUMMARY OF PRODUCT LINES SALES BY INDUSTRY

SALES (MILLIONS OF U.S. DOLLARS)

Main Category	Sub Category	U.S. Industry	Year			
			2016	2017	2018	2019
Lawn & Garden	--	Home centers	844	846	850	860
Lawn & Garden	--	Hardware stores	2,361	2,427	2,478	2,545
Lawn & Garden	--	Supermarkets & grocery stores	562	570	580	594
Lawn & Garden	--	Beer, wine, & liquor stores	1	1	1	1
Lawn & Garden	--	Pharmacies & drug stores	58	59	61	62
Lawn & Garden	--	Gas stations w/ conven. stores	31	31	32	33
Lawn & Garden	--	Department stores	186	181	178	177
Lawn & Garden	--	Warehouse clubs & supercntrs	161	169	176	179
Lawn & Garden	--	Electronic shopping & mail-order	1,053	1,117	1,182	1,240
	Cut Flowers	Home centers	0	0	0	0
	Cut Flowers	Hardware stores	15	16	16	17
	Cut Flowers	Department stores	1	1	1	1
	Cut Flowers	Warehouse clubs & supercntrs	27	29	30	30
	Indoor Plants	Home centers	45	45	45	46
	Indoor Plants	Hardware stores	33	34	35	36
	Indoor Plants	Department stores	7	6	6	6
	Indoor Plants	Warehouse clubs & supercntrs	7	8	8	8
	Outdoor Plants	Home centers	208	208	209	212
	Outdoor Plants	Hardware stores	158	162	166	170
	Outdoor Plants	Department stores	35	34	33	33
	Outdoor Plants	Warehouse clubs & supercntrs	24	25	26	27
	Fertilizers	Home centers	162	163	164	166
	Fertilizers	Hardware stores	377	388	396	407
	Fertilizers	Department stores	18	18	18	17
	Fertilizers	Warehouse clubs & supercntrs	22	23	24	25
	Lawn Tools	Home centers	72	72	72	73
	Lawn Tools	Hardware stores	412	423	432	444
	Lawn Tools	Department stores	4	4	4	4
	Lawn Tools	Warehouse clubs & supercntrs	5	5	5	6
	Lawn Machinery	Home centers	191	192	193	195
	Lawn Machinery	Hardware stores	609	626	639	656
	Lawn Machinery	Department stores	76	74	73	73
	Lawn Machinery	Warehouse clubs & supercntrs	53	55	57	59

SUMMARY OF PRODUCT LINES SALES BY INDUSTRY

Sales (Millions of U.S. Dollars)

Main Category	Sub Category	U.S. Industry	Year			
			2016	2017	2018	2019
	Farm Machinery	Home Centers	4	4	4	4
	Farm Machinery	Hardware Stores	98	101	103	106
	Farm Machinery	Department Stores	0	0	0	0
	Other Farm Supplies	Home Centers	2	2	2	2
	Other Farm Supplies	Hardware Stores	291	299	306	314
	Other Farm Supplies	Department Stores	0	0	0	0
	Other Farm Supplies	Warehouse clubs & supercntrs	0	0	0	0
	Other Lawn Supplies	Home Centers	161	161	162	164
	Other Lawn Supplies	Hardware Stores	368	378	386	396
	Other Lawn Supplies	Department Stores	45	43	43	43
	Other Lawn Supplies	Warehouse clubs & supercntrs	22	23	24	25

SUMMARY OF PRODUCT LINES SALES BY INDUSTRY

SALES (MILLIONS OF U.S. DOLLARS)

Main Category	Sub Category	U.S. Industry	Year			
			2016	2017	2018	2019
Lumber & Bldg Mat.	--	Home centers	2,414	2,419	2,433	2,461
Lumber & Bldg Mat.	--	Hardware stores	1,061	1,091	1,114	1,145
Lumber & Bldg Mat.	--	Gas stations w/ conven. stores	1	1	1	1
Lumber & Bldg Mat.	--	Department stores	0	0	0	0
Lumber & Bldg Mat.	--	Warehouse clubs & supercntrs	1	1	1	1
Lumber & Bldg Mat.	--	Electronic shopping & mail-order	128	136	144	151
	Nontreated Lumber	Home centers	188	188	189	191
	Nontreated Lumber	Hardware stores	99	102	104	107
	Treated Lumber	Home centers	194	195	196	198
	Treated Lumber	Hardware stores	64	66	67	69
	Bldg. Boards	Home centers	77	77	77	78
	Bldg. Boards	Hardware stores	40	41	42	43
	Gypsum	Home centers	141	141	142	143
	Gypsum	Hardware stores	35	36	37	38
	Engin'd. Wood Prod.	Home centers	16	16	16	16
	Engin'd. Wood Prod.	Hardware stores	4	4	4	4
	Structural Panels	Home centers	142	142	143	144
	Structural Panels	Hardware stores	32	32	33	34
	Other Panel Prods.	Home centers	137	137	138	140
	Other Panel Prods.	Hardware stores	36	37	37	38
	Bldg. Components	Home centers	12	13	13	13
	Bldg. Components	Hardware stores	6	7	7	7
	Connectors	Home centers	16	16	16	16
	Connectors	Hardware stores	24	25	26	26
	Steel Studs	Home centers	6	6	6	6
	Steel Studs	Hardware stores	4	4	5	5
	Doors & Moulding	Home centers	350	350	352	356
	Doors & Moulding	Hardware stores	75	77	79	81
	Windows & Skylights	Home centers	205	205	206	209
	Windows & Skylights	Hardware stores	35	36	37	38
	Glass	Home centers	11	11	11	11
	Glass	Hardware stores	66	68	69	71
	Masonry Supplies	Home centers	108	108	109	110
	Masonry Supplies	Hardware stores	128	131	134	138

SUMMARY OF PRODUCT LINES SALES BY INDUSTRY

SALES (MILLIONS OF U.S. DOLLARS)

Main Category	Sub Category	U.S. Industry	Year			
			2016	2017	2018	2019
	Insulation Products	Home centers	55	55	55	56
	Insulation Products	Hardware stores	45	46	47	48
	Siding & Exter. Trim	Home centers	30	30	31	31
	Siding & Exter. Trim	Hardware stores	12	12	12	12
	Roofing Supplies	Home centers	94	95	95	96
	Roofing Supplies	Hardware stores	46	48	49	50
	Ceilings	Home centers	19	19	19	19
	Ceilings	Hardware stores	7	8	8	8
	Kitchen & Cabinets	Home centers	389	390	392	397
	Kitchen & Cabinets	Hardware stores	94	97	99	101
	Heating & HVAC	Home centers	97	97	98	99
	Heating & HVAC	Hardware stores	100	103	105	108
	Refrigeration	Home centers	0	0	0	0
	Refrigeration	Hardware stores	10	11	11	11
	Other Bldg. Supplies	Home centers	128	128	129	130
	Other Bldg. Supplies	Hardware stores	99	102	104	107

SUMMARY OF PRODUCT LINES SALES BY INDUSTRY

SALES (MILLIONS OF U.S. DOLLARS)

Main Category	Sub Category	U.S. Industry	Year			
			2016	2017	2018	2019
Paint & Wallpaper	--	Home centers	523	524	527	533
Paint & Wallpaper	--	Hardware stores	1,853	1,905	1,945	1,998
Paint & Wallpaper	--	Supermarkets & grocery stores	0	0	0	0
Paint & Wallpaper	--	Gas stations w/ conven. stores	0	0	0	0
Paint & Wallpaper	--	Department stores	37	36	35	35
Paint & Wallpaper	--	Warehouse clubs & supercntrs	25	26	27	28
Paint & Wallpaper	--	Electronic shopping & mail-order	5	5	6	6
	Interior Paint	Home centers	195	196	197	199
	Interior Paint	Hardware stores	610	628	641	658
	Exterior Paint	Home centers	59	60	60	61
	Exterior Paint	Hardware stores	394	405	413	425
	Stains & Varnishes	Home centers	50	50	50	51
	Stains & Varnishes	Hardware stores	202	208	212	218
	Painting Equipment	Home centers	93	93	94	95
	Painting Equipment	Hardware stores	389	400	409	420
	Painting Supplies	Home centers	125	126	126	128
	Painting Supplies	Hardware stores	257	265	270	278

SALES (MILLIONS OF U.S. DOLLARS)

Main Category	Sub Category	U.S. Industry	Year			
			2016	2017	2018	2019
Gasoline & Fuels	--	Home centers	0	0	0	0
Gasoline & Fuels	--	Hardware stores	21	22	22	23
Gasoline & Fuels	--	Supermarkets & grocery stores	456	463	471	482
Gasoline & Fuels	--	Beer, wine, & liquor stores	94	96	99	102
Gasoline & Fuels	--	Gas stations w/ conven. stores	64,533	65,589	66,777	68,400
Gasoline & Fuels	--	Department stores	1	1	1	1
Gasoline & Fuels	--	Warehouse clubs & supercntrs	4	4	4	4
Gasoline & Fuels	--	Electronic shopping & mail-order	1	1	1	1
	Unleaded Regular	Gas stations w/ conven. stores	44,055	44,776	45,587	46,694
	Unleaded Mid-Grade	Gas stations w/ conven. stores	9,268	9,420	9,590	9,823
	Unleaded Premium	Gas stations w/ conven. stores	7,136	7,253	7,384	7,564
	Leaded Gasoline	Gas stations w/ conven. stores	138	140	143	146
	Diesel Fuel	Gas stations w/ conven. stores	3,597	3,656	3,722	3,813
	Other Fuels	Gas stations w/ conven. stores	339	344	351	359
Tires & Other Parts	--	Home centers	6	6	6	6
Tires & Other Parts	--	Hardware stores	129	132	135	139
Tires & Other Parts	--	Supermarkets & grocery stores	5	5	5	6
Tires & Other Parts	--	Beer, wine, & liquor stores	0	0	0	0
Tires & Other Parts	--	Pharmacies & drug stores	5	5	5	6
Tires & Other Parts	--	Gas stations w/ conven. stores	506	515	524	537
Tires & Other Parts	--	Department stores	93	90	89	89
Tires & Other Parts	--	Warehouse clubs & supercntrs	123	129	135	138
Tires & Other Parts	--	Electronic shopping & mail-order	2,120	2,248	2,378	2,496
	Tires & Tubes	Gas stations w/ conven. stores	101	103	105	107
	Tires & Tubes	Department stores	11	11	11	10
	Tires & Tubes	Warehouse clubs & supercntrs	52	54	56	58
	Auto Parts	Department stores	70	68	67	67
	Auto Parts	Warehouse clubs & supercntrs	54	56	59	60
	Auto Parts	Gas stations w/ conven. stores	211	215	219	224
	Batteries	Gas stations w/ conven. stores	22	23	23	24
	Batteries	Department stores	12	11	11	11
	Batteries	Warehouse clubs & supercntrs	18	19	20	20
	Auto Accessories	Gas stations w/ conven. stores	42	43	43	44
	Other Auto Parts	Gas stations w/ conven. stores	130	132	134	137

SUMMARY OF PRODUCT LINES SALES BY INDUSTRY

Sales (Millions of U.S. Dollars)

Main Category	Sub Category	U.S. Industry	Year			
			2016	2017	2018	2019
Pets & Pet Foods	--	Home centers	22	22	22	22
Pets & Pet Foods	--	Hardware stores	89	92	94	96
Pets & Pet Foods	--	Supermarkets & grocery stores	707	717	730	748
Pets & Pet Foods	--	Beer, wine, & liquor stores	8	8	8	9
Pets & Pet Foods	--	Pharmacies & drug stores	50	51	52	53
Pets & Pet Foods	--	Gas stations w/ conven. stores	70	71	72	74
Pets & Pet Foods	--	Department Stores	105	102	100	100
Pets & Pet Foods	--	Warehouse Clubs & Superctrs	125	131	136	139
Pets & Pet Foods	--	Electronic Shopping/Mail-Order	332	352	373	391
Pets & Pet Foods	--	Book Stores	1	1	1	1
	Stationery Products	Supermarkets & grocery stores	34	35	36	36
	Stationery Products	Beer, wine, & liquor stores	2	2	3	3
	Stationery Products	Pharmacies & drug stores	77	78	80	82
	Stationery Products	Department stores	29	28	27	27
	Stationery Products	Warehouse clubs & supercntrs	28	30	31	31
	Stationery Products	Office supply/stationery stores	830	803	776	755
	Stationery Products	Electronic shopping & mail-order	836	887	938	984
	Stationery Products	Book stores	58	56	56	55
	Office Paper	Supermarkets & grocery stores	8	8	8	8
	Office Paper	Beer, wine, & liquor stores	0	0	0	0
	Office Paper	Pharmacies & drug stores	24	24	25	25
	Office Paper	Department stores	25	24	24	24
	Office Paper	Warehouse clubs & supercntrs	27	28	30	30
	Office Paper	Office supply/stationery stores	1,611	1,559	1,508	1,466
	Office Paper	Electronic shopping & mail-order	734	778	823	864
	Office Paper	Book stores	20	19	19	19
	Office Supplies	Supermarkets & grocery stores	64	65	66	68
	Office Supplies	Beer, wine, & liquor stores	4	4	4	4
	Office Supplies	Pharmacies & drug stores	140	143	146	150
	Office Supplies	Department stores	33	32	32	31
	Office Supplies	Warehouse clubs & supercntrs	63	66	68	70
	Office Supplies	Office supply/stationery stores	2,280	2,206	2,133	2,075
	Office Supplies	Electronic shopping & mail-order	2,828	3,000	3,173	3,330
	Office Supplies	Book stores	115	111	110	110

SUMMARY OF PRODUCT LINES SALES BY INDUSTRY

SALES (MILLIONS OF U.S. DOLLARS)

Main Category	Sub Category	U.S. Industry	Year			
			2016	2017	2018	2019
	Office Equipment	Pharmacies & drug stores	3	3	3	3
	Office Equipment	Department stores	12	12	12	12
	Office Equipment	Warehouse clubs & supercntrs	10	10	11	11
	Office Equipment	Office supply/stationery stores	1,054	1,020	987	960
	Office Equipment	Electronic shopping & mail-order	519	551	583	612
	Office Equipment	Book stores	3	2	2	2
	Greeting Cards	Supermarkets & grocery stores	208	211	215	220
	Greeting Cards	Beer, wine, & liquor stores	3	3	4	4
	Greeting Cards	Warehouse clubs & supercntrs	402	410	418	430
	Greeting Cards	Pharmacies & drug stores	49	48	47	47
	Greeting Cards	Department stores	25	26	27	28
	Greeting Cards	Office supply/stationery stores	21	21	20	19
	Greeting Cards	Electronic shopping & mail-order	71	75	79	83
	Greeting Cards	Book stores	149	145	144	143
	Magazine/Newpaper	Supermarkets & grocery stores	298	302	308	315
	Magazine/Newpaper	Beer, wine, & liquor stores	45	46	47	49
	Magazine/Newpaper	Pharmacies & drug stores	80	81	83	85
	Magazine/Newpaper	Gas stations w/ conven. stores	413	420	427	438
	Magazine/Newpaper	Prerecorded Tape & CDs stores	0	0	0	0
	Magazine/Newpaper	Department stores	22	21	21	21
	Magazine/Newpaper	Warehouse clubs & supercntrs	16	17	17	18
	Magazine/Newpaper	Office supply/stationery stores	3	3	3	3
	Magazine/Newpaper	Electronic shopping & mail-order	546	580	613	643
	Magazine/Newpaper	Office supply/stationery stores	353	343	339	337

SALES (MILLIONS OF U.S. DOLLARS)

Main Category	Sub Category	U.S. Industry	Year			
			2016	2017	2018	2019
Souvenirs & Novelty	--	Supermarkets & grocery stores	70	71	73	74
Souvenirs & Novelty	--	Beer, wine, & liquor stores	21	21	22	23
Souvenirs & Novelty	--	Pharmacies & drug stores	77	79	80	83
Souvenirs & Novelty	--	Men's clothing stores	13	13	13	13
Souvenirs & Novelty	--	Women's clothing stores	27	28	28	29
Souvenirs & Novelty	--	Family clothing stores	92	92	94	96
Souvenirs & Novelty	--	Department stores	35	34	34	33
Souvenirs & Novelty	--	Warehouse Clubs & Superctrs	11	11	12	12
Souvenirs & Novelty	--	Office Supplies/Stationery Store	8	8	8	7
Souvenirs & Novelty	--	Electronic Shopping/Mail-Order	1,143	1,213	1,283	1,346
Souvenirs & Novelty	--	Book Stores	279	271	268	266

INDUSTRY: HOME CENTERS INDUSTRY (NAICS 44411)
PRODUCT LINE: GROCERY FOODS (Main Category)

NAICS 44411: Home Centers. This industry comprises establishments known as home centers primarily engaged in retailing a general line of new home repair and improvement materials and supplies, such as lumber, plumbing goods, electrical goods, tools, housewares, hardware, and lawn and garden supplies, with no one merchandise line predominating. The merchandise lines are normally arranged in separate departments.

5-YEAR TREND — ESTIMATED INDUSTRY SALES ($MILLIONS)

Year	Employee Size of Establishment									Total Industry Sales
	1-4 Emps.	5-9 Emps.	10-19 Emps.	20-49 Emps.	50-99 Emps.	100-249 Emps.	250-499 Emps.	500-999 Emps.	Unknown Emps.	
2015	0.0	0.0	0.1	0.2	0.1	8.6	0.7	0.0	0.0	9.7
2016	0.0	0.0	0.1	0.2	0.1	8.8	0.7	0.0	0.0	9.9
2017	0.0	0.0	0.1	0.2	0.1	9.0	0.7	0.0	0.0	10.2
2018	0.0	0.0	0.1	0.2	0.1	9.4	0.7	0.0	0.0	10.6
2019	0.0	0.0	0.1	0.2	0.1	9.8	0.8	0.0	0.0	11.1

INDUSTRY: HARDWARE STORES (NAICS 44413)
PRODUCT LINE: GROCERY FOODS (Main Category)

NAICS 44413: Hardware Stores. Establishments primarily engaged in the retail sale of a number of basic hardware lines, such as tools, builders' hardware, paint and glass, housewares and household appliances, and cutlery.

5-YEAR TREND — ESTIMATED INDUSTRY SALES ($MILLIONS)

Year	Employee Size of Establishment									Total Industry Sales
	1-4 Emps.	5-9 Emps.	10-19 Emps.	20-49 Emps.	50-99 Emps.	100-249 Emps.	250-499 Emps.	500-999 Emps.	Unknown Emps.	
2015	7.4	12.5	25.2	36.0	7.2	2.3	0.4	0.0	0.6	91.7
2016	7.5	12.6	25.4	36.4	7.2	2.4	0.4	0.0	0.7	92.6
2017	7.6	12.8	25.8	37.0	7.3	2.4	0.4	0.0	0.7	94.1
2018	7.9	13.4	26.9	38.4	7.6	2.5	0.4	0.0	0.7	97.8
2019	8.3	14.0	28.2	40.3	8.0	2.6	0.5	0.0	0.7	102.7

INDUSTRY: SUPERMARKETS & GROCERY STORES (NAICS 44511)
PRODUCT LINE: GROCERY FOODS (Main Category)

NAICS 44511: Grocery Stores Industry. This industry comprises establishments generally known as supermarkets and grocery stores primarily engaged in retailing a general line of food, such as canned and frozen foods; fresh fruits and vegetables; and fresh and prepared meats, fish, and poultry. Included in this industry are delicatessen-type establishments primarily engaged in retailing a general line of food.

5-YEAR TREND – ESTIMATED INDUSTRY SALES ($MILLIONS)

Year	Employee Size of Establishment									Total Industry Sales
	1-4 Emps.	5-9 Emps.	10-19 Emps.	20-49 Emps.	50-99 Emps.	100-249 Emps.	250-499 Emps.	500-999 Emps.	Unknown Emps.	
2015	6,059	4,374	11,287	37,195	88,152	219,149	68,442	8,189	1,137	443,984
2016	6,021	4,346	11,215	36,959	87,592	217,759	68,008	8,137	1,130	441,167
2017	6,018	4,345	11,211	36,946	87,562	217,684	67,984	8,134	1,130	441,014
2018	6,143	4,434	11,442	37,708	89,367	222,172	69,386	8,297	1,153	450,102
2019	6,332	4,571	11,796	38,873	92,130	229,039	71,531	8,547	1,189	464,008

INDUSTRY: BEER & WINE & LIQUOR STORES (NAICS 44531)
PRODUCT LINE: GROCERY FOODS (Main Category)

NAICS 44531: Beer & Wine & Liquor Stores. Establishments primarily engaged in the retail sale of packaged alcoholic beverages, such as ale, beer, wine, and liquor, for consumption off the premises. Stores selling prepared drinks for consumption on the premises are classified in SIC 5813.

5-YEAR TREND – ESTIMATED INDUSTRY SALES ($MILLIONS)

Year	Employee Size of Establishment									Total Industry Sales
	1-4 Emps.	5-9 Emps.	10-19 Emps.	20-49 Emps.	50-99 Emps.	100-249 Emps.	250-499 Emps.	500-999 Emps.	Unknown Emps.	
2015	523.9	528.0	451.3	330.7	47.4	27.5	0.1	15.6	29.4	1,954.0
2016	535.9	540.1	461.7	338.3	48.4	28.2	0.1	16.0	30.1	1,998.9
2017	551.1	555.4	474.8	347.9	49.8	29.0	0.1	16.4	31.0	2,055.5
2018	583.2	587.8	502.4	368.2	52.7	30.6	0.1	17.4	32.8	2,175.3
2019	622.7	627.5	536.4	393.1	56.3	32.7	0.1	18.5	35.0	2,322.4

INDUSTRY: PHARMACIES & DRUG STORES (NAICS 44611)
PRODUCT LINE: GROCERY FOODS (Main Category)

NAICS 44611 Pharmacies and Drug Stores – This industry comprises
establishments known as pharmacies and drug stores engaged in retailing
prescription or nonprescription drugs and medicines.

5-YEAR TREND – ESTIMATED INDUSTRY SALES ($MILLIONS)

Year	Employee Size of Establishment									Total Industry Sales
	1-4 Emps.	5-9 Emps.	10-19 Emps.	20-49 Emps.	50-99 Emps.	100-249 Emps.	250-499 Emps.	500-999 Emps.	Unknown Emps.	
2015	125.3	310.3	1,255.7	3,688.1	373.0	149.3	57.1	19.0	9.6	5,987.6
2016	129.2	320.1	1,295.1	3,803.7	384.7	154.0	58.9	19.6	9.9	6,175.2
2017	133.9	331.7	1,342.0	3,941.3	398.6	159.6	61.0	20.4	10.2	6,398.7
2018	141.8	351.3	1,421.3	4,174.4	422.2	169.0	64.6	21.6	10.9	6,777.1
2019	151.5	375.1	1,517.8	4,457.7	450.9	180.5	69.0	23.0	11.6	7,237.0

INDUSTRY: GAS STATIONS WITH CONVENIENCE STORES (NAICS 44711)
PRODUCT LINE: GROCERY FOODS (Main Category)

NAICS 44711: Gas Stations with Convenience Stores. This industry
comprises establishments primarily engaged in selling gasoline and
lubricating oils. These establishments frequently sell other merchandise,
such as tires, batteries, and other automobile parts, or perform minor repair
work. Gasoline stations combined with other activities, such as grocery
stores, convenience stores, or carwashes, are classified according to the
primary activity.

5-YEAR TREND – ESTIMATED INDUSTRY SALES ($MILLIONS)

Year	Employee Size of Establishment									Total Industry Sales
	1-4 Emps.	5-9 Emps.	10-19 Emps.	20-49 Emps.	50-99 Emps.	100-249 Emps.	250-499 Emps.	500-999 Emps.	Unknown Emps.	
2015	4,316	11,151	18,666	12,880	1,210	663	263	2	47	49,199
2016	4,497	11,618	19,447	13,419	1,261	691	274	2	49	51,259
2017	4,704	12,152	20,341	14,036	1,319	722	286	2	52	53,614
2018	5,013	12,950	21,676	14,957	1,405	770	305	3	55	57,134
2019	5,381	13,902	23,271	16,058	1,509	826	328	3	59	61,337

	INDUSTRY: DEPARTMENT STORES (NAICS 45211)
	PRODUCT LINE: GROCERY FOODS (Main Category)

NAICS 45211: Department Stores Industry . This industry comprises establishments known as department stores primarily engaged in retailing a wide range of the following new products with no one merchandise line predominating: apparel, furniture, appliances and home furnishings; and selected additional items, such as paint, hardware, toiletries, cosmetics, photographic equipment, jewelry, toys, and sporting goods. Merchandise lines are normally arranged in separate departments.

5-YEAR TREND – ESTIMATED INDUSTRY SALES ($MILLIONS)

Year	Employee Size of Establishment									Total
	1-4 Emps.	5-9 Emps.	10-19 Emps.	20-49 Emps.	50-99 Emps.	100-249 Emps.	250-499 Emps.	500-999 Emps.	Unknown Emps.	Industry Sales
2015	0	0	1	50	906	2,908	1,204	174	7	5,251
2016	0	0	1	50	909	2,920	1,209	175	7	5,271
2017	0	0	1	51	918	2,949	1,221	177	8	5,323
2018	0	0	1	51	918	2,949	1,221	177	8	5,324
2019	0	0	1	51	927	2,978	1,233	179	8	5,377

	INDUSTRY: WAREHOUSE CLUBS & SUPERCENTERS (NAICS 45291)
	PRODUCT LINE: GROCERY FOODS (Main Category)

NAICS 45291: Warehouse Clubs and Superstores This industry comprises establishments known as warehouse clubs, superstores or supercenters primarily engaged in retailing a general line of groceries in combination with general lines of new merchandise, such as apparel, furniture, and appliances.

5-YEAR TREND – ESTIMATED INDUSTRY SALES ($MILLIONS)

Year	Employee Size of Establishment									Total
	1-4 Emps.	5-9 Emps.	10-19 Emps.	20-49 Emps.	50-99 Emps.	100-249 Emps.	250-499 Emps.	500-999 Emps.	Unknown Emps.	Industry Sales
2015	3	1	3	104	197	11,239	49,477	1,247	19	62,289
2016	3	1	3	107	202	11,549	50,840	1,281	19	64,005
2017	4	1	3	110	209	11,926	52,501	1,323	20	66,096
2018	4	1	3	118	225	12,835	56,503	1,424	22	71,134
2019	4	1	3	126	238	13,595	59,850	1,508	23	75,348

INDUSTRY: OFFICE SUPPLIES & STATIONERY STORES (NAICS 45321)
PRODUCT LINE: GROCERY FOODS (Main Category)

NAICS 45321: Office Supplies and Stationery Stores . This industry comprises establishments primarily engaged in one or more of the following: (1) retailing new stationery, school supplies, and office supplies; (2) selling a combination of new office equipment, furniture, and supplies; and (3) selling new office equipment, furniture, and supplies in combination with selling new computers.

5-YEAR TREND – ESTIMATED INDUSTRY SALES ($MILLIONS)

Year	Employee Size of Establishment									Total
	1-4 Emps.	5-9 Emps.	10-19 Emps.	20-49 Emps.	50-99 Emps.	100-249 Emps.	250-499 Emps.	500-999 Emps.	Unknown Emps.	Industry Sales
2015	1.7	1.4	8.9	22.3	0.5	0.3	0.0	0.0	0.4	35.6
2016	1.7	1.4	8.8	22.1	0.5	0.3	0.0	0.0	0.4	35.3
2017	1.7	1.4	8.8	22.1	0.5	0.3	0.0	0.0	0.4	35.2
2018	1.7	1.3	8.5	21.4	0.4	0.3	0.0	0.0	0.4	34.1
2019	1.6	1.3	8.3	20.9	0.4	0.3	0.0	0.0	0.4	33.3

INDUSTRY: ELECTRONIC SHOPPING & MAIL-ORDER (NAICS 45411)
PRODUCT LINE: GROCERY FOODS (Main Category)

NAICS 45411: Electronic Shopping and Mail-Order Houses This industry comprises establishments primarily engaged in retailing all types of merchandise by means of mail or by electronic media, such as interactive television or computer. Included in this industry are establishments primarily engaged in retailing from catalogue showrooms of mail-order houses.

5-YEAR TREND – ESTIMATED INDUSTRY SALES ($MILLIONS)

Year	Employee Size of Establishment									Total
	1-4 Emps.	5-9 Emps.	10-19 Emps.	20-49 Emps.	50-99 Emps.	100-249 Emps.	250-499 Emps.	500-999 Emps.	Unknown Emps.	Industry Sales
2015	1,533.4	789.9	1,141.2	1,915.6	1,441.9	2,667.7	3,596.5	5,076.9	215.5	18,378.6
2016	1,621.9	835.5	1,207.1	2,026.2	1,525.1	2,821.6	3,804.1	5,369.9	228.0	19,439.4
2017	1,719.6	885.8	1,279.8	2,148.2	1,617.0	2,991.6	4,033.2	5,693.4	241.7	20,610.4
2018	1,927.1	992.7	1,434.3	2,407.5	1,812.2	3,352.7	4,520.1	6,265.0	270.9	22,982.5
2019	2,142.6	1,103.7	1,594.7	2,676.7	2,014.8	3,727.6	5,025.4	6,860.8	301.2	25,447.4

INDUSTRY: BOOK STORES (NAICS 451211)
PRODUCT LINE: GROCERY FOODS (Main Category)

NAICS 451211: Book Stores. This industry comprises establishments primarily engaged in the retail sale of new books and magazines. Establishments primarily engaged in the retail sale of used books are classified in 5932.

5-YEAR TREND — ESTIMATED INDUSTRY SALES ($MILLIONS)

Year	Employee Size of Establishment									Total Industry Sales
	1-4 Emps.	5-9 Emps.	10-19 Emps.	20-49 Emps.	50-99 Emps.	100-249 Emps.	250-499 Emps.	500-999 Emps.	Unknown Emps.	
2015	52.1	79.0	157.2	418.0	182.0	83.8	20.7	49.7	26.3	1,068.7
2016	54.4	82.6	164.3	437.0	190.2	87.6	21.6	52.0	27.5	1,117.3
2017	57.1	86.6	172.4	458.6	199.6	91.9	22.7	54.5	28.9	1,172.3
2018	59.3	89.9	179.0	476.1	207.2	95.4	23.5	56.9	30.0	1,217.4
2019	62.0	94.0	187.1	497.8	216.7	99.8	24.6	59.7	31.3	1,273.1

INDUSTRY: SUPERMARKETS & GROCERY STORES (NAICS 44511)
PRODUCT LINE: MEAT, FISH & POULTRY (Sub Category)

NAICS 44511: Grocery Stores Industry. This industry comprises establishments generally known as supermarkets and grocery stores primarily engaged in retailing a general line of food, such as canned and frozen foods; fresh fruits and vegetables; and fresh and prepared meats, fish, and poultry. Included in this industry are delicatessen-type establishments primarily engaged in retailing a general line of food.

5-YEAR TREND — ESTIMATED INDUSTRY SALES ($MILLIONS)

Year	Employee Size of Establishment									Total Industry Sales
	1-4 Emps.	5-9 Emps.	10-19 Emps.	20-49 Emps.	50-99 Emps.	100-249 Emps.	250-499 Emps.	500-999 Emps.	Unknown Emps.	
2015	2	2	4	14	32	80	25	3	0	162
2016	2	2	4	14	32	80	25	3	0	161
2017	2	2	4	14	32	80	25	3	0	161
2018	2	2	4	14	33	81	25	3	0	165
2019	2	2	4	14	34	84	26	3	0	170

INDUSTRY: WAREHOUSE CLUBS & SUPERCENTERS (NAICS 45291)
PRODUCT LINE: MEAT, FISH & POULTRY (Sub Category)

NAICS 45291: Warehouse Clubs and Superstores This industry comprises establishments known as warehouse clubs, superstores or supercenters primarily engaged in retailing a general line of groceries in combination with general lines of new merchandise, such as apparel, furniture, and appliances.

5-Year Trend — Estimated Industry Sales ($Millions)

Year	Employee Size of Establishment									Total Industry Sales
	1-4 Emps.	5-9 Emps.	10-19 Emps.	20-49 Emps.	50-99 Emps.	100-249 Emps.	250-499 Emps.	500-999 Emps.	Unknown Emps.	
2015	1.1	0.3	1.0	36.1	68.5	3,912.4	17,223.3	434.0	6.6	21,683.4
2016	1.2	0.3	1.0	37.1	70.4	4,020.2	17,698.0	446.0	6.7	22,281.0
2017	1.2	0.3	1.1	38.3	72.7	4,151.5	18,276.1	460.5	7.0	23,008.7
2018	1.3	0.3	1.1	41.3	78.2	4,468.0	19,669.2	495.6	7.5	24,762.6
2019	1.4	0.4	1.2	43.7	82.9	4,732.7	20,834.4	525.0	7.9	26,229.5

INDUSTRY: SUPERMARKETS & GROCERY STORES (NAICS 44511)
PRODUCT LINE: PRODUCE, FRESH & PREPACKAGED (Sub Category)

NAICS 44511: Grocery Stores Industry. This industry comprises establishments generally known as supermarkets and grocery stores primarily engaged in retailing a general line of food, such as canned and frozen foods; fresh fruits and vegetables; and fresh and prepared meats, fish, and poultry. Included in this industry are delicatessen-type establishments primarily engaged in retailing a general line of food.

5-Year Trend — Estimated Industry Sales ($Millions)

Year	Employee Size of Establishment									Total Industry Sales
	1-4 Emps.	5-9 Emps.	10-19 Emps.	20-49 Emps.	50-99 Emps.	100-249 Emps.	250-499 Emps.	500-999 Emps.	Unknown Emps.	
2015	834.7	602.6	1,554.9	5,124.0	12,143.8	30,190.1	9,428.6	1,128.1	156.7	61,163.5
2016	829.4	598.8	1,545.0	5,091.5	12,066.8	29,998.6	9,368.8	1,121.0	155.7	60,775.4
2017	829.1	598.5	1,544.5	5,089.7	12,062.6	29,988.2	9,365.6	1,120.6	155.6	60,754.4
2018	846.2	610.9	1,576.3	5,194.6	12,311.3	30,606.5	9,558.7	1,143.0	158.8	62,006.2
2019	872.4	629.8	1,625.0	5,355.2	12,691.8	31,552.6	9,854.1	1,177.4	163.7	63,922.0

INDUSTRY: WAREHOUSE CLUBS & SUPERCENTERS (NAICS 45291)
PRODUCT LINE: PRODUCE, FRESH & PREPACKAGED (Sub Category)

NAICS 45291: Warehouse Clubs and Superstores This industry comprises establishments known as warehouse clubs, superstores or supercenters primarily engaged in retailing a general line of groceries in combination with general lines of new merchandise, such as apparel, furniture, and appliances.

5-Year Trend – Estimated Industry Sales ($Millions)

Year	Employee Size of Establishment									Total
	1-4 Emps.	5-9 Emps.	10-19 Emps.	20-49 Emps.	50-99 Emps.	100-249 Emps.	250-499 Emps.	500-999 Emps.	Unknown Emps.	Industry Sales
2015	0.8	0.2	0.7	26.3	49.9	2,851.6	12,553.6	316.3	4.8	15,804.5
2016	0.9	0.2	0.7	27.1	51.3	2,930.2	12,899.6	325.1	4.9	16,240.0
2017	0.9	0.2	0.8	27.9	53.0	3,025.9	13,320.9	335.7	5.1	16,770.5
2018	1.0	0.3	0.8	30.1	57.0	3,256.6	14,336.4	361.3	5.5	18,048.8
2019	1.0	0.3	0.9	31.8	60.4	3,449.5	15,185.6	382.7	5.8	19,118.0

INDUSTRY: SUPERMARKETS & GROCERY STORES (NAICS 44511)
PRODUCT LINE: FROZEN FOODS (Sub Category)

NAICS 44511: Grocery Stores Industry. This industry comprises establishments generally known as supermarkets and grocery stores primarily engaged in retailing a general line of food, such as canned and frozen foods; fresh fruits and vegetables; and fresh and prepared meats, fish, and poultry. Included in this industry are delicatessen-type establishments primarily engaged in retailing a general line of food.

5-Year Trend – Estimated Industry Sales ($Millions)

Year	Employee Size of Establishment									Total
	1-4 Emps.	5-9 Emps.	10-19 Emps.	20-49 Emps.	50-99 Emps.	100-249 Emps.	250-499 Emps.	500-999 Emps.	Unknown Emps.	Industry Sales
2015	472	341	880	2,899	6,870	17,078	5,334	638	89	34,599
2016	469	339	874	2,880	6,826	16,970	5,300	634	88	34,379
2017	469	339	874	2,879	6,824	16,964	5,298	634	88	34,368
2018	479	346	892	2,939	6,964	17,313	5,407	647	90	35,076
2019	493	356	919	3,029	7,180	17,849	5,574	666	93	36,159

INDUSTRY: WAREHOUSE CLUBS & SUPERCENTERS (NAICS 45291)
PRODUCT LINE: FROZEN FOODS (Sub Category)

NAICS 45291: Warehouse Clubs and Superstores This industry comprises establishments known as warehouse clubs, superstores or supercenters primarily engaged in retailing a general line of groceries in combination with general lines of new merchandise, such as apparel, furniture, and appliances.

5-YEAR TREND — ESTIMATED INDUSTRY SALES ($MILLIONS)

Year	Employee Size of Establishment									Total
	1-4 Emps.	5-9 Emps.	10-19 Emps.	20-49 Emps.	50-99 Emps.	100-249 Emps.	250-499 Emps.	500-999 Emps.	Unknown Emps.	Industry Sales
2016	0.9	0.2	0.8	29.2	55.3	3,159.8	13,910.2	350.5	5.3	17,512.3
2017	1.0	0.3	0.8	30.0	56.9	3,246.9	14,293.6	360.2	5.4	17,995.0
2018	1.0	0.3	0.8	31.0	58.7	3,352.9	14,760.4	372.0	5.6	18,582.7
2019	1.1	0.3	0.9	33.3	63.2	3,608.5	15,885.6	400.3	6.1	19,999.2
2019	1.1	0.3	1.0	35.3	66.9	3,822.3	16,826.6	424.0	6.4	21,183.9

INDUSTRY: SUPERMARKETS & GROCERY STORES (NAICS 44511)
PRODUCT LINE: DAIRY PRODUCTS (Sub Category)

NAICS 44511: Grocery Stores Industry. This industry comprises establishments generally known as supermarkets and grocery stores primarily engaged in retailing a general line of food, such as canned and frozen foods; fresh fruits and vegetables; and fresh and prepared meats, fish, and poultry. Included in this industry are delicatessen-type establishments primarily engaged in retailing a general line of food.

5-YEAR TREND — ESTIMATED INDUSTRY SALES ($MILLIONS)

Year	Employee Size of Establishment									Total
	1-4 Emps.	5-9 Emps.	10-19 Emps.	20-49 Emps.	50-99 Emps.	100-249 Emps.	250-499 Emps.	500-999 Emps.	Unknown Emps.	Industry Sales
2015	721	521	1,343	4,426	10,490	26,078	8,144	974	135	52,833
2016	716	517	1,335	4,398	10,423	25,913	8,093	968	134	52,498
2017	716	517	1,334	4,397	10,420	25,904	8,090	968	134	52,480
2018	731	528	1,362	4,487	10,635	26,438	8,257	987	137	53,561
2019	754	544	1,404	4,626	10,963	27,255	8,512	1,017	141	55,216

INDUSTRY: GASOLINE STATIONS W/ CONVEN. STORES (NAICS 44771)
PRODUCT LINE: DAIRY PRODUCTS (Sub Category)

NAICS 44711: Gas Stations with Convenience Stores. This industry comprises establishments primarily engaged in selling gasoline and lubricating oils. These establishments frequently sell other merchandise, such as tires, batteries, and other automobile parts, or perform minor repair work. Gasoline stations combined with other activities, such as grocery stores, convenience stores, or carwashes, are classified according to the primary activity.

5-YEAR TREND — ESTIMATED INDUSTRY SALES ($MILLIONS)

Year	Employee Size of Establishment									Total Industry Sales
	1-4 Emps.	5-9 Emps.	10-19 Emps.	20-49 Emps.	50-99 Emps.	100-249 Emps.	250-499 Emps.	500-999 Emps.	Unknown Emps.	
2015	495.5	1,280.2	2,142.8	1,478.6	138.9	76.1	30.2	0.3	5.4	5,648.1
2016	516.3	1,333.8	2,232.6	1,540.6	144.8	79.3	31.4	0.3	5.7	5,884.6
2017	540.0	1,395.1	2,335.1	1,611.3	151.4	82.9	32.9	0.3	5.9	6,154.9
2018	575.4	1,486.6	2,488.4	1,717.1	161.3	88.4	35.0	0.3	6.3	6,559.0
2019	617.8	1,596.0	2,671.5	1,843.4	173.2	94.9	37.6	0.3	6.8	7,041.5

INDUSTRY: WAREHOUSE CLUBS & SUPERCENTERS (NAICS 45291)
PRODUCT LINE: DAIRY PRODUCTS (Sub Category)

NAICS 45291: Warehouse Clubs and Superstores This industry comprises establishments known as warehouse clubs, superstores or supercenters primarily engaged in retailing a general line of groceries in combination with general lines of new merchandise, such as apparel, furniture, and appliances.

5-YEAR TREND — ESTIMATED INDUSTRY SALES ($MILLIONS)

Year	Employee Size of Establishment									Total Industry Sales
	1-4 Emps.	5-9 Emps.	10-19 Emps.	20-49 Emps.	50-99 Emps.	100-249 Emps.	250-499 Emps.	500-999 Emps.	Unknown Emps.	
2015	0.7	0.2	0.6	22.7	43.0	2,454.2	10,803.8	272.2	4.1	13,601.4
2016	0.7	0.2	0.6	23.3	44.2	2,521.8	11,101.5	279.7	4.2	13,976.3
2017	0.8	0.2	0.7	24.0	45.6	2,604.2	11,464.1	288.9	4.4	14,432.8
2018	0.8	0.2	0.7	25.9	49.1	2,802.7	12,338.0	310.9	4.7	15,533.0
2019	0.9	0.2	0.8	27.4	52.0	2,968.7	13,068.9	329.3	5.0	16,453.1

INDUSTRY: SUPERMARKETS & GROCERY STORES (NAICS 44511)
PRODUCT LINE: IN-STORE BAKED GOODS (Sub Category)

NAICS 44511: Grocery Stores Industry. This industry comprises establishments generally known as supermarkets and grocery stores primarily engaged in retailing a general line of food, such as canned and frozen foods; fresh fruits and vegetables; and fresh and prepared meats, fish, and poultry. Included in this industry are delicatessen-type establishments primarily engaged in retailing a general line of food.

5-YEAR TREND – ESTIMATED INDUSTRY SALES ($MILLIONS)

Year	Employee Size of Establishment									Total
	1-4 Emps.	5-9 Emps.	10-19 Emps.	20-49 Emps.	50-99 Emps.	100-249 Emps.	250-499 Emps.	500-999 Emps.	Unknown Emps.	Industry Sales
2015	135	98	252	830	1,967	4,889	1,527	183	25	9,905
2016	134	97	250	825	1,954	4,858	1,517	182	25	9,842
2017	134	97	250	824	1,953	4,856	1,517	181	25	9,839
2018	137	99	255	841	1,994	4,956	1,548	185	26	10,041
2019	141	102	263	867	2,055	5,110	1,596	191	27	10,352

INDUSTRY: WAREHOUSE CLUBS & SUPERCENTERS (NAICS 45291)
PRODUCT LINE: IN-STORE BAKED GOODS (Sub Category)

NAICS 45291: Warehouse Clubs and Superstores This industry comprises establishments known as warehouse clubs, superstores or supercenters primarily engaged in retailing a general line of groceries in combination with general lines of new merchandise, such as apparel, furniture, and appliances.

5-YEAR TREND – ESTIMATED INDUSTRY SALES ($MILLIONS)

Year	Employee Size of Establishment									Total
	1-4 Emps.	5-9 Emps.	10-19 Emps.	20-49 Emps.	50-99 Emps.	100-249 Emps.	250-499 Emps.	500-999 Emps.	Unknown Emps.	Industry Sales
2015	0.2	0.1	0.2	6.7	12.8	730.4	3,215.3	81.0	1.2	4,047.9
2016	0.2	0.1	0.2	6.9	13.1	750.5	3,303.9	83.3	1.3	4,159.5
2017	0.2	0.1	0.2	7.2	13.6	775.0	3,411.8	86.0	1.3	4,295.3
2018	0.2	0.1	0.2	7.7	14.6	834.1	3,671.9	92.5	1.4	4,622.8
2019	0.3	0.1	0.2	8.2	15.5	883.5	3,889.4	98.0	1.5	4,896.6

	INDUSTRY: SUPERMARKETS & GROCERY STORES (NAICS 44511)
	PRODUCT LINE: BAKED GOODS-OFF PREMISES (Sub Category)

NAICS 44511: Grocery Stores Industry. This industry comprises establishments generally known as supermarkets and grocery stores primarily engaged in retailing a general line of food, such as canned and frozen foods; fresh fruits and vegetables; and fresh and prepared meats, fish, and poultry. Included in this industry are delicatessen-type establishments primarily engaged in retailing a general line of food.

5-YEAR TREND – ESTIMATED INDUSTRY SALES ($MILLIONS)

Year	Employee Size of Establishment									Total
	1-4 Emps.	5-9 Emps.	10-19 Emps.	20-49 Emps.	50-99 Emps.	100-249 Emps.	250-499 Emps.	500-999 Emps.	Unknown Emps.	Industry Sales
2015	226	163	422	1,390	3,295	8,191	2,558	306	43	16,594
2016	225	162	419	1,381	3,274	8,139	2,542	304	42	16,489
2017	225	162	419	1,381	3,273	8,136	2,541	304	42	16,483
2018	230	166	428	1,409	3,340	8,304	2,593	310	43	16,823
2019	237	171	441	1,453	3,443	8,560	2,673	319	44	17,342

	INDUSTRY: GASOLINE STATIONS W/ CONVEN. STORES (NAICS 44711)
	PRODUCT LINE: BAKED GOODS-OFF PREMISES (Sub Category)

NAICS 44711: Gas Stations with Convenience Stores. This industry comprises establishments primarily engaged in selling gasoline and lubricating oils. These establishments frequently sell other merchandise, such as tires, batteries, and other automobile parts, or perform minor repair work. Gasoline stations combined with other activities, such as grocery stores, convenience stores, or carwashes, are classified according to the primary activity.

5-YEAR TREND – ESTIMATED INDUSTRY SALES ($MILLIONS)

Year	Employee Size of Establishment									Total
	1-4 Emps.	5-9 Emps.	10-19 Emps.	20-49 Emps.	50-99 Emps.	100-249 Emps.	250-499 Emps.	500-999 Emps.	Unknown Emps.	Industry Sales
2015	178.9	462.2	773.7	533.9	50.2	27.5	10.9	0.1	2.0	2,039.2
2016	186.4	481.5	806.0	556.2	52.3	28.6	11.3	0.1	2.0	2,124.6
2017	195.0	503.7	843.1	581.8	54.7	29.9	11.9	0.1	2.1	2,222.2
2018	207.8	536.7	898.4	619.9	58.3	31.9	12.6	0.1	2.3	2,368.0
2019	223.0	576.2	964.5	665.6	62.5	34.2	13.6	0.1	2.5	2,542.2

INDUSTRY: WAREHOUSE CLUBS & SUPERCENTERS (NAICS 45291)
PRODUCT LINE: BAKED GOODS-OFF PREMISE (Sub Category)

NAICS 45291: Warehouse Clubs and Superstores This industry comprises establishments known as warehouse clubs, superstores or supercenters primarily engaged in retailing a general line of groceries in combination with general lines of new merchandise, such as apparel, furniture, and appliances.

5-Year Trend – Estimated Industry Sales ($Millions)

Year	Employee Size of Establishment									Total
	1-4 Emps.	5-9 Emps.	10-19 Emps.	20-49 Emps.	50-99 Emps.	100-249 Emps.	250-499 Emps.	500-999 Emps.	Unknown Emps.	Industry Sales
2015	0.3	0.1	0.2	8.8	16.7	951.1	4,186.8	105.5	1.6	5,270.9
2016	0.3	0.1	0.2	9.0	17.1	977.3	4,302.2	108.4	1.6	5,416.2
2017	0.3	0.1	0.3	9.3	17.7	1,009.2	4,442.7	112.0	1.7	5,593.1
2018	0.3	0.1	0.3	10.0	19.0	1,086.1	4,781.3	120.5	1.8	6,019.5
2019	0.3	0.1	0.3	10.6	20.1	1,150.4	5,064.6	127.6	1.9	6,376.0

INDUSTRY: SUPERMARKETS & GROCERY STORES (NAICS 44511)
PRODUCT LINE: DELICATESSEN FOODS (Sub Category)

NAICS 44511: Grocery Stores Industry. This industry comprises establishments generally known as supermarkets and grocery stores primarily engaged in retailing a general line of food, such as canned and frozen foods; fresh fruits and vegetables; and fresh and prepared meats, fish, and poultry. Included in this industry are delicatessen-type establishments primarily engaged in retailing a general line of food.

5-Year Trend – Estimated Industry Sales ($Millions)

Year	Employee Size of Establishment									Total
	1-4 Emps.	5-9 Emps.	10-19 Emps.	20-49 Emps.	50-99 Emps.	100-249 Emps.	250-499 Emps.	500-999 Emps.	Unknown Emps.	Industry Sales
2015	302	218	563	1,857	4,401	10,940	3,417	409	57	22,164
2016	301	217	560	1,845	4,373	10,871	3,395	406	56	22,024
2017	300	217	560	1,844	4,371	10,867	3,394	406	56	22,016
2018	307	221	571	1,882	4,461	11,091	3,464	414	58	22,470
2019	316	228	589	1,941	4,599	11,434	3,571	427	59	23,164

INDUSTRY: WAREHOUSE CLUBS & SUPERCENTERS (NAICS 45291)
PRODUCT LINE: DELICATESSEN FOODS (Sub Category)

NAICS 45291: Warehouse Clubs and Superstores This industry comprises establishments known as warehouse clubs, superstores or supercenters primarily engaged in retailing a general line of groceries in combination with general lines of new merchandise, such as apparel, furniture, and appliances.

5-YEAR TREND – ESTIMATED INDUSTRY SALES ($MILLIONS)

Year	Employee Size of Establishment									Total Industry Sales
	1-4 Emps.	5-9 Emps.	10-19 Emps.	20-49 Emps.	50-99 Emps.	100-249 Emps.	250-499 Emps.	500-999 Emps.	Unknown Emps.	
2015	0.3	0.1	0.2	9.1	17.3	987.1	4,345.3	109.5	1.7	5,470.5
2016	0.3	0.1	0.3	9.4	17.8	1,014.3	4,465.0	112.5	1.7	5,621.3
2017	0.3	0.1	0.3	9.7	18.3	1,047.4	4,610.8	116.2	1.8	5,804.8
2018	0.3	0.1	0.3	10.4	19.7	1,127.2	4,962.3	125.0	1.9	6,247.3
2019	0.4	0.1	0.3	11.0	20.9	1,194.0	5,256.3	132.5	2.0	6,617.4

INDUSTRY: SUPERMARKETS & GROCERY STORES (NAICS 44511)
PRODUCT LINE: SOFT DRINKS (Sub Category)

NAICS 44511: Grocery Stores Industry. This industry comprises establishments generally known as supermarkets and grocery stores primarily engaged in retailing a general line of food, such as canned and frozen foods; fresh fruits and vegetables; and fresh and prepared meats, fish, and poultry. Included in this industry are delicatessen-type establishments primarily engaged in retailing a general line of food.

5-YEAR TREND – ESTIMATED INDUSTRY SALES ($MILLIONS)

Year	Employee Size of Establishment									Total Industry Sales
	1-4 Emps.	5-9 Emps.	10-19 Emps.	20-49 Emps.	50-99 Emps.	100-249 Emps.	250-499 Emps.	500-999 Emps.	Unknown Emps.	
2015	241	174	449	1,478	3,504	8,711	2,720	325	45	17,647
2016	239	173	446	1,469	3,482	8,655	2,703	323	45	17,535
2017	239	173	446	1,469	3,480	8,652	2,702	323	45	17,529
2018	244	176	455	1,499	3,552	8,831	2,758	330	46	17,890
2019	252	182	469	1,545	3,662	9,104	2,843	340	47	18,443

INDUSTRY: BEER, WINE & LIQUOR STORES (NAICS 44531)
PRODUCT LINE: SOFT DRINKS (Sub Category)

NAICS 44531: Beer & Wine & Liquor Stores. Establishments primarily engaged in the retail sale of packaged alcoholic beverages, such as ale, beer, wine, and liquor, for consumption off the premises. Stores selling prepared drinks for consumption on the premises are classified in SIC 5813.

5-YEAR TREND – ESTIMATED INDUSTRY SALES ($MILLIONS)

Year	Employee Size of Establishment									Total
	1-4 Emps.	5-9 Emps.	10-19 Emps.	20-49 Emps.	50-99 Emps.	100-249 Emps.	250-499 Emps.	500-999 Emps.	Unknown Emps.	Industry Sales
2015	211.5	213.2	182.2	133.5	19.1	11.1	0.0	6.3	11.9	789.0
2016	216.4	218.1	186.4	136.6	19.6	11.4	0.0	6.5	12.2	807.1
2017	222.5	224.3	191.7	140.5	20.1	11.7	0.0	6.6	12.5	830.0
2018	235.5	237.3	202.9	148.7	21.3	12.4	0.0	7.0	13.2	878.4
2019	251.4	253.4	216.6	158.7	22.7	13.2	0.0	7.5	14.1	937.7

INDUSTRY: PHARMACIES & DRUG STORES (NAICS 44611)
PRODUCT LINE: SOFT DRINKS (Sub Category)

NAICS 44611 Pharmacies and Drug Stores – This industry comprises establishments known as pharmacies and drug stores engaged in retailing prescription or nonprescription drugs and medicines.

5-YEAR TREND – ESTIMATED INDUSTRY SALES ($MILLIONS)

Year	Employee Size of Establishment									Total
	1-4 Emps.	5-9 Emps.	10-19 Emps.	20-49 Emps.	50-99 Emps.	100-249 Emps.	250-499 Emps.	500-999 Emps.	Unknown Emps.	Industry Sales
2015	37.5	93.0	376.2	1,104.9	111.8	44.7	17.1	5.7	2.9	1,793.8
2016	38.7	95.9	388.0	1,139.6	115.3	46.1	17.6	5.9	3.0	1,850.0
2017	40.1	99.4	402.0	1,180.8	119.4	47.8	18.3	6.1	3.1	1,917.0
2018	42.5	105.2	425.8	1,250.6	126.5	50.6	19.4	6.5	3.3	2,030.4
2019	45.4	112.4	454.7	1,335.5	135.1	54.1	20.7	6.9	3.5	2,168.2

INDUSTRY: GAS STATIONS W/ CONVEN. STORES (NAICS 44711)
PRODUCT LINE: SOFT DRINKS (Sub Category)

NAICS 44711: Gas Stations with Convenience Stores. This industry comprises establishments primarily engaged in selling gasoline and lubricating oils. These establishments frequently sell other merchandise, such as tires, batteries, and other automobile parts, or perform minor repair work. Gasoline stations combined with other activities, such as grocery stores, convenience stores, or carwashes, are classified according to the primary activity.

5-YEAR TREND — ESTIMATED INDUSTRY SALES ($MILLIONS)

Year	Employee Size of Establishment									Total
	1-4 Emps.	5-9 Emps.	10-19 Emps.	20-49 Emps.	50-99 Emps.	100-249 Emps.	250-499 Emps.	500-999 Emps.	Unknown Emps.	Industry Sales
2015	1,339.7	3,461.0	5,793.2	3,997.6	375.6	205.7	81.6	0.7	14.7	15,269.8
2016	1,395.8	3,605.9	6,035.8	4,164.9	391.4	214.3	85.0	0.7	15.3	15,909.1
2017	1,459.9	3,771.6	6,313.1	4,356.3	409.3	224.2	88.9	0.8	16.1	16,640.0
2018	1,555.7	4,019.1	6,727.5	4,642.3	436.2	238.9	94.7	0.8	17.1	17,732.3
2019	1,670.2	4,314.8	7,222.4	4,983.8	468.3	256.4	101.7	0.8	18.4	19,036.8

INDUSTRY: WAREHOUSE CLUBS & SUPERCENTERS (NAICS 45291)
PRODUCT LINE: SOFT DRINKS (Sub Category)

NAICS 45291: Warehouse Clubs and Superstores This industry comprises establishments known as warehouse clubs, superstores or supercenters primarily engaged in retailing a general line of groceries in combination with general lines of new merchandise, such as apparel, furniture, and appliances.

5-YEAR TREND — ESTIMATED INDUSTRY SALES ($MILLIONS)

Year	Employee Size of Establishment									Total
	1-4 Emps.	5-9 Emps.	10-19 Emps.	20-49 Emps.	50-99 Emps.	100-249 Emps.	250-499 Emps.	500-999 Emps.	Unknown Emps.	Industry Sales
2015	0.7	0.2	0.6	20.5	38.8	2,215.3	9,752.4	245.8	3.7	12,277.9
2016	0.7	0.2	0.6	21.0	39.9	2,276.4	10,021.2	252.5	3.8	12,616.3
2017	0.7	0.2	0.6	21.7	41.2	2,350.7	10,348.5	260.8	3.9	13,028.3
2018	0.7	0.2	0.6	23.4	44.3	2,529.9	11,137.4	280.6	4.2	14,021.4
2019	0.8	0.2	0.7	24.7	46.9	2,679.8	11,797.1	297.3	4.5	14,852.0

INDUSTRY: SUPERMARKETS & GROCERY STORES (NAICS 44511)
PRODUCT LINE: CANDY (Sub Category)

NAICS 44511: Grocery Stores Industry. This industry comprises establishments generally known as supermarkets and grocery stores primarily engaged in retailing a general line of food, such as canned and frozen foods; fresh fruits and vegetables; and fresh and prepared meats, fish, and poultry. Included in this industry are delicatessen-type establishments primarily engaged in retailing a general line of food.

5-Year Trend — Estimated Industry Sales ($Millions)

Year	Employee Size of Establishment									Total
	1-4 Emps.	5-9 Emps.	10-19 Emps.	20-49 Emps.	50-99 Emps.	100-249 Emps.	250-499 Emps.	500-999 Emps.	Unknown Emps.	Industry Sales
2015	79.9	57.7	148.8	490.4	1,162.1	2,889.1	902.3	108.0	15.0	5,853.2
2016	79.4	57.3	147.9	487.2	1,154.8	2,870.8	896.6	107.3	14.9	5,816.0
2017	79.3	57.3	147.8	487.1	1,154.4	2,869.8	896.3	107.2	14.9	5,814.0
2018	81.0	58.5	150.8	497.1	1,178.2	2,929.0	914.7	109.4	15.2	5,933.8
2019	83.5	60.3	155.5	512.5	1,214.6	3,019.5	943.0	112.7	15.7	6,117.2

INDUSTRY: GAS STATIONS W/ CONVEN. STORES (NAICS 44711)
PRODUCT LINE: CANDY (Sub Category)

NAICS 44711: Gas Stations with Convenience Stores. This industry comprises establishments primarily engaged in selling gasoline and lubricating oils. These establishments frequently sell other merchandise, such as tires, batteries, and other automobile parts, or perform minor repair work. Gasoline stations combined with other activities, such as grocery stores, convenience stores, or carwashes, are classified according to the primary activity.

5-Year Trend — Estimated Industry Sales ($Millions)

Year	Employee Size of Establishment									Total
	1-4 Emps.	5-9 Emps.	10-19 Emps.	20-49 Emps.	50-99 Emps.	100-249 Emps.	250-499 Emps.	500-999 Emps.	Unknown Emps.	Industry Sales
2015	542.7	1,402.1	2,347.0	1,619.5	152.2	83.3	33.0	0.3	6.0	6,186.2
2016	565.5	1,460.9	2,445.3	1,687.3	158.5	86.8	34.4	0.3	6.2	6,445.2
2017	591.4	1,528.0	2,557.6	1,764.9	165.8	90.8	36.0	0.3	6.5	6,741.4
2018	630.3	1,628.3	2,725.5	1,880.7	176.7	96.8	38.4	0.3	6.9	7,183.9
2019	676.6	1,748.1	2,926.0	2,019.1	189.7	103.9	41.2	0.3	7.4	7,712.4

INDUSTRY: WAREHOUSE CLUBS & GROCERY STORES (NAICS 45291)
PRODUCT LINE: CANDY (Sub Category)

NAICS 45291: Warehouse Clubs and Superstores This industry comprises establishments known as warehouse clubs, superstores or supercenters primarily engaged in retailing a general line of groceries in combination with general lines of new merchandise, such as apparel, furniture, and appliances.

5-Year Trend – Estimated Industry Sales ($Millions)

Year	Employee Size of Establishment									Total
	1-4 Emps.	5-9 Emps.	10-19 Emps.	20-49 Emps.	50-99 Emps.	100-249 Emps.	250-499 Emps.	500-999 Emps.	Unknown Emps.	Industry Sales
2015	0.6	0.2	0.6	20.1	38.1	2,172.8	9,565.0	241.0	3.6	12,041.9
2016	0.7	0.2	0.6	20.6	39.1	2,232.6	9,828.6	247.7	3.7	12,373.8
2017	0.7	0.2	0.6	21.3	40.4	2,305.6	10,149.6	255.8	3.9	12,777.9
2018	0.7	0.2	0.6	22.9	43.5	2,481.3	10,923.3	275.3	4.2	13,752.0
2019	0.8	0.2	0.7	24.3	46.0	2,628.3	11,570.4	291.6	4.4	14,566.6

INDUSTRY: SUPERMARKETS & GROCERY STORES (NAICS 44511)
PRODUCT LINE: ALL OTHER FOODS (Sub Category)

NAICS 44511: Grocery Stores Industry. This industry comprises establishments generally known as supermarkets and grocery stores primarily engaged in retailing a general line of food, such as canned and frozen foods; fresh fruits and vegetables; and fresh and prepared meats, fish, and poultry. Included in this industry are delicatessen-type establishments primarily engaged in retailing a general line of food.

5-Year Trend – Estimated Industry Sales ($Millions)

Year	Employee Size of Establishment									Total
	1-4 Emps.	5-9 Emps.	10-19 Emps.	20-49 Emps.	50-99 Emps.	100-249 Emps.	250-499 Emps.	500-999 Emps.	Unknown Emps.	Industry Sales
2015	1,988	1,435	3,704	12,207	28,930	71,921	22,462	2,687	373	145,708
2016	1,976	1,426	3,681	12,129	28,746	71,465	22,319	2,670	371	144,784
2017	1,975	1,426	3,679	12,125	28,736	71,440	22,311	2,670	371	144,733
2018	2,016	1,455	3,755	12,375	29,329	72,913	22,771	2,723	378	147,716
2019	2,078	1,500	3,871	12,758	30,235	75,167	23,475	2,805	390	152,280

INDUSTRY: BEER, WINE & LIQUOR STORES (NAICS 44531)
PRODUCT LINE: ALL OTHER FOODS (Sub Category)

NAICS 44531: Beer & Wine & Liquor Stores. Establishments primarily engaged in the retail sale of packaged alcoholic beverages, such as ale, beer, wine, and liquor, for consumption off the premises. Stores selling prepared drinks for consumption on the premises are classified in SIC 5813.

5-Year Trend — Estimated Industry Sales ($Millions)

Year	Employee Size of Establishment									Total
	1-4 Emps.	5-9 Emps.	10-19 Emps.	20-49 Emps.	50-99 Emps.	100-249 Emps.	250-499 Emps.	500-999 Emps.	Unknown Emps.	Industry Sales
2015	131.6	132.6	113.4	83.1	11.9	6.9	0.0	3.9	7.4	490.8
2016	134.6	135.7	116.0	85.0	12.2	7.1	0.0	4.0	7.6	502.0
2017	138.4	139.5	119.2	87.4	12.5	7.3	0.0	4.1	7.8	516.3
2018	146.5	147.6	126.2	92.5	13.2	7.7	0.0	4.4	8.2	546.4
2019	156.4	157.6	134.7	98.7	14.1	8.2	0.0	4.7	8.8	583.3

INDUSTRY: WAREHOUSE CLUBS & SUPERCENTERS (NAICS 45291)
PRODUCT LINE: ALL OTHER FOODS (Sub Category)

NAICS 45291: Warehouse Clubs and Superstores This industry comprises establishments known as warehouse clubs, superstores or supercenters primarily engaged in retailing a general line of groceries in combination with general lines of new merchandise, such as apparel, furniture, and appliances.

5-Year Trend — Estimated Industry Sales ($Millions)

Year	Employee Size of Establishment									Total
	1-4 Emps.	5-9 Emps.	10-19 Emps.	20-49 Emps.	50-99 Emps.	100-249 Emps.	250-499 Emps.	500-999 Emps.	Unknown Emps.	Industry Sales
2015	3	1	3	100	190	10,871	47,856	1,206	18	60,249
2016	3	1	3	103	196	11,171	49,175	1,239	19	61,909
2017	3	1	3	106	202	11,535	50,781	1,280	19	63,931
2018	4	1	3	115	217	12,415	54,652	1,377	21	68,805
2019	4	1	3	121	230	13,150	57,890	1,459	22	72,881

INDUSTRY: GAS STATIONS W/ CONVEN. STORES (NAICS 44711)

PRODUCT LINE: ALL OTHER FOODS (Sub Category)

NAICS 44711: Gas Stations with Convenience Stores. This industry comprises establishments primarily engaged in selling gasoline and lubricating oils. These establishments frequently sell other merchandise, such as tires, batteries, and other automobile parts, or perform minor repair work. Gasoline stations combined with other activities, such as grocery stores, convenience stores, or carwashes, are classified according to the primary activity.

5-Year Trend – Estimated Industry Sales ($Millions)

Year	Employee Size of Establishment									Total
	1-4 Emps.	5-9 Emps.	10-19 Emps.	20-49 Emps.	50-99 Emps.	100-249 Emps.	250-499 Emps.	500-999 Emps.	Unknown Emps.	Industry Sales
2015	1,759.6	4,545.9	7,609.2	5,250.6	493.4	270.2	107.1	0.9	19.3	20,056.2
2016	1,833.3	4,736.2	7,927.7	5,470.5	514.0	281.5	111.6	0.9	20.2	20,895.9
2017	1,917.5	4,953.8	8,292.0	5,721.8	537.6	294.4	116.7	1.0	21.1	21,855.9
2018	2,043.4	5,279.0	8,836.3	6,097.4	572.9	313.8	124.4	1.0	22.5	23,290.6
2019	2,193.7	5,667.3	9,486.3	6,546.0	615.1	336.8	133.6	1.1	24.1	25,004.0

INDUSTRY: PHARMACIES & DRUG STORES (NAICS 44611)

PRODUCT LINE: ALL OTHER FOODS (Sub Category)

NAICS 44611 Pharmacies and Drug Stores – This industry comprises establishments known as pharmacies and drug stores engaged in retailing prescription or nonprescription drugs and medicines.

5-Year Trend – Estimated Industry Sales ($Millions)

Year	Employee Size of Establishment									Total
	1-4 Emps.	5-9 Emps.	10-19 Emps.	20-49 Emps.	50-99 Emps.	100-249 Emps.	250-499 Emps.	500-999 Emps.	Unknown Emps.	Industry Sales
2015	87.8	217.4	879.5	2,583.2	261.3	104.6	40.0	13.3	6.7	4,193.7
2016	90.5	224.2	907.1	2,664.1	269.5	107.9	41.2	13.8	6.9	4,325.1
2017	93.8	232.3	939.9	2,760.5	279.2	111.8	42.7	14.3	7.2	4,481.7
2018	99.3	246.0	995.5	2,923.8	295.7	118.4	45.3	15.1	7.6	4,746.7
2019	106.1	262.7	1,063.0	3,122.2	315.8	126.4	48.3	16.1	8.1	5,068.8

INDUSTRY: ELECTRONIC SHOPPING & MAIL-ORDER (NAICS 45411)
PRODUCT LINE: ALL OTHER FOODS (Sub Category)

NAICS 45411: Electronic Shopping and Mail-Order Houses This industry comprises establishments primarily engaged in retailing all types of merchandise by means of mail or by electronic media, such as interactive television or computer. Included in this industry are establishments primarily engaged in retailing from catalogue showrooms of mail-order houses.

5-Year Trend — Estimated Industry Sales ($Millions)

Year	Employee Size of Establishment									Total
	1-4 Emps.	5-9 Emps.	10-19 Emps.	20-49 Emps.	50-99 Emps.	100-249 Emps.	250-499 Emps.	500-999 Emps.	Unknown Emps.	Industry Sales
2015	363.1	187.0	270.2	453.6	341.4	631.7	851.6	1,202.2	51.0	4,352.0
2016	384.1	197.8	285.8	479.8	361.2	668.2	900.8	1,271.6	54.0	4,603.2
2017	407.2	209.8	303.1	508.7	382.9	708.4	955.1	1,348.2	57.2	4,880.5
2018	456.3	235.1	339.6	570.1	429.1	793.9	1,070.3	1,483.5	64.1	5,442.2
2019	507.4	261.4	377.6	633.8	477.1	882.7	1,190.0	1,624.6	71.3	6,025.9

INDUSTRY: SUPERMARKETS & GROCERY STORES (NAICS 44511)
PRODUCT LINE: BEER, WINE & LIQUOR (Main Category)

NAICS 44511: Grocery Stores Industry. This industry comprises establishments generally known as supermarkets and grocery stores primarily engaged in retailing a general line of food, such as canned and frozen foods; fresh fruits and vegetables; and fresh and prepared meats, fish, and poultry. Included in this industry are delicatessen-type establishments primarily engaged in retailing a general line of food.

5-Year Trend — Estimated Industry Sales ($Millions)

Year	Employee Size of Establishment									Total
	1-4 Emps.	5-9 Emps.	10-19 Emps.	20-49 Emps.	50-99 Emps.	100-249 Emps.	250-499 Emps.	500-999 Emps.	Unknown Emps.	Industry Sales
2015	284	205	529	1,744	4,133	10,274	3,209	384	53	20,815
2016	282	204	526	1,733	4,106	10,209	3,188	381	53	20,683
2017	282	204	526	1,732	4,105	10,205	3,187	381	53	20,675
2018	288	208	536	1,768	4,190	10,416	3,253	389	54	21,101
2019	297	214	553	1,822	4,319	10,738	3,353	401	56	21,753

INDUSTRY: BEER, WINE & LIQUOR STORES (NAICS 44531)
PRODUCT LINE: BEER, WINE & LIQUOR (Main Category)

NAICS 44531: Beer & Wine & Liquor Stores. Establishments primarily engaged in the retail sale of packaged alcoholic beverages, such as ale, beer, wine, and liquor, for consumption off the premises. Stores selling prepared drinks for consumption on the premises are classified in SIC 5813.

5-YEAR TREND – ESTIMATED INDUSTRY SALES ($MILLIONS)

Year	Employee Size of Establishment									Total Industry Sales
	1-4 Emps.	5-9 Emps.	10-19 Emps.	20-49 Emps.	50-99 Emps.	100-249 Emps.	250-499 Emps.	500-999 Emps.	Unknown Emps.	
2015	10,161	10,240	8,753	6,415	918	534	2	303	571	37,897
2016	10,395	10,476	8,954	6,562	940	546	2	310	584	38,769
2017	10,689	10,773	9,208	6,748	966	562	2	319	601	39,867
2018	11,312	11,401	9,745	7,142	1,023	594	2	337	636	42,191
2019	12,077	12,171	10,404	7,624	1,092	635	2	360	679	45,043

INDUSTRY: PHARMACIES & DRUG STORES (NAICS 44611)
PRODUCT LINE: BEER, WINE & LIQUOR (Main Category)

NAICS 44611 Pharmacies and Drug Stores – This industry comprises establishments known as pharmacies and drug stores engaged in retailing prescription or nonprescription drugs and medicines.

5-YEAR TREND – ESTIMATED INDUSTRY SALES ($MILLIONS)

Year	Employee Size of Establishment									Total Industry Sales
	1-4 Emps.	5-9 Emps.	10-19 Emps.	20-49 Emps.	50-99 Emps.	100-249 Emps.	250-499 Emps.	500-999 Emps.	Unknown Emps.	
2015	42.9	106.4	430.3	1,263.9	127.8	51.2	19.6	6.5	3.3	2,052.0
2016	44.3	109.7	443.8	1,303.5	131.8	52.8	20.2	6.7	3.4	2,116.3
2017	45.9	113.7	459.9	1,350.7	136.6	54.7	20.9	7.0	3.5	2,192.9
2018	48.6	120.4	487.1	1,430.6	144.7	57.9	22.1	7.4	3.7	2,322.6
2019	51.9	128.6	520.1	1,527.7	154.5	61.9	23.6	7.9	4.0	2,480.2

INDUSTRY: GASOLINE STATIONS W/ CONVEN. STORES (NAICS 44711)
PRODUCT LINE: BEER, WINE & LIQUOR (Main Category)

NAICS 44711: Gas Stations with Convenience Stores. This industry comprises establishments primarily engaged in selling gasoline and lubricating oils. These establishments frequently sell other merchandise, such as tires, batteries, and other automobile parts, or perform minor repair work. Gasoline stations combined with other activities, such as grocery stores, convenience stores, or carwashes, are classified according to the primary activity.

5-YEAR TREND – ESTIMATED INDUSTRY SALES ($MILLIONS)

Year	Employee Size of Establishment									Total
	1-4 Emps.	5-9 Emps.	10-19 Emps.	20-49 Emps.	50-99 Emps.	100-249 Emps.	250-499 Emps.	500-999 Emps.	Unknown Emps.	Industry Sales
2015	1,380.4	3,566.3	5,969.6	4,119.2	387.1	212.0	84.0	0.7	15.2	15,734.5
2016	1,438.2	3,715.6	6,219.5	4,291.7	403.3	220.8	87.6	0.7	15.8	16,393.3
2017	1,504.3	3,886.3	6,505.2	4,488.9	421.8	231.0	91.6	0.8	16.5	17,146.4
2018	1,603.1	4,141.5	6,932.3	4,783.5	449.5	246.1	97.6	0.8	17.6	18,272.0
2019	1,721.0	4,446.1	7,442.2	5,135.5	482.5	264.3	104.8	0.9	18.9	19,616.2

INDUSTRY: WAREHOUSE CLUBS & SUPERCENTERS (NAICS 45291)
PRODUCT LINE: BEER, WINE & LIQUOR (Main Category)

NAICS 45291: Warehouse Clubs and Superstores This industry comprises establishments known as warehouse clubs, superstores or supercenters primarily engaged in retailing a general line of groceries in combination with general lines of new merchandise, such as apparel, furniture, and appliances.

Year	Employee Size of Establishment									Total
	1-4 Emps.	5-9 Emps.	10-19 Emps.	20-49 Emps.	50-99 Emps.	100-249 Emps.	250-499 Emps.	500-999 Emps.	Unknown Emps.	Industry Sales
2015	0.4	0.1	0.3	12.7	24.0	1,373.0	6,044.1	152.3	2.3	7,609.2
2016	0.4	0.1	0.4	13.0	24.7	1,410.8	6,210.6	156.5	2.4	7,818.9
2017	0.4	0.1	0.4	13.5	25.5	1,456.9	6,413.5	161.6	2.4	8,074.3
2018	0.5	0.1	0.4	14.5	27.5	1,567.9	6,902.4	173.9	2.6	8,689.8
2019	0.5	0.1	0.4	15.3	29.1	1,660.8	7,311.3	184.2	2.8	9,204.5

INDUSTRY: ELECTRONIC SHOPPING & MAIL ORDER (NAICS 45411)
PRODUCT LINE: BEER, WINE & LIQUOR (Main Category)

NAICS 45411: Electronic Shopping and Mail-Order Houses This industry comprises establishments primarily engaged in retailing all types of merchandise by means of mail or by electronic media, such as interactive television or computer. Included in this industry are establishments primarily engaged in retailing from catalogue showrooms of mail-order houses.

5-YEAR TREND – ESTIMATED INDUSTRY SALES ($MILLIONS)

Year	Employee Size of Establishment									Total
	1-4 Emps.	5-9 Emps.	10-19 Emps.	20-49 Emps.	50-99 Emps.	100-249 Emps.	250-499 Emps.	500-999 Emps.	Unknown Emps.	Industry Sales
2015	60.4	31.1	45.0	75.5	56.8	105.1	141.7	200.0	8.5	724.1
2016	63.9	32.9	47.6	79.8	60.1	111.2	149.9	211.6	9.0	765.9
2017	67.7	34.9	50.4	84.6	63.7	117.9	158.9	224.3	9.5	812.0
2018	75.9	39.1	56.5	94.9	71.4	132.1	178.1	246.8	10.7	905.5
2019	84.4	43.5	62.8	105.5	79.4	146.9	198.0	270.3	11.9	1,002.6

INDUSTRY: SUPERMARKETS & GROCERY STORES (NAICS 44511)
PRODUCT LINE: LIQUOR, BRANDIES & LIQUEURS (Sub Category)

NAICS 44511: Grocery Stores Industry. This industry comprises establishments generally known as supermarkets and grocery stores primarily engaged in retailing a general line of food, such as canned and frozen foods; fresh fruits and vegetables; and fresh and prepared meats, fish, and poultry. Included in this industry are delicatessen-type establishments primarily engaged in retailing a general line of food.

5-YEAR TREND – ESTIMATED INDUSTRY SALES ($MILLIONS)

Year	Employee Size of Establishment									Total
	1-4 Emps.	5-9 Emps.	10-19 Emps.	20-49 Emps.	50-99 Emps.	100-249 Emps.	250-499 Emps.	500-999 Emps.	Unknown Emps.	Industry Sales
2015	55.4	40.0	103.2	340.2	806.2	2,004.3	626.0	74.9	10.4	4,060.6
2016	55.1	39.8	102.6	338.0	801.1	1,991.6	622.0	74.4	10.3	4,034.8
2017	55.0	39.7	102.5	337.9	800.8	1,990.9	621.8	74.4	10.3	4,033.4
2018	56.2	40.6	104.6	344.9	817.3	2,031.9	634.6	75.9	10.5	4,116.5
2019	57.9	41.8	107.9	355.5	842.6	2,094.7	654.2	78.2	10.9	4,243.7

<table>
<tr><td colspan="2">INDUSTRY: BEER, WINE & LIQUOR STORES (NAICS 44531)</td></tr>
<tr><td colspan="2">PRODUCT LINE: LIQUOR, BRANDIES & LIQUEURS (Sub Category)</td></tr>
</table>

NAICS 44531: Beer & Wine & Liquor Stores. Establishments primarily engaged in the retail sale of packaged alcoholic beverages, such as ale, beer, wine, and liquor, for consumption off the premises. Stores selling prepared drinks for consumption on the premises are classified in SIC 5813.

5-YEAR TREND — ESTIMATED INDUSTRY SALES ($MILLIONS)

Year	1-4 Emps.	5-9 Emps.	10-19 Emps.	20-49 Emps.	50-99 Emps.	100-249 Emps.	250-499 Emps.	500-999 Emps.	Unknown Emps.	Total Industry Sales
2015	4,298.8	4,332.5	3,703.3	2,713.9	388.6	225.9	0.7	128.2	241.6	16,033.4
2016	4,397.6	4,432.1	3,788.4	2,776.3	397.5	231.1	0.7	131.1	247.1	16,402.0
2017	4,522.2	4,557.6	3,895.7	2,855.0	408.8	237.6	0.7	134.8	254.2	16,866.7
2018	4,785.9	4,823.3	4,122.8	3,021.4	432.6	251.5	0.8	142.6	269.0	17,849.9
2019	5,109.4	5,149.4	4,401.5	3,225.7	461.8	268.5	0.8	152.2	287.1	19,056.4

<table>
<tr><td colspan="2">INDUSTRY: GASOLINE STATIONS W/ CONVEN. STORES (NAICS 44711)</td></tr>
<tr><td colspan="2">PRODUCT LINE: LIQUOR, BRANDIES & LIQUEURS (Sub Category)</td></tr>
</table>

NAICS 44711: Gas Stations with Convenience Stores. This industry comprises establishments primarily engaged in selling gasoline and lubricating oils. These establishments frequently sell other merchandise, such as tires, batteries, and other automobile parts, or perform minor repair work. Gasoline stations combined with other activities, such as grocery stores, convenience stores, or carwashes, are classified according to the primary activity.

5-YEAR TREND — ESTIMATED INDUSTRY SALES ($MILLIONS)

Year	1-4 Emps.	5-9 Emps.	10-19 Emps.	20-49 Emps.	50-99 Emps.	100-249 Emps.	250-499 Emps.	500-999 Emps.	Unknown Emps.	Total Industry Sales
2015	46.3	119.6	200.2	138.2	13.0	7.1	2.8	0.0	0.5	527.7
2016	48.2	124.6	208.6	143.9	13.5	7.4	2.9	0.0	0.5	549.8
2017	50.5	130.3	218.2	150.6	14.1	7.7	3.1	0.0	0.6	575.1
2018	53.8	138.9	232.5	160.4	15.1	8.3	3.3	0.0	0.6	612.8
2019	57.7	149.1	249.6	172.2	16.2	8.9	3.5	0.0	0.6	657.9

INDUSTRY: WAREHOUSE CLUBS & SUPERCENTERS (NAICS 45291)
PRODUCT LINE: LIQUOR, BRANDIES & LIQUEURS (Sub Category)

NAICS 45291: Warehouse Clubs and Superstores This industry comprises establishments known as warehouse clubs, superstores or supercenters primarily engaged in retailing a general line of groceries in combination with general lines of new merchandise, such as apparel, furniture, and appliances.

5-YEAR TREND – ESTIMATED INDUSTRY SALES ($MILLIONS)

Year	Employee Size of Establishment									Total
	1-4 Emps.	5-9 Emps.	10-19 Emps.	20-49 Emps.	50-99 Emps.	100-249 Emps.	250-499 Emps.	500-999 Emps.	Unknown Emps.	Industry Sales
2015	0.0	0.0	0.0	1.3	2.5	142.1	625.5	15.8	0.2	787.4
2016	0.0	0.0	0.0	1.3	2.6	146.0	642.7	16.2	0.2	809.1
2017	0.0	0.0	0.0	1.4	2.6	150.8	663.7	16.7	0.3	835.5
2018	0.0	0.0	0.0	1.5	2.8	162.3	714.3	18.0	0.3	899.2
2019	0.1	0.0	0.0	1.6	3.0	171.9	756.6	19.1	0.3	952.5

INDUSTRY: SUPERMARKETS & GROCERY STORES (NAICS 44511)
PRODUCT LINE: WINE PRODUCTS (Sub Category)

NAICS 44511: Grocery Stores Industry. This industry comprises establishments generally known as supermarkets and grocery stores primarily engaged in retailing a general line of food, such as canned and frozen foods; fresh fruits and vegetables; and fresh and prepared meats, fish, and poultry. Included in this industry are delicatessen-type establishments primarily engaged in retailing a general line of food.

5-YEAR TREND – ESTIMATED INDUSTRY SALES ($MILLIONS)

Year	Employee Size of Establishment									Total
	1-4 Emps.	5-9 Emps.	10-19 Emps.	20-49 Emps.	50-99 Emps.	100-249 Emps.	250-499 Emps.	500-999 Emps.	Unknown Emps.	Industry Sales
2015	94	68	174	575	1,363	3,387	1,058	127	18	6,862
2016	93	67	173	571	1,354	3,366	1,051	126	17	6,819
2017	93	67	173	571	1,353	3,365	1,051	126	17	6,817
2018	95	69	177	583	1,381	3,434	1,072	128	18	6,957
2019	98	71	182	601	1,424	3,540	1,106	132	18	7,172

INDUSTRY: BEER, WINE & LIQUOR STORES (NAICS 44531)
PRODUCT LINE: WINE PRODUCTS (Sub Category)

NAICS 44531: Beer & Wine & Liquor Stores. Establishments primarily engaged in the retail sale of packaged alcoholic beverages, such as ale, beer, wine, and liquor, for consumption off the premises. Stores selling prepared drinks for consumption on the premises are classified in SIC 5813.

5-YEAR TREND — ESTIMATED INDUSTRY SALES ($MILLIONS)

Year	Employee Size of Establishment									Total
	1-4 Emps.	5-9 Emps.	10-19 Emps.	20-49 Emps.	50-99 Emps.	100-249 Emps.	250-499 Emps.	500-999 Emps.	Unknown Emps.	Industry Sales
2015	2,953.5	2,976.6	2,544.3	1,864.6	267.0	155.2	0.5	88.0	166.0	11,015.8
2016	3,021.4	3,045.1	2,602.8	1,907.5	273.1	158.8	0.5	90.1	169.8	11,269.0
2017	3,107.0	3,131.3	2,676.6	1,961.5	280.8	163.3	0.5	92.6	174.6	11,588.3
2018	3,288.1	3,313.9	2,832.6	2,075.9	297.2	172.8	0.5	98.0	184.8	12,263.8
2019	3,510.4	3,537.9	3,024.1	2,216.2	317.3	184.5	0.6	104.5	197.3	13,092.7

INDUSTRY: GASOLINE STATIONS W/ CONVEN. STORES (NAICS 44711)
PRODUCT LINE: WINE PRODUCTS (Sub Category)

NAICS 44711: Gas Stations with Convenience Stores. This industry comprises establishments primarily engaged in selling gasoline and lubricating oils. These establishments frequently sell other merchandise, such as tires, batteries, and other automobile parts, or perform minor repair work. Gasoline stations combined with other activities, such as grocery stores, convenience stores, or carwashes, are classified according to the primary activity.

5-YEAR TREND — ESTIMATED INDUSTRY SALES ($MILLIONS)

Year	Employee Size of Establishment									Total
	1-4 Emps.	5-9 Emps.	10-19 Emps.	20-49 Emps.	50-99 Emps.	100-249 Emps.	250-499 Emps.	500-999 Emps.	Unknown Emps.	Industry Sales
2015	71.1	183.7	307.5	212.2	19.9	10.9	4.3	0.0	0.8	810.6
2016	74.1	191.4	320.4	221.1	20.8	11.4	4.5	0.0	0.8	844.6
2017	77.5	200.2	335.1	231.3	21.7	11.9	4.7	0.0	0.9	883.4
2018	82.6	213.4	357.1	246.4	23.2	12.7	5.0	0.0	0.9	941.4
2019	88.7	229.1	383.4	264.6	24.9	13.6	5.4	0.0	1.0	1,010.6

INDUSTRY: WAREHOUSE CLUBS & SUPERCENTERS (NAICS 45291)
PRODUCT LINE: WINE PRODUCTS (Sub Category)

NAICS 45291: Warehouse Clubs and Superstores This industry comprises establishments known as warehouse clubs, superstores or supercenters primarily engaged in retailing a general line of groceries in combination with general lines of new merchandise, such as apparel, furniture, and appliances.

5-YEAR TREND — ESTIMATED INDUSTRY SALES ($MILLIONS)

Year	Employee Size of Establishment									Total Industry Sales
	1-4 Emps.	5-9 Emps.	10-19 Emps.	20-49 Emps.	50-99 Emps.	100-249 Emps.	250-499 Emps.	500-999 Emps.	Unknown Emps.	
2015	0.2	0.0	0.2	5.5	10.5	597.7	2,631.2	66.3	1.0	3,312.6
2016	0.2	0.0	0.2	5.7	10.8	614.2	2,703.7	68.1	1.0	3,403.9
2017	0.2	0.0	0.2	5.9	11.1	634.2	2,792.0	70.4	1.1	3,515.0
2018	0.2	0.1	0.2	6.3	12.0	682.6	3,004.9	75.7	1.1	3,783.0
2019	0.2	0.1	0.2	6.7	12.7	723.0	3,182.9	80.2	1.2	4,007.1

INDUSTRY: SUPERMARKETS & GROCERY STORES (NAICS 44511)
PRODUCT LINE: BEER & ALE PRODUCTS (Sub Category)

NAICS 44511: Grocery Stores Industry. This industry comprises establishments generally known as supermarkets and grocery stores primarily engaged in retailing a general line of food, such as canned and frozen foods; fresh fruits and vegetables; and fresh and prepared meats, fish, and poultry. Included in this industry are delicatessen-type establishments primarily engaged in retailing a general line of food.

5-YEAR TREND — ESTIMATED INDUSTRY SALES ($MILLIONS)

Year	Employee Size of Establishment									Total Industry Sales
	1-4 Emps.	5-9 Emps.	10-19 Emps.	20-49 Emps.	50-99 Emps.	100-249 Emps.	250-499 Emps.	500-999 Emps.	Unknown Emps.	
2015	135	97	251	829	1,964	4,882	1,525	182	25	9,892
2016	134	97	250	823	1,951	4,851	1,515	181	25	9,829
2017	134	97	250	823	1,951	4,850	1,515	181	25	9,825
2018	137	99	255	840	1,991	4,950	1,546	185	26	10,028
2019	141	102	263	866	2,053	5,103	1,594	190	26	10,338

INDUSTRY: BEER, WINE & LIQUOR STORES (NAICS 44531)
PRODUCT LINE: BEER & ALE PRODUCTS (Sub Category)

NAICS 44531: Beer & Wine & Liquor Stores. Establishments primarily engaged in the retail sale of packaged alcoholic beverages, such as ale, beer, wine, and liquor, for consumption off the premises. Stores selling prepared drinks for consumption on the premises are classified in SIC 5813.

5-YEAR TREND – ESTIMATED INDUSTRY SALES ($MILLIONS)

Year	Employee Size of Establishment									Total
	1-4 Emps.	5-9 Emps.	10-19 Emps.	20-49 Emps.	50-99 Emps.	100-249 Emps.	250-499 Emps.	500-999 Emps.	Unknown Emps.	Industry Sales
2015	2,908.6	2,931.4	2,505.7	1,836.3	262.9	152.8	0.5	86.7	163.5	10,848.3
2016	2,975.5	2,998.8	2,563.3	1,878.5	269.0	156.3	0.5	88.7	167.2	11,097.7
2017	3,059.8	3,083.7	2,635.9	1,931.7	276.6	160.8	0.5	91.2	172.0	11,412.2
2018	3,238.1	3,263.5	2,789.5	2,044.3	292.7	170.2	0.5	96.5	182.0	12,077.4
2019	3,457.0	3,484.1	2,978.1	2,182.5	312.5	181.7	0.6	103.0	194.3	12,893.7

INDUSTRY: GASOLINE STATIONS W/ CONVEN. STORES (NAICS 44711)
PRODUCT LINE: BEER & ALE PRODUCTS (Sub Category)

NAICS 44711: Gas Stations with Convenience Stores. This industry comprises establishments primarily engaged in selling gasoline and lubricating oils. These establishments frequently sell other merchandise, such as tires, batteries, and other automobile parts, or perform minor repair work. Gasoline stations combined with other activities, such as grocery stores, convenience stores, or carwashes, are classified according to the primary activity.

5-YEAR TREND – ESTIMATED INDUSTRY SALES ($MILLIONS)

Year	Employee Size of Establishment									Total
	1-4 Emps.	5-9 Emps.	10-19 Emps.	20-49 Emps.	50-99 Emps.	100-249 Emps.	250-499 Emps.	500-999 Emps.	Unknown Emps.	Industry Sales
2015	1,263.0	3,263.0	5,461.8	3,768.9	354.1	193.9	76.9	0.7	13.9	14,396.2
2016	1,315.9	3,399.6	5,690.5	3,926.7	369.0	202.1	80.1	0.7	14.5	14,998.9
2017	1,376.4	3,555.8	5,951.9	4,107.1	385.9	211.3	83.8	0.7	15.1	15,688.0
2018	1,466.7	3,789.2	6,342.6	4,376.7	411.2	225.2	89.3	0.8	16.1	16,717.8
2019	1,574.6	4,068.0	6,809.2	4,698.6	441.5	241.8	95.9	0.8	17.3	17,947.7

INDUSTRY: WAREHOUSE CLUBS & SUPERCENTERS (NAICS 45291)
PRODUCT LINE: BEER & ALE PRODUCTS (Sub Category)

NAICS 45291: Warehouse Clubs and Superstores This industry comprises establishments known as warehouse clubs, superstores or supercenters primarily engaged in retailing a general line of groceries in combination with general lines of new merchandise, such as apparel, furniture, and appliances.

5-YEAR TREND — ESTIMATED INDUSTRY SALES ($MILLIONS)

Year	Employee Size of Establishment									Total
	1-4 Emps.	5-9 Emps.	10-19 Emps.	20-49 Emps.	50-99 Emps.	100-249 Emps.	250-499 Emps.	500-999 Emps.	Unknown Emps.	Industry Sales
2015	0	0	0	6	11	633	2,787	70	1	3,509
2016	0	0	0	6	11	651	2,864	72	1	3,606
2017	0	0	0	6	12	672	2,958	75	1	3,724
2018	0	0	0	7	13	723	3,183	80	1	4,008
2019	0	0	0	7	13	766	3,372	85	1	4,245

INDUSTRY: SUPERMARKETS & GROCERY STORES (NAICS 44511)
PRODUCT LINE: DRUGS & HEALTH/BEAUTY AIDS (Main Category)

NAICS 44511: Grocery Stores Industry. This industry comprises establishments generally known as supermarkets and grocery stores primarily engaged in retailing a general line of food, such as canned and frozen foods; fresh fruits and vegetables; and fresh and prepared meats, fish, and poultry. Included in this industry are delicatessen-type establishments primarily engaged in retailing a general line of food.

5-YEAR TREND — ESTIMATED INDUSTRY SALES ($MILLIONS)

Year	Employee Size of Establishment									Total
	1-4 Emps.	5-9 Emps.	10-19 Emps.	20-49 Emps.	50-99 Emps.	100-249 Emps.	250-499 Emps.	500-999 Emps.	Unknown Emps.	Industry Sales
2015	745	538	1,389	4,576	10,845	26,961	8,420	1,007	140	54,621
2016	741	535	1,380	4,547	10,776	26,790	8,367	1,001	139	54,275
2017	740	535	1,379	4,545	10,772	26,781	8,364	1,001	139	54,256
2018	756	546	1,408	4,639	10,994	27,333	8,536	1,021	142	55,374
2019	779	562	1,451	4,782	11,334	28,178	8,800	1,051	146	57,085

INDUSTRY: BEER, WINE & LIQUOR STORES (NAICS 44531)
PRODUCT LINE: DRUGS & HEALTH/BEAUTY AIDS (Main Category)

NAICS 44531: Beer & Wine & Liquor Stores. Establishments primarily engaged in the retail sale of packaged alcoholic beverages, such as ale, beer, wine, and liquor, for consumption off the premises. Stores selling prepared drinks for consumption on the premises are classified in SIC 5813.

5-YEAR TREND — ESTIMATED INDUSTRY SALES ($MILLIONS)

Year	Employee Size of Establishment									Total
	1-4 Emps.	5-9 Emps.	10-19 Emps.	20-49 Emps.	50-99 Emps.	100-249 Emps.	250-499 Emps.	500-999 Emps.	Unknown Emps.	Industry Sales
2015	36.7	37.0	31.6	23.2	3.3	1.9	0.0	1.1	2.1	136.9
2016	37.5	37.8	32.3	23.7	3.4	2.0	0.0	1.1	2.1	140.0
2017	38.6	38.9	33.3	24.4	3.5	2.0	0.0	1.2	2.2	144.0
2018	40.9	41.2	35.2	25.8	3.7	2.1	0.0	1.2	2.3	152.4
2019	43.6	44.0	37.6	27.5	3.9	2.3	0.0	1.3	2.5	162.7

INDUSTRY: PHARMACIES & DRUG STORES (NAICS 44611)
PRODUCT LINE: DRUGS & HEALTH/BEAUTY AIDS (Main Category)

NAICS 44611 Pharmacies and Drug Stores – This industry comprises establishments known as pharmacies and drug stores engaged in retailing prescription or nonprescription drugs and medicines.

5-YEAR TREND — ESTIMATED INDUSTRY SALES ($MILLIONS)

Year	Employee Size of Establishment									Total
	1-4 Emps.	5-9 Emps.	10-19 Emps.	20-49 Emps.	50-99 Emps.	100-249 Emps.	250-499 Emps.	500-999 Emps.	Unknown Emps.	Industry Sales
2015	3,578	8,862	35,856	105,310	10,651	4,264	1,630	544	274	170,969
2016	3,690	9,139	36,980	108,610	10,985	4,398	1,681	561	282	176,327
2017	3,824	9,470	38,318	112,542	11,383	4,557	1,742	581	293	182,710
2018	4,050	10,030	40,584	119,197	12,056	4,827	1,845	616	310	193,514
2019	4,325	10,711	43,338	127,285	12,874	5,154	1,970	657	331	206,645

INDUSTRY: GASOLINE STATIONS W/ CONVEN. STORES (NAICS 44711)
PRODUCT LINE: DRUGS & HEALTH/BEAUTY AIDS (Main Category)

NAICS 44711: Gas Stations with Convenience Stores. This industry comprises establishments primarily engaged in selling gasoline and lubricating oils. These establishments frequently sell other merchandise, such as tires, batteries, and other automobile parts, or perform minor repair work. Gasoline stations combined with other activities, such as grocery stores, convenience stores, or carwashes, are classified according to the primary activity.

5-YEAR TREND – ESTIMATED INDUSTRY SALES ($MILLIONS)

Year	Employee Size of Establishment									Total
	1-4 Emps.	5-9 Emps.	10-19 Emps.	20-49 Emps.	50-99 Emps.	100-249 Emps.	250-499 Emps.	500-999 Emps.	Unknown Emps.	Industry Sales
2015	158.6	409.6	685.7	473.1	44.5	24.3	9.7	0.1	1.7	1,807.3
2016	165.2	426.8	714.4	493.0	46.3	25.4	10.1	0.1	1.8	1,883.0
2017	172.8	446.4	747.2	515.6	48.4	26.5	10.5	0.1	1.9	1,969.5
2018	184.1	475.7	796.3	549.4	51.6	28.3	11.2	0.1	2.0	2,098.8
2019	197.7	510.7	854.8	589.9	55.4	30.4	12.0	0.1	2.2	2,253.2

INDUSTRY: WOMEN'S CLOTHING STORES (NAICS 44812)
PRODUCT LINE: DRUGS & HEALTH/BEAUTY AIDS (Main Category)

NAICS 44812: Women's Clothing Stores . This industry comprises establishments primarily engaged in retailing a general line of new women's, misses' and juniors' clothing, including maternity wear. These establishments may provide basic alterations, such as hemming, taking in or letting out seams, or lengthening or shortening sleeves.

5-YEAR TREND – ESTIMATED INDUSTRY SALES ($MILLIONS)

Year	Employee Size of Establishment									Total
	1-4 Emps.	5-9 Emps.	10-19 Emps.	20-49 Emps.	50-99 Emps.	100-249 Emps.	250-499 Emps.	500-999 Emps.	Unknown Emps.	Industry Sales
2015	57.0	127.3	271.6	191.6	67.7	62.5	25.3	24.5	12.7	840.3
2016	58.7	131.1	279.7	197.3	69.7	64.4	26.1	25.3	13.1	865.2
2017	60.7	135.6	289.3	204.1	72.1	66.6	27.0	26.1	13.6	895.1
2018	64.1	143.1	305.3	215.3	76.0	70.3	28.5	27.4	14.3	944.2
2019	68.2	152.2	324.8	229.1	80.9	74.7	30.3	28.8	15.2	1,004.3

INDUSTRY: DEPARTMENT STORES (NAICS 45211)
PRODUCT LINE: DRUGS & HEALTH/BEAUTY AIDS (Main Category)

NAICS 45211: Department Stores Industry . This industry comprises establishments known as department stores primarily engaged in retailing a wide range of the following new products with no one merchandise line predominating: apparel, furniture, appliances and home furnishings; and selected additional items, such as paint, hardware, toiletries, cosmetics, photographic equipment, jewelry, toys, and sporting goods. Merchandise lines are normally arranged in separate departments.

5-Year Trend – Estimated Industry Sales ($Millions)

Year	Employee Size of Establishment									Total
	1-4 Emps.	5-9 Emps.	10-19 Emps.	20-49 Emps.	50-99 Emps.	100-249 Emps.	250-499 Emps.	500-999 Emps.	Unknown Emps.	Industry Sales
2015		1	1	2	156	2,831	9,091	3,763	544	23	16,412
2016		1	1	2	157	2,842	9,127	3,778	547	23	16,476
2017		1	1	2	158	2,870	9,217	3,815	552	23	16,639
2018		1	1	2	158	2,871	9,218	3,816	553	23	16,643
2019		1	1	2	160	2,899	9,309	3,853	560	24	16,808

INDUSTRY: WAREHOUSE CLUBS & SUPERCENTERS (NAICS 45291)
PRODUCT LINE: DRUGS & HEALTH/BEAUTY AIDS (Main Category)

NAICS 45291: Warehouse Clubs and Superstores This industry comprises establishments known as warehouse clubs, superstores or supercenters primarily engaged in retailing a general line of groceries in combination with general lines of new merchandise, such as apparel, furniture, and appliances.

5-Year Trend – Estimated Industry Sales ($Millions)

Year	Employee Size of Establishment									Total
	1-4 Emps.	5-9 Emps.	10-19 Emps.	20-49 Emps.	50-99 Emps.	100-249 Emps.	250-499 Emps.	500-999 Emps.	Unknown Emps.	Industry Sales
2015	3	1	2	89	169	9,637	42,426	1,069	16	53,412
2016	3	1	3	91	173	9,903	43,595	1,099	17	54,884
2017	3	1	3	94	179	10,226	45,019	1,134	17	56,677
2018	3	1	3	102	193	11,006	48,451	1,221	18	60,997
2019	3	1	3	108	204	11,658	51,321	1,293	20	64,610

INDUSTRY: ELECTRONIC SHOPPING & MAIL ORDER (NAICS 45411)
PRODUCT LINE: DRUGS & HEALTH/BEAUTY AIDS (Main Category)

NAICS 45411: Electronic Shopping and Mail-Order Houses This industry comprises establishments primarily engaged in retailing all types of merchandise by means of mail or by electronic media, such as interactive television or computer. Included in this industry are establishments primarily engaged in retailing from catalogue showrooms of mail-order houses.

5-YEAR TREND – ESTIMATED INDUSTRY SALES ($MILLIONS)

Year	Employee Size of Establishment									Total
	1-4 Emps.	5-9 Emps.	10-19 Emps.	20-49 Emps.	50-99 Emps.	100-249 Emps.	250-499 Emps.	500-999 Emps.	Unknown Emps.	Industry Sales
2015	8,437	4,346	6,279	10,540	7,934	14,678	19,788	27,933	1,186	101,120
2016	8,924	4,597	6,642	11,148	8,391	15,525	20,930	29,546	1,254	106,957
2017	9,461	4,874	7,042	11,820	8,897	16,460	22,191	31,326	1,330	113,400
2018	10,603	5,462	7,892	13,246	9,971	18,447	24,870	34,470	1,490	126,451
2019	11,789	6,073	8,774	14,727	11,086	20,509	27,650	37,749	1,657	140,013

INDUSTRY: SUPERMARKETS & GROCERY STORES (NAICS 44511)
PRODUCT LINE: PRESCRIPTIONS (Sub Category)

NAICS 44511: Grocery Stores Industry. This industry comprises establishments generally known as supermarkets and grocery stores primarily engaged in retailing a general line of food, such as canned and frozen foods; fresh fruits and vegetables; and fresh and prepared meats, fish, and poultry. Included in this industry are delicatessen-type establishments primarily engaged in retailing a general line of food.

5-YEAR TREND – ESTIMATED INDUSTRY SALES ($MILLIONS)

Year	Employee Size of Establishment									Total
	1-4 Emps.	5-9 Emps.	10-19 Emps.	20-49 Emps.	50-99 Emps.	100-249 Emps.	250-499 Emps.	500-999 Emps.	Unknown Emps.	Industry Sales
2015	381	275	710	2,338	5,542	13,777	4,303	515	71	27,911
2016	378	273	705	2,323	5,506	13,689	4,275	512	71	27,734
2017	378	273	705	2,323	5,505	13,685	4,274	511	71	27,724
2018	386	279	719	2,370	5,618	13,967	4,362	522	72	28,295
2019	398	287	742	2,444	5,792	14,398	4,497	537	75	29,170

INDUSTRY: PHARMACIES & DRUG STORES (NAICS 44611)
PRODUCT LINE: PRESCRIPTIONS (Sub Category)

NAICS 44611 Pharmacies and Drug Stores – This industry comprises establishments known as pharmacies and drug stores engaged in retailing prescription or nonprescription drugs and medicines.

5-Year Trend – Estimated Industry Sales ($Millions)

Year	Employee Size of Establishment									Total
	1-4 Emps.	5-9 Emps.	10-19 Emps.	20-49 Emps.	50-99 Emps.	100-249 Emps.	250-499 Emps.	500-999 Emps.	Unknown Emps.	Industry Sales
2015	3,007	7,448	30,136	88,511	8,952	3,584	1,370	457	230	143,697
2016	3,102	7,681	31,081	91,285	9,233	3,696	1,413	471	237	148,200
2017	3,214	7,959	32,206	94,589	9,567	3,830	1,464	489	246	153,564
2018	3,404	8,430	34,110	100,183	10,133	4,057	1,551	517	261	162,646
2019	3,635	9,002	36,425	106,981	10,820	4,332	1,656	552	278	173,682

INDUSTRY: DEPARTMENT STORES (NAICS 45211)
PRODUCT LINE: PRESCRIPTIONS (Sub Category)

NAICS 45211: Department Stores Industry . This industry comprises establishments known as department stores primarily engaged in retailing a wide range of the following new products with no one merchandise line predominating: apparel, furniture, appliances and home furnishings; and selected additional items, such as paint, hardware, toiletries, cosmetics, photographic equipment, jewelry, toys, and sporting goods. Merchandise lines are normally arranged in separate departments.

5-Year Trend – Estimated Industry Sales ($Millions)

Year	Employee Size of Establishment									Total
	1-4 Emps.	5-9 Emps.	10-19 Emps.	20-49 Emps.	50-99 Emps.	100-249 Emps.	250-499 Emps.	500-999 Emps.	Unknown Emps.	Industry Sales
2015	0	0	1	45	815	2,616	1,083	157	7	4,723
2016	0	0	1	45	818	2,626	1,087	157	7	4,742
2017	0	0	1	46	826	2,652	1,098	159	7	4,788
2018	0	0	1	46	826	2,653	1,098	159	7	4,789
2019	0	0	1	46	834	2,679	1,109	161	7	4,837

INDUSTRY: WAREHOUSE CLUBS & SUPERCENTERS (NAICS 45291)
PRODUCT LINE: PRESCRIPTIONS (Sub Category)

NAICS 45291: Warehouse Clubs and Superstores This industry comprises establishments known as warehouse clubs, superstores or supercenters primarily engaged in retailing a general line of groceries in combination with general lines of new merchandise, such as apparel, furniture, and appliances.

5-YEAR TREND – ESTIMATED INDUSTRY SALES ($MILLIONS)

Year	Employee Size of Establishment									Total
	1-4 Emps.	5-9 Emps.	10-19 Emps.	20-49 Emps.	50-99 Emps.	100-249 Emps.	250-499 Emps.	500-999 Emps.	Unknown Emps.	Industry Sales
2015	0.9	0.2	0.8	27.7	52.5	3,000.2	13,207.8	332.8	5.0	16,628.0
2016	0.9	0.2	0.8	28.5	54.0	3,082.9	13,571.8	342.0	5.2	17,086.3
2017	0.9	0.2	0.8	29.4	55.8	3,183.6	14,015.1	353.2	5.3	17,644.3
2018	1.0	0.3	0.9	31.6	60.0	3,426.3	15,083.4	380.1	5.7	18,989.3
2019	1.1	0.3	0.9	33.5	63.6	3,629.3	15,976.9	402.6	6.1	20,114.2

INDUSTRY: ELECTRONIC SHOPPING & MAIL ORDER (NAICS 45411)
PRODUCT LINE: PRESCRIPTIONS (Sub Category)

NAICS 45411: Electronic Shopping and Mail-Order Houses This industry comprises establishments primarily engaged in retailing all types of merchandise by means of mail or by electronic media, such as interactive television or computer. Included in this industry are establishments primarily engaged in retailing from catalogue showrooms of mail-order houses.

5-YEAR TREND – ESTIMATED INDUSTRY SALES ($MILLIONS)

Year	Employee Size of Establishment									Total
	1-4 Emps.	5-9 Emps.	10-19 Emps.	20-49 Emps.	50-99 Emps.	100-249 Emps.	250-499 Emps.	500-999 Emps.	Unknown Emps.	Industry Sales
2015	6,534	3,366	4,863	8,163	6,144	11,367	15,325	21,633	918	78,312
2016	6,911	3,560	5,144	8,634	6,499	12,023	16,209	22,882	971	82,833
2017	7,327	3,774	5,453	9,154	6,890	12,748	17,186	24,260	1,030	87,822
2018	8,212	4,230	6,112	10,259	7,722	14,286	19,260	26,696	1,154	97,930
2019	9,130	4,703	6,795	11,406	8,585	15,883	21,414	29,234	1,283	108,433

INDUSTRY: SUPERMARKETS & GROCERY STORES (NAICS 44511)
PRODUCT LINE: NON-PRESCRIPTION MEDICINES (Sub Category)

NAICS 44511: Grocery Stores Industry. This industry comprises establishments generally known as supermarkets and grocery stores primarily engaged in retailing a general line of food, such as canned and frozen foods; fresh fruits and vegetables; and fresh and prepared meats, fish, and poultry. Included in this industry are delicatessen-type establishments primarily engaged in retailing a general line of food.

5-YEAR TREND – ESTIMATED INDUSTRY SALES ($MILLIONS)

Year	Employee Size of Establishment									Total Industry Sales
	1-4 Emps.	5-9 Emps.	10-19 Emps.	20-49 Emps.	50-99 Emps.	100-249 Emps.	250-499 Emps.	500-999 Emps.	Unknown Emps.	
2015	55.8	40.3	104.0	342.6	812.0	2,018.7	630.4	75.4	10.5	4,089.7
2016	55.5	40.0	103.3	340.4	806.8	2,005.9	626.4	75.0	10.4	4,063.8
2017	55.4	40.0	103.3	340.3	806.6	2,005.2	626.2	74.9	10.4	4,062.4
2018	56.6	40.8	105.4	347.3	823.2	2,046.5	639.1	76.4	10.6	4,146.1
2019	58.3	42.1	108.7	358.1	848.6	2,109.8	658.9	78.7	10.9	4,274.2

INDUSTRY: PHARMACIES & DRUG STORES (NAICS 44611)
PRODUCT LINE: NON-PRESCRIPTION MEDICINES (Sub Category)

NAICS 44611 Pharmacies and Drug Stores – This industry comprises establishments known as pharmacies and drug stores engaged in retailing prescription or nonprescription drugs and medicines.

5-YEAR TREND – ESTIMATED INDUSTRY SALES ($MILLIONS)

Year	Employee Size of Establishment									Total Industry Sales
	1-4 Emps.	5-9 Emps.	10-19 Emps.	20-49 Emps.	50-99 Emps.	100-249 Emps.	250-499 Emps.	500-999 Emps.	Unknown Emps.	
2015	237.1	587.2	2,375.8	6,977.7	705.7	282.6	108.0	36.0	18.1	11,328.2
2016	244.5	605.6	2,450.2	7,196.3	727.9	291.4	111.4	37.2	18.7	11,683.2
2017	253.4	627.5	2,538.9	7,456.9	754.2	302.0	115.4	38.5	19.4	12,106.1
2018	268.3	664.6	2,689.1	7,897.8	798.8	319.8	122.2	40.8	20.5	12,822.0
2019	286.6	709.7	2,871.5	8,433.7	853.0	341.5	130.5	43.5	21.9	13,692.0

INDUSTRY: DEPARTMENT STORES (NAICS 45211)
PRODUCT LINE: NON-PRESCRIPTION MEDICINES (Sub Category)

NAICS 45211: Department Stores Industry . This industry comprises establishments known as department stores primarily engaged in retailing a wide range of the following new products with no one merchandise line predominating: apparel, furniture, appliances and home furnishings; and selected additional items, such as paint, hardware, toiletries, cosmetics, photographic equipment, jewelry, toys, and sporting goods. Merchandise lines are normally arranged in separate departments.

5-YEAR TREND – ESTIMATED INDUSTRY SALES ($MILLIONS)

Year	Employee Size of Establishment									Total
	1-4 Emps.	5-9 Emps.	10-19 Emps.	20-49 Emps.	50-99 Emps.	100-249 Emps.	250-499 Emps.	500-999 Emps.	Unknown Emps.	Industry Sales
2015	0.0	0.0	0.1	7.7	140.0	449.4	186.0	26.9	1.1	811.4
2016	0.0	0.0	0.1	7.7	140.5	451.2	186.8	27.0	1.1	814.5
2017	0.0	0.0	0.1	7.8	141.9	455.6	188.6	27.3	1.2	822.6
2018	0.0	0.0	0.1	7.8	141.9	455.7	188.6	27.4	1.2	822.8
2019	0.0	0.0	0.1	7.9	143.3	460.2	190.5	27.7	1.2	830.9

INDUSTRY: WAREHOUSE CLUBS & SUPERCENTERS (NAICS 45291)
PRODUCT LINE: NON-PRESCRIPTION MEDICINES (Sub Category)

NAICS 45291: Warehouse Clubs and Superstores This industry comprises establishments known as warehouse clubs, superstores or supercenters primarily engaged in retailing a general line of groceries in combination with general lines of new merchandise, such as apparel, furniture, and appliances.

5-YEAR TREND – ESTIMATED INDUSTRY SALES ($MILLIONS)

Year	Employee Size of Establishment									Total
	1-4 Emps.	5-9 Emps.	10-19 Emps.	20-49 Emps.	50-99 Emps.	100-249 Emps.	250-499 Emps.	500-999 Emps.	Unknown Emps.	Industry Sales
2015	0.3	0.1	0.3	9.6	18.2	1,041.7	4,585.8	115.6	1.7	5,773.3
2016	0.3	0.1	0.3	9.9	18.7	1,070.4	4,712.1	118.7	1.8	5,932.4
2017	0.3	0.1	0.3	10.2	19.4	1,105.4	4,866.0	122.6	1.9	6,126.1
2018	0.3	0.1	0.3	11.0	20.8	1,189.6	5,237.0	132.0	2.0	6,593.1
2019	0.4	0.1	0.3	11.6	22.1	1,260.1	5,547.2	139.8	2.1	6,983.7

INDUSTRY: ELECTRONIC SHOPPING & MAIL ORDER (NAICS 45411)
PRODUCT LINE: NON-PRESCRIPTION MEDICINES (Sub Category)

NAICS 45411: Electronic Shopping and Mail-Order Houses This industry comprises establishments primarily engaged in retailing all types of merchandise by means of mail or by electronic media, such as interactive television or computer. Included in this industry are establishments primarily engaged in retailing from catalogue showrooms of mail-order houses.

5-YEAR TREND — ESTIMATED INDUSTRY SALES ($MILLIONS)

Year	Employee Size of Establishment									Total
	1-4 Emps.	5-9 Emps.	10-19 Emps.	20-49 Emps.	50-99 Emps.	100-249 Emps.	250-499 Emps.	500-999 Emps.	Unknown Emps.	Industry Sales
2015	160.7	82.8	119.6	200.8	151.2	279.6	377.0	532.2	22.6	1,926.6
2016	170.0	87.6	126.5	212.4	159.9	295.8	398.8	562.9	23.9	2,037.8
2017	180.3	92.9	134.2	225.2	169.5	313.6	422.8	596.8	25.3	2,160.5
2018	202.0	104.1	150.4	252.4	190.0	351.5	473.8	656.7	28.4	2,409.2
2019	224.6	115.7	167.2	280.6	211.2	390.8	526.8	719.2	31.6	2,667.6

INDUSTRY: SUPERMARKETS & GROCERY STORES (NAICS 44511)
PRODUCT LINE: VITAMINS, MINERALS & SUPPLEMENTS (Sub Category)

NAICS 44511: Grocery Stores Industry. This industry comprises establishments generally known as supermarkets and grocery stores primarily engaged in retailing a general line of food, such as canned and frozen foods; fresh fruits and vegetables; and fresh and prepared meats, fish, and poultry. Included in this industry are delicatessen-type establishments primarily engaged in retailing a general line of food.

5-YEAR TREND — ESTIMATED INDUSTRY SALES ($MILLIONS)

Year	Employee Size of Establishment									Total
	1-4 Emps.	5-9 Emps.	10-19 Emps.	20-49 Emps.	50-99 Emps.	100-249 Emps.	250-499 Emps.	500-999 Emps.	Unknown Emps.	Industry Sales
2015	44.8	32.3	83.4	275.0	651.7	1,620.1	506.0	60.5	8.4	3,282.3
2016	44.5	32.1	82.9	273.2	647.6	1,609.9	502.8	60.2	8.4	3,261.5
2017	44.5	32.1	82.9	273.1	647.3	1,609.3	502.6	60.1	8.4	3,260.3
2018	45.4	32.8	84.6	278.8	660.7	1,642.5	513.0	61.3	8.5	3,327.5
2019	46.8	33.8	87.2	287.4	681.1	1,693.2	528.8	63.2	8.8	3,430.3

INDUSTRY: PHARMACIES & DRUG STORES (NAICS 44611)
PRODUCT LINE: VITAMINS, MINERALS & SUPPLEMENTS (Sub Category)

NAICS 44611 Pharmacies and Drug Stores – This industry comprises establishments known as pharmacies and drug stores engaged in retailing prescription or nonprescription drugs and medicines.

5-YEAR TREND – ESTIMATED INDUSTRY SALES ($MILLIONS)

Year	Employee Size of Establishment									Total
	1-4 Emps.	5-9 Emps.	10-19 Emps.	20-49 Emps.	50-99 Emps.	100-249 Emps.	250-499 Emps.	500-999 Emps.	Unknown Emps.	Industry Sales
2015	45.1	111.6	451.5	1,325.9	134.1	53.7	20.5	6.8	3.4	2,152.6
2016	46.5	115.1	465.6	1,367.5	138.3	55.4	21.2	7.1	3.6	2,220.1
2017	48.1	119.2	482.5	1,417.0	143.3	57.4	21.9	7.3	3.7	2,300.5
2018	51.0	126.3	511.0	1,500.8	151.8	60.8	23.2	7.8	3.9	2,436.5
2019	54.5	134.9	545.7	1,602.6	162.1	64.9	24.8	8.3	4.2	2,601.8

INDUSTRY: DEPARTMENT STORES (NAICS 45211)
PRODUCT LINE: VITAMINS, MINERALS & SUPPLEMENTS (Sub Category)

NAICS 45211: Department Stores Industry . This industry comprises establishments known as department stores primarily engaged in retailing a wide range of the following new products with no one merchandise line predominating: apparel, furniture, appliances and home furnishings; and selected additional items, such as paint, hardware, toiletries, cosmetics, photographic equipment, jewelry, toys, and sporting goods. Merchandise lines are normally arranged in separate departments.

5-YEAR TREND – ESTIMATED INDUSTRY SALES ($MILLIONS)

Year	Employee Size of Establishment									Total
	1-4 Emps.	5-9 Emps.	10-19 Emps.	20-49 Emps.	50-99 Emps.	100-249 Emps.	250-499 Emps.	500-999 Emps.	Unknown Emps.	Industry Sales
2015	0.0	0.0	0.1	5.9	107.8	346.0	143.2	20.7	0.9	624.7
2016	0.0	0.0	0.1	6.0	108.2	347.4	143.8	20.8	0.9	627.1
2017	0.0	0.0	0.1	6.0	109.2	350.8	145.2	21.0	0.9	633.3
2018	0.0	0.0	0.1	6.0	109.3	350.8	145.2	21.1	0.9	633.5
2019	0.0	0.0	0.1	6.1	110.3	354.3	146.7	21.3	0.9	639.8

	INDUSTRY: WAREHOUSE CLUBS & SUPERCENTERS (NAICS 45291)
	PRODUCT LINE: VITAMINS, MINERALS & SUPPLEMENTS (Sub Category)

NAICS 45291: Warehouse Clubs and Superstores This industry comprises establishments known as warehouse clubs, superstores or supercenters primarily engaged in retailing a general line of groceries in combination with general lines of new merchandise, such as apparel, furniture, and appliances.

5-YEAR TREND – ESTIMATED INDUSTRY SALES ($MILLIONS)

Year	Employee Size of Establishment									Total
	1-4 Emps.	5-9 Emps.	10-19 Emps.	20-49 Emps.	50-99 Emps.	100-249 Emps.	250-499 Emps.	500-999 Emps.	Unknown Emps.	Industry Sales
2015	0.2	0.1	0.2	6.4	12.1	688.2	3,029.6	76.3	1.2	3,814.2
2016	0.2	0.1	0.2	6.5	12.4	707.2	3,113.1	78.4	1.2	3,919.3
2017	0.2	0.1	0.2	6.7	12.8	730.3	3,214.8	81.0	1.2	4,047.3
2018	0.2	0.1	0.2	7.3	13.8	785.9	3,459.8	87.2	1.3	4,355.8
2019	0.2	0.1	0.2	7.7	14.6	832.5	3,664.8	92.3	1.4	4,613.8

	INDUSTRY: ELECTRONIC SHOPPING & MAIL ORDER (NAICS 45411)
	PRODUCT LINE: VITAMINS, MINERALS & SUPPLEMENTS (Sub Category)

NAICS 45411: Electronic Shopping and Mail-Order Houses This industry comprises establishments primarily engaged in retailing all types of merchandise by means of mail or by electronic media, such as interactive television or computer. Included in this industry are establishments primarily engaged in retailing from catalogue showrooms of mail-order houses.

5-YEAR TREND – ESTIMATED INDUSTRY SALES ($MILLIONS)

Year	Employee Size of Establishment									Total
	1-4 Emps.	5-9 Emps.	10-19 Emps.	20-49 Emps.	50-99 Emps.	100-249 Emps.	250-499 Emps.	500-999 Emps.	Unknown Emps.	Industry Sales
2015	960.5	494.8	714.8	1,199.9	903.2	1,671.0	2,252.8	3,180.0	135.0	11,511.9
2016	1,015.9	523.3	756.1	1,269.1	955.3	1,767.4	2,382.8	3,363.6	142.8	12,176.4
2017	1,077.1	554.8	801.7	1,345.6	1,012.9	1,873.9	2,526.3	3,566.2	151.4	12,909.9
2018	1,207.1	621.8	898.4	1,508.0	1,135.1	2,100.1	2,831.3	3,924.2	169.7	14,395.7
2019	1,342.1	691.3	998.9	1,676.6	1,262.0	2,334.9	3,147.8	4,297.4	188.6	15,939.6

INDUSTRY: SUPERMARKETS & GROCERY STORES (NAICS 44511)
PRODUCT LINE: HEALTH AIDS/FIRST-AID PRODUCTS (Sub Category)

NAICS 44511: Grocery Stores Industry. This industry comprises establishments generally known as supermarkets and grocery stores primarily engaged in retailing a general line of food, such as canned and frozen foods; fresh fruits and vegetables; and fresh and prepared meats, fish, and poultry. Included in this industry are delicatessen-type establishments primarily engaged in retailing a general line of food.

5-YEAR TREND – ESTIMATED INDUSTRY SALES ($MILLIONS)

Year	Employee Size of Establishment									Total
	1-4 Emps.	5-9 Emps.	10-19 Emps.	20-49 Emps.	50-99 Emps.	100-249 Emps.	250-499 Emps.	500-999 Emps.	Unknown Emps.	Industry Sales
2015	42.4	30.6	78.9	260.2	616.6	1,532.9	478.7	57.3	8.0	3,105.5
2016	42.1	30.4	78.4	258.5	612.7	1,523.2	475.7	56.9	7.9	3,085.8
2017	42.1	30.4	78.4	258.4	612.5	1,522.6	475.5	56.9	7.9	3,084.7
2018	43.0	31.0	80.0	263.8	625.1	1,554.0	485.3	58.0	8.1	3,148.3
2019	44.3	32.0	82.5	271.9	644.4	1,602.1	500.3	59.8	8.3	3,245.6

INDUSTRY: PHARMACIES & DRUG STORES (NAICS 44611)
PRODUCT LINE: HEALTH AIDS/FIRST-AID PRODUCTS (Sub Category)

NAICS 44611 Pharmacies and Drug Stores – This industry comprises establishments known as pharmacies and drug stores engaged in retailing prescription or nonprescription drugs and medicines.

5-YEAR TREND – ESTIMATED INDUSTRY SALES ($MILLIONS)

Year	Employee Size of Establishment									Total
	1-4 Emps.	5-9 Emps.	10-19 Emps.	20-49 Emps.	50-99 Emps.	100-249 Emps.	250-499 Emps.	500-999 Emps.	Unknown Emps.	Industry Sales
2015	76.6	189.8	768.1	2,255.9	228.2	91.4	34.9	11.7	5.9	3,662.5
2016	79.1	195.8	792.2	2,326.6	235.3	94.2	36.0	12.0	6.1	3,777.2
2017	81.9	202.9	820.8	2,410.8	243.8	97.6	37.3	12.5	6.3	3,914.0
2018	86.8	214.9	869.4	2,553.4	258.3	103.4	39.5	13.2	6.6	4,145.4
2019	92.6	229.4	928.4	2,726.7	275.8	110.4	42.2	14.1	7.1	4,426.7

INDUSTRY: DEPARTMENT STORES (NAICS 45211)
PRODUCT LINE: HEALTH AIDS/FIRST-AID PRODUCTS (Sub Category)

NAICS 45211: Department Stores Industry . This industry comprises establishments known as department stores primarily engaged in retailing a wide range of the following new products with no one merchandise line predominating: apparel, furniture, appliances and home furnishings; and selected additional items, such as paint, hardware, toiletries, cosmetics, photographic equipment, jewelry, toys, and sporting goods. Merchandise lines are normally arranged in separate departments.

5-YEAR TREND — ESTIMATED INDUSTRY SALES ($MILLIONS)

Year	Employee Size of Establishment									Total
	1-4 Emps.	5-9 Emps.	10-19 Emps.	20-49 Emps.	50-99 Emps.	100-249 Emps.	250-499 Emps.	500-999 Emps.	Unknown Emps.	Industry Sales
2015	0.0	0.0	0.1	5.0	90.6	291.0	120.5	17.4	0.7	525.4
2016	0.0	0.0	0.1	5.0	91.0	292.2	120.9	17.5	0.7	527.5
2017	0.0	0.0	0.1	5.1	91.9	295.1	122.1	17.7	0.8	532.7
2018	0.0	0.0	0.1	5.1	91.9	295.1	122.2	17.7	0.8	532.8
2019	0.0	0.0	0.1	5.1	92.8	298.0	123.4	17.9	0.8	538.1

INDUSTRY: WAREHOUSE CLUBS & SUPERCENTERS (NAICS 45291)
PRODUCT LINE: HEALTH AIDS/FIRST-AID PRODUCTS (Sub Category)

NAICS 45291: Warehouse Clubs and Superstores This industry comprises establishments known as warehouse clubs, superstores or supercenters primarily engaged in retailing a general line of groceries in combination with general lines of new merchandise, such as apparel, furniture, and appliances.

5-YEAR TREND — ESTIMATED INDUSTRY SALES ($MILLIONS)

Year	Employee Size of Establishment									Total
	1-4 Emps.	5-9 Emps.	10-19 Emps.	20-49 Emps.	50-99 Emps.	100-249 Emps.	250-499 Emps.	500-999 Emps.	Unknown Emps.	Industry Sales
2015	0.2	0.1	0.2	7.4	13.9	796.5	3,506.6	88.4	1.3	4,414.6
2016	0.2	0.1	0.2	7.6	14.3	818.5	3,603.2	90.8	1.4	4,536.3
2017	0.2	0.1	0.2	7.8	14.8	845.2	3,720.9	93.8	1.4	4,684.4
2018	0.3	0.1	0.2	8.4	15.9	909.7	4,004.5	100.9	1.5	5,041.5
2019	0.3	0.1	0.2	8.9	16.9	963.5	4,241.7	106.9	1.6	5,340.2

INDUSTRY: ELECTRONIC SHOPPING & MAIL ORDER (NAICS 45411)
PRODUCT LINE: HEALTH AIDS/FIRST-AID PRODUCTS (Sub Category)

NAICS 45411: Electronic Shopping and Mail-Order Houses This
industry comprises establishments primarily engaged in retailing all
types of merchandise by means of mail or by electronic media, such
as interactive television or computer. Included in this industry are
establishments primarily engaged in retailing from catalogue showrooms
of mail-order houses.

5-YEAR TREND — ESTIMATED INDUSTRY SALES ($MILLIONS)

| Year | Employee Size of Establishment | | | | | | | | | Total |
	1-4 Emps.	5-9 Emps.	10-19 Emps.	20-49 Emps.	50-99 Emps.	100-249 Emps.	250-499 Emps.	500-999 Emps.	Unknown Emps.	Industry Sales
2015	337.9	174.1	251.5	422.1	317.7	587.8	792.5	1,118.7	47.5	4,049.8
2016	357.4	184.1	266.0	446.5	336.1	621.8	838.3	1,183.3	50.2	4,283.6
2017	378.9	195.2	282.0	473.4	356.3	659.2	888.7	1,254.6	53.3	4,541.6
2018	424.7	218.8	316.1	530.5	399.3	738.8	996.0	1,380.5	59.7	5,064.3
2019	472.1	243.2	351.4	589.8	444.0	821.4	1,107.4	1,511.8	66.4	5,607.5

INDUSTRY: SUPERMARKETS & GROCERY STORES (NAICS 44511)
PRODUCT LINE: COSMETICS/PERFUMES PRODUCTS (Sub Category)

NAICS 44511: Grocery Stores Industry. This industry comprises
establishments generally known as supermarkets and grocery stores
primarily engaged in retailing a general line of food, such as canned and
frozen foods; fresh fruits and vegetables; and fresh and prepared meats,
fish, and poultry. Included in this industry are delicatessen-type
establishments primarily engaged in retailing a general line of food.

5-YEAR TREND — ESTIMATED INDUSTRY SALES ($MILLIONS)

| Year | Employee Size of Establishment | | | | | | | | | Total |
	1-4 Emps.	5-9 Emps.	10-19 Emps.	20-49 Emps.	50-99 Emps.	100-249 Emps.	250-499 Emps.	500-999 Emps.	Unknown Emps.	Industry Sales
2015	37.7	27.2	70.1	231.1	547.8	1,361.8	425.3	50.9	7.1	2,759.0
2016	37.4	27.0	69.7	229.7	544.3	1,353.2	422.6	50.6	7.0	2,741.5
2017	37.4	27.0	69.7	229.6	544.1	1,352.7	422.5	50.5	7.0	2,740.5
2018	38.2	27.6	71.1	234.3	555.3	1,380.6	431.2	51.6	7.2	2,797.0
2019	39.4	28.4	73.3	241.6	572.5	1,423.3	444.5	53.1	7.4	2,883.4

INDUSTRY: PHARMACIES & DRUG STORES (NAICS 44611)
PRODUCT LINE: COSMETICS/PERFUMES PRODUCTS (Sub Category)

NAICS 44611 Pharmacies and Drug Stores – This industry comprises
establishments known as pharmacies and drug stores engaged in retailing
prescription or nonprescription drugs and medicines.

5-YEAR TREND – ESTIMATED INDUSTRY SALES ($MILLIONS)

Year	Employee Size of Establishment									Total
	1-4 Emps.	5-9 Emps.	10-19 Emps.	20-49 Emps.	50-99 Emps.	100-249 Emps.	250-499 Emps.	500-999 Emps.	Unknown Emps.	Industry Sales
2015	88.7	219.6	888.4	2,609.4	263.9	105.7	40.4	13.5	6.8	4,236.3
2016	91.4	226.5	916.3	2,691.1	272.2	109.0	41.7	13.9	7.0	4,369.0
2017	94.7	234.7	949.4	2,788.6	282.0	112.9	43.2	14.4	7.3	4,527.2
2018	100.3	248.5	1,005.6	2,953.5	298.7	119.6	45.7	15.3	7.7	4,794.9
2019	107.2	265.4	1,073.8	3,153.9	319.0	127.7	48.8	16.3	8.2	5,120.2

INDUSTRY: DEPARTMENT STORES (NAICS 45211)
PRODUCT LINE: COSMETICS/PERFUMES PRODUCTS (Sub Category)

NAICS 45211: Department Stores Industry . This industry comprises
establishments known as department stores primarily engaged in retailing
a wide range of the following new products with no one merchandise line
predominating: apparel, furniture, appliances and home furnishings; and
selected additional items, such as paint, hardware, toiletries, cosmetics,
photographic equipment, jewelry, toys, and sporting goods. Merchandise lines
are normally arranged in separate departments.

5-YEAR TREND – ESTIMATED INDUSTRY SALES ($MILLIONS)

Year	Employee Size of Establishment									Total
	1-4 Emps.	5-9 Emps.	10-19 Emps.	20-49 Emps.	50-99 Emps.	100-249 Emps.	250-499 Emps.	500-999 Emps.	Unknown Emps.	Industry Sales
2015	0	0	1	52	946	3,037	1,257	182	8	5,483
2016	0	0	1	52	950	3,049	1,262	183	8	5,504
2017	0	0	1	53	959	3,079	1,275	184	8	5,559
2018	0	0	1	53	959	3,079	1,275	185	8	5,560
2019	0	0	1	53	969	3,110	1,287	187	8	5,615

INDUSTRY: WAREHOUSE CLUBS & SUPERCENTERS (NAICS 45291)
PRODUCT LINE: COSMETICS/PERFUMES PRODUCTS (Sub Category)

NAICS 45291: Warehouse Clubs and Superstores This industry comprises establishments known as warehouse clubs, superstores or supercenters primarily engaged in retailing a general line of groceries in combination with general lines of new merchandise, such as apparel, furniture, and appliances.

5-YEAR TREND – ESTIMATED INDUSTRY SALES ($MILLIONS)

Year	Employee Size of Establishment									Total
	1-4 Emps.	5-9 Emps.	10-19 Emps.	20-49 Emps.	50-99 Emps.	100-249 Emps.	250-499 Emps.	500-999 Emps.	Unknown Emps.	Industry Sales
2015	0.3	0.1	0.2	8.1	15.4	878.9	3,869.3	97.5	1.5	4,871.3
2016	0.3	0.1	0.2	8.3	15.8	903.2	3,975.9	100.2	1.5	5,005.5
2017	0.3	0.1	0.2	8.6	16.3	932.7	4,105.8	103.5	1.6	5,169.0
2018	0.3	0.1	0.3	9.3	17.6	1,003.8	4,418.8	111.3	1.7	5,563.0
2019	0.3	0.1	0.3	9.8	18.6	1,063.2	4,680.5	117.9	1.8	5,892.6

INDUSTRY: ELECTRONIC SHOPPING & MAIL ORDER (NAICS 45411)
PRODUCT LINE: COSMETICS/PERFUMES PRODUCTS (Sub Category)

NAICS 45411: Electronic Shopping and Mail-Order Houses This industry comprises establishments primarily engaged in retailing all types of merchandise by means of mail or by electronic media, such as interactive television or computer. Included in this industry are establishments primarily engaged in retailing from catalogue showrooms of mail-order houses.

5-YEAR TREND – ESTIMATED INDUSTRY SALES ($MILLIONS)

Year	Employee Size of Establishment									Total
	1-4 Emps.	5-9 Emps.	10-19 Emps.	20-49 Emps.	50-99 Emps.	100-249 Emps.	250-499 Emps.	500-999 Emps.	Unknown Emps.	Industry Sales
2015	361.5	186.2	269.1	451.6	340.0	629.0	848.0	1,197.0	50.8	4,333.2
2016	382.4	197.0	284.6	477.7	359.6	665.3	896.9	1,266.1	53.7	4,583.3
2017	405.4	208.8	301.7	506.5	381.2	705.3	950.9	1,342.4	57.0	4,859.4
2018	454.4	234.1	338.2	567.6	427.3	790.5	1,065.7	1,477.1	63.9	5,418.6
2019	505.2	260.2	376.0	631.1	475.0	878.9	1,184.9	1,617.6	71.0	5,999.8

INDUSTRY: SUPERMARKETS & GROCERY STORES (NAICS 44511)
PRODUCT LINE: HYGIENIC/DEORDANTS/HAIR PRODUCTS (Sub Category)

NAICS 44511: Grocery Stores Industry. This industry comprises establishments generally known as supermarkets and grocery stores primarily engaged in retailing a general line of food, such as canned and frozen foods; fresh fruits and vegetables; and fresh and prepared meats, fish, and poultry. Included in this industry are delicatessen-type establishments primarily engaged in retailing a general line of food.

5-YEAR TREND – ESTIMATED INDUSTRY SALES ($MILLIONS)

Year	Employee Size of Establishment									Total
	1-4 Emps.	5-9 Emps.	10-19 Emps.	20-49 Emps.	50-99 Emps.	100-249 Emps.	250-499 Emps.	500-999 Emps.	Unknown Emps.	Industry Sales
2015	184	133	343	1,129	2,675	6,651	2,077	249	35	13,474
2016	183	132	340	1,122	2,658	6,609	2,064	247	34	13,389
2017	183	132	340	1,121	2,657	6,606	2,063	247	34	13,384
2018	186	135	347	1,144	2,712	6,743	2,106	252	35	13,660
2019	192	139	358	1,180	2,796	6,951	2,171	259	36	14,082

INDUSTRY: PHARMACIES & DRUG STORES (NAICS 44611)
PRODUCT LINE: HYGIENIC/DEORDANTS/HAIR PRODUCTS (Sub Category)

NAICS 44611 Pharmacies and Drug Stores – This industry comprises establishments known as pharmacies and drug stores engaged in retailing prescription or nonprescription drugs and medicines.

5-YEAR TREND – ESTIMATED INDUSTRY SALES ($MILLIONS)

Year	Employee Size of Establishment									Total
	1-4 Emps.	5-9 Emps.	10-19 Emps.	20-49 Emps.	50-99 Emps.	100-249 Emps.	250-499 Emps.	500-999 Emps.	Unknown Emps.	Industry Sales
2015	121.7	301.4	1,219.6	3,581.9	362.3	145.0	55.4	18.5	9.3	5,815.2
2016	125.5	310.9	1,257.8	3,694.2	373.6	149.6	57.2	19.1	9.6	5,997.4
2017	130.1	322.1	1,303.3	3,827.9	387.2	155.0	59.2	19.8	10.0	6,214.5
2018	137.8	341.2	1,380.4	4,054.3	410.1	164.2	62.7	20.9	10.5	6,582.0
2019	147.1	364.3	1,474.1	4,329.4	437.9	175.3	67.0	22.4	11.3	7,028.6

	INDUSTRY: DEPARTMENT STORES (NAICS 45211)
	PRODUCT LINE: HYGIENIC/DEORDANTS/HAIR PRODUCTS (Sub Category)

NAICS 45211: Department Stores Industry . This industry comprises establishments known as department stores primarily engaged in retailing a wide range of the following new products with no one merchandise line predominating: apparel, furniture, appliances and home furnishings; and selected additional items, such as paint, hardware, toiletries, cosmetics, photographic equipment, jewelry, toys, and sporting goods. Merchandise lines are normally arranged in separate departments.

5-YEAR TREND – ESTIMATED INDUSTRY SALES ($MILLIONS)

Year	Employee Size of Establishment									Total
	1-4 Emps.	5-9 Emps.	10-19 Emps.	20-49 Emps.	50-99 Emps.	100-249 Emps.	250-499 Emps.	500-999 Emps.	Unknown Emps.	Industry Sales
2015	0.2	0.2	0.5	40.3	732.2	2,351.3	973.3	140.8	6.0	4,244.8
2016	0.2	0.2	0.5	40.5	735.1	2,360.5	977.1	141.4	6.0	4,261.4
2017	0.2	0.2	0.5	40.9	742.4	2,383.8	986.8	142.7	6.1	4,303.5
2018	0.2	0.2	0.5	40.9	742.4	2,384.1	986.9	143.1	6.1	4,304.4
2019	0.2	0.2	0.5	41.3	749.8	2,407.7	996.6	144.8	6.1	4,347.2

	INDUSTRY: WAREHOUSE CLUBS & SUPERSTORES (NAICS 45291)
	PRODUCT LINE: HYGIENIC/DEORDANTS/HAIR PRODUCTS (Sub Category)

NAICS 45291: Warehouse Clubs and Superstores This industry comprises establishments known as warehouse clubs, superstores or supercenters primarily engaged in retailing a general line of groceries in combination with general lines of new merchandise, such as apparel, furniture, and appliances.

5-YEAR TREND – ESTIMATED INDUSTRY SALES ($MILLIONS)

Year	Employee Size of Establishment									Total
	1-4 Emps.	5-9 Emps.	10-19 Emps.	20-49 Emps.	50-99 Emps.	100-249 Emps.	250-499 Emps.	500-999 Emps.	Unknown Emps.	Industry Sales
2015	0.9	0.3	0.8	29.8	56.6	3,231.7	14,226.7	358.5	5.4	17,910.8
2016	1.0	0.3	0.8	30.7	58.2	3,320.8	14,618.8	368.4	5.6	18,404.5
2017	1.0	0.3	0.9	31.7	60.1	3,429.2	15,096.3	380.4	5.8	19,005.6
2018	1.1	0.3	0.9	34.1	64.6	3,690.6	16,247.1	409.4	6.2	20,454.3
2019	1.1	0.3	1.0	36.1	68.5	3,909.3	17,209.5	433.7	6.6	21,666.0

	INDUSTRY: ELECTRONIC SHOPPING & MAIL ORDER (NAICS 45411)
	PRODUCT LINE: DRUGS & HEALTH/BEAUTY AIDS (Main Category)

NAICS 45411: Electronic Shopping and Mail-Order Houses This industry comprises establishments primarily engaged in retailing all types of merchandise by means of mail or by electronic media, such as interactive television or computer. Included in this industry are establishments primarily engaged in retailing from catalogue showrooms of mail-order houses.

5-YEAR TREND — ESTIMATED INDUSTRY SALES ($MILLIONS)

Year	Employee Size of Establishment									Total Industry Sales
	1-4 Emps.	5-9 Emps.	10-19 Emps.	20-49 Emps.	50-99 Emps.	100-249 Emps.	250-499 Emps.	500-999 Emps.	Unknown Emps.	
2015	63.7	32.8	47.4	79.6	59.9	110.8	149.4	211.0	9.0	763.7
2016	67.4	34.7	50.2	84.2	63.4	117.2	158.1	223.1	9.5	807.7
2017	71.5	36.8	53.2	89.3	67.2	124.3	167.6	236.6	10.0	856.4
2018	80.1	41.2	59.6	100.0	75.3	139.3	187.8	260.3	11.3	955.0
2019	89.0	45.9	66.3	111.2	83.7	154.9	208.8	285.1	12.5	1,057.4

	INDUSTRY: PHARMACIES & DRUG STORES (NAICS 44611)
	PRODUCT LINE: HEARING AIDS & SUPPLIES (Sub Category)

NAICS 44611 Pharmacies and Drug Stores – This industry comprises establishments known as pharmacies and drug stores engaged in retailing prescription or nonprescription drugs and medicines.

5-YEAR TREND — ESTIMATED INDUSTRY SALES ($MILLIONS)

Year	Employee Size of Establishment									Total Industry Sales
	1-4 Emps.	5-9 Emps.	10-19 Emps.	20-49 Emps.	50-99 Emps.	100-249 Emps.	250-499 Emps.	500-999 Emps.	Unknown Emps.	
2015	1.6	4.0	16.3	47.9	4.8	1.9	0.7	0.2	0.1	77.7
2016	1.7	4.2	16.8	49.4	5.0	2.0	0.8	0.3	0.1	80.1
2017	1.7	4.3	17.4	51.2	5.2	2.1	0.8	0.3	0.1	83.0
2018	1.8	4.6	18.4	54.2	5.5	2.2	0.8	0.3	0.1	88.0
2019	2.0	4.9	19.7	57.9	5.9	2.3	0.9	0.3	0.2	93.9

	INDUSTRY: ELECTRONIC SHOPPING & MAIL ORDER (NAICS 45411)
	PRODUCT LINE: HEARING AIDS & SUPPLIES (Sub Category)

NAICS 45411: Electronic Shopping and Mail-Order Houses This
industry comprises establishments primarily engaged in retailing all
types of merchandise by means of mail or by electronic media, such
as interactive television or computer. Included in this industry are
establishments primarily engaged in retailing from catalogue showrooms
of mail-order houses.

5-YEAR TREND – ESTIMATED INDUSTRY SALES ($MILLIONS)

Year	Employee Size of Establishment									Total
	1-4 Emps.	5-9 Emps.	10-19 Emps.	20-49 Emps.	50-99 Emps.	100-249 Emps.	250-499 Emps.	500-999 Emps.	Unknown Emps.	Industry Sales
2015	18.6	9.6	13.8	23.2	17.5	32.3	43.6	61.5	2.6	222.6
2016	19.6	10.1	14.6	24.5	18.5	34.2	46.1	65.1	2.8	235.5
2017	20.8	10.7	15.5	26.0	19.6	36.2	48.9	69.0	2.9	249.7
2018	23.3	12.0	17.4	29.2	22.0	40.6	54.8	75.9	3.3	278.4
2019	26.0	13.4	19.3	32.4	24.4	45.2	60.9	83.1	3.6	308.3

	INDUSTRY: HOME CENTERS INDUSTRY (NAICS 44411)
	PRODUCT LINE: SOAPS & CLEANERS (Main Category)

NAICS 44411: Home Centers. This industry comprises establishments
known as home centers primarily engaged in retailing a general line of
new home repair and improvement materials and supplies, such as
lumber, plumbing goods, electrical goods, tools, housewares, hardware,
and lawn and garden supplies, with no one merchandise line predominating.
The merchandise lines are normally arranged in separate departments.

5-YEAR TREND – ESTIMATED INDUSTRY SALES ($MILLIONS)

Year	Employee Size of Establishment									Total
	1-4 Emps.	5-9 Emps.	10-19 Emps.	20-49 Emps.	50-99 Emps.	100-249 Emps.	250-499 Emps.	500-999 Emps.	Unknown Emps.	Industry Sales
2015	2.5	5.0	12.6	25.7	19.5	1,286.6	100.5	2.1	0.9	1,455.4
2016	2.6	5.1	12.9	26.3	20.0	1,317.5	102.9	2.1	0.9	1,490.3
2017	2.7	5.2	13.3	27.1	20.6	1,356.0	105.9	2.2	0.9	1,534.0
2018	2.8	5.4	13.8	28.1	21.3	1,406.4	109.8	2.3	1.0	1,590.9
2019	2.9	5.7	14.4	29.4	22.3	1,471.3	114.9	2.4	1.0	1,664.4

NAICS 44413: Hardware Stores. Establishments primarily engaged
in the retail sale of a number of basic hardware lines, such as tools,
builders' hardware, paint and glass, housewares and household appliances,
and cutlery.

5-YEAR TREND – ESTIMATED INDUSTRY SALES ($MILLIONS)

| Year | Employee Size of Establishment | | | | | | | | | Total |
	1-4 Emps.	5-9 Emps.	10-19 Emps.	20-49 Emps.	50-99 Emps.	100-249 Emps.	250-499 Emps.	500-999 Emps.	Unknown Emps.	Industry Sales
2015	17.4	29.5	59.4	84.9	16.9	5.5	1.0	0.0	1.5	216.2
2016	17.6	29.8	60.0	85.8	17.0	5.6	1.0	0.0	1.5	218.3
2017	17.9	30.3	60.9	87.1	17.3	5.6	1.0	0.1	1.6	221.8
2018	18.6	31.5	63.4	90.6	18.0	5.9	1.0	0.1	1.6	230.6
2019	19.5	33.0	66.5	95.1	18.9	6.2	1.1	0.1	1.7	242.0

NAICS 44511: Grocery Stores Industry. This industry comprises
establishments generally known as supermarkets and grocery stores
primarily engaged in retailing a general line of food, such as canned and
frozen foods; fresh fruits and vegetables; and fresh and prepared meats,
fish, and poultry. Included in this industry are delicatessen-type
establishments primarily engaged in retailing a general line of food.

5-YEAR TREND – ESTIMATED INDUSTRY SALES ($MILLIONS)

| Year | Employee Size of Establishment | | | | | | | | | Total |
	1-4 Emps.	5-9 Emps.	10-19 Emps.	20-49 Emps.	50-99 Emps.	100-249 Emps.	250-499 Emps.	500-999 Emps.	Unknown Emps.	Industry Sales
2015	206.6	149.2	384.9	1,268.3	3,005.9	7,472.9	2,333.9	279.2	38.8	15,139.7
2016	205.3	148.2	382.4	1,260.3	2,986.9	7,425.5	2,319.0	277.5	38.5	15,043.6
2017	205.2	148.2	382.3	1,259.8	2,985.8	7,422.9	2,318.2	277.4	38.5	15,038.4
2018	209.5	151.2	390.2	1,285.8	3,047.4	7,576.0	2,366.0	282.9	39.3	15,348.3
2019	215.9	155.9	402.2	1,325.6	3,141.6	7,810.1	2,439.2	291.4	40.5	15,822.5

INDUSTRY: BEER, WINE & LIQUOR STORES INDUSTRY (NAICS 44531)
PRODUCT LINE: SOAPS & CLEANERS (Main Category)

NAICS 44531: Beer & Wine & Liquor Stores. Establishments primarily engaged in the retail sale of packaged alcoholic beverages, such as ale, beer, wine, and liquor, for consumption off the premises. Stores selling prepared drinks for consumption on the premises are classified in SIC 5813.

5-Year Trend – Estimated Industry Sales ($Millions)

Year	Employee Size of Establishment									Total Industry Sales
	1-4 Emps.	5-9 Emps.	10-19 Emps.	20-49 Emps.	50-99 Emps.	100-249 Emps.	250-499 Emps.	500-999 Emps.	Unknown Emps.	
2015	19.6	19.7	16.9	12.4	1.8	1.0	0.0	0.6	1.1	73.0
2016	20.0	20.2	17.3	12.6	1.8	1.1	0.0	0.6	1.1	74.7
2017	20.6	20.8	17.7	13.0	1.9	1.1	0.0	0.6	1.2	76.8
2018	21.8	22.0	18.8	13.8	2.0	1.1	0.0	0.6	1.2	81.3
2019	23.3	23.5	20.0	14.7	2.1	1.2	0.0	0.7	1.3	86.8

INDUSTRY: PHARMACIES & DRUG STORES INDUSTRY (NAICS 44611)
PRODUCT LINE: SOAPS & CLEANERS (Main Category)

NAICS 44611 Pharmacies and Drug Stores – This industry comprises establishments known as pharmacies and drug stores engaged in retailing prescription or nonprescription drugs and medicines.

5-Year Trend – Estimated Industry Sales ($Millions)

Year	Employee Size of Establishment									Total Industry Sales
	1-4 Emps.	5-9 Emps.	10-19 Emps.	20-49 Emps.	50-99 Emps.	100-249 Emps.	250-499 Emps.	500-999 Emps.	Unknown Emps.	
2015	20.1	49.7	201.2	591.0	59.8	23.9	9.1	3.1	1.5	959.4
2016	20.7	51.3	207.5	609.5	61.6	24.7	9.4	3.1	1.6	989.5
2017	21.5	53.1	215.0	631.5	63.9	25.6	9.8	3.3	1.6	1,025.3
2018	22.7	56.3	227.7	668.9	67.7	27.1	10.4	3.5	1.7	1,085.9
2019	24.3	60.1	243.2	714.3	72.2	28.9	11.1	3.7	1.9	1,159.6

INDUSTRY: GAS STATIONS W/CONVENIENCE STORES (NAICS 44711)
PRODUCT LINE: SOAPS & CLEANERS (Main Category)

NAICS 44711: Gas Stations with Convenience Stores. This industry comprises establishments primarily engaged in selling gasoline and lubricating oils. These establishments frequently sell other merchandise, such as tires, batteries, and other automobile parts, or perform minor repair work. Gasoline stations combined with other activities, such as grocery stores, convenience stores, or carwashes, are classified according to the primary activity.

5-YEAR TREND – ESTIMATED INDUSTRY SALES ($MILLIONS)

Year	Employee Size of Establishment									Total
	1-4 Emps.	5-9 Emps.	10-19 Emps.	20-49 Emps.	50-99 Emps.	100-249 Emps.	250-499 Emps.	500-999 Emps.	Unknown Emps.	Industry Sales
2015	50.1	129.3	216.5	149.4	14.0	7.7	3.0	0.0	0.6	570.6
2016	52.2	134.8	225.6	155.6	14.6	8.0	3.2	0.0	0.6	594.5
2017	54.6	140.9	235.9	162.8	15.3	8.4	3.3	0.0	0.6	621.8
2018	58.1	150.2	251.4	173.5	16.3	8.9	3.5	0.0	0.6	662.7
2019	62.4	161.2	269.9	186.2	17.5	9.6	3.8	0.0	0.7	711.4

INDUSTRY: DEPARTMENT STORES INDUSTRY (NAICS 45211)
PRODUCT LINE: SOAPS & CLEANERS (Main Category)

NAICS 45211: Department Stores Industry . This industry comprises establishments known as department stores primarily engaged in retailing a wide range of the following new products with no one merchandise line predominating: apparel, furniture, appliances and home furnishings; and selected additional items, such as paint, hardware, toiletries, cosmetics, photographic equipment, jewelry, toys, and sporting goods. Merchandise lines are normally arranged in separate departments.

5-YEAR TREND – ESTIMATED INDUSTRY SALES ($MILLIONS)

Year	Employee Size of Establishment									Total
	1-4 Emps.	5-9 Emps.	10-19 Emps.	20-49 Emps.	50-99 Emps.	100-249 Emps.	250-499 Emps.	500-999 Emps.	Unknown Emps.	Industry Sales
2015	0.1	0.1	0.3	21.4	388.4	1,247.2	516.3	74.7	3.2	2,251.5
2016	0.1	0.1	0.3	21.5	389.9	1,252.0	518.3	75.0	3.2	2,260.3
2017	0.1	0.1	0.3	21.7	393.8	1,264.4	523.4	75.7	3.2	2,282.7
2018	0.1	0.1	0.3	21.7	393.8	1,264.6	523.5	75.9	3.2	2,283.1
2019	0.1	0.1	0.3	21.9	397.7	1,277.1	528.6	76.8	3.2	2,305.8

INDUSTRY: WAREHOUSE CLUBS & SUPERCENTERS (NAICS 45291)
PRODUCT LINE: SOAPS & CLEANERS (Main Category)

NAICS 45291: Warehouse Clubs and Superstores This industry comprises establishments known as warehouse clubs, superstores or supercenters primarily engaged in retailing a general line of groceries in combination with general lines of new merchandise, such as apparel, furniture, and appliances.

5-YEAR TREND – ESTIMATED INDUSTRY SALES ($MILLIONS)

Year	1-4 Emps.	5-9 Emps.	10-19 Emps.	20-49 Emps.	50-99 Emps.	100-249 Emps.	250-499 Emps.	500-999 Emps.	Unknown Emps.	Total Industry Sales
2016	0.7	0.2	0.6	22.8	43.3	2,471.2	10,878.8	274.1	4.1	13,695.9
2017	0.7	0.2	0.6	23.4	44.5	2,539.3	11,178.6	281.7	4.3	14,073.4
2018	0.8	0.2	0.7	24.2	45.9	2,622.2	11,543.7	290.9	4.4	14,533.0
2019	0.8	0.2	0.7	26.1	49.4	2,822.1	12,423.7	313.1	4.7	15,640.8
2019	0.9	0.2	0.8	27.6	52.3	2,989.3	13,159.6	331.6	5.0	16,567.4

INDUSTRY: ELECTRONIC SHOPPING & MAIL-ORDER (NAICS 45411)
PRODUCT LINE: SOAPS & CLEANERS (Main Category)

NAICS 45411: Electronic Shopping and Mail-Order Houses This industry comprises establishments primarily engaged in retailing all types of merchandise by means of mail or by electronic media, such as interactive television or computer. Included in this industry are establishments primarily engaged in retailing from catalogue showrooms of mail-order houses.

5-YEAR TREND – ESTIMATED INDUSTRY SALES ($MILLIONS)

Year	1-4 Emps.	5-9 Emps.	10-19 Emps.	20-49 Emps.	50-99 Emps.	100-249 Emps.	250-499 Emps.	500-999 Emps.	Unknown Emps.	Total Industry Sales
2015	23.9	12.3	17.8	29.9	22.5	41.6	56.1	79.2	3.4	286.6
2016	25.3	13.0	18.8	31.6	23.8	44.0	59.3	83.7	3.6	303.1
2017	26.8	13.8	20.0	33.5	25.2	46.7	62.9	88.8	3.8	321.4
2018	30.1	15.5	22.4	37.5	28.3	52.3	70.5	97.7	4.2	358.4
2019	33.4	17.2	24.9	41.7	31.4	58.1	78.4	107.0	4.7	396.8

INDUSTRY: SUPERMARKETS INDUSTRY (NAICS 44511)
PRODUCT LINE: PAPER & TISSUE PRODUCTS (Main Category)

NAICS 44511: Grocery Stores Industry. This industry comprises establishments generally known as supermarkets and grocery stores primarily engaged in retailing a general line of food, such as canned and frozen foods; fresh fruits and vegetables; and fresh and prepared meats, fish, and poultry. Included in this industry are delicatessen-type establishments primarily engaged in retailing a general line of food.

5-YEAR TREND — ESTIMATED INDUSTRY SALES ($MILLIONS)

Year	Employee Size of Establishment									Total Industry Sales
	1-4 Emps.	5-9 Emps.	10-19 Emps.	20-49 Emps.	50-99 Emps.	100-249 Emps.	250-499 Emps.	500-999 Emps.	Unknown Emps.	
2015	212.2	153.2	395.2	1,302.4	3,086.8	7,673.9	2,396.6	286.8	39.8	15,546.9
2016	210.8	152.2	392.7	1,294.2	3,067.2	7,625.2	2,381.4	284.9	39.6	15,448.2
2017	210.7	152.1	392.6	1,293.7	3,066.1	7,622.6	2,380.6	284.8	39.6	15,442.9
2018	215.1	155.3	400.7	1,320.4	3,129.3	7,779.7	2,429.7	290.5	40.4	15,761.1
2019	221.7	160.1	413.1	1,361.2	3,226.1	8,020.2	2,504.8	299.3	41.6	16,248.1

INDUSTRY: BEER, WINE & LIQUOR STORES (NAICS 44531)
PRODUCT LINE: PAPER & TISSUE PRODUCTS (Main Category)

NAICS 44531: Beer & Wine & Liquor Stores. Establishments primarily engaged in the retail sale of packaged alcoholic beverages, such as ale, beer, wine, and liquor, for consumption off the premises. Stores selling prepared drinks for consumption on the premises are classified in SIC 5813.

5-YEAR TREND — ESTIMATED INDUSTRY SALES ($MILLIONS)

Year	Employee Size of Establishment									Total Industry Sales
	1-4 Emps.	5-9 Emps.	10-19 Emps.	20-49 Emps.	50-99 Emps.	100-249 Emps.	250-499 Emps.	500-999 Emps.	Unknown Emps.	
2015	11.9	12.0	10.3	7.5	1.1	0.6	0.0	0.4	0.7	44.5
2016	12.2	12.3	10.5	7.7	1.1	0.6	0.0	0.4	0.7	45.5
2017	12.5	12.6	10.8	7.9	1.1	0.7	0.0	0.4	0.7	46.8
2018	13.3	13.4	11.4	8.4	1.2	0.7	0.0	0.4	0.7	49.5
2019	14.2	14.3	12.2	8.9	1.3	0.7	0.0	0.4	0.8	52.9

INDUSTRY: PHARMACIES & DRUG STORES INDUSTRY (NAICS 44611)
PRODUCT LINE: PAPER & TISSUE PRODUCTS (Main Category)

NAICS 44611 Pharmacies and Drug Stores – This industry comprises establishments known as pharmacies and drug stores engaged in retailing prescription or nonprescription drugs and medicines.

5-YEAR TREND – ESTIMATED INDUSTRY SALES ($MILLIONS)

Year	Employee Size of Establishment									Total
	1-4 Emps.	5-9 Emps.	10-19 Emps.	20-49 Emps.	50-99 Emps.	100-249 Emps.	250-499 Emps.	500-999 Emps.	Unknown Emps.	Industry Sales
2015	16.1	39.8	161.2	473.5	47.9	19.2	7.3	2.4	1.2	768.7
2016	16.6	41.1	166.3	488.3	49.4	19.8	7.6	2.5	1.3	792.8
2017	17.2	42.6	172.3	506.0	51.2	20.5	7.8	2.6	1.3	821.5
2018	18.2	45.1	182.5	535.9	54.2	21.7	8.3	2.8	1.4	870.0
2019	19.4	48.2	194.8	572.3	57.9	23.2	8.9	3.0	1.5	929.1

INDUSTRY: GAS STATIONS W/CONVENIENCE STORES (NAICS 44711)
PRODUCT LINE: PAPER & TISSUE PRODUCTS (Main Category)

NAICS 44711: Gas Stations with Convenience Stores. This industry comprises establishments primarily engaged in selling gasoline and lubricating oils. These establishments frequently sell other merchandise, such as tires, batteries, and other automobile parts, or perform minor repair work. Gasoline stations combined with other activities, such as grocery stores, convenience stores, or carwashes, are classified according to the primary activity.

5-YEAR TREND – ESTIMATED INDUSTRY SALES ($MILLIONS)

Year	Employee Size of Establishment									Total
	1-4 Emps.	5-9 Emps.	10-19 Emps.	20-49 Emps.	50-99 Emps.	100-249 Emps.	250-499 Emps.	500-999 Emps.	Unknown Emps.	Industry Sales
2015	61.2	158.2	264.7	182.7	17.2	9.4	3.7	0.0	0.7	697.8
2016	63.8	164.8	275.8	190.3	17.9	9.8	3.9	0.0	0.7	727.0
2017	66.7	172.4	288.5	199.1	18.7	10.2	4.1	0.0	0.7	760.4
2018	71.1	183.7	307.4	212.1	19.9	10.9	4.3	0.0	0.8	810.4
2019	76.3	197.2	330.1	227.8	21.4	11.7	4.6	0.0	0.8	870.0

INDUSTRY: DEPARTMENT STORES INDUSTRY (NAICS 45211)
PRODUCT LINE: PAPER & TISSUE PRODUCTS (Main Category)

NAICS 45211: Department Stores Industry . This industry comprises establishments known as department stores primarily engaged in retailing a wide range of the following new products with no one merchandise line predominating: apparel, furniture, appliances and home furnishings; and selected additional items, such as paint, hardware, toiletries, cosmetics, photographic equipment, jewelry, toys, and sporting goods. Merchandise lines are normally arranged in separate departments.

5-YEAR TREND – ESTIMATED INDUSTRY SALES ($MILLIONS)

Year	Employee Size of Establishment									Total
	1-4 Emps.	5-9 Emps.	10-19 Emps.	20-49 Emps.	50-99 Emps.	100-249 Emps.	250-499 Emps.	500-999 Emps.	Unknown Emps.	Industry Sales
2015	0.1	0.1	0.2	16.6	301.9	969.5	401.3	58.1	2.5	1,750.3
2016	0.1	0.1	0.2	16.7	303.1	973.3	402.9	58.3	2.5	1,757.2
2017	0.1	0.1	0.2	16.9	306.1	982.9	406.9	58.9	2.5	1,774.5
2018	0.1	0.1	0.2	16.9	306.1	983.1	406.9	59.0	2.5	1,774.9
2019	0.1	0.1	0.2	17.0	309.2	992.8	411.0	59.7	2.5	1,792.6

INDUSTRY: WAREHOUSE CLUBS & SUPERCENTERS (NAICS 45291)
PRODUCT LINE: PAPER & TISSUE PRODUCTS (Main Category)

NAICS 45291: Warehouse Clubs and Superstores This industry comprises establishments known as warehouse clubs, superstores or supercenters primarily engaged in retailing a general line of groceries in combination with general lines of new merchandise, such as apparel, furniture, and appliances.

5-YEAR TREND – ESTIMATED INDUSTRY SALES ($MILLIONS)

Year	Employee Size of Establishment									Total
	1-4 Emps.	5-9 Emps.	10-19 Emps.	20-49 Emps.	50-99 Emps.	100-249 Emps.	250-499 Emps.	500-999 Emps.	Unknown Emps.	Industry Sales
2015	0.7	0.2	0.6	20.5	38.9	2,220.5	9,775.2	246.3	3.7	12,306.6
2016	0.7	0.2	0.6	21.1	40.0	2,281.7	10,044.6	253.1	3.8	12,645.7
2017	0.7	0.2	0.6	21.8	41.3	2,356.2	10,372.7	261.4	4.0	13,058.7
2018	0.7	0.2	0.6	23.4	44.4	2,535.8	11,163.4	281.3	4.3	14,054.2
2019	0.8	0.2	0.7	24.8	47.0	2,686.1	11,824.7	298.0	4.5	14,886.7

INDUSTRY: OFFICE SUPPLIES & STATIONERY STORES (NAICS 45321)
PRODUCT LINE: PAPER & TISSUE PRODUCTS (Main Category)

NAICS 45321: Office Supplies and Stationery Stores . This industry comprises establishments primarily engaged in one or more of the following: (1) retailing new stationery, school supplies, and office supplies; (2) selling a combination of new office equipment, furniture, and supplies; and (3) selling new office equipment, furniture, and supplies in combination with selling new computers.

5-YEAR TREND — ESTIMATED INDUSTRY SALES ($MILLIONS)

Year	Employee Size of Establishment									Total
	1-4 Emps.	5-9 Emps.	10-19 Emps.	20-49 Emps.	50-99 Emps.	100-249 Emps.	250-499 Emps.	500-999 Emps.	Unknown Emps.	Industry Sales
2015	1.0	0.8	5.2	12.9	0.3	0.2	0.0	0.0	0.2	20.6
2016	1.0	0.8	5.1	12.8	0.3	0.2	0.0	0.0	0.2	20.4
2017	1.0	0.8	5.1	12.8	0.3	0.2	0.0	0.0	0.2	20.3
2018	1.0	0.8	4.9	12.3	0.3	0.2	0.0	0.0	0.2	19.7
2019	0.9	0.8	4.8	12.1	0.3	0.2	0.0	0.0	0.2	19.2

INDUSTRY: ELECTRONIC SHOPPING & MAIL-ORDER (NAICS 45411)
PRODUCT LINE: PAPER & TISSUE PRODUCTS (Main Category)

NAICS 45411: Electronic Shopping and Mail-Order Houses This industry comprises establishments primarily engaged in retailing all types of merchandise by means of mail or by electronic media, such as interactive television or computer. Included in this industry are establishments primarily engaged in retailing from catalogue showrooms of mail-order houses.

5-YEAR TREND — ESTIMATED INDUSTRY SALES ($MILLIONS)

Year	Employee Size of Establishment									Total
	1-4 Emps.	5-9 Emps.	10-19 Emps.	20-49 Emps.	50-99 Emps.	100-249 Emps.	250-499 Emps.	500-999 Emps.	Unknown Emps.	Industry Sales
2015	147.7	76.1	109.9	184.5	138.9	257.0	346.5	489.1	20.8	1,770.6
2016	156.3	80.5	116.3	195.2	146.9	271.8	366.5	517.3	22.0	1,872.8
2017	165.7	85.3	123.3	207.0	155.8	288.2	388.6	548.5	23.3	1,985.6
2018	185.7	95.6	138.2	231.9	174.6	323.0	435.5	603.6	26.1	2,214.1
2019	206.4	106.3	153.6	257.9	194.1	359.1	484.1	661.0	29.0	2,451.6

INDUSTRY: HARDWARE STORES (NAICS 44413)
PRODUCT LINE: MEN'S WEAR (Main Category)

NAICS 44413: Hardware Stores. Establishments primarily engaged
in the retail sale of a number of basic hardware lines, such as tools,
builders' hardware, paint and glass, housewares and household appliances,
and cutlery.

5-Year Trend — Estimated Industry Sales ($Millions)

Year	Employee Size of Establishment									Total
	1-4 Emps.	5-9 Emps.	10-19 Emps.	20-49 Emps.	50-99 Emps.	100-249 Emps.	250-499 Emps.	500-999 Emps.	Unknown Emps.	Industry Sales
2015	3.7	6.3	12.6	18.1	3.6	1.2	0.2	0.0	0.3	46.0
2016	3.7	6.3	12.8	18.2	3.6	1.2	0.2	0.0	0.3	46.5
2017	3.8	6.4	13.0	18.5	3.7	1.2	0.2	0.0	0.3	47.2
2018	4.0	6.7	13.5	19.3	3.8	1.2	0.2	0.0	0.3	49.1
2019	4.1	7.0	14.1	20.2	4.0	1.3	0.2	0.0	0.4	51.5

INDUSTRY: MEN'S CLOTHING STORES (NAICS 44811)
PRODUCT LINE: MEN'S WEAR (Main Category)

NAICS 44811: Men's Clothing Stores. This industry comprises
establishments primarily engaged in retailing a general line of new
men's and boys' clothing. These establishments may provide basic
alterations, such as hemming, taking in or letting out seams, or lengthening
or shortening sleeves.

5-Year Trend — Estimated Industry Sales ($Millions)

Year	Employee Size of Establishment									Total
	1-4 Emps.	5-9 Emps.	10-19 Emps.	20-49 Emps.	50-99 Emps.	100-249 Emps.	250-499 Emps.	500-999 Emps.	Unknown Emps.	Industry Sales
2015	731	1,284	2,391	1,260	274	246	83	4	126	6,400
2016	758	1,332	2,479	1,306	284	255	86	5	131	6,636
2017	789	1,387	2,582	1,361	296	266	90	5	136	6,912
2018	814	1,430	2,663	1,403	305	274	92	5	140	7,128
2019	846	1,487	2,767	1,458	317	285	96	5	146	7,408

INDUSTRY: WOMEN'S CLOTHING STORES (NAICS 44812)
PRODUCT LINE: MEN'S WEAR (Main Category)

NAICS 44812: Women's Clothing Stores . This industry comprises establishments primarily engaged in retailing a general line of new women's, misses' and juniors' clothing, including maternity wear. These establishments may provide basic alterations, such as hemming, taking in or letting out seams, or lengthening or shortening sleeves.

5-YEAR TREND – ESTIMATED INDUSTRY SALES ($MILLIONS)

Year	Employee Size of Establishment									Total
	1-4 Emps.	5-9 Emps.	10-19 Emps.	20-49 Emps.	50-99 Emps.	100-249 Emps.	250-499 Emps.	500-999 Emps.	Unknown Emps.	Industry Sales
2015	91.2	203.7	434.6	306.5	108.3	100.0	40.6	39.3	20.4	1,344.5
2016	93.9	209.7	447.5	315.6	111.5	103.0	41.8	40.4	21.0	1,384.2
2017	97.2	217.0	462.9	326.5	115.3	106.5	43.2	41.8	21.7	1,432.1
2018	102.5	228.9	488.4	344.5	121.7	112.4	45.6	43.8	22.9	1,510.7
2019	109.1	243.6	519.6	366.5	129.4	119.6	48.5	46.1	24.3	1,606.8

INDUSTRY: FAMILY CLOTHING STORES (NAICS 44814)
PRODUCT LINE: MEN'S WEAR (Main Category)

NAICS 44814: Family Clothing Stores . This industry comprises establishments primarily engaged in retailing a general line of new clothing for men, women, and children, without specializing in sales for an individual gender or age group. These establishments may provide basic alterations, such as hemming, taking in or letting out seams, or lengthening or shortening sleeves.

5-YEAR TREND – ESTIMATED INDUSTRY SALES ($MILLIONS)

Year	Employee Size of Establishment									Total
	1-4 Emps.	5-9 Emps.	10-19 Emps.	20-49 Emps.	50-99 Emps.	100-249 Emps.	250-499 Emps.	500-999 Emps.	Unknown Emps.	Industry Sales
2015	362	749	2,829	9,402	8,305	2,286	2,156	1,248	99	27,437
2016	372	769	2,905	9,654	8,528	2,347	2,214	1,282	102	28,172
2017	384	794	2,998	9,963	8,800	2,422	2,285	1,323	105	29,073
2018	405	836	3,159	10,501	9,276	2,553	2,408	1,389	111	30,638
2019	430	889	3,359	11,163	9,860	2,714	2,560	1,470	118	32,563

INDUSTRY: DEPARTMENT STORES (NAICS 45211)
PRODUCT LINE: MEN'S WEAR (Main Category)

NAICS 45211: Department Stores Industry . This industry comprises establishments known as department stores primarily engaged in retailing a wide range of the following new products with no one merchandise line predominating: apparel, furniture, appliances and home furnishings; and selected additional items, such as paint, hardware, toiletries, cosmetics, photographic equipment, jewelry, toys, and sporting goods. Merchandise lines are normally arranged in separate departments.

5-YEAR TREND – ESTIMATED INDUSTRY SALES ($MILLIONS)

Year	Employee Size of Establishment									Total
	1-4 Emps.	5-9 Emps.	10-19 Emps.	20-49 Emps.	50-99 Emps.	100-249 Emps.	250-499 Emps.	500-999 Emps.	Unknown Emps.	Industry Sales
2015	0	1	1	105	1,902	6,106	2,528	366	16	11,024
2016	0	1	1	105	1,909	6,130	2,538	367	16	11,067
2017	0	1	1	106	1,928	6,191	2,563	371	16	11,176
2018	0	1	1	106	1,928	6,191	2,563	372	16	11,178
2019	0	1	1	107	1,947	6,253	2,588	376	16	11,290

INDUSTRY: WAREHOUSE CLUBS & SUPERCENTERS (NAICS 45291)
PRODUCT LINE: MEN'S WEAR (Main Category)

NAICS 45291: Warehouse Clubs and Superstores This industry comprises establishments known as warehouse clubs, superstores or supercenters primarily engaged in retailing a general line of groceries in combination with general lines of new merchandise, such as apparel, furniture, and appliances.

5-YEAR TREND – ESTIMATED INDUSTRY SALES ($MILLIONS)

Year	Employee Size of Establishment									Total
	1-4 Emps.	5-9 Emps.	10-19 Emps.	20-49 Emps.	50-99 Emps.	100-249 Emps.	250-499 Emps.	500-999 Emps.	Unknown Emps.	Industry Sales
2015	0.6	0.2	0.5	18.4	34.9	1,993.9	8,777.8	221.2	3.3	11,050.9
2016	0.6	0.2	0.5	18.9	35.9	2,048.9	9,019.8	227.3	3.4	11,355.5
2017	0.6	0.2	0.5	19.5	37.1	2,115.8	9,314.3	234.7	3.6	11,726.3
2018	0.7	0.2	0.6	21.0	39.9	2,277.1	10,024.4	252.6	3.8	12,620.2
2019	0.7	0.2	0.6	22.3	42.2	2,412.0	10,618.2	267.6	4.0	13,367.8

INDUSTRY: ELECTRONIC SHOPPING & MAIL ORDER (NAICS 45411)

PRODUCT LINE: MEN'S WEAR (Main Category)

NAICS 45411: Electronic Shopping and Mail-Order Houses This
industry comprises establishments primarily engaged in retailing all
types of merchandise by means of mail or by electronic media, such
as interactive television or computer. Included in this industry are
establishments primarily engaged in retailing from catalogue showrooms
of mail-order houses.

5-YEAR TREND – ESTIMATED INDUSTRY SALES ($MILLIONS)

Year	Employee Size of Establishment									Total
	1-4 Emps.	5-9 Emps.	10-19 Emps.	20-49 Emps.	50-99 Emps.	100-249 Emps.	250-499 Emps.	500-999 Emps.	Unknown Emps.	Industry Sales
2015	660.8	340.4	491.8	825.6	621.4	1,149.7	1,550.0	2,188.0	92.9	7,920.7
2016	699.0	360.1	520.2	873.2	657.3	1,216.1	1,639.5	2,314.3	98.2	8,377.9
2017	741.1	381.8	551.6	925.8	696.9	1,289.3	1,738.2	2,453.7	104.2	8,882.6
2018	830.6	427.8	618.1	1,037.6	781.0	1,444.9	1,948.0	2,700.1	116.7	9,904.9
2019	923.4	475.7	687.3	1,153.6	868.3	1,606.5	2,165.8	2,956.8	129.8	10,967.2

INDUSTRY: BOOK STORES (NAICS 451211)

PRODUCT LINE: MEN'S WEAR (Main Category)

NAICS 451211: Book Stores. This industry comprises
establishments primarily engaged in the retail sale of new books and
magazines. Establishments primarily engaged in the retail sale of used
books are classified in 5932.

5-YEAR TREND – ESTIMATED INDUSTRY SALES ($MILLIONS)

Year	Employee Size of Establishment									Total
	1-4 Emps.	5-9 Emps.	10-19 Emps.	20-49 Emps.	50-99 Emps.	100-249 Emps.	250-499 Emps.	500-999 Emps.	Unknown Emps.	Industry Sales
2015	6.0	9.1	18.1	48.1	20.9	9.6	2.4	5.7	3.0	123.0
2016	6.3	9.5	18.9	50.3	21.9	10.1	2.5	6.0	3.2	128.6
2017	6.6	10.0	19.8	52.8	23.0	10.6	2.6	6.3	3.3	134.9
2018	6.8	10.3	20.6	54.8	23.8	11.0	2.7	6.6	3.4	140.1
2019	7.1	10.8	21.5	57.3	24.9	11.5	2.8	6.9	3.6	146.5

INDUSTRY: MEN'S CLOTHING STORES (NAICS 44811)
PRODUCT LINE: MEN'S OVERCOATS & OUTERWEAR (Sub Category)

NAICS 44811: Men's Clothing Stores. This industry comprises establishments primarily engaged in retailing a general line of new men's and boys' clothing. These establishments may provide basic alterations, such as hemming, taking in or letting out seams, or lengthening or shortening sleeves.

5-YEAR TREND – ESTIMATED INDUSTRY SALES ($MILLIONS)

Year	Employee Size of Establishment									Total
	1-4 Emps.	5-9 Emps.	10-19 Emps.	20-49 Emps.	50-99 Emps.	100-249 Emps.	250-499 Emps.	500-999 Emps.	Unknown Emps.	Industry Sales
2015	33.3	58.5	109.0	57.4	12.5	11.2	3.8	0.2	5.7	291.7
2016	34.6	60.7	113.0	59.5	13.0	11.6	3.9	0.2	6.0	302.5
2017	36.0	63.2	117.7	62.0	13.5	12.1	4.1	0.2	6.2	315.0
2018	37.1	65.2	121.4	64.0	13.9	12.5	4.2	0.2	6.4	324.9
2019	38.6	67.8	126.1	66.5	14.5	13.0	4.4	0.2	6.6	337.7

INDUSTRY: WOMEN'S CLOTHING STORES (NAICS 44812)
PRODUCT LINE: MEN'S OVERCOATS & OUTERWEAR (Sub Category)

NAICS 44812: Women's Clothing Stores . This industry comprises establishments primarily engaged in retailing a general line of new women's, misses' and juniors' clothing, including maternity wear. These establishments may provide basic alterations, such as hemming, taking in or letting out seams, or lengthening or shortening sleeves.

5-YEAR TREND – ESTIMATED INDUSTRY SALES ($MILLIONS)

Year	Employee Size of Establishment									Total
	1-4 Emps.	5-9 Emps.	10-19 Emps.	20-49 Emps.	50-99 Emps.	100-249 Emps.	250-499 Emps.	500-999 Emps.	Unknown Emps.	Industry Sales
2015	6.6	14.7	31.3	22.1	7.8	7.2	2.9	2.8	1.5	96.9
2016	6.8	15.1	32.3	22.7	8.0	7.4	3.0	2.9	1.5	99.8
2017	7.0	15.6	33.4	23.5	8.3	7.7	3.1	3.0	1.6	103.2
2018	7.4	16.5	35.2	24.8	8.8	8.1	3.3	3.2	1.6	108.9
2019	7.9	17.6	37.5	26.4	9.3	8.6	3.5	3.3	1.8	115.8

INDUSTRY: FAMILY CLOTHING STORES (NAICS 44814)
PRODUCT LINE: MEN'S OVERCOATS & OUTERWEAR (Sub Category)

NAICS 44814: Family Clothing Stores . This industry comprises establishments primarily engaged in retailing a general line of new clothing for men, women, and children, without specializing in sales for an individual gender or age group. These establishments may provide basic alterations, such as hemming, taking in or letting out seams, or lengthening or shortening sleeves.

5-YEAR TREND – ESTIMATED INDUSTRY SALES ($MILLIONS)

Year	Employee Size of Establishment									Total
	1-4 Emps.	5-9 Emps.	10-19 Emps.	20-49 Emps.	50-99 Emps.	100-249 Emps.	250-499 Emps.	500-999 Emps.	Unknown Emps.	Industry Sales
2015	23.0	47.5	179.4	596.2	526.7	145.0	136.7	79.2	6.3	1,740.0
2016	23.6	48.8	184.2	612.2	540.8	148.8	140.4	81.3	6.5	1,786.6
2017	24.3	50.3	190.1	631.8	558.1	153.6	144.9	83.9	6.7	1,843.7
2018	25.7	53.0	200.4	665.9	588.2	161.9	152.7	88.1	7.0	1,943.0
2019	27.3	56.4	213.0	707.9	625.3	172.1	162.3	93.2	7.5	2,065.0

INDUSTRY: DEPARTMENT STORES (NAICS 45211)
PRODUCT LINE: MEN'S OVERCOATS & OUTERWEAR (Sub Category)

NAICS 45211: Department Stores Industry . This industry comprises establishments known as department stores primarily engaged in retailing a wide range of the following new products with no one merchandise line predominating: apparel, furniture, appliances and home furnishings; and selected additional items, such as paint, hardware, toiletries, cosmetics, photographic equipment, jewelry, toys, and sporting goods. Merchandise lines are normally arranged in separate departments.

5-YEAR TREND – ESTIMATED INDUSTRY SALES ($MILLIONS)

Year	Employee Size of Establishment									Total
	1-4 Emps.	5-9 Emps.	10-19 Emps.	20-49 Emps.	50-99 Emps.	100-249 Emps.	250-499 Emps.	500-999 Emps.	Unknown Emps.	Industry Sales
2015	0.0	0.0	0.1	4.8	87.7	281.5	116.5	16.9	0.7	508.2
2016	0.0	0.0	0.1	4.8	88.0	282.6	117.0	16.9	0.7	510.2
2017	0.0	0.0	0.1	4.9	88.9	285.4	118.1	17.1	0.7	515.2
2018	0.0	0.0	0.1	4.9	88.9	285.4	118.1	17.1	0.7	515.3
2019	0.0	0.0	0.1	4.9	89.8	288.2	119.3	17.3	0.7	520.4

INDUSTRY: WAREHOUSE CLUBS & SUPERCENTERS (NAICS 45291)
PRODUCT LINE: MEN'S OVERCOATS & OUTERWEAR (Sub Category)

NAICS 45291: Warehouse Clubs and Superstores This industry comprises establishments known as warehouse clubs, superstores or supercenters primarily engaged in retailing a general line of groceries in combination with general lines of new merchandise, such as apparel, furniture, and appliances.

5-YEAR TREND – ESTIMATED INDUSTRY SALES ($MILLIONS)

Year	Employee Size of Establishment									Total
	1-4 Emps.	5-9 Emps.	10-19 Emps.	20-49 Emps.	50-99 Emps.	100-249 Emps.	250-499 Emps.	500-999 Emps.	Unknown Emps.	Industry Sales
2015	0.0	0.0	0.0	1.1	2.1	122.3	538.5	13.6	0.2	677.9
2016	0.0	0.0	0.0	1.2	2.2	125.7	553.3	13.9	0.2	696.6
2017	0.0	0.0	0.0	1.2	2.3	129.8	571.4	14.4	0.2	719.4
2018	0.0	0.0	0.0	1.3	2.4	139.7	615.0	15.5	0.2	774.2
2019	0.0	0.0	0.0	1.4	2.6	148.0	651.4	16.4	0.2	820.1

INDUSTRY: MEN'S CLOTHING STORES (NAICS 44811)
PRODUCT LINE: MEN'S SUITS & FORMAL WEAR (Sub Category)

NAICS 44811: Men's Clothing Stores. This industry comprises establishments primarily engaged in retailing a general line of new men's and boys' clothing. These establishments may provide basic alterations, such as hemming, taking in or letting out seams, or lengthening or shortening sleeves.

5-YEAR TREND – ESTIMATED INDUSTRY SALES ($MILLIONS)

Year	Employee Size of Establishment									Total
	1-4 Emps.	5-9 Emps.	10-19 Emps.	20-49 Emps.	50-99 Emps.	100-249 Emps.	250-499 Emps.	500-999 Emps.	Unknown Emps.	Industry Sales
2015	71.7	126.0	234.5	123.6	26.9	24.2	8.1	0.4	12.4	627.7
2016	74.4	130.6	243.2	128.1	27.9	25.1	8.4	0.5	12.8	650.9
2017	77.4	136.0	253.2	133.4	29.0	26.1	8.8	0.5	13.3	677.9
2018	79.9	140.3	261.2	137.6	30.0	26.9	9.1	0.5	13.8	699.1
2019	83.0	145.8	271.4	143.0	31.1	28.0	9.4	0.5	14.3	726.6

INDUSTRY: FAMILY CLOTHING STORES (NAICS 44814)
PRODUCT LINE: MEN'S SUITS & FORMAL WEAR (Sub Category)

NAICS 44814: Family Clothing Stores . This industry comprises
establishments primarily engaged in retailing a general line of new clothing
for men, women, and children, without specializing in sales for an individual
gender or age group. These establishments may provide basic alterations,
such as hemming, taking in or letting out seams, or lengthening or shortening sleeves.

5-YEAR TREND — ESTIMATED INDUSTRY SALES ($MILLIONS)

Year	Employee Size of Establishment									Total
	1-4 Emps.	5-9 Emps.	10-19 Emps.	20-49 Emps.	50-99 Emps.	100-249 Emps.	250-499 Emps.	500-999 Emps.	Unknown Emps.	Industry Sales
2015	13.3	27.5	104.0	345.6	305.2	84.0	79.2	45.9	3.6	1,008.4
2016	13.7	28.3	106.8	354.8	313.4	86.3	81.4	47.1	3.7	1,035.5
2017	14.1	29.2	110.2	366.2	323.4	89.0	84.0	48.6	3.9	1,068.5
2018	14.9	30.7	116.1	385.9	340.9	93.8	88.5	51.1	4.1	1,126.1
2019	15.8	32.7	123.4	410.3	362.4	99.7	94.1	54.0	4.3	1,196.8

INDUSTRY: DEPARTMENT STORES (NAICS 45211)
PRODUCT LINE: MEN'S SUITS & FORMAL WEAR (Sub Category)

NAICS 45211: Department Stores Industry . **This industry comprises**
establishments known as department stores primarily engaged in retailing
a wide range of the following new products with no one merchandise line
predominating: apparel, furniture, appliances and home furnishings; and
selected additional items, such as paint, hardware, toiletries, cosmetics,
photographic equipment, jewelry, toys, and sporting goods. Merchandise lines
are normally arranged in separate departments.

5-YEAR TREND — ESTIMATED INDUSTRY SALES ($MILLIONS)

Year	Employee Size of Establishment									Total
	1-4 Emps.	5-9 Emps.	10-19 Emps.	20-49 Emps.	50-99 Emps.	100-249 Emps.	250-499 Emps.	500-999 Emps.	Unknown Emps.	Industry Sales
2015	0.0	0.0	0.1	4.6	83.5	268.0	110.9	16.1	0.7	483.9
2016	0.0	0.0	0.1	4.6	83.8	269.1	111.4	16.1	0.7	485.8
2017	0.0	0.0	0.1	4.7	84.6	271.7	112.5	16.3	0.7	490.6
2018	0.0	0.0	0.1	4.7	84.6	271.8	112.5	16.3	0.7	490.7
2019	0.0	0.0	0.1	4.7	85.5	274.5	113.6	16.5	0.7	495.5

INDUSTRY: MEN'S CLOTHING STORES (NAICS 44811)
PRODUCT LINE: MEN'S SPORT COATS & BLAZERS (Sub Category)

NAICS 44811: Men's Clothing Stores. This industry comprises establishments primarily engaged in retailing a general line of new men's and boys' clothing. These establishments may provide basic alterations, such as hemming, taking in or letting out seams, or lengthening or shortening sleeves.

5-YEAR TREND — ESTIMATED INDUSTRY SALES ($MILLIONS)

Year	Employee Size of Establishment									Total
	1-4 Emps.	5-9 Emps.	10-19 Emps.	20-49 Emps.	50-99 Emps.	100-249 Emps.	250-499 Emps.	500-999 Emps.	Unknown Emps.	Industry Sales
2015	60.3	106.0	197.3	103.9	22.6	20.3	6.9	0.4	10.4	528.0
2016	62.5	109.9	204.6	107.8	23.5	21.1	7.1	0.4	10.8	547.6
2017	65.1	114.4	213.0	112.3	24.4	22.0	7.4	0.4	11.2	570.3
2018	67.2	118.0	219.7	115.8	25.2	22.6	7.6	0.4	11.6	588.1
2019	69.8	122.7	228.3	120.3	26.2	23.5	7.9	0.4	12.0	611.3

INDUSTRY: FAMILY CLOTHING STORES (NAICS 44814)
PRODUCT LINE: MEN'S SPORT COATS & BLAZERS (Sub Category)

NAICS 44814: Family Clothing Stores . This industry comprises establishments primarily engaged in retailing a general line of new clothing for men, women, and children, without specializing in sales for an individual gender or age group. These establishments may provide basic alterations, such as hemming, taking in or letting out seams, or lengthening or shortening sleeves.

5-YEAR TREND — ESTIMATED INDUSTRY SALES ($MILLIONS)

Year	Employee Size of Establishment									Total
	1-4 Emps.	5-9 Emps.	10-19 Emps.	20-49 Emps.	50-99 Emps.	100-249 Emps.	250-499 Emps.	500-999 Emps.	Unknown Emps.	Industry Sales
2015	7.9	16.4	61.9	205.6	181.6	50.0	47.1	27.3	2.2	599.9
2016	8.1	16.8	63.5	211.1	186.5	51.3	48.4	28.0	2.2	616.0
2017	8.4	17.4	65.5	217.8	192.4	53.0	50.0	28.9	2.3	635.7
2018	8.8	18.3	69.1	229.6	202.8	55.8	52.7	30.4	2.4	669.9
2019	9.4	19.4	73.4	244.1	215.6	59.3	56.0	32.2	2.6	712.0

INDUSTRY: DEPARTMENT STORES (NAICS 45211)
PRODUCT LINE: MEN'S SPORT COATS & BLAZERS (Sub Category)

NAICS 45211: Department Stores Industry . This industry comprises establishments known as department stores primarily engaged in retailing a wide range of the following new products with no one merchandise line predominating: apparel, furniture, appliances and home furnishings; and selected additional items, such as paint, hardware, toiletries, cosmetics, photographic equipment, jewelry, toys, and sporting goods. Merchandise lines are normally arranged in separate departments.

5-YEAR TREND – ESTIMATED INDUSTRY SALES ($MILLIONS)

Year	Employee Size of Establishment									Total
	1-4 Emps.	5-9 Emps.	10-19 Emps.	20-49 Emps.	50-99 Emps.	100-249 Emps.	250-499 Emps.	500-999 Emps.	Unknown Emps.	Industry Sales
2015	0.0	0.0	0.0	1.6	29.0	93.2	38.6	5.6	0.2	168.3
2016	0.0	0.0	0.0	1.6	29.1	93.6	38.7	5.6	0.2	168.9
2017	0.0	0.0	0.0	1.6	29.4	94.5	39.1	5.7	0.2	170.6
2018	0.0	0.0	0.0	1.6	29.4	94.5	39.1	5.7	0.2	170.6
2019	0.0	0.0	0.0	1.6	29.7	95.4	39.5	5.7	0.2	172.3

INDUSTRY: MEN'S CLOTHING STORES (NAICS 44811)
PRODUCT LINE: MEN'S DRESS SLACKS (Sub Category)

NAICS 44811: Men's Clothing Stores. This industry comprises establishments primarily engaged in retailing a general line of new men's and boys' clothing. These establishments may provide basic alterations, such as hemming, taking in or letting out seams, or lengthening or shortening sleeves.

5-YEAR TREND – ESTIMATED INDUSTRY SALES ($MILLIONS)

Year	Employee Size of Establishment									Total
	1-4 Emps.	5-9 Emps.	10-19 Emps.	20-49 Emps.	50-99 Emps.	100-249 Emps.	250-499 Emps.	500-999 Emps.	Unknown Emps.	Industry Sales
2015	58.4	102.7	191.1	100.7	21.9	19.7	6.6	0.4	10.1	511.7
2016	60.6	106.5	198.2	104.4	22.7	20.4	6.9	0.4	10.4	530.6
2017	63.1	110.9	206.4	108.8	23.7	21.3	7.2	0.4	10.9	552.6
2018	65.1	114.4	212.9	112.2	24.4	21.9	7.4	0.4	11.2	569.9
2019	67.7	118.9	221.3	116.6	25.4	22.8	7.7	0.4	11.7	592.3

INDUSTRY: WOMEN'S CLOTHING STORES (NAICS 44812)
PRODUCT LINE: MEN'S DRESS SLACKS (Sub Category)

NAICS 44812: Women's Clothing Stores . This industry comprises establishments primarily engaged in retailing a general line of new women's, misses' and juniors' clothing, including maternity wear. These establishments may provide basic alterations, such as hemming, taking in or letting out seams, or lengthening or shortening sleeves.

5-YEAR TREND – ESTIMATED INDUSTRY SALES ($MILLIONS)

Year	Employee Size of Establishment									Total
	1-4 Emps.	5-9 Emps.	10-19 Emps.	20-49 Emps.	50-99 Emps.	100-249 Emps.	250-499 Emps.	500-999 Emps.	Unknown Emps.	Industry Sales
2015	4.1	9.3	19.8	13.9	4.9	4.5	1.8	1.8	0.9	61.2
2016	4.3	9.5	20.4	14.4	5.1	4.7	1.9	1.8	1.0	63.0
2017	4.4	9.9	21.1	14.9	5.2	4.8	2.0	1.9	1.0	65.1
2018	4.7	10.4	22.2	15.7	5.5	5.1	2.1	2.0	1.0	68.7
2019	5.0	11.1	23.6	16.7	5.9	5.4	2.2	2.1	1.1	73.1

INDUSTRY: FAMILY CLOTHING STORES (NAICS 44814)
PRODUCT LINE: MEN'S DRESS SLACKS (Sub Category)

NAICS 44814: Family Clothing Stores . This industry comprises establishments primarily engaged in retailing a general line of new clothing for men, women, and children, without specializing in sales for an individual gender or age group. These establishments may provide basic alterations, such as hemming, taking in or letting out seams, or lengthening or shortening sleeves.

5-YEAR TREND – ESTIMATED INDUSTRY SALES ($MILLIONS)

Year	Employee Size of Establishment									Total
	1-4 Emps.	5-9 Emps.	10-19 Emps.	20-49 Emps.	50-99 Emps.	100-249 Emps.	250-499 Emps.	500-999 Emps.	Unknown Emps.	Industry Sales
2015	21.4	44.2	167.0	554.9	490.2	134.9	127.3	73.7	5.9	1,619.4
2016	22.0	45.4	171.4	569.8	503.3	138.5	130.7	75.7	6.0	1,662.8
2017	22.7	46.8	176.9	588.0	519.4	142.9	134.8	78.1	6.2	1,715.9
2018	23.9	49.4	186.5	619.8	547.5	150.7	142.1	82.0	6.5	1,808.3
2019	25.4	52.5	198.2	658.8	582.0	160.2	151.1	86.8	7.0	1,921.9

INDUSTRY: DEPARTMENT STORES (NAICS 45211)
PRODUCT LINE: MEN'S DRESS SLACKS (Sub Category)

NAICS 45211: Department Stores Industry . This industry comprises establishments known as department stores primarily engaged in retailing a wide range of the following new products with no one merchandise line predominating: apparel, furniture, appliances and home furnishings; and selected additional items, such as paint, hardware, toiletries, cosmetics, photographic equipment, jewelry, toys, and sporting goods. Merchandise lines are normally arranged in separate departments.

5-YEAR TREND – ESTIMATED INDUSTRY SALES ($MILLIONS)

Year	Employee Size of Establishment									Total
	1-4 Emps.	5-9 Emps.	10-19 Emps.	20-49 Emps.	50-99 Emps.	100-249 Emps.	250-499 Emps.	500-999 Emps.	Unknown Emps.	Industry Sales
2015	0.0	0.0	0.0	0.1	1.3	4.3	1.8	0.3	0.0	7.8
2016	0.0	0.0	0.0	0.1	1.3	4.3	1.8	0.3	0.0	7.8
2017	0.0	0.0	0.0	0.1	1.4	4.4	1.8	0.3	0.0	7.9
2018	0.0	0.0	0.0	0.1	1.4	4.4	1.8	0.3	0.0	7.9
2019	0.0	0.0	0.0	0.1	1.4	4.4	1.8	0.3	0.0	8.0

INDUSTRY: MEN'S CLOTHING STORES (NAICS 44811)
PRODUCT LINE: MEN'S CASUAL SLACKS & JEANS (Sub Category)

NAICS 44811: Men's Clothing Stores. This industry comprises establishments primarily engaged in retailing a general line of new men's and boys' clothing. These establishments may provide basic alterations, such as hemming, taking in or letting out seams, or lengthening or shortening sleeves.

5-YEAR TREND – ESTIMATED INDUSTRY SALES ($MILLIONS)

Year	Employee Size of Establishment									Total
	1-4 Emps.	5-9 Emps.	10-19 Emps.	20-49 Emps.	50-99 Emps.	100-249 Emps.	250-499 Emps.	500-999 Emps.	Unknown Emps.	Industry Sales
2015	95.6	168.0	312.7	164.8	35.9	32.2	10.9	0.6	16.5	837.2
2016	99.2	174.2	324.3	170.9	37.2	33.4	11.3	0.6	17.1	868.2
2017	103.3	181.4	337.8	178.0	38.7	34.8	11.7	0.6	17.8	904.1
2018	106.5	187.1	348.3	183.5	39.9	35.9	12.1	0.7	18.4	932.4
2019	110.7	194.5	362.0	190.8	41.5	37.3	12.6	0.7	19.1	969.1

INDUSTRY: WOMEN'S CLOTHING STORES (NAICS 44812)

PRODUCT LINE: MEN'S CASUAL SLACKS & JEANS (Sub Category)

NAICS 44812: Women's Clothing Stores . This industry comprises establishments primarily engaged in retailing a general line of new women's, misses' and juniors' clothing, including maternity wear. These establishments may provide basic alterations, such as hemming, taking in or letting out seams, or lengthening or shortening sleeves.

5-Year Trend – Estimated Industry Sales ($Millions)

Year	Employee Size of Establishment									Total Industry Sales
	1-4 Emps.	5-9 Emps.	10-19 Emps.	20-49 Emps.	50-99 Emps.	100-249 Emps.	250-499 Emps.	500-999 Emps.	Unknown Emps.	
2015	20.1	44.9	95.8	67.6	23.9	22.0	8.9	8.7	4.5	296.4
2016	20.7	46.2	98.6	69.6	24.6	22.7	9.2	8.9	4.6	305.2
2017	21.4	47.8	102.1	72.0	25.4	23.5	9.5	9.2	4.8	315.7
2018	22.6	50.5	107.7	75.9	26.8	24.8	10.0	9.7	5.0	333.0
2019	24.0	53.7	114.6	80.8	28.5	26.4	10.7	10.2	5.4	354.2

INDUSTRY: FAMILY CLOTHING STORES (NAICS 44814)

PRODUCT LINE: MEN'S CASUAL SLACKS & JEANS (Sub Category)

NAICS 44814: Family Clothing Stores . This industry comprises establishments primarily engaged in retailing a general line of new clothing for men, women, and children, without specializing in sales for an individual gender or age group. These establishments may provide basic alterations, such as hemming, taking in or letting out seams, or lengthening or shortening sleeves.

5-Year Trend – Estimated Industry Sales ($Millions)

Year	Employee Size of Establishment									Total Industry Sales
	1-4 Emps.	5-9 Emps.	10-19 Emps.	20-49 Emps.	50-99 Emps.	100-249 Emps.	250-499 Emps.	500-999 Emps.	Unknown Emps.	
2015	75.9	156.8	592.4	1,969.0	1,739.3	478.7	451.6	261.5	20.8	5,745.9
2016	77.9	161.0	608.3	2,021.8	1,785.9	491.5	463.7	268.5	21.3	5,900.0
2017	80.4	166.2	627.8	2,086.4	1,843.0	507.2	478.5	277.0	22.0	6,088.5
2018	84.8	175.2	661.7	2,199.1	1,942.5	534.6	504.3	291.0	23.2	6,416.4
2019	90.1	186.2	703.4	2,337.7	2,065.0	568.3	536.1	307.9	24.7	6,819.4

INDUSTRY: DEPARTMENT STORES (NAICS 45211)
PRODUCT LINE: MEN'S CASUAL SLACKS & JEANS (Sub Category)

NAICS 45211: Department Stores Industry . This industry comprises establishments known as department stores primarily engaged in retailing a wide range of the following new products with no one merchandise line predominating: apparel, furniture, appliances and home furnishings; and selected additional items, such as paint, hardware, toiletries, cosmetics, photographic equipment, jewelry, toys, and sporting goods. Merchandise lines are normally arranged in separate departments.

5-Year Trend — Estimated Industry Sales ($Millions)

Year	Employee Size of Establishment									Total
	1-4 Emps.	5-9 Emps.	10-19 Emps.	20-49 Emps.	50-99 Emps.	100-249 Emps.	250-499 Emps.	500-999 Emps.	Unknown Emps.	Industry Sales
2015	6.2	12.1	30.6	62.5	47.4	3,125.6	244.1	5.1	2.2	3,535.6
2016	6.3	12.3	31.3	64.0	48.5	3,200.5	250.0	5.2	2.2	3,620.4
2017	6.5	12.7	32.2	65.9	50.0	3,294.3	257.3	5.4	2.3	3,726.4
2018	6.8	13.2	33.4	68.3	51.8	3,416.6	266.8	5.6	2.4	3,864.8
2019	7.1	13.8	35.0	71.5	54.2	3,574.3	279.1	5.8	2.5	4,043.3

INDUSTRY: WAREHOUSE CLUBS & SUPERCENTERS (NAICS 45291)
PRODUCT LINE: MEN'S CASUAL SLACKS & JEANS (Sub Category)

NAICS 45291: Warehouse Clubs and Superstores This industry comprises establishments known as warehouse clubs, superstores or supercenters primarily engaged in retailing a general line of groceries in combination with general lines of new merchandise, such as apparel, furniture, and appliances.

5-Year Trend — Estimated Industry Sales ($Millions)

Year	Employee Size of Establishment									Total
	1-4 Emps.	5-9 Emps.	10-19 Emps.	20-49 Emps.	50-99 Emps.	100-249 Emps.	250-499 Emps.	500-999 Emps.	Unknown Emps.	Industry Sales
2015	0.2	0.0	0.1	4.9	9.2	525.8	2,314.9	58.3	0.9	2,914.3
2016	0.2	0.0	0.1	5.0	9.5	540.3	2,378.7	59.9	0.9	2,994.6
2017	0.2	0.0	0.1	5.2	9.8	558.0	2,456.4	61.9	0.9	3,092.4
2018	0.2	0.0	0.2	5.5	10.5	600.5	2,643.6	66.6	1.0	3,328.2
2019	0.2	0.0	0.2	5.9	11.1	636.1	2,800.2	70.6	1.1	3,525.3

INDUSTRY: MEN'S CLOTHING STORES (NAICS 44811)
PRODUCT LINE: MEN'S WORK UNIFORMS (Sub Category)

NAICS 44811: Men's Clothing Stores. This industry comprises establishments primarily engaged in retailing a general line of new men's and boys' clothing. These establishments may provide basic alterations, such as hemming, taking in or letting out seams, or lengthening or shortening sleeves.

5-YEAR TREND – ESTIMATED INDUSTRY SALES ($MILLIONS)

Year	Employee Size of Establishment									Total
	1-4 Emps.	5-9 Emps.	10-19 Emps.	20-49 Emps.	50-99 Emps.	100-249 Emps.	250-499 Emps.	500-999 Emps.	Unknown Emps.	Industry Sales
2015	9.9	17.4	32.5	17.1	3.7	3.3	1.1	0.1	1.7	86.9
2016	10.3	18.1	33.7	17.7	3.9	3.5	1.2	0.1	1.8	90.1
2017	10.7	18.8	35.0	18.5	4.0	3.6	1.2	0.1	1.8	93.8
2018	11.1	19.4	36.1	19.0	4.1	3.7	1.3	0.1	1.9	96.8
2019	11.5	20.2	37.6	19.8	4.3	3.9	1.3	0.1	2.0	100.6

INDUSTRY: FAMILY CLOTHING STORES (NAICS 44814)
PRODUCT LINE: MEN'S WORK UNIFORMS (Sub Category)

NAICS 44814: Family Clothing Stores . This industry comprises establishments primarily engaged in retailing a general line of new clothing for men, women, and children, without specializing in sales for an individual gender or age group. These establishments may provide basic alterations, such as hemming, taking in or letting out seams, or lengthening or shortening sleeves.

5-YEAR TREND – ESTIMATED INDUSTRY SALES ($MILLIONS)

Year	Employee Size of Establishment									Total
	1-4 Emps.	5-9 Emps.	10-19 Emps.	20-49 Emps.	50-99 Emps.	100-249 Emps.	250-499 Emps.	500-999 Emps.	Unknown Emps.	Industry Sales
2015	10.5	21.7	81.8	271.9	240.2	66.1	62.4	36.1	2.9	793.4
2016	10.8	22.2	84.0	279.2	246.6	67.9	64.0	37.1	2.9	814.7
2017	11.1	22.9	86.7	288.1	254.5	70.0	66.1	38.3	3.0	840.7
2018	11.7	24.2	91.4	303.7	268.2	73.8	69.6	40.2	3.2	886.0
2019	12.4	25.7	97.1	322.8	285.1	78.5	74.0	42.5	3.4	941.6

INDUSTRY: MEN'S CLOTHING STORES (NAICS 44811)
PRODUCT LINE: MEN'S DRESS SHIRTS (Sub Category)

NAICS 44811: Men's Clothing Stores. This industry comprises establishments primarily engaged in retailing a general line of new men's and boys' clothing. These establishments may provide basic alterations, such as hemming, taking in or letting out seams, or lengthening or shortening sleeves.

5-YEAR TREND – ESTIMATED INDUSTRY SALES ($MILLIONS)

Year	Employee Size of Establishment									Total Industry Sales
	1-4 Emps.	5-9 Emps.	10-19 Emps.	20-49 Emps.	50-99 Emps.	100-249 Emps.	250-499 Emps.	500-999 Emps.	Unknown Emps.	
2015	54.9	96.5	179.6	94.6	20.6	18.5	6.2	0.3	9.5	480.7
2016	56.9	100.0	186.2	98.1	21.4	19.2	6.5	0.3	9.8	498.5
2017	59.3	104.2	194.0	102.2	22.2	20.0	6.7	0.4	10.2	519.2
2018	61.2	107.4	200.0	105.4	22.9	20.6	6.9	0.4	10.5	535.4
2019	63.6	111.7	207.9	109.5	23.8	21.4	7.2	0.4	11.0	556.5

INDUSTRY: FAMILY CLOTHING STORES (NAICS 44814)
PRODUCT LINE: MEN'S DRESS SHIRTS (Sub Category)

NAICS 44814: Family Clothing Stores . This industry comprises establishments primarily engaged in retailing a general line of new clothing for men, women, and children, without specializing in sales for an individual gender or age group. These establishments may provide basic alterations, such as hemming, taking in or letting out seams, or lengthening or shortening sleeves.

5-YEAR TREND – ESTIMATED INDUSTRY SALES ($MILLIONS)

Year	Employee Size of Establishment									Total Industry Sales
	1-4 Emps.	5-9 Emps.	10-19 Emps.	20-49 Emps.	50-99 Emps.	100-249 Emps.	250-499 Emps.	500-999 Emps.	Unknown Emps.	
2015	25.9	53.6	202.3	672.5	594.0	163.5	154.2	89.3	7.1	1,962.5
2016	26.6	55.0	207.8	690.5	610.0	167.9	158.4	91.7	7.3	2,015.1
2017	27.5	56.8	214.4	712.6	629.5	173.2	163.4	94.6	7.5	2,079.5
2018	28.9	59.8	226.0	751.1	663.5	182.6	172.2	99.4	7.9	2,191.5
2019	30.8	63.6	240.2	798.4	705.3	194.1	183.1	105.2	8.4	2,329.1

INDUSTRY: DEPARTMENT STORES (NAICS 45211)
PRODUCT LINE: MEN'S DRESS SHIRTS (Sub Category)

NAICS 45211: Department Stores Industry . This industry comprises
establishments known as department stores primarily engaged in retailing
a wide range of the following new products with no one merchandise line
predominating: apparel, furniture, appliances and home furnishings; and
selected additional items, such as paint, hardware, toiletries, cosmetics,
photographic equipment, jewelry, toys, and sporting goods. Merchandise lines
are normally arranged in separate departments.

5-YEAR TREND — ESTIMATED INDUSTRY SALES ($MILLIONS)

| Year | Employee Size of Establishment | | | | | | | | | Total |
	1-4 Emps.	5-9 Emps.	10-19 Emps.	20-49 Emps.	50-99 Emps.	100-249 Emps.	250-499 Emps.	500-999 Emps.	Unknown Emps.	Industry Sales
2015	0.0	0.0	0.1	4.6	84.0	269.7	111.6	16.2	0.7	486.9
2016	0.0	0.0	0.1	4.6	84.3	270.8	112.1	16.2	0.7	488.8
2017	0.0	0.0	0.1	4.7	85.2	273.4	113.2	16.4	0.7	493.6
2018	0.0	0.0	0.1	4.7	85.2	273.5	113.2	16.4	0.7	493.7
2019	0.0	0.0	0.1	4.7	86.0	276.2	114.3	16.6	0.7	498.7

INDUSTRY: MEN'S CLOTHING STORES (NAICS 44811)
PRODUCT LINE: MEN'S SPORT SHIRTS & T-SHIRTS (Sub Category)

NAICS 44811: Men's Clothing Stores. This industry comprises
establishments primarily engaged in retailing a general line of new
men's and boys' clothing. These establishments may provide basic
alterations, such as hemming, taking in or letting out seams, or lengthening
or shortening sleeves.

5-YEAR TREND — ESTIMATED INDUSTRY SALES ($MILLIONS)

| Year | Employee Size of Establishment | | | | | | | | | Total |
	1-4 Emps.	5-9 Emps.	10-19 Emps.	20-49 Emps.	50-99 Emps.	100-249 Emps.	250-499 Emps.	500-999 Emps.	Unknown Emps.	Industry Sales
2015	107.1	188.1	350.3	184.6	40.2	36.1	12.2	0.7	18.5	937.6
2016	111.1	195.1	363.2	191.4	41.7	37.4	12.6	0.7	19.1	972.3
2017	115.7	203.2	378.3	199.3	43.4	39.0	13.1	0.7	19.9	1,012.6
2018	119.3	209.6	390.1	205.6	44.7	40.2	13.5	0.7	20.6	1,044.3
2019	124.0	217.8	405.5	213.6	46.5	41.8	14.1	0.8	21.4	1,085.4

INDUSTRY: WOMEN'S CLOTHING STORES (NAICS 44812)
PRODUCT LINE: MEN'S SPORT SHIRTS & T-SHIRTS (Sub Category)

NAICS 44812: Women's Clothing Stores . This industry comprises establishments primarily engaged in retailing a general line of new women's, misses' and juniors' clothing, including maternity wear. These establishments may provide basic alterations, such as hemming, taking in or letting out seams, or lengthening or shortening sleeves.

5-YEAR TREND – ESTIMATED INDUSTRY SALES ($MILLIONS)

Year	Employee Size of Establishment									Total
	1-4 Emps.	5-9 Emps.	10-19 Emps.	20-49 Emps.	50-99 Emps.	100-249 Emps.	250-499 Emps.	500-999 Emps.	Unknown Emps.	Industry Sales
2015	29.4	65.6	140.0	98.8	34.9	32.2	13.1	12.6	6.6	433.1
2016	30.3	67.6	144.2	101.7	35.9	33.2	13.5	13.0	6.8	446.0
2017	31.3	69.9	149.1	105.2	37.2	34.3	13.9	13.5	7.0	461.4
2018	33.0	73.8	157.4	111.0	39.2	36.2	14.7	14.1	7.4	486.7
2019	35.1	78.5	167.4	118.1	41.7	38.5	15.6	14.9	7.8	517.7

INDUSTRY: FAMILY CLOTHING STORES (NAICS 44814)
PRODUCT LINE: MEN'S SPORT SHIRTS & T-SHIRTS (Sub Category)

NAICS 44814: Family Clothing Stores . This industry comprises establishments primarily engaged in retailing a general line of new clothing for men, women, and children, without specializing in sales for an individual gender or age group. These establishments may provide basic alterations, such as hemming, taking in or letting out seams, or lengthening or shortening sleeves.

5-YEAR TREND – ESTIMATED INDUSTRY SALES ($MILLIONS)

Year	Employee Size of Establishment									Total
	1-4 Emps.	5-9 Emps.	10-19 Emps.	20-49 Emps.	50-99 Emps.	100-249 Emps.	250-499 Emps.	500-999 Emps.	Unknown Emps.	Industry Sales
2015	85.5	176.7	667.5	2,218.4	1,959.6	539.3	508.7	294.6	23.4	6,473.7
2016	87.8	181.4	685.4	2,277.9	2,012.1	553.8	522.4	302.5	24.1	6,647.3
2017	90.6	187.2	707.3	2,350.7	2,076.4	571.5	539.1	312.1	24.8	6,859.7
2018	95.5	197.4	745.5	2,477.7	2,188.6	602.3	568.2	327.8	26.2	7,229.1
2019	101.5	209.8	792.5	2,633.8	2,326.5	640.3	604.0	346.9	27.8	7,683.2

INDUSTRY: DEPARTMENT STORES (NAICS 45211)
PRODUCT LINE: MEN'S SPORT SHIRTS & T-SHIRTS (Sub Category)

NAICS 45211: Department Stores Industry . This industry comprises establishments known as department stores primarily engaged in retailing a wide range of the following new products with no one merchandise line predominating: apparel, furniture, appliances and home furnishings; and selected additional items, such as paint, hardware, toiletries, cosmetics, photographic equipment, jewelry, toys, and sporting goods. Merchandise lines are normally arranged in separate departments.

5-YEAR TREND – ESTIMATED INDUSTRY SALES ($MILLIONS)

Year	Employee Size of Establishment									Total
	1-4 Emps.	5-9 Emps.	10-19 Emps.	20-49 Emps.	50-99 Emps.	100-249 Emps.	250-499 Emps.	500-999 Emps.	Unknown Emps.	Industry Sales
2015	0.1	0.1	0.3	23.8	431.4	1,385.3	573.4	83.0	3.5	2,501.0
2016	0.1	0.1	0.3	23.9	433.1	1,390.7	575.7	83.3	3.5	2,510.7
2017	0.1	0.1	0.3	24.1	437.4	1,404.5	581.4	84.1	3.6	2,535.5
2018	0.1	0.1	0.3	24.1	437.4	1,404.6	581.4	84.3	3.6	2,536.1
2019	0.1	0.1	0.3	24.3	441.8	1,418.6	587.2	85.3	3.6	2,561.3

INDUSTRY: WAREHOUSE CLUBS & SUPERCENTERS (NAICS 45291)
PRODUCT LINE: MEN'S SPORT SHIRTS & T-SHIRTS (Sub Category)

NAICS 45291: Warehouse Clubs and Superstores This industry comprises establishments known as warehouse clubs, superstores or supercenters primarily engaged in retailing a general line of groceries in combination with general lines of new merchandise, such as apparel, furniture, and appliances.

5-YEAR TREND – ESTIMATED INDUSTRY SALES ($MILLIONS)

Year	Employee Size of Establishment									Total
	1-4 Emps.	5-9 Emps.	10-19 Emps.	20-49 Emps.	50-99 Emps.	100-249 Emps.	250-499 Emps.	500-999 Emps.	Unknown Emps.	Industry Sales
2015	0.1	0.0	0.1	3.2	6.2	352.0	1,549.7	39.1	0.6	1,951.0
2016	0.1	0.0	0.1	3.3	6.3	361.7	1,592.4	40.1	0.6	2,004.7
2017	0.1	0.0	0.1	3.4	6.5	373.5	1,644.4	41.4	0.6	2,070.2
2018	0.1	0.0	0.1	3.7	7.0	402.0	1,769.7	44.6	0.7	2,228.0
2019	0.1	0.0	0.1	3.9	7.5	425.8	1,874.6	47.2	0.7	2,360.0

INDUSTRY: MEN'S CLOTHING STORES (NAICS 44811)
PRODUCT LINE: MEN'S SWEATERS (Sub Category)

NAICS 44811: Men's Clothing Stores. This industry comprises establishments primarily engaged in retailing a general line of new men's and boys' clothing. These establishments may provide basic alterations, such as hemming, taking in or letting out seams, or lengthening or shortening sleeves.

5-YEAR TREND – ESTIMATED INDUSTRY SALES ($MILLIONS)

Year	Employee Size of Establishment									Total
	1-4 Emps.	5-9 Emps.	10-19 Emps.	20-49 Emps.	50-99 Emps.	100-249 Emps.	250-499 Emps.	500-999 Emps.	Unknown Emps.	Industry Sales
2015	24.9	43.8	81.5	43.0	9.3	8.4	2.8	0.2	4.3	218.2
2016	25.8	45.4	84.5	44.5	9.7	8.7	2.9	0.2	4.5	226.3
2017	26.9	47.3	88.0	46.4	10.1	9.1	3.1	0.2	4.6	235.7
2018	27.8	48.8	90.8	47.8	10.4	9.4	3.2	0.2	4.8	243.1
2019	28.9	50.7	94.4	49.7	10.8	9.7	3.3	0.2	5.0	252.6

INDUSTRY: FAMILY CLOTHING STORES (NAICS 44814)
PRODUCT LINE: MEN'S SWEATERS (Sub Category)

NAICS 44814: Family Clothing Stores . This industry comprises establishments primarily engaged in retailing a general line of new clothing for men, women, and children, without specializing in sales for an individual gender or age group. These establishments may provide basic alterations, such as hemming, taking in or letting out seams, or lengthening or shortening sleeves.

5-YEAR TREND – ESTIMATED INDUSTRY SALES ($MILLIONS)

Year	Employee Size of Establishment									Total
	1-4 Emps.	5-9 Emps.	10-19 Emps.	20-49 Emps.	50-99 Emps.	100-249 Emps.	250-499 Emps.	500-999 Emps.	Unknown Emps.	Industry Sales
2015	25.2	52.1	196.9	654.4	578.1	159.1	150.1	86.9	6.9	1,909.8
2016	25.9	53.5	202.2	672.0	593.6	163.4	154.1	89.2	7.1	1,961.0
2017	26.7	55.2	208.6	693.5	612.6	168.6	159.0	92.1	7.3	2,023.6
2018	28.2	58.2	219.9	730.9	645.6	177.7	167.6	96.7	7.7	2,132.6
2019	29.9	61.9	233.8	777.0	686.3	188.9	178.2	102.4	8.2	2,266.6

INDUSTRY: DEPARTMENT STORES (NAICS 45211)
PRODUCT LINE: MEN'S SWEATERS (Sub Category)

NAICS 45211: Department Stores Industry . This industry comprises establishments known as department stores primarily engaged in retailing a wide range of the following new products with no one merchandise line predominating: apparel, furniture, appliances and home furnishings; and selected additional items, such as paint, hardware, toiletries, cosmetics, photographic equipment, jewelry, toys, and sporting goods. Merchandise lines are normally arranged in separate departments.

5-YEAR TREND — ESTIMATED INDUSTRY SALES ($MILLIONS)

Year	Employee Size of Establishment									Total
	1-4 Emps.	5-9 Emps.	10-19 Emps.	20-49 Emps.	50-99 Emps.	100-249 Emps.	250-499 Emps.	500-999 Emps.	Unknown Emps.	Industry Sales
2015	0.0	0.0	0.0	3.4	61.7	198.2	82.1	11.9	0.5	357.9
2016	0.0	0.0	0.0	3.4	62.0	199.0	82.4	11.9	0.5	359.3
2017	0.0	0.0	0.0	3.4	62.6	201.0	83.2	12.0	0.5	362.8
2018	0.0	0.0	0.0	3.4	62.6	201.0	83.2	12.1	0.5	362.9
2019	0.0	0.0	0.0	3.5	63.2	203.0	84.0	12.2	0.5	366.5

INDUSTRY: MEN'S CLOTHING STORES (NAICS 44811)
PRODUCT LINE: MEN'S SOCKS & UNDERWEAR (Sub Category)

NAICS 44811: Men's Clothing Stores. This industry comprises establishments primarily engaged in retailing a general line of new men's and boys' clothing. These establishments may provide basic alterations, such as hemming, taking in or letting out seams, or lengthening or shortening sleeves.

5-YEAR TREND — ESTIMATED INDUSTRY SALES ($MILLIONS)

Year	Employee Size of Establishment									Total
	1-4 Emps.	5-9 Emps.	10-19 Emps.	20-49 Emps.	50-99 Emps.	100-249 Emps.	250-499 Emps.	500-999 Emps.	Unknown Emps.	Industry Sales
2015	16.3	28.7	53.4	28.1	6.1	5.5	1.9	0.1	2.8	143.0
2016	16.9	29.8	55.4	29.2	6.4	5.7	1.9	0.1	2.9	148.3
2017	17.6	31.0	57.7	30.4	6.6	5.9	2.0	0.1	3.0	154.4
2018	18.2	32.0	59.5	31.3	6.8	6.1	2.1	0.1	3.1	159.2
2019	18.9	33.2	61.8	32.6	7.1	6.4	2.1	0.1	3.3	165.5

INDUSTRY: FAMILY CLOTHING STORES (NAICS 44814)
PRODUCT LINE: MEN'S SOCKS & UNDERWEAR (Sub Category)

NAICS 44814: Family Clothing Stores . This industry comprises
establishments primarily engaged in retailing a general line of new clothing
for men, women, and children, without specializing in sales for an individual
gender or age group. These establishments may provide basic alterations,
such as hemming, taking in or letting out seams, or lengthening or shortening sleeves.

5-YEAR TREND – ESTIMATED INDUSTRY SALES ($MILLIONS)

Year	Employee Size of Establishment									Total
	1-4 Emps.	5-9 Emps.	10-19 Emps.	20-49 Emps.	50-99 Emps.	100-249 Emps.	250-499 Emps.	500-999 Emps.	Unknown Emps.	Industry Sales
2015	17.6	36.5	137.8	457.8	404.4	111.3	105.0	60.8	4.8	1,336.1
2016	18.1	37.4	141.4	470.1	415.3	114.3	107.8	62.4	5.0	1,371.9
2017	18.7	38.6	146.0	485.1	428.5	117.9	111.3	64.4	5.1	1,415.7
2018	19.7	40.7	153.9	511.3	451.7	124.3	117.3	67.7	5.4	1,492.0
2019	20.9	43.3	163.6	543.6	480.2	132.1	124.7	71.6	5.7	1,585.7

INDUSTRY: DEPARTMENT STORES (NAICS 45211)
PRODUCT LINE: MEN'S SOCKS & UNDERWEAR (Sub Category)

NAICS 45211: Department Stores Industry . This industry comprises
establishments known as department stores primarily engaged in retailing
a wide range of the following new products with no one merchandise line
predominating: apparel, furniture, appliances and home furnishings; and
selected additional items, such as paint, hardware, toiletries, cosmetics,
photographic equipment, jewelry, toys, and sporting goods. Merchandise lines
are normally arranged in separate departments.

5-YEAR TREND – ESTIMATED INDUSTRY SALES ($MILLIONS)

Year	Employee Size of Establishment									Total
	1-4 Emps.	5-9 Emps.	10-19 Emps.	20-49 Emps.	50-99 Emps.	100-249 Emps.	250-499 Emps.	500-999 Emps.	Unknown Emps.	Industry Sales
2015	0.1	0.1	0.2	13.0	236.9	760.6	314.9	45.5	1.9	1,373.2
2016	0.1	0.1	0.2	13.1	237.8	763.6	316.1	45.7	1.9	1,378.5
2017	0.1	0.1	0.2	13.2	240.1	771.1	319.2	46.2	2.0	1,392.2
2018	0.1	0.1	0.2	13.2	240.2	771.2	319.2	46.3	2.0	1,392.5
2019	0.1	0.1	0.2	13.4	242.6	778.9	322.4	46.8	2.0	1,406.3

INDUSTRY: WAREHOUSE CLUBS & SUPERCENTERS (NAICS 45291)
PRODUCT LINE: MEN'S SOCKS & UNDERWEAR (Sub Category)

NAICS 45291: Warehouse Clubs and Superstores This industry comprises establishments known as warehouse clubs, superstores or supercenters primarily engaged in retailing a general line of groceries in combination with general lines of new merchandise, such as apparel, furniture, and appliances.

5-YEAR TREND – ESTIMATED INDUSTRY SALES ($MILLIONS)

Year	Employee Size of Establishment									Total
	1-4 Emps.	5-9 Emps.	10-19 Emps.	20-49 Emps.	50-99 Emps.	100-249 Emps.	250-499 Emps.	500-999 Emps.	Unknown Emps.	Industry Sales
2015	0.1	0.0	0.1	3.5	6.6	375.4	1,652.5	41.6	0.6	2,080.4
2016	0.1	0.0	0.1	3.6	6.8	385.7	1,698.1	42.8	0.6	2,137.8
2017	0.1	0.0	0.1	3.7	7.0	398.3	1,753.5	44.2	0.7	2,207.6
2018	0.1	0.0	0.1	4.0	7.5	428.7	1,887.2	47.6	0.7	2,375.9
2019	0.1	0.0	0.1	4.2	8.0	454.1	1,999.0	50.4	0.8	2,516.6

INDUSTRY: MEN'S CLOTHING STORES (NAICS 44811)
PRODUCT LINE: MEN'S SPORTS APPAREL (Sub Category)

NAICS 44811: Men's Clothing Stores. This industry comprises establishments primarily engaged in retailing a general line of new men's and boys' clothing. These establishments may provide basic alterations, such as hemming, taking in or letting out seams, or lengthening or shortening sleeves.

5-YEAR TREND – ESTIMATED INDUSTRY SALES ($MILLIONS)

Year	Employee Size of Establishment									Total
	1-4 Emps.	5-9 Emps.	10-19 Emps.	20-49 Emps.	50-99 Emps.	100-249 Emps.	250-499 Emps.	500-999 Emps.	Unknown Emps.	Industry Sales
2015	32.7	57.5	107.0	56.4	12.3	11.0	3.7	0.2	5.6	286.5
2016	33.9	59.6	111.0	58.5	12.7	11.4	3.9	0.2	5.9	297.1
2017	35.3	62.1	115.6	60.9	13.3	11.9	4.0	0.2	6.1	309.5
2018	36.5	64.0	119.2	62.8	13.7	12.3	4.1	0.2	6.3	319.2
2019	37.9	66.6	123.9	65.3	14.2	12.8	4.3	0.2	6.5	331.7

INDUSTRY: FAMILY CLOTHING STORES (NAICS 44814)
PRODUCT LINE: MEN'S SPORTS APPAREL (Sub Category)

NAICS 44814: Family Clothing Stores . This industry comprises
establishments primarily engaged in retailing a general line of new clothing
for men, women, and children, without specializing in sales for an individual
gender or age group. These establishments may provide basic alterations,
such as hemming, taking in or letting out seams, or lengthening or shortening sleeves.

5-YEAR TREND – ESTIMATED INDUSTRY SALES ($MILLIONS)

Year	Employee Size of Establishment									Total Industry Sales
	1-4 Emps.	5-9 Emps.	10-19 Emps.	20-49 Emps.	50-99 Emps.	100-249 Emps.	250-499 Emps.	500-999 Emps.	Unknown Emps.	
2015	12.4	25.5	96.5	320.6	283.2	78.0	73.5	42.6	3.4	935.7
2016	12.7	26.2	99.1	329.2	290.8	80.0	75.5	43.7	3.5	960.8
2017	13.1	27.1	102.2	339.8	300.1	82.6	77.9	45.1	3.6	991.5
2018	13.8	28.5	107.8	358.1	316.3	87.1	82.1	47.4	3.8	1,044.9
2019	14.7	30.3	114.5	380.7	336.3	92.5	87.3	50.1	4.0	1,110.5

INDUSTRY: DEPARTMENT STORES (NAICS 45211)
PRODUCT LINE: MEN'S SPORTS APPAREL (Sub Category)

NAICS 45211: Department Stores Industry . This industry comprises
establishments known as department stores primarily engaged in retailing
a wide range of the following new products with no one merchandise line
predominating: apparel, furniture, appliances and home furnishings; and
selected additional items, such as paint, hardware, toiletries, cosmetics,
photographic equipment, jewelry, toys, and sporting goods. Merchandise lines
are normally arranged in separate departments.

5-YEAR TREND – ESTIMATED INDUSTRY SALES ($MILLIONS)

Year	Employee Size of Establishment									Total Industry Sales
	1-4 Emps.	5-9 Emps.	10-19 Emps.	20-49 Emps.	50-99 Emps.	100-249 Emps.	250-499 Emps.	500-999 Emps.	Unknown Emps.	
2015	0.0	0.0	0.1	6.1	110.0	353.2	146.2	21.2	0.9	637.7
2016	0.0	0.0	0.1	6.1	110.4	354.6	146.8	21.2	0.9	640.2
2017	0.0	0.0	0.1	6.1	111.5	358.1	148.2	21.4	0.9	646.5
2018	0.0	0.0	0.1	6.1	111.5	358.2	148.3	21.5	0.9	646.7
2019	0.0	0.0	0.1	6.2	112.6	361.7	149.7	21.7	0.9	653.1

INDUSTRY: MEN'S CLOTHING STORES (NAICS 44811)
PRODUCT LINE: MEN'S ACCESSORIES (Sub Category)

NAICS 44811: Men's Clothing Stores. This industry comprises establishments primarily engaged in retailing a general line of new men's and boys' clothing. These establishments may provide basic alterations, such as hemming, taking in or letting out seams, or lengthening or shortening sleeves.

5-YEAR TREND – ESTIMATED INDUSTRY SALES ($MILLIONS)

Year	Employee Size of Establishment									Total
	1-4 Emps.	5-9 Emps.	10-19 Emps.	20-49 Emps.	50-99 Emps.	100-249 Emps.	250-499 Emps.	500-999 Emps.	Unknown Emps.	Industry Sales
2015	62.9	110.4	205.6	108.3	23.6	21.2	7.1	0.4	10.8	550.3
2016	65.2	114.5	213.2	112.3	24.4	22.0	7.4	0.4	11.2	570.7
2017	67.9	119.3	222.0	117.0	25.5	22.9	7.7	0.4	11.7	594.3
2018	70.0	123.0	229.0	120.7	26.3	23.6	8.0	0.4	12.1	612.9
2019	72.8	127.8	238.0	125.4	27.3	24.5	8.3	0.4	12.5	637.0

INDUSTRY: FAMILY CLOTHING STORES (NAICS 44814)
PRODUCT LINE: MEN'S ACCESSORIES (Sub Category)

NAICS 44814: Family Clothing Stores . This industry comprises establishments primarily engaged in retailing a general line of new clothing for men, women, and children, without specializing in sales for an individual gender or age group. These establishments may provide basic alterations, such as hemming, taking in or letting out seams, or lengthening or shortening sleeves.

5-YEAR TREND – ESTIMATED INDUSTRY SALES ($MILLIONS)

Year	Employee Size of Establishment									Total
	1-4 Emps.	5-9 Emps.	10-19 Emps.	20-49 Emps.	50-99 Emps.	100-249 Emps.	250-499 Emps.	500-999 Emps.	Unknown Emps.	Industry Sales
2015	24.1	49.7	187.9	624.4	551.6	151.8	143.2	82.9	6.6	1,822.2
2016	24.7	51.1	192.9	641.2	566.4	155.9	147.0	85.1	6.8	1,871.1
2017	25.5	52.7	199.1	661.7	584.5	160.9	151.7	87.9	7.0	1,930.9
2018	26.9	55.6	209.8	697.4	616.0	169.5	159.9	92.3	7.4	2,034.8
2019	28.6	59.1	223.1	741.4	654.9	180.2	170.0	97.7	7.8	2,162.6

INDUSTRY: DEPARTMENT STORES (NAICS 45211)
PRODUCT LINE: MEN'S ACCESSORIES (Sub Category)

NAICS 45211: Department Stores Industry . This industry comprises
establishments known as department stores primarily engaged in retailing
a wide range of the following new products with no one merchandise line
predominating: apparel, furniture, appliances and home furnishings; and
selected additional items, such as paint, hardware, toiletries, cosmetics,
photographic equipment, jewelry, toys, and sporting goods. Merchandise lines
are normally arranged in separate departments.

5-YEAR TREND — ESTIMATED INDUSTRY SALES ($MILLIONS)

Year	Employee Size of Establishment									Total
	1-4 Emps.	5-9 Emps.	10-19 Emps.	20-49 Emps.	50-99 Emps.	100-249 Emps.	250-499 Emps.	500-999 Emps.	Unknown Emps.	Industry Sales
2015	0.0	0.0	0.1	6.2	111.8	359.1	148.6	21.5	0.9	648.2
2016	0.0	0.0	0.1	6.2	112.3	360.5	149.2	21.6	0.9	650.8
2017	0.0	0.0	0.1	6.2	113.4	364.0	150.7	21.8	0.9	657.2
2018	0.0	0.0	0.1	6.2	113.4	364.1	150.7	21.9	0.9	657.3
2019	0.0	0.0	0.1	6.3	114.5	367.7	152.2	22.1	0.9	663.9

INDUSTRY: MEN'S CLOTHING STORES (NAICS 44811)
PRODUCT LINE: MEN'S CUSTOM-MADE GARMENTS Category)

NAICS 44811: Men's Clothing Stores. This industry comprises
establishments primarily engaged in retailing a general line of new
men's and boys' clothing. These establishments may provide basic
alterations, such as hemming, taking in or letting out seams, or lengthening
or shortening sleeves.

5-YEAR TREND — ESTIMATED INDUSTRY SALES ($MILLIONS)

Year	Employee Size of Establishment									Total
	1-4 Emps.	5-9 Emps.	10-19 Emps.	20-49 Emps.	50-99 Emps.	100-249 Emps.	250-499 Emps.	500-999 Emps.	Unknown Emps.	Industry Sales
2015	8.2	14.5	26.9	14.2	3.1	2.8	0.9	0.1	1.4	72.0
2016	8.5	15.0	27.9	14.7	3.2	2.9	1.0	0.1	1.5	74.7
2017	8.9	15.6	29.1	15.3	3.3	3.0	1.0	0.1	1.5	77.8
2018	9.2	16.1	30.0	15.8	3.4	3.1	1.0	0.1	1.6	80.2
2019	9.5	16.7	31.1	16.4	3.6	3.2	1.1	0.1	1.6	83.4

INDUSTRY: MEN'S CLOTHING STORES (NAICS 44811)
PRODUCT LINE: MEN'S SWEAT TOPS & PANTS (Sub Category)

NAICS 44811: Men's Clothing Stores. This industry comprises establishments primarily engaged in retailing a general line of new men's and boys' clothing. These establishments may provide basic alterations, such as hemming, taking in or letting out seams, or lengthening or shortening sleeves.

5-YEAR TREND — ESTIMATED INDUSTRY SALES ($MILLIONS)

Year	Employee Size of Establishment									Total
	1-4 Emps.	5-9 Emps.	10-19 Emps.	20-49 Emps.	50-99 Emps.	100-249 Emps.	250-499 Emps.	500-999 Emps.	Unknown Emps.	Industry Sales
2015	8.5	14.8	27.6	14.6	3.2	2.8	1.0	0.1	1.5	74.0
2016	8.8	15.4	28.7	15.1	3.3	3.0	1.0	0.1	1.5	76.7
2017	9.1	16.0	29.9	15.7	3.4	3.1	1.0	0.1	1.6	79.9
2018	9.4	16.5	30.8	16.2	3.5	3.2	1.1	0.1	1.6	82.4
2019	9.8	17.2	32.0	16.9	3.7	3.3	1.1	0.1	1.7	85.7

INDUSTRY: FAMILY CLOTHING STORES (NAICS 44814)
PRODUCT LINE: MEN'S SWEAT TOPS & PANTS (Sub Category)

NAICS 44814: Family Clothing Stores . This industry comprises establishments primarily engaged in retailing a general line of new clothing for men, women, and children, without specializing in sales for an individual gender or age group. These establishments may provide basic alterations, such as hemming, taking in or letting out seams, or lengthening or shortening sleeves.

5-YEAR TREND — ESTIMATED INDUSTRY SALES ($MILLIONS)

Year	Employee Size of Establishment									Total
	1-4 Emps.	5-9 Emps.	10-19 Emps.	20-49 Emps.	50-99 Emps.	100-249 Emps.	250-499 Emps.	500-999 Emps.	Unknown Emps.	Industry Sales
2015	19.3	39.9	150.8	501.3	442.8	121.9	115.0	66.6	5.3	1,462.9
2016	19.8	41.0	154.9	514.8	454.7	125.1	118.1	68.4	5.4	1,502.2
2017	20.5	42.3	159.8	531.2	469.2	129.1	121.8	70.5	5.6	1,550.2
2018	21.6	44.6	168.5	559.9	494.6	136.1	128.4	74.1	5.9	1,633.7
2019	22.9	47.4	179.1	595.2	525.8	144.7	136.5	78.4	6.3	1,736.3

INDUSTRY: DEPARTMENT STORES (NAICS 45211)
PRODUCT LINE: MEN'S SWEAT TOPS & PANTS (Sub Category)

NAICS 45211: Department Stores Industry . This industry comprises establishments known as department stores primarily engaged in retailing a wide range of the following new products with no one merchandise line predominating: apparel, furniture, appliances and home furnishings; and selected additional items, such as paint, hardware, toiletries, cosmetics, photographic equipment, jewelry, toys, and sporting goods. Merchandise lines are normally arranged in separate departments.

5-YEAR TREND – ESTIMATED INDUSTRY SALES ($MILLIONS)

Year	Employee Size of Establishment									Total
	1-4 Emps.	5-9 Emps.	10-19 Emps.	20-49 Emps.	50-99 Emps.	100-249 Emps.	250-499 Emps.	500-999 Emps.	Unknown Emps.	Industry Sales
2015	0.0	0.0	0.1	6.3	114.7	368.2	152.4	22.0	0.9	664.7
2016	0.0	0.0	0.1	6.3	115.1	369.6	153.0	22.1	0.9	667.2
2017	0.0	0.0	0.1	6.4	116.2	373.3	154.5	22.4	0.9	673.8
2018	0.0	0.0	0.1	6.4	116.3	373.3	154.5	22.4	0.9	674.0
2019	0.0	0.0	0.1	6.5	117.4	377.0	156.1	22.7	1.0	680.7

INDUSTRY: MEN'S CLOTHING STORES (NAICS 44811)
PRODUCT LINE: WOMEN'S WEAR (Main Category)

NAICS 44811: Men's Clothing Stores. This industry comprises establishments primarily engaged in retailing a general line of new men's and boys' clothing. These establishments may provide basic alterations, such as hemming, taking in or letting out seams, or lengthening or shortening sleeves.

5-YEAR TREND – ESTIMATED INDUSTRY SALES ($MILLIONS)

Year	Employee Size of Establishment									Total
	1-4 Emps.	5-9 Emps.	10-19 Emps.	20-49 Emps.	50-99 Emps.	100-249 Emps.	250-499 Emps.	500-999 Emps.	Unknown Emps.	Industry Sales
2015	18.1	31.8	59.2	31.2	6.8	6.1	2.1	0.1	3.1	158.5
2016	18.8	33.0	61.4	32.4	7.0	6.3	2.1	0.1	3.2	164.4
2017	19.6	34.4	64.0	33.7	7.3	6.6	2.2	0.1	3.4	171.2
2018	20.2	35.4	66.0	34.8	7.6	6.8	2.3	0.1	3.5	176.6
2019	21.0	36.8	68.6	36.1	7.9	7.1	2.4	0.1	3.6	183.5

INDUSTRY: WOMEN'S CLOTHING STORES (NAICS 44812)
PRODUCT LINE: WOMEN'S WEAR (Main Category)

NAICS 44812: Women's Clothing Stores . This industry comprises establishments primarily engaged in retailing a general line of new women's, misses' and juniors' clothing, including maternity wear. These establishments may provide basic alterations, such as hemming, taking in or letting out seams, or lengthening or shortening sleeves.

5-YEAR TREND — ESTIMATED INDUSTRY SALES ($MILLIONS)

Year	Employee Size of Establishment									Total
	1-4 Emps.	5-9 Emps.	10-19 Emps.	20-49 Emps.	50-99 Emps.	100-249 Emps.	250-499 Emps.	500-999 Emps.	Unknown Emps.	Industry Sales
2015	2,644	5,905	12,600	8,887	3,139	2,900	1,176	1,138	590	38,978
2016	2,723	6,080	12,973	9,150	3,231	2,985	1,210	1,172	608	40,132
2017	2,817	6,290	13,421	9,466	3,343	3,089	1,252	1,212	629	41,519
2018	2,972	6,637	14,161	9,988	3,527	3,259	1,321	1,270	663	43,797
2019	3,162	7,061	15,066	10,626	3,753	3,467	1,406	1,338	706	46,583

INDUSTRY: FAMILY CLOTHING STORES (NAICS 44814)
PRODUCT LINE: WOMEN'S WEAR (Main Category)

NAICS 44814: Family Clothing Stores . This industry comprises establishments primarily engaged in retailing a general line of new clothing for men, women, and children, without specializing in sales for an individual gender or age group. These establishments may provide basic alterations, such as hemming, taking in or letting out seams, or lengthening or shortening sleeves.

5-YEAR TREND — ESTIMATED INDUSTRY SALES ($MILLIONS)

Year	Employee Size of Establishment									Total
	1-4 Emps.	5-9 Emps.	10-19 Emps.	20-49 Emps.	50-99 Emps.	100-249 Emps.	250-499 Emps.	500-999 Emps.	Unknown Emps.	Industry Sales
2015	595	1,229	4,641	15,427	13,627	3,750	3,538	2,048	163	45,017
2016	610	1,262	4,766	15,840	13,992	3,851	3,633	2,103	167	46,224
2017	630	1,302	4,918	16,346	14,439	3,974	3,749	2,171	173	47,701
2018	664	1,372	5,184	17,229	15,219	4,189	3,951	2,280	182	50,270
2019	706	1,459	5,511	18,315	16,178	4,453	4,200	2,413	193	53,428

INDUSTRY: DEPARTMENT STORES (NAICS 45211)
PRODUCT LINE: WOMEN'S WEAR (Main Category)

NAICS 45211: Department Stores Industry . This industry comprises establishments known as department stores primarily engaged in retailing a wide range of the following new products with no one merchandise line predominating: apparel, furniture, appliances and home furnishings; and selected additional items, such as paint, hardware, toiletries, cosmetics, photographic equipment, jewelry, toys, and sporting goods. Merchandise lines are normally arranged in separate departments.

5-Year Trend – Estimated Industry Sales ($Millions)

Year	Employee Size of Establishment									Total
	1-4 Emps.	5-9 Emps.	10-19 Emps.	20-49 Emps.	50-99 Emps.	100-249 Emps.	250-499 Emps.	500-999 Emps.	Unknown Emps.	Industry Sales
2015	0.9	1.2	2.5	211.5	3,839.2	12,328.0	5,103.1	738.2	31.4	22,255.9
2016	0.9	1.2	2.5	212.3	3,854.2	12,376.1	5,123.0	741.1	31.5	22,342.9
2017	0.9	1.2	2.5	214.4	3,892.2	12,498.3	5,173.6	748.4	31.8	22,563.4
2018	0.9	1.2	2.5	214.4	3,892.7	12,499.8	5,174.3	750.5	31.8	22,568.2
2019	0.9	1.2	2.6	216.6	3,931.2	12,623.6	5,225.5	759.0	32.1	22,792.7

INDUSTRY: WAREHOUSE CLUBS & SUPERCENTERS (NAICS 45291)
PRODUCT LINE: WOMEN'S WEAR (Main Category)

NAICS 45291: Warehouse Clubs and Superstores This industry comprises establishments known as warehouse clubs, superstores or supercenters primarily engaged in retailing a general line of groceries in combination with general lines of new merchandise, such as apparel, furniture, and appliances.

5-Year Trend – Estimated Industry Sales ($Millions)

Year	Employee Size of Establishment									Total
	1-4 Emps.	5-9 Emps.	10-19 Emps.	20-49 Emps.	50-99 Emps.	100-249 Emps.	250-499 Emps.	500-999 Emps.	Unknown Emps.	Industry Sales
2015	0.8	0.2	0.7	24.4	46.3	2,641.1	11,626.8	293.0	4.4	14,637.7
2016	0.8	0.2	0.7	25.1	47.5	2,713.9	11,947.3	301.1	4.6	15,041.1
2017	0.8	0.2	0.7	25.9	49.1	2,802.5	12,337.5	310.9	4.7	15,532.3
2018	0.9	0.2	0.8	27.8	52.8	3,016.2	13,277.9	334.6	5.1	16,716.3
2019	0.9	0.3	0.8	29.5	55.9	3,194.8	14,064.5	354.4	5.4	17,706.6

INDUSTRY: ELECTRONIC SHOPPING & MAIL ORDER (NAICS 45411)
PRODUCT LINE: WOMEN'S WEAR (Main Category)

NAICS 45411: Electronic Shopping and Mail-Order Houses This industry comprises establishments primarily engaged in retailing all types of merchandise by means of mail or by electronic media, such as interactive television or computer. Included in this industry are establishments primarily engaged in retailing from catalogue showrooms of mail-order houses.

5-YEAR TREND – ESTIMATED INDUSTRY SALES ($MILLIONS)

Year	Employee Size of Establishment									Total Industry Sales
	1-4 Emps.	5-9 Emps.	10-19 Emps.	20-49 Emps.	50-99 Emps.	100-249 Emps.	250-499 Emps.	500-999 Emps.	Unknown Emps.	
2015	2,272	1,171	1,691	2,839	2,137	3,953	5,330	7,524	319	27,237
2016	2,404	1,238	1,789	3,003	2,260	4,182	5,638	7,958	338	28,809
2017	2,548	1,313	1,897	3,184	2,396	4,434	5,977	8,438	358	30,544
2018	2,856	1,471	2,126	3,568	2,686	4,969	6,699	9,285	401	34,060
2019	3,175	1,636	2,363	3,967	2,986	5,524	7,448	10,168	446	37,713

INDUSTRY: BOOK STORES (NAICS 451211)
PRODUCT LINE: WOMEN'S WEAR (Main Category)

NAICS 451211: Book Stores. This industry comprises establishments primarily engaged in the retail sale of new books and magazines. Establishments primarily engaged in the retail sale of used books are classified in 5932.

5-YEAR TREND – ESTIMATED INDUSTRY SALES ($MILLIONS)

Year	Employee Size of Establishment									Total Industry Sales
	1-4 Emps.	5-9 Emps.	10-19 Emps.	20-49 Emps.	50-99 Emps.	100-249 Emps.	250-499 Emps.	500-999 Emps.	Unknown Emps.	
2015	3.1	4.6	9.2	24.5	10.7	4.9	1.2	2.9	1.5	62.6
2016	3.2	4.8	9.6	25.6	11.2	5.1	1.3	3.0	1.6	65.5
2017	3.3	5.1	10.1	26.9	11.7	5.4	1.3	3.2	1.7	68.7
2018	3.5	5.3	10.5	27.9	12.1	5.6	1.4	3.3	1.8	71.4
2019	3.6	5.5	11.0	29.2	12.7	5.8	1.4	3.5	1.8	74.6

INDUSTRY: WOMEN'S CLOTHING STORES (NAICS 44812)

PRODUCT LINE: FURS (Sub Category)

NAICS 44812: Women's Clothing Stores . This industry comprises establishments primarily engaged in retailing a general line of new women's, misses' and juniors' clothing, including maternity wear. These establishments may provide basic alterations, such as hemming, taking in or letting out seams, or lengthening or shortening sleeves.

5-YEAR TREND – ESTIMATED INDUSTRY SALES ($MILLIONS)

Year	Employee Size of Establishment									Total
	1-4 Emps.	5-9 Emps.	10-19 Emps.	20-49 Emps.	50-99 Emps.	100-249 Emps.	250-499 Emps.	500-999 Emps.	Unknown Emps.	Industry Sales
2015	3.6	8.1	17.2	12.1	4.3	4.0	1.6	1.6	0.8	53.2
2016	3.7	8.3	17.7	12.5	4.4	4.1	1.7	1.6	0.8	54.8
2017	3.8	8.6	18.3	12.9	4.6	4.2	1.7	1.7	0.9	56.7
2018	4.1	9.1	19.3	13.6	4.8	4.4	1.8	1.7	0.9	59.8
2019	4.3	9.6	20.6	14.5	5.1	4.7	1.9	1.8	1.0	63.6

INDUSTRY: WOMEN'S CLOTHING STORES (NAICS 44812)

PRODUCT LINE: DRESSES (Sub Category)

NAICS 44812: Women's Clothing Stores . This industry comprises establishments primarily engaged in retailing a general line of new women's, misses' and juniors' clothing, including maternity wear. These establishments may provide basic alterations, such as hemming, taking in or letting out seams, or lengthening or shortening sleeves.

5-YEAR TREND – ESTIMATED INDUSTRY SALES ($MILLIONS)

Year	Employee Size of Establishment									Total
	1-4 Emps.	5-9 Emps.	10-19 Emps.	20-49 Emps.	50-99 Emps.	100-249 Emps.	250-499 Emps.	500-999 Emps.	Unknown Emps.	Industry Sales
2015	320.6	716.0	1,527.7	1,077.5	380.6	351.6	142.6	138.0	71.5	4,726.2
2016	330.1	737.2	1,573.0	1,109.4	391.8	362.0	146.8	142.1	73.7	4,866.1
2017	341.5	762.7	1,627.3	1,147.8	405.4	374.5	151.8	147.0	76.2	5,034.3
2018	360.4	804.7	1,717.0	1,211.0	427.7	395.1	160.2	154.0	80.4	5,310.5
2019	383.4	856.2	1,826.7	1,288.4	455.0	420.4	170.5	162.2	85.6	5,648.3

<table>
<tr><td colspan="2">INDUSTRY: FAMILY CLOTHING STORES (NAICS 44814)</td></tr>
<tr><td colspan="2">PRODUCT LINE: DRESSES (Sub Category)</td></tr>
</table>

NAICS 44814: Family Clothing Stores . This industry comprises establishments primarily engaged in retailing a general line of new clothing for men, women, and children, without specializing in sales for an individual gender or age group. These establishments may provide basic alterations, such as hemming, taking in or letting out seams, or lengthening or shortening sleeves.

5-YEAR TREND – ESTIMATED INDUSTRY SALES ($MILLIONS)

| Year | Employee Size of Establishment | | | | | | | | | Total |
	1-4 Emps.	5-9 Emps.	10-19 Emps.	20-49 Emps.	50-99 Emps.	100-249 Emps.	250-499 Emps.	500-999 Emps.	Unknown Emps.	Industry Sales
2015	38.9	80.4	303.8	1,009.7	891.9	245.5	231.6	134.1	10.7	2,946.5
2016	40.0	82.6	311.9	1,036.8	915.8	252.0	237.8	137.7	10.9	3,025.5
2017	41.2	85.2	321.9	1,069.9	945.1	260.1	245.4	142.1	11.3	3,122.2
2018	43.5	89.8	339.3	1,127.7	996.1	274.2	258.6	149.2	11.9	3,290.3
2019	46.2	95.5	360.7	1,198.8	1,058.9	291.4	274.9	157.9	12.7	3,497.0

<table>
<tr><td colspan="2">INDUSTRY: DEPARTMENT STORES (NAICS 45211)</td></tr>
<tr><td colspan="2">PRODUCT LINE: DRESSES (Sub Category)</td></tr>
</table>

NAICS 45211: Department Stores Industry . This industry comprises establishments known as department stores primarily engaged in retailing a wide range of the following new products with no one merchandise line predominating: apparel, furniture, appliances and home furnishings; and selected additional items, such as paint, hardware, toiletries, cosmetics, photographic equipment, jewelry, toys, and sporting goods. Merchandise lines are normally arranged in separate departments.

5-YEAR TREND – ESTIMATED INDUSTRY SALES ($MILLIONS)

| Year | Employee Size of Establishment | | | | | | | | | Total |
	1-4 Emps.	5-9 Emps.	10-19 Emps.	20-49 Emps.	50-99 Emps.	100-249 Emps.	250-499 Emps.	500-999 Emps.	Unknown Emps.	Industry Sales
2015	0.1	0.1	0.2	16.1	292.4	939.0	388.7	56.2	2.4	1,695.2
2016	0.1	0.1	0.2	16.2	293.6	942.6	390.2	56.4	2.4	1,701.8
2017	0.1	0.1	0.2	16.3	296.5	952.0	394.1	57.0	2.4	1,718.6
2018	0.1	0.1	0.2	16.3	296.5	952.1	394.1	57.2	2.4	1,718.9
2019	0.1	0.1	0.2	16.5	299.4	961.5	398.0	57.8	2.4	1,736.0

INDUSTRY: WAREHOUSE CLUBS & SUPERCENTERS (NAICS 45291)
PRODUCT LINE: DRESSES (Sub Category)

NAICS 45291: Warehouse Clubs and Superstores This industry comprises establishments known as warehouse clubs, superstores or supercenters primarily engaged in retailing a general line of groceries in combination with general lines of new merchandise, such as apparel, furniture, and appliances.

5-YEAR TREND – ESTIMATED INDUSTRY SALES ($MILLIONS)

Year	Employee Size of Establishment									Total
	1-4 Emps.	5-9 Emps.	10-19 Emps.	20-49 Emps.	50-99 Emps.	100-249 Emps.	250-499 Emps.	500-999 Emps.	Unknown Emps.	Industry Sales
2015	0.0	0.0	0.0	0.9	1.7	98.2	432.2	10.9	0.2	544.2
2016	0.0	0.0	0.0	0.9	1.8	100.9	444.2	11.2	0.2	559.2
2017	0.0	0.0	0.0	1.0	1.8	104.2	458.7	11.6	0.2	577.4
2018	0.0	0.0	0.0	1.0	2.0	112.1	493.6	12.4	0.2	621.4
2019	0.0	0.0	0.0	1.1	2.1	118.8	522.9	13.2	0.2	658.3

INDUSTRY: WOMEN'S CLOTHING STORES (NAICS 44812)
PRODUCT LINE: COATS & OUTERWEAR (Sub Category)

NAICS 44812: Women's Clothing Stores . This industry comprises establishments primarily engaged in retailing a general line of new women's, misses' and juniors' clothing, including maternity wear. These establishments may provide basic alterations, such as hemming, taking in or letting out seams, or lengthening or shortening sleeves.

5-YEAR TREND – ESTIMATED INDUSTRY SALES ($MILLIONS)

Year	Employee Size of Establishment									Total
	1-4 Emps.	5-9 Emps.	10-19 Emps.	20-49 Emps.	50-99 Emps.	100-249 Emps.	250-499 Emps.	500-999 Emps.	Unknown Emps.	Industry Sales
2015	121.5	271.4	579.0	408.4	144.2	133.2	54.0	52.3	27.1	1,791.1
2016	125.1	279.4	596.1	420.4	148.5	137.2	55.6	53.8	27.9	1,844.1
2017	129.4	289.1	616.7	435.0	153.6	141.9	57.5	55.7	28.9	1,907.9
2018	136.6	305.0	650.7	459.0	162.1	149.7	60.7	58.3	30.5	2,012.6
2019	145.3	324.5	692.3	488.3	172.4	159.3	64.6	61.5	32.4	2,140.6

INDUSTRY: FAMILY CLOTHING STORES (NAICS 44814)
PRODUCT LINE: COATS & OUTERWEAR (Sub Category)

NAICS 44814: Family Clothing Stores . This industry comprises
establishments primarily engaged in retailing a general line of new clothing
for men, women, and children, without specializing in sales for an individual
gender or age group. These establishments may provide basic alterations,
such as hemming, taking in or letting out seams, or lengthening or shortening sleeves.

5-YEAR TREND – ESTIMATED INDUSTRY SALES ($MILLIONS)

Year	Employee Size of Establishment									Total
	1-4 Emps.	5-9 Emps.	10-19 Emps.	20-49 Emps.	50-99 Emps.	100-249 Emps.	250-499 Emps.	500-999 Emps.	Unknown Emps.	Industry Sales
2015	29.3	60.5	228.7	760.0	671.3	184.8	174.3	100.9	8.0	2,217.8
2016	30.1	62.2	234.8	780.4	689.3	189.7	179.0	103.6	8.2	2,277.3
2017	31.0	64.1	242.3	805.3	711.4	195.8	184.7	106.9	8.5	2,350.0
2018	32.7	67.6	255.4	848.8	749.8	206.4	194.7	112.3	9.0	2,476.6
2019	34.8	71.9	271.5	902.3	797.0	219.4	206.9	118.9	9.5	2,632.1

INDUSTRY: DEPARTMENT STORES (NAICS 45211)
PRODUCT LINE: COATS & OUTERWEAR (Sub Category)

NAICS 45211: Department Stores Industry . This industry comprises
establishments known as department stores primarily engaged in retailing
a wide range of the following new products with no one merchandise line
predominating: apparel, furniture, appliances and home furnishings; and
selected additional items, such as paint, hardware, toiletries, cosmetics,
photographic equipment, jewelry, toys, and sporting goods. Merchandise lines
are normally arranged in separate departments.

5-YEAR TREND – ESTIMATED INDUSTRY SALES ($MILLIONS)

Year	Employee Size of Establishment									Total
	1-4 Emps.	5-9 Emps.	10-19 Emps.	20-49 Emps.	50-99 Emps.	100-249 Emps.	250-499 Emps.	500-999 Emps.	Unknown Emps.	Industry Sales
2015	0.0	0.0	0.1	8.5	153.6	493.3	204.2	29.5	1.3	890.6
2016	0.0	0.0	0.1	8.5	154.2	495.3	205.0	29.7	1.3	894.1
2017	0.0	0.0	0.1	8.6	155.8	500.1	207.0	29.9	1.3	902.9
2018	0.0	0.0	0.1	8.6	155.8	500.2	207.1	30.0	1.3	903.1
2019	0.0	0.0	0.1	8.7	157.3	505.2	209.1	30.4	1.3	912.1

INDUSTRY: MEN'S CLOTHING STORES (NAICS 44811)
PRODUCT LINE: SUITS & BLAZERS (Sub Category)

NAICS 44811: Men's Clothing Stores. This industry comprises establishments primarily engaged in retailing a general line of new men's and boys' clothing. These establishments may provide basic alterations, such as hemming, taking in or letting out seams, or lengthening or shortening sleeves.

5-YEAR TREND – ESTIMATED INDUSTRY SALES ($MILLIONS)

Year	Employee Size of Establishment									Total
	1-4 Emps.	5-9 Emps.	10-19 Emps.	20-49 Emps.	50-99 Emps.	100-249 Emps.	250-499 Emps.	500-999 Emps.	Unknown Emps.	Industry Sales
2015	2.8	5.0	9.2	4.9	1.1	1.0	0.3	0.0	0.5	24.7
2016	2.9	5.1	9.6	5.0	1.1	1.0	0.3	0.0	0.5	25.6
2017	3.1	5.4	10.0	5.3	1.1	1.0	0.3	0.0	0.5	26.7
2018	3.1	5.5	10.3	5.4	1.2	1.1	0.4	0.0	0.5	27.5
2019	3.3	5.7	10.7	5.6	1.2	1.1	0.4	0.0	0.6	28.6

INDUSTRY: WOMEN'S CLOTHING STORES (NAICS 44812)
PRODUCT LINE: SUITS & BLAZERS (Sub Category)

NAICS 44812: Women's Clothing Stores . This industry comprises establishments primarily engaged in retailing a general line of new women's, misses' and juniors' clothing, including maternity wear. These establishments may provide basic alterations, such as hemming, taking in or letting out seams, or lengthening or shortening sleeves.

5-YEAR TREND – ESTIMATED INDUSTRY SALES ($MILLIONS)

Year	Employee Size of Establishment									Total
	1-4 Emps.	5-9 Emps.	10-19 Emps.	20-49 Emps.	50-99 Emps.	100-249 Emps.	250-499 Emps.	500-999 Emps.	Unknown Emps.	Industry Sales
2015	185.4	413.9	883.2	622.9	220.0	203.2	82.4	79.8	41.4	2,732.2
2016	190.8	426.2	909.3	641.3	226.5	209.3	84.8	82.1	42.6	2,813.0
2017	197.4	440.9	940.7	663.5	234.3	216.5	87.8	85.0	44.1	2,910.3
2018	208.3	465.2	992.6	700.1	247.2	228.4	92.6	89.0	46.5	3,070.0
2019	221.6	494.9	1,056.0	744.8	263.0	243.0	98.5	93.8	49.5	3,265.2

INDUSTRY: FAMILY CLOTHING STORES (NAICS 44814)
PRODUCT LINE: SUITS & BLAZERS (Sub Category)

NAICS 44814: Family Clothing Stores . This industry comprises establishments primarily engaged in retailing a general line of new clothing for men, women, and children, without specializing in sales for an individual gender or age group. These establishments may provide basic alterations, such as hemming, taking in or letting out seams, or lengthening or shortening sleeves.

5-YEAR TREND – ESTIMATED INDUSTRY SALES ($MILLIONS)

Year	Employee Size of Establishment									Total
	1-4 Emps.	5-9 Emps.	10-19 Emps.	20-49 Emps.	50-99 Emps.	100-249 Emps.	250-499 Emps.	500-999 Emps.	Unknown Emps.	Industry Sales
2015	52.7	109.0	411.6	1,367.8	1,208.3	332.5	313.7	181.6	14.4	3,991.6
2016	54.1	111.9	422.6	1,404.5	1,240.6	341.4	322.1	186.5	14.8	4,098.6
2017	55.9	115.5	436.1	1,449.4	1,280.3	352.4	332.4	192.5	15.3	4,229.6
2018	58.9	121.7	459.6	1,527.7	1,349.5	371.4	350.3	202.1	16.1	4,457.4
2019	62.6	129.4	488.6	1,624.0	1,434.5	394.8	372.4	213.9	17.1	4,737.3

INDUSTRY: DEPARTMENT STORES (NAICS 45211)
PRODUCT LINE: SUITS & BLAZERS (Sub Category)

NAICS 45211: Department Stores Industry . This industry comprises establishments known as department stores primarily engaged in retailing a wide range of the following new products with no one merchandise line predominating: apparel, furniture, appliances and home furnishings; and selected additional items, such as paint, hardware, toiletries, cosmetics, photographic equipment, jewelry, toys, and sporting goods. Merchandise lines are normally arranged in separate departments.

5-YEAR TREND – ESTIMATED INDUSTRY SALES ($MILLIONS)

Year	Employee Size of Establishment									Total
	1-4 Emps.	5-9 Emps.	10-19 Emps.	20-49 Emps.	50-99 Emps.	100-249 Emps.	250-499 Emps.	500-999 Emps.	Unknown Emps.	Industry Sales
2015	0	0	0	32	579	1,858	769	111	5	3,354
2016	0	0	0	32	581	1,865	772	112	5	3,367
2017	0	0	0	32	587	1,883	780	113	5	3,400
2018	0	0	0	32	587	1,884	780	113	5	3,401
2019	0	0	0	33	592	1,902	787	114	5	3,435

INDUSTRY: MEN'S CLOTHING STORES (NAICS 44811)
PRODUCT LINE: SLACKS & JEANS & SKIRTS (Sub Category)

NAICS 44811: Men's Clothing Stores. This industry comprises establishments primarily engaged in retailing a general line of new men's and boys' clothing. These establishments may provide basic alterations, such as hemming, taking in or letting out seams, or lengthening or shortening sleeves.

5-YEAR TREND — ESTIMATED INDUSTRY SALES ($MILLIONS)

Year	Employee Size of Establishment									Total Industry Sales
	1-4 Emps.	5-9 Emps.	10-19 Emps.	20-49 Emps.	50-99 Emps.	100-249 Emps.	250-499 Emps.	500-999 Emps.	Unknown Emps.	
2015	4.2	7.4	13.8	7.3	1.6	1.4	0.5	0.0	0.7	37.0
2016	4.4	7.7	14.3	7.5	1.6	1.5	0.5	0.0	0.8	38.4
2017	4.6	8.0	14.9	7.9	1.7	1.5	0.5	0.0	0.8	39.9
2018	4.7	8.3	15.4	8.1	1.8	1.6	0.5	0.0	0.8	41.2
2019	4.9	8.6	16.0	8.4	1.8	1.6	0.6	0.0	0.8	42.8

INDUSTRY: WOMEN'S CLOTHING STORES (NAICS 44812)
PRODUCT LINE: SLACKS & JEANS & SKIRTS (Sub Category)

NAICS 44812: Women's Clothing Stores . This industry comprises establishments primarily engaged in retailing a general line of new women's, misses' and juniors' clothing, including maternity wear. These establishments may provide basic alterations, such as hemming, taking in or letting out seams, or lengthening or shortening sleeves.

5-YEAR TREND — ESTIMATED INDUSTRY SALES ($MILLIONS)

Year	Employee Size of Establishment									Total Industry Sales
	1-4 Emps.	5-9 Emps.	10-19 Emps.	20-49 Emps.	50-99 Emps.	100-249 Emps.	250-499 Emps.	500-999 Emps.	Unknown Emps.	
2015	711.4	1,588.8	3,389.9	2,390.9	844.4	780.1	316.3	306.2	158.8	10,486.8
2016	732.5	1,635.8	3,490.2	2,461.7	869.4	803.2	325.7	315.3	163.5	10,797.2
2017	757.8	1,692.4	3,610.9	2,546.8	899.4	831.0	336.9	326.2	169.1	11,170.4
2018	799.6	1,785.6	3,809.8	2,687.1	949.0	876.7	355.5	341.6	178.4	11,783.4
2019	850.7	1,899.7	4,053.3	2,858.8	1,009.7	932.8	378.2	359.9	189.8	12,532.9

INDUSTRY: FAMILY CLOTHING STORES (NAICS 44814)
PRODUCT LINE: SLACKS & JEANS & SKIRTS (Sub Category)

NAICS 44814: Family Clothing Stores . This industry comprises establishments primarily engaged in retailing a general line of new clothing for men, women, and children, without specializing in sales for an individual gender or age group. These establishments may provide basic alterations, such as hemming, taking in or letting out seams, or lengthening or shortening sleeves.

5-YEAR TREND – ESTIMATED INDUSTRY SALES ($MILLIONS)

Year	Employee Size of Establishment									Total
	1-4 Emps.	5-9 Emps.	10-19 Emps.	20-49 Emps.	50-99 Emps.	100-249 Emps.	250-499 Emps.	500-999 Emps.	Unknown Emps.	Industry Sales
2015	116.3	240.4	908.2	3,018.5	2,666.4	733.8	692.2	400.8	31.9	8,808.6
2016	119.5	246.9	932.6	3,099.5	2,737.9	753.5	710.8	411.6	32.7	9,044.8
2017	123.3	254.8	962.4	3,198.5	2,825.3	777.6	733.5	424.7	33.8	9,333.8
2018	129.9	268.5	1,014.3	3,371.3	2,978.0	819.6	773.1	446.1	35.6	9,836.5
2019	138.1	285.5	1,078.3	3,583.8	3,165.6	871.2	821.9	472.1	37.8	10,454.3

INDUSTRY: DEPARTMENT STORES (NAICS 45211)
PRODUCT LINE: SLACKS & JEANS & SKIRTS (Sub Category)

NAICS 45211: Department Stores Industry . This industry comprises establishments known as department stores primarily engaged in retailing a wide range of the following new products with no one merchandise line predominating: apparel, furniture, appliances and home furnishings; and selected additional items, such as paint, hardware, toiletries, cosmetics, photographic equipment, jewelry, toys, and sporting goods. Merchandise lines are normally arranged in separate departments.

5-YEAR TREND – ESTIMATED INDUSTRY SALES ($MILLIONS)

Year	Employee Size of Establishment									Total
	1-4 Emps.	5-9 Emps.	10-19 Emps.	20-49 Emps.	50-99 Emps.	100-249 Emps.	250-499 Emps.	500-999 Emps.	Unknown Emps.	Industry Sales
2015	0	0	0	32	577	1,852	767	111	5	3,344
2016	0	0	0	32	579	1,860	770	111	5	3,357
2017	0	0	0	32	585	1,878	777	112	5	3,390
2018	0	0	0	32	585	1,878	777	113	5	3,391
2019	0	0	0	33	591	1,897	785	114	5	3,425

INDUSTRY: WAREHOUSE CLUBS & SUPERCENTERS (NAICS 45291)
PRODUCT LINE: SLACKS & JEANS & SKIRTS (Sub Category)

NAICS 45291: Warehouse Clubs and Superstores This industry comprises establishments known as warehouse clubs, superstores or supercenters primarily engaged in retailing a general line of groceries in combination with general lines of new merchandise, such as apparel, furniture, and appliances.

5-YEAR TREND — ESTIMATED INDUSTRY SALES ($MILLIONS)

Year	Employee Size of Establishment									Total Industry Sales
	1-4 Emps.	5-9 Emps.	10-19 Emps.	20-49 Emps.	50-99 Emps.	100-249 Emps.	250-499 Emps.	500-999 Emps.	Unknown Emps.	
2015	0.2	0.1	0.2	6.4	12.1	688.6	3,031.3	76.4	1.2	3,816.2
2016	0.2	0.1	0.2	6.5	12.4	707.5	3,114.8	78.5	1.2	3,921.4
2017	0.2	0.1	0.2	6.7	12.8	730.7	3,216.5	81.1	1.2	4,049.5
2018	0.2	0.1	0.2	7.3	13.8	786.4	3,461.7	87.2	1.3	4,358.2
2019	0.2	0.1	0.2	7.7	14.6	832.9	3,666.8	92.4	1.4	4,616.3

INDUSTRY: MEN'S CLOTHING STORES (NAICS 44811)
PRODUCT LINE: SHIRTS & SWEATERS (Sub Category)

NAICS 44811: Men's Clothing Stores. This industry comprises establishments primarily engaged in retailing a general line of new men's and boys' clothing. These establishments may provide basic alterations, such as hemming, taking in or letting out seams, or lengthening or shortening sleeves.

5-YEAR TREND — ESTIMATED INDUSTRY SALES ($MILLIONS)

Year	Employee Size of Establishment									Total Industry Sales
	1-4 Emps.	5-9 Emps.	10-19 Emps.	20-49 Emps.	50-99 Emps.	100-249 Emps.	250-499 Emps.	500-999 Emps.	Unknown Emps.	
2015	4.7	8.3	15.5	8.2	1.8	1.6	0.5	0.0	0.8	41.5
2016	4.9	8.6	16.1	8.5	1.8	1.7	0.6	0.0	0.8	43.0
2017	5.1	9.0	16.7	8.8	1.9	1.7	0.6	0.0	0.9	44.8
2018	5.3	9.3	17.3	9.1	2.0	1.8	0.6	0.0	0.9	46.2
2019	5.5	9.6	17.9	9.4	2.1	1.8	0.6	0.0	0.9	48.0

INDUSTRY: WOMEN'S CLOTHING STORES (NAICS 44812)
PRODUCT LINE: SHIRTS & SWEATERS (Sub Category)

NAICS 44812: Women's Clothing Stores . This industry comprises establishments primarily engaged in retailing a general line of new women's, misses' and juniors' clothing, including maternity wear. These establishments may provide basic alterations, such as hemming, taking in or letting out seams, or lengthening or shortening sleeves.

5-Year Trend – Estimated Industry Sales ($Millions)

Year	Employee Size of Establishment									Total
	1-4 Emps.	5-9 Emps.	10-19 Emps.	20-49 Emps.	50-99 Emps.	100-249 Emps.	250-499 Emps.	500-999 Emps.	Unknown Emps.	Industry Sales
2015	932	2,082	4,442	3,133	1,107	1,022	415	401	208	13,743
2016	960	2,144	4,574	3,226	1,139	1,053	427	413	214	14,149
2017	993	2,218	4,732	3,337	1,179	1,089	442	427	222	14,639
2018	1,048	2,340	4,993	3,521	1,244	1,149	466	448	234	15,442
2019	1,115	2,490	5,312	3,746	1,323	1,222	496	472	249	16,424

INDUSTRY: FAMILY CLOTHING STORES (NAICS 44814)
PRODUCT LINE: SHIRTS & SWEATERS (Sub Category)

NAICS 44814: Family Clothing Stores . This industry comprises establishments primarily engaged in retailing a general line of new clothing for men, women, and children, without specializing in sales for an individual gender or age group. These establishments may provide basic alterations, such as hemming, taking in or letting out seams, or lengthening or shortening sleeves.

5-Year Trend – Estimated Industry Sales ($Millions)

Year	Employee Size of Establishment									Total
	1-4 Emps.	5-9 Emps.	10-19 Emps.	20-49 Emps.	50-99 Emps.	100-249 Emps.	250-499 Emps.	500-999 Emps.	Unknown Emps.	Industry Sales
2015	191.0	394.8	1,491.2	4,956.2	4,378.0	1,204.9	1,136.6	658.1	52.3	14,463.2
2016	196.1	405.4	1,531.2	5,089.1	4,495.4	1,237.2	1,167.1	675.8	53.7	14,851.0
2017	202.4	418.3	1,580.1	5,251.7	4,639.0	1,276.7	1,204.4	697.3	55.5	15,325.5
2018	213.3	440.9	1,665.5	5,535.4	4,889.6	1,345.7	1,269.4	732.5	58.4	16,150.8
2019	226.8	468.7	1,770.5	5,884.3	5,197.8	1,430.5	1,349.4	775.1	62.1	17,165.2

INDUSTRY: DEPARTMENT STORES (NAICS 45211)
PRODUCT LINE: SHIRTS & SWEATERS (Sub Category)

NAICS 45211: Department Stores Industry . This industry comprises establishments known as department stores primarily engaged in retailing a wide range of the following new products with no one merchandise line predominating: apparel, furniture, appliances and home furnishings; and selected additional items, such as paint, hardware, toiletries, cosmetics, photographic equipment, jewelry, toys, and sporting goods. Merchandise lines are normally arranged in separate departments.

5-YEAR TREND – ESTIMATED INDUSTRY SALES ($MILLIONS)

Year	Employee Size of Establishment									Total
	1-4 Emps.	5-9 Emps.	10-19 Emps.	20-49 Emps.	50-99 Emps.	100-249 Emps.	250-499 Emps.	500-999 Emps.	Unknown Emps.	Industry Sales
2015	0	0	0	31	562	1,805	747	108	5	3,259
2016	0	0	0	31	564	1,812	750	109	5	3,272
2017	0	0	0	31	570	1,830	758	110	5	3,304
2018	0	0	0	31	570	1,830	758	110	5	3,305
2019	0	0	0	32	576	1,848	765	111	5	3,337

INDUSTRY: WAREHOUSE CLUBS & SUPERSTORES (NAICS 45291)
PRODUCT LINE: SHIRTS & SWEATERS (Sub Category)

NAICS 45291: Warehouse Clubs and Superstores This industry comprises establishments known as warehouse clubs, superstores or supercenters primarily engaged in retailing a general line of groceries in combination with general lines of new merchandise, such as apparel, furniture, and appliances.

5-YEAR TREND – ESTIMATED INDUSTRY SALES ($MILLIONS)

Year	Employee Size of Establishment									Total
	1-4 Emps.	5-9 Emps.	10-19 Emps.	20-49 Emps.	50-99 Emps.	100-249 Emps.	250-499 Emps.	500-999 Emps.	Unknown Emps.	Industry Sales
2015	0.2	0.0	0.1	5.0	9.6	545.6	2,402.0	60.5	0.9	3,024.0
2016	0.2	0.0	0.1	5.2	9.8	560.7	2,468.2	62.2	0.9	3,107.4
2017	0.2	0.0	0.1	5.3	10.1	579.0	2,548.8	64.2	1.0	3,208.9
2018	0.2	0.0	0.2	5.8	10.9	623.1	2,743.1	69.1	1.0	3,453.5
2019	0.2	0.1	0.2	6.1	11.6	660.0	2,905.6	73.2	1.1	3,658.1

| INDUSTRY: WOMEN'S CLOTHING STORES (NAICS 44812) |
| PRODUCT LINE: SPORTS APPAREL (Sub Category) |

NAICS 44812: Women's Clothing Stores . This industry comprises establishments primarily engaged in retailing a general line of new women's, misses' and juniors' clothing, including maternity wear. These establishments may provide basic alterations, such as hemming, taking in or letting out seams, or lengthening or shortening sleeves.

5-YEAR TREND – ESTIMATED INDUSTRY SALES ($MILLIONS)

Year	Employee Size of Establishment									Total
	1-4 Emps.	5-9 Emps.	10-19 Emps.	20-49 Emps.	50-99 Emps.	100-249 Emps.	250-499 Emps.	500-999 Emps.	Unknown Emps.	Industry Sales
2015	35.6	79.5	169.7	119.7	42.3	39.1	15.8	15.3	7.9	525.0
2016	36.7	81.9	174.7	123.2	43.5	40.2	16.3	15.8	8.2	540.6
2017	37.9	84.7	180.8	127.5	45.0	41.6	16.9	16.3	8.5	559.3
2018	40.0	89.4	190.7	134.5	47.5	43.9	17.8	17.1	8.9	589.9
2019	42.6	95.1	202.9	143.1	50.5	46.7	18.9	18.0	9.5	627.5

| INDUSTRY: FAMILY CLOTHING STORES (NAICS 44814) |
| PRODUCT LINE: SPORTS APPAREL (Sub Category) |

NAICS 44814: Family Clothing Stores . This industry comprises establishments primarily engaged in retailing a general line of new clothing for men, women, and children, without specializing in sales for an individual gender or age group. These establishments may provide basic alterations, such as hemming, taking in or letting out seams, or lengthening or shortening sleeves.

5-YEAR TREND – ESTIMATED INDUSTRY SALES ($MILLIONS)

Year	Employee Size of Establishment									Total
	1-4 Emps.	5-9 Emps.	10-19 Emps.	20-49 Emps.	50-99 Emps.	100-249 Emps.	250-499 Emps.	500-999 Emps.	Unknown Emps.	Industry Sales
2015	17.2	35.5	134.1	445.6	393.6	108.3	102.2	59.2	4.7	1,300.2
2016	17.6	36.4	137.7	457.5	404.1	111.2	104.9	60.7	4.8	1,335.1
2017	18.2	37.6	142.0	472.1	417.0	114.8	108.3	62.7	5.0	1,377.7
2018	19.2	39.6	149.7	497.6	439.6	121.0	114.1	65.8	5.3	1,451.9
2019	20.4	42.1	159.2	529.0	467.3	128.6	121.3	69.7	5.6	1,543.1

INDUSTRY: DEPARTMENT STORES (NAICS 45211)
PRODUCT LINE: SPORTS APPAREL (Sub Category)

NAICS 45211: Department Stores Industry . This industry comprises establishments known as department stores primarily engaged in retailing a wide range of the following new products with no one merchandise line predominating: apparel, furniture, appliances and home furnishings; and selected additional items, such as paint, hardware, toiletries, cosmetics, photographic equipment, jewelry, toys, and sporting goods. Merchandise lines are normally arranged in separate departments.

5-YEAR TREND – ESTIMATED INDUSTRY SALES ($MILLIONS)

Year	Employee Size of Establishment									Total
	1-4 Emps.	5-9 Emps.	10-19 Emps.	20-49 Emps.	50-99 Emps.	100-249 Emps.	250-499 Emps.	500-999 Emps.	Unknown Emps.	Industry Sales
2015	0.1	0.1	0.3	24.4	442.0	1,419.4	587.5	85.0	3.6	2,562.4
2016	0.1	0.1	0.3	24.4	443.8	1,424.9	589.8	85.3	3.6	2,572.5
2017	0.1	0.1	0.3	24.7	448.1	1,439.0	595.7	86.2	3.7	2,597.9
2018	0.1	0.1	0.3	24.7	448.2	1,439.2	595.7	86.4	3.7	2,598.4
2019	0.1	0.1	0.3	24.9	452.6	1,453.4	601.6	87.4	3.7	2,624.3

INDUSTRY: WAREHOUSE CLUBS & SUPERCENTERS (NAICS 45291)
PRODUCT LINE: SPORTS APPAREL (Sub Category)

NAICS 45291: Warehouse Clubs and Superstores This industry comprises establishments known as warehouse clubs, superstores or supercenters primarily engaged in retailing a general line of groceries in combination with general lines of new merchandise, such as apparel, furniture, and appliances.

5-YEAR TREND – ESTIMATED INDUSTRY SALES ($MILLIONS)

Year	Employee Size of Establishment									Total
	1-4 Emps.	5-9 Emps.	10-19 Emps.	20-49 Emps.	50-99 Emps.	100-249 Emps.	250-499 Emps.	500-999 Emps.	Unknown Emps.	Industry Sales
2015	0.1	0.0	0.0	1.7	3.2	181.7	800.0	20.2	0.3	1,007.1
2016	0.1	0.0	0.0	1.7	3.3	186.7	822.0	20.7	0.3	1,034.9
2017	0.1	0.0	0.0	1.8	3.4	192.8	848.9	21.4	0.3	1,068.7
2018	0.1	0.0	0.1	1.9	3.6	207.5	913.6	23.0	0.3	1,150.1
2019	0.1	0.0	0.1	2.0	3.8	219.8	967.7	24.4	0.4	1,218.3

INDUSTRY: WOMEN'S CLOTHING STORES (NAICS 44812)
PRODUCT LINE: HOSIERY & SOCKS (Sub Category)

NAICS 44812: Women's Clothing Stores . This industry comprises establishments primarily engaged in retailing a general line of new women's, misses' and juniors' clothing, including maternity wear. These establishments may provide basic alterations, such as hemming, taking in or letting out seams, or lengthening or shortening sleeves.

5-YEAR TREND – ESTIMATED INDUSTRY SALES ($MILLIONS)

Year	Employee Size of Establishment									Total
	1-4 Emps.	5-9 Emps.	10-19 Emps.	20-49 Emps.	50-99 Emps.	100-249 Emps.	250-499 Emps.	500-999 Emps.	Unknown Emps.	Industry Sales
2015	24.5	54.6	116.5	82.2	29.0	26.8	10.9	10.5	5.5	360.5
2016	25.2	56.2	120.0	84.6	29.9	27.6	11.2	10.8	5.6	371.2
2017	26.1	58.2	124.1	87.6	30.9	28.6	11.6	11.2	5.8	384.0
2018	27.5	61.4	131.0	92.4	32.6	30.1	12.2	11.7	6.1	405.1
2019	29.2	65.3	139.3	98.3	34.7	32.1	13.0	12.4	6.5	430.9

INDUSTRY: FAMILY CLOTHING STORES (NAICS 44814)
PRODUCT LINE: HOSIERY & SOCKS (Sub Category)

NAICS 44814: Family Clothing Stores . This industry comprises establishments primarily engaged in retailing a general line of new clothing for men, women, and children, without specializing in sales for an individual gender or age group. These establishments may provide basic alterations, such as hemming, taking in or letting out seams, or lengthening or shortening sleeves.

5-YEAR TREND – ESTIMATED INDUSTRY SALES ($MILLIONS)

Year	Employee Size of Establishment									Total
	1-4 Emps.	5-9 Emps.	10-19 Emps.	20-49 Emps.	50-99 Emps.	100-249 Emps.	250-499 Emps.	500-999 Emps.	Unknown Emps.	Industry Sales
2015	13.6	28.2	106.5	353.9	312.6	86.0	81.2	47.0	3.7	1,032.6
2016	14.0	28.9	109.3	363.3	321.0	88.3	83.3	48.2	3.8	1,060.3
2017	14.5	29.9	112.8	375.0	331.2	91.2	86.0	49.8	4.0	1,094.2
2018	15.2	31.5	118.9	395.2	349.1	96.1	90.6	52.3	4.2	1,153.1
2019	16.2	33.5	126.4	420.1	371.1	102.1	96.3	55.3	4.4	1,225.5

INDUSTRY: DEPARTMENT STORES (NAICS 45211)
PRODUCT LINE: HOSIERY & SOCKS (Sub Category)

NAICS 45211: Department Stores Industry . This industry comprises establishments known as department stores primarily engaged in retailing a wide range of the following new products with no one merchandise line predominating: apparel, furniture, appliances and home furnishings; and selected additional items, such as paint, hardware, toiletries, cosmetics, photographic equipment, jewelry, toys, and sporting goods. Merchandise lines are normally arranged in separate departments.

5-YEAR TREND – ESTIMATED INDUSTRY SALES ($MILLIONS)

Year	Employee Size of Establishment									Total
	1-4 Emps.	5-9 Emps.	10-19 Emps.	20-49 Emps.	50-99 Emps.	100-249 Emps.	250-499 Emps.	500-999 Emps.	Unknown Emps.	Industry Sales
2015	0.0	0.0	0.1	6.5	118.4	380.2	157.4	22.8	1.0	686.4
2016	0.0	0.0	0.1	6.5	118.9	381.7	158.0	22.9	1.0	689.1
2017	0.0	0.0	0.1	6.6	120.0	385.5	159.6	23.1	1.0	695.9
2018	0.0	0.0	0.1	6.6	120.1	385.5	159.6	23.1	1.0	696.0
2019	0.0	0.0	0.1	6.7	121.2	389.3	161.2	23.4	1.0	703.0

INDUSTRY: WAREHOUSE CLUBS & SUPERCENTERS (NAICS 45291)
PRODUCT LINE: HOSIERY & SOCKS (Sub Category)

NAICS 45291: Warehouse Clubs and Superstores This industry comprises establishments known as warehouse clubs, superstores or supercenters primarily engaged in retailing a general line of groceries in combination with general lines of new merchandise, such as apparel, furniture, and appliances.

5-YEAR TREND – ESTIMATED INDUSTRY SALES ($MILLIONS)

Year	Employee Size of Establishment									Total
	1-4 Emps.	5-9 Emps.	10-19 Emps.	20-49 Emps.	50-99 Emps.	100-249 Emps.	250-499 Emps.	500-999 Emps.	Unknown Emps.	Industry Sales
2015	0.1	0.0	0.1	1.8	3.5	199.1	876.7	22.1	0.3	1,103.7
2016	0.1	0.0	0.1	1.9	3.6	204.6	900.8	22.7	0.3	1,134.1
2017	0.1	0.0	0.1	2.0	3.7	211.3	930.3	23.4	0.4	1,171.2
2018	0.1	0.0	0.1	2.1	4.0	227.4	1,001.2	25.2	0.4	1,260.4
2019	0.1	0.0	0.1	2.2	4.2	240.9	1,060.5	26.7	0.4	1,335.1

INDUSTRY: WOMEN'S CLOTHING STORES (NAICS 44812)
PRODUCT LINE: BRAS & UNDERWEAR (Sub Category)

NAICS 44812: Women's Clothing Stores . This industry comprises establishments primarily engaged in retailing a general line of new women's, misses' and juniors' clothing, including maternity wear. These establishments may provide basic alterations, such as hemming, taking in or letting out seams, or lengthening or shortening sleeves.

5-YEAR TREND – ESTIMATED INDUSTRY SALES ($MILLIONS)

Year	Employee Size of Establishment									Total
	1-4 Emps.	5-9 Emps.	10-19 Emps.	20-49 Emps.	50-99 Emps.	100-249 Emps.	250-499 Emps.	500-999 Emps.	Unknown Emps.	Industry Sales
2015	41.4	92.5	197.4	139.2	49.2	45.4	18.4	17.8	9.2	610.7
2016	42.7	95.3	203.2	143.3	50.6	46.8	19.0	18.4	9.5	628.7
2017	44.1	98.5	210.3	148.3	52.4	48.4	19.6	19.0	9.8	650.5
2018	46.6	104.0	221.8	156.5	55.3	51.1	20.7	19.9	10.4	686.2
2019	49.5	110.6	236.0	166.5	58.8	54.3	22.0	21.0	11.1	729.8

INDUSTRY: FAMILY CLOTHING STORES (NAICS 44814)
PRODUCT LINE: BRAS & UNDERWEAR (Sub Category)

NAICS 44814: Family Clothing Stores . This industry comprises establishments primarily engaged in retailing a general line of new clothing for men, women, and children, without specializing in sales for an individual gender or age group. These establishments may provide basic alterations, such as hemming, taking in or letting out seams, or lengthening or shortening sleeves.

5-YEAR TREND – ESTIMATED INDUSTRY SALES ($MILLIONS)

Year	Employee Size of Establishment									Total
	1-4 Emps.	5-9 Emps.	10-19 Emps.	20-49 Emps.	50-99 Emps.	100-249 Emps.	250-499 Emps.	500-999 Emps.	Unknown Emps.	Industry Sales
2015	20.8	43.1	162.6	540.5	477.5	131.4	124.0	71.8	5.7	1,577.3
2016	21.4	44.2	167.0	555.0	490.3	134.9	127.3	73.7	5.9	1,619.6
2017	22.1	45.6	172.3	572.7	505.9	139.2	131.3	76.1	6.0	1,671.3
2018	23.3	48.1	181.6	603.7	533.2	146.8	138.4	79.9	6.4	1,761.4
2019	24.7	51.1	193.1	641.7	566.9	156.0	147.2	84.5	6.8	1,872.0

INDUSTRY: DEPARTMENT STORES (NAICS 45211)
PRODUCT LINE: BRAS & UNDERWEAR (Sub Category)

NAICS 45211: Department Stores Industry . This industry comprises establishments known as department stores primarily engaged in retailing a wide range of the following new products with no one merchandise line predominating: apparel, furniture, appliances and home furnishings; and selected additional items, such as paint, hardware, toiletries, cosmetics, photographic equipment, jewelry, toys, and sporting goods. Merchandise lines are normally arranged in separate departments.

5-YEAR TREND – ESTIMATED INDUSTRY SALES ($MILLIONS)

Year	Employee Size of Establishment									Total
	1-4 Emps.	5-9 Emps.	10-19 Emps.	20-49 Emps.	50-99 Emps.	100-249 Emps.	250-499 Emps.	500-999 Emps.	Unknown Emps.	Industry Sales
2015	0	0	0	27	486	1,560	646	93	4	2,817
2016	0	0	0	27	488	1,566	648	94	4	2,828
2017	0	0	0	27	493	1,582	655	95	4	2,855
2018	0	0	0	27	493	1,582	655	95	4	2,856
2019	0	0	0	27	498	1,598	661	96	4	2,884

INDUSTRY: WAREHOUSE CLUBS & SUPERCENTERS (NAICS 45291)
PRODUCT LINE: BRAS & UNDERWEAR (Sub Category)

NAICS 45291: Warehouse Clubs and Superstores This industry comprises establishments known as warehouse clubs, superstores or supercenters primarily engaged in retailing a general line of groceries in combination with general lines of new merchandise, such as apparel, furniture, and appliances.

5-YEAR TREND – ESTIMATED INDUSTRY SALES ($MILLIONS)

Year	Employee Size of Establishment									Total
	1-4 Emps.	5-9 Emps.	10-19 Emps.	20-49 Emps.	50-99 Emps.	100-249 Emps.	250-499 Emps.	500-999 Emps.	Unknown Emps.	Industry Sales
2015	0.1	0.0	0.1	3.2	6.0	342.4	1,507.5	38.0	0.6	1,897.9
2016	0.1	0.0	0.1	3.2	6.2	351.9	1,549.0	39.0	0.6	1,950.2
2017	0.1	0.0	0.1	3.4	6.4	363.4	1,599.6	40.3	0.6	2,013.9
2018	0.1	0.0	0.1	3.6	6.8	391.1	1,721.6	43.4	0.7	2,167.4
2019	0.1	0.0	0.1	3.8	7.3	414.2	1,823.5	46.0	0.7	2,295.8

INDUSTRY: WOMEN'S CLOTHING STORES (NAICS 44812)
PRODUCT LINE: LINGERIE & SLEEPWEAR (Sub Category)

NAICS 44812: Women's Clothing Stores . This industry comprises establishments primarily engaged in retailing a general line of new women's, misses' and juniors' clothing, including maternity wear. These establishments may provide basic alterations, such as hemming, taking in or letting out seams, or lengthening or shortening sleeves.

5-YEAR TREND – ESTIMATED INDUSTRY SALES ($MILLIONS)

| Year | Employee Size of Establishment | | | | | | | | | Total |
	1-4 Emps.	5-9 Emps.	10-19 Emps.	20-49 Emps.	50-99 Emps.	100-249 Emps.	250-499 Emps.	500-999 Emps.	Unknown Emps.	Industry Sales
2015	65.5	146.3	312.1	220.1	77.7	71.8	29.1	28.2	14.6	965.5
2016	67.4	150.6	321.3	226.7	80.0	74.0	30.0	29.0	15.0	994.1
2017	69.8	155.8	332.5	234.5	82.8	76.5	31.0	30.0	15.6	1,028.5
2018	73.6	164.4	350.8	247.4	87.4	80.7	32.7	31.5	16.4	1,084.9
2019	78.3	174.9	373.2	263.2	93.0	85.9	34.8	33.1	17.5	1,153.9

INDUSTRY: FAMILY CLOTHING STORES (NAICS 44814)
PRODUCT LINE: LINGERIE & SLEEPWEAR (Sub Category)

NAICS 44814: Family Clothing Stores . This industry comprises establishments primarily engaged in retailing a general line of new clothing for men, women, and children, without specializing in sales for an individual gender or age group. These establishments may provide basic alterations, such as hemming, taking in or letting out seams, or lengthening or shortening sleeves.

5-YEAR TREND – ESTIMATED INDUSTRY SALES ($MILLIONS)

| Year | Employee Size of Establishment | | | | | | | | | Total |
	1-4 Emps.	5-9 Emps.	10-19 Emps.	20-49 Emps.	50-99 Emps.	100-249 Emps.	250-499 Emps.	500-999 Emps.	Unknown Emps.	Industry Sales
2015	17.5	36.2	136.8	454.7	401.7	110.5	104.3	60.4	4.8	1,326.9
2016	18.0	37.2	140.5	466.9	412.4	113.5	107.1	62.0	4.9	1,362.5
2017	18.6	38.4	145.0	481.8	425.6	117.1	110.5	64.0	5.1	1,406.0
2018	19.6	40.5	152.8	507.8	448.6	123.5	116.5	67.2	5.4	1,481.7
2019	20.8	43.0	162.4	539.8	476.9	131.2	123.8	71.1	5.7	1,574.8

INDUSTRY: DEPARTMENT STORES (NAICS 45211)
PRODUCT LINE: LINGERIE & SLEEPWEAR (Sub Category)

NAICS 45211: Department Stores Industry . This industry comprises establishments known as department stores primarily engaged in retailing a wide range of the following new products with no one merchandise line predominating: apparel, furniture, appliances and home furnishings; and selected additional items, such as paint, hardware, toiletries, cosmetics, photographic equipment, jewelry, toys, and sporting goods. Merchandise lines are normally arranged in separate departments.

5-YEAR TREND – ESTIMATED INDUSTRY SALES ($MILLIONS)

	Employee Size of Establishment									Total
Year	1-4 Emps.	5-9 Emps.	10-19 Emps.	20-49 Emps.	50-99 Emps.	100-249 Emps.	250-499 Emps.	500-999 Emps.	Unknown Emps.	Industry Sales
2015	0.1	0.1	0.2	14.6	264.9	850.6	352.1	50.9	2.2	1,535.6
2016	0.1	0.1	0.2	14.6	265.9	853.9	353.5	51.1	2.2	1,541.6
2017	0.1	0.1	0.2	14.8	268.6	862.4	357.0	51.6	2.2	1,556.8
2018	0.1	0.1	0.2	14.8	268.6	862.5	357.0	51.8	2.2	1,557.2
2019	0.1	0.1	0.2	14.9	271.2	871.0	360.5	52.4	2.2	1,572.7

INDUSTRY: WAREHOUSE CLUBS & SUPERCENTERS (NAICS 45291)
PRODUCT LINE: LINGERIE & SLEEPWEAR (Sub Category)

NAICS 45291: Warehouse Clubs and Superstores This industry comprises establishments known as warehouse clubs, superstores or supercenters primarily engaged in retailing a general line of groceries in combination with general lines of new merchandise, such as apparel, furniture, and appliances.

5-YEAR TREND – ESTIMATED INDUSTRY SALES ($MILLIONS)

	Employee Size of Establishment									Total
Year	1-4 Emps.	5-9 Emps.	10-19 Emps.	20-49 Emps.	50-99 Emps.	100-249 Emps.	250-499 Emps.	500-999 Emps.	Unknown Emps.	Industry Sales
2015	0.1	0.0	0.1	2.4	4.5	256.4	1,128.6	28.4	0.4	1,420.8
2016	0.1	0.0	0.1	2.4	4.6	263.4	1,159.7	29.2	0.4	1,460.0
2017	0.1	0.0	0.1	2.5	4.8	272.0	1,197.6	30.2	0.5	1,507.7
2018	0.1	0.0	0.1	2.7	5.1	292.8	1,288.8	32.5	0.5	1,622.6
2019	0.1	0.0	0.1	2.9	5.4	310.1	1,365.2	34.4	0.5	1,718.7

INDUSTRY: WOMEN'S CLOTHING STORES (NAICS 44812)
PRODUCT LINE: HATS & WIGS (Sub Category)

NAICS 44812: Women's Clothing Stores . This industry comprises establishments primarily engaged in retailing a general line of new women's, misses' and juniors' clothing, including maternity wear. These establishments may provide basic alterations, such as hemming, taking in or letting out seams, or lengthening or shortening sleeves.

5-YEAR TREND — ESTIMATED INDUSTRY SALES ($MILLIONS)

Year	Employee Size of Establishment									Total
	1-4 Emps.	5-9 Emps.	10-19 Emps.	20-49 Emps.	50-99 Emps.	100-249 Emps.	250-499 Emps.	500-999 Emps.	Unknown Emps.	Industry Sales
2015	5.3	11.9	25.4	17.9	6.3	5.8	2.4	2.3	1.2	78.5
2016	5.5	12.3	26.1	18.4	6.5	6.0	2.4	2.4	1.2	80.9
2017	5.7	12.7	27.0	19.1	6.7	6.2	2.5	2.4	1.3	83.7
2018	6.0	13.4	28.5	20.1	7.1	6.6	2.7	2.6	1.3	88.2
2019	6.4	14.2	30.4	21.4	7.6	7.0	2.8	2.7	1.4	93.9

INDUSTRY: FAMILY CLOTHING STORES (NAICS 44814)
PRODUCT LINE: HATS & WIGS (Sub Category)

NAICS 44814: Family Clothing Stores . This industry comprises establishments primarily engaged in retailing a general line of new clothing for men, women, and children, without specializing in sales for an individual gender or age group. These establishments may provide basic alterations, such as hemming, taking in or letting out seams, or lengthening or shortening sleeves.

5-YEAR TREND — ESTIMATED INDUSTRY SALES ($MILLIONS)

Year	Employee Size of Establishment									Total
	1-4 Emps.	5-9 Emps.	10-19 Emps.	20-49 Emps.	50-99 Emps.	100-249 Emps.	250-499 Emps.	500-999 Emps.	Unknown Emps.	Industry Sales
2015	9.8	20.3	76.8	255.1	225.4	62.0	58.5	33.9	2.7	744.5
2016	10.1	20.9	78.8	262.0	231.4	63.7	60.1	34.8	2.8	764.5
2017	10.4	21.5	81.3	270.3	238.8	65.7	62.0	35.9	2.9	788.9
2018	11.0	22.7	85.7	284.9	251.7	69.3	65.3	37.7	3.0	831.4
2019	11.7	24.1	91.1	302.9	267.6	73.6	69.5	39.9	3.2	883.6

INDUSTRY: WOMEN'S CLOTHING STORES (NAICS 44812)
PRODUCT LINE: ACCESSORIES & HANDBAGS (Sub Category)

NAICS 44812: Women's Clothing Stores . This industry comprises establishments primarily engaged in retailing a general line of new women's, misses' and juniors' clothing, including maternity wear. These establishments may provide basic alterations, such as hemming, taking in or letting out seams, or lengthening or shortening sleeves.

5-YEAR TREND — ESTIMATED INDUSTRY SALES ($MILLIONS)

Year	Employee Size of Establishment									Total
	1-4 Emps.	5-9 Emps.	10-19 Emps.	20-49 Emps.	50-99 Emps.	100-249 Emps.	250-499 Emps.	500-999 Emps.	Unknown Emps.	Industry Sales
2015	140.4	313.6	669.1	471.9	166.7	154.0	62.4	60.4	31.3	2,069.9
2016	144.6	322.9	688.9	485.9	171.6	158.5	64.3	62.2	32.3	2,131.2
2017	149.6	334.0	712.7	502.7	177.5	164.0	66.5	64.4	33.4	2,204.9
2018	157.8	352.5	752.0	530.4	187.3	173.1	70.2	67.4	35.2	2,325.8
2019	167.9	375.0	800.1	564.3	199.3	184.1	74.7	71.0	37.5	2,473.8

INDUSTRY: FAMILY CLOTHING STORES (NAICS 44814)
PRODUCT LINE: ACCESSORIES & HANDBAGS (Sub Category)

NAICS 44814: Family Clothing Stores . This industry comprises establishments primarily engaged in retailing a general line of new clothing for men, women, and children, without specializing in sales for an individual gender or age group. These establishments may provide basic alterations, such as hemming, taking in or letting out seams, or lengthening or shortening sleeves.

5-YEAR TREND — ESTIMATED INDUSTRY SALES ($MILLIONS)

Year	Employee Size of Establishment									Total
	1-4 Emps.	5-9 Emps.	10-19 Emps.	20-49 Emps.	50-99 Emps.	100-249 Emps.	250-499 Emps.	500-999 Emps.	Unknown Emps.	Industry Sales
2015	54.2	112.1	423.5	1,407.6	1,243.4	342.2	322.8	186.9	14.9	4,107.7
2016	55.7	115.1	434.9	1,445.4	1,276.7	351.4	331.5	191.9	15.3	4,217.8
2017	57.5	118.8	448.8	1,491.5	1,317.5	362.6	342.1	198.1	15.7	4,352.6
2018	60.6	125.2	473.0	1,572.1	1,388.7	382.2	360.5	208.0	16.6	4,587.0
2019	64.4	133.1	502.8	1,671.2	1,476.2	406.3	383.3	220.1	17.6	4,875.1

INDUSTRY: DEPARTMENT STORES (NAICS 45211)
PRODUCT LINE: ACCESSORIES & HANDBAGS (Sub Category)

NAICS 45211: Department Stores Industry . This industry comprises establishments known as department stores primarily engaged in retailing a wide range of the following new products with no one merchandise line predominating: apparel, furniture, appliances and home furnishings; and selected additional items, such as paint, hardware, toiletries, cosmetics, photographic equipment, jewelry, toys, and sporting goods. Merchandise lines are normally arranged in separate departments.

5-Year Trend – Estimated Industry Sales ($Millions)

Year	Employee Size of Establishment									Total
	1-4 Emps.	5-9 Emps.	10-19 Emps.	20-49 Emps.	50-99 Emps.	100-249 Emps.	250-499 Emps.	500-999 Emps.	Unknown Emps.	Industry Sales
2015	0.1	0.1	0.2	17.5	316.9	1,017.5	421.2	60.9	2.6	1,837.0
2016	0.1	0.1	0.2	17.5	318.1	1,021.5	422.8	61.2	2.6	1,844.2
2017	0.1	0.1	0.2	17.7	321.3	1,031.6	427.0	61.8	2.6	1,862.4
2018	0.1	0.1	0.2	17.7	321.3	1,031.7	427.1	61.9	2.6	1,862.8
2019	0.1	0.1	0.2	17.9	324.5	1,041.9	431.3	62.6	2.7	1,881.3

INDUSTRY: WAREHOUSE CLUBS & SUPERCENTERS (NAICS 45291)
PRODUCT LINE: ACCESSORIES & HANDBAGS (Sub Category)

NAICS 45291: Warehouse Clubs and Superstores This industry comprises establishments known as warehouse clubs, superstores or supercenters primarily engaged in retailing a general line of groceries in combination with general lines of new merchandise, such as apparel, furniture, and appliances.

5-Year Trend – Estimated Industry Sales ($Millions)

Year	Employee Size of Establishment									Total
	1-4 Emps.	5-9 Emps.	10-19 Emps.	20-49 Emps.	50-99 Emps.	100-249 Emps.	250-499 Emps.	500-999 Emps.	Unknown Emps.	Industry Sales
2015	0.0	0.0	0.0	1.6	3.0	169.2	745.1	18.8	0.3	938.0
2016	0.1	0.0	0.0	1.6	3.0	173.9	765.6	19.3	0.3	963.9
2017	0.1	0.0	0.0	1.7	3.1	179.6	790.6	19.9	0.3	995.3
2018	0.1	0.0	0.0	1.8	3.4	193.3	850.9	21.4	0.3	1,071.2
2019	0.1	0.0	0.1	1.9	3.6	204.7	901.3	22.7	0.3	1,134.7

INDUSTRY: WOMEN'S CLOTHING STORES (NAICS 44812)
PRODUCT LINE: WOMEN'S SWEAT TOPS & PANTS (Sub Category)

NAICS 44812: Women's Clothing Stores . This industry comprises establishments primarily engaged in retailing a general line of new women's, misses' and juniors' clothing, including maternity wear. These establishments may provide basic alterations, such as hemming, taking in or letting out seams, or lengthening or shortening sleeves.

5-YEAR TREND – ESTIMATED INDUSTRY SALES ($MILLIONS)

Year	Employee Size of Establishment									Total
	1-4 Emps.	5-9 Emps.	10-19 Emps.	20-49 Emps.	50-99 Emps.	100-249 Emps.	250-499 Emps.	500-999 Emps.	Unknown Emps.	Industry Sales
2015	38.1	85.1	181.5	128.0	45.2	41.8	16.9	16.4	8.5	561.5
2016	39.2	87.6	186.9	131.8	46.5	43.0	17.4	16.9	8.8	578.1
2017	40.6	90.6	193.3	136.4	48.2	44.5	18.0	17.5	9.1	598.1
2018	42.8	95.6	204.0	143.9	50.8	46.9	19.0	18.3	9.6	630.9
2019	45.5	101.7	217.0	153.1	54.1	49.9	20.2	19.3	10.2	671.0

INDUSTRY: FAMILY CLOTHING STORES (NAICS 44814)
PRODUCT LINE: WOMEN'S SWEAT TOPS & PANTS (Sub Category)

NAICS 44814: Family Clothing Stores . This industry comprises establishments primarily engaged in retailing a general line of new clothing for men, women, and children, without specializing in sales for an individual gender or age group. These establishments may provide basic alterations, such as hemming, taking in or letting out seams, or lengthening or shortening sleeves.

5-YEAR TREND – ESTIMATED INDUSTRY SALES ($MILLIONS)

Year	Employee Size of Establishment									Total
	1-4 Emps.	5-9 Emps.	10-19 Emps.	20-49 Emps.	50-99 Emps.	100-249 Emps.	250-499 Emps.	500-999 Emps.	Unknown Emps.	Industry Sales
2015	26.4	54.6	206.2	685.2	605.2	166.6	157.1	91.0	7.2	1,999.5
2016	27.1	56.0	211.7	703.6	621.5	171.0	161.3	93.4	7.4	2,053.1
2017	28.0	57.8	218.4	726.0	641.3	176.5	166.5	96.4	7.7	2,118.7
2018	29.5	61.0	230.2	765.3	676.0	186.0	175.5	101.3	8.1	2,232.8
2019	31.4	64.8	244.8	813.5	718.6	197.8	186.6	107.2	8.6	2,373.0

NAICS 44812: Women's Clothing Stores . This industry comprises establishments primarily engaged in retailing a general line of new women's, misses' and juniors' clothing, including maternity wear. These establishments may provide basic alterations, such as hemming, taking in or letting out seams, or lengthening or shortening sleeves.

5-Year Trend – Estimated Industry Sales ($Millions)

Year	Employee Size of Establishment									Total
	1-4 Emps.	5-9 Emps.	10-19 Emps.	20-49 Emps.	50-99 Emps.	100-249 Emps.	250-499 Emps.	500-999 Emps.	Unknown Emps.	Industry Sales
2015	17.7	39.5	84.3	59.4	21.0	19.4	7.9	7.6	3.9	260.7
2016	18.2	40.7	86.8	61.2	21.6	20.0	8.1	7.8	4.1	268.4
2017	18.8	42.1	89.8	63.3	22.4	20.7	8.4	8.1	4.2	277.7
2018	19.9	44.4	94.7	66.8	23.6	21.8	8.8	8.5	4.4	292.9
2019	21.1	47.2	100.8	71.1	25.1	23.2	9.4	8.9	4.7	311.6

NAICS 44814: Family Clothing Stores . This industry comprises establishments primarily engaged in retailing a general line of new clothing for men, women, and children, without specializing in sales for an individual gender or age group. These establishments may provide basic alterations, such as hemming, taking in or letting out seams, or lengthening or shortening sleeves.

5-Year Trend – Estimated Industry Sales ($Millions)

Year	Employee Size of Establishment									Total
	1-4 Emps.	5-9 Emps.	10-19 Emps.	20-49 Emps.	50-99 Emps.	100-249 Emps.	250-499 Emps.	500-999 Emps.	Unknown Emps.	Industry Sales
2015	2.1	4.3	16.3	54.0	47.7	13.1	12.4	7.2	0.6	157.7
2016	2.1	4.4	16.7	55.5	49.0	13.5	12.7	7.4	0.6	161.9
2017	2.2	4.6	17.2	57.2	50.6	13.9	13.1	7.6	0.6	167.1
2018	2.3	4.8	18.2	60.3	53.3	14.7	13.8	8.0	0.6	176.1
2019	2.5	5.1	19.3	64.1	56.7	15.6	14.7	8.4	0.7	187.1

INDUSTRY: DEPARTMENT STORES (NAICS 45211)
PRODUCT LINE: UNIFORMS & OTHER APPAREL (Sub Category)

NAICS 45211: Department Stores Industry . This industry comprises establishments known as department stores primarily engaged in retailing a wide range of the following new products with no one merchandise line predominating: apparel, furniture, appliances and home furnishings; and selected additional items, such as paint, hardware, toiletries, cosmetics, photographic equipment, jewelry, toys, and sporting goods. Merchandise lines are normally arranged in separate departments.

5-YEAR TREND – ESTIMATED INDUSTRY SALES ($MILLIONS)

Year	Employee Size of Establishment									Total
	1-4 Emps.	5-9 Emps.	10-19 Emps.	20-49 Emps.	50-99 Emps.	100-249 Emps.	250-499 Emps.	500-999 Emps.	Unknown Emps.	Industry Sales
2015	0.0	0.0	0.0	1.6	29.6	95.2	39.4	5.7	0.2	171.8
2016	0.0	0.0	0.0	1.6	29.7	95.5	39.5	5.7	0.2	172.5
2017	0.0	0.0	0.0	1.7	30.0	96.5	39.9	5.8	0.2	174.2
2018	0.0	0.0	0.0	1.7	30.0	96.5	39.9	5.8	0.2	174.2
2019	0.0	0.0	0.0	1.7	30.3	97.4	40.3	5.9	0.2	175.9

INDUSTRY: SUPERMARKETS & GROCERY STORES (NAICS 44511)
PRODUCT LINE: CHILDREN'S WEAR (Main Category)

NAICS 44511: Grocery Stores Industry. This industry comprises establishments generally known as supermarkets and grocery stores primarily engaged in retailing a general line of food, such as canned and frozen foods; fresh fruits and vegetables; and fresh and prepared meats, fish, and poultry. Included in this industry are delicatessen-type establishments primarily engaged in retailing a general line of food.

5-YEAR TREND – ESTIMATED INDUSTRY SALES ($MILLIONS)

Year	Employee Size of Establishment									Total
	1-4 Emps.	5-9 Emps.	10-19 Emps.	20-49 Emps.	50-99 Emps.	100-249 Emps.	250-499 Emps.	500-999 Emps.	Unknown Emps.	Industry Sales
2015	0.8	0.6	1.5	5.0	11.9	29.5	9.2	1.1	0.2	59.8
2016	0.8	0.6	1.5	5.0	11.8	29.3	9.2	1.1	0.2	59.4
2017	0.8	0.6	1.5	5.0	11.8	29.3	9.2	1.1	0.2	59.4
2018	0.8	0.6	1.5	5.1	12.0	29.9	9.3	1.1	0.2	60.6
2019	0.9	0.6	1.6	5.2	12.4	30.8	9.6	1.2	0.2	62.5

INDUSTRY: PHARMACIES & DRUG STORES (NAICS 44611)
PRODUCT LINE: CHILDREN'S WEAR (Main Category)

NAICS 44611 Pharmacies and Drug Stores – This industry comprises establishments known as pharmacies and drug stores engaged in retailing prescription or nonprescription drugs and medicines.

5-Year Trend – Estimated Industry Sales ($Millions)

Year	Employee Size of Establishment									Total
	1-4 Emps.	5-9 Emps.	10-19 Emps.	20-49 Emps.	50-99 Emps.	100-249 Emps.	250-499 Emps.	500-999 Emps.	Unknown Emps.	Industry Sales
2015	0.6	1.5	6.0	17.7	1.8	0.7	0.3	0.1	0.0	28.7
2016	0.6	1.5	6.2	18.2	1.8	0.7	0.3	0.1	0.0	29.6
2017	0.6	1.6	6.4	18.9	1.9	0.8	0.3	0.1	0.0	30.6
2018	0.7	1.7	6.8	20.0	2.0	0.8	0.3	0.1	0.1	32.4
2019	0.7	1.8	7.3	21.3	2.2	0.9	0.3	0.1	0.1	34.6

INDUSTRY: MEN'S CLOTHING STORES (NAICS 44811)
PRODUCT LINE: CHILDREN'S WEAR (Main Category)

NAICS 44811: Men's Clothing Stores. This industry comprises establishments primarily engaged in retailing a general line of new men's and boys' clothing. These establishments may provide basic alterations, such as hemming, taking in or letting out seams, or lengthening or shortening sleeves.

5-Year Trend – Estimated Industry Sales ($Millions)

Year	Employee Size of Establishment									Total
	1-4 Emps.	5-9 Emps.	10-19 Emps.	20-49 Emps.	50-99 Emps.	100-249 Emps.	250-499 Emps.	500-999 Emps.	Unknown Emps.	Industry Sales
2015	10.5	18.4	34.2	18.0	3.9	3.5	1.2	0.1	1.8	91.6
2016	10.8	19.1	35.5	18.7	4.1	3.7	1.2	0.1	1.9	95.0
2017	11.3	19.8	37.0	19.5	4.2	3.8	1.3	0.1	1.9	98.9
2018	11.7	20.5	38.1	20.1	4.4	3.9	1.3	0.1	2.0	102.0
2019	12.1	21.3	39.6	20.9	4.5	4.1	1.4	0.1	2.1	106.0

INDUSTRY: WOMEN'S CLOTHING STORES (NAICS 44812)
PRODUCT LINE: CHILDREN'S WEAR (Main Category)

NAICS 44812: Women's Clothing Stores . This industry comprises establishments primarily engaged in retailing a general line of new women's, misses' and juniors' clothing, including maternity wear. These establishments may provide basic alterations, such as hemming, taking in or letting out seams, or lengthening or shortening sleeves.

5-YEAR TREND – ESTIMATED INDUSTRY SALES ($MILLIONS)

| Year | Employee Size of Establishment | | | | | | | | | Total |
	1-4 Emps.	5-9 Emps.	10-19 Emps.	20-49 Emps.	50-99 Emps.	100-249 Emps.	250-499 Emps.	500-999 Emps.	Unknown Emps.	Industry Sales
2015	16.6	37.1	79.2	55.9	19.7	18.2	7.4	7.2	3.7	245.1
2016	17.1	38.2	81.6	57.5	20.3	18.8	7.6	7.4	3.8	252.4
2017	17.7	39.6	84.4	59.5	21.0	19.4	7.9	7.6	4.0	261.1
2018	18.7	41.7	89.1	62.8	22.2	20.5	8.3	8.0	4.2	275.5
2019	19.9	44.4	94.8	66.8	23.6	21.8	8.8	8.4	4.4	293.0

INDUSTRY: FAMILY CLOTHING STORES (NAICS 44814)
PRODUCT LINE: CHILDREN'S WEAR (Main Category)

NAICS 44814: Family Clothing Stores . This industry comprises establishments primarily engaged in retailing a general line of new clothing for men, women, and children, without specializing in sales for an individual gender or age group. These establishments may provide basic alterations, such as hemming, taking in or letting out seams, or lengthening or shortening sleeves.

5-YEAR TREND – ESTIMATED INDUSTRY SALES ($MILLIONS)

| Year | Employee Size of Establishment | | | | | | | | | Total |
	1-4 Emps.	5-9 Emps.	10-19 Emps.	20-49 Emps.	50-99 Emps.	100-249 Emps.	250-499 Emps.	500-999 Emps.	Unknown Emps.	Industry Sales
2015	147.3	304.4	1,149.9	3,821.9	3,376.0	929.1	876.5	507.5	40.4	11,152.9
2016	151.2	312.6	1,180.7	3,924.3	3,466.5	954.0	900.0	521.1	41.4	11,451.9
2017	156.1	322.6	1,218.5	4,049.7	3,577.2	984.5	928.7	537.7	42.8	11,817.8
2018	164.5	340.0	1,284.3	4,268.5	3,770.5	1,037.7	978.9	564.8	45.1	12,454.2
2019	174.9	361.4	1,365.2	4,537.5	4,008.1	1,103.1	1,040.6	597.7	47.9	13,236.5

INDUSTRY: DEPARTMENT STORES (NAICS 45211)
PRODUCT LINE: CHILDREN'S WEAR (Main Category)

NAICS 45211: Department Stores Industry . This industry comprises establishments known as department stores primarily engaged in retailing a wide range of the following new products with no one merchandise line predominating: apparel, furniture, appliances and home furnishings; and selected additional items, such as paint, hardware, toiletries, cosmetics, photographic equipment, jewelry, toys, and sporting goods. Merchandise lines are normally arranged in separate departments.

5-YEAR TREND – ESTIMATED INDUSTRY SALES ($MILLIONS)

Year	Employee Size of Establishment									Total Industry Sales
	1-4 Emps.	5-9 Emps.	10-19 Emps.	20-49 Emps.	50-99 Emps.	100-249 Emps.	250-499 Emps.	500-999 Emps.	Unknown Emps.	
2015	0.3	0.4	0.9	76.6	1,390.5	4,465.0	1,848.2	267.4	11.4	8,060.7
2016	0.3	0.4	0.9	76.9	1,395.9	4,482.4	1,855.5	268.4	11.4	8,092.2
2017	0.3	0.4	0.9	77.7	1,409.7	4,526.7	1,873.8	271.1	11.5	8,172.0
2018	0.3	0.4	0.9	77.7	1,409.9	4,527.2	1,874.0	271.8	11.5	8,173.8
2019	0.3	0.4	0.9	78.4	1,423.8	4,572.0	1,892.6	274.9	11.6	8,255.1

INDUSTRY: WAREHOUSE CLUBS & SUPERCENTERS (NAICS 45291)
PRODUCT LINE: CHILDREN'S WEAR (Main Category)

NAICS 45291: Warehouse Clubs and Superstores This industry comprises establishments known as warehouse clubs, superstores or supercenters primarily engaged in retailing a general line of groceries in combination with general lines of new merchandise, such as apparel, furniture, and appliances.

5-YEAR TREND – ESTIMATED INDUSTRY SALES ($MILLIONS)

Year	Employee Size of Establishment									Total Industry Sales
	1-4 Emps.	5-9 Emps.	10-19 Emps.	20-49 Emps.	50-99 Emps.	100-249 Emps.	250-499 Emps.	500-999 Emps.	Unknown Emps.	
2015	0.6	0.1	0.5	17.5	33.2	1,894.9	8,341.6	210.2	3.2	10,501.7
2016	0.6	0.2	0.5	18.0	34.1	1,947.1	8,571.5	216.0	3.3	10,791.2
2017	0.6	0.2	0.5	18.6	35.2	2,010.7	8,851.5	223.0	3.4	11,143.6
2018	0.6	0.2	0.5	20.0	37.9	2,163.9	9,526.2	240.0	3.6	11,993.0
2019	0.7	0.2	0.6	21.2	40.1	2,292.1	10,090.5	254.3	3.8	12,703.5

INDUSTRY: ELECTRONIC SHOPPING & MAIL ORDER (NAICS 45411)
PRODUCT LINE: CHILDREN'S WEAR (Main Category)

NAICS 45411: Electronic Shopping and Mail-Order Houses This industry comprises establishments primarily engaged in retailing all types of merchandise by means of mail or by electronic media, such as interactive television or computer. Included in this industry are establishments primarily engaged in retailing from catalogue showrooms of mail-order houses.

5-YEAR TREND – ESTIMATED INDUSTRY SALES ($MILLIONS)

Year	Employee Size of Establishment									Total Industry Sales
	1-4 Emps.	5-9 Emps.	10-19 Emps.	20-49 Emps.	50-99 Emps.	100-249 Emps.	250-499 Emps.	500-999 Emps.	Unknown Emps.	
2015	285.2	146.9	212.2	356.2	268.1	496.1	668.8	944.1	40.1	3,417.8
2016	301.6	155.4	224.5	376.8	283.6	524.7	707.4	998.6	42.4	3,615.1
2017	319.8	164.7	238.0	399.5	300.7	556.3	750.0	1,058.8	44.9	3,832.9
2018	358.4	184.6	266.7	447.7	337.0	623.5	840.6	1,165.1	50.4	4,274.0
2019	398.5	205.3	296.6	497.8	374.7	693.2	934.6	1,275.9	56.0	4,732.4

INDUSTRY: BOOK STORES (NAICS 451211)
PRODUCT LINE: CHILDREN'S WEAR (Main Category)

NAICS 451211: Book Stores. This industry comprises establishments primarily engaged in the retail sale of new books and magazines. Establishments primarily engaged in the retail sale of used books are classified in 5932.

5-YEAR TREND – ESTIMATED INDUSTRY SALES ($MILLIONS)

Year	Employee Size of Establishment									Total Industry Sales
	1-4 Emps.	5-9 Emps.	10-19 Emps.	20-49 Emps.	50-99 Emps.	100-249 Emps.	250-499 Emps.	500-999 Emps.	Unknown Emps.	
2015	0.4	0.6	1.2	3.2	1.4	0.6	0.2	0.4	0.2	8.1
2016	0.4	0.6	1.2	3.3	1.4	0.7	0.2	0.4	0.2	8.5
2017	0.4	0.7	1.3	3.5	1.5	0.7	0.2	0.4	0.2	8.9
2018	0.4	0.7	1.4	3.6	1.6	0.7	0.2	0.4	0.2	9.2
2019	0.5	0.7	1.4	3.8	1.6	0.8	0.2	0.5	0.2	9.6

	INDUSTRY: MEN'S CLOTHING STORES (NAICS 44811)
	PRODUCT LINE: BOYS' WEAR & ACCESSORIES (Sub Category)

NAICS 44811: Men's Clothing Stores. This industry comprises establishments primarily engaged in retailing a general line of new men's and boys' clothing. These establishments may provide basic alterations, such as hemming, taking in or letting out seams, or lengthening or shortening sleeves.

5-YEAR TREND — ESTIMATED INDUSTRY SALES ($MILLIONS)

Year	Employee Size of Establishment									Total
	1-4 Emps.	5-9 Emps.	10-19 Emps.	20-49 Emps.	50-99 Emps.	100-249 Emps.	250-499 Emps.	500-999 Emps.	Unknown Emps.	Industry Sales
2015	7.6	13.3	24.8	13.1	2.8	2.6	0.9	0.0	1.3	66.3
2016	7.9	13.8	25.7	13.5	2.9	2.6	0.9	0.0	1.4	68.8
2017	8.2	14.4	26.8	14.1	3.1	2.8	0.9	0.0	1.4	71.6
2018	8.4	14.8	27.6	14.5	3.2	2.8	1.0	0.1	1.5	73.9
2019	8.8	15.4	28.7	15.1	3.3	3.0	1.0	0.1	1.5	76.8

	INDUSTRY: WOMEN'S CLOTHING STORES (NAICS 44812)
	PRODUCT LINE: BOYS' WEAR & ACCESSORIES (Sub Category)

NAICS 44812: Women's Clothing Stores . This industry comprises establishments primarily engaged in retailing a general line of new women's, misses' and juniors' clothing, including maternity wear. These establishments may provide basic alterations, such as hemming, taking in or letting out seams, or lengthening or shortening sleeves.

5-YEAR TREND — ESTIMATED INDUSTRY SALES ($MILLIONS)

Year	Employee Size of Establishment									Total
	1-4 Emps.	5-9 Emps.	10-19 Emps.	20-49 Emps.	50-99 Emps.	100-249 Emps.	250-499 Emps.	500-999 Emps.	Unknown Emps.	Industry Sales
2015	3.4	7.6	16.3	11.5	4.1	3.8	1.5	1.5	0.8	50.5
2016	3.5	7.9	16.8	11.9	4.2	3.9	1.6	1.5	0.8	52.0
2017	3.6	8.1	17.4	12.3	4.3	4.0	1.6	1.6	0.8	53.8
2018	3.8	8.6	18.3	12.9	4.6	4.2	1.7	1.6	0.9	56.7
2019	4.1	9.1	19.5	13.8	4.9	4.5	1.8	1.7	0.9	60.3

INDUSTRY: FAMILY CLOTHING STORES (NAICS 44814)
PRODUCT LINE: BOYS' WEAR & ACCESSORIES (Sub Category)

NAICS 44814: Family Clothing Stores . This industry comprises establishments primarily engaged in retailing a general line of new clothing for men, women, and children, without specializing in sales for an individual gender or age group. These establishments may provide basic alterations, such as hemming, taking in or letting out seams, or lengthening or shortening sleeves.

5-YEAR TREND — ESTIMATED INDUSTRY SALES ($MILLIONS)

| Year | Employee Size of Establishment | | | | | | | | | Total |
	1-4 Emps.	5-9 Emps.	10-19 Emps.	20-49 Emps.	50-99 Emps.	100-249 Emps.	250-499 Emps.	500-999 Emps.	Unknown Emps.	Industry Sales
2015	53.4	110.3	416.7	1,384.8	1,223.3	336.7	317.6	183.9	14.6	4,041.2
2016	54.8	113.3	427.8	1,422.0	1,256.1	345.7	326.1	188.8	15.0	4,149.5
2017	56.6	116.9	441.5	1,467.4	1,296.2	356.7	336.5	194.8	15.5	4,282.1
2018	59.6	123.2	465.4	1,546.7	1,366.2	376.0	354.7	204.7	16.3	4,512.7
2019	63.4	131.0	494.7	1,644.1	1,452.3	399.7	377.1	216.6	17.4	4,796.2

INDUSTRY: DEPARTMENT STORES (NAICS 45211)
PRODUCT LINE: BOYS' WEAR & ACCESSORIES (Sub Category)

NAICS 45211: Department Stores Industry . This industry comprises establishments known as department stores primarily engaged in retailing a wide range of the following new products with no one merchandise line predominating: apparel, furniture, appliances and home furnishings; and selected additional items, such as paint, hardware, toiletries, cosmetics, photographic equipment, jewelry, toys, and sporting goods. Merchandise lines are normally arranged in separate departments.

5-YEAR TREND — ESTIMATED INDUSTRY SALES ($MILLIONS)

| Year | Employee Size of Establishment | | | | | | | | | Total |
	1-4 Emps.	5-9 Emps.	10-19 Emps.	20-49 Emps.	50-99 Emps.	100-249 Emps.	250-499 Emps.	500-999 Emps.	Unknown Emps.	Industry Sales
2015	0.1	0.1	0.3	23.8	431.1	1,384.4	573.1	82.9	3.5	2,499.3
2016	0.1	0.1	0.3	23.8	432.8	1,389.8	575.3	83.2	3.5	2,509.1
2017	0.1	0.1	0.3	24.1	437.1	1,403.6	581.0	84.0	3.6	2,533.9
2018	0.1	0.1	0.3	24.1	437.1	1,403.7	581.1	84.3	3.6	2,534.4
2019	0.1	0.1	0.3	24.3	441.5	1,417.6	586.8	85.2	3.6	2,559.6

INDUSTRY: WAREHOUSE CLUBS & SUPERCENTERS (NAICS 45291)
PRODUCT LINE: BOYS' WEAR & ACCESSORIES (Sub Category)

NAICS 45291: Warehouse Clubs and Superstores This industry comprises establishments known as warehouse clubs, superstores or supercenters primarily engaged in retailing a general line of groceries in combination with general lines of new merchandise, such as apparel, furniture, and appliances.

5-YEAR TREND – ESTIMATED INDUSTRY SALES ($MILLIONS)

Year	Employee Size of Establishment									Total
	1-4 Emps.	5-9 Emps.	10-19 Emps.	20-49 Emps.	50-99 Emps.	100-249 Emps.	250-499 Emps.	500-999 Emps.	Unknown Emps.	Industry Sales
2015	0.1	0.0	0.1	4.3	8.1	463.3	2,039.4	51.4	0.8	2,567.6
2016	0.1	0.0	0.1	4.4	8.3	476.0	2,095.7	52.8	0.8	2,638.3
2017	0.1	0.0	0.1	4.5	8.6	491.6	2,164.1	54.5	0.8	2,724.5
2018	0.2	0.0	0.1	4.9	9.3	529.1	2,329.1	58.7	0.9	2,932.2
2019	0.2	0.0	0.1	5.2	9.8	560.4	2,467.0	62.2	0.9	3,105.9

INDUSTRY: MEN'S CLOTHING STORES (NAICS 44811)
PRODUCT LINE: GIRLS' WEAR & ACCESSORIES (Sub Category)

NAICS 44811: Men's Clothing Stores. This industry comprises establishments primarily engaged in retailing a general line of new men's and boys' clothing. These establishments may provide basic alterations, such as hemming, taking in or letting out seams, or lengthening or shortening sleeves.

5-YEAR TREND – ESTIMATED INDUSTRY SALES ($MILLIONS)

Year	Employee Size of Establishment									Total
	1-4 Emps.	5-9 Emps.	10-19 Emps.	20-49 Emps.	50-99 Emps.	100-249 Emps.	250-499 Emps.	500-999 Emps.	Unknown Emps.	Industry Sales
2015	2.5	4.3	8.1	4.3	0.9	0.8	0.3	0.0	0.4	21.6
2016	2.6	4.5	8.4	4.4	1.0	0.9	0.3	0.0	0.4	22.4
2017	2.7	4.7	8.7	4.6	1.0	0.9	0.3	0.0	0.5	23.3
2018	2.7	4.8	9.0	4.7	1.0	0.9	0.3	0.0	0.5	24.1
2019	2.9	5.0	9.3	4.9	1.1	1.0	0.3	0.0	0.5	25.0

INDUSTRY: WOMEN'S CLOTHING STORES (NAICS 44812)
PRODUCT LINE: GIRLS' WEAR & ACCESSORIES (Sub Category)

NAICS 44812: Women's Clothing Stores . This industry comprises establishments primarily engaged in retailing a general line of new women's, misses' and juniors' clothing, including maternity wear. These establishments may provide basic alterations, such as hemming, taking in or letting out seams, or lengthening or shortening sleeves.

5-YEAR TREND – ESTIMATED INDUSTRY SALES ($MILLIONS)

Year	Employee Size of Establishment									Total
	1-4 Emps.	5-9 Emps.	10-19 Emps.	20-49 Emps.	50-99 Emps.	100-249 Emps.	250-499 Emps.	500-999 Emps.	Unknown Emps.	Industry Sales
2015	0.7	1.4	3.5	7.1	5.4	352.9	27.6	0.6	0.2	399.1
2016	0.7	1.4	3.5	7.2	5.5	361.3	28.2	0.6	0.3	408.7
2017	0.7	1.4	3.6	7.4	5.6	371.9	29.0	0.6	0.3	420.7
2018	0.8	1.5	3.8	7.7	5.8	385.7	30.1	0.6	0.3	436.3
2019	0.8	1.6	3.9	8.1	6.1	403.5	31.5	0.7	0.3	456.5

INDUSTRY: FAMILY CLOTHING STORES (NAICS 44814)
PRODUCT LINE: GIRLS' WEAR & ACCESSORIES (Sub Category)

NAICS 44814: Family Clothing Stores . This industry comprises establishments primarily engaged in retailing a general line of new clothing for men, women, and children, without specializing in sales for an individual gender or age group. These establishments may provide basic alterations, such as hemming, taking in or letting out seams, or lengthening or shortening sleeves.

5-YEAR TREND – ESTIMATED INDUSTRY SALES ($MILLIONS)

Year	Employee Size of Establishment									Total
	1-4 Emps.	5-9 Emps.	10-19 Emps.	20-49 Emps.	50-99 Emps.	100-249 Emps.	250-499 Emps.	500-999 Emps.	Unknown Emps.	Industry Sales
2015	57.3	118.4	447.0	1,485.8	1,312.4	361.2	340.7	197.3	15.7	4,335.8
2016	58.8	121.5	459.0	1,525.6	1,347.6	370.9	349.9	202.6	16.1	4,452.0
2017	60.7	125.4	473.7	1,574.4	1,390.7	382.7	361.0	209.1	16.6	4,594.3
2018	64.0	132.2	499.3	1,659.4	1,465.8	403.4	380.6	219.6	17.5	4,841.7
2019	68.0	140.5	530.7	1,764.0	1,558.2	428.8	404.5	232.4	18.6	5,145.8

INDUSTRY: DEPARTMENT STORES (NAICS 45211)
PRODUCT LINE: GIRLS' WEAR & ACCESSORIES (Sub Category)

NAICS 45211: Department Stores Industry . This industry comprises establishments known as department stores primarily engaged in retailing a wide range of the following new products with no one merchandise line predominating: apparel, furniture, appliances and home furnishings; and selected additional items, such as paint, hardware, toiletries, cosmetics, photographic equipment, jewelry, toys, and sporting goods. Merchandise lines are normally arranged in separate departments.

5-Year Trend – Estimated Industry Sales ($Millions)

Year	Employee Size of Establishment									Total
	1-4 Emps.	5-9 Emps.	10-19 Emps.	20-49 Emps.	50-99 Emps.	100-249 Emps.	250-499 Emps.	500-999 Emps.	Unknown Emps.	Industry Sales
2015	0.1	0.1	0.3	22.8	414.0	1,329.4	550.3	79.6	3.4	2,400.0
2016	0.1	0.1	0.3	22.9	415.6	1,334.6	552.5	79.9	3.4	2,409.4
2017	0.1	0.1	0.3	23.1	419.7	1,347.8	557.9	80.7	3.4	2,433.2
2018	0.1	0.1	0.3	23.1	419.8	1,348.0	558.0	80.9	3.4	2,433.7
2019	0.1	0.1	0.3	23.4	423.9	1,361.3	563.5	81.9	3.5	2,457.9

INDUSTRY: WAREHOUSE CLUBS & SUPERCENTERS (NAICS 45291)
PRODUCT LINE: GIRLS' WEAR & ACCESSORIES (Sub Category)

NAICS 45291: Warehouse Clubs and Superstores This industry comprises establishments known as warehouse clubs, superstores or supercenters primarily engaged in retailing a general line of groceries in combination with general lines of new merchandise, such as apparel, furniture, and appliances.

5-Year Trend – Estimated Industry Sales ($Millions)

Year	Employee Size of Establishment									Total
	1-4 Emps.	5-9 Emps.	10-19 Emps.	20-49 Emps.	50-99 Emps.	100-249 Emps.	250-499 Emps.	500-999 Emps.	Unknown Emps.	Industry Sales
2015	0.0	0.0	0.0	0.1	0.1	5.5	24.1	0.6	0.0	30.4
2016	0.0	0.0	0.0	0.1	0.1	5.6	24.8	0.6	0.0	31.2
2017	0.0	0.0	0.0	0.1	0.1	5.8	25.6	0.6	0.0	32.2
2018	0.0	0.0	0.0	0.1	0.1	6.3	27.6	0.7	0.0	34.7
2019	0.0	0.0	0.0	0.1	0.1	6.6	29.2	0.7	0.0	36.7

INDUSTRY: MEN'S CLOTHING STORES (NAICS 44811)
PRODUCT LINE: INFANTS' & TODDLERS' WEAR (Sub Category)

NAICS 44811: Men's Clothing Stores. This industry comprises establishments primarily engaged in retailing a general line of new men's and boys' clothing. These establishments may provide basic alterations, such as hemming, taking in or letting out seams, or lengthening or shortening sleeves.

5-YEAR TREND – ESTIMATED INDUSTRY SALES ($MILLIONS)

Year	Employee Size of Establishment									Total
	1-4 Emps.	5-9 Emps.	10-19 Emps.	20-49 Emps.	50-99 Emps.	100-249 Emps.	250-499 Emps.	500-999 Emps.	Unknown Emps.	Industry Sales
2015	0.4	0.7	1.4	0.7	0.2	0.1	0.0	0.0	0.1	3.7
2016	0.4	0.8	1.4	0.7	0.2	0.1	0.0	0.0	0.1	3.8
2017	0.5	0.8	1.5	0.8	0.2	0.2	0.1	0.0	0.1	4.0
2018	0.5	0.8	1.5	0.8	0.2	0.2	0.1	0.0	0.1	4.1
2019	0.5	0.9	1.6	0.8	0.2	0.2	0.1	0.0	0.1	4.3

INDUSTRY: WOMEN'S CLOTHING STORES (NAICS 44812)
PRODUCT LINE: INFANTS' & TODDLERS' WEAR (Sub Category)

NAICS 44812: Women's Clothing Stores . This industry comprises establishments primarily engaged in retailing a general line of new women's, misses' and juniors' clothing, including maternity wear. These establishments may provide basic alterations, such as hemming, taking in or letting out seams, or lengthening or shortening sleeves.

5-YEAR TREND – ESTIMATED INDUSTRY SALES ($MILLIONS)

Year	Employee Size of Establishment									Total
	1-4 Emps.	5-9 Emps.	10-19 Emps.	20-49 Emps.	50-99 Emps.	100-249 Emps.	250-499 Emps.	500-999 Emps.	Unknown Emps.	Industry Sales
2015	5.5	12.2	26.0	18.3	6.5	6.0	2.4	2.3	1.2	80.5
2016	5.6	12.5	26.8	18.9	6.7	6.2	2.5	2.4	1.3	82.8
2017	5.8	13.0	27.7	19.5	6.9	6.4	2.6	2.5	1.3	85.7
2018	6.1	13.7	29.2	20.6	7.3	6.7	2.7	2.6	1.4	90.4
2019	6.5	14.6	31.1	21.9	7.7	7.2	2.9	2.8	1.5	96.2

INDUSTRY: FAMILY CLOTHING STORES (NAICS 44814)
PRODUCT LINE: INFANTS' & TODDLERS' WEAR (Sub Category)

NAICS 44814: Family Clothing Stores . This industry comprises establishments primarily engaged in retailing a general line of new clothing for men, women, and children, without specializing in sales for an individual gender or age group. These establishments may provide basic alterations, such as hemming, taking in or letting out seams, or lengthening or shortening sleeves.

5-YEAR TREND – ESTIMATED INDUSTRY SALES ($MILLIONS)

Year	Employee Size of Establishment									Total
	1-4 Emps.	5-9 Emps.	10-19 Emps.	20-49 Emps.	50-99 Emps.	100-249 Emps.	250-499 Emps.	500-999 Emps.	Unknown Emps.	Industry Sales
2015	36.7	75.8	286.2	951.2	840.3	231.3	218.1	126.3	10.0	2,775.9
2016	37.6	77.8	293.9	976.7	862.8	237.5	224.0	129.7	10.3	2,850.3
2017	38.8	80.3	303.3	1,008.0	890.4	245.0	231.2	133.8	10.6	2,941.4
2018	40.9	84.6	319.7	1,062.4	938.5	258.3	243.6	140.6	11.2	3,099.8
2019	43.5	90.0	339.8	1,129.4	997.6	274.6	259.0	148.8	11.9	3,294.5

INDUSTRY: DEPARTMENT STORES (NAICS 45211)
PRODUCT LINE: INFANTS' & TODDLERS' WEAR (Sub Category)

NAICS 45211: Department Stores Industry . This industry comprises establishments known as department stores primarily engaged in retailing a wide range of the following new products with no one merchandise line predominating: apparel, furniture, appliances and home furnishings; and selected additional items, such as paint, hardware, toiletries, cosmetics, photographic equipment, jewelry, toys, and sporting goods. Merchandise lines are normally arranged in separate departments.

5-YEAR TREND – ESTIMATED INDUSTRY SALES ($MILLIONS)

Year	Employee Size of Establishment									Total
	1-4 Emps.	5-9 Emps.	10-19 Emps.	20-49 Emps.	50-99 Emps.	100-249 Emps.	250-499 Emps.	500-999 Emps.	Unknown Emps.	Industry Sales
2015	0.1	0.2	0.4	30.0	545.3	1,751.1	724.9	104.9	4.5	3,161.3
2016	0.1	0.2	0.4	30.2	547.5	1,757.9	727.7	105.3	4.5	3,173.7
2017	0.1	0.2	0.4	30.5	552.9	1,775.3	734.9	106.3	4.5	3,205.0
2018	0.1	0.2	0.4	30.5	552.9	1,775.5	735.0	106.6	4.5	3,205.7
2019	0.1	0.2	0.4	30.8	558.4	1,793.1	742.2	107.8	4.6	3,237.6

INDUSTRY: WAREHOUSE CLUBS & SUPERCENTERS (NAICS 45291)
PRODUCT LINE: INFANTS' & TODDLERS' WEAR (Sub Category)

NAICS 45291: Warehouse Clubs and Superstores This industry comprises establishments known as warehouse clubs, superstores or supercenters primarily engaged in retailing a general line of groceries in combination with general lines of new merchandise, such as apparel, furniture, and appliances.

5-YEAR TREND – ESTIMATED INDUSTRY SALES ($MILLIONS)

Year	Employee Size of Establishment									Total
	1-4 Emps.	5-9 Emps.	10-19 Emps.	20-49 Emps.	50-99 Emps.	100-249 Emps.	250-499 Emps.	500-999 Emps.	Unknown Emps.	Industry Sales
2015	0.3	0.1	0.3	9.2	17.5	997.8	4,392.7	110.7	1.7	5,530.2
2016	0.3	0.1	0.3	9.5	18.0	1,025.3	4,513.8	113.7	1.7	5,682.6
2017	0.3	0.1	0.3	9.8	18.5	1,058.8	4,661.2	117.5	1.8	5,868.2
2018	0.3	0.1	0.3	10.5	20.0	1,139.5	5,016.5	126.4	1.9	6,315.5
2019	0.4	0.1	0.3	11.1	21.1	1,207.0	5,313.7	133.9	2.0	6,689.7

INDUSTRY: HARDWARE STORES (NAICS 44413)
PRODUCT LINE: FOOTWEAR (Main Category)

NAICS 44413: Hardware Stores. Establishments primarily engaged in the retail sale of a number of basic hardware lines, such as tools, builders' hardware, paint and glass, housewares and household appliances, and cutlery.

5-YEAR TREND – ESTIMATED INDUSTRY SALES ($MILLIONS)

Year	Employee Size of Establishment									Total
	1-4 Emps.	5-9 Emps.	10-19 Emps.	20-49 Emps.	50-99 Emps.	100-249 Emps.	250-499 Emps.	500-999 Emps.	Unknown Emps.	Industry Sales
2015	2.4	4.1	8.3	11.8	2.4	0.8	0.1	0.0	0.2	30.1
2016	2.4	4.2	8.4	11.9	2.4	0.8	0.1	0.0	0.2	30.4
2017	2.5	4.2	8.5	12.1	2.4	0.8	0.1	0.0	0.2	30.9
2018	2.6	4.4	8.8	12.6	2.5	0.8	0.1	0.0	0.2	32.1
2019	2.7	4.6	9.3	13.2	2.6	0.9	0.2	0.0	0.2	33.7

INDUSTRY: SUPERMARKETS & GROCERY STORES (NAICS 44511)
PRODUCT LINE: FOOTWEAR (Main Category)

NAICS 44511: Grocery Stores Industry. This industry comprises establishments generally known as supermarkets and grocery stores primarily engaged in retailing a general line of food, such as canned and frozen foods; fresh fruits and vegetables; and fresh and prepared meats, fish, and poultry. Included in this industry are delicatessen-type establishments primarily engaged in retailing a general line of food.

5-YEAR TREND — ESTIMATED INDUSTRY SALES ($MILLIONS)

Year	Employee Size of Establishment									Total
	1-4 Emps.	5-9 Emps.	10-19 Emps.	20-49 Emps.	50-99 Emps.	100-249 Emps.	250-499 Emps.	500-999 Emps.	Unknown Emps.	Industry Sales
2015	0.5	0.4	1.0	3.3	7.8	19.3	6.0	0.7	0.1	39.0
2016	0.5	0.4	1.0	3.2	7.7	19.1	6.0	0.7	0.1	38.8
2017	0.5	0.4	1.0	3.2	7.7	19.1	6.0	0.7	0.1	38.8
2018	0.5	0.4	1.0	3.3	7.9	19.5	6.1	0.7	0.1	39.6
2019	0.6	0.4	1.0	3.4	8.1	20.1	6.3	0.8	0.1	40.8

INDUSTRY: PHARMACIES & DRUG STORES (NAICS 44611)
PRODUCT LINE: FOOTWEAR (Main Category)

NAICS 44611 Pharmacies and Drug Stores – This industry comprises establishments known as pharmacies and drug stores engaged in retailing prescription or nonprescription drugs and medicines.

5-YEAR TREND — ESTIMATED INDUSTRY SALES ($MILLIONS)

Year	Employee Size of Establishment									Total
	1-4 Emps.	5-9 Emps.	10-19 Emps.	20-49 Emps.	50-99 Emps.	100-249 Emps.	250-499 Emps.	500-999 Emps.	Unknown Emps.	Industry Sales
2015	4.4	10.9	44.0	129.1	13.1	5.2	2.0	0.7	0.3	209.6
2016	4.5	11.2	45.3	133.2	13.5	5.4	2.1	0.7	0.3	216.2
2017	4.7	11.6	47.0	138.0	14.0	5.6	2.1	0.7	0.4	224.0
2018	5.0	12.3	49.8	146.1	14.8	5.9	2.3	0.8	0.4	237.3
2019	5.3	13.1	53.1	156.1	15.8	6.3	2.4	0.8	0.4	253.4

INDUSTRY: MEN'S CLOTHING STORES (NAICS 44811)
PRODUCT LINE: FOOTWEAR (Main Category)

NAICS 44811: Men's Clothing Stores. This industry comprises establishments primarily engaged in retailing a general line of new men's and boys' clothing. These establishments may provide basic alterations, such as hemming, taking in or letting out seams, or lengthening or shortening sleeves.

5-YEAR TREND — ESTIMATED INDUSTRY SALES ($MILLIONS)

Year	Employee Size of Establishment									Total Industry Sales
	1-4 Emps.	5-9 Emps.	10-19 Emps.	20-49 Emps.	50-99 Emps.	100-249 Emps.	250-499 Emps.	500-999 Emps.	Unknown Emps.	
2015	35.9	63.1	117.4	61.9	13.5	12.1	4.1	0.2	6.2	314.2
2016	37.2	65.4	121.7	64.1	14.0	12.5	4.2	0.2	6.4	325.9
2017	38.8	68.1	126.8	66.8	14.5	13.1	4.4	0.2	6.7	339.4
2018	40.0	70.2	130.7	68.9	15.0	13.5	4.5	0.2	6.9	350.0
2019	41.6	73.0	135.9	71.6	15.6	14.0	4.7	0.3	7.2	363.8

INDUSTRY: WOMEN'S CLOTHING STORES (NAICS 44812)
PRODUCT LINE: FOOTWEAR (Main Category)

NAICS 44812: Women's Clothing Stores . This industry comprises establishments primarily engaged in retailing a general line of new women's, misses' and juniors' clothing, including maternity wear. These establishments may provide basic alterations, such as hemming, taking in or letting out seams, or lengthening or shortening sleeves.

5-YEAR TREND — ESTIMATED INDUSTRY SALES ($MILLIONS)

Year	Employee Size of Establishment									Total Industry Sales
	1-4 Emps.	5-9 Emps.	10-19 Emps.	20-49 Emps.	50-99 Emps.	100-249 Emps.	250-499 Emps.	500-999 Emps.	Unknown Emps.	
2015	92.0	205.4	438.3	309.2	109.2	100.9	40.9	39.6	20.5	1,356.0
2016	94.7	211.5	451.3	318.3	112.4	103.9	42.1	40.8	21.1	1,396.1
2017	98.0	218.8	466.9	329.3	116.3	107.4	43.6	42.2	21.9	1,444.4
2018	103.4	230.9	492.6	347.4	122.7	113.4	46.0	44.2	23.1	1,523.6
2019	110.0	245.6	524.1	369.7	130.6	120.6	48.9	46.5	24.5	1,620.5

<table>
<tr><td colspan="2">INDUSTRY: FAMILY CLOTHING STORES (NAICS 44814)</td></tr>
<tr><td colspan="2">PRODUCT LINE: FOOTWEAR (Main Category)</td></tr>
</table>

NAICS 44814: Family Clothing Stores . This industry comprises establishments primarily engaged in retailing a general line of new clothing for men, women, and children, without specializing in sales for an individual gender or age group. These establishments may provide basic alterations, such as hemming, taking in or letting out seams, or lengthening or shortening sleeves.

5-YEAR TREND – ESTIMATED INDUSTRY SALES ($MILLIONS)

Year	Employee Size of Establishment									Total
	1-4 Emps.	5-9 Emps.	10-19 Emps.	20-49 Emps.	50-99 Emps.	100-249 Emps.	250-499 Emps.	500-999 Emps.	Unknown Emps.	Industry Sales
2015	74.0	153.0	577.8	1,920.3	1,696.3	466.8	440.4	255.0	20.3	5,603.9
2016	76.0	157.1	593.3	1,971.8	1,741.8	479.4	452.2	261.8	20.8	5,754.1
2017	78.4	162.1	612.2	2,034.8	1,797.4	494.7	466.6	270.2	21.5	5,938.0
2018	82.7	170.8	645.3	2,144.7	1,894.5	521.4	491.9	283.8	22.6	6,257.8
2019	87.9	181.6	686.0	2,279.9	2,013.9	554.3	522.9	300.3	24.1	6,650.8

<table>
<tr><td colspan="2">INDUSTRY: DEPARTMENT STORES (NAICS 45211)</td></tr>
<tr><td colspan="2">PRODUCT LINE: FOOTWEAR (Main Category)</td></tr>
</table>

NAICS 45211: Department Stores Industry . This industry comprises establishments known as department stores primarily engaged in retailing a wide range of the following new products with no one merchandise line predominating: apparel, furniture, appliances and home furnishings; and selected additional items, such as paint, hardware, toiletries, cosmetics, photographic equipment, jewelry, toys, and sporting goods. Merchandise lines are normally arranged in separate departments.

5-YEAR TREND – ESTIMATED INDUSTRY SALES ($MILLIONS)

Year	Employee Size of Establishment									Total
	1-4 Emps.	5-9 Emps.	10-19 Emps.	20-49 Emps.	50-99 Emps.	100-249 Emps.	250-499 Emps.	500-999 Emps.	Unknown Emps.	Industry Sales
2015	0.2	0.2	0.5	44.5	808.4	2,595.9	1,074.6	155.4	6.6	4,686.5
2016	0.2	0.2	0.5	44.7	811.6	2,606.1	1,078.8	156.1	6.6	4,704.8
2017	0.2	0.2	0.5	45.2	819.6	2,631.8	1,089.4	157.6	6.7	4,751.2
2018	0.2	0.2	0.5	45.2	819.7	2,632.1	1,089.6	158.0	6.7	4,752.2
2019	0.2	0.2	0.5	45.6	827.8	2,658.2	1,100.3	159.8	6.8	4,799.5

INDUSTRY: WAREHOUSE CLUBS & SUPERCENTERS (NAICS 45291)
PRODUCT LINE: FOOTWEAR (Main Category)

NAICS 45291: Warehouse Clubs and Superstores This industry comprises establishments known as warehouse clubs, superstores or supercenters primarily engaged in retailing a general line of groceries in combination with general lines of new merchandise, such as apparel, furniture, and appliances.

5-YEAR TREND – ESTIMATED INDUSTRY SALES ($MILLIONS)

Year	Employee Size of Establishment									Total Industry Sales
	1-4 Emps.	5-9 Emps.	10-19 Emps.	20-49 Emps.	50-99 Emps.	100-249 Emps.	250-499 Emps.	500-999 Emps.	Unknown Emps.	
2015	0.2	0.1	0.2	6.3	11.9	678.4	2,986.3	75.3	1.1	3,759.7
2016	0.2	0.1	0.2	6.4	12.2	697.1	3,068.6	77.3	1.2	3,863.3
2017	0.2	0.1	0.2	6.6	12.6	719.8	3,168.9	79.9	1.2	3,989.5
2018	0.2	0.1	0.2	7.2	13.6	774.7	3,410.4	85.9	1.3	4,293.6
2019	0.2	0.1	0.2	7.6	14.4	820.6	3,612.5	91.0	1.4	4,547.9

INDUSTRY: ELECTRONIC SHOPPING & MAIL ORDER (NAICS 45411)
PRODUCT LINE: FOOTWEAR (Main Category)

NAICS 45411: Electronic Shopping and Mail-Order Houses This industry comprises establishments primarily engaged in retailing all types of merchandise by means of mail or by electronic media, such as interactive television or computer. Included in this industry are establishments primarily engaged in retailing from catalogue showrooms of mail-order houses.

5-YEAR TREND – ESTIMATED INDUSTRY SALES ($MILLIONS)

Year	Employee Size of Establishment									Total Industry Sales
	1-4 Emps.	5-9 Emps.	10-19 Emps.	20-49 Emps.	50-99 Emps.	100-249 Emps.	250-499 Emps.	500-999 Emps.	Unknown Emps.	
2015	492.7	253.8	366.7	615.5	463.3	857.1	1,155.5	1,631.2	69.2	5,904.9
2016	521.1	268.4	387.8	651.0	490.0	906.6	1,222.2	1,725.3	73.2	6,245.8
2017	552.5	284.6	411.2	690.2	519.5	961.2	1,295.9	1,829.3	77.7	6,622.0
2018	619.2	319.0	460.8	773.5	582.3	1,077.2	1,452.3	2,012.9	87.0	7,384.2
2019	688.4	354.6	512.4	860.0	647.3	1,197.6	1,614.6	2,204.3	96.8	8,176.1

© Barnes Reports: 2018 U.S. Product & Retail Outlook

INDUSTRY: MEN'S CLOTHING STORES (NAICS 44811)
PRODUCT LINE: MEN'S FOOTWEAR (Sub Category)

NAICS 44811: Men's Clothing Stores. This industry comprises establishments primarily engaged in retailing a general line of new men's and boys' clothing. These establishments may provide basic alterations, such as hemming, taking in or letting out seams, or lengthening or shortening sleeves.

5-YEAR TREND – ESTIMATED INDUSTRY SALES ($MILLIONS)

Year	Employee Size of Establishment									Total Industry Sales
	1-4 Emps.	5-9 Emps.	10-19 Emps.	20-49 Emps.	50-99 Emps.	100-249 Emps.	250-499 Emps.	500-999 Emps.	Unknown Emps.	
2015	28.0	49.2	91.7	48.3	10.5	9.4	3.2	0.2	4.8	245.4
2016	29.1	51.1	95.1	50.1	10.9	9.8	3.3	0.2	5.0	254.4
2017	30.3	53.2	99.0	52.2	11.4	10.2	3.4	0.2	5.2	265.0
2018	31.2	54.8	102.1	53.8	11.7	10.5	3.5	0.2	5.4	273.3
2019	32.4	57.0	106.1	55.9	12.2	10.9	3.7	0.2	5.6	284.0

INDUSTRY: WOMEN'S CLOTHING STORES (NAICS 44812)
PRODUCT LINE: MEN'S FOOTWEAR (Sub Category)

NAICS 44812: Women's Clothing Stores . This industry comprises establishments primarily engaged in retailing a general line of new women's, misses' and juniors' clothing, including maternity wear. These establishments may provide basic alterations, such as hemming, taking in or letting out seams, or lengthening or shortening sleeves.

5-YEAR TREND – ESTIMATED INDUSTRY SALES ($MILLIONS)

Year	Employee Size of Establishment									Total Industry Sales
	1-4 Emps.	5-9 Emps.	10-19 Emps.	20-49 Emps.	50-99 Emps.	100-249 Emps.	250-499 Emps.	500-999 Emps.	Unknown Emps.	
2015	1.9	4.2	8.9	6.3	2.2	2.0	0.8	0.8	0.4	27.4
2016	1.9	4.3	9.1	6.4	2.3	2.1	0.9	0.8	0.4	28.2
2017	2.0	4.4	9.4	6.7	2.4	2.2	0.9	0.9	0.4	29.2
2018	2.1	4.7	10.0	7.0	2.5	2.3	0.9	0.9	0.5	30.8
2019	2.2	5.0	10.6	7.5	2.6	2.4	1.0	0.9	0.5	32.8

INDUSTRY: FAMILY CLOTHING STORES (NAICS 44814)
PRODUCT LINE: MEN'S FOOTWEAR (Sub Category)

NAICS 44814: Family Clothing Stores . This industry comprises
establishments primarily engaged in retailing a general line of new clothing
for men, women, and children, without specializing in sales for an individual
gender or age group. These establishments may provide basic alterations,
such as hemming, taking in or letting out seams, or lengthening or shortening sleeves.

5-YEAR TREND – ESTIMATED INDUSTRY SALES ($MILLIONS)

Year	Employee Size of Establishment									Total
	1-4 Emps.	5-9 Emps.	10-19 Emps.	20-49 Emps.	50-99 Emps.	100-249 Emps.	250-499 Emps.	500-999 Emps.	Unknown Emps.	Industry Sales
2015	14.4	29.7	112.4	373.4	329.9	90.8	85.6	49.6	3.9	1,089.8
2016	14.8	30.5	115.4	383.5	338.7	93.2	87.9	50.9	4.0	1,119.0
2017	15.3	31.5	119.1	395.7	349.5	96.2	90.7	52.5	4.2	1,154.8
2018	16.1	33.2	125.5	417.1	368.4	101.4	95.7	55.2	4.4	1,217.0
2019	17.1	35.3	133.4	443.4	391.7	107.8	101.7	58.4	4.7	1,293.4

INDUSTRY: DEPARTMENT STORES (NAICS 45211)
PRODUCT LINE: MEN'S FOOTWEAR (Sub Category)

NAICS 45211: Department Stores Industry . This industry comprises
establishments known as department stores primarily engaged in retailing
a wide range of the following new products with no one merchandise line
predominating: apparel, furniture, appliances and home furnishings; and
selected additional items, such as paint, hardware, toiletries, cosmetics,
photographic equipment, jewelry, toys, and sporting goods. Merchandise lines
are normally arranged in separate departments.

5-YEAR TREND – ESTIMATED INDUSTRY SALES ($MILLIONS)

Year	Employee Size of Establishment									Total
	1-4 Emps.	5-9 Emps.	10-19 Emps.	20-49 Emps.	50-99 Emps.	100-249 Emps.	250-499 Emps.	500-999 Emps.	Unknown Emps.	Industry Sales
2015	0.0	0.0	0.1	8.1	146.5	470.4	194.7	28.2	1.2	849.2
2016	0.0	0.0	0.1	8.1	147.1	472.2	195.5	28.3	1.2	852.5
2017	0.0	0.0	0.1	8.2	148.5	476.9	197.4	28.6	1.2	860.9
2018	0.0	0.0	0.1	8.2	148.5	476.9	197.4	28.6	1.2	861.1
2019	0.0	0.0	0.1	8.3	150.0	481.7	199.4	29.0	1.2	869.7

INDUSTRY: MEN'S CLOTHING STORES (NAICS 44811)
PRODUCT LINE: WOMEN'S FOOTWEAR (Sub Category)

NAICS 44811: Men's Clothing Stores. This industry comprises
establishments primarily engaged in retailing a general line of new
men's and boys' clothing. These establishments may provide basic
alterations, such as hemming, taking in or letting out seams, or lengthening
or shortening sleeves.

5-YEAR TREND — ESTIMATED INDUSTRY SALES ($MILLIONS)

Year	Employee Size of Establishment									Total
	1-4 Emps.	5-9 Emps.	10-19 Emps.	20-49 Emps.	50-99 Emps.	100-249 Emps.	250-499 Emps.	500-999 Emps.	Unknown Emps.	Industry Sales
2015	1.3	2.3	4.3	2.3	0.5	0.4	0.1	0.0	0.2	11.5
2016	1.4	2.4	4.4	2.3	0.5	0.5	0.2	0.0	0.2	11.9
2017	1.4	2.5	4.6	2.4	0.5	0.5	0.2	0.0	0.2	12.4
2018	1.5	2.6	4.8	2.5	0.5	0.5	0.2	0.0	0.3	12.8
2019	1.5	2.7	5.0	2.6	0.6	0.5	0.2	0.0	0.3	13.3

INDUSTRY: WOMEN'S CLOTHING STORES (NAICS 44812)
PRODUCT LINE: WOMEN'S FOOTWEAR (Sub Category)

NAICS 44812: Women's Clothing Stores . This industry comprises
establishments primarily engaged in retailing a general line of new
women's, misses' and juniors' clothing, including maternity wear.
These establishments may provide basic alterations, such as hemming,
taking in or letting out seams, or lengthening or shortening sleeves.

5-YEAR TREND — ESTIMATED INDUSTRY SALES ($MILLIONS)

Year	Employee Size of Establishment									Total
	1-4 Emps.	5-9 Emps.	10-19 Emps.	20-49 Emps.	50-99 Emps.	100-249 Emps.	250-499 Emps.	500-999 Emps.	Unknown Emps.	Industry Sales
2015	87.9	196.3	418.9	295.4	104.3	96.4	39.1	37.8	19.6	1,295.8
2016	90.5	202.1	431.3	304.2	107.4	99.2	40.2	39.0	20.2	1,334.2
2017	93.6	209.1	446.2	314.7	111.1	102.7	41.6	40.3	20.9	1,380.3
2018	98.8	220.6	470.8	332.0	117.3	108.3	43.9	42.2	22.0	1,456.0
2019	105.1	234.7	500.8	353.3	124.8	115.3	46.7	44.5	23.5	1,548.6

INDUSTRY: FAMILY CLOTHING STORES (NAICS 44814)
PRODUCT LINE: WOMEN'S FOOTWEAR (Sub Category)

NAICS 44814: Family Clothing Stores . This industry comprises establishments primarily engaged in retailing a general line of new clothing for men, women, and children, without specializing in sales for an individual gender or age group. These establishments may provide basic alterations, such as hemming, taking in or letting out seams, or lengthening or shortening sleeves.

5-Year Trend – Estimated Industry Sales ($Millions)

Year	Employee Size of Establishment									Total
	1-4 Emps.	5-9 Emps.	10-19 Emps.	20-49 Emps.	50-99 Emps.	100-249 Emps.	250-499 Emps.	500-999 Emps.	Unknown Emps.	Industry Sales
2015	32.3	66.9	252.5	839.3	741.3	204.0	192.5	111.4	8.9	2,449.1
2016	33.2	68.6	259.3	861.8	761.2	209.5	197.6	114.4	9.1	2,514.8
2017	34.3	70.8	267.6	889.3	785.5	216.2	203.9	118.1	9.4	2,595.1
2018	36.1	74.7	282.0	937.3	828.0	227.9	215.0	124.0	9.9	2,734.9
2019	38.4	79.4	299.8	996.4	880.2	242.2	228.5	131.3	10.5	2,906.7

INDUSTRY: DEPARTMENT STORES (NAICS 45211)
PRODUCT LINE: WOMEN'S FOOTWEAR (Sub Category)

NAICS 45211: Department Stores Industry . This industry comprises establishments known as department stores primarily engaged in retailing a wide range of the following new products with no one merchandise line predominating: apparel, furniture, appliances and home furnishings; and selected additional items, such as paint, hardware, toiletries, cosmetics, photographic equipment, jewelry, toys, and sporting goods. Merchandise lines are normally arranged in separate departments.

5-Year Trend – Estimated Industry Sales ($Millions)

Year	Employee Size of Establishment									Total
	1-4 Emps.	5-9 Emps.	10-19 Emps.	20-49 Emps.	50-99 Emps.	100-249 Emps.	250-499 Emps.	500-999 Emps.	Unknown Emps.	Industry Sales
2015	5.2	10.1	25.6	52.3	39.7	2,614.5	204.2	4.3	1.8	2,957.5
2016	5.3	10.3	26.2	53.5	40.6	2,677.2	209.1	4.4	1.9	3,028.4
2017	5.5	10.6	26.9	55.1	41.8	2,755.6	215.2	4.5	1.9	3,117.1
2018	5.7	11.0	27.9	57.1	43.3	2,857.9	223.2	4.6	2.0	3,232.8
2019	5.9	11.5	29.2	59.8	45.3	2,989.9	233.5	4.9	2.1	3,382.1

INDUSTRY: FAMILY CLOTHING STORES (NAICS 44814)
PRODUCT LINE: CHILDREN'S FOOTWEAR (Sub Category)

NAICS 44814: Family Clothing Stores . This industry comprises
establishments primarily engaged in retailing a general line of new clothing
for men, women, and children, without specializing in sales for an individual
gender or age group. These establishments may provide basic alterations,
such as hemming, taking in or letting out seams, or lengthening or shortening sleeves.

5-YEAR TREND – ESTIMATED INDUSTRY SALES ($MILLIONS)

Year	Employee Size of Establishment									Total
	1-4 Emps.	5-9 Emps.	10-19 Emps.	20-49 Emps.	50-99 Emps.	100-249 Emps.	250-499 Emps.	500-999 Emps.	Unknown Emps.	Industry Sales
2015	5.8	12.0	45.4	150.9	133.3	36.7	34.6	20.0	1.6	440.5
2016	6.0	12.3	46.6	155.0	136.9	37.7	35.5	20.6	1.6	452.3
2017	6.2	12.7	48.1	159.9	141.3	38.9	36.7	21.2	1.7	466.7
2018	6.5	13.4	50.7	168.6	148.9	41.0	38.7	22.3	1.8	491.9
2019	6.9	14.3	53.9	179.2	158.3	43.6	41.1	23.6	1.9	522.8

INDUSTRY: DEPARTMENT STORES (NAICS 45211)
PRODUCT LINE: CHILDREN'S FOOTWEAR (Sub Category)

NAICS 45211: Department Stores Industry . This industry comprises
establishments known as department stores primarily engaged in retailing
a wide range of the following new products with no one merchandise line
predominating: apparel, furniture, appliances and home furnishings; and
selected additional items, such as paint, hardware, toiletries, cosmetics,
photographic equipment, jewelry, toys, and sporting goods. Merchandise lines
are normally arranged in separate departments.

5-YEAR TREND – ESTIMATED INDUSTRY SALES ($MILLIONS)

Year	Employee Size of Establishment									Total
	1-4 Emps.	5-9 Emps.	10-19 Emps.	20-49 Emps.	50-99 Emps.	100-249 Emps.	250-499 Emps.	500-999 Emps.	Unknown Emps.	Industry Sales
2015	0.0	0.0	0.0	4.1	74.2	238.3	98.6	14.3	0.6	430.2
2016	0.0	0.0	0.0	4.1	74.5	239.2	99.0	14.3	0.6	431.8
2017	0.0	0.0	0.0	4.1	75.2	241.6	100.0	14.5	0.6	436.1
2018	0.0	0.0	0.0	4.1	75.2	241.6	100.0	14.5	0.6	436.2
2019	0.0	0.0	0.0	4.2	76.0	244.0	101.0	14.7	0.6	440.5

INDUSTRY: MEN'S CLOTHING STORES (NAICS 44811)
PRODUCT LINE: MEN'S ATHLETIC FOOTWEAR (Sub Category)

NAICS 44811: Men's Clothing Stores. This industry comprises establishments primarily engaged in retailing a general line of new men's and boys' clothing. These establishments may provide basic alterations, such as hemming, taking in or letting out seams, or lengthening or shortening sleeves.

5-YEAR TREND – ESTIMATED INDUSTRY SALES ($MILLIONS)

Year	Employee Size of Establishment									Total
	1-4 Emps.	5-9 Emps.	10-19 Emps.	20-49 Emps.	50-99 Emps.	100-249 Emps.	250-499 Emps.	500-999 Emps.	Unknown Emps.	Industry Sales
2015	5.9	10.3	19.2	10.1	2.2	2.0	0.7	0.0	1.0	51.3
2016	6.1	10.7	19.9	10.5	2.3	2.0	0.7	0.0	1.0	53.2
2017	6.3	11.1	20.7	10.9	2.4	2.1	0.7	0.0	1.1	55.4
2018	6.5	11.5	21.4	11.3	2.4	2.2	0.7	0.0	1.1	57.2
2019	6.8	11.9	22.2	11.7	2.5	2.3	0.8	0.0	1.2	59.4

INDUSTRY: FAMILY CLOTHING STORES (NAICS 44814)
PRODUCT LINE: MEN'S ATHLETIC FOOTWEAR (Sub Category)

NAICS 44814: Family Clothing Stores . This industry comprises establishments primarily engaged in retailing a general line of new clothing for men, women, and children, without specializing in sales for an individual gender or age group. These establishments may provide basic alterations, such as hemming, taking in or letting out seams, or lengthening or shortening sleeves.

5-YEAR TREND – ESTIMATED INDUSTRY SALES ($MILLIONS)

Year	Employee Size of Establishment									Total
	1-4 Emps.	5-9 Emps.	10-19 Emps.	20-49 Emps.	50-99 Emps.	100-249 Emps.	250-499 Emps.	500-999 Emps.	Unknown Emps.	Industry Sales
2015	10.7	22.1	83.6	277.8	245.4	67.5	63.7	36.9	2.9	810.7
2016	11.0	22.7	85.8	285.2	252.0	69.3	65.4	37.9	3.0	832.4
2017	11.3	23.4	88.6	294.4	260.0	71.6	67.5	39.1	3.1	859.0
2018	12.0	24.7	93.4	310.3	274.1	75.4	71.2	41.1	3.3	905.3
2019	12.7	26.3	99.2	329.8	291.3	80.2	75.6	43.4	3.5	962.1

INDUSTRY: DEPARTMENT STORES (NAICS 45211)
PRODUCT LINE: MEN'S ATHLETIC FOOTWEAR (Sub Category)

NAICS 45211: Department Stores Industry . This industry comprises establishments known as department stores primarily engaged in retailing a wide range of the following new products with no one merchandise line predominating: apparel, furniture, appliances and home furnishings; and selected additional items, such as paint, hardware, toiletries, cosmetics, photographic equipment, jewelry, toys, and sporting goods. Merchandise lines are normally arranged in separate departments.

5-YEAR TREND – ESTIMATED INDUSTRY SALES ($MILLIONS)

Year	Employee Size of Establishment									Total
	1-4 Emps.	5-9 Emps.	10-19 Emps.	20-49 Emps.	50-99 Emps.	100-249 Emps.	250-499 Emps.	500-999 Emps.	Unknown Emps.	Industry Sales
2015	0.0	0.0	0.1	4.4	80.8	259.4	107.4	15.5	0.7	468.2
2016	0.0	0.0	0.1	4.5	81.1	260.4	107.8	15.6	0.7	470.1
2017	0.0	0.0	0.1	4.5	81.9	262.9	108.8	15.7	0.7	474.7
2018	0.0	0.0	0.1	4.5	81.9	263.0	108.9	15.8	0.7	474.8
2019	0.0	0.0	0.1	4.6	82.7	265.6	109.9	16.0	0.7	479.5

INDUSTRY: WOMEN'S CLOTHING STORES (NAICS 44812)
PRODUCT LINE: WOMEN'S ATHLETIC FOOTWEAR (Sub Category)

NAICS 44812: Women's Clothing Stores . This industry comprises establishments primarily engaged in retailing a general line of new women's, misses' and juniors' clothing, including maternity wear. These establishments may provide basic alterations, such as hemming, taking in or letting out seams, or lengthening or shortening sleeves.

5-YEAR TREND – ESTIMATED INDUSTRY SALES ($MILLIONS)

Year	Employee Size of Establishment									Total
	1-4 Emps.	5-9 Emps.	10-19 Emps.	20-49 Emps.	50-99 Emps.	100-249 Emps.	250-499 Emps.	500-999 Emps.	Unknown Emps.	Industry Sales
2015	1.4	3.1	6.6	4.7	1.6	1.5	0.6	0.6	0.3	20.4
2016	1.4	3.2	6.8	4.8	1.7	1.6	0.6	0.6	0.3	21.0
2017	1.5	3.3	7.0	5.0	1.8	1.6	0.7	0.6	0.3	21.7
2018	1.6	3.5	7.4	5.2	1.8	1.7	0.7	0.7	0.3	22.9
2019	1.7	3.7	7.9	5.6	2.0	1.8	0.7	0.7	0.4	24.4

INDUSTRY: FAMILY CLOTHING STORES (NAICS 44814)
PRODUCT LINE: WOMEN'S ATHLETIC FOOTWEAR (Sub Category)

NAICS 44814: Family Clothing Stores . This industry comprises
establishments primarily engaged in retailing a general line of new clothing
for men, women, and children, without specializing in sales for an individual
gender or age group. These establishments may provide basic alterations,
such as hemming, taking in or letting out seams, or lengthening or shortening sleeves.

5-Year Trend – Estimated Industry Sales ($Millions)

Year	Employee Size of Establishment									Total Industry Sales
	1-4 Emps.	5-9 Emps.	10-19 Emps.	20-49 Emps.	50-99 Emps.	100-249 Emps.	250-499 Emps.	500-999 Emps.	Unknown Emps.	
2015	8.2	17.0	64.3	213.6	188.6	51.9	49.0	28.4	2.3	623.2
2016	8.5	17.5	66.0	219.3	193.7	53.3	50.3	29.1	2.3	639.9
2017	8.7	18.0	68.1	226.3	199.9	55.0	51.9	30.0	2.4	660.3
2018	9.2	19.0	71.8	238.5	210.7	58.0	54.7	31.6	2.5	695.9
2019	9.8	20.2	76.3	253.5	224.0	61.6	58.1	33.4	2.7	739.6

INDUSTRY: DEPARTMENT STORES (NAICS 45211)
PRODUCT LINE: WOMEN'S ATHLETIC FOOTWEAR (Sub Category)

NAICS 45211: Department Stores Industry . This industry comprises
establishments known as department stores primarily engaged in retailing
a wide range of the following new products with no one merchandise line
predominating: apparel, furniture, appliances and home furnishings; and
selected additional items, such as paint, hardware, toiletries, cosmetics,
photographic equipment, jewelry, toys, and sporting goods. Merchandise lines
are normally arranged in separate departments.

5-Year Trend – Estimated Industry Sales ($Millions)

Year	Employee Size of Establishment									Total Industry Sales
	1-4 Emps.	5-9 Emps.	10-19 Emps.	20-49 Emps.	50-99 Emps.	100-249 Emps.	250-499 Emps.	500-999 Emps.	Unknown Emps.	
2015	0.0	0.0	0.1	4.4	80.3	257.7	106.7	15.4	0.7	465.3
2016	0.0	0.0	0.1	4.4	80.6	258.8	107.1	15.5	0.7	467.1
2017	0.0	0.0	0.1	4.5	81.4	261.3	108.2	15.6	0.7	471.7
2018	0.0	0.0	0.1	4.5	81.4	261.3	108.2	15.7	0.7	471.8
2019	0.0	0.0	0.1	4.5	82.2	263.9	109.3	15.9	0.7	476.5

	INDUSTRY: FAMILY CLOTHING STORES (NAICS 44814)
	PRODUCT LINE: CHILDREN'S ATHLETIC FOOTWEAR (Sub Category)

NAICS 44814: Family Clothing Stores . This industry comprises
establishments primarily engaged in retailing a general line of new clothing
for men, women, and children, without specializing in sales for an individual
gender or age group. These establishments may provide basic alterations,
such as hemming, taking in or letting out seams, or lengthening or shortening sleeves.

5-YEAR TREND — ESTIMATED INDUSTRY SALES ($MILLIONS)

Year	Employee Size of Establishment									Total
	1-4 Emps.	5-9 Emps.	10-19 Emps.	20-49 Emps.	50-99 Emps.	100-249 Emps.	250-499 Emps.	500-999 Emps.	Unknown Emps.	Industry Sales
2015	2.3	4.7	17.9	59.4	52.5	14.4	13.6	7.9	0.6	173.4
2016	2.4	4.9	18.4	61.0	53.9	14.8	14.0	8.1	0.6	178.1
2017	2.4	5.0	18.9	63.0	55.6	15.3	14.4	8.4	0.7	183.8
2018	2.6	5.3	20.0	66.4	58.6	16.1	15.2	8.8	0.7	193.7
2019	2.7	5.6	21.2	70.6	62.3	17.2	16.2	9.3	0.7	205.8

	INDUSTRY: DEPARTMENT STORES (NAICS 45211)
	PRODUCT LINE: CHILDREN'S ATHLETIC FOOTWEAR (Sub Category)

NAICS 45211: Department Stores Industry . This industry comprises
establishments known as department stores primarily engaged in retailing
a wide range of the following new products with no one merchandise line
predominating: apparel, furniture, appliances and home furnishings; and
selected additional items, such as paint, hardware, toiletries, cosmetics,
photographic equipment, jewelry, toys, and sporting goods. Merchandise lines
are normally arranged in separate departments.

5-YEAR TREND — ESTIMATED INDUSTRY SALES ($MILLIONS)

Year	Employee Size of Establishment									Total
	1-4 Emps.	5-9 Emps.	10-19 Emps.	20-49 Emps.	50-99 Emps.	100-249 Emps.	250-499 Emps.	500-999 Emps.	Unknown Emps.	Industry Sales
2015	0.0	0.0	0.0	0.9	15.4	49.6	20.5	3.0	0.1	89.5
2016	0.0	0.0	0.0	0.9	15.5	49.8	20.6	3.0	0.1	89.9
2017	0.0	0.0	0.0	0.9	15.7	50.3	20.8	3.0	0.1	90.8
2018	0.0	0.0	0.0	0.9	15.7	50.3	20.8	3.0	0.1	90.8
2019	0.0	0.0	0.0	0.9	15.8	50.8	21.0	3.1	0.1	91.7

INDUSTRY: FAMILY CLOTHING STORES (NAICS 44814)
PRODUCT LINE: FOOTWEAR ACCESSORIES (Sub Category)

NAICS 44814: Family Clothing Stores . This industry comprises
establishments primarily engaged in retailing a general line of new clothing
for men, women, and children, without specializing in sales for an individual
gender or age group. These establishments may provide basic alterations,
such as hemming, taking in or letting out seams, or lengthening or shortening sleeves.

5-YEAR TREND – ESTIMATED INDUSTRY SALES ($MILLIONS)

Year	Employee Size of Establishment									Total
	1-4 Emps.	5-9 Emps.	10-19 Emps.	20-49 Emps.	50-99 Emps.	100-249 Emps.	250-499 Emps.	500-999 Emps.	Unknown Emps.	Industry Sales
2015	0.2	0.5	1.8	5.9	5.2	1.4	1.4	0.8	0.1	17.2
2016	0.2	0.5	1.8	6.1	5.3	1.5	1.4	0.8	0.1	17.7
2017	0.2	0.5	1.9	6.2	5.5	1.5	1.4	0.8	0.1	18.2
2018	0.3	0.5	2.0	6.6	5.8	1.6	1.5	0.9	0.1	19.2
2019	0.3	0.6	2.1	7.0	6.2	1.7	1.6	0.9	0.1	20.4

INDUSTRY: DEPARTMENT STORES (NAICS 45211)
PRODUCT LINE: FOOTWEAR ACCESSORIES (Sub Category)

NAICS 45211: Department Stores Industry . This industry comprises
establishments known as department stores primarily engaged in retailing
a wide range of the following new products with no one merchandise line
predominating: apparel, furniture, appliances and home furnishings; and
selected additional items, such as paint, hardware, toiletries, cosmetics,
photographic equipment, jewelry, toys, and sporting goods. Merchandise lines
are normally arranged in separate departments.

5-YEAR TREND – ESTIMATED INDUSTRY SALES ($MILLIONS)

Year	Employee Size of Establishment									Total
	1-4 Emps.	5-9 Emps.	10-19 Emps.	20-49 Emps.	50-99 Emps.	100-249 Emps.	250-499 Emps.	500-999 Emps.	Unknown Emps.	Industry Sales
2015	0.0	0.0	0.0	0.1	2.0	6.3	2.6	0.4	0.0	11.3
2016	0.0	0.0	0.0	0.1	2.0	6.3	2.6	0.4	0.0	11.4
2017	0.0	0.0	0.0	0.1	2.0	6.4	2.6	0.4	0.0	11.5
2018	0.0	0.0	0.0	0.1	2.0	6.4	2.6	0.4	0.0	11.5
2019	0.0	0.0	0.0	0.1	2.0	6.4	2.7	0.4	0.0	11.6

<table>
<tr><td colspan="2">INDUSTRY: HOME CENTERS INDUSTRY (NAICS 44411)</td></tr>
<tr><td colspan="2">PRODUCT LINE: HOUSEHOLD APPLIANCES (Main Category)</td></tr>
</table>

NAICS 44411: Home Centers. This industry comprises establishments known as home centers primarily engaged in retailing a general line of new home repair and improvement materials and supplies, such as lumber, plumbing goods, electrical goods, tools, housewares, hardware, and lawn and garden supplies, with no one merchandise line predominating. The merchandise lines are normally arranged in separate departments.

5-Year Trend — Estimated Industry Sales ($Millions)

Year	Employee Size of Establishment									Total
	1-4 Emps.	5-9 Emps.	10-19 Emps.	20-49 Emps.	50-99 Emps.	100-249 Emps.	250-499 Emps.	500-999 Emps.	Unknown Emps.	Industry Sales
2015	12	23	59	120	91	6,007	469	10	4	6,795
2016	12	24	60	123	93	6,151	480	10	4	6,958
2017	13	24	62	127	96	6,331	494	10	4	7,161
2018	13	25	64	131	100	6,566	513	11	5	7,427
2019	14	26	67	137	104	6,869	536	11	5	7,770

<table>
<tr><td colspan="2">INDUSTRY: HARDWARE STORES (NAICS 44413)</td></tr>
<tr><td colspan="2">PRODUCT LINE: HOUSEHOLD APPLIANCES (Main Category)</td></tr>
</table>

NAICS 44413: Hardware Stores. Establishments primarily engaged in the retail sale of a number of basic hardware lines, such as tools, builders' hardware, paint and glass, housewares and household appliances, and cutlery.

5-Year Trend — Estimated Industry Sales ($Millions)

Year	Employee Size of Establishment									Total
	1-4 Emps.	5-9 Emps.	10-19 Emps.	20-49 Emps.	50-99 Emps.	100-249 Emps.	250-499 Emps.	500-999 Emps.	Unknown Emps.	Industry Sales
2015	33.7	57.1	114.9	164.3	32.6	10.6	1.9	0.1	2.9	418.2
2016	34.0	57.7	116.0	165.9	33.0	10.8	1.9	0.1	3.0	422.3
2017	34.5	58.6	117.9	168.5	33.5	10.9	1.9	0.1	3.0	428.9
2018	35.9	60.9	122.5	175.2	34.8	11.4	2.0	0.1	3.1	446.0
2019	37.7	63.9	128.6	183.9	36.5	11.9	2.1	0.1	3.3	468.1

INDUSTRY: DEPARTMENT STORES (NAICS 45211)
PRODUCT LINE: HOUSEHOLD APPLIANCES (Main Category)

NAICS 45211: Department Stores Industry . This industry comprises
establishments known as department stores primarily engaged in retailing
a wide range of the following new products with no one merchandise line
predominating: apparel, furniture, appliances and home furnishings; and
selected additional items, such as paint, hardware, toiletries, cosmetics,
photographic equipment, jewelry, toys, and sporting goods. Merchandise lines
are normally arranged in separate departments.

5-YEAR TREND – ESTIMATED INDUSTRY SALES ($MILLIONS)

Year	Employee Size of Establishment									Total
	1-4 Emps.	5-9 Emps.	10-19 Emps.	20-49 Emps.	50-99 Emps.	100-249 Emps.	250-499 Emps.	500-999 Emps.	Unknown Emps.	Industry Sales
2015	0	0	1	45	814	2,615	1,082	157	7	4,720
2016	0	0	1	45	817	2,625	1,087	157	7	4,739
2017	0	0	1	45	825	2,651	1,097	159	7	4,785
2018	0	0	1	45	826	2,651	1,097	159	7	4,786
2019	0	0	1	46	834	2,677	1,108	161	7	4,834

INDUSTRY: WAREHOUSE CLUBS & SUPERCENTERS (NAICS 45211)
PRODUCT LINE: HOUSEHOLD APPLIANCES (Main Category)

NAICS 45291: Warehouse Clubs and Superstores This industry
comprises establishments known as warehouse clubs, superstores or
supercenters primarily engaged in retailing a general line of groceries
in combination with general lines of new merchandise, such as apparel,
furniture, and appliances.

5-YEAR TREND – ESTIMATED INDUSTRY SALES ($MILLIONS)

Year	Employee Size of Establishment									Total
	1-4 Emps.	5-9 Emps.	10-19 Emps.	20-49 Emps.	50-99 Emps.	100-249 Emps.	250-499 Emps.	500-999 Emps.	Unknown Emps.	Industry Sales
2015	0.1	0.1	0.1	12.3	222.7	715.2	296.1	42.8	1.8	1,291.2
2016	0.1	0.1	0.1	12.3	223.6	718.0	297.2	43.0	1.8	1,296.2
2017	0.1	0.1	0.1	12.4	225.8	725.1	300.2	43.4	1.8	1,309.0
2018	0.1	0.1	0.1	12.4	225.8	725.2	300.2	43.5	1.8	1,309.3
2019	0.1	0.1	0.1	12.6	228.1	732.4	303.2	44.0	1.9	1,322.3

<table>
<tr><td colspan="2">INDUSTRY: ELECTRONIC SHOPPING & MAIL ORDER (NAICS 45291)</td></tr>
<tr><td colspan="2">PRODUCT LINE: HOUSEHOLD APPLIANCES (Main Category)</td></tr>
</table>

NAICS 45411: Electronic Shopping and Mail-Order Houses This industry comprises establishments primarily engaged in retailing all types of merchandise by means of mail or by electronic media, such as interactive television or computer. Included in this industry are establishments primarily engaged in retailing from catalogue showrooms of mail-order houses.

5-YEAR TREND – ESTIMATED INDUSTRY SALES ($MILLIONS)

Year	Employee Size of Establishment									Total
	1-4 Emps.	5-9 Emps.	10-19 Emps.	20-49 Emps.	50-99 Emps.	100-249 Emps.	250-499 Emps.	500-999 Emps.	Unknown Emps.	Industry Sales
2015	0.1	0.0	0.1	4.3	8.1	464.0	2,042.7	51.5	0.8	2,571.7
2016	0.1	0.0	0.1	4.4	8.4	476.8	2,099.0	52.9	0.8	2,642.6
2017	0.1	0.0	0.1	4.5	8.6	492.4	2,167.6	54.6	0.8	2,728.9
2018	0.2	0.0	0.1	4.9	9.3	529.9	2,332.8	58.8	0.9	2,936.9
2019	0.2	0.0	0.1	5.2	9.8	561.3	2,471.0	62.3	0.9	3,110.9

<table>
<tr><td colspan="2">INDUSTRY: DEPARTMENT STORES (NAICS 45211)</td></tr>
<tr><td colspan="2">PRODUCT LINE: KITCHEN APPLIANCES (Sub Category)</td></tr>
</table>

NAICS 45211: Department Stores Industry . This industry comprises establishments known as department stores primarily engaged in retailing a wide range of the following new products with no one merchandise line predominating: apparel, furniture, appliances and home furnishings; and selected additional items, such as paint, hardware, toiletries, cosmetics, photographic equipment, jewelry, toys, and sporting goods. Merchandise lines are normally arranged in separate departments.

5-YEAR TREND – ESTIMATED INDUSTRY SALES ($MILLIONS)

Year	Employee Size of Establishment									Total
	1-4 Emps.	5-9 Emps.	10-19 Emps.	20-49 Emps.	50-99 Emps.	100-249 Emps.	250-499 Emps.	500-999 Emps.	Unknown Emps.	Industry Sales
2015	0	0	0	30	552	1,772	734	106	5	3,199
2016	0	0	0	31	554	1,779	736	107	5	3,212
2017	0	0	0	31	559	1,797	744	108	5	3,243
2018	0	0	0	31	560	1,797	744	108	5	3,244
2019	0	0	0	31	565	1,815	751	109	5	3,276

INDUSTRY: WAREHOUSE CLUBS & SUPERCENTERS (NAICS 45291)
PRODUCT LINE: KITCHEN APPLIANCES (Sub Category)

NAICS 45291: Warehouse Clubs and Superstores This industry comprises establishments known as warehouse clubs, superstores or supercenters primarily engaged in retailing a general line of groceries in combination with general lines of new merchandise, such as apparel, furniture, and appliances.

5-YEAR TREND — ESTIMATED INDUSTRY SALES ($MILLIONS)

Year	Employee Size of Establishment									Total
	1-4 Emps.	5-9 Emps.	10-19 Emps.	20-49 Emps.	50-99 Emps.	100-249 Emps.	250-499 Emps.	500-999 Emps.	Unknown Emps.	Industry Sales
2015	0.1	0.0	0.1	2.7	5.2	296.8	1,306.8	32.9	0.5	1,645.2
2016	0.1	0.0	0.1	2.8	5.3	305.0	1,342.8	33.8	0.5	1,690.5
2017	0.1	0.0	0.1	2.9	5.5	315.0	1,386.7	34.9	0.5	1,745.8
2018	0.1	0.0	0.1	3.1	5.9	339.0	1,492.4	37.6	0.6	1,878.8
2019	0.1	0.0	0.1	3.3	6.3	359.1	1,580.8	39.8	0.6	1,990.1

INDUSTRY: DEPARTMENT STORES (NAICS 45211)
PRODUCT LINE: LAUNDRY APPLIANCES (Sub Category)

NAICS 45211: Department Stores Industry . This industry comprises establishments known as department stores primarily engaged in retailing a wide range of the following new products with no one merchandise line predominating: apparel, furniture, appliances and home furnishings; and selected additional items, such as paint, hardware, toiletries, cosmetics, photographic equipment, jewelry, toys, and sporting goods. Merchandise lines are normally arranged in separate departments.

5-YEAR TREND — ESTIMATED INDUSTRY SALES ($MILLIONS)

Year	Employee Size of Establishment									Total
	1-4 Emps.	5-9 Emps.	10-19 Emps.	20-49 Emps.	50-99 Emps.	100-249 Emps.	250-499 Emps.	500-999 Emps.	Unknown Emps.	Industry Sales
2015	0.0	0.0	0.0	0.3	5.0	16.1	6.7	1.0	0.0	29.1
2016	0.0	0.0	0.0	0.3	5.0	16.2	6.7	1.0	0.0	29.2
2017	0.0	0.0	0.0	0.3	5.1	16.4	6.8	1.0	0.0	29.5
2018	0.0	0.0	0.0	0.3	5.1	16.4	6.8	1.0	0.0	29.5
2019	0.0	0.0	0.0	0.3	5.1	16.5	6.8	1.0	0.0	29.8

INDUSTRY: DEPARTMENT STORES (NAICS 45211)
PRODUCT LINE: OTHER APPLIANCES (Sub Category)

NAICS 45211: Department Stores Industry . This industry comprises establishments known as department stores primarily engaged in retailing a wide range of the following new products with no one merchandise line predominating: apparel, furniture, appliances and home furnishings; and selected additional items, such as paint, hardware, toiletries, cosmetics, photographic equipment, jewelry, toys, and sporting goods. Merchandise lines are normally arranged in separate departments.

5-YEAR TREND — ESTIMATED INDUSTRY SALES ($MILLIONS)

Year	Employee Size of Establishment									Total
	1-4 Emps.	5-9 Emps.	10-19 Emps.	20-49 Emps.	50-99 Emps.	100-249 Emps.	250-499 Emps.	500-999 Emps.	Unknown Emps.	Industry Sales
2015	0.1	0.1	0.2	14.5	262.4	842.5	348.8	50.5	2.1	1,521.0
2016	0.1	0.1	0.2	14.5	263.4	845.8	350.1	50.7	2.2	1,527.0
2017	0.1	0.1	0.2	14.7	266.0	854.2	353.6	51.2	2.2	1,542.1
2018	0.1	0.1	0.2	14.7	266.0	854.3	353.6	51.3	2.2	1,542.4
2019	0.1	0.1	0.2	14.8	268.7	862.7	357.1	51.9	2.2	1,557.7

INDUSTRY: WAREHOUSE CLUBS & SUPERCENTERS (NAICS 45291)
PRODUCT LINE: OTHER APPLIANCES (Sub Category)

NAICS 45291: Warehouse Clubs and Superstores This industry comprises establishments known as warehouse clubs, superstores or supercenters primarily engaged in retailing a general line of groceries in combination with general lines of new merchandise, such as apparel, furniture, and appliances.

5-YEAR TREND — ESTIMATED INDUSTRY SALES ($MILLIONS)

Year	Employee Size of Establishment									Total
	1-4 Emps.	5-9 Emps.	10-19 Emps.	20-49 Emps.	50-99 Emps.	100-249 Emps.	250-499 Emps.	500-999 Emps.	Unknown Emps.	Industry Sales
2015	0.2	0.0	0.2	5.5	10.4	593.2	2,611.3	65.8	1.0	3,287.5
2016	0.2	0.0	0.2	5.6	10.7	609.5	2,683.2	67.6	1.0	3,378.1
2017	0.2	0.0	0.2	5.8	11.0	629.4	2,770.9	69.8	1.1	3,488.4
2018	0.2	0.1	0.2	6.3	11.9	677.4	2,982.1	75.1	1.1	3,754.3
2019	0.2	0.1	0.2	6.6	12.6	717.5	3,158.7	79.6	1.2	3,976.7

INDUSTRY: HOME CENTERS INDUSTRY (NAICS 44411)
PRODUCT LINE: SMALL ELECTRICAL APPLIANCES (Main Category)

NAICS 44411: Home Centers. This industry comprises establishments
known as home centers primarily engaged in retailing a general line of
new home repair and improvement materials and supplies, such as
lumber, plumbing goods, electrical goods, tools, housewares, hardware,
and lawn and garden supplies, with no one merchandise line predominating.
The merchandise lines are normally arranged in separate departments.

5-YEAR TREND – ESTIMATED INDUSTRY SALES ($MILLIONS)

| Year | Employee Size of Establishment | | | | | | | | | Total |
	1-4 Emps.	5-9 Emps.	10-19 Emps.	20-49 Emps.	50-99 Emps.	100-249 Emps.	250-499 Emps.	500-999 Emps.	Unknown Emps.	Industry Sales
2015	1.0	1.9	4.7	9.6	7.3	481.3	37.6	0.8	0.3	544.4
2016	1.0	1.9	4.8	9.9	7.5	492.8	38.5	0.8	0.3	557.5
2017	1.0	2.0	5.0	10.1	7.7	507.2	39.6	0.8	0.4	573.8
2018	1.0	2.0	5.1	10.5	8.0	526.1	41.1	0.9	0.4	595.1
2019	1.1	2.1	5.4	11.0	8.3	550.4	43.0	0.9	0.4	622.6

INDUSTRY: HARDWARE STORES (NAICS 44413)
PRODUCT LINE: SMALL ELECTRICAL APPLIANCES (Main Category)

NAICS 44413: Hardware Stores. Establishments primarily engaged
in the retail sale of a number of basic hardware lines, such as tools,
builders' hardware, paint and glass, housewares and household appliances,
and cutlery.

5-YEAR TREND – ESTIMATED INDUSTRY SALES ($MILLIONS)

| Year | Employee Size of Establishment | | | | | | | | | Total |
	1-4 Emps.	5-9 Emps.	10-19 Emps.	20-49 Emps.	50-99 Emps.	100-249 Emps.	250-499 Emps.	500-999 Emps.	Unknown Emps.	Industry Sales
2015	25.9	44.0	88.5	126.5	25.1	8.2	1.5	0.1	2.3	322.1
2016	26.2	44.4	89.4	127.8	25.4	8.3	1.5	0.1	2.3	325.2
2017	26.6	45.1	90.8	129.8	25.8	8.4	1.5	0.1	2.3	330.3
2018	27.7	46.9	94.4	134.9	26.8	8.7	1.6	0.1	2.4	343.5
2019	29.0	49.2	99.1	141.6	28.1	9.2	1.6	0.1	2.5	360.5

INDUSTRY: SUPERMARKETS INDUSTRY (NAICS 44511)
PRODUCT LINE: SMALL ELECTRICAL APPLIANCES (Main Category)

NAICS 44511: Grocery Stores Industry. This industry comprises establishments generally known as supermarkets and grocery stores primarily engaged in retailing a general line of food, such as canned and frozen foods; fresh fruits and vegetables; and fresh and prepared meats, fish, and poultry. Included in this industry are delicatessen-type establishments primarily engaged in retailing a general line of food.

5-YEAR TREND – ESTIMATED INDUSTRY SALES ($MILLIONS)

Year	Employee Size of Establishment									Total Industry Sales
	1-4 Emps.	5-9 Emps.	10-19 Emps.	20-49 Emps.	50-99 Emps.	100-249 Emps.	250-499 Emps.	500-999 Emps.	Unknown Emps.	
2015	2.9	2.1	5.3	17.5	41.6	103.3	32.3	3.9	0.5	209.3
2016	2.8	2.0	5.3	17.4	41.3	102.7	32.1	3.8	0.5	208.0
2017	2.8	2.0	5.3	17.4	41.3	102.6	32.0	3.8	0.5	207.9
2018	2.9	2.1	5.4	17.8	42.1	104.7	32.7	3.9	0.5	212.2
2019	3.0	2.2	5.6	18.3	43.4	108.0	33.7	4.0	0.6	218.7

INDUSTRY: PHARMACIES & DRUG STORES INDUSTRY (NAICS 44611)
PRODUCT LINE: SMALL ELECTRICAL APPLIANCES (Main Category)

NAICS 44611 Pharmacies and Drug Stores – This industry comprises establishments known as pharmacies and drug stores engaged in retailing prescription or nonprescription drugs and medicines.

5-YEAR TREND – ESTIMATED INDUSTRY SALES ($MILLIONS)

Year	Employee Size of Establishment									Total Industry Sales
	1-4 Emps.	5-9 Emps.	10-19 Emps.	20-49 Emps.	50-99 Emps.	100-249 Emps.	250-499 Emps.	500-999 Emps.	Unknown Emps.	
2015	19.6	48.6	196.7	577.7	58.4	23.4	8.9	3.0	1.5	937.9
2016	20.2	50.1	202.9	595.8	60.3	24.1	9.2	3.1	1.5	967.3
2017	21.0	52.0	210.2	617.4	62.4	25.0	9.6	3.2	1.6	1,002.3
2018	22.2	55.0	222.6	653.9	66.1	26.5	10.1	3.4	1.7	1,061.6
2019	23.7	58.8	237.8	698.3	70.6	28.3	10.8	3.6	1.8	1,133.6

INDUSTRY: DEPARTMENT STORES INDUSTRY (NAICS 45211)
PRODUCT LINE: SMALL ELECTRICAL APPLIANCES (Main Category)

NAICS 45211: Department Stores Industry . This industry comprises
establishments known as department stores primarily engaged in retailing
a wide range of the following new products with no one merchandise line
predominating: apparel, furniture, appliances and home furnishings; and
selected additional items, such as paint, hardware, toiletries, cosmetics,
photographic equipment, jewelry, toys, and sporting goods. Merchandise lines
are normally arranged in separate departments.

5-Year Trend — Estimated Industry Sales ($Millions)

Year	Employee Size of Establishment									Total
	1-4 Emps.	5-9 Emps.	10-19 Emps.	20-49 Emps.	50-99 Emps.	100-249 Emps.	250-499 Emps.	500-999 Emps.	Unknown Emps.	Industry Sales
2015	0.1	0.1	0.2	16.8	305.8	982.1	406.5	58.8	2.5	1,772.9
2016	0.1	0.1	0.2	16.9	307.0	985.9	408.1	59.0	2.5	1,779.9
2017	0.1	0.1	0.2	17.1	310.1	995.6	412.1	59.6	2.5	1,797.4
2018	0.1	0.1	0.2	17.1	310.1	995.8	412.2	59.8	2.5	1,797.8
2019	0.1	0.1	0.2	17.3	313.2	1,005.6	416.3	60.5	2.6	1,815.7

INDUSTRY: WAREHOUSE CLUBS & SUPERCENTERS (NAICS 45291)
PRODUCT LINE: SMALL ELECTRICAL APPLIANCES (Main Category)

NAICS 45291: Warehouse Clubs and Superstores This industry
comprises establishments known as warehouse clubs, superstores or
supercenters primarily engaged in retailing a general line of groceries
in combination with general lines of new merchandise, such as apparel,
furniture, and appliances.

5-Year Trend — Estimated Industry Sales ($Millions)

Year	Employee Size of Establishment									Total
	1-4 Emps.	5-9 Emps.	10-19 Emps.	20-49 Emps.	50-99 Emps.	100-249 Emps.	250-499 Emps.	500-999 Emps.	Unknown Emps.	Industry Sales
2015	0.3	0.1	0.2	8.7	16.5	941.4	4,144.3	104.4	1.6	5,217.5
2016	0.3	0.1	0.2	8.9	16.9	967.4	4,258.6	107.3	1.6	5,361.3
2017	0.3	0.1	0.3	9.2	17.5	999.0	4,397.6	110.8	1.7	5,536.4
2018	0.3	0.1	0.3	9.9	18.8	1,075.1	4,732.9	119.3	1.8	5,958.5
2019	0.3	0.1	0.3	10.5	19.9	1,138.8	5,013.2	126.3	1.9	6,311.4

INDUSTRY: ELECTRONIC SHOPPING & MAIL-ORDER (NAICS 45411)
PRODUCT LINE: SMALL ELECTRICAL APPLIANCES (Main Category)

NAICS 45411: Electronic Shopping and Mail-Order Houses This industry comprises establishments primarily engaged in retailing all types of merchandise by means of mail or by electronic media, such as interactive television or computer. Included in this industry are establishments primarily engaged in retailing from catalogue showrooms of mail-order houses.

5-YEAR TREND – ESTIMATED INDUSTRY SALES ($MILLIONS)

Year	Employee Size of Establishment									Total
	1-4 Emps.	5-9 Emps.	10-19 Emps.	20-49 Emps.	50-99 Emps.	100-249 Emps.	250-499 Emps.	500-999 Emps.	Unknown Emps.	Industry Sales
2015	110.2	56.8	82.0	137.7	103.7	191.8	258.5	364.9	15.5	1,321.1
2016	116.6	60.1	86.8	145.6	109.6	202.8	273.5	386.0	16.4	1,397.4
2017	123.6	63.7	92.0	154.4	116.2	215.0	289.9	409.3	17.4	1,481.6
2018	138.5	71.4	103.1	173.1	130.3	241.0	324.9	450.4	19.5	1,652.1
2019	154.0	79.3	114.6	192.4	144.8	268.0	361.2	493.2	21.6	1,829.3

INDUSTRY: HARDWARE CENTERS INDUSTRY (NAICS 44413)
PRODUCT LINE: TVs & VIDEO EQUIPMENT (Main Category)

NAICS 44413: Hardware Stores. Establishments primarily engaged in the retail sale of a number of basic hardware lines, such as tools, builders' hardware, paint and glass, housewares and household appliances, and cutlery.

5-YEAR TREND – ESTIMATED INDUSTRY SALES ($MILLIONS)

Year	Employee Size of Establishment									Total
	1-4 Emps.	5-9 Emps.	10-19 Emps.	20-49 Emps.	50-99 Emps.	100-249 Emps.	250-499 Emps.	500-999 Emps.	Unknown Emps.	Industry Sales
2015	2.6	4.4	8.8	12.5	2.5	0.8	0.1	0.0	0.2	31.9
2016	2.6	4.4	8.8	12.6	2.5	0.8	0.1	0.0	0.2	32.2
2017	2.6	4.5	9.0	12.8	2.6	0.8	0.1	0.0	0.2	32.7
2018	2.7	4.6	9.3	13.4	2.7	0.9	0.2	0.0	0.2	34.0
2019	2.9	4.9	9.8	14.0	2.8	0.9	0.2	0.0	0.3	35.7

INDUSTRY: PHARMACIES & DRUG STORES (NAICS 44611)
PRODUCT LINE: TVs & VIDEO EQUIPMENT (Main Category)

NAICS 44611 Pharmacies and Drug Stores – this industry comprises establishments known as pharmacies and drug stores engaged in retailing prescription or nonprescription drugs and medicines.

5-YEAR TREND – ESTIMATED INDUSTRY SALES ($MILLIONS)

Year	Employee Size of Establishment									Total Industry Sales
	1-4 Emps.	5-9 Emps.	10-19 Emps.	20-49 Emps.	50-99 Emps.	100-249 Emps.	250-499 Emps.	500-999 Emps.	Unknown Emps.	
2015	4.4	10.8	43.7	128.3	13.0	5.2	2.0	0.7	0.3	208.4
2016	4.5	11.1	45.1	132.4	13.4	5.4	2.0	0.7	0.3	214.9
2017	4.7	11.5	46.7	137.2	13.9	5.6	2.1	0.7	0.4	222.7
2018	4.9	12.2	49.5	145.3	14.7	5.9	2.2	0.8	0.4	235.8
2019	5.3	13.1	52.8	155.1	15.7	6.3	2.4	0.8	0.4	251.8

INDUSTRY: PRERECORDED TAPE/CDs STORES (NAICS 45122)
PRODUCT LINE: TVs & VIDEO EQUIPMENT (Main Category)

NAICS 45122: Prerecorded Tape, Compact Disc, and Record Stores .
This industry comprises establishments primarily engaged in retailing new prerecorded audio and video tapes, compact discs (CDs), and phonograph records.

5-YEAR TREND – ESTIMATED INDUSTRY SALES ($MILLIONS)

Year	Employee Size of Establishment									Total Industry Sales
	1-4 Emps.	5-9 Emps.	10-19 Emps.	20-49 Emps.	50-99 Emps.	100-249 Emps.	250-499 Emps.	500-999 Emps.	Unknown Emps.	
2015	59.2	115.1	291.9	596.8	452.7	29,847.3	2,331.0	48.5	20.7	33,763.0
2016	60.6	117.8	298.9	611.1	463.5	30,563.1	2,386.9	49.7	21.2	34,572.7
2017	62.3	121.3	307.6	629.0	477.1	31,458.0	2,456.8	51.1	21.8	35,585.0
2018	64.7	125.8	319.0	652.3	494.8	32,626.0	2,548.0	53.0	22.6	36,906.2
2019	67.6	131.6	333.8	682.5	517.7	34,132.6	2,665.6	55.5	23.6	38,610.5

INDUSTRY: WAREHOUSE CLUBS & SUPERCENTERS (NAICS 45291)
PRODUCT LINE: TVs & VIDEO EQUIPMENT (Main Category)

NAICS 45291: Warehouse Clubs and Superstores This industry comprises establishments known as warehouse clubs, superstores or supercenters primarily engaged in retailing a general line of groceries in combination with general lines of new merchandise, such as apparel, furniture, and appliances.

5-YEAR TREND – ESTIMATED INDUSTRY SALES ($MILLIONS)

Year	Employee Size of Establishment									Total
	1-4 Emps.	5-9 Emps.	10-19 Emps.	20-49 Emps.	50-99 Emps.	100-249 Emps.	250-499 Emps.	500-999 Emps.	Unknown Emps.	Industry Sales
2015	0.6	0.2	0.5	19.5	37.0	2,112.2	9,298.3	234.3	3.5	11,706.1
2016	0.6	0.2	0.5	20.0	38.0	2,170.4	9,554.6	240.8	3.6	12,028.7
2017	0.7	0.2	0.6	20.7	39.2	2,241.3	9,866.6	248.6	3.8	12,421.6
2018	0.7	0.2	0.6	22.3	42.2	2,412.1	10,618.7	267.6	4.0	13,368.5
2019	0.8	0.2	0.6	23.6	44.7	2,555.0	11,247.8	283.4	4.3	14,160.4

INDUSTRY: ELECTRONIC SHOPPING & MAIL-ORDER (NAICS 45411)
PRODUCT LINE: TVs & VIDEO EQUIPMENT (Main Category)

NAICS 45411: Electronic Shopping and Mail-Order Houses This industry comprises establishments primarily engaged in retailing all types of merchandise by means of mail or by electronic media, such as interactive television or computer. Included in this industry are establishments primarily engaged in retailing from catalogue showrooms of mail-order houses.

5-YEAR TREND – ESTIMATED INDUSTRY SALES ($MILLIONS)

Year	Employee Size of Establishment									Total
	1-4 Emps.	5-9 Emps.	10-19 Emps.	20-49 Emps.	50-99 Emps.	100-249 Emps.	250-499 Emps.	500-999 Emps.	Unknown Emps.	Industry Sales
2015	723.8	372.8	538.7	904.2	680.6	1,259.2	1,697.6	2,396.4	101.7	8,675.0
2016	765.6	394.4	569.8	956.4	719.9	1,331.9	1,795.6	2,534.7	107.6	9,175.7
2017	811.7	418.1	604.1	1,014.0	763.3	1,412.1	1,903.8	2,687.4	114.1	9,728.5
2018	909.6	468.6	677.0	1,136.4	855.4	1,582.5	2,133.5	2,957.2	127.9	10,848.2
2019	1,011.3	521.0	752.7	1,263.4	951.0	1,759.5	2,372.1	3,238.4	142.2	12,011.6

INDUSTRY: BOOK STORES INDUSTRY (NAICS 451211)
PRODUCT LINE: TVs & VIDEO EQUIPMENT (Main Category)

NAICS 451211: Book Stores. this industry comprises establishments primarily engaged in the retail sale of new books and magazines. Establishments primarily engaged in the retail sale of used books are classified in 5932.

5-YEAR TREND — ESTIMATED INDUSTRY SALES ($MILLIONS)

Year	Employee Size of Establishment									Total
	1-4 Emps.	5-9 Emps.	10-19 Emps.	20-49 Emps.	50-99 Emps.	100-249 Emps.	250-499 Emps.	500-999 Emps.	Unknown Emps.	Industry Sales
2015	16.5	25.0	49.7	132.2	57.6	26.5	6.5	15.7	8.3	338.1
2016	17.2	26.1	52.0	138.2	60.2	27.7	6.8	16.4	8.7	353.4
2017	18.1	27.4	54.5	145.1	63.1	29.1	7.2	17.3	9.1	370.8
2018	18.8	28.5	56.6	150.6	65.6	30.2	7.4	18.0	9.5	385.1
2019	19.6	29.7	59.2	157.5	68.5	31.6	7.8	18.9	9.9	402.7

INDUSTRY: DEPARTMENT STORES INDUSTRY (NAICS 45211)
PRODUCT LINE: TELEVISIONS (Sub Category)

NAICS 45211: Department Stores Industry . this industry comprises establishments known as department stores primarily engaged in retailing a wide range of the following new products with no one merchandise line predominating: apparel, furniture, appliances and home furnishings; and selected additional items, such as paint, hardware, toiletries, cosmetics, photographic equipment, jewelry, toys, and sporting goods. merchandise lines are normally arranged in separate departments.

5-YEAR TREND — ESTIMATED INDUSTRY SALES ($MILLIONS)

Year	Employee Size of Establishment									Total
	1-4 Emps.	5-9 Emps.	10-19 Emps.	20-49 Emps.	50-99 Emps.	100-249 Emps.	250-499 Emps.	500-999 Emps.	Unknown Emps.	Industry Sales
2015	0.1	0.1	0.2	13.2	238.9	767.2	317.6	45.9	2.0	1,385.1
2016	0.1	0.1	0.2	13.2	239.9	770.2	318.8	46.1	2.0	1,390.5
2017	0.1	0.1	0.2	13.3	242.2	777.8	322.0	46.6	2.0	1,404.2
2018	0.1	0.1	0.2	13.3	242.3	777.9	322.0	46.7	2.0	1,404.5
2019	0.1	0.1	0.2	13.5	244.7	785.6	325.2	47.2	2.0	1,418.5

INDUSTRY: WAREHOUSE CLUBS & SUPERCENTERS (NAICS 45291)
PRODUCT LINE: TELEVISIONS (Sub Category)

NAICS 45291: Warehouse Clubs and Superstores This industry comprises establishments known as warehouse clubs, superstores or supercenters primarily engaged in retailing a general line of groceries in combination with general lines of new merchandise, such as apparel, furniture, and appliances.

5-YEAR TREND – ESTIMATED INDUSTRY SALES ($MILLIONS)

Year	Employee Size of Establishment									Total
	1-4 Emps.	5-9 Emps.	10-19 Emps.	20-49 Emps.	50-99 Emps.	100-249 Emps.	250-499 Emps.	500-999 Emps.	Unknown Emps.	Industry Sales
2015	0.3	0.1	0.2	8.8	16.7	951.0	4,186.5	105.5	1.6	5,270.7
2016	0.3	0.1	0.2	9.0	17.1	977.2	4,301.9	108.4	1.6	5,415.9
2017	0.3	0.1	0.3	9.3	17.7	1,009.1	4,442.4	111.9	1.7	5,592.8
2018	0.3	0.1	0.3	10.0	19.0	1,086.1	4,781.1	120.5	1.8	6,019.1
2019	0.3	0.1	0.3	10.6	20.1	1,150.4	5,064.3	127.6	1.9	6,375.7

INDUSTRY: ELECTRONIC SHOPPING & MAIL-ORDER (NAICS 45411)
PRODUCT LINE: TELEVISIONS (Sub Category)

NAICS 45411: Electronic Shopping and Mail-Order Houses This industry comprises establishments primarily engaged in retailing all types of merchandise by means of mail or by electronic media, such as interactive television or computer. Included in this industry are establishments primarily engaged in retailing from catalogue showrooms of mail-order houses.

5-YEAR TREND – ESTIMATED INDUSTRY SALES ($MILLIONS)

Year	Employee Size of Establishment									Total
	1-4 Emps.	5-9 Emps.	10-19 Emps.	20-49 Emps.	50-99 Emps.	100-249 Emps.	250-499 Emps.	500-999 Emps.	Unknown Emps.	Industry Sales
2015	83.4	43.0	62.1	104.2	78.4	145.1	195.6	276.2	11.7	999.8
2016	88.2	45.4	65.7	110.2	83.0	153.5	206.9	292.1	12.4	1,057.5
2017	93.5	48.2	69.6	116.9	88.0	162.7	219.4	309.7	13.1	1,121.2
2018	104.8	54.0	78.0	131.0	98.6	182.4	245.9	340.8	14.7	1,250.2
2019	116.6	60.0	86.7	145.6	109.6	202.8	273.4	373.2	16.4	1,384.3

INDUSTRY: PRERECORDED TAPE/CDs STORES (NAICS 45122)
PRODUCT LINE: VIDEO RECORDERS & CAMERAS (Sub Category)

NAICS 45122: Prerecorded Tape, Compact Disc, and Record Stores .
This industry comprises establishments primarily engaged in retailing new
prerecorded audio and video tapes, compact discs (CDs), and phonograph
records.

5-YEAR TREND – ESTIMATED INDUSTRY SALES ($MILLIONS)

| Year | Employee Size of Establishment | | | | | | | | | Total |
	1-4 Emps.	5-9 Emps.	10-19 Emps.	20-49 Emps.	50-99 Emps.	100-249 Emps.	250-499 Emps.	500-999 Emps.	Unknown Emps.	Industry Sales
2015	3.4	6.5	16.6	33.9	25.7	1,693.8	132.3	2.8	1.2	1,916.1
2016	3.4	6.7	17.0	34.7	26.3	1,734.5	135.5	2.8	1.2	1,962.0
2017	3.5	6.9	17.5	35.7	27.1	1,785.2	139.4	2.9	1.2	2,019.5
2018	3.7	7.1	18.1	37.0	28.1	1,851.5	144.6	3.0	1.3	2,094.4
2019	3.8	7.5	18.9	38.7	29.4	1,937.0	151.3	3.1	1.3	2,191.2

INDUSTRY: PRERECORDED TAPE/CDs STORES (NAICS 45122)
PRODUCT LINE: VIDEO TAPES & DISCS (Sub Category)

NAICS 45122: Prerecorded Tape, Compact Disc, and Record Stores .
This industry comprises establishments primarily engaged in retailing new
prerecorded audio and video tapes, compact discs (CDs), and phonograph
records.

5-YEAR TREND – ESTIMATED INDUSTRY SALES ($MILLIONS)

| Year | Employee Size of Establishment | | | | | | | | | Total |
	1-4 Emps.	5-9 Emps.	10-19 Emps.	20-49 Emps.	50-99 Emps.	100-249 Emps.	250-499 Emps.	500-999 Emps.	Unknown Emps.	Industry Sales
2015	55.8	108.5	275.1	562.5	426.7	28,134.9	2,197.2	45.7	19.5	31,826.0
2016	57.1	111.1	281.7	576.0	436.9	28,809.7	2,249.9	46.8	19.9	32,589.2
2017	58.8	114.3	290.0	592.9	449.7	29,653.2	2,315.8	48.2	20.5	33,543.5
2018	60.9	118.6	300.7	614.9	466.4	30,754.2	2,401.8	50.0	21.3	34,788.9
2019	63.8	124.0	314.6	643.3	488.0	32,174.4	2,512.7	52.3	22.3	36,395.4

© Barnes Reports: 2018 U.S. Product & Retail Outlook

	INDUSTRY: DEPARTMENT STORES INDUSTRY (NAICS 45211)
	PRODUCT LINE: OTHER VIDEO EQUIPMENT (Sub Category)

NAICS 45211: Department Stores Industry . this industry comprises establishments known as department stores primarily engaged in retailing a wide range of the following new products with no one merchandise line predominating: apparel, furniture, appliances and home furnishings; and selected additional items, such as paint, hardware, toiletries, cosmetics, photographic equipment, jewelry, toys, and sporting goods. merchandise lines are normally arranged in separate departments.

5-YEAR TREND – ESTIMATED INDUSTRY SALES ($MILLIONS)

Year	Employee Size of Establishment									Total
	1-4 Emps.	5-9 Emps.	10-19 Emps.	20-49 Emps.	50-99 Emps.	100-249 Emps.	250-499 Emps.	500-999 Emps.	Unknown Emps.	Industry Sales
2015	0.1	0.1	0.3	21.2	384.4	1,234.5	511.0	73.9	3.1	2,228.7
2016	0.1	0.1	0.3	21.3	385.9	1,239.3	513.0	74.2	3.2	2,237.4
2017	0.1	0.1	0.3	21.5	389.8	1,251.6	518.1	74.9	3.2	2,259.4
2018	0.1	0.1	0.3	21.5	389.8	1,251.7	518.1	75.2	3.2	2,259.9
2019	0.1	0.1	0.3	21.7	393.7	1,264.1	523.3	76.0	3.2	2,282.4

	INDUSTRY: WAREHOUSE CLUBS & SUPERCENTERS (NAICS 45291)
	PRODUCT LINE: OTHER VIDEO EQUIPMENT (Sub Category)

NAICS 45291: Warehouse Clubs and Superstores This industry comprises establishments known as warehouse clubs, superstores or supercenters primarily engaged in retailing a general line of groceries in combination with general lines of new merchandise, such as apparel, furniture, and appliances.

5-YEAR TREND – ESTIMATED INDUSTRY SALES ($MILLIONS)

Year	Employee Size of Establishment									Total
	1-4 Emps.	5-9 Emps.	10-19 Emps.	20-49 Emps.	50-99 Emps.	100-249 Emps.	250-499 Emps.	500-999 Emps.	Unknown Emps.	Industry Sales
2015	0.3	0.1	0.3	10.7	20.3	1,161.2	5,111.7	128.8	1.9	6,435.5
2016	0.4	0.1	0.3	11.0	20.9	1,193.2	5,252.6	132.4	2.0	6,612.8
2017	0.4	0.1	0.3	11.4	21.6	1,232.1	5,424.2	136.7	2.1	6,828.8
2018	0.4	0.1	0.3	12.2	23.2	1,326.1	5,837.7	147.1	2.2	7,349.3
2019	0.4	0.1	0.4	13.0	24.6	1,404.6	6,183.5	155.8	2.4	7,784.7

INDUSTRY: ELECTRONIC SHOPPING & MAIL-ORDER (NAICS 45411)
PRODUCT LINE: OTHER VIDEO EQUIPMENT (Sub Category)

NAICS 45411: Electronic Shopping and Mail-Order Houses This industry comprises establishments primarily engaged in retailing all types of merchandise by means of mail or by electronic media, such as interactive television or computer. Included in this industry are establishments primarily engaged in retailing from catalogue showrooms of mail-order houses.

5-YEAR TREND – ESTIMATED INDUSTRY SALES ($MILLIONS)

Year	Employee Size of Establishment									Total
	1-4 Emps.	5-9 Emps.	10-19 Emps.	20-49 Emps.	50-99 Emps.	100-249 Emps.	250-499 Emps.	500-999 Emps.	Unknown Emps.	Industry Sales
2015	640.4	329.9	476.6	800.0	602.2	1,114.1	1,502.0	2,120.2	90.0	7,675.3
2016	677.3	348.9	504.1	846.2	636.9	1,178.4	1,588.7	2,242.6	95.2	8,118.3
2017	718.1	369.9	534.5	897.1	675.3	1,249.4	1,684.4	2,377.7	100.9	8,607.3
2018	804.8	414.6	599.0	1,005.4	756.8	1,400.2	1,887.7	2,616.4	113.1	9,598.0
2019	894.8	460.9	666.0	1,117.8	841.4	1,556.7	2,098.7	2,865.2	125.8	10,627.3

INDUSTRY: HARDWARE STORES (NAICS 44413)
PRODUCT LINE: AUDIO EQUIPMENT (Main Category)

NAICS 44413: Hardware Stores. Establishments primarily engaged in the retail sale of a number of basic hardware lines, such as tools, builders' hardware, paint and glass, housewares and household appliances, and cutlery.

5-YEAR TREND – ESTIMATED INDUSTRY SALES ($MILLIONS)

Year	Employee Size of Establishment									Total
	1-4 Emps.	5-9 Emps.	10-19 Emps.	20-49 Emps.	50-99 Emps.	100-249 Emps.	250-499 Emps.	500-999 Emps.	Unknown Emps.	Industry Sales
2015	1.7	2.8	5.7	8.2	1.6	0.5	0.1	0.0	0.1	20.8
2016	1.7	2.9	5.8	8.3	1.6	0.5	0.1	0.0	0.1	21.0
2017	1.7	2.9	5.9	8.4	1.7	0.5	0.1	0.0	0.2	21.4
2018	1.8	3.0	6.1	8.7	1.7	0.6	0.1	0.0	0.2	22.2
2019	1.9	3.2	6.4	9.2	1.8	0.6	0.1	0.0	0.2	23.3

INDUSTRY: SUPERMARKETS INDUSTRY (NAICS 44511)
PRODUCT LINE: AUDIO EQUIPMENT (Main Category)

NAICS 44511: Grocery Stores Industry. this industry comprises establishments generally known as supermarkets and grocery stores primarily engaged in retailing a general line of food, such as canned and frozen foods; fresh fruits and vegetables; and fresh and prepared meats, fish, and poultry. Included in this industry are delicatessen-type establishments primarily engaged in retailing a general line of food.

5-YEAR TREND – ESTIMATED INDUSTRY SALES ($MILLIONS)

Year	Employee Size of Establishment									Total
	1-4 Emps.	5-9 Emps.	10-19 Emps.	20-49 Emps.	50-99 Emps.	100-249 Emps.	250-499 Emps.	500-999 Emps.	Unknown Emps.	Industry Sales
2015	5.4	3.9	10.0	33.1	78.4	194.9	60.9	7.3	1.0	394.8
2016	5.4	3.9	10.0	32.9	77.9	193.6	60.5	7.2	1.0	392.3
2017	5.4	3.9	10.0	32.9	77.9	193.6	60.4	7.2	1.0	392.1
2018	5.5	3.9	10.2	33.5	79.5	197.5	61.7	7.4	1.0	400.2
2019	5.6	4.1	10.5	34.6	81.9	203.7	63.6	7.6	1.1	412.6

INDUSTRY: PHARMACIES & DRUG STORES INDUSTRY (NAICS 44611)
PRODUCT LINE: AUDIO EQUIPMENT (Main Category)

NAICS 44611 Pharmacies and Drug Stores – this industry comprises establishments known as pharmacies and drug stores engaged in retailing prescription or nonprescription drugs and medicines.

5-YEAR TREND – ESTIMATED INDUSTRY SALES ($MILLIONS)

Year	Employee Size of Establishment									Total
	1-4 Emps.	5-9 Emps.	10-19 Emps.	20-49 Emps.	50-99 Emps.	100-249 Emps.	250-499 Emps.	500-999 Emps.	Unknown Emps.	Industry Sales
2015	14.5	35.9	145.2	426.5	43.1	17.3	6.6	2.2	1.1	692.4
2016	14.9	37.0	149.8	439.9	44.5	17.8	6.8	2.3	1.1	714.1
2017	15.5	38.4	155.2	455.8	46.1	18.5	7.1	2.4	1.2	740.0
2018	16.4	40.6	164.4	482.8	48.8	19.5	7.5	2.5	1.3	783.7
2019	17.5	43.4	175.5	515.5	52.1	20.9	8.0	2.7	1.3	836.9

INDUSTRY: PRERECORDED TAPES & CDs STORES (NAICS 45122)
PRODUCT LINE: AUDIO EQUIPMENT (Main Category)

NAICS 45122: Prerecorded Tape, Compact Disc, and Record Stores .
This industry comprises establishments primarily engaged in retailing new
prerecorded audio and video tapes, compact discs (CDs), and phonograph
records.

5-YEAR TREND – ESTIMATED INDUSTRY SALES ($MILLIONS)

Year	Employee Size of Establishment									Total
	1-4 Emps.	5-9 Emps.	10-19 Emps.	20-49 Emps.	50-99 Emps.	100-249 Emps.	250-499 Emps.	500-999 Emps.	Unknown Emps.	Industry Sales
2015	170.7	332.1	842.3	1,722.2	1,306.3	86,135.9	6,726.9	140.1	59.6	97,436.2
2016	174.8	340.1	862.5	1,763.5	1,337.7	88,201.7	6,888.3	143.4	61.1	99,773.0
2017	179.9	350.0	887.7	1,815.2	1,376.8	90,784.3	7,090.0	147.6	62.9	102,694.5
2018	186.6	363.0	920.7	1,882.6	1,427.9	94,154.9	7,353.2	153.1	65.2	106,507.2
2019	195.2	379.8	963.2	1,969.5	1,493.9	98,503.0	7,692.8	160.1	68.2	111,425.7

INDUSTRY: DEPARTMENT STORES INDUSTRY (NAICS 45211)
PRODUCT LINE: AUDIO EQUIPMENT (Main Category)

NAICS 45211: Department Stores Industry . this industry comprises
establishments known as department stores primarily engaged in retailing
a wide range of the following new products with no one merchandise line
predominating: apparel, furniture, appliances and home furnishings; and
selected additional items, such as paint, hardware, toiletries, cosmetics,
photographic equipment, jewelry, toys, and sporting goods. merchandise lines
are normally arranged in separate departments.

5-YEAR TREND – ESTIMATED INDUSTRY SALES ($MILLIONS)

Year	Employee Size of Establishment									Total
	1-4 Emps.	5-9 Emps.	10-19 Emps.	20-49 Emps.	50-99 Emps.	100-249 Emps.	250-499 Emps.	500-999 Emps.	Unknown Emps.	Industry Sales
2015	0.1	0.2	0.3	28.7	520.1	1,670.2	691.4	100.0	4.2	3,015.2
2016	0.1	0.2	0.3	28.8	522.2	1,676.7	694.1	100.4	4.3	3,027.0
2017	0.1	0.2	0.3	29.0	527.3	1,693.3	700.9	101.4	4.3	3,056.9
2018	0.1	0.2	0.3	29.1	527.4	1,693.5	701.0	101.7	4.3	3,057.5
2019	0.1	0.2	0.3	29.3	532.6	1,710.2	707.9	102.8	4.4	3,087.9

INDUSTRY: WAREHOUSE CLUBS & SUPERCENTERS (NAICS 45291)
PRODUCT LINE: AUDIO EQUIPMENT (Main Category)

NAICS 45291: Warehouse Clubs and Superstores This industry comprises establishments known as warehouse clubs, superstores or supercenters primarily engaged in retailing a general line of groceries in combination with general lines of new merchandise, such as apparel, furniture, and appliances.

5-Year Trend – Estimated Industry Sales ($Millions)

Year	Employee Size of Establishment									Total Industry Sales
	1-4 Emps.	5-9 Emps.	10-19 Emps.	20-49 Emps.	50-99 Emps.	100-249 Emps.	250-499 Emps.	500-999 Emps.	Unknown Emps.	
2015	0.5	0.1	0.5	17.2	32.7	1,868.1	8,224.0	207.2	3.1	10,353.6
2016	0.6	0.2	0.5	17.7	33.6	1,919.6	8,450.7	212.9	3.2	10,639.0
2017	0.6	0.2	0.5	18.3	34.7	1,982.3	8,726.7	219.9	3.3	10,986.5
2018	0.6	0.2	0.5	19.7	37.4	2,133.4	9,391.9	236.7	3.6	11,823.9
2019	0.7	0.2	0.6	20.9	39.6	2,259.8	9,948.2	250.7	3.8	12,524.4

INDUSTRY: OFFICE SUPPLIES & STATIONERY STORES (NAICS 45321)
PRODUCT LINE: AUDIO EQUIPMENT (Main Category)

NAICS 45321: Office Supplies and Stationery Stores . this industry comprises establishments primarily engaged in one or more of the following: (1) retailing new stationery, school supplies, and office supplies; (2) selling a combination of new office equipment, furniture, and supplies; and (3) selling new office equipment, furniture, and supplies in combination with selling new computers.

5-Year Trend – Estimated Industry Sales ($Millions)

Year	Employee Size of Establishment									Total Industry Sales
	1-4 Emps.	5-9 Emps.	10-19 Emps.	20-49 Emps.	50-99 Emps.	100-249 Emps.	250-499 Emps.	500-999 Emps.	Unknown Emps.	
2015	0.2	0.2	1.1	2.6	0.1	0.0	0.0	0.0	0.1	4.2
2016	0.2	0.2	1.0	2.6	0.1	0.0	0.0	0.0	0.0	4.2
2017	0.2	0.2	1.0	2.6	0.1	0.0	0.0	0.0	0.0	4.2
2018	0.2	0.2	1.0	2.5	0.1	0.0	0.0	0.0	0.0	4.0
2019	0.2	0.2	1.0	2.5	0.1	0.0	0.0	0.0	0.0	3.9

INDUSTRY: ELECTRONIC SHOPPING & MAIL-ORDER (NAICS 45411)

PRODUCT LINE: AUDIO EQUIPMENT (Main Category)

NAICS 45411: Electronic Shopping and Mail-Order Houses This industry comprises establishments primarily engaged in retailing all types of merchandise by means of mail or by electronic media, such as interactive television or computer. Included in this industry are establishments primarily engaged in retailing from catalogue showrooms of mail-order houses.

5-YEAR TREND — ESTIMATED INDUSTRY SALES ($MILLIONS)

Year	Employee Size of Establishment									Total
	1-4 Emps.	5-9 Emps.	10-19 Emps.	20-49 Emps.	50-99 Emps.	100-249 Emps.	250-499 Emps.	500-999 Emps.	Unknown Emps.	Industry Sales
2015	1,046.6	539.1	778.9	1,307.4	984.1	1,820.7	2,454.7	3,465.1	147.1	12,543.8
2016	1,107.0	570.2	823.9	1,382.9	1,040.9	1,925.8	2,596.4	3,665.1	155.6	13,267.8
2017	1,173.7	604.6	873.5	1,466.2	1,103.7	2,041.9	2,752.8	3,885.9	165.0	14,067.1
2018	1,315.3	677.6	978.9	1,643.2	1,236.9	2,288.3	3,085.0	4,276.0	184.9	15,686.1
2019	1,462.4	753.3	1,088.4	1,826.9	1,375.2	2,544.1	3,430.0	4,682.7	205.5	17,368.4

INDUSTRY: BOOK STORES INDUSTRY (NAICS 451211)

PRODUCT LINE: AUDIO EQUIPMENT (Main Category)

NAICS 451211: Book Stores. this industry comprises establishments primarily engaged in the retail sale of new books and magazines. Establishments primarily engaged in the retail sale of used books are classified in 5932.

5-YEAR TREND — ESTIMATED INDUSTRY SALES ($MILLIONS)

Year	Employee Size of Establishment									Total
	1-4 Emps.	5-9 Emps.	10-19 Emps.	20-49 Emps.	50-99 Emps.	100-249 Emps.	250-499 Emps.	500-999 Emps.	Unknown Emps.	Industry Sales
2015	29.9	45.4	90.3	240.1	104.5	48.1	11.9	28.6	15.1	613.8
2016	31.3	47.4	94.4	251.0	109.3	50.3	12.4	29.9	15.8	641.7
2017	32.8	49.8	99.0	263.4	114.6	52.8	13.0	31.3	16.6	673.3
2018	34.1	51.7	102.8	273.5	119.0	54.8	13.5	32.7	17.2	699.2
2019	35.6	54.0	107.5	285.9	124.5	57.3	14.1	34.3	18.0	731.2

INDUSTRY: PRERECORDED TAPES & CDs STORES (NAICS 45122)
PRODUCT LINE: STEREO & COMPONENT EQUIPMENT (Sub Category)

NAICS 45122: Prerecorded Tape, Compact Disc, and Record Stores .
This industry comprises establishments primarily engaged in retailing new prerecorded audio and video tapes, compact discs (CDs), and phonograph records.

5-YEAR TREND – ESTIMATED INDUSTRY SALES ($MILLIONS)

Year	Employee Size of Establishment									Total
	1-4 Emps.	5-9 Emps.	10-19 Emps.	20-49 Emps.	50-99 Emps.	100-249 Emps.	250-499 Emps.	500-999 Emps.	Unknown Emps.	Industry Sales
2015	1.3	2.5	6.2	12.7	9.7	636.8	49.7	1.0	0.4	720.4
2016	1.3	2.5	6.4	13.0	9.9	652.1	50.9	1.1	0.5	737.7
2017	1.3	2.6	6.6	13.4	10.2	671.2	52.4	1.1	0.5	759.3
2018	1.4	2.7	6.8	13.9	10.6	696.1	54.4	1.1	0.5	787.5
2019	1.4	2.8	7.1	14.6	11.0	728.3	56.9	1.2	0.5	823.8

INDUSTRY: DEPARTMENT STORES INDUSTRY (NAICS 45211)
PRODUCT LINE: STEREO & COMPONENT EQUIPMENT (Sub Category)

NAICS 45211: Department Stores Industry . this industry comprises establishments known as department stores primarily engaged in retailing a wide range of the following new products with no one merchandise line predominating: apparel, furniture, appliances and home furnishings; and selected additional items, such as paint, hardware, toiletries, cosmetics, photographic equipment, jewelry, toys, and sporting goods. merchandise lines are normally arranged in separate departments.

5-YEAR TREND – ESTIMATED INDUSTRY SALES ($MILLIONS)

Year	Employee Size of Establishment									Total
	1-4 Emps.	5-9 Emps.	10-19 Emps.	20-49 Emps.	50-99 Emps.	100-249 Emps.	250-499 Emps.	500-999 Emps.	Unknown Emps.	Industry Sales
2015	0.1	0.1	0.2	14.4	262.0	841.2	348.2	50.4	2.1	1,518.6
2016	0.1	0.1	0.2	14.5	263.0	844.4	349.6	50.6	2.1	1,524.5
2017	0.1	0.1	0.2	14.6	265.6	852.8	353.0	51.1	2.2	1,539.5
2018	0.1	0.1	0.2	14.6	265.6	852.9	353.0	51.2	2.2	1,539.9
2019	0.1	0.1	0.2	14.8	268.2	861.3	356.5	51.8	2.2	1,555.2

INDUSTRY: WAREHOUSE CLUBS & SUPERCENTERS (NAICS 45291)
PRODUCT LINE: STEREO & COMPONENT EQUIPMENT (Sub Category)

NAICS 45291: Warehouse Clubs and Superstores This industry comprises establishments known as warehouse clubs, superstores or supercenters primarily engaged in retailing a general line of groceries in combination with general lines of new merchandise, such as apparel, furniture, and appliances.

5-YEAR TREND – ESTIMATED INDUSTRY SALES ($MILLIONS)

Year	Employee Size of Establishment									Total
	1-4 Emps.	5-9 Emps.	10-19 Emps.	20-49 Emps.	50-99 Emps.	100-249 Emps.	250-499 Emps.	500-999 Emps.	Unknown Emps.	Industry Sales
2015	0.2	0.1	0.2	7.6	14.5	828.0	3,645.0	91.9	1.4	4,588.9
2016	0.2	0.1	0.2	7.9	14.9	850.8	3,745.5	94.4	1.4	4,715.4
2017	0.3	0.1	0.2	8.1	15.4	878.6	3,867.8	97.5	1.5	4,869.4
2018	0.3	0.1	0.2	8.7	16.6	945.6	4,162.6	104.9	1.6	5,240.6
2019	0.3	0.1	0.3	9.2	17.5	1,001.6	4,409.2	111.1	1.7	5,551.0

INDUSTRY: ELECTRONIC SHOPPING & MAIL-ORDER (NAICS 45411)
PRODUCT LINE: STEREO & COMPONENT EQUIPMENT (Sub Category)

NAICS 45411: Electronic Shopping and Mail-Order Houses This industry comprises establishments primarily engaged in retailing all types of merchandise by means of mail or by electronic media, such as interactive television or computer. Included in this industry are establishments primarily engaged in retailing from catalogue showrooms of mail-order houses.

5-YEAR TREND – ESTIMATED INDUSTRY SALES ($MILLIONS)

Year	Employee Size of Establishment									Total
	1-4 Emps.	5-9 Emps.	10-19 Emps.	20-49 Emps.	50-99 Emps.	100-249 Emps.	250-499 Emps.	500-999 Emps.	Unknown Emps.	Industry Sales
2015	288.2	148.5	214.5	360.1	271.0	501.4	676.0	954.3	40.5	3,454.4
2016	304.8	157.0	226.9	380.8	286.7	530.4	715.0	1,009.3	42.8	3,653.8
2017	323.2	166.5	240.6	403.8	303.9	562.3	758.1	1,070.1	45.4	3,873.9
2018	362.2	186.6	269.6	452.5	340.6	630.2	849.6	1,177.6	50.9	4,319.8
2019	402.7	207.5	299.7	503.1	378.7	700.6	944.6	1,289.6	56.6	4,783.1

INDUSTRY: PRERECORDED TAPES & CDs STORES (NAICS 45122)
PRODUCT LINE: TAPES & CDs (Sub Category)

NAICS 45122: Prerecorded Tape, Compact Disc, and Record Stores .
This industry comprises establishments primarily engaged in retailing new
prerecorded audio and video tapes, compact discs (CDs), and phonograph
records.

5-YEAR TREND — ESTIMATED INDUSTRY SALES ($MILLIONS)

Year	Employee Size of Establishment									Total
	1-4 Emps.	5-9 Emps.	10-19 Emps.	20-49 Emps.	50-99 Emps.	100-249 Emps.	250-499 Emps.	500-999 Emps.	Unknown Emps.	Industry Sales
2015	168.6	328.1	832.1	1,701.4	1,290.5	85,092.3	6,645.4	138.4	58.9	96,255.6
2016	172.7	335.9	852.0	1,742.2	1,321.4	87,133.0	6,804.8	141.7	60.3	98,564.1
2017	177.7	345.8	877.0	1,793.2	1,360.1	89,684.4	7,004.1	145.8	62.1	101,450.2
2018	184.3	358.6	909.6	1,859.8	1,410.6	93,014.1	7,264.1	151.2	64.4	105,216.8
2019	192.9	375.2	951.6	1,945.7	1,475.8	97,309.5	7,599.6	158.2	67.4	110,075.6

INDUSTRY: DEPARTMENT STORES INDUSTRY (NAICS 45211)
PRODUCT LINE: TAPES & CDs (Sub Category)

NAICS 45211: Department Stores Industry . this industry comprises
establishments known as department stores primarily engaged in retailing
a wide range of the following new products with no one merchandise line
predominating: apparel, furniture, appliances and home furnishings; and
selected additional items, such as paint, hardware, toiletries, cosmetics,
photographic equipment, jewelry, toys, and sporting goods. merchandise lines
are normally arranged in separate departments.

5-YEAR TREND — ESTIMATED INDUSTRY SALES ($MILLIONS)

Year	Employee Size of Establishment									Total
	1-4 Emps.	5-9 Emps.	10-19 Emps.	20-49 Emps.	50-99 Emps.	100-249 Emps.	250-499 Emps.	500-999 Emps.	Unknown Emps.	Industry Sales
2015	0.1	0.1	0.2	14.2	258.1	828.9	343.1	49.6	2.1	1,496.4
2016	0.1	0.1	0.2	14.3	259.1	832.1	344.5	49.8	2.1	1,502.3
2017	0.1	0.1	0.2	14.4	261.7	840.4	347.9	50.3	2.1	1,517.1
2018	0.1	0.1	0.2	14.4	261.7	840.5	347.9	50.5	2.1	1,517.4
2019	0.1	0.1	0.2	14.6	264.3	848.8	351.3	51.0	2.2	1,532.5

INDUSTRY: WAREHOUSE CLUBS & SUPERCENTERS (NAICS 45291)
PRODUCT LINE: TAPES & CDs (Sub Category)

NAICS 45291: Warehouse Clubs and Superstores This industry comprises establishments known as warehouse clubs, superstores or supercenters primarily engaged in retailing a general line of groceries in combination with general lines of new merchandise, such as apparel, furniture, and appliances.

5-Year Trend – Estimated Industry Sales ($Millions)

Year	Employee Size of Establishment									Total
	1-4 Emps.	5-9 Emps.	10-19 Emps.	20-49 Emps.	50-99 Emps.	100-249 Emps.	250-499 Emps.	500-999 Emps.	Unknown Emps.	Industry Sales
2015	0.3	0.1	0.3	9.5	17.9	1,024.9	4,511.7	113.7	1.7	5,680.1
2016	0.3	0.1	0.3	9.7	18.4	1,053.1	4,636.1	116.8	1.8	5,836.6
2017	0.3	0.1	0.3	10.0	19.0	1,087.5	4,787.5	120.6	1.8	6,027.3
2018	0.3	0.1	0.3	10.8	20.5	1,170.4	5,152.5	129.8	2.0	6,486.7
2019	0.4	0.1	0.3	11.4	21.7	1,239.7	5,457.7	137.5	2.1	6,871.0

INDUSTRY: ELECTRONIC SHOPPING & MAIL-ORDER (NAICS 45411)
PRODUCT LINE: TAPES & CDs (Sub Category)

NAICS 45411: Electronic Shopping and Mail-Order Houses This industry comprises establishments primarily engaged in retailing all types of merchandise by means of mail or by electronic media, such as interactive television or computer. Included in this industry are establishments primarily engaged in retailing from catalogue showrooms of mail-order houses.

5-Year Trend – Estimated Industry Sales ($Millions)

Year	Employee Size of Establishment									Total
	1-4 Emps.	5-9 Emps.	10-19 Emps.	20-49 Emps.	50-99 Emps.	100-249 Emps.	250-499 Emps.	500-999 Emps.	Unknown Emps.	Industry Sales
2015	372.5	191.9	277.2	465.3	350.3	648.0	873.7	1,233.3	52.4	4,464.5
2016	394.0	203.0	293.2	492.2	370.5	685.4	924.1	1,304.5	55.4	4,722.2
2017	417.7	215.2	310.9	521.8	392.8	726.7	979.8	1,383.0	58.7	5,006.7
2018	468.1	241.2	348.4	584.8	440.2	814.4	1,098.0	1,521.9	65.8	5,582.9
2019	520.5	268.1	387.4	650.2	489.4	905.5	1,220.8	1,666.6	73.2	6,181.7

INDUSTRY: PRERECORDED TAPES & CDs STORES (NAICS 45122)
PRODUCT LINE: SHEET MUSIC & RELATED ITEMS (Sub Category)

NAICS 45122: Prerecorded Tape, Compact Disc, and Record Stores .
This industry comprises establishments primarily engaged in retailing new
prerecorded audio and video tapes, compact discs (CDs), and phonograph
records.

5-Year Trend – Estimated Industry Sales ($Millions)

| Year | Employee Size of Establishment | | | | | | | | | Total |
	1-4 Emps.	5-9 Emps.	10-19 Emps.	20-49 Emps.	50-99 Emps.	100-249 Emps.	250-499 Emps.	500-999 Emps.	Unknown Emps.	Industry Sales
2015	0.7	1.4	3.6	7.3	5.5	363.8	28.4	0.6	0.3	411.6
2016	0.7	1.4	3.6	7.4	5.7	372.6	29.1	0.6	0.3	421.4
2017	0.8	1.5	3.7	7.7	5.8	383.5	29.9	0.6	0.3	433.8
2018	0.8	1.5	3.9	8.0	6.0	397.7	31.1	0.6	0.3	449.9
2019	0.8	1.6	4.1	8.3	6.3	416.1	32.5	0.7	0.3	470.6

INDUSTRY: WAREHOUSE CLUBS & SUPERCENTERS (NAICS 45291)
PRODUCT LINE: OTHER AUDIO & MUSIC ITEMS (Sub Category)

NAICS 45291: Warehouse Clubs and Superstores This industry
comprises establishments known as warehouse clubs, superstores or
supercenters primarily engaged in retailing a general line of groceries
in combination with general lines of new merchandise, such as apparel,
furniture, and appliances.

5-Year Trend – Estimated Industry Sales ($Millions)

| Year | Employee Size of Establishment | | | | | | | | | Total |
	1-4 Emps.	5-9 Emps.	10-19 Emps.	20-49 Emps.	50-99 Emps.	100-249 Emps.	250-499 Emps.	500-999 Emps.	Unknown Emps.	Industry Sales
2015	0.0	0.0	0.0	0.1	0.3	15.3	67.2	1.7	0.0	84.6
2016	0.0	0.0	0.0	0.1	0.3	15.7	69.1	1.7	0.0	87.0
2017	0.0	0.0	0.0	0.1	0.3	16.2	71.3	1.8	0.0	89.8
2018	0.0	0.0	0.0	0.2	0.3	17.4	76.8	1.9	0.0	96.7
2019	0.0	0.0	0.0	0.2	0.3	18.5	81.3	2.0	0.0	102.4

INDUSTRY: ELECTRONIC SHOPPING & MAIL-ORDER (NAICS 45411)
PRODUCT LINE: OTHER AUDIO & MUSIC ITEMS (Sub Category)

NAICS 45411: Electronic Shopping and Mail-Order Houses This industry comprises establishments primarily engaged in retailing all types of merchandise by means of mail or by electronic media, such as interactive television or computer. Included in this industry are establishments primarily engaged in retailing from catalogue showrooms of mail-order houses.

5-YEAR TREND – ESTIMATED INDUSTRY SALES ($MILLIONS)

Year	Employee Size of Establishment									Total
	1-4 Emps.	5-9 Emps.	10-19 Emps.	20-49 Emps.	50-99 Emps.	100-249 Emps.	250-499 Emps.	500-999 Emps.	Unknown Emps.	Industry Sales
2015	385.9	198.8	287.2	482.0	362.8	671.3	905.0	1,277.6	54.2	4,624.8
2016	408.1	210.2	303.8	509.9	383.8	710.0	957.3	1,351.3	57.4	4,891.8
2017	432.7	222.9	322.1	540.6	406.9	752.8	1,014.9	1,432.7	60.8	5,186.5
2018	485.0	249.8	360.9	605.8	456.0	843.7	1,137.4	1,576.5	68.2	5,783.4
2019	539.2	277.7	401.3	673.6	507.0	938.0	1,264.6	1,726.5	75.8	6,403.7

INDUSTRY: HOME CENTERS INDUSTRY (NAICS 44411)
PRODUCT LINE: FURNITURE (Main Category)

NAICS 44411: Home Centers. This industry comprises establishments known as home centers primarily engaged in retailing a general line of new home repair and improvement materials and supplies, such as lumber, plumbing goods, electrical goods, tools, housewares, hardware, and lawn and garden supplies, with no one merchandise line predominating. The merchandise lines are normally arranged in separate departments.

5-YEAR TREND – ESTIMATED INDUSTRY SALES ($MILLIONS)

Year	Employee Size of Establishment									Total
	1-4 Emps.	5-9 Emps.	10-19 Emps.	20-49 Emps.	50-99 Emps.	100-249 Emps.	250-499 Emps.	500-999 Emps.	Unknown Emps.	Industry Sales
2015	4.8	9.3	23.5	48.0	36.4	2,399.7	187.4	3.9	1.7	2,714.5
2016	4.9	9.5	24.0	49.1	37.3	2,457.2	191.9	4.0	1.7	2,779.6
2017	5.0	9.8	24.7	50.6	38.4	2,529.2	197.5	4.1	1.8	2,861.0
2018	5.2	10.1	25.7	52.4	39.8	2,623.1	204.9	4.3	1.8	2,967.2
2019	5.4	10.6	26.8	54.9	41.6	2,744.2	214.3	4.5	1.9	3,104.2

INDUSTRY: HARDWARE STORES (NAICS 44413)
PRODUCT LINE: FURNITURE (Main Category)

NAICS 44413: Hardware Stores. Establishments primarily engaged
in the retail sale of a number of basic hardware lines, such as tools,
builders' hardware, paint and glass, housewares and household appliances,
and cutlery.

5-YEAR TREND – ESTIMATED INDUSTRY SALES ($MILLIONS)

Year	Employee Size of Establishment									Total
	1-4 Emps.	5-9 Emps.	10-19 Emps.	20-49 Emps.	50-99 Emps.	100-249 Emps.	250-499 Emps.	500-999 Emps.	Unknown Emps.	Industry Sales
2015	27.8	47.1	94.8	135.5	26.9	8.8	1.6	0.1	2.4	344.9
2016	28.0	47.6	95.7	136.8	27.2	8.9	1.6	0.1	2.5	348.2
2017	28.5	48.3	97.2	138.9	27.6	9.0	1.6	0.1	2.5	353.7
2018	29.6	50.2	101.1	144.5	28.7	9.4	1.7	0.1	2.6	367.8
2019	31.1	52.7	106.1	151.6	30.1	9.8	1.7	0.1	2.7	386.0

INDUSTRY: WOMEN'S CLOTHING STORES INDUSTRY (NAICS 44812)
PRODUCT LINE: FURNITURE (Main Category)

NAICS 44812: Women's Clothing Stores . this industry comprises
establishments primarily engaged in retailing a general line of new
women's, misses' and juniors' clothing, including maternity wear.
These establishments may provide basic alterations, such as hemming,
taking in or letting out seams, or lengthening or shortening sleeves.

5-YEAR TREND – ESTIMATED INDUSTRY SALES ($MILLIONS)

Year	Employee Size of Establishment									Total
	1-4 Emps.	5-9 Emps.	10-19 Emps.	20-49 Emps.	50-99 Emps.	100-249 Emps.	250-499 Emps.	500-999 Emps.	Unknown Emps.	Industry Sales
2015	2.0	4.5	9.6	6.8	2.4	2.2	0.9	0.9	0.5	29.8
2016	2.1	4.6	9.9	7.0	2.5	2.3	0.9	0.9	0.5	30.7
2017	2.2	4.8	10.3	7.2	2.6	2.4	1.0	0.9	0.5	31.7
2018	2.3	5.1	10.8	7.6	2.7	2.5	1.0	1.0	0.5	33.5
2019	2.4	5.4	11.5	8.1	2.9	2.7	1.1	1.0	0.5	35.6

NAICS 44814: Family Clothing Stores . this industry comprises
establishments primarily engaged in retailing a general line of new clothing
for men, women, and children, without specializing in sales for an individual
gender or age group. These establishments may provide basic alterations,
such as hemming, taking in or letting out seams, or lengthening or shortening sleeves.

5-YEAR TREND – ESTIMATED INDUSTRY SALES ($MILLIONS)

Year	Employee Size of Establishment									Total
	1-4 Emps.	5-9 Emps.	10-19 Emps.	20-49 Emps.	50-99 Emps.	100-249 Emps.	250-499 Emps.	500-999 Emps.	Unknown Emps.	Industry Sales
2015	0.3	0.7	2.6	8.5	7.5	2.1	1.9	1.1	0.1	24.8
2016	0.3	0.7	2.6	8.7	7.7	2.1	2.0	1.2	0.1	25.4
2017	0.3	0.7	2.7	9.0	7.9	2.2	2.1	1.2	0.1	26.2
2018	0.4	0.8	2.9	9.5	8.4	2.3	2.2	1.3	0.1	27.6
2019	0.4	0.8	3.0	10.1	8.9	2.4	2.3	1.3	0.1	29.4

INDUSTRY: DEPARTMENT STORES INDUSTRY (NAICS 45211)
PRODUCT LINE: FURNITURE (Main Category)

NAICS 45211: Department Stores Industry . this industry comprises
establishments known as department stores primarily engaged in retailing
a wide range of the following new products with no one merchandise line
predominating: apparel, furniture, appliances and home furnishings; and
selected additional items, such as paint, hardware, toiletries, cosmetics,
photographic equipment, jewelry, toys, and sporting goods. merchandise lines
are normally arranged in separate departments.

5-YEAR TREND – ESTIMATED INDUSTRY SALES ($MILLIONS)

Year	Employee Size of Establishment									Total
	1-4 Emps.	5-9 Emps.	10-19 Emps.	20-49 Emps.	50-99 Emps.	100-249 Emps.	250-499 Emps.	500-999 Emps.	Unknown Emps.	Industry Sales
2015	0.1	0.1	0.3	23.6	428.3	1,375.4	569.4	82.4	3.5	2,483.1
2016	0.1	0.1	0.3	23.7	430.0	1,380.8	571.6	82.7	3.5	2,492.8
2017	0.1	0.1	0.3	23.9	434.3	1,394.4	577.2	83.5	3.5	2,517.4
2018	0.1	0.1	0.3	23.9	434.3	1,394.6	577.3	83.7	3.5	2,518.0
2019	0.1	0.1	0.3	24.2	438.6	1,408.4	583.0	84.7	3.6	2,543.0

INDUSTRY: WAREHOUSE CLUBS & SUPERCENTERS (NAICS 45291)
PRODUCT LINE: FURNITURE (Main Category)

NAICS 45291: Warehouse Clubs and Superstores This industry comprises establishments known as warehouse clubs, superstores or supercenters primarily engaged in retailing a general line of groceries in combination with general lines of new merchandise, such as apparel, furniture, and appliances.

5-YEAR TREND – ESTIMATED INDUSTRY SALES ($MILLIONS)

Year	Employee Size of Establishment									Total
	1-4 Emps.	5-9 Emps.	10-19 Emps.	20-49 Emps.	50-99 Emps.	100-249 Emps.	250-499 Emps.	500-999 Emps.	Unknown Emps.	Industry Sales
2015	0.3	0.1	0.3	9.8	18.7	1,066.2	4,693.5	118.3	1.8	5,908.8
2016	0.3	0.1	0.3	10.1	19.2	1,095.5	4,822.8	121.5	1.8	6,071.7
2017	0.3	0.1	0.3	10.4	19.8	1,131.3	4,980.3	125.5	1.9	6,270.0
2018	0.4	0.1	0.3	11.2	21.3	1,217.6	5,360.0	135.1	2.0	6,747.9
2019	0.4	0.1	0.3	11.9	22.6	1,289.7	5,677.5	143.1	2.2	7,147.7

INDUSTRY: OFFICE SUPPLIES & STATIONERY STORES (NAICS 45321)
PRODUCT LINE: FURNITURE (Main Category)

NAICS 45321: Office Supplies and Stationery Stores . this industry comprises establishments primarily engaged in one or more of the following: (1) retailing new stationery, school supplies, and office supplies; (2) selling a combination of new office equipment, furniture, and supplies; and (3) selling new office equipment, furniture, and supplies in combination with selling new computers.

5-YEAR TREND – ESTIMATED INDUSTRY SALES ($MILLIONS)

Year	Employee Size of Establishment									Total
	1-4 Emps.	5-9 Emps.	10-19 Emps.	20-49 Emps.	50-99 Emps.	100-249 Emps.	250-499 Emps.	500-999 Emps.	Unknown Emps.	Industry Sales
2015	61.5	49.4	316.4	792.0	16.5	11.1	0.1	0.5	15.1	1,262.7
2016	61.0	49.0	313.8	785.4	16.4	11.0	0.1	0.5	15.0	1,252.3
2017	60.8	48.8	313.1	783.6	16.4	11.0	0.1	0.5	15.0	1,249.4
2018	58.9	47.3	302.9	758.2	15.8	10.7	0.1	0.5	14.5	1,208.9
2019	57.5	46.2	296.1	741.0	15.5	10.4	0.1	0.5	14.2	1,181.5

INDUSTRY: ELECTRONIC SHOPPING & MAIL-ORDER (NAICS 45411)
PRODUCT LINE: FURNITURE (Main Category)

NAICS 45411: Electronic Shopping and Mail-Order Houses This industry comprises establishments primarily engaged in retailing all types of merchandise by means of mail or by electronic media, such as interactive television or computer. Included in this industry are establishments primarily engaged in retailing from catalogue showrooms of mail-order houses.

5-YEAR TREND – ESTIMATED INDUSTRY SALES ($MILLIONS)

Year	Employee Size of Establishment									Total
	1-4 Emps.	5-9 Emps.	10-19 Emps.	20-49 Emps.	50-99 Emps.	100-249 Emps.	250-499 Emps.	500-999 Emps.	Unknown Emps.	Industry Sales
2015	509.8	262.6	379.4	636.9	479.4	886.9	1,195.7	1,687.8	71.7	6,110.1
2016	539.2	277.8	401.3	673.6	507.0	938.1	1,264.7	1,785.3	75.8	6,462.7
2017	571.7	294.5	425.5	714.2	537.6	994.6	1,340.9	1,892.8	80.4	6,852.0
2018	640.7	330.0	476.8	800.4	602.5	1,114.6	1,502.7	2,082.8	90.1	7,640.7
2019	712.3	366.9	530.2	889.9	669.8	1,239.2	1,670.7	2,280.9	100.1	8,460.1

INDUSTRY: DEPARTMENT STORES INDUSTRY (NAICS 45211)
PRODUCT LINE: UPHOLSTERED FURNITURE (Sub Category)

NAICS 45211: Department Stores Industry . this industry comprises establishments known as department stores primarily engaged in retailing a wide range of the following new products with no one merchandise line predominating: apparel, furniture, appliances and home furnishings; and selected additional items, such as paint, hardware, toiletries, cosmetics, photographic equipment, jewelry, toys, and sporting goods. merchandise lines are normally arranged in separate departments.

5-YEAR TREND – ESTIMATED INDUSTRY SALES ($MILLIONS)

Year	Employee Size of Establishment									Total
	1-4 Emps.	5-9 Emps.	10-19 Emps.	20-49 Emps.	50-99 Emps.	100-249 Emps.	250-499 Emps.	500-999 Emps.	Unknown Emps.	Industry Sales
2015	0.0	0.0	0.0	3.3	59.3	190.5	78.9	11.4	0.5	344.0
2016	0.0	0.0	0.0	3.3	59.6	191.3	79.2	11.5	0.5	345.3
2017	0.0	0.0	0.0	3.3	60.2	193.2	80.0	11.6	0.5	348.7
2018	0.0	0.0	0.0	3.3	60.2	193.2	80.0	11.6	0.5	348.8
2019	0.0	0.0	0.0	3.3	60.8	195.1	80.8	11.7	0.5	352.3

INDUSTRY: WAREHOUSE CLUBS & SUPERCENTERS (NAICS 45291)
PRODUCT LINE: UPHOLSTERED FURNITURE (Sub Category)

NAICS 45291: Warehouse Clubs and Superstores This industry comprises establishments known as warehouse clubs, superstores or supercenters primarily engaged in retailing a general line of groceries in combination with general lines of new merchandise, such as apparel, furniture, and appliances.

5-YEAR TREND — ESTIMATED INDUSTRY SALES ($MILLIONS)

Year	Employee Size of Establishment									Total
	1-4 Emps.	5-9 Emps.	10-19 Emps.	20-49 Emps.	50-99 Emps.	100-249 Emps.	250-499 Emps.	500-999 Emps.	Unknown Emps.	Industry Sales
2015	0.0	0.0	0.0	0.4	0.7	38.0	167.3	4.2	0.1	210.7
2016	0.0	0.0	0.0	0.4	0.7	39.1	171.9	4.3	0.1	216.5
2017	0.0	0.0	0.0	0.4	0.7	40.3	177.6	4.5	0.1	223.5
2018	0.0	0.0	0.0	0.4	0.8	43.4	191.1	4.8	0.1	240.6
2019	0.0	0.0	0.0	0.4	0.8	46.0	202.4	5.1	0.1	254.8

INDUSTRY: DEPARTMENT STORES INDUSTRY (NAICS 45211)
PRODUCT LINE: SLEEP SOFAS & FUTONS (Sub Category)

NAICS 45211: Department Stores Industry . this industry comprises establishments known as department stores primarily engaged in retailing a wide range of the following new products with no one merchandise line predominating: apparel, furniture, appliances and home furnishings; and selected additional items, such as paint, hardware, toiletries, cosmetics, photographic equipment, jewelry, toys, and sporting goods. merchandise lines are normally arranged in separate departments.

5-YEAR TREND — ESTIMATED INDUSTRY SALES ($MILLIONS)

Year	Employee Size of Establishment									Total
	1-4 Emps.	5-9 Emps.	10-19 Emps.	20-49 Emps.	50-99 Emps.	100-249 Emps.	250-499 Emps.	500-999 Emps.	Unknown Emps.	Industry Sales
2015	0.0	0.0	0.0	0.4	6.4	20.6	8.5	1.2	0.1	37.2
2016	0.0	0.0	0.0	0.4	6.4	20.7	8.6	1.2	0.1	37.3
2017	0.0	0.0	0.0	0.4	6.5	20.9	8.6	1.2	0.1	37.7
2018	0.0	0.0	0.0	0.4	6.5	20.9	8.6	1.3	0.1	37.7
2019	0.0	0.0	0.0	0.4	6.6	21.1	8.7	1.3	0.1	38.1

INDUSTRY: WAREHOUSE CLUBS & SUPERCENTERS (NAICS 45291)
PRODUCT LINE: SLEEP SOFAS & FUTONS (Sub Category)

NAICS 45291: Warehouse Clubs and Superstores This industry comprises establishments known as warehouse clubs, superstores or supercenters primarily engaged in retailing a general line of groceries in combination with general lines of new merchandise, such as apparel, furniture, and appliances.

5-YEAR TREND – ESTIMATED INDUSTRY SALES ($MILLIONS)

Year	Employee Size of Establishment									Total
	1-4 Emps.	5-9 Emps.	10-19 Emps.	20-49 Emps.	50-99 Emps.	100-249 Emps.	250-499 Emps.	500-999 Emps.	Unknown Emps.	Industry Sales
2015	0.0	0.0	0.0	0.3	0.5	30.0	132.0	3.3	0.1	166.2
2016	0.0	0.0	0.0	0.3	0.5	30.8	135.6	3.4	0.1	170.7
2017	0.0	0.0	0.0	0.3	0.6	31.8	140.0	3.5	0.1	176.3
2018	0.0	0.0	0.0	0.3	0.6	34.2	150.7	3.8	0.1	189.8
2019	0.0	0.0	0.0	0.3	0.6	36.3	159.7	4.0	0.1	201.0

INDUSTRY: DEPARTMENT STORES INDUSTRY (NAICS 45211)
PRODUCT LINE: MATTRESSES & SLEEP FURNITURE (Sub Category)

NAICS 45211: Department Stores Industry . this industry comprises establishments known as department stores primarily engaged in retailing a wide range of the following new products with no one merchandise line predominating: apparel, furniture, appliances and home furnishings; and selected additional items, such as paint, hardware, toiletries, cosmetics, photographic equipment, jewelry, toys, and sporting goods. merchandise lines are normally arranged in separate departments.

5-YEAR TREND – ESTIMATED INDUSTRY SALES ($MILLIONS)

Year	Employee Size of Establishment									Total
	1-4 Emps.	5-9 Emps.	10-19 Emps.	20-49 Emps.	50-99 Emps.	100-249 Emps.	250-499 Emps.	500-999 Emps.	Unknown Emps.	Industry Sales
2015	0.0	0.0	0.0	2.9	52.2	167.6	69.4	10.0	0.4	302.5
2016	0.0	0.0	0.0	2.9	52.4	168.2	69.6	10.1	0.4	303.7
2017	0.0	0.0	0.0	2.9	52.9	169.9	70.3	10.2	0.4	306.7
2018	0.0	0.0	0.0	2.9	52.9	169.9	70.3	10.2	0.4	306.7
2019	0.0	0.0	0.0	2.9	53.4	171.6	71.0	10.3	0.4	309.8

INDUSTRY: WAREHOUSE CLUBS & SUPERCENTERS (NAICS 45291)
PRODUCT LINE: MATTRESSES & SLEEP FURNITURE (Sub Category)

NAICS 45291: Warehouse Clubs and Superstores This industry comprises establishments known as warehouse clubs, superstores or supercenters primarily engaged in retailing a general line of groceries in combination with general lines of new merchandise, such as apparel, furniture, and appliances.

5-YEAR TREND – ESTIMATED INDUSTRY SALES ($MILLIONS)

Year	Employee Size of Establishment									Total
	1-4 Emps.	5-9 Emps.	10-19 Emps.	20-49 Emps.	50-99 Emps.	100-249 Emps.	250-499 Emps.	500-999 Emps.	Unknown Emps.	Industry Sales
2015	0.1	0.0	0.1	2.4	4.5	256.6	1,129.6	28.5	0.4	1,422.1
2016	0.1	0.0	0.1	2.4	4.6	263.7	1,160.7	29.2	0.4	1,461.3
2017	0.1	0.0	0.1	2.5	4.8	272.3	1,198.7	30.2	0.5	1,509.0
2018	0.1	0.0	0.1	2.7	5.1	293.0	1,290.0	32.5	0.5	1,624.1
2019	0.1	0.0	0.1	2.9	5.4	310.4	1,366.4	34.4	0.5	1,720.3

INDUSTRY: DEPARTMENT STORES INDUSTRY (NAICS 45211)
PRODUCT LINE: OTHER HOME FURNITURE (Sub Category)

NAICS 45211: Department Stores Industry . this industry comprises establishments known as department stores primarily engaged in retailing a wide range of the following new products with no one merchandise line predominating: apparel, furniture, appliances and home furnishings; and selected additional items, such as paint, hardware, toiletries, cosmetics, photographic equipment, jewelry, toys, and sporting goods. merchandise lines are normally arranged in separate departments.

5-YEAR TREND – ESTIMATED INDUSTRY SALES ($MILLIONS)

Year	Employee Size of Establishment									Total
	1-4 Emps.	5-9 Emps.	10-19 Emps.	20-49 Emps.	50-99 Emps.	100-249 Emps.	250-499 Emps.	500-999 Emps.	Unknown Emps.	Industry Sales
2015	0.0	0.0	0.1	5.5	99.2	318.6	131.9	19.1	0.8	575.1
2016	0.0	0.0	0.1	5.5	99.6	319.8	132.4	19.2	0.8	577.4
2017	0.0	0.0	0.1	5.5	100.6	323.0	133.7	19.3	0.8	583.1
2018	0.0	0.0	0.1	5.5	100.6	323.0	133.7	19.4	0.8	583.2
2019	0.0	0.0	0.1	5.6	101.6	326.2	135.0	19.6	0.8	589.0

INDUSTRY: WAREHOUSE CLUBS & SUPERCENTERS (NAICS 45291)
PRODUCT LINE: OTHER HOME FURNITURE (Sub Category)

NAICS 45291: Warehouse Clubs and Superstores This industry comprises establishments known as warehouse clubs, superstores or supercenters primarily engaged in retailing a general line of groceries in combination with general lines of new merchandise, such as apparel, furniture, and appliances.

5-YEAR TREND – ESTIMATED INDUSTRY SALES ($MILLIONS)

Year	Employee Size of Establishment									Total
	1-4 Emps.	5-9 Emps.	10-19 Emps.	20-49 Emps.	50-99 Emps.	100-249 Emps.	250-499 Emps.	500-999 Emps.	Unknown Emps.	Industry Sales
2015	0.0	0.0	0.0	0.8	1.5	87.6	385.6	9.7	0.1	485.4
2016	0.0	0.0	0.0	0.8	1.6	90.0	396.2	10.0	0.2	498.8
2017	0.0	0.0	0.0	0.9	1.6	92.9	409.1	10.3	0.2	515.1
2018	0.0	0.0	0.0	0.9	1.8	100.0	440.3	11.1	0.2	554.3
2019	0.0	0.0	0.0	1.0	1.9	105.9	466.4	11.8	0.2	587.2

INDUSTRY: DEPARTMENT STORES INDUSTRY (NAICS 45211)
PRODUCT LINE: OTHER OFFICE FURNITURE (Sub Category)

NAICS 45211: Department Stores Industry . this industry comprises establishments known as department stores primarily engaged in retailing a wide range of the following new products with no one merchandise line predominating: apparel, furniture, appliances and home furnishings; and selected additional items, such as paint, hardware, toiletries, cosmetics, photographic equipment, jewelry, toys, and sporting goods. merchandise lines are normally arranged in separate departments.

5-YEAR TREND – ESTIMATED INDUSTRY SALES ($MILLIONS)

Year	Employee Size of Establishment									Total
	1-4 Emps.	5-9 Emps.	10-19 Emps.	20-49 Emps.	50-99 Emps.	100-249 Emps.	250-499 Emps.	500-999 Emps.	Unknown Emps.	Industry Sales
2015	0.1	0.1	0.1	11.6	211.2	678.2	280.7	40.6	1.7	1,224.4
2016	0.1	0.1	0.1	11.7	212.0	680.9	281.8	40.8	1.7	1,229.2
2017	0.1	0.1	0.1	11.8	214.1	687.6	284.6	41.2	1.7	1,241.3
2018	0.1	0.1	0.1	11.8	214.2	687.7	284.7	41.3	1.7	1,241.6
2019	0.1	0.1	0.1	11.9	216.3	694.5	287.5	41.8	1.8	1,253.9

INDUSTRY: WAREHOUSE CLUBS & SUPERCENTERS (NAICS 45291)
PRODUCT LINE: OTHER OFFICE FURNITURE (Sub Category)

NAICS 45291: Warehouse Clubs and Superstores This industry comprises establishments known as warehouse clubs, superstores or supercenters primarily engaged in retailing a general line of groceries in combination with general lines of new merchandise, such as apparel, furniture, and appliances.

5-Year Trend — Estimated Industry Sales ($Millions)

Year	Employee Size of Establishment									Total
	1-4 Emps.	5-9 Emps.	10-19 Emps.	20-49 Emps.	50-99 Emps.	100-249 Emps.	250-499 Emps.	500-999 Emps.	Unknown Emps.	Industry Sales
2015	0.2	0.1	0.2	6.0	11.5	654.0	2,879.0	72.5	1.1	3,624.5
2016	0.2	0.1	0.2	6.2	11.8	672.0	2,958.3	74.5	1.1	3,724.4
2017	0.2	0.1	0.2	6.4	12.2	693.9	3,054.9	77.0	1.2	3,846.0
2018	0.2	0.1	0.2	6.9	13.1	746.8	3,287.8	82.8	1.3	4,139.2
2019	0.2	0.1	0.2	7.3	13.9	791.1	3,482.6	87.8	1.3	4,384.4

INDUSTRY: HOME CENTERS INDUSTRY (NAICS 44411)
PRODUCT LINE: FLOORING & COVERINGS (Main Category)

NAICS 44411: Home Centers. This industry comprises establishments known as home centers primarily engaged in retailing a general line of new home repair and improvement materials and supplies, such as lumber, plumbing goods, electrical goods, tools, housewares, hardware, and lawn and garden supplies, with no one merchandise line predominating. The merchandise lines are normally arranged in separate departments.

5-Year Trend — Estimated Industry Sales ($Millions)

Year	Employee Size of Establishment									Total
	1-4 Emps.	5-9 Emps.	10-19 Emps.	20-49 Emps.	50-99 Emps.	100-249 Emps.	250-499 Emps.	500-999 Emps.	Unknown Emps.	Industry Sales
2015	15.4	30.0	76.1	155.5	118.0	7,778.8	607.5	12.6	5.4	8,799.4
2016	15.8	30.7	77.9	159.3	120.8	7,965.4	622.1	13.0	5.5	9,010.4
2017	16.2	31.6	80.2	163.9	124.3	8,198.6	640.3	13.3	5.7	9,274.2
2018	16.9	32.8	83.1	170.0	129.0	8,503.0	664.1	13.8	5.9	9,618.6
2019	17.6	34.3	87.0	177.9	134.9	8,895.7	694.7	14.5	6.2	10,062.7

INDUSTRY: HARDWARE STORES (NAICS 44413)
PRODUCT LINE: FLOORING & COVERINGS (Main Category)

NAICS 44413: Hardware Stores. Establishments primarily engaged
in the retail sale of a number of basic hardware lines, such as tools,
builders' hardware, paint and glass, housewares and household appliances,
and cutlery.

5-YEAR TREND – ESTIMATED INDUSTRY SALES ($MILLIONS)

Year	Employee Size of Establishment									Total
	1-4 Emps.	5-9 Emps.	10-19 Emps.	20-49 Emps.	50-99 Emps.	100-249 Emps.	250-499 Emps.	500-999 Emps.	Unknown Emps.	Industry Sales
2015	6.3	10.7	21.5	30.7	6.1	2.0	0.4	0.0	0.6	78.2
2016	6.4	10.8	21.7	31.0	6.2	2.0	0.4	0.0	0.6	79.0
2017	6.5	11.0	22.0	31.5	6.3	2.0	0.4	0.0	0.6	80.2
2018	6.7	11.4	22.9	32.8	6.5	2.1	0.4	0.0	0.6	83.4
2019	7.1	12.0	24.1	34.4	6.8	2.2	0.4	0.0	0.6	87.5

INDUSTRY: DEPARTMENT STORES INDUSTRY (NAICS 45211)
PRODUCT LINE: FLOORING & COVERINGS (Main Category)

NAICS 45211: Department Stores Industry . this industry comprises
establishments known as department stores primarily engaged in retailing
a wide range of the following new products with no one merchandise line
predominating: apparel, furniture, appliances and home furnishings; and
selected additional items, such as paint, hardware, toiletries, cosmetics,
photographic equipment, jewelry, toys, and sporting goods. merchandise lines
are normally arranged in separate departments.

5-YEAR TREND – ESTIMATED INDUSTRY SALES ($MILLIONS)

Year	Employee Size of Establishment									Total
	1-4 Emps.	5-9 Emps.	10-19 Emps.	20-49 Emps.	50-99 Emps.	100-249 Emps.	250-499 Emps.	500-999 Emps.	Unknown Emps.	Industry Sales
2015	0.0	0.0	0.0	3.7	67.7	217.4	90.0	13.0	0.6	392.4
2016	0.0	0.0	0.0	3.7	68.0	218.2	90.3	13.1	0.6	394.0
2017	0.0	0.0	0.0	3.8	68.6	220.4	91.2	13.2	0.6	397.8
2018	0.0	0.0	0.0	3.8	68.6	220.4	91.2	13.2	0.6	397.9
2019	0.0	0.0	0.0	3.8	69.3	222.6	92.1	13.4	0.6	401.9

INDUSTRY: WAREHOUSE CLUBS & SUPERCENTERS (NAICS 45291)
PRODUCT LINE: FLOORING & COVERINGS (Main Category)

NAICS 45291: Warehouse Clubs and Superstores This industry comprises establishments known as warehouse clubs, superstores or supercenters primarily engaged in retailing a general line of groceries in combination with general lines of new merchandise, such as apparel, furniture, and appliances.

5-YEAR TREND – ESTIMATED INDUSTRY SALES ($MILLIONS)

Year	Employee Size of Establishment									Total
	1-4 Emps.	5-9 Emps.	10-19 Emps.	20-49 Emps.	50-99 Emps.	100-249 Emps.	250-499 Emps.	500-999 Emps.	Unknown Emps.	Industry Sales
2015	0.0	0.0	0.0	0.1	0.2	13.1	57.5	1.5	0.0	72.4
2016	0.0	0.0	0.0	0.1	0.2	13.4	59.1	1.5	0.0	74.4
2017	0.0	0.0	0.0	0.1	0.2	13.9	61.1	1.5	0.0	76.9
2018	0.0	0.0	0.0	0.1	0.3	14.9	65.7	1.7	0.0	82.7
2019	0.0	0.0	0.0	0.1	0.3	15.8	69.6	1.8	0.0	87.6

INDUSTRY: ELECTRONIC SHOPPING & MAIL-ORDER (NAICS 45411)
PRODUCT LINE: FLOORING & COVERINGS (Main Category)

NAICS 45411: Electronic Shopping and Mail-Order Houses This industry comprises establishments primarily engaged in retailing all types of merchandise by means of mail or by electronic media, such as interactive television or computer. Included in this industry are establishments primarily engaged in retailing from catalogue showrooms of mail-order houses.

5-YEAR TREND – ESTIMATED INDUSTRY SALES ($MILLIONS)

Year	Employee Size of Establishment									Total
	1-4 Emps.	5-9 Emps.	10-19 Emps.	20-49 Emps.	50-99 Emps.	100-249 Emps.	250-499 Emps.	500-999 Emps.	Unknown Emps.	Industry Sales
2015	88.1	45.4	65.5	110.0	82.8	153.2	206.6	291.6	12.4	1,055.6
2016	93.2	48.0	69.3	116.4	87.6	162.1	218.5	308.4	13.1	1,116.5
2017	98.8	50.9	73.5	123.4	92.9	171.8	231.7	327.0	13.9	1,183.8
2018	110.7	57.0	82.4	138.3	104.1	192.6	259.6	359.8	15.6	1,320.0
2019	123.1	63.4	91.6	153.7	115.7	214.1	288.6	394.1	17.3	1,461.6

INDUSTRY: HOME CENTERS INDUSTRY (NAICS 44411)
PRODUCT LINE: SOFT FLOOR COVERINGS (Sub Category)

NAICS 44411: Home Centers. This industry comprises establishments known as home centers primarily engaged in retailing a general line of new home repair and improvement materials and supplies, such as lumber, plumbing goods, electrical goods, tools, housewares, hardware, and lawn and garden supplies, with no one merchandise line predominating. The merchandise lines are normally arranged in separate departments.

5-Year Trend – Estimated Industry Sales ($Millions)

Year	Employee Size of Establishment									Total
	1-4 Emps.	5-9 Emps.	10-19 Emps.	20-49 Emps.	50-99 Emps.	100-249 Emps.	250-499 Emps.	500-999 Emps.	Unknown Emps.	Industry Sales
2015	5.5	10.7	27.0	55.3	41.9	2,764.2	215.9	4.5	1.9	3,126.8
2016	5.6	10.9	27.7	56.6	42.9	2,830.5	221.1	4.6	2.0	3,201.8
2017	5.8	11.2	28.5	58.3	44.2	2,913.3	227.5	4.7	2.0	3,295.6
2018	6.0	11.6	29.5	60.4	45.8	3,021.5	236.0	4.9	2.1	3,417.9
2019	6.3	12.2	30.9	63.2	47.9	3,161.0	246.9	5.1	2.2	3,575.7

INDUSTRY: HOME CENTERS INDUSTRY (NAICS 44413)
PRODUCT LINE: SOFT FLOOR COVERINGS (Sub Category)

NAICS 44411: Home Centers. This industry comprises establishments known as home centers primarily engaged in retailing a general line of new home repair and improvement materials and supplies, such as lumber, plumbing goods, electrical goods, tools, housewares, hardware, and lawn and garden supplies, with no one merchandise line predominating. The merchandise lines are normally arranged in separate departments.

5-Year Trend – Estimated Industry Sales ($Millions)

Year	Employee Size of Establishment									Total
	1-4 Emps.	5-9 Emps.	10-19 Emps.	20-49 Emps.	50-99 Emps.	100-249 Emps.	250-499 Emps.	500-999 Emps.	Unknown Emps.	Industry Sales
2015	2.3	4.0	8.0	11.5	2.3	0.7	0.1	0.0	0.2	29.2
2016	2.4	4.0	8.1	11.6	2.3	0.7	0.1	0.0	0.2	29.5
2017	2.4	4.1	8.2	11.8	2.3	0.8	0.1	0.0	0.2	29.9
2018	2.5	4.2	8.5	12.2	2.4	0.8	0.1	0.0	0.2	31.1
2019	2.6	4.5	9.0	12.8	2.5	0.8	0.1	0.0	0.2	32.6

INDUSTRY: DEPARTMENT STORES INDUSTRY (NAICS 45211)
PRODUCT LINE: SOFT FLOOR COVERINGS (Sub Category)

NAICS 45211: Department Stores Industry . this industry comprises establishments known as department stores primarily engaged in retailing a wide range of the following new products with no one merchandise line predominating: apparel, furniture, appliances and home furnishings; and selected additional items, such as paint, hardware, toiletries, cosmetics, photographic equipment, jewelry, toys, and sporting goods. merchandise lines are normally arranged in separate departments.

5-YEAR TREND – ESTIMATED INDUSTRY SALES ($MILLIONS)

| Year | Employee Size of Establishment | | | | | | | | | Total |
	1-4 Emps.	5-9 Emps.	10-19 Emps.	20-49 Emps.	50-99 Emps.	100-249 Emps.	250-499 Emps.	500-999 Emps.	Unknown Emps.	Industry Sales
2015	0.0	0.0	0.0	3.6	65.9	211.5	87.5	12.7	0.5	381.8
2016	0.0	0.0	0.0	3.6	66.1	212.3	87.9	12.7	0.5	383.3
2017	0.0	0.0	0.0	3.7	66.8	214.4	88.8	12.8	0.5	387.1
2018	0.0	0.0	0.0	3.7	66.8	214.4	88.8	12.9	0.5	387.1
2019	0.0	0.0	0.0	3.7	67.4	216.6	89.6	13.0	0.6	391.0

INDUSTRY: WAREHOUSE CLUBS & SUPERCENTERS (NAICS 45291)
PRODUCT LINE: SOFT FLOOR COVERINGS (Sub Category)

NAICS 45291: Warehouse Clubs and Superstores This industry comprises establishments known as warehouse clubs, superstores or supercenters primarily engaged in retailing a general line of groceries in combination with general lines of new merchandise, such as apparel, furniture, and appliances.

5-YEAR TREND – ESTIMATED INDUSTRY SALES ($MILLIONS)

| Year | Employee Size of Establishment | | | | | | | | | Total |
	1-4 Emps.	5-9 Emps.	10-19 Emps.	20-49 Emps.	50-99 Emps.	100-249 Emps.	250-499 Emps.	500-999 Emps.	Unknown Emps.	Industry Sales
2015	0.0	0.0	0.0	0.1	0.2	12.1	53.4	1.3	0.0	67.2
2016	0.0	0.0	0.0	0.1	0.2	12.5	54.9	1.4	0.0	69.1
2017	0.0	0.0	0.0	0.1	0.2	12.9	56.6	1.4	0.0	71.3
2018	0.0	0.0	0.0	0.1	0.2	13.8	61.0	1.5	0.0	76.7
2019	0.0	0.0	0.0	0.1	0.3	14.7	64.6	1.6	0.0	81.3

INDUSTRY: HOME CENTERS INDUSTRY (NAICS 44411)
PRODUCT LINE: HARDWOOD FLOORING (Sub Category)

NAICS 44411: Home Centers. This industry comprises establishments
known as home centers primarily engaged in retailing a general line of
new home repair and improvement materials and supplies, such as
lumber, plumbing goods, electrical goods, tools, housewares, hardware,
and lawn and garden supplies, with no one merchandise line predominating.
The merchandise lines are normally arranged in separate departments.

5-YEAR TREND – ESTIMATED INDUSTRY SALES ($MILLIONS)

Year	Employee Size of Establishment									Total
	1-4 Emps.	5-9 Emps.	10-19 Emps.	20-49 Emps.	50-99 Emps.	100-249 Emps.	250-499 Emps.	500-999 Emps.	Unknown Emps.	Industry Sales
2015	0.9	1.7	4.3	8.7	6.6	436.0	34.0	0.7	0.3	493.2
2016	0.9	1.7	4.4	8.9	6.8	446.4	34.9	0.7	0.3	505.0
2017	0.9	1.8	4.5	9.2	7.0	459.5	35.9	0.7	0.3	519.8
2018	0.9	1.8	4.7	9.5	7.2	476.5	37.2	0.8	0.3	539.1
2019	1.0	1.9	4.9	10.0	7.6	498.6	38.9	0.8	0.3	564.0

INDUSTRY: HARDWARE STORES INDUSTRY (NAICS 44413)
PRODUCT LINE: HARDWOOD FLOORING (Sub Category)

NAICS 44413: Hardware Stores. Establishments primarily engaged
in the retail sale of a number of basic hardware lines, such as tools,
builders' hardware, paint and glass, housewares and household appliances,
and cutlery.

5-YEAR TREND – ESTIMATED INDUSTRY SALES ($MILLIONS)

Year	Employee Size of Establishment									Total
	1-4 Emps.	5-9 Emps.	10-19 Emps.	20-49 Emps.	50-99 Emps.	100-249 Emps.	250-499 Emps.	500-999 Emps.	Unknown Emps.	Industry Sales
2015	0.7	1.2	2.4	3.4	0.7	0.2	0.0	0.0	0.1	8.7
2016	0.7	1.2	2.4	3.5	0.7	0.2	0.0	0.0	0.1	8.8
2017	0.7	1.2	2.5	3.5	0.7	0.2	0.0	0.0	0.1	9.0
2018	0.8	1.3	2.6	3.7	0.7	0.2	0.0	0.0	0.1	9.3
2019	0.8	1.3	2.7	3.8	0.8	0.2	0.0	0.0	0.1	9.8

INDUSTRY: HOME CENTERS INDUSTRY (NAICS 44411)
PRODUCT LINE: OTHER HARD FLOORING (Sub Category)

NAICS 44411: Home Centers. This industry comprises establishments known as home centers primarily engaged in retailing a general line of new home repair and improvement materials and supplies, such as lumber, plumbing goods, electrical goods, tools, housewares, hardware, and lawn and garden supplies, with no one merchandise line predominating. The merchandise lines are normally arranged in separate departments.

5-YEAR TREND – ESTIMATED INDUSTRY SALES ($MILLIONS)

Year	Employee Size of Establishment									Total Industry Sales
	1-4 Emps.	5-9 Emps.	10-19 Emps.	20-49 Emps.	50-99 Emps.	100-249 Emps.	250-499 Emps.	500-999 Emps.	Unknown Emps.	
2015	9.1	17.7	44.8	91.5	69.4	4,578.7	357.6	7.4	3.2	5,179.4
2016	9.3	18.1	45.8	93.7	71.1	4,688.5	366.2	7.6	3.2	5,303.6
2017	9.6	18.6	47.2	96.5	73.2	4,825.8	376.9	7.8	3.3	5,458.9
2018	9.9	19.3	48.9	100.1	75.9	5,005.0	390.9	8.1	3.5	5,661.6
2019	10.4	20.2	51.2	104.7	79.4	5,236.1	408.9	8.5	3.6	5,923.0

INDUSTRY: HARDWARE STORES INDUSTRY (NAICS 44413)
PRODUCT LINE: OTHER HARD FLOORING (Sub Category)

NAICS 44413: Hardware Stores. Establishments primarily engaged in the retail sale of a number of basic hardware lines, such as tools, builders' hardware, paint and glass, housewares and household appliances, and cutlery.

5-YEAR TREND – ESTIMATED INDUSTRY SALES ($MILLIONS)

Year	Employee Size of Establishment									Total Industry Sales
	1-4 Emps.	5-9 Emps.	10-19 Emps.	20-49 Emps.	50-99 Emps.	100-249 Emps.	250-499 Emps.	500-999 Emps.	Unknown Emps.	
2015	3.2	5.5	11.1	15.8	3.1	1.0	0.2	0.0	0.3	40.3
2016	3.3	5.6	11.2	16.0	3.2	1.0	0.2	0.0	0.3	40.7
2017	3.3	5.6	11.3	16.2	3.2	1.1	0.2	0.0	0.3	41.3
2018	3.5	5.9	11.8	16.9	3.4	1.1	0.2	0.0	0.3	42.9
2019	3.6	6.2	12.4	17.7	3.5	1.1	0.2	0.0	0.3	45.1

INDUSTRY: DEPARTMENT STORES INDUSTRY (NAICS 45211)
PRODUCT LINE: OTHER HARD FLOORING (Sub Category)

NAICS 45211: Department Stores Industry . this industry comprises establishments known as department stores primarily engaged in retailing a wide range of the following new products with no one merchandise line predominating: apparel, furniture, appliances and home furnishings; and selected additional items, such as paint, hardware, toiletries, cosmetics, photographic equipment, jewelry, toys, and sporting goods. merchandise lines are normally arranged in separate departments.

5-YEAR TREND – ESTIMATED INDUSTRY SALES ($MILLIONS)

Year	Employee Size of Establishment									Total Industry Sales
	1-4 Emps.	5-9 Emps.	10-19 Emps.	20-49 Emps.	50-99 Emps.	100-249 Emps.	250-499 Emps.	500-999 Emps.	Unknown Emps.	
2015	0.0	0.0	0.0	0.0	0.7	2.3	0.9	0.1	0.0	4.1
2016	0.0	0.0	0.0	0.0	0.7	2.3	0.9	0.1	0.0	4.1
2017	0.0	0.0	0.0	0.0	0.7	2.3	1.0	0.1	0.0	4.2
2018	0.0	0.0	0.0	0.0	0.7	2.3	1.0	0.1	0.0	4.2
2019	0.0	0.0	0.0	0.0	0.7	2.3	1.0	0.1	0.0	4.2

INDUSTRY: HOME CENTERS INDUSTRY (NAICS 44411)
PRODUCT LINE: COMPUTER HARDWARE & SOFTWARE (Main Category)

NAICS 44411: Home Centers. This industry comprises establishments known as home centers primarily engaged in retailing a general line of new home repair and improvement materials and supplies, such as lumber, plumbing goods, electrical goods, tools, housewares, hardware, and lawn and garden supplies, with no one merchandise line predominating. The merchandise lines are normally arranged in separate departments.

5-YEAR TREND – ESTIMATED INDUSTRY SALES ($MILLIONS)

Year	Employee Size of Establishment									Total Industry Sales
	1-4 Emps.	5-9 Emps.	10-19 Emps.	20-49 Emps.	50-99 Emps.	100-249 Emps.	250-499 Emps.	500-999 Emps.	Unknown Emps.	
2015	1.0	2.0	5.0	10.2	7.8	512.5	40.0	0.8	0.4	579.7
2016	1.0	2.0	5.1	10.5	8.0	524.7	41.0	0.9	0.4	593.6
2017	1.1	2.1	5.3	10.8	8.2	540.1	42.2	0.9	0.4	611.0
2018	1.1	2.2	5.5	11.2	8.5	560.2	43.7	0.9	0.4	633.7
2019	1.2	2.3	5.7	11.7	8.9	586.0	45.8	1.0	0.4	662.9

INDUSTRY: PRERECORDED TAPES/CDs STORES (NAICS 45122)
PRODUCT LINE: COMPUTER HARDWARE & SOFTWARE (Main Category)

NAICS 45122: Prerecorded Tape, Compact Disc, and Record Stores .
This industry comprises establishments primarily engaged in retailing new
prerecorded audio and video tapes, compact discs (CDs), and phonograph
records.

5-YEAR TREND – ESTIMATED INDUSTRY SALES ($MILLIONS)

Year	Employee Size of Establishment									Total
	1-4 Emps.	5-9 Emps.	10-19 Emps.	20-49 Emps.	50-99 Emps.	100-249 Emps.	250-499 Emps.	500-999 Emps.	Unknown Emps.	Industr y Sales
2015	2.7	5.2	13.2	26.9	20.4	1,347.3	105.2	2.2	0.9	1,524.1
2016	2.7	5.3	13.5	27.6	20.9	1,379.7	107.7	2.2	1.0	1,560.6
2017	2.8	5.5	13.9	28.4	21.5	1,420.0	110.9	2.3	1.0	1,606.3
2018	2.9	5.7	14.4	29.4	22.3	1,472.8	115.0	2.4	1.0	1,666.0
2019	3.1	5.9	15.1	30.8	23.4	1,540.8	120.3	2.5	1.1	1,742.9

INDUSTRY: DEPARTMENT STORES INDUSTRY (NAICS 45211)
PRODUCT LINE: COMPUTER HARDWARE & SOFTWARE (Main Category)

NAICS 45211: Department Stores Industry . this industry comprises
establishments known as department stores primarily engaged in retailing
a wide range of the following new products with no one merchandise line
predominating: apparel, furniture, appliances and home furnishings; and
selected additional items, such as paint, hardware, toiletries, cosmetics,
photographic equipment, jewelry, toys, and sporting goods. merchandise lines
are normally arranged in separate departments.

5-YEAR TREND – ESTIMATED INDUSTRY SALES ($MILLIONS)

Year	Employee Size of Establishment									Total
	1-4 Emps.	5-9 Emps.	10-19 Emps.	20-49 Emps.	50-99 Emps.	100-249 Emps.	250-499 Emps.	500-999 Emps.	Unknown Emps.	Industr y Sales
2015	0.0	0.0	0.1	5.1	92.4	296.8	122.9	17.8	0.8	535.8
2016	0.0	0.0	0.1	5.1	92.8	297.9	123.3	17.8	0.8	537.9
2017	0.0	0.0	0.1	5.2	93.7	300.9	124.5	18.0	0.8	543.2
2018	0.0	0.0	0.1	5.2	93.7	300.9	124.6	18.1	0.8	543.3
2019	0.0	0.0	0.1	5.2	94.6	303.9	125.8	18.3	0.8	548.7

INDUSTRY: WAREHOUSE CLUBS & SUPERCENTERS (NAICS 45291)
PRODUCT LINE: COMPUTER HARDWARE & SOFTWARE (Main Category)

NAICS 45291: Warehouse Clubs and Superstores This industry comprises establishments known as warehouse clubs, superstores or supercenters primarily engaged in retailing a general line of groceries in combination with general lines of new merchandise, such as apparel, furniture, and appliances.

5-YEAR TREND – ESTIMATED INDUSTRY SALES ($MILLIONS)

Year	Employee Size of Establishment									Total
	1-4 Emps.	5-9 Emps.	10-19 Emps.	20-49 Emps.	50-99 Emps.	100-249 Emps.	250-499 Emps.	500-999 Emps.	Unknown Emps.	Industry Sales
2015	0.4	0.1	0.3	12.2	23.1	1,321.9	5,819.1	146.6	2.2	7,326.0
2016	0.4	0.1	0.3	12.5	23.8	1,358.3	5,979.5	150.7	2.3	7,527.9
2017	0.4	0.1	0.4	12.9	24.6	1,402.6	6,174.8	155.6	2.4	7,773.8
2018	0.4	0.1	0.4	13.9	26.4	1,509.6	6,645.5	167.5	2.5	8,366.4
2019	0.5	0.1	0.4	14.8	28.0	1,599.0	7,039.1	177.4	2.7	8,862.0

INDUSTRY: OFFICE SUPPLY & STATIONERY STORES (NAICS 45321)
PRODUCT LINE: COMPUTER HARDWARE & SOFTWARE (Main Category)

NAICS 45321: Office Supplies and Stationery Stores . this industry comprises establishments primarily engaged in one or more of the following: (1) retailing new stationery, school supplies, and office supplies; (2) selling a combination of new office equipment, furniture, and supplies; and (3) selling new office equipment, furniture, and supplies in combination with selling new computers.

5-YEAR TREND – ESTIMATED INDUSTRY SALES ($MILLIONS)

Year	Employee Size of Establishment									Total
	1-4 Emps.	5-9 Emps.	10-19 Emps.	20-49 Emps.	50-99 Emps.	100-249 Emps.	250-499 Emps.	500-999 Emps.	Unknown Emps.	Industry Sales
2015	87.9	70.5	452.3	1,131.9	23.6	15.9	0.1	0.7	21.6	1,804.7
2016	87.2	70.0	448.5	1,122.6	23.4	15.8	0.1	0.7	21.5	1,789.7
2017	87.0	69.8	447.5	1,120.0	23.4	15.8	0.1	0.7	21.4	1,785.6
2018	84.1	67.5	433.0	1,083.6	22.6	15.2	0.1	0.7	20.7	1,727.7
2019	82.2	66.0	423.2	1,059.1	22.1	14.9	0.1	0.7	20.3	1,688.6

INDUSTRY: ELECTRONIC SHOPPING & MAIL-ORDER (NAICS 45411)
PRODUCT LINE: COMPUTER HARDWARE & SOFTWARE (Main Category)

NAICS 45411: Electronic Shopping and Mail-Order Houses This industry comprises establishments primarily engaged in retailing all types of merchandise by means of mail or by electronic media, such as interactive television or computer. Included in this industry are establishments primarily engaged in retailing from catalogue showrooms of mail-order houses.

5-YEAR TREND — ESTIMATED INDUSTRY SALES ($MILLIONS)

Year	Employee Size of Establishment									Total
	1-4 Emps.	5-9 Emps.	10-19 Emps.	20-49 Emps.	50-99 Emps.	100-249 Emps.	250-499 Emps.	500-999 Emps.	Unknown Emps.	Industry Sales
2015	5,563.2	2,865.7	4,140.5	6,949.9	5,231.4	9,678.5	13,048.3	18,419.3	781.9	66,678.7
2016	5,884.3	3,031.1	4,379.5	7,351.1	5,533.3	10,237.1	13,801.4	19,482.4	827.1	70,527.2
2017	6,238.8	3,213.7	4,643.3	7,793.9	5,866.6	10,853.8	14,632.8	20,656.1	876.9	74,775.9
2018	6,991.8	3,601.7	5,203.7	8,734.6	6,574.8	12,163.9	16,399.0	22,729.8	982.7	83,382.1
2019	7,773.5	4,004.3	5,785.5	9,711.2	7,309.8	13,523.8	18,232.5	24,891.4	1,092.6	92,324.7

INDUSTRY: BOOK STORES INDUSTRY (NAICS 451211)
PRODUCT LINE: COMPUTER HARDWARE & SOFTWARE (Main Category)

NAICS 451211: Book Stores. this industry comprises establishments primarily engaged in the retail sale of new books and magazines. Establishments primarily engaged in the retail sale of used books are classified in 5932.

5-YEAR TREND — ESTIMATED INDUSTRY SALES ($MILLIONS)

Year	Employee Size of Establishment									Total
	1-4 Emps.	5-9 Emps.	10-19 Emps.	20-49 Emps.	50-99 Emps.	100-249 Emps.	250-499 Emps.	500-999 Emps.	Unknown Emps.	Industry Sales
2015	4.1	6.2	12.4	32.9	14.3	6.6	1.6	3.9	2.1	84.0
2016	4.3	6.5	12.9	34.4	15.0	6.9	1.7	4.1	2.2	87.8
2017	4.5	6.8	13.6	36.0	15.7	7.2	1.8	4.3	2.3	92.2
2018	4.7	7.1	14.1	37.4	16.3	7.5	1.8	4.5	2.4	95.7
2019	4.9	7.4	14.7	39.1	17.0	7.8	1.9	4.7	2.5	100.1

INDUSTRY: DEPARTMENT STORES INDUSTRY (NAICS 45211)
PRODUCT LINE: COMPUTER HARDWARE & PERIPHERALS (Sub Category)

NAICS 45211: Department Stores Industry . this industry comprises establishments known as department stores primarily engaged in retailing a wide range of the following new products with no one merchandise line predominating: apparel, furniture, appliances and home furnishings; and selected additional items, such as paint, hardware, toiletries, cosmetics, photographic equipment, jewelry, toys, and sporting goods. merchandise lines are normally arranged in separate departments.

5-YEAR TREND – ESTIMATED INDUSTRY SALES ($MILLIONS)

Year	Employee Size of Establishment									Total
	1-4 Emps.	5-9 Emps.	10-19 Emps.	20-49 Emps.	50-99 Emps.	100-249 Emps.	250-499 Emps.	500-999 Emps.	Unknown Emps.	Industry Sales
2015	0.0	0.0	0.0	3.8	68.1	218.7	90.5	13.1	0.6	394.9
2016	0.0	0.0	0.0	3.8	68.4	219.6	90.9	13.1	0.6	396.4
2017	0.0	0.0	0.0	3.8	69.1	221.7	91.8	13.3	0.6	400.3
2018	0.0	0.0	0.0	3.8	69.1	221.8	91.8	13.3	0.6	400.4
2019	0.0	0.0	0.0	3.8	69.7	224.0	92.7	13.5	0.6	404.4

INDUSTRY: WAREHOUSE CLUBS & SUPERCENTERS (NAICS 45291)
PRODUCT LINE: COMPUTER HARDWARE & PERIPHERALS (Sub Category)

NAICS 45291: Warehouse Clubs and Superstores This industry comprises establishments known as warehouse clubs, superstores or supercenters primarily engaged in retailing a general line of groceries in combination with general lines of new merchandise, such as apparel, furniture, and appliances.

5-YEAR TREND – ESTIMATED INDUSTRY SALES ($MILLIONS)

Year	Employee Size of Establishment									Total
	1-4 Emps.	5-9 Emps.	10-19 Emps.	20-49 Emps.	50-99 Emps.	100-249 Emps.	250-499 Emps.	500-999 Emps.	Unknown Emps.	Industry Sales
2015	0.3	0.1	0.2	8.3	15.7	898.7	3,956.2	99.7	1.5	4,980.7
2016	0.3	0.1	0.2	8.5	16.2	923.5	4,065.3	102.4	1.5	5,118.0
2017	0.3	0.1	0.2	8.8	16.7	953.6	4,198.0	105.8	1.6	5,285.1
2018	0.3	0.1	0.3	9.5	18.0	1,026.3	4,518.0	113.8	1.7	5,688.0
2019	0.3	0.1	0.3	10.0	19.0	1,087.1	4,785.7	120.6	1.8	6,025.0

INDUSTRY: ELECTRONIC SHOPPING & MAIL-ORDER (NAICS 45411)
PRODUCT LINE: COMPUTER HARDWARE & PERIPHERALS (Sub Category)

NAICS 45411: Electronic Shopping and Mail-Order Houses This industry comprises establishments primarily engaged in retailing all types of merchandise by means of mail or by electronic media, such as interactive television or computer. Included in this industry are establishments primarily engaged in retailing from catalogue showrooms of mail-order houses.

5-YEAR TREND – ESTIMATED INDUSTRY SALES ($MILLIONS)

Year	Employee Size of Establishment									Total
	1-4 Emps.	5-9 Emps.	10-19 Emps.	20-49 Emps.	50-99 Emps.	100-249 Emps.	250-499 Emps.	500-999 Emps.	Unknown Emps.	Industry Sales
2015	5,133.3	2,644.3	3,820.5	6,412.8	4,827.1	8,930.5	12,039.9	16,995.9	721.5	61,525.8
2016	5,429.5	2,796.9	4,041.0	6,783.0	5,105.7	9,446.0	12,734.8	17,976.8	763.2	65,076.9
2017	5,756.6	2,965.4	4,284.4	7,191.6	5,413.3	10,015.0	13,502.0	19,059.8	809.1	68,997.2
2018	6,451.5	3,323.3	4,801.6	8,059.6	6,066.7	11,223.8	15,131.7	20,973.3	906.8	76,938.3
2019	7,172.8	3,694.9	5,338.4	8,960.7	6,744.9	12,478.7	16,823.5	22,967.8	1,008.2	85,189.9

INDUSTRY: BOOK STORES INDUSTRY (NAICS 451211)
PRODUCT LINE: COMPUTER HARDWARE & PERIPHERALS (Sub Category)

NAICS 451211: Book Stores. this industry comprises establishments primarily engaged in the retail sale of new books and magazines. Establishments primarily engaged in the retail sale of used books are classified in 5932.

5-YEAR TREND – ESTIMATED INDUSTRY SALES ($MILLIONS)

Year	Employee Size of Establishment									Total
	1-4 Emps.	5-9 Emps.	10-19 Emps.	20-49 Emps.	50-99 Emps.	100-249 Emps.	250-499 Emps.	500-999 Emps.	Unknown Emps.	Industry Sales
2015	2.0	3.0	6.0	16.0	7.0	3.2	0.8	1.9	1.0	40.8
2016	2.1	3.2	6.3	16.7	7.3	3.3	0.8	2.0	1.1	42.7
2017	2.2	3.3	6.6	17.5	7.6	3.5	0.9	2.1	1.1	44.8
2018	2.3	3.4	6.8	18.2	7.9	3.6	0.9	2.2	1.1	46.5
2019	2.4	3.6	7.2	19.0	8.3	3.8	0.9	2.3	1.2	48.7

INDUSTRY: DEPARTMENT STORES INDUSTRY (NAICS 45211)
PRODUCT LINE: COMPUTER PREPACKAGED SOFTWARE (Sub Category)

NAICS 45211: Department Stores Industry . this industry comprises establishments known as department stores primarily engaged in retailing a wide range of the following new products with no one merchandise line predominating: apparel, furniture, appliances and home furnishings; and selected additional items, such as paint, hardware, toiletries, cosmetics, photographic equipment, jewelry, toys, and sporting goods. merchandise lines are normally arranged in separate departments.

5-YEAR TREND — ESTIMATED INDUSTRY SALES ($MILLIONS)

Year	Employee Size of Establishment									Total
	1-4 Emps.	5-9 Emps.	10-19 Emps.	20-49 Emps.	50-99 Emps.	100-249 Emps.	250-499 Emps.	500-999 Emps.	Unknown Emps.	Industry Sales
2015	0.0	0.0	0.0	1.3	24.3	78.1	32.3	4.7	0.2	140.9
2016	0.0	0.0	0.0	1.3	24.4	78.4	32.4	4.7	0.2	141.5
2017	0.0	0.0	0.0	1.4	24.6	79.1	32.8	4.7	0.2	142.9
2018	0.0	0.0	0.0	1.4	24.7	79.2	32.8	4.8	0.2	142.9
2019	0.0	0.0	0.0	1.4	24.9	79.9	33.1	4.8	0.2	144.3

INDUSTRY: WAREHOUSE CLUBS & SUPERCENTERS (NAICS 45291)
PRODUCT LINE: COMPUTER PREPACKAGED SOFTWARE (Sub Category)

NAICS 45291: Warehouse Clubs and Superstores This industry comprises establishments known as warehouse clubs, superstores or supercenters primarily engaged in retailing a general line of groceries in combination with general lines of new merchandise, such as apparel, furniture, and appliances.

5-YEAR TREND — ESTIMATED INDUSTRY SALES ($MILLIONS)

Year	Employee Size of Establishment									Total
	1-4 Emps.	5-9 Emps.	10-19 Emps.	20-49 Emps.	50-99 Emps.	100-249 Emps.	250-499 Emps.	500-999 Emps.	Unknown Emps.	Industry Sales
2015	0.1	0.0	0.1	3.9	7.4	423.2	1,862.9	46.9	0.7	2,345.3
2016	0.1	0.0	0.1	4.0	7.6	434.8	1,914.2	48.2	0.7	2,409.9
2017	0.1	0.0	0.1	4.1	7.9	449.0	1,976.8	49.8	0.8	2,488.6
2018	0.1	0.0	0.1	4.5	8.5	483.3	2,127.4	53.6	0.8	2,678.3
2019	0.2	0.0	0.1	4.7	9.0	511.9	2,253.5	56.8	0.9	2,837.0

	INDUSTRY: ELECTRONIC SHOPPING & MAIL-ORDER (NAICS 45411)
	PRODUCT LINE: COMPUTER PREPACKAGED SOFTWARE (Sub Category)

NAICS 45411: Electronic Shopping and Mail-Order Houses This industry comprises establishments primarily engaged in retailing all types of merchandise by means of mail or by electronic media, such as interactive television or computer. Included in this industry are establishments primarily engaged in retailing from catalogue showrooms of mail-order houses.

5-YEAR TREND – ESTIMATED INDUSTRY SALES ($MILLIONS)

Year	Employee Size of Establishment									Total
	1-4 Emps.	5-9 Emps.	10-19 Emps.	20-49 Emps.	50-99 Emps.	100-249 Emps.	250-499 Emps.	500-999 Emps.	Unknown Emps.	Industry Sales
2015	429.9	221.5	320.0	537.1	404.3	748.0	1,008.4	1,423.4	60.4	5,152.9
2016	454.7	234.2	338.4	568.1	427.6	791.1	1,066.6	1,505.6	63.9	5,450.3
2017	482.1	248.4	358.8	602.3	453.4	838.8	1,130.8	1,596.3	67.8	5,778.7
2018	540.3	278.3	402.1	675.0	508.1	940.0	1,267.3	1,756.6	75.9	6,443.8
2019	600.7	309.5	447.1	750.5	564.9	1,045.1	1,409.0	1,923.6	84.4	7,134.9

	INDUSTRY: BOOK STORES INDUSTRY (NAICS 451211)
	PRODUCT LINE: COMPUTER PREPACKAGED SOFTWARE (Sub Category)

NAICS 451211: Book Stores. this industry comprises establishments primarily engaged in the retail sale of new books and magazines. Establishments primarily engaged in the retail sale of used books are classified in 5932.

5-YEAR TREND – ESTIMATED INDUSTRY SALES ($MILLIONS)

Year	Employee Size of Establishment									Total
	1-4 Emps.	5-9 Emps.	10-19 Emps.	20-49 Emps.	50-99 Emps.	100-249 Emps.	250-499 Emps.	500-999 Emps.	Unknown Emps.	Industry Sales
2015	2.1	3.2	6.3	16.9	7.4	3.4	0.8	2.0	1.1	43.2
2016	2.2	3.3	6.6	17.7	7.7	3.5	0.9	2.1	1.1	45.1
2017	2.3	3.5	7.0	18.5	8.1	3.7	0.9	2.2	1.2	47.4
2018	2.4	3.6	7.2	19.2	8.4	3.9	1.0	2.3	1.2	49.2
2019	2.5	3.8	7.6	20.1	8.8	4.0	1.0	2.4	1.3	51.4

INDUSTRY: HOME CENTERS INDUSTRY (NAICS 44411)
PRODUCT LINE: KITCHENWARE & HOME FURNISHINGS (Main Category)

NAICS 44411: Home Centers. This industry comprises establishments known as home centers primarily engaged in retailing a general line of new home repair and improvement materials and supplies, such as lumber, plumbing goods, electrical goods, tools, housewares, hardware, and lawn and garden supplies, with no one merchandise line predominating. The merchandise lines are normally arranged in separate departments.

5-YEAR TREND – ESTIMATED INDUSTRY SALES ($MILLIONS)

Year	Employee Size of Establishment									Total
	1-4 Emps.	5-9 Emps.	10-19 Emps.	20-49 Emps.	50-99 Emps.	100-249 Emps.	250-499 Emps.	500-999 Emps.	Unknown Emps.	Industry Sales
2015	6.6	12.9	32.6	66.7	50.6	3,334.6	260.4	5.4	2.3	3,772.1
2016	6.8	13.2	33.4	68.3	51.8	3,414.6	266.7	5.6	2.4	3,862.6
2017	7.0	13.6	34.4	70.3	53.3	3,514.6	274.5	5.7	2.4	3,975.7
2018	7.2	14.1	35.6	72.9	55.3	3,645.1	284.7	5.9	2.5	4,123.3
2019	7.6	14.7	37.3	76.2	57.8	3,813.4	297.8	6.2	2.6	4,313.7

INDUSTRY: HARDWARE STORES (NAICS 44413)
PRODUCT LINE: KITCHENWARE & HOME FURNISHINGS (Main Category)

NAICS 44413: Hardware Stores. Establishments primarily engaged in the retail sale of a number of basic hardware lines, such as tools, builders' hardware, paint and glass, housewares and household appliances, and cutlery.

5-YEAR TREND – ESTIMATED INDUSTRY SALES ($MILLIONS)

Year	Employee Size of Establishment									Total
	1-4 Emps.	5-9 Emps.	10-19 Emps.	20-49 Emps.	50-99 Emps.	100-249 Emps.	250-499 Emps.	500-999 Emps.	Unknown Emps.	Industry Sales
2015	36.7	62.3	125.3	179.1	35.6	11.6	2.1	0.1	3.2	455.9
2016	37.1	62.9	126.5	180.9	35.9	11.7	2.1	0.1	3.2	460.4
2017	37.7	63.9	128.5	183.7	36.5	11.9	2.1	0.1	3.3	467.6
2018	39.2	66.4	133.6	191.0	37.9	12.4	2.2	0.1	3.4	486.2
2019	41.1	69.7	140.2	200.5	39.8	13.0	2.3	0.1	3.6	510.4

INDUSTRY: SUPERMARKETS INDUSTRY (NAICS 44511)
PRODUCT LINE: KITCHENWARE & HOME FURNISHINGS (Main Category)

NAICS 44511: Grocery Stores Industry. this industry comprises establishments generally known as supermarkets and grocery stores primarily engaged in retailing a general line of food, such as canned and frozen foods; fresh fruits and vegetables; and fresh and prepared meats, fish, and poultry. Included in this industry are delicatessen-type establishments primarily engaged in retailing a general line of food.

5-YEAR TREND — ESTIMATED INDUSTRY SALES ($MILLIONS)

Year	Employee Size of Establishment									Total
	1-4 Emps.	5-9 Emps.	10-19 Emps.	20-49 Emps.	50-99 Emps.	100-249 Emps.	250-499 Emps.	500-999 Emps.	Unknown Emps.	Industry Sales
2015	27.1	19.5	50.4	166.1	393.7	978.8	305.7	36.6	5.1	1,983.0
2016	26.9	19.4	50.1	165.1	391.2	972.6	303.7	36.3	5.0	1,970.4
2017	26.9	19.4	50.1	165.0	391.1	972.2	303.6	36.3	5.0	1,969.7
2018	27.4	19.8	51.1	168.4	399.1	992.3	309.9	37.1	5.1	2,010.3
2019	28.3	20.4	52.7	173.6	411.5	1,023.0	319.5	38.2	5.3	2,072.4

INDUSTRY: BEER, WINE & LIQUOR STORES (NAICS 44531)
PRODUCT LINE: KITCHENWARE & HOME FURNISHINGS (Main Category)

NAICS 44531: Beer & Wine & Liquor Stores. Establishments primarily engaged in the retail sale of packaged alcoholic beverages, such as ale, beer, wine, and liquor, for consumption off the premises. Stores selling prepared drinks for consumption on the premises are classified in SIC 5813.

5-YEAR TREND — ESTIMATED INDUSTRY SALES ($MILLIONS)

Year	Employee Size of Establishment									Total
	1-4 Emps.	5-9 Emps.	10-19 Emps.	20-49 Emps.	50-99 Emps.	100-249 Emps.	250-499 Emps.	500-999 Emps.	Unknown Emps.	Industry Sales
2015	9.7	9.8	8.4	6.1	0.9	0.5	0.0	0.3	0.5	36.2
2016	9.9	10.0	8.6	6.3	0.9	0.5	0.0	0.3	0.6	37.0
2017	10.2	10.3	8.8	6.4	0.9	0.5	0.0	0.3	0.6	38.1
2018	10.8	10.9	9.3	6.8	1.0	0.6	0.0	0.3	0.6	40.3
2019	11.5	11.6	9.9	7.3	1.0	0.6	0.0	0.3	0.6	43.0

INDUSTRY: PHARMACIES & DRUG STORES INDUSTRY (NAICS 44611)
PRODUCT LINE: KITCHENWARE & HOME FURNISHINGS (Main Category)

NAICS 44611 Pharmacies and Drug Stores – this industry comprises
establishments known as pharmacies and drug stores engaged in retailing
prescription or nonprescription drugs and medicines.

5-YEAR TREND – ESTIMATED INDUSTRY SALES ($MILLIONS)

Year	Employee Size of Establishment									Total
	1-4 Emps.	5-9 Emps.	10-19 Emps.	20-49 Emps.	50-99 Emps.	100-249 Emps.	250-499 Emps.	500-999 Emps.	Unknown Emps.	Industry Sales
2015	12.2	30.3	122.6	360.0	36.4	14.6	5.6	1.9	0.9	584.5
2016	12.6	31.2	126.4	371.3	37.6	15.0	5.7	1.9	1.0	602.8
2017	13.1	32.4	131.0	384.7	38.9	15.6	6.0	2.0	1.0	624.6
2018	13.8	34.3	138.7	407.5	41.2	16.5	6.3	2.1	1.1	661.5
2019	14.8	36.6	148.2	435.1	44.0	17.6	6.7	2.2	1.1	706.4

INDUSTRY: MEN'S CLOTHING STORES INDUSTRY (NAICS 44811)
PRODUCT LINE: KITCHENWARE & HOME FURNISHINGS (Main Category)

NAICS 44811: Men's Clothing Stores. this industry comprises
establishments primarily engaged in retailing a general line of new
men's and boys' clothing. These establishments may provide basic
alterations, such as hemming, taking in or letting out seams, or lengthening
or shortening sleeves.

5-YEAR TREND – ESTIMATED INDUSTRY SALES ($MILLIONS)

Year	Employee Size of Establishment									Total
	1-4 Emps.	5-9 Emps.	10-19 Emps.	20-49 Emps.	50-99 Emps.	100-249 Emps.	250-499 Emps.	500-999 Emps.	Unknown Emps.	Industry Sales
2015	1.4	2.5	4.7	2.5	0.5	0.5	0.2	0.0	0.2	12.6
2016	1.5	2.6	4.9	2.6	0.6	0.5	0.2	0.0	0.3	13.0
2017	1.6	2.7	5.1	2.7	0.6	0.5	0.2	0.0	0.3	13.6
2018	1.6	2.8	5.2	2.8	0.6	0.5	0.2	0.0	0.3	14.0
2019	1.7	2.9	5.4	2.9	0.6	0.6	0.2	0.0	0.3	14.6

INDUSTRY: WOMEN'S CLOTHING STORES INDUSTRY (NAICS 44812)
PRODUCT LINE: KITCHENWARE & HOME FURNISHINGS (Main Category)

NAICS 44812: Women's Clothing Stores . this industry comprises establishments primarily engaged in retailing a general line of new women's, misses' and juniors' clothing, including maternity wear. These establishments may provide basic alterations, such as hemming, taking in or letting out seams, or lengthening or shortening sleeves.

5-YEAR TREND – ESTIMATED INDUSTRY SALES ($MILLIONS)

Year	Employee Size of Establishment									Total
	1-4 Emps.	5-9 Emps.	10-19 Emps.	20-49 Emps.	50-99 Emps.	100-249 Emps.	250-499 Emps.	500-999 Emps.	Unknown Emps.	Industry Sales
2015	8.3	18.5	39.6	27.9	9.9	9.1	3.7	3.6	1.9	122.4
2016	8.6	19.1	40.7	28.7	10.1	9.4	3.8	3.7	1.9	126.0
2017	8.8	19.8	42.2	29.7	10.5	9.7	3.9	3.8	2.0	130.4
2018	9.3	20.8	44.5	31.4	11.1	10.2	4.2	4.0	2.1	137.6
2019	9.9	22.2	47.3	33.4	11.8	10.9	4.4	4.2	2.2	146.3

INDUSTRY: FAMILY CLOTHING STORES INDUSTRY (NAICS 44814)
PRODUCT LINE: KITCHENWARE & HOME FURNISHINGS (Main Category)

NAICS 44814: Family Clothing Stores . this industry comprises establishments primarily engaged in retailing a general line of new clothing for men, women, and children, without specializing in sales for an individual gender or age group. These establishments may provide basic alterations, such as hemming, taking in or letting out seams, or lengthening or shortening sleeves.

5-YEAR TREND – ESTIMATED INDUSTRY SALES ($MILLIONS)

Year	Employee Size of Establishment									Total
	1-4 Emps.	5-9 Emps.	10-19 Emps.	20-49 Emps.	50-99 Emps.	100-249 Emps.	250-499 Emps.	500-999 Emps.	Unknown Emps.	Industry Sales
2015	53.6	110.8	418.6	1,391.2	1,228.9	338.2	319.0	184.7	14.7	4,059.8
2016	55.1	113.8	429.8	1,428.5	1,261.8	347.3	327.6	189.7	15.1	4,168.6
2017	56.8	117.4	443.5	1,474.1	1,302.2	358.4	338.1	195.7	15.6	4,301.8
2018	59.9	123.8	467.5	1,553.8	1,372.5	377.7	356.3	205.6	16.4	4,533.5
2019	63.7	131.6	497.0	1,651.7	1,459.0	401.5	378.8	217.6	17.4	4,818.2

INDUSTRY: PRERECORDED TAPES & CDs STORES (NAICS 45122)
PRODUCT LINE: KITCHENWARE & HOME FURNISHINGS (Main Category)

NAICS 45122: Prerecorded Tape, Compact Disc, and Record Stores .
This industry comprises establishments primarily engaged in retailing new
prerecorded audio and video tapes, compact discs (CDs), and phonograph
records.

5-Year Trend – Estimated Industry Sales ($Millions)

| Year | Employee Size of Establishment | | | | | | | | | Total |
	1-4 Emps.	5-9 Emps.	10-19 Emps.	20-49 Emps.	50-99 Emps.	100-249 Emps.	250-499 Emps.	500-999 Emps.	Unknown Emps.	Industry Sales
2015	0.1	0.3	0.7	1.4	1.0	67.7	5.3	0.1	0.0	76.6
2016	0.1	0.3	0.7	1.4	1.1	69.3	5.4	0.1	0.0	78.4
2017	0.1	0.3	0.7	1.4	1.1	71.4	5.6	0.1	0.0	80.7
2018	0.1	0.3	0.7	1.5	1.1	74.0	5.8	0.1	0.1	83.7
2019	0.2	0.3	0.8	1.5	1.2	77.4	6.0	0.1	0.1	87.6

INDUSTRY: DEPARTMENT STORES INDUSTRY (NAICS 45211)
PRODUCT LINE: KITCHENWARE & HOME FURNISHINGS (Main Category)

NAICS 45211: Department Stores Industry . this industry comprises
establishments known as department stores primarily engaged in retailing
a wide range of the following new products with no one merchandise line
predominating: apparel, furniture, appliances and home furnishings; and
selected additional items, such as paint, hardware, toiletries, cosmetics,
photographic equipment, jewelry, toys, and sporting goods. merchandise lines
are normally arranged in separate departments.

5-Year Trend – Estimated Industry Sales ($Millions)

| Year | Employee Size of Establishment | | | | | | | | | Total |
	1-4 Emps.	5-9 Emps.	10-19 Emps.	20-49 Emps.	50-99 Emps.	100-249 Emps.	250-499 Emps.	500-999 Emps.	Unknown Emps.	Industry Sales
2015	0.2	0.3	0.6	46.9	851.5	2,734.4	1,131.9	163.7	7.0	4,936.4
2016	0.2	0.3	0.6	47.1	854.9	2,745.1	1,136.3	164.4	7.0	4,955.7
2017	0.2	0.3	0.6	47.6	863.3	2,772.2	1,147.5	166.0	7.1	5,004.6
2018	0.2	0.3	0.6	47.6	863.4	2,772.5	1,147.7	166.5	7.1	5,005.7
2019	0.2	0.3	0.6	48.0	872.0	2,799.9	1,159.0	168.4	7.1	5,055.5

	INDUSTRY: WAREHOUSE CLUBS & SUPERCENTERS (NAICS 45291)
	PRODUCT LINE: KITCHENWARE & HOME FURNISHINGS (Main Category)

NAICS 45291: Warehouse Clubs and Superstores This industry comprises establishments known as warehouse clubs, superstores or supercenters primarily engaged in retailing a general line of groceries in combination with general lines of new merchandise, such as apparel, furniture, and appliances.

5-YEAR TREND — ESTIMATED INDUSTRY SALES ($MILLIONS)

Year	Employee Size of Establishment									Total
	1-4 Emps.	5-9 Emps.	10-19 Emps.	20-49 Emps.	50-99 Emps.	100-249 Emps.	250-499 Emps.	500-999 Emps.	Unknown Emps.	Industry Sales
2015	0.5	0.1	0.4	14.3	27.1	1,546.9	6,809.8	171.6	2.6	8,573.2
2016	0.5	0.1	0.4	14.7	27.8	1,589.5	6,997.5	176.3	2.7	8,809.5
2017	0.5	0.1	0.4	15.2	28.7	1,641.4	7,226.0	182.1	2.8	9,097.2
2018	0.5	0.1	0.4	16.3	30.9	1,766.6	7,776.9	196.0	3.0	9,790.7
2019	0.5	0.1	0.5	17.3	32.8	1,871.2	8,237.5	207.6	3.1	10,370.7

	INDUSTRY: OFFICE SUPPLY & STATIONERY STORES (NAICS 45321)
	PRODUCT LINE: KITCHENWARE & HOME FURNISHINGS (Main Category)

NAICS 45321: Office Supplies and Stationery Stores . this industry comprises establishments primarily engaged in one or more of the following: (1) retailing new stationery, school supplies, and office supplies; (2) selling a combination of new office equipment, furniture, and supplies; and (3) selling new office equipment, furniture, and supplies in combination with selling new computers.

5-YEAR TREND — ESTIMATED INDUSTRY SALES ($MILLIONS)

Year	Employee Size of Establishment									Total
	1-4 Emps.	5-9 Emps.	10-19 Emps.	20-49 Emps.	50-99 Emps.	100-249 Emps.	250-499 Emps.	500-999 Emps.	Unknown Emps.	Industry Sales
2015	0.4	0.4	2.3	5.8	0.1	0.1	0.0	0.0	0.1	9.2
2016	0.4	0.4	2.3	5.7	0.1	0.1	0.0	0.0	0.1	9.1
2017	0.4	0.4	2.3	5.7	0.1	0.1	0.0	0.0	0.1	9.1
2018	0.4	0.3	2.2	5.5	0.1	0.1	0.0	0.0	0.1	8.8
2019	0.4	0.3	2.2	5.4	0.1	0.1	0.0	0.0	0.1	8.6

INDUSTRY: ELECTRONIC SHOPPING & MAIL-ORDER (NAICS 45411)
PRODUCT LINE: KITCHENWARE & HOME FURNISHINGS (Main Category)

NAICS 45411: Electronic Shopping and Mail-Order Houses This
industry comprises establishments primarily engaged in retailing all
types of merchandise by means of mail or by electronic media, such
as interactive television or computer. Included in this industry are
establishments primarily engaged in retailing from catalogue showrooms
of mail-order houses.

5-YEAR TREND – ESTIMATED INDUSTRY SALES ($MILLIONS)

| Year | Employee Size of Establishment | | | | | | | | | Total |
	1-4 Emps.	5-9 Emps.	10-19 Emps.	20-49 Emps.	50-99 Emps.	100-249 Emps.	250-499 Emps.	500-999 Emps.	Unknown Emps.	Industry Sales
2015	1,526.1	786.2	1,135.9	1,906.6	1,435.1	2,655.1	3,579.5	5,053.0	214.5	18,291.9
2016	1,614.2	831.5	1,201.4	2,016.6	1,518.0	2,808.3	3,786.1	5,344.6	226.9	19,347.7
2017	1,711.5	881.6	1,273.8	2,138.1	1,609.4	2,977.5	4,014.2	5,666.6	240.6	20,513.2
2018	1,918.1	988.0	1,427.5	2,396.2	1,803.7	3,336.9	4,498.7	6,235.5	269.6	22,874.2
2019	2,132.5	1,098.5	1,587.1	2,664.1	2,005.3	3,710.0	5,001.7	6,828.5	299.7	25,327.4

INDUSTRY: BOOK STORES INDUSTRY (NAICS 451211)
PRODUCT LINE: KITCHENWARE & HOME FURNISHINGS (Main Category)

NAICS 451211: Book Stores. this industry comprises
establishments primarily engaged in the retail sale of new books and
magazines. Establishments primarily engaged in the retail sale of used
books are classified in 5932.

5-YEAR TREND – ESTIMATED INDUSTRY SALES ($MILLIONS)

| Year | Employee Size of Establishment | | | | | | | | | Total |
	1-4 Emps.	5-9 Emps.	10-19 Emps.	20-49 Emps.	50-99 Emps.	100-249 Emps.	250-499 Emps.	500-999 Emps.	Unknown Emps.	Industry Sales
2015	2.9	4.4	8.8	23.4	10.2	4.7	1.2	2.8	1.5	59.7
2016	3.0	4.6	9.2	24.4	10.6	4.9	1.2	2.9	1.5	62.4
2017	3.2	4.8	9.6	25.6	11.2	5.1	1.3	3.0	1.6	65.5
2018	3.3	5.0	10.0	26.6	11.6	5.3	1.3	3.2	1.7	68.0
2019	3.5	5.3	10.5	27.8	12.1	5.6	1.4	3.3	1.8	71.1

INDUSTRY: DEPARTMENT STORES INDUSTRY (NAICS 45211)
PRODUCT LINE: COOKWARE & COOKING ACCESSORIES (Sub Category)

NAICS 45211: Department Stores Industry . this industry comprises establishments known as department stores primarily engaged in retailing a wide range of the following new products with no one merchandise line predominating: apparel, furniture, appliances and home furnishings; and selected additional items, such as paint, hardware, toiletries, cosmetics, photographic equipment, jewelry, toys, and sporting goods. merchandise lines are normally arranged in separate departments.

5-YEAR TREND – ESTIMATED INDUSTRY SALES ($MILLIONS)

Year	Employee Size of Establishment									Total
	1-4 Emps.	5-9 Emps.	10-19 Emps.	20-49 Emps.	50-99 Emps.	100-249 Emps.	250-499 Emps.	500-999 Emps.	Unknown Emps.	Industry Sales
2015	0.1	0.1	0.2	12.8	232.7	747.4	309.4	44.8	1.9	1,349.2
2016	0.1	0.1	0.2	12.9	233.7	750.3	310.6	44.9	1.9	1,354.5
2017	0.1	0.1	0.2	13.0	236.0	757.7	313.6	45.4	1.9	1,367.9
2018	0.1	0.1	0.2	13.0	236.0	757.8	313.7	45.5	1.9	1,368.2
2019	0.1	0.1	0.2	13.1	238.3	765.3	316.8	46.0	1.9	1,381.8

INDUSTRY: WAREHOUSE CLUBS & SUPERCENTERS (NAICS 45291)
PRODUCT LINE: COOKWARE & COOKING ACCESSORIES (Sub Category)

NAICS 45291: Warehouse Clubs and Superstores This industry comprises establishments known as warehouse clubs, superstores or supercenters primarily engaged in retailing a general line of groceries in combination with general lines of new merchandise, such as apparel, furniture, and appliances.

5-YEAR TREND – ESTIMATED INDUSTRY SALES ($MILLIONS)

Year	Employee Size of Establishment									Total
	1-4 Emps.	5-9 Emps.	10-19 Emps.	20-49 Emps.	50-99 Emps.	100-249 Emps.	250-499 Emps.	500-999 Emps.	Unknown Emps.	Industry Sales
2015	0.2	0.1	0.2	6.0	11.4	649.5	2,859.1	72.0	1.1	3,599.5
2016	0.2	0.1	0.2	6.2	11.7	667.4	2,937.9	74.0	1.1	3,698.7
2017	0.2	0.1	0.2	6.4	12.1	689.2	3,033.8	76.5	1.2	3,819.5
2018	0.2	0.1	0.2	6.8	13.0	741.7	3,265.1	82.3	1.2	4,110.6
2019	0.2	0.1	0.2	7.3	13.8	785.6	3,458.5	87.1	1.3	4,354.1

	INDUSTRY: DEPARTMENT STORES INDUSTRY (NAICS 45211)
	PRODUCT LINE: DINNERWARE & GLASSWARE (Sub Category)

NAICS 45211: Department Stores Industry . this industry comprises establishments known as department stores primarily engaged in retailing a wide range of the following new products with no one merchandise line predominating: apparel, furniture, appliances and home furnishings; and selected additional items, such as paint, hardware, toiletries, cosmetics, photographic equipment, jewelry, toys, and sporting goods. merchandise lines are normally arranged in separate departments.

5-YEAR TREND – ESTIMATED INDUSTRY SALES ($MILLIONS)

Year	Employee Size of Establishment									Total Industry Sales
	1-4 Emps.	5-9 Emps.	10-19 Emps.	20-49 Emps.	50-99 Emps.	100-249 Emps.	250-499 Emps.	500-999 Emps.	Unknown Emps.	
2015	0.1	0.1	0.1	11.8	213.8	686.6	284.2	41.1	1.7	1,239.5
2016	0.1	0.1	0.1	11.8	214.6	689.3	285.3	41.3	1.8	1,244.3
2017	0.1	0.1	0.1	11.9	216.8	696.1	288.1	41.7	1.8	1,256.6
2018	0.1	0.1	0.1	11.9	216.8	696.1	288.2	41.8	1.8	1,256.9
2019	0.1	0.1	0.1	12.1	218.9	703.0	291.0	42.3	1.8	1,269.4

	INDUSTRY: WAREHOUSE CLUBS & SUPERCENTERS (NAICS 45291)
	PRODUCT LINE: DINNERWARE & GLASSWARE (Sub Category)

NAICS 45291: Warehouse Clubs and Superstores This industry comprises establishments known as warehouse clubs, superstores or supercenters primarily engaged in retailing a general line of groceries in combination with general lines of new merchandise, such as apparel, furniture, and appliances.

5-YEAR TREND – ESTIMATED INDUSTRY SALES ($MILLIONS)

Year	Employee Size of Establishment									Total Industry Sales
	1-4 Emps.	5-9 Emps.	10-19 Emps.	20-49 Emps.	50-99 Emps.	100-249 Emps.	250-499 Emps.	500-999 Emps.	Unknown Emps.	
2015	0.0	0.0	0.0	1.5	2.8	157.3	692.7	17.5	0.3	872.1
2016	0.0	0.0	0.0	1.5	2.8	161.7	711.8	17.9	0.3	896.1
2017	0.0	0.0	0.0	1.5	2.9	167.0	735.0	18.5	0.3	925.4
2018	0.1	0.0	0.0	1.7	3.1	179.7	791.0	19.9	0.3	995.9
2019	0.1	0.0	0.0	1.8	3.3	190.3	837.9	21.1	0.3	1,054.9

INDUSTRY: DEPARTMENT STORES INDUSTRY (NAICS 45211)
PRODUCT LINE: DECORATIVE ACCESSORIES (Sub Category)

NAICS 45211: Department Stores Industry . this industry comprises establishments known as department stores primarily engaged in retailing a wide range of the following new products with no one merchandise line predominating: apparel, furniture, appliances and home furnishings; and selected additional items, such as paint, hardware, toiletries, cosmetics, photographic equipment, jewelry, toys, and sporting goods. merchandise lines are normally arranged in separate departments.

5-YEAR TREND — ESTIMATED INDUSTRY SALES ($MILLIONS)

Year	Employee Size of Establishment									Total
	1-4 Emps.	5-9 Emps.	10-19 Emps.	20-49 Emps.	50-99 Emps.	100-249 Emps.	250-499 Emps.	500-999 Emps.	Unknown Emps.	Industry Sales
2015	0.1	0.1	0.1	12.1	219.0	703.3	291.1	42.1	1.8	1,269.8
2016	0.1	0.1	0.1	12.1	219.9	706.1	292.3	42.3	1.8	1,274.7
2017	0.1	0.1	0.1	12.2	222.1	713.1	295.2	42.7	1.8	1,287.3
2018	0.1	0.1	0.1	12.2	222.1	713.2	295.2	42.8	1.8	1,287.6
2019	0.1	0.1	0.1	12.4	224.3	720.2	298.1	43.3	1.8	1,300.4

INDUSTRY: WAREHOUSE CLUBS & SUPERCENTERS (NAICS 45291)
PRODUCT LINE: DECORATIVE ACCESSORIES (Sub Category)

NAICS 45291: Warehouse Clubs and Superstores This industry comprises establishments known as warehouse clubs, superstores or supercenters primarily engaged in retailing a general line of groceries in combination with general lines of new merchandise, such as apparel, furniture, and appliances.

5-YEAR TREND — ESTIMATED INDUSTRY SALES ($MILLIONS)

Year	Employee Size of Establishment									Total
	1-4 Emps.	5-9 Emps.	10-19 Emps.	20-49 Emps.	50-99 Emps.	100-249 Emps.	250-499 Emps.	500-999 Emps.	Unknown Emps.	Industry Sales
2015	0.1	0.0	0.1	4.2	8.0	458.8	2,019.6	50.9	0.8	2,542.6
2016	0.1	0.0	0.1	4.4	8.3	471.4	2,075.3	52.3	0.8	2,612.7
2017	0.1	0.0	0.1	4.5	8.5	486.8	2,143.0	54.0	0.8	2,698.0
2018	0.2	0.0	0.1	4.8	9.2	523.9	2,306.4	58.1	0.9	2,903.7
2019	0.2	0.0	0.1	5.1	9.7	555.0	2,443.0	61.6	0.9	3,075.7

INDUSTRY: DEPARTMENT STORES INDUSTRY (NAICS 45211)
PRODUCT LINE: OTHER KITCHENWARE (Sub Category)

NAICS 45211: Department Stores Industry . this industry comprises establishments known as department stores primarily engaged in retailing a wide range of the following new products with no one merchandise line predominating: apparel, furniture, appliances and home furnishings; and selected additional items, such as paint, hardware, toiletries, cosmetics, photographic equipment, jewelry, toys, and sporting goods. merchandise lines are normally arranged in separate departments.

5-YEAR TREND – ESTIMATED INDUSTRY SALES ($MILLIONS)

Year	Employee Size of Establishment									Total
	1-4 Emps.	5-9 Emps.	10-19 Emps.	20-49 Emps.	50-99 Emps.	100-249 Emps.	250-499 Emps.	500-999 Emps.	Unknown Emps.	Industry Sales
2015	0.0	0.1	0.1	10.2	185.9	597.1	247.2	35.8	1.5	1,078.0
2016	0.0	0.1	0.1	10.3	186.7	599.4	248.1	35.9	1.5	1,082.2
2017	0.0	0.1	0.1	10.4	188.5	605.3	250.6	36.2	1.5	1,092.8
2018	0.0	0.1	0.1	10.4	188.5	605.4	250.6	36.4	1.5	1,093.1
2019	0.0	0.1	0.1	10.5	190.4	611.4	253.1	36.8	1.6	1,104.0

INDUSTRY: WAREHOUSE CLUBS & SUPERCENTERS (NAICS 45291)
PRODUCT LINE: OTHER KITCHENWARE (Sub Category)

NAICS 45291: Warehouse Clubs and Superstores This industry comprises establishments known as warehouse clubs, superstores or supercenters primarily engaged in retailing a general line of groceries in combination with general lines of new merchandise, such as apparel, furniture, and appliances.

5-YEAR TREND – ESTIMATED INDUSTRY SALES ($MILLIONS)

Year	Employee Size of Establishment									Total
	1-4 Emps.	5-9 Emps.	10-19 Emps.	20-49 Emps.	50-99 Emps.	100-249 Emps.	250-499 Emps.	500-999 Emps.	Unknown Emps.	Industry Sales
2015	0.1	0.0	0.1	2.6	4.9	281.3	1,238.4	31.2	0.5	1,559.1
2016	0.1	0.0	0.1	2.7	5.1	289.1	1,272.6	32.1	0.5	1,602.1
2017	0.1	0.0	0.1	2.8	5.2	298.5	1,314.1	33.1	0.5	1,654.4
2018	0.1	0.0	0.1	3.0	5.6	321.3	1,414.3	35.6	0.5	1,780.5
2019	0.1	0.0	0.1	3.1	6.0	340.3	1,498.1	37.7	0.6	1,886.0

<table>
<tr><td colspan="2">INDUSTRY: OFFICE SUPPLY & STATIONERY STORES (NAICS 45321)</td></tr>
<tr><td colspan="2">PRODUCT LINE: GIFTWARE (Sub Category)</td></tr>
</table>

NAICS 45321: Office Supplies and Stationery Stores . this industry comprises establishments primarily engaged in one or more of the following: (1) retailing new stationery, school supplies, and office supplies; (2) selling a combination of new office equipment, furniture, and supplies; and (3) selling new office equipment, furniture, and supplies in combination with selling new computers.

5-YEAR TREND – ESTIMATED INDUSTRY SALES ($MILLIONS)

| Year | Employee Size of Establishment | | | | | | | | | Total |
	1-4 Emps.	5-9 Emps.	10-19 Emps.	20-49 Emps.	50-99 Emps.	100-249 Emps.	250-499 Emps.	500-999 Emps.	Unknown Emps.	Industry Sales
2015	0.3	0.3	1.8	4.5	0.1	0.1	0.0	0.0	0.1	7.2
2016	0.3	0.3	1.8	4.5	0.1	0.1	0.0	0.0	0.1	7.1
2017	0.3	0.3	1.8	4.4	0.1	0.1	0.0	0.0	0.1	7.1
2018	0.3	0.3	1.7	4.3	0.1	0.1	0.0	0.0	0.1	6.9
2019	0.3	0.3	1.7	4.2	0.1	0.1	0.0	0.0	0.1	6.7

<table>
<tr><td colspan="2">INDUSTRY: BOOK STORES INDUSTRY (NAICS 451211)</td></tr>
<tr><td colspan="2">PRODUCT LINE: GIFTWARE (Sub Category)</td></tr>
</table>

NAICS 451211: Book Stores. this industry comprises establishments primarily engaged in the retail sale of new books and magazines. Establishments primarily engaged in the retail sale of used books are classified in 5932.

5-YEAR TREND – ESTIMATED INDUSTRY SALES ($MILLIONS)

| Year | Employee Size of Establishment | | | | | | | | | Total |
	1-4 Emps.	5-9 Emps.	10-19 Emps.	20-49 Emps.	50-99 Emps.	100-249 Emps.	250-499 Emps.	500-999 Emps.	Unknown Emps.	Industry Sales
2015	2.0	3.1	6.1	16.3	7.1	3.3	0.8	1.9	1.0	41.8
2016	2.1	3.2	6.4	17.1	7.4	3.4	0.8	2.0	1.1	43.7
2017	2.2	3.4	6.7	17.9	7.8	3.6	0.9	2.1	1.1	45.8
2018	2.3	3.5	7.0	18.6	8.1	3.7	0.9	2.2	1.2	47.6
2019	2.4	3.7	7.3	19.5	8.5	3.9	1.0	2.3	1.2	49.8

INDUSTRY: BOOK STORES INDUSTRY (NAICS 451211)
PRODUCT LINE: OTHER HOME FURNISHINGS (Sub Category)

NAICS 451211: Book Stores. this industry comprises
establishments primarily engaged in the retail sale of new books and
magazines. Establishments primarily engaged in the retail sale of used
books are classified in 5932.

5-YEAR TREND — ESTIMATED INDUSTRY SALES ($MILLIONS)

Year	Employee Size of Establishment									Total Industry Sales
	1-4 Emps.	5-9 Emps.	10-19 Emps.	20-49 Emps.	50-99 Emps.	100-249 Emps.	250-499 Emps.	500-999 Emps.	Unknown Emps.	
2015	0.9	1.3	2.6	7.0	3.1	1.4	0.3	0.8	0.4	17.9
2016	0.9	1.4	2.8	7.3	3.2	1.5	0.4	0.9	0.5	18.7
2017	1.0	1.5	2.9	7.7	3.3	1.5	0.4	0.9	0.5	19.7
2018	1.0	1.5	3.0	8.0	3.5	1.6	0.4	1.0	0.5	20.4
2019	1.0	1.6	3.1	8.4	3.6	1.7	0.4	1.0	0.5	21.4

INDUSTRY: SUPERMARKETS INDUSTRY (NAICS 44511)
PRODUCT LINE: JEWELRY & WATCHES (Main Category)

NAICS 44511: Grocery Stores Industry. this industry comprises
establishments generally known as supermarkets and grocery stores
primarily engaged in retailing a general line of food, such as canned and
frozen foods; fresh fruits and vegetables; and fresh and prepared meats,
fish, and poultry. Included in this industry are delicatessen-type
establishments primarily engaged in retailing a general line of food.

5-YEAR TREND — ESTIMATED INDUSTRY SALES ($MILLIONS)

Year	Employee Size of Establishment									Total Industry Sales
	1-4 Emps.	5-9 Emps.	10-19 Emps.	20-49 Emps.	50-99 Emps.	100-249 Emps.	250-499 Emps.	500-999 Emps.	Unknown Emps.	
2015	2.8	2.0	5.2	17.3	41.0	101.8	31.8	3.8	0.5	206.3
2016	2.8	2.0	5.2	17.2	40.7	101.2	31.6	3.8	0.5	205.0
2017	2.8	2.0	5.2	17.2	40.7	101.1	31.6	3.8	0.5	204.9
2018	2.9	2.1	5.3	17.5	41.5	103.2	32.2	3.9	0.5	209.1
2019	2.9	2.1	5.5	18.1	42.8	106.4	33.2	4.0	0.6	215.6

INDUSTRY: BEER, WINE & LIQUOR STORES (NAICS 44531)
PRODUCT LINE: JEWELRY & WATCHES (Main Category)

NAICS 44531: Beer & Wine & Liquor Stores. Establishments primarily engaged in the retail sale of packaged alcoholic beverages, such as ale, beer, wine, and liquor, for consumption off the premises. Stores selling prepared drinks for consumption on the premises are classified in SIC 5813.

5-YEAR TREND – ESTIMATED INDUSTRY SALES ($MILLIONS)

Year	Employee Size of Establishment									Total Industry Sales
	1-4 Emps.	5-9 Emps.	10-19 Emps.	20-49 Emps.	50-99 Emps.	100-249 Emps.	250-499 Emps.	500-999 Emps.	Unknown Emps.	
2015	2.8	2.8	2.4	1.7	0.2	0.1	0.0	0.1	0.2	10.3
2016	2.8	2.8	2.4	1.8	0.3	0.1	0.0	0.1	0.2	10.5
2017	2.9	2.9	2.5	1.8	0.3	0.2	0.0	0.1	0.2	10.8
2018	3.1	3.1	2.6	1.9	0.3	0.2	0.0	0.1	0.2	11.5
2019	3.3	3.3	2.8	2.1	0.3	0.2	0.0	0.1	0.2	12.2

INDUSTRY: PHARMACIES & DRUG STORES (NAICS 44611)
PRODUCT LINE: JEWELRY & WATCHES (Main Category)

NAICS 44611 Pharmacies and Drug Stores – this industry comprises establishments known as pharmacies and drug stores engaged in retailing prescription or nonprescription drugs and medicines.

5-YEAR TREND – ESTIMATED INDUSTRY SALES ($MILLIONS)

Year	Employee Size of Establishment									Total Industry Sales
	1-4 Emps.	5-9 Emps.	10-19 Emps.	20-49 Emps.	50-99 Emps.	100-249 Emps.	250-499 Emps.	500-999 Emps.	Unknown Emps.	
2015	5.2	13.0	52.5	154.3	15.6	6.2	2.4	0.8	0.4	250.5
2016	5.4	13.4	54.2	159.2	16.1	6.4	2.5	0.8	0.4	258.4
2017	5.6	13.9	56.2	164.9	16.7	6.7	2.6	0.9	0.4	267.8
2018	5.9	14.7	59.5	174.7	17.7	7.1	2.7	0.9	0.5	283.6
2019	6.3	15.7	63.5	186.5	18.9	7.6	2.9	1.0	0.5	302.8

INDUSTRY: MEN'S CLOTHING STORES INDUSTRY (NAICS 44811)
PRODUCT LINE: JEWELRY & WATCHES (Main Category)

NAICS 44811: Men's Clothing Stores. this industry comprises
establishments primarily engaged in retailing a general line of new
men's and boys' clothing. These establishments may provide basic
alterations, such as hemming, taking in or letting out seams, or lengthening
or shortening sleeves.

5-YEAR TREND — ESTIMATED INDUSTRY SALES ($MILLIONS)

Year	Employee Size of Establishment									Total
	1-4 Emps.	5-9 Emps.	10-19 Emps.	20-49 Emps.	50-99 Emps.	100-249 Emps.	250-499 Emps.	500-999 Emps.	Unknown Emps.	Industry Sales
2015	1.0	1.7	3.2	1.7	0.4	0.3	0.1	0.0	0.2	8.6
2016	1.0	1.8	3.3	1.8	0.4	0.3	0.1	0.0	0.2	8.9
2017	1.1	1.9	3.5	1.8	0.4	0.4	0.1	0.0	0.2	9.3
2018	1.1	1.9	3.6	1.9	0.4	0.4	0.1	0.0	0.2	9.6
2019	1.1	2.0	3.7	2.0	0.4	0.4	0.1	0.0	0.2	10.0

INDUSTRY: WOMEN'S CLOTHING STORES INDUSTRY (NAICS 44812)
PRODUCT LINE: JEWELRY & WATCHES (Main Category)

NAICS 44812: Women's Clothing Stores . this industry comprises
establishments primarily engaged in retailing a general line of new
women's, misses' and juniors' clothing, including maternity wear.
These establishments may provide basic alterations, such as hemming,
taking in or letting out seams, or lengthening or shortening sleeves.

5-YEAR TREND — ESTIMATED INDUSTRY SALES ($MILLIONS)

Year	Employee Size of Establishment									Total
	1-4 Emps.	5-9 Emps.	10-19 Emps.	20-49 Emps.	50-99 Emps.	100-249 Emps.	250-499 Emps.	500-999 Emps.	Unknown Emps.	Industry Sales
2015	78.0	174.1	371.5	262.0	92.5	85.5	34.7	33.6	17.4	1,149.3
2016	80.3	179.3	382.5	269.8	95.3	88.0	35.7	34.6	17.9	1,183.4
2017	83.1	185.5	395.7	279.1	98.6	91.1	36.9	35.7	18.5	1,224.3
2018	87.6	195.7	417.6	294.5	104.0	96.1	39.0	37.4	19.6	1,291.4
2019	93.2	208.2	444.2	313.3	110.7	102.2	41.5	39.4	20.8	1,373.6

	INDUSTRY: FAMILY CLOTHING STORES INDUSTRY (NAICS 44814)
	PRODUCT LINE: JEWELRY & WATCHES (Main Category)

NAICS 44814: Family Clothing Stores . this industry comprises establishments primarily engaged in retailing a general line of new clothing for men, women, and children, without specializing in sales for an individual gender or age group. These establishments may provide basic alterations, such as hemming, taking in or letting out seams, or lengthening or shortening sleeves.

5-YEAR TREND — ESTIMATED INDUSTRY SALES ($MILLIONS)

Year	Employee Size of Establishment									Total
	1-4 Emps.	5-9 Emps.	10-19 Emps.	20-49 Emps.	50-99 Emps.	100-249 Emps.	250-499 Emps.	500-999 Emps.	Unknown Emps.	Industry Sales
2015	17.8	36.8	139.1	462.4	408.5	112.4	106.0	61.4	4.9	1,349.5
2016	18.3	37.8	142.9	474.8	419.4	115.4	108.9	63.0	5.0	1,385.6
2017	18.9	39.0	147.4	490.0	432.8	119.1	112.4	65.1	5.2	1,429.9
2018	19.9	41.1	155.4	516.5	456.2	125.6	118.4	68.3	5.5	1,506.9
2019	21.2	43.7	165.2	549.0	485.0	133.5	125.9	72.3	5.8	1,601.6

	INDUSTRY: PRERECORDED TAPES & CDs STORES (NAICS 45122)
	PRODUCT LINE: JEWELRY & WATCHES (Main Category)

NAICS 45122: Prerecorded Tape, Compact Disc, and Record Stores . This industry comprises establishments primarily engaged in retailing new prerecorded audio and video tapes, compact discs (CDs), and phonograph records.

5-YEAR TREND — ESTIMATED INDUSTRY SALES ($MILLIONS)

Year	Employee Size of Establishment									Total
	1-4 Emps.	5-9 Emps.	10-19 Emps.	20-49 Emps.	50-99 Emps.	100-249 Emps.	250-499 Emps.	500-999 Emps.	Unknown Emps.	Industry Sales
2015	0.5	1.0	2.6	5.4	4.1	271.0	21.2	0.4	0.2	306.5
2016	0.5	1.1	2.7	5.5	4.2	277.5	21.7	0.5	0.2	313.9
2017	0.6	1.1	2.8	5.7	4.3	285.6	22.3	0.5	0.2	323.1
2018	0.6	1.1	2.9	5.9	4.5	296.2	23.1	0.5	0.2	335.1
2019	0.6	1.2	3.0	6.2	4.7	309.9	24.2	0.5	0.2	350.5

INDUSTRY: DEPARTMENT STORES INDUSTRY (NAICS 45211)
PRODUCT LINE: JEWELRY & WATCHES (Main Category)

NAICS 45211: Department Stores Industry . this industry comprises establishments known as department stores primarily engaged in retailing a wide range of the following new products with no one merchandise line predominating: apparel, furniture, appliances and home furnishings; and selected additional items, such as paint, hardware, toiletries, cosmetics, photographic equipment, jewelry, toys, and sporting goods. merchandise lines are normally arranged in separate departments.

5-YEAR TREND – ESTIMATED INDUSTRY SALES ($MILLIONS)

Year	Employee Size of Establishment									Total Industry Sales
	1-4 Emps.	5-9 Emps.	10-19 Emps.	20-49 Emps.	50-99 Emps.	100-249 Emps.	250-499 Emps.	500-999 Emps.	Unknown Emps.	
2015	0.1	0.2	0.4	29.7	538.7	1,729.9	716.1	103.6	4.4	3,123.0
2016	0.1	0.2	0.4	29.8	540.8	1,736.6	718.9	104.0	4.4	3,135.2
2017	0.1	0.2	0.4	30.1	546.2	1,753.8	726.0	105.0	4.5	3,166.1
2018	0.1	0.2	0.4	30.1	546.2	1,754.0	726.1	105.3	4.5	3,166.8
2019	0.1	0.2	0.4	30.4	551.6	1,771.4	733.3	106.5	4.5	3,198.3

INDUSTRY: WAREHOUSE CLUBS & SUPERCENTERS (NAICS 45291)
PRODUCT LINE: JEWELRY & WATCHES (Main Category)

NAICS 45291: Warehouse Clubs and Superstores This industry comprises establishments known as warehouse clubs, superstores or supercenters primarily engaged in retailing a general line of groceries in combination with general lines of new merchandise, such as apparel, furniture, and appliances.

5-YEAR TREND – ESTIMATED INDUSTRY SALES ($MILLIONS)

Year	Employee Size of Establishment									Total Industry Sales
	1-4 Emps.	5-9 Emps.	10-19 Emps.	20-49 Emps.	50-99 Emps.	100-249 Emps.	250-499 Emps.	500-999 Emps.	Unknown Emps.	
2015	0.3	0.1	0.2	8.1	15.4	876.6	3,858.9	97.2	1.5	4,858.2
2016	0.3	0.1	0.2	8.3	15.8	900.7	3,965.3	99.9	1.5	4,992.1
2017	0.3	0.1	0.2	8.6	16.3	930.2	4,094.8	103.2	1.6	5,155.2
2018	0.3	0.1	0.3	9.2	17.5	1,001.1	4,406.9	111.0	1.7	5,548.1
2019	0.3	0.1	0.3	9.8	18.6	1,060.4	4,668.0	117.6	1.8	5,876.8

INDUSTRY: ELECTRONIC SHOPPING & MAIL-ORDER (NAICS 45411)
PRODUCT LINE: JEWELRY & WATCHES (Main Category)

NAICS 45411: Electronic Shopping and Mail-Order Houses This industry comprises establishments primarily engaged in retailing all types of merchandise by means of mail or by electronic media, such as interactive television or computer. Included in this industry are establishments primarily engaged in retailing from catalogue showrooms of mail-order houses.

5-Year Trend – Estimated Industry Sales ($Millions)

| Year | Employee Size of Establishment | | | | | | | | | Total |
	1-4 Emps.	5-9 Emps.	10-19 Emps.	20-49 Emps.	50-99 Emps.	100-249 Emps.	250-499 Emps.	500-999 Emps.	Unknown Emps.	Industry Sales
2015	1,283.7	661.3	955.4	1,603.7	1,207.1	2,233.3	3,010.9	4,250.2	180.4	15,386.0
2016	1,357.8	699.4	1,010.6	1,696.2	1,276.8	2,362.2	3,184.7	4,495.6	190.8	16,274.1
2017	1,439.6	741.6	1,071.4	1,798.4	1,353.7	2,504.5	3,376.5	4,766.4	202.3	17,254.5
2018	1,613.4	831.1	1,200.8	2,015.5	1,517.1	2,806.8	3,784.1	5,244.9	226.8	19,240.3
2019	1,793.7	924.0	1,335.0	2,240.8	1,686.7	3,120.6	4,207.1	5,743.7	252.1	21,303.8

INDUSTRY: BOOK STORES INDUSTRY (NAICS 451211)
PRODUCT LINE: JEWELRY & WATCHES (Main Category)

NAICS 451211: Book Stores. this industry comprises establishments primarily engaged in the retail sale of new books and magazines. Establishments primarily engaged in the retail sale of used books are classified in 5932.

5-Year Trend – Estimated Industry Sales ($Millions)

| Year | Employee Size of Establishment | | | | | | | | | Total |
	1-4 Emps.	5-9 Emps.	10-19 Emps.	20-49 Emps.	50-99 Emps.	100-249 Emps.	250-499 Emps.	500-999 Emps.	Unknown Emps.	Industry Sales
2015	0.9	1.3	2.6	7.0	3.1	1.4	0.3	0.8	0.4	18.0
2016	0.9	1.4	2.8	7.4	3.2	1.5	0.4	0.9	0.5	18.8
2017	1.0	1.5	2.9	7.7	3.4	1.5	0.4	0.9	0.5	19.7
2018	1.0	1.5	3.0	8.0	3.5	1.6	0.4	1.0	0.5	20.5
2019	1.0	1.6	3.2	8.4	3.6	1.7	0.4	1.0	0.5	21.4

INDUSTRY: DEPARTMENT STORES INDUSTRY (NAICS 45211)
PRODUCT LINE: GOLD JEWELRY (Sub Category)

NAICS 45211: Department Stores Industry . this industry comprises
establishments known as department stores primarily engaged in retailing
a wide range of the following new products with no one merchandise line
predominating: apparel, furniture, appliances and home furnishings; and
selected additional items, such as paint, hardware, toiletries, cosmetics,
photographic equipment, jewelry, toys, and sporting goods. merchandise lines
are normally arranged in separate departments.

5-YEAR TREND – ESTIMATED INDUSTRY SALES ($MILLIONS)

| Year | Employee Size of Establishment | | | | | | | | | Total |
	1-4 Emps.	5-9 Emps.	10-19 Emps.	20-49 Emps.	50-99 Emps.	100-249 Emps.	250-499 Emps.	500-999 Emps.	Unknown Emps.	Industry Sales
2015	0.0	0.0	0.1	4.7	86.1	276.5	114.4	16.6	0.7	499.1
2016	0.0	0.0	0.1	4.8	86.4	277.6	114.9	16.6	0.7	501.1
2017	0.0	0.0	0.1	4.8	87.3	280.3	116.0	16.8	0.7	506.0
2018	0.0	0.0	0.1	4.8	87.3	280.3	116.0	16.8	0.7	506.1
2019	0.0	0.0	0.1	4.9	88.2	283.1	117.2	17.0	0.7	511.2

INDUSTRY: WAREHOUSE CLUBS & SUPERCENTERS (NAICS 45291)
PRODUCT LINE: GOLD JEWELRY (Sub Category)

NAICS 45291: Warehouse Clubs and Superstores This industry
comprises establishments known as warehouse clubs, superstores or
supercenters primarily engaged in retailing a general line of groceries
in combination with general lines of new merchandise, such as apparel,
furniture, and appliances.

5-YEAR TREND – ESTIMATED INDUSTRY SALES ($MILLIONS)

| Year | Employee Size of Establishment | | | | | | | | | Total |
	1-4 Emps.	5-9 Emps.	10-19 Emps.	20-49 Emps.	50-99 Emps.	100-249 Emps.	250-499 Emps.	500-999 Emps.	Unknown Emps.	Industry Sales
2015	0.1	0.0	0.1	2.2	4.2	241.3	1,062.1	26.8	0.4	1,337.1
2016	0.1	0.0	0.1	2.3	4.3	247.9	1,091.3	27.5	0.4	1,373.9
2017	0.1	0.0	0.1	2.4	4.5	256.0	1,127.0	28.4	0.4	1,418.8
2018	0.1	0.0	0.1	2.5	4.8	275.5	1,212.9	30.6	0.5	1,527.0
2019	0.1	0.0	0.1	2.7	5.1	291.8	1,284.7	32.4	0.5	1,617.4

	INDUSTRY: DEPARTMENT STORES INDUSTRY (NAICS 45211)
	PRODUCT LINE: DIAMOND & GEMSTONE JEWELRY (Sub Category)

NAICS 45211: Department Stores Industry . this industry comprises establishments known as department stores primarily engaged in retailing a wide range of the following new products with no one merchandise line predominating: apparel, furniture, appliances and home furnishings; and selected additional items, such as paint, hardware, toiletries, cosmetics, photographic equipment, jewelry, toys, and sporting goods. merchandise lines are normally arranged in separate departments.

5-YEAR TREND – ESTIMATED INDUSTRY SALES ($MILLIONS)

Year	Employee Size of Establishment									Total
	1-4 Emps.	5-9 Emps.	10-19 Emps.	20-49 Emps.	50-99 Emps.	100-249 Emps.	250-499 Emps.	500-999 Emps.	Unknown Emps.	Industry Sales
2015	0.0	0.0	0.1	8.6	155.8	500.3	207.1	30.0	1.3	903.1
2016	0.0	0.0	0.1	8.6	156.4	502.2	207.9	30.1	1.3	906.6
2017	0.0	0.0	0.1	8.7	157.9	507.2	209.9	30.4	1.3	915.6
2018	0.0	0.0	0.1	8.7	158.0	507.2	210.0	30.5	1.3	915.8
2019	0.0	0.0	0.1	8.8	159.5	512.3	212.0	30.8	1.3	924.9

	INDUSTRY: WAREHOUSE CLUBS & SUPERCENTERS (NAICS 45291)
	PRODUCT LINE: DIAMOND & GEMSTONE JEWELRY (Sub Category)

NAICS 45291: Warehouse Clubs and Superstores This industry comprises establishments known as warehouse clubs, superstores or supercenters primarily engaged in retailing a general line of groceries in combination with general lines of new merchandise, such as apparel, furniture, and appliances.

5-YEAR TREND – ESTIMATED INDUSTRY SALES ($MILLIONS)

Year	Employee Size of Establishment									Total
	1-4 Emps.	5-9 Emps.	10-19 Emps.	20-49 Emps.	50-99 Emps.	100-249 Emps.	250-499 Emps.	500-999 Emps.	Unknown Emps.	Industry Sales
2015	0.1	0.0	0.1	2.0	3.8	218.4	961.5	24.2	0.4	1,210.5
2016	0.1	0.0	0.1	2.1	3.9	224.4	988.0	24.9	0.4	1,243.8
2017	0.1	0.0	0.1	2.1	4.1	231.8	1,020.2	25.7	0.4	1,284.4
2018	0.1	0.0	0.1	2.3	4.4	249.4	1,098.0	27.7	0.4	1,382.3
2019	0.1	0.0	0.1	2.4	4.6	264.2	1,163.1	29.3	0.4	1,464.2

INDUSTRY: DEPARTMENT STORES INDUSTRY (NAICS 45211)
PRODUCT LINE: OTHER FINE JEWELRY (Sub Category)

NAICS 45211: Department Stores Industry . this industry comprises establishments known as department stores primarily engaged in retailing a wide range of the following new products with no one merchandise line predominating: apparel, furniture, appliances and home furnishings; and selected additional items, such as paint, hardware, toiletries, cosmetics, photographic equipment, jewelry, toys, and sporting goods. merchandise lines are normally arranged in separate departments.

5-YEAR TREND – ESTIMATED INDUSTRY SALES ($MILLIONS)

Year	Employee Size of Establishment									Total
	1-4 Emps.	5-9 Emps.	10-19 Emps.	20-49 Emps.	50-99 Emps.	100-249 Emps.	250-499 Emps.	500-999 Emps.	Unknown Emps.	Industry Sales
2015	0.1	0.1	0.2	16.4	296.8	953.2	394.6	57.1	2.4	1,720.8
2016	0.1	0.1	0.2	16.4	298.0	956.9	396.1	57.3	2.4	1,727.5
2017	0.1	0.1	0.2	16.6	300.9	966.3	400.0	57.9	2.5	1,744.5
2018	0.1	0.1	0.2	16.6	301.0	966.4	400.1	58.0	2.5	1,744.9
2019	0.1	0.1	0.2	16.7	304.0	976.0	404.0	58.7	2.5	1,762.3

INDUSTRY: WAREHOUSE CLUBS & SUPERCENTERS (NAICS 45291)
PRODUCT LINE: OTHER FINE JEWELRY (Sub Category)

NAICS 45291: Warehouse Clubs and Superstores This industry comprises establishments known as warehouse clubs, superstores or supercenters primarily engaged in retailing a general line of groceries in combination with general lines of new merchandise, such as apparel, furniture, and appliances.

5-YEAR TREND – ESTIMATED INDUSTRY SALES ($MILLIONS)

Year	Employee Size of Establishment									Total
	1-4 Emps.	5-9 Emps.	10-19 Emps.	20-49 Emps.	50-99 Emps.	100-249 Emps.	250-499 Emps.	500-999 Emps.	Unknown Emps.	Industry Sales
2015	0.1	0.0	0.1	3.8	7.3	416.9	1,835.4	46.3	0.7	2,310.7
2016	0.1	0.0	0.1	4.0	7.5	428.4	1,886.0	47.5	0.7	2,374.4
2017	0.1	0.0	0.1	4.1	7.7	442.4	1,947.6	49.1	0.7	2,451.9
2018	0.1	0.0	0.1	4.4	8.3	476.1	2,096.0	52.8	0.8	2,638.8
2019	0.1	0.0	0.1	4.7	8.8	504.3	2,220.2	55.9	0.8	2,795.1

INDUSTRY: MEN'S CLOTHING STORES INDUSTRY (NAICS 44811)
PRODUCT LINE: COSTUME & NOVELTY JEWELRY (Sub Category)

NAICS 44811: Men's Clothing Stores. this industry comprises establishments primarily engaged in retailing a general line of new men's and boys' clothing. These establishments may provide basic alterations, such as hemming, taking in or letting out seams, or lengthening or shortening sleeves.

5-YEAR TREND – ESTIMATED INDUSTRY SALES ($MILLIONS)

Year	Employee Size of Establishment									Total
	1-4 Emps.	5-9 Emps.	10-19 Emps.	20-49 Emps.	50-99 Emps.	100-249 Emps.	250-499 Emps.	500-999 Emps.	Unknown Emps.	Industry Sales
2015	0.5	0.9	1.7	0.9	0.2	0.2	0.1	0.0	0.1	4.4
2016	0.5	0.9	1.7	0.9	0.2	0.2	0.1	0.0	0.1	4.6
2017	0.5	1.0	1.8	0.9	0.2	0.2	0.1	0.0	0.1	4.8
2018	0.6	1.0	1.8	1.0	0.2	0.2	0.1	0.0	0.1	4.9
2019	0.6	1.0	1.9	1.0	0.2	0.2	0.1	0.0	0.1	5.1

INDUSTRY: WOMEN'S CLOTHING STORES INDUSTRY (NAICS 44812)
PRODUCT LINE: COSTUME & NOVELTY JEWELRY (Sub Category)

NAICS 44812: Women's Clothing Stores . this industry comprises establishments primarily engaged in retailing a general line of new women's, misses' and juniors' clothing, including maternity wear. These establishments may provide basic alterations, such as hemming, taking in or letting out seams, or lengthening or shortening sleeves.

5-YEAR TREND – ESTIMATED INDUSTRY SALES ($MILLIONS)

Year	Employee Size of Establishment									Total
	1-4 Emps.	5-9 Emps.	10-19 Emps.	20-49 Emps.	50-99 Emps.	100-249 Emps.	250-499 Emps.	500-999 Emps.	Unknown Emps.	Industry Sales
2015	67.2	150.1	320.2	225.9	79.8	73.7	29.9	28.9	15.0	990.7
2016	69.2	154.5	329.7	232.6	82.1	75.9	30.8	29.8	15.4	1,020.0
2017	71.6	159.9	341.1	240.6	85.0	78.5	31.8	30.8	16.0	1,055.3
2018	75.5	168.7	359.9	253.9	89.7	82.8	33.6	32.3	16.9	1,113.2
2019	80.4	179.5	382.9	270.1	95.4	88.1	35.7	34.0	17.9	1,184.0

INDUSTRY: FAMILY CLOTHING STORES INDUSTRY (NAICS 44814)
PRODUCT LINE: COSTUME & NOVELTY JEWELRY (Sub Category)

NAICS 44814: Family Clothing Stores . this industry comprises establishments primarily engaged in retailing a general line of new clothing for men, women, and children, without specializing in sales for an individual gender or age group. These establishments may provide basic alterations, such as hemming, taking in or letting out seams, or lengthening or shortening sleeves.

5-Year Trend – Estimated Industry Sales ($Millions)

| Year | Employee Size of Establishment | | | | | | | | | Total |
	1-4 Emps.	5-9 Emps.	10-19 Emps.	20-49 Emps.	50-99 Emps.	100-249 Emps.	250-499 Emps.	500-999 Emps.	Unknown Emps.	Industry Sales
2015	6.7	13.8	52.0	172.8	152.6	42.0	39.6	22.9	1.8	504.2
2016	6.8	14.1	53.4	177.4	156.7	43.1	40.7	23.6	1.9	517.7
2017	7.1	14.6	55.1	183.1	161.7	44.5	42.0	24.3	1.9	534.2
2018	7.4	15.4	58.1	193.0	170.4	46.9	44.3	25.5	2.0	563.0
2019	7.9	16.3	61.7	205.1	181.2	49.9	47.0	27.0	2.2	598.4

INDUSTRY: MEN'S CLOTHING STORES INDUSTRY (NAICS 44811)
PRODUCT LINE: OTHER JEWELRY (Sub Category)

NAICS 44811: Men's Clothing Stores. this industry comprises establishments primarily engaged in retailing a general line of new men's and boys' clothing. These establishments may provide basic alterations, such as hemming, taking in or letting out seams, or lengthening or shortening sleeves.

5-Year Trend – Estimated Industry Sales ($Millions)

| Year | Employee Size of Establishment | | | | | | | | | Total |
	1-4 Emps.	5-9 Emps.	10-19 Emps.	20-49 Emps.	50-99 Emps.	100-249 Emps.	250-499 Emps.	500-999 Emps.	Unknown Emps.	Industry Sales
2015	0.5	0.8	1.6	0.8	0.2	0.2	0.1	0.0	0.1	4.2
2016	0.5	0.9	1.6	0.9	0.2	0.2	0.1	0.0	0.1	4.3
2017	0.5	0.9	1.7	0.9	0.2	0.2	0.1	0.0	0.1	4.5
2018	0.5	0.9	1.7	0.9	0.2	0.2	0.1	0.0	0.1	4.7
2019	0.6	1.0	1.8	1.0	0.2	0.2	0.1	0.0	0.1	4.8

INDUSTRY: WOMEN'S CLOTHING STORES INDUSTRY (NAICS 44812)
PRODUCT LINE: OTHER JEWELRY (Sub Category)

NAICS 44812: Women's Clothing Stores . this industry comprises establishments primarily engaged in retailing a general line of new women's, misses' and juniors' clothing, including maternity wear. These establishments may provide basic alterations, such as hemming, taking in or letting out seams, or lengthening or shortening sleeves.

5-YEAR TREND – ESTIMATED INDUSTRY SALES ($MILLIONS)

Year	Employee Size of Establishment									Total
	1-4 Emps.	5-9 Emps.	10-19 Emps.	20-49 Emps.	50-99 Emps.	100-249 Emps.	250-499 Emps.	500-999 Emps.	Unknown Emps.	Industry Sales
2015	10.8	24.0	51.3	36.2	12.8	11.8	4.8	4.6	2.4	158.6
2016	11.1	24.7	52.8	37.2	13.2	12.2	4.9	4.8	2.5	163.3
2017	11.5	25.6	54.6	38.5	13.6	12.6	5.1	4.9	2.6	169.0
2018	12.1	27.0	57.6	40.6	14.4	13.3	5.4	5.2	2.7	178.3
2019	12.9	28.7	61.3	43.2	15.3	14.1	5.7	5.4	2.9	189.6

INDUSTRY: FAMILY CLOTHING STORES INDUSTRY (NAICS 44814)
PRODUCT LINE: OTHER JEWELRY (Sub Category)

NAICS 44814: Family Clothing Stores . this industry comprises establishments primarily engaged in retailing a general line of new clothing for men, women, and children, without specializing in sales for an individual gender or age group. These establishments may provide basic alterations, such as hemming, taking in or letting out seams, or lengthening or shortening sleeves.

5-YEAR TREND – ESTIMATED INDUSTRY SALES ($MILLIONS)

Year	Employee Size of Establishment									Total
	1-4 Emps.	5-9 Emps.	10-19 Emps.	20-49 Emps.	50-99 Emps.	100-249 Emps.	250-499 Emps.	500-999 Emps.	Unknown Emps.	Industry Sales
2015	11.2	23.1	87.2	289.7	255.9	70.4	66.4	38.5	3.1	845.3
2016	11.5	23.7	89.5	297.4	262.7	72.3	68.2	39.5	3.1	867.9
2017	11.8	24.4	92.3	306.9	271.1	74.6	70.4	40.8	3.2	895.7
2018	12.5	25.8	97.3	323.5	285.8	78.6	74.2	42.8	3.4	943.9
2019	13.3	27.4	103.5	343.9	303.8	83.6	78.9	45.3	3.6	1,003.2

NAICS 44511: Grocery Stores Industry. this industry comprises establishments generally known as supermarkets and grocery stores primarily engaged in retailing a general line of food, such as canned and frozen foods; fresh fruits and vegetables; and fresh and prepared meats, fish, and poultry. Included in this industry are delicatessen-type establishments primarily engaged in retailing a general line of food.

5-YEAR TREND – ESTIMATED INDUSTRY SALES ($MILLIONS)

Year	Employee Size of Establishment									Total
	1-4 Emps.	5-9 Emps.	10-19 Emps.	20-49 Emps.	50-99 Emps.	100-249 Emps.	250-499 Emps.	500-999 Emps.	Unknown Emps.	Industry Sales
2015	13.4	9.7	24.9	82.2	194.7	484.2	151.2	18.1	2.5	980.9
2016	13.3	9.6	24.8	81.7	193.5	481.1	150.2	18.0	2.5	974.6
2017	13.3	9.6	24.8	81.6	193.4	480.9	150.2	18.0	2.5	974.3
2018	13.6	9.8	25.3	83.3	197.4	490.8	153.3	18.3	2.5	994.4
2019	14.0	10.1	26.1	85.9	203.5	506.0	158.0	18.9	2.6	1,025.1

NAICS 44611 Pharmacies and Drug Stores – this industry comprises establishments known as pharmacies and drug stores engaged in retailing prescription or nonprescription drugs and medicines.

5-YEAR TREND – ESTIMATED INDUSTRY SALES ($MILLIONS)

Year	Employee Size of Establishment									Total
	1-4 Emps.	5-9 Emps.	10-19 Emps.	20-49 Emps.	50-99 Emps.	100-249 Emps.	250-499 Emps.	500-999 Emps.	Unknown Emps.	Industry Sales
2015	4.6	11.5	46.6	136.8	13.8	5.5	2.1	0.7	0.4	222.1
2016	4.8	11.9	48.0	141.1	14.3	5.7	2.2	0.7	0.4	229.1
2017	5.0	12.3	49.8	146.2	14.8	5.9	2.3	0.8	0.4	237.4
2018	5.3	13.0	52.7	154.9	15.7	6.3	2.4	0.8	0.4	251.4
2019	5.6	13.9	56.3	165.4	16.7	6.7	2.6	0.9	0.4	268.5

INDUSTRY: GAS STATIONS W/CONVENIENCE STORES (NAICS 44711)
PRODUCT LINE: BOOKS (Main Category)

NAICS 44711: Gas Stations with Convenience Stores. this industry comprises establishments primarily engaged in selling gasoline and lubricating oils. These establishments frequently sell other merchandise, such as tires, batteries, and other automobile parts, or perform minor repair work. Gasoline stations combined with other activities, such as grocery stores, convenience stores, or carwashes, are classified according to the primary activity.

5-YEAR TREND – ESTIMATED INDUSTRY SALES ($MILLIONS)

| Year | Employee Size of Establishment | | | | | | | | | Total |
	1-4 Emps.	5-9 Emps.	10-19 Emps.	20-49 Emps.	50-99 Emps.	100-249 Emps.	250-499 Emps.	500-999 Emps.	Unknown Emps.	Industry Sales
2015	8.1	20.8	34.9	24.1	2.3	1.2	0.5	0.0	0.1	91.9
2016	8.4	21.7	36.3	25.1	2.4	1.3	0.5	0.0	0.1	95.8
2017	8.8	22.7	38.0	26.2	2.5	1.3	0.5	0.0	0.1	100.2
2018	9.4	24.2	40.5	27.9	2.6	1.4	0.6	0.0	0.1	106.8
2019	10.1	26.0	43.5	30.0	2.8	1.5	0.6	0.0	0.1	114.6

INDUSTRY: PRERECORDED TAPES & CDs STORES (NAICS 45122)
PRODUCT LINE: BOOKS (Main Category)

NAICS 45122: Prerecorded Tape, Compact Disc, and Record Stores .
This industry comprises establishments primarily engaged in retailing new prerecorded audio and video tapes, compact discs (CDs), and phonograph records.

5-YEAR TREND – ESTIMATED INDUSTRY SALES ($MILLIONS)

| Year | Employee Size of Establishment | | | | | | | | | Total |
	1-4 Emps.	5-9 Emps.	10-19 Emps.	20-49 Emps.	50-99 Emps.	100-249 Emps.	250-499 Emps.	500-999 Emps.	Unknown Emps.	Industry Sales
2015	6.5	12.7	32.2	65.9	50.0	3,294.6	257.3	5.4	2.3	3,726.8
2016	6.7	13.0	33.0	67.5	51.2	3,373.6	263.5	5.5	2.3	3,816.2
2017	6.9	13.4	34.0	69.4	52.7	3,472.4	271.2	5.6	2.4	3,927.9
2018	7.1	13.9	35.2	72.0	54.6	3,601.3	281.2	5.9	2.5	4,073.7
2019	7.5	14.5	36.8	75.3	57.1	3,767.6	294.2	6.1	2.6	4,261.9

INDUSTRY: DEPARTMENT STORES INDUSTRY (NAICS 45211)
PRODUCT LINE: BOOKS (Main Category)

NAICS 45211: Department Stores Industry . this industry comprises establishments known as department stores primarily engaged in retailing a wide range of the following new products with no one merchandise line predominating: apparel, furniture, appliances and home furnishings; and selected additional items, such as paint, hardware, toiletries, cosmetics, photographic equipment, jewelry, toys, and sporting goods. merchandise lines are normally arranged in separate departments.

5-YEAR TREND – ESTIMATED INDUSTRY SALES ($MILLIONS)

Year	Employee Size of Establishment									Total
	1-4 Emps.	5-9 Emps.	10-19 Emps.	20-49 Emps.	50-99 Emps.	100-249 Emps.	250-499 Emps.	500-999 Emps.	Unknown Emps.	Industry Sales
2015	0.0	0.0	0.0	3.4	61.6	197.9	81.9	11.9	0.5	357.3
2016	0.0	0.0	0.0	3.4	61.9	198.7	82.3	11.9	0.5	358.7
2017	0.0	0.0	0.0	3.4	62.5	200.7	83.1	12.0	0.5	362.3
2018	0.0	0.0	0.0	3.4	62.5	200.7	83.1	12.0	0.5	362.3
2019	0.0	0.0	0.0	3.5	63.1	202.7	83.9	12.2	0.5	365.9

INDUSTRY: WAREHOUSE CLUBS & SUPERCENTERS (NAICS 45291)
PRODUCT LINE: BOOKS (Main Category)

NAICS 45291: Warehouse Clubs and Superstores This industry comprises establishments known as warehouse clubs, superstores or supercenters primarily engaged in retailing a general line of groceries in combination with general lines of new merchandise, such as apparel, furniture, and appliances.

5-YEAR TREND – ESTIMATED INDUSTRY SALES ($MILLIONS)

Year	Employee Size of Establishment									Total
	1-4 Emps.	5-9 Emps.	10-19 Emps.	20-49 Emps.	50-99 Emps.	100-249 Emps.	250-499 Emps.	500-999 Emps.	Unknown Emps.	Industry Sales
2015	0.3	0.1	0.2	7.9	14.9	853.4	3,757.1	94.7	1.4	4,730.0
2016	0.3	0.1	0.2	8.1	15.4	877.0	3,860.6	97.3	1.5	4,860.4
2017	0.3	0.1	0.2	8.4	15.9	905.6	3,986.7	100.5	1.5	5,019.1
2018	0.3	0.1	0.2	9.0	17.1	974.6	4,290.6	108.1	1.6	5,401.7
2019	0.3	0.1	0.3	9.5	18.1	1,032.4	4,544.8	114.5	1.7	5,721.7

INDUSTRY: OFFICE SUPPLY & STATIONERY STORES (NAICS 45321)
PRODUCT LINE: BOOKS (Main Category)

NAICS 45321: Office Supplies and Stationery Stores . this industry comprises establishments primarily engaged in one or more of the following: (1) retailing new stationery, school supplies, and office supplies; (2) selling a combination of new office equipment, furniture, and supplies; and (3) selling new office equipment, furniture, and supplies in combination with selling new computers.

5-YEAR TREND – ESTIMATED INDUSTRY SALES ($MILLIONS)

Year	Employee Size of Establishment									Total
	1-4 Emps.	5-9 Emps.	10-19 Emps.	20-49 Emps.	50-99 Emps.	100-249 Emps.	250-499 Emps.	500-999 Emps.	Unknown Emps.	Industry Sales
2015	1.4	1.2	7.4	18.6	0.4	0.3	0.0	0.0	0.4	29.6
2016	1.4	1.1	7.4	18.4	0.4	0.3	0.0	0.0	0.4	29.4
2017	1.4	1.1	7.3	18.4	0.4	0.3	0.0	0.0	0.4	29.3
2018	1.4	1.1	7.1	17.8	0.4	0.3	0.0	0.0	0.3	28.3
2019	1.3	1.1	6.9	17.4	0.4	0.2	0.0	0.0	0.3	27.7

INDUSTRY: ELECTRONIC SHOPPING & MAIL-ORDER (NAICS 45411)
PRODUCT LINE: BOOKS (Main Category)

NAICS 45411: Electronic Shopping and Mail-Order Houses This industry comprises establishments primarily engaged in retailing all types of merchandise by means of mail or by electronic media, such as interactive television or computer. Included in this industry are establishments primarily engaged in retailing from catalogue showrooms of mail-order houses.

5-YEAR TREND – ESTIMATED INDUSTRY SALES ($MILLIONS)

Year	Employee Size of Establishment									Total
	1-4 Emps.	5-9 Emps.	10-19 Emps.	20-49 Emps.	50-99 Emps.	100-249 Emps.	250-499 Emps.	500-999 Emps.	Unknown Emps.	Industry Sales
2015	1,155.2	595.1	859.7	1,443.1	1,086.3	2,009.7	2,709.4	3,824.6	162.4	13,845.4
2016	1,221.8	629.4	909.4	1,526.4	1,149.0	2,125.7	2,865.8	4,045.4	171.7	14,644.5
2017	1,295.4	667.3	964.1	1,618.3	1,218.2	2,253.7	3,038.4	4,289.1	182.1	15,526.7
2018	1,451.8	747.9	1,080.5	1,813.7	1,365.2	2,525.7	3,405.1	4,719.7	204.1	17,313.7
2019	1,614.1	831.5	1,201.3	2,016.5	1,517.8	2,808.1	3,785.9	5,168.5	226.9	19,170.6

INDUSTRY: BOOK STORES INDUSTRY (NAICS 451211)
PRODUCT LINE: BOOKS (Main Category)

NAICS 451211: Book Stores. this industry comprises
establishments primarily engaged in the retail sale of new books and
magazines. Establishments primarily engaged in the retail sale of used
books are classified in 5932.

5-YEAR TREND — ESTIMATED INDUSTRY SALES ($MILLIONS)

| Year | Employee Size of Establishment | | | | | | | | | Total |
	1-4 Emps.	5-9 Emps.	10-19 Emps.	20-49 Emps.	50-99 Emps.	100-249 Emps.	250-499 Emps.	500-999 Emps.	Unknown Emps.	Industry Sales
2015	375.9	570.2	1,134.7	3,018.3	1,313.9	604.9	149.2	359.1	190.0	7,716.3
2016	393.0	596.1	1,186.3	3,155.6	1,373.6	632.4	156.0	375.4	198.7	8,067.1
2017	412.4	625.5	1,244.7	3,310.9	1,441.2	663.6	163.6	393.9	208.5	8,464.2
2018	428.2	649.4	1,292.3	3,437.6	1,496.3	689.0	169.9	411.2	216.4	8,790.2
2019	447.7	679.0	1,351.2	3,594.4	1,564.6	720.4	177.7	431.0	226.3	9,192.2

INDUSTRY: BOOK STORES INDUSTRY (NAICS 451211)
PRODUCT LINE: TRADE BOOKS (Sub Category)

NAICS 451211: Book Stores. this industry comprises
establishments primarily engaged in the retail sale of new books and
magazines. Establishments primarily engaged in the retail sale of used
books are classified in 5932.

5-YEAR TREND — ESTIMATED INDUSTRY SALES ($MILLIONS)

| Year | Employee Size of Establishment | | | | | | | | | Total |
	1-4 Emps.	5-9 Emps.	10-19 Emps.	20-49 Emps.	50-99 Emps.	100-249 Emps.	250-499 Emps.	500-999 Emps.	Unknown Emps.	Industry Sales
2015	200.0	303.4	603.7	1,605.9	699.0	321.8	79.4	191.0	101.1	4,105.3
2016	209.1	317.2	631.1	1,678.9	730.8	336.5	83.0	199.7	105.7	4,291.9
2017	219.4	332.8	662.2	1,761.5	766.8	353.0	87.1	209.5	110.9	4,503.2
2018	227.8	345.5	687.5	1,828.9	796.1	366.5	90.4	218.7	115.1	4,676.6
2019	238.2	361.3	718.9	1,912.3	832.4	383.3	94.5	229.3	120.4	4,890.5

INDUSTRY: BOOK STORES INDUSTRY (NAICS 451211)
PRODUCT LINE: MASS MARKET PAPERBACK BOOKS (Sub Category)

NAICS 451211: Book Stores. this industry comprises establishments primarily engaged in the retail sale of new books and magazines. Establishments primarily engaged in the retail sale of used books are classified in 5932.

5-YEAR TREND – ESTIMATED INDUSTRY SALES ($MILLIONS)

| Year | Employee Size of Establishment | | | | | | | | | Total |
	1-4 Emps.	5-9 Emps.	10-19 Emps.	20-49 Emps.	50-99 Emps.	100-249 Emps.	250-499 Emps.	500-999 Emps.	Unknown Emps.	Industry Sales
2015	12.2	18.4	36.7	97.6	42.5	19.6	4.8	11.6	6.1	249.4
2016	12.7	19.3	38.3	102.0	44.4	20.4	5.0	12.1	6.4	260.8
2017	13.3	20.2	40.2	107.0	46.6	21.4	5.3	12.7	6.7	273.6
2018	13.8	21.0	41.8	111.1	48.4	22.3	5.5	13.3	7.0	284.1
2019	14.5	21.9	43.7	116.2	50.6	23.3	5.7	13.9	7.3	297.1

INDUSTRY: BOOK STORES INDUSTRY (NAICS 451211)
PRODUCT LINE: RELIGIOUS BOOKS (Sub Category)

NAICS 451211: Book Stores. this industry comprises establishments primarily engaged in the retail sale of new books and magazines. Establishments primarily engaged in the retail sale of used books are classified in 5932.

5-YEAR TREND – ESTIMATED INDUSTRY SALES ($MILLIONS)

| Year | Employee Size of Establishment | | | | | | | | | Total |
	1-4 Emps.	5-9 Emps.	10-19 Emps.	20-49 Emps.	50-99 Emps.	100-249 Emps.	250-499 Emps.	500-999 Emps.	Unknown Emps.	Industry Sales
2015	23.2	35.3	70.2	186.6	81.2	37.4	9.2	22.2	11.8	477.1
2016	24.3	36.9	73.4	195.1	84.9	39.1	9.6	23.2	12.3	498.8
2017	25.5	38.7	77.0	204.7	89.1	41.0	10.1	24.4	12.9	523.4
2018	26.5	40.2	79.9	212.6	92.5	42.6	10.5	25.4	13.4	543.5
2019	27.7	42.0	83.6	222.2	96.7	44.5	11.0	26.6	14.0	568.4

INDUSTRY: BOOK STORES INDUSTRY (NAICS 451211)
PRODUCT LINE: GENERAL REFERENCE BOOKS (Sub Category)

NAICS 451211: Book Stores. this industry comprises establishments primarily engaged in the retail sale of new books and magazines. Establishments primarily engaged in the retail sale of used books are classified in 5932.

5-YEAR TREND — ESTIMATED INDUSTRY SALES ($MILLIONS)

| Year | Employee Size of Establishment | | | | | | | | | Total |
	1-4 Emps.	5-9 Emps.	10-19 Emps.	20-49 Emps.	50-99 Emps.	100-249 Emps.	250-499 Emps.	500-999 Emps.	Unknown Emps.	Industry Sales
2015	3.1	4.7	9.4	25.0	10.9	5.0	1.2	3.0	1.6	63.8
2016	3.3	4.9	9.8	26.1	11.4	5.2	1.3	3.1	1.6	66.7
2017	3.4	5.2	10.3	27.4	11.9	5.5	1.4	3.3	1.7	70.0
2018	3.5	5.4	10.7	28.4	12.4	5.7	1.4	3.4	1.8	72.7
2019	3.7	5.6	11.2	29.7	12.9	6.0	1.5	3.6	1.9	76.0

INDUSTRY: BOOK STORES INDUSTRY (NAICS 451211)
PRODUCT LINE: TEXTBOOKS (Sub Category)

NAICS 451211: Book Stores. this industry comprises establishments primarily engaged in the retail sale of new books and magazines. Establishments primarily engaged in the retail sale of used books are classified in 5932.

5-YEAR TREND — ESTIMATED INDUSTRY SALES ($MILLIONS)

| Year | Employee Size of Establishment | | | | | | | | | Total |
	1-4 Emps.	5-9 Emps.	10-19 Emps.	20-49 Emps.	50-99 Emps.	100-249 Emps.	250-499 Emps.	500-999 Emps.	Unknown Emps.	Industry Sales
2015	124.3	188.5	375.1	997.8	434.3	200.0	49.3	118.7	62.8	2,550.9
2016	129.9	197.1	392.2	1,043.2	454.1	209.1	51.6	124.1	65.7	2,666.9
2017	136.3	206.8	411.5	1,094.6	476.5	219.4	54.1	130.2	68.9	2,798.2
2018	141.5	214.7	427.2	1,136.4	494.7	227.8	56.2	135.9	71.5	2,906.0
2019	148.0	224.5	446.7	1,188.3	517.2	238.2	58.7	142.5	74.8	3,038.9

<table>
<tr><td colspan="2" align="center">INDUSTRY: BOOK STORES INDUSTRY (NAICS 451211)</td></tr>
<tr><td colspan="2" align="center">PRODUCT LINE: PROFESSIONAL BOOKS (Sub Category)</td></tr>
</table>

NAICS 451211: Book Stores. this industry comprises
establishments primarily engaged in the retail sale of new books and
magazines. Establishments primarily engaged in the retail sale of used
books are classified in 5932.

5-YEAR TREND — ESTIMATED INDUSTRY SALES ($MILLIONS)

Year	Employee Size of Establishment									Total
	1-4 Emps.	5-9 Emps.	10-19 Emps.	20-49 Emps.	50-99 Emps.	100-249 Emps.	250-499 Emps.	500-999 Emps.	Unknown Emps.	Industry Sales
2015	3.7	5.7	11.3	30.0	13.1	6.0	1.5	3.6	1.9	76.7
2016	3.9	5.9	11.8	31.4	13.6	6.3	1.5	3.7	2.0	80.2
2017	4.1	6.2	12.4	32.9	14.3	6.6	1.6	3.9	2.1	84.1
2018	4.3	6.5	12.8	34.2	14.9	6.8	1.7	4.1	2.2	87.3
2019	4.4	6.7	13.4	35.7	15.5	7.2	1.8	4.3	2.2	91.3

<table>
<tr><td colspan="2" align="center">INDUSTRY: BOOK STORES INDUSTRY (NAICS 451211)</td></tr>
<tr><td colspan="2" align="center">PRODUCT LINE: OTHER BOOKS (Sub Category)</td></tr>
</table>

NAICS 451211: Book Stores. this industry comprises
establishments primarily engaged in the retail sale of new books and
magazines. Establishments primarily engaged in the retail sale of used
books are classified in 5932.

5-YEAR TREND — ESTIMATED INDUSTRY SALES ($MILLIONS)

Year	Employee Size of Establishment									Total
	1-4 Emps.	5-9 Emps.	10-19 Emps.	20-49 Emps.	50-99 Emps.	100-249 Emps.	250-499 Emps.	500-999 Emps.	Unknown Emps.	Industry Sales
2015	9.4	14.3	28.4	75.5	32.9	15.1	3.7	9.0	4.8	193.0
2016	9.8	14.9	29.7	78.9	34.4	15.8	3.9	9.4	5.0	201.8
2017	10.3	15.6	31.1	82.8	36.1	16.6	4.1	9.9	5.2	211.7
2018	10.7	16.2	32.3	86.0	37.4	17.2	4.3	10.3	5.4	219.9
2019	11.2	17.0	33.8	89.9	39.1	18.0	4.4	10.8	5.7	230.0

INDUSTRY: HOME CENTERS INDUSTRY (NAICS 44411)
PRODUCT LINE: TOYS & GAMES (Main Category)

NAICS 44411: Home Centers. This industry comprises establishments known as home centers primarily engaged in retailing a general line of new home repair and improvement materials and supplies, such as lumber, plumbing goods, electrical goods, tools, housewares, hardware, and lawn and garden supplies, with no one merchandise line predominating. The merchandise lines are normally arranged in separate departments.

5-YEAR TREND – ESTIMATED INDUSTRY SALES ($MILLIONS)

Year	Employee Size of Establishment									Total
	1-4 Emps.	5-9 Emps.	10-19 Emps.	20-49 Emps.	50-99 Emps.	100-249 Emps.	250-499 Emps.	500-999 Emps.	Unknown Emps.	Industry Sales
2015	0.0	0.0	0.1	0.1	0.1	5.5	0.4	0.0	0.0	6.2
2016	0.0	0.0	0.1	0.1	0.1	5.6	0.4	0.0	0.0	6.4
2017	0.0	0.0	0.1	0.1	0.1	5.8	0.5	0.0	0.0	6.6
2018	0.0	0.0	0.1	0.1	0.1	6.0	0.5	0.0	0.0	6.8
2019	0.0	0.0	0.1	0.1	0.1	6.3	0.5	0.0	0.0	7.1

INDUSTRY: HARDWARE STORES (NAICS 44413)
PRODUCT LINE: TOYS & GAMES (Main Category)

NAICS 44413: Hardware Stores. Establishments primarily engaged in the retail sale of a number of basic hardware lines, such as tools, builders' hardware, paint and glass, housewares and household appliances, and cutlery.

5-YEAR TREND – ESTIMATED INDUSTRY SALES ($MILLIONS)

Year	Employee Size of Establishment									Total
	1-4 Emps.	5-9 Emps.	10-19 Emps.	20-49 Emps.	50-99 Emps.	100-249 Emps.	250-499 Emps.	500-999 Emps.	Unknown Emps.	Industry Sales
2016	6.1	10.4	20.9	29.9	5.9	1.9	0.3	0.0	0.5	76.0
2017	6.2	10.5	21.1	30.2	6.0	2.0	0.3	0.0	0.5	76.8
2018	6.3	10.6	21.4	30.6	6.1	2.0	0.4	0.0	0.5	78.0
2019	6.5	11.1	22.3	31.9	6.3	2.1	0.4	0.0	0.6	81.1
2019	6.9	11.6	23.4	33.4	6.6	2.2	0.4	0.0	0.6	85.1

NAICS 44511: Grocery Stores Industry. this industry comprises establishments generally known as supermarkets and grocery stores primarily engaged in retailing a general line of food, such as canned and frozen foods; fresh fruits and vegetables; and fresh and prepared meats, fish, and poultry. Included in this industry are delicatessen-type establishments primarily engaged in retailing a general line of food.

5-YEAR TREND – ESTIMATED INDUSTRY SALES ($MILLIONS)

Year	Employee Size of Establishment									Total
	1-4 Emps.	5-9 Emps.	10-19 Emps.	20-49 Emps.	50-99 Emps.	100-249 Emps.	250-499 Emps.	500-999 Emps.	Unknown Emps.	Industry Sales
2016	7.0	5.1	13.0	42.9	101.8	253.1	79.0	9.5	1.3	512.7
2017	7.0	5.0	13.0	42.7	101.1	251.4	78.5	9.4	1.3	509.4
2018	6.9	5.0	12.9	42.7	101.1	251.4	78.5	9.4	1.3	509.2
2019	7.1	5.1	13.2	43.5	103.2	256.5	80.1	9.6	1.3	519.7
2019	7.3	5.3	13.6	44.9	106.4	264.5	82.6	9.9	1.4	535.8

NAICS 44611 Pharmacies and Drug Stores – this industry comprises establishments known as pharmacies and drug stores engaged in retailing prescription or nonprescription drugs and medicines.

5-YEAR TREND – ESTIMATED INDUSTRY SALES ($MILLIONS)

Year	Employee Size of Establishment									Total
	1-4 Emps.	5-9 Emps.	10-19 Emps.	20-49 Emps.	50-99 Emps.	100-249 Emps.	250-499 Emps.	500-999 Emps.	Unknown Emps.	Industry Sales
2016	14.7	36.5	147.6	433.5	43.8	17.6	6.7	2.2	1.1	703.8
2017	15.2	37.6	152.2	447.1	45.2	18.1	6.9	2.3	1.2	725.9
2018	15.7	39.0	157.7	463.3	46.9	18.8	7.2	2.4	1.2	752.1
2019	16.7	41.3	167.1	490.7	49.6	19.9	7.6	2.5	1.3	796.6
2019	17.8	44.1	178.4	524.0	53.0	21.2	8.1	2.7	1.4	850.7

INDUSTRY: GAS STATIONS W/CONVENIENCE STORES (NAICS 44711)
PRODUCT LINE: TOYS & GAMES (Main Category)

NAICS 44711: Gas Stations with Convenience Stores. this industry comprises establishments primarily engaged in selling gasoline and lubricating oils. These establishments frequently sell other merchandise, such as tires, batteries, and other automobile parts, or perform minor repair work. Gasoline stations combined with other activities, such as grocery stores, convenience stores, or carwashes, are classified according to the primary activity.

5-YEAR TREND — ESTIMATED INDUSTRY SALES ($MILLIONS)

Year	Employee Size of Establishment									Total
	1-4 Emps.	5-9 Emps.	10-19 Emps.	20-49 Emps.	50-99 Emps.	100-249 Emps.	250-499 Emps.	500-999 Emps.	Unknown Emps.	Industry Sales
2016	1.2	3.0	5.1	3.5	0.3	0.2	0.1	0.0	0.0	13.4
2017	1.2	3.2	5.3	3.6	0.3	0.2	0.1	0.0	0.0	13.9
2018	1.3	3.3	5.5	3.8	0.4	0.2	0.1	0.0	0.0	14.6
2019	1.4	3.5	5.9	4.1	0.4	0.2	0.1	0.0	0.0	15.5
2019	1.5	3.8	6.3	4.4	0.4	0.2	0.1	0.0	0.0	16.7

INDUSTRY: FAMILY CLOTHING STORES INDUSTRY (NAICS 44814)
PRODUCT LINE: TOYS & GAMES (Main Category)

NAICS 44814: Family Clothing Stores . this industry comprises establishments primarily engaged in retailing a general line of new clothing for men, women, and children, without specializing in sales for an individual gender or age group. These establishments may provide basic alterations, such as hemming, taking in or letting out seams, or lengthening or shortening sleeves.

5-YEAR TREND — ESTIMATED INDUSTRY SALES ($MILLIONS)

Year	Employee Size of Establishment									Total
	1-4 Emps.	5-9 Emps.	10-19 Emps.	20-49 Emps.	50-99 Emps.	100-249 Emps.	250-499 Emps.	500-999 Emps.	Unknown Emps.	Industry Sales
2016	28.5	58.9	222.4	739.0	652.8	179.7	169.5	98.1	7.8	2,156.6
2017	29.2	60.4	228.3	758.8	670.3	184.5	174.0	100.8	8.0	2,214.4
2018	30.2	62.4	235.6	783.1	691.7	190.4	179.6	104.0	8.3	2,285.2
2019	31.8	65.7	248.3	825.4	729.1	200.7	189.3	109.2	8.7	2,408.3
2019	33.8	69.9	264.0	877.4	775.0	213.3	201.2	115.6	9.3	2,559.5

INDUSTRY: PRERECORDED TAPES & CDs STORES (NAICS 45122)
PRODUCT LINE: TOYS & GAMES (Main Category)

NAICS 45122: Prerecorded Tape, Compact Disc, and Record Stores .
This industry comprises establishments primarily engaged in retailing new prerecorded audio and video tapes, compact discs (CDs), and phonograph records.

5-YEAR TREND – ESTIMATED INDUSTRY SALES ($MILLIONS)

Year	Employee Size of Establishment									Total
	1-4 Emps.	5-9 Emps.	10-19 Emps.	20-49 Emps.	50-99 Emps.	100-249 Emps.	250-499 Emps.	500-999 Emps.	Unknown Emps.	Industry Sales
2016	8.0	15.6	39.6	80.9	61.4	4,047.8	316.1	6.6	2.8	4,578.8
2017	8.2	16.0	40.5	82.9	62.9	4,144.8	323.7	6.7	2.9	4,688.6
2018	8.5	16.4	41.7	85.3	64.7	4,266.2	333.2	6.9	3.0	4,825.9
2019	8.8	17.1	43.3	88.5	67.1	4,424.6	345.5	7.2	3.1	5,005.1
2019	9.2	17.8	45.3	92.6	70.2	4,628.9	361.5	7.5	3.2	5,236.2

INDUSTRY: DEPARTMENT STORES INDUSTRY (NAICS 45211)
PRODUCT LINE: TOYS & GAMES (Main Category)

NAICS 45211: Department Stores Industry . this industry comprises establishments known as department stores primarily engaged in retailing a wide range of the following new products with no one merchandise line predominating: apparel, furniture, appliances and home furnishings; and selected additional items, such as paint, hardware, toiletries, cosmetics, photographic equipment, jewelry, toys, and sporting goods. merchandise lines are normally arranged in separate departments.

5-YEAR TREND – ESTIMATED INDUSTRY SALES ($MILLIONS)

Year	Employee Size of Establishment									Total
	1-4 Emps.	5-9 Emps.	10-19 Emps.	20-49 Emps.	50-99 Emps.	100-249 Emps.	250-499 Emps.	500-999 Emps.	Unknown Emps.	Industry Sales
2016	0.2	0.2	0.5	40.2	729.9	2,343.6	970.1	140.3	6.0	4,231.0
2017	0.2	0.2	0.5	40.4	732.7	2,352.8	973.9	140.9	6.0	4,247.5
2018	0.2	0.2	0.5	40.8	739.9	2,376.0	983.5	142.3	6.0	4,289.5
2019	0.2	0.2	0.5	40.8	740.0	2,376.3	983.7	142.7	6.0	4,290.4
2019	0.2	0.2	0.5	41.2	747.4	2,399.8	993.4	144.3	6.1	4,333.1

INDUSTRY: WAREHOUSE CLUBS & SUPERCENTERS (NAICS 45291)
PRODUCT LINE: TOYS & GAMES (Main Category)

NAICS 45291: Warehouse Clubs and Superstores This industry comprises establishments known as warehouse clubs, superstores or supercenters primarily engaged in retailing a general line of groceries in combination with general lines of new merchandise, such as apparel, furniture, and appliances.

5-YEAR TREND – ESTIMATED INDUSTRY SALES ($MILLIONS)

Year	Employee Size of Establishment									Total
	1-4 Emps.	5-9 Emps.	10-19 Emps.	20-49 Emps.	50-99 Emps.	100-249 Emps.	250-499 Emps.	500-999 Emps.	Unknown Emps.	Industry Sales
2016	0.7	0.2	0.6	21.9	41.5	2,367.4	10,422.0	262.6	4.0	13,120.9
2017	0.7	0.2	0.6	22.5	42.6	2,432.7	10,709.3	269.9	4.1	13,482.5
2018	0.7	0.2	0.6	23.2	44.0	2,512.1	11,059.1	278.7	4.2	13,922.8
2019	0.8	0.2	0.7	25.0	47.3	2,703.6	11,902.1	299.9	4.5	14,984.1
2019	0.8	0.2	0.7	26.4	50.2	2,863.8	12,607.1	317.7	4.8	15,871.8

INDUSTRY: OFFICE SUPPLY & STATIONERY STORES (NAICS 45321)
PRODUCT LINE: TOYS & GAMES (Main Category)

NAICS 45321: Office Supplies and Stationery Stores . this industry comprises establishments primarily engaged in one or more of the following: (1) retailing new stationery, school supplies, and office supplies; (2) selling a combination of new office equipment, furniture, and supplies; and (3) selling new office equipment, furniture, and supplies in combination with selling new computers.

5-YEAR TREND – ESTIMATED INDUSTRY SALES ($MILLIONS)

Year	Employee Size of Establishment									Total
	1-4 Emps.	5-9 Emps.	10-19 Emps.	20-49 Emps.	50-99 Emps.	100-249 Emps.	250-499 Emps.	500-999 Emps.	Unknown Emps.	Industry Sales
2016	0.7	0.6	3.8	9.4	0.2	0.1	0.0	0.0	0.2	15.1
2017	0.7	0.6	3.7	9.4	0.2	0.1	0.0	0.0	0.2	14.9
2018	0.7	0.6	3.7	9.3	0.2	0.1	0.0	0.0	0.2	14.9
2019	0.7	0.6	3.6	9.0	0.2	0.1	0.0	0.0	0.2	14.4
2019	0.7	0.6	3.5	8.8	0.2	0.1	0.0	0.0	0.2	14.1

INDUSTRY: ELECTRONIC SHOPPING & MAIL-ORDER (NAICS 45411)
PRODUCT LINE: TOYS & GAMES (Main Category)

NAICS 45411: Electronic Shopping and Mail-Order Houses This industry comprises establishments primarily engaged in retailing all types of merchandise by means of mail or by electronic media, such as interactive television or computer. Included in this industry are establishments primarily engaged in retailing from catalogue showrooms of mail-order houses.

5-Year Trend – Estimated Industry Sales ($Millions)

Year	Employee Size of Establishment									Total
	1-4 Emps.	5-9 Emps.	10-19 Emps.	20-49 Emps.	50-99 Emps.	100-249 Emps.	250-499 Emps.	500-999 Emps.	Unknown Emps.	Industry Sales
2016	722.8	372.3	538.0	903.0	679.7	1,257.5	1,695.4	2,393.2	101.6	8,663.5
2017	764.5	393.8	569.0	955.1	718.9	1,330.1	1,793.2	2,531.3	107.5	9,163.6
2018	810.6	417.6	603.3	1,012.7	762.3	1,410.2	1,901.2	2,683.8	113.9	9,715.6
2019	908.4	468.0	676.1	1,134.9	854.3	1,580.4	2,130.7	2,953.3	127.7	10,833.8
2019	1,010.0	520.3	751.7	1,261.8	949.8	1,757.1	2,368.9	3,234.1	142.0	11,995.7

INDUSTRY: BOOK STORES INDUSTRY (NAICS 451211)
PRODUCT LINE: TOYS & GAMES (Main Category)

NAICS 451211: Book Stores. this industry comprises establishments primarily engaged in the retail sale of new books and magazines. Establishments primarily engaged in the retail sale of used books are classified in 5932.

5-Year Trend – Estimated Industry Sales ($Millions)

Year	Employee Size of Establishment									Total
	1-4 Emps.	5-9 Emps.	10-19 Emps.	20-49 Emps.	50-99 Emps.	100-249 Emps.	250-499 Emps.	500-999 Emps.	Unknown Emps.	Industry Sales
2016	1.2	1.8	3.5	9.4	4.1	1.9	0.5	1.1	0.6	24.1
2017	1.2	1.9	3.7	9.9	4.3	2.0	0.5	1.2	0.6	25.2
2018	1.3	2.0	3.9	10.3	4.5	2.1	0.5	1.2	0.7	26.4
2019	1.3	2.0	4.0	10.7	4.7	2.2	0.5	1.3	0.7	27.5
2019	1.4	2.1	4.2	11.2	4.9	2.3	0.6	1.3	0.7	28.7

INDUSTRY: PHARMACIES & DRUG STORES (NAICS 44611)
PRODUCT LINE: TOYS (Sub Category)

NAICS 44611 Pharmacies and Drug Stores – this industry comprises establishments known as pharmacies and drug stores engaged in retailing prescription or nonprescription drugs and medicines.

5-YEAR TREND – ESTIMATED INDUSTRY SALES ($MILLIONS)

Year	Employee Size of Establishment									Total
	1-4 Emps.	5-9 Emps.	10-19 Emps.	20-49 Emps.	50-99 Emps.	100-249 Emps.	250-499 Emps.	500-999 Emps.	Unknown Emps.	Industry Sales
2016	13.0	32.2	130.1	382.1	38.7	15.5	5.9	2.0	1.0	620.4
2017	13.4	33.2	134.2	394.1	39.9	16.0	6.1	2.0	1.0	639.8
2018	13.9	34.4	139.0	408.4	41.3	16.5	6.3	2.1	1.1	663.0
2019	14.7	36.4	147.3	432.5	43.7	17.5	6.7	2.2	1.1	702.2
2019	15.7	38.9	157.3	461.9	46.7	18.7	7.1	2.4	1.2	749.8

INDUSTRY: DEPARTMENT STORES INDUSTRY (NAICS 45211)
PRODUCT LINE: TOYS (Sub Category)

NAICS 45211: Department Stores Industry . this industry comprises establishments known as department stores primarily engaged in retailing a wide range of the following new products with no one merchandise line predominating: apparel, furniture, appliances and home furnishings; and selected additional items, such as paint, hardware, toiletries, cosmetics, photographic equipment, jewelry, toys, and sporting goods. merchandise lines are normally arranged in separate departments.

5-YEAR TREND – ESTIMATED INDUSTRY SALES ($MILLIONS)

Year	Employee Size of Establishment									Total
	1-4 Emps.	5-9 Emps.	10-19 Emps.	20-49 Emps.	50-99 Emps.	100-249 Emps.	250-499 Emps.	500-999 Emps.	Unknown Emps.	Industry Sales
2016	0.1	0.1	0.3	27.0	490.9	1,576.5	652.6	94.4	4.0	2,846.0
2017	0.1	0.1	0.3	27.2	492.9	1,582.6	655.1	94.8	4.0	2,857.1
2018	0.1	0.2	0.3	27.4	497.7	1,598.2	661.6	95.7	4.1	2,885.3
2019	0.1	0.2	0.3	27.4	497.8	1,598.4	661.7	96.0	4.1	2,885.9
2019	0.1	0.2	0.3	27.7	502.7	1,614.3	668.2	97.1	4.1	2,914.6

	INDUSTRY: ELECTRONIC SHOPPING & MAIL-ORDER (NAICS 45411)
PRODUCT LINE: TOYS (Sub Category)

NAICS 45411: Electronic Shopping and Mail-Order Houses This industry comprises establishments primarily engaged in retailing all types of merchandise by means of mail or by electronic media, such as interactive television or computer. Included in this industry are establishments primarily engaged in retailing from catalogue showrooms of mail-order houses.

5-Year Trend – Estimated Industry Sales ($Millions)

Year	Employee Size of Establishment									Total
	1-4 Emps.	5-9 Emps.	10-19 Emps.	20-49 Emps.	50-99 Emps.	100-249 Emps.	250-499 Emps.	500-999 Emps.	Unknown Emps.	Industry Sales
2016	375.4	193.4	279.4	468.9	353.0	653.0	880.4	1,242.8	52.8	4,498.9
2017	397.0	204.5	295.5	496.0	373.3	690.7	931.2	1,314.5	55.8	4,758.6
2018	420.9	216.8	313.3	525.9	395.8	732.3	987.3	1,393.7	59.2	5,045.3
2019	471.8	243.0	351.1	589.3	443.6	820.7	1,106.5	1,533.6	66.3	5,626.0
2019	524.5	270.2	390.4	655.2	493.2	912.5	1,230.2	1,679.5	73.7	6,229.3

	INDUSTRY: PHARMACIES & DRUG STORES (NAICS 44611)
PRODUCT LINE: GAMES (Sub Category)

NAICS 44611 Pharmacies and Drug Stores – this industry comprises establishments known as pharmacies and drug stores engaged in retailing prescription or nonprescription drugs and medicines.

5-Year Trend – Estimated Industry Sales ($Millions)

Year	Employee Size of Establishment									Total
	1-4 Emps.	5-9 Emps.	10-19 Emps.	20-49 Emps.	50-99 Emps.	100-249 Emps.	250-499 Emps.	500-999 Emps.	Unknown Emps.	Industry Sales
2016	0.6	1.4	5.6	16.5	1.7	0.7	0.3	0.1	0.0	26.9
2017	0.6	1.4	5.8	17.1	1.7	0.7	0.3	0.1	0.0	27.7
2018	0.6	1.5	6.0	17.7	1.8	0.7	0.3	0.1	0.0	28.7
2019	0.6	1.6	6.4	18.7	1.9	0.8	0.3	0.1	0.0	30.4
2019	0.7	1.7	6.8	20.0	2.0	0.8	0.3	0.1	0.1	32.5

NAICS 45211: Department Stores Industry . this industry comprises establishments known as department stores primarily engaged in retailing a wide range of the following new products with no one merchandise line predominating: apparel, furniture, appliances and home furnishings; and selected additional items, such as paint, hardware, toiletries, cosmetics, photographic equipment, jewelry, toys, and sporting goods. merchandise lines are normally arranged in separate departments.

5-YEAR TREND – ESTIMATED INDUSTRY SALES ($MILLIONS)

Year	Employee Size of Establishment									Total
	1-4 Emps.	5-9 Emps.	10-19 Emps.	20-49 Emps.	50-99 Emps.	100-249 Emps.	250-499 Emps.	500-999 Emps.	Unknown Emps.	Industry Sales
2016	0.1	0.1	0.2	13.1	238.3	765.2	316.8	45.8	1.9	1,381.5
2017	0.1	0.1	0.2	13.2	239.2	768.2	318.0	46.0	2.0	1,386.9
2018	0.1	0.1	0.2	13.3	241.6	775.8	321.1	46.5	2.0	1,400.6
2019	0.1	0.1	0.2	13.3	241.6	775.9	321.2	46.6	2.0	1,400.9
2019	0.1	0.1	0.2	13.4	244.0	783.6	324.4	47.1	2.0	1,414.8

NAICS 45411: Electronic Shopping and Mail-Order Houses This industry comprises establishments primarily engaged in retailing all types of merchandise by means of mail or by electronic media, such as interactive television or computer. Included in this industry are establishments primarily engaged in retailing from catalogue showrooms of mail-order houses.

5-YEAR TREND – ESTIMATED INDUSTRY SALES ($MILLIONS)

Year	Employee Size of Establishment									Total
	1-4 Emps.	5-9 Emps.	10-19 Emps.	20-49 Emps.	50-99 Emps.	100-249 Emps.	250-499 Emps.	500-999 Emps.	Unknown Emps.	Industry Sales
2016	93.2	48.0	69.4	116.5	87.7	162.2	218.6	308.6	13.1	1,117.3
2017	98.6	50.8	73.4	123.2	92.7	171.5	231.3	326.5	13.9	1,181.8
2018	104.5	53.9	77.8	130.6	98.3	181.9	245.2	346.1	14.7	1,253.0
2019	117.2	60.4	87.2	146.4	110.2	203.8	274.8	380.9	16.5	1,397.2
2019	130.3	67.1	96.9	162.7	122.5	226.6	305.5	417.1	18.3	1,547.1

INDUSTRY: PHARMACIES & DRUG STORES (NAICS 44611)
PRODUCT LINE: HOBBY GOODS (Sub Category)

NAICS 44611 Pharmacies and Drug Stores – this industry comprises establishments known as pharmacies and drug stores engaged in retailing prescription or nonprescription drugs and medicines.

5-YEAR TREND – ESTIMATED INDUSTRY SALES ($MILLIONS)

Year	Employee Size of Establishment									Total
	1-4 Emps.	5-9 Emps.	10-19 Emps.	20-49 Emps.	50-99 Emps.	100-249 Emps.	250-499 Emps.	500-999 Emps.	Unknown Emps.	Industry Sales
2016	1.2	2.9	11.9	34.8	3.5	1.4	0.5	0.2	0.1	56.6
2017	1.2	3.0	12.2	35.9	3.6	1.5	0.6	0.2	0.1	58.3
2018	1.3	3.1	12.7	37.2	3.8	1.5	0.6	0.2	0.1	60.5
2019	1.3	3.3	13.4	39.4	4.0	1.6	0.6	0.2	0.1	64.0
2019	1.4	3.5	14.3	42.1	4.3	1.7	0.7	0.2	0.1	68.4

INDUSTRY: ELECTRONIC SHOPPING & MAIL-ORDER (NAICS 45411)
PRODUCT LINE: HOBBY GOODS (Sub Category)

NAICS 45411: Electronic Shopping and Mail-Order Houses This industry comprises establishments primarily engaged in retailing all types of merchandise by means of mail or by electronic media, such as interactive television or computer. Included in this industry are establishments primarily engaged in retailing from catalogue showrooms of mail-order houses.

5-YEAR TREND – ESTIMATED INDUSTRY SALES ($MILLIONS)

Year	Employee Size of Establishment									Total
	1-4 Emps.	5-9 Emps.	10-19 Emps.	20-49 Emps.	50-99 Emps.	100-249 Emps.	250-499 Emps.	500-999 Emps.	Unknown Emps.	Industry Sales
2016	254.2	131.0	189.2	317.6	239.1	442.3	596.3	841.8	35.7	3,047.2
2017	268.9	138.5	200.1	335.9	252.9	467.8	630.7	890.3	37.8	3,223.1
2018	285.1	146.9	212.2	356.2	268.1	496.0	668.7	944.0	40.1	3,417.3
2019	319.5	164.6	237.8	399.2	300.5	555.9	749.4	1,038.8	44.9	3,810.6
2019	355.2	183.0	264.4	443.8	334.1	618.0	833.2	1,137.5	49.9	4,219.2

INDUSTRY: HOME CENTERS INDUSTRY (NAICS 44411)
PRODUCT LINE: SPORTING & RECREATION GOODS (Main Category)

NAICS 44411: Home Centers. This industry comprises establishments
known as home centers primarily engaged in retailing a general line of
new home repair and improvement materials and supplies, such as
lumber, plumbing goods, electrical goods, tools, housewares, hardware,
and lawn and garden supplies, with no one merchandise line predominating.
The merchandise lines are normally arranged in separate departments.

5-Year Trend – Estimated Industry Sales ($Millions)

Year	Employee Size of Establishment									Total Industry Sales
	1-4 Emps.	5-9 Emps.	10-19 Emps.	20-49 Emps.	50-99 Emps.	100-249 Emps.	250-499 Emps.	500-999 Emps.	Unknown Emps.	
2016	0.2	0.5	1.2	2.5	1.9	124.2	9.7	0.2	0.1	140.5
2017	0.3	0.5	1.2	2.5	1.9	127.2	9.9	0.2	0.1	143.9
2018	0.3	0.5	1.3	2.6	2.0	130.9	10.2	0.2	0.1	148.1
2019	0.3	0.5	1.3	2.7	2.1	135.8	10.6	0.2	0.1	153.6
2019	0.3	0.5	1.4	2.8	2.2	142.0	11.1	0.2	0.1	160.7

INDUSTRY: HARDWARE STORES (NAICS 44413)
PRODUCT LINE: SPORTING & RECREATION GOODS (Main Category)

NAICS 44413: Hardware Stores. Establishments primarily engaged
in the retail sale of a number of basic hardware lines, such as tools,
builders' hardware, paint and glass, housewares and household appliances,
and cutlery.

5-Year Trend – Estimated Industry Sales ($Millions)

Year	Employee Size of Establishment									Total Industry Sales
	1-4 Emps.	5-9 Emps.	10-19 Emps.	20-49 Emps.	50-99 Emps.	100-249 Emps.	250-499 Emps.	500-999 Emps.	Unknown Emps.	
2016	16.6	28.1	56.6	81.0	16.1	5.2	0.9	0.0	1.5	206.1
2017	16.8	28.4	57.2	81.8	16.2	5.3	0.9	0.0	1.5	208.1
2018	17.0	28.9	58.1	83.0	16.5	5.4	1.0	0.0	1.5	211.4
2019	17.7	30.0	60.4	86.3	17.2	5.6	1.0	0.0	1.5	219.8
2019	18.6	31.5	63.4	90.6	18.0	5.9	1.0	0.1	1.6	230.7

INDUSTRY: SUPERMARKETS INDUSTRY (NAICS 44511)
PRODUCT LINE: SPORTING & RECREATION GOODS (Main Category)

NAICS 44511: Grocery Stores Industry. this industry comprises establishments generally known as supermarkets and grocery stores primarily engaged in retailing a general line of food, such as canned and frozen foods; fresh fruits and vegetables; and fresh and prepared meats, fish, and poultry. Included in this industry are delicatessen-type establishments primarily engaged in retailing a general line of food.

5-YEAR TREND – ESTIMATED INDUSTRY SALES ($MILLIONS)

Year	Employee Size of Establishment									Total Industry Sales
	1-4 Emps.	5-9 Emps.	10-19 Emps.	20-49 Emps.	50-99 Emps.	100-249 Emps.	250-499 Emps.	500-999 Emps.	Unknown Emps.	
2016	87.2	63.0	162.4	535.3	1,268.7	3,154.0	985.0	117.9	16.4	6,389.9
2017	86.6	62.6	161.4	531.9	1,260.6	3,134.0	978.8	117.1	16.3	6,349.3
2018	86.6	62.5	161.4	531.7	1,260.2	3,132.9	978.4	117.1	16.3	6,347.1
2019	88.4	63.8	164.7	542.7	1,286.2	3,197.5	998.6	119.4	16.6	6,477.9
2019	91.1	65.8	169.8	559.5	1,325.9	3,296.4	1,029.5	123.0	17.1	6,678.1

INDUSTRY: PHARMACIES & DRUG STORES (NAICS 44611)
PRODUCT LINE: SPORTING & RECREATION GOODS (Main Category)

NAICS 44611 Pharmacies and Drug Stores – this industry comprises establishments known as pharmacies and drug stores engaged in retailing prescription or nonprescription drugs and medicines.

5-YEAR TREND – ESTIMATED INDUSTRY SALES ($MILLIONS)

Year	Employee Size of Establishment									Total Industry Sales
	1-4 Emps.	5-9 Emps.	10-19 Emps.	20-49 Emps.	50-99 Emps.	100-249 Emps.	250-499 Emps.	500-999 Emps.	Unknown Emps.	
2016	0.6	1.6	6.5	18.9	1.9	0.8	0.3	0.1	0.0	30.8
2017	0.7	1.6	6.7	19.5	2.0	0.8	0.3	0.1	0.1	31.7
2018	0.7	1.7	6.9	20.2	2.0	0.8	0.3	0.1	0.1	32.9
2019	0.7	1.8	7.3	21.4	2.2	0.9	0.3	0.1	0.1	34.8
2019	0.8	1.9	7.8	22.9	2.3	0.9	0.4	0.1	0.1	37.2

INDUSTRY: GAS STATIONS W/CONVENIENCE STORES (NAICS 44711)
PRODUCT LINE: SPORTING & RECREATION GOODS (Main Category)

NAICS 44711: Gas Stations with Convenience Stores. this industry comprises establishments primarily engaged in selling gasoline and lubricating oils. These establishments frequently sell other merchandise, such as tires, batteries, and other automobile parts, or perform minor repair work. Gasoline stations combined with other activities, such as grocery stores, convenience stores, or carwashes, are classified according to the primary activity.

5-YEAR TREND – ESTIMATED INDUSTRY SALES ($MILLIONS)

Year	Employee Size of Establishment									Total
	1-4 Emps.	5-9 Emps.	10-19 Emps.	20-49 Emps.	50-99 Emps.	100-249 Emps.	250-499 Emps.	500-999 Emps.	Unknown Emps.	Industry Sales
2016	18.3	47.4	79.3	54.7	5.1	2.8	1.1	0.0	0.2	209.0
2017	19.1	49.4	82.6	57.0	5.4	2.9	1.2	0.0	0.2	217.8
2018	20.0	51.6	86.4	59.6	5.6	3.1	1.2	0.0	0.2	227.8
2019	21.3	55.0	92.1	63.6	6.0	3.3	1.3	0.0	0.2	242.8
2019	22.9	59.1	98.9	68.2	6.4	3.5	1.4	0.0	0.3	260.6

INDUSTRY: MEN'S CLOTHING STORES INDUSTRY (NAICS 44811)
PRODUCT LINE: SPORTING & RECREATION GOODS (Main Category)

NAICS 44811: Men's Clothing Stores. this industry comprises establishments primarily engaged in retailing a general line of new men's and boys' clothing. These establishments may provide basic alterations, such as hemming, taking in or letting out seams, or lengthening or shortening sleeves.

5-YEAR TREND – ESTIMATED INDUSTRY SALES ($MILLIONS)

Year	Employee Size of Establishment									Total
	1-4 Emps.	5-9 Emps.	10-19 Emps.	20-49 Emps.	50-99 Emps.	100-249 Emps.	250-499 Emps.	500-999 Emps.	Unknown Emps.	Industry Sales
2016	1.2	2.1	3.9	2.0	0.4	0.4	0.1	0.0	0.2	10.4
2017	1.2	2.2	4.0	2.1	0.5	0.4	0.1	0.0	0.2	10.8
2018	1.3	2.3	4.2	2.2	0.5	0.4	0.1	0.0	0.2	11.2
2019	1.3	2.3	4.3	2.3	0.5	0.4	0.2	0.0	0.2	11.6
2019	1.4	2.4	4.5	2.4	0.5	0.5	0.2	0.0	0.2	12.0

INDUSTRY: FAMILY CLOTHING STORES INDUSTRY (NAICS 44814)
PRODUCT LINE: SPORTING & RECREATION GOODS (Main Category)

NAICS 44814: Family Clothing Stores . this industry comprises
establishments primarily engaged in retailing a general line of new clothing
for men, women, and children, without specializing in sales for an individual
gender or age group. These establishments may provide basic alterations,
such as hemming, taking in or letting out seams, or lengthening or shortening sleeves.

5-YEAR TREND – ESTIMATED INDUSTRY SALES ($MILLIONS)

Year	Employee Size of Establishment									Total
	1-4 Emps.	5-9 Emps.	10-19 Emps.	20-49 Emps.	50-99 Emps.	100-249 Emps.	250-499 Emps.	500-999 Emps.	Unknown Emps.	Industry Sales
2016	2.0	4.1	15.5	51.6	45.6	12.6	11.8	6.9	0.5	150.7
2017	2.0	4.2	16.0	53.0	46.8	12.9	12.2	7.0	0.6	154.7
2018	2.1	4.4	16.5	54.7	48.3	13.3	12.5	7.3	0.6	159.7
2019	2.2	4.6	17.4	57.7	50.9	14.0	13.2	7.6	0.6	168.3
2019	2.4	4.9	18.4	61.3	54.2	14.9	14.1	8.1	0.6	178.8

INDUSTRY: DEPARTMENT STORES INDUSTRY (NAICS 45211)
PRODUCT LINE: SPORTING & RECREATION GOODS (Main Category)

NAICS 45211: Department Stores Industry . this industry comprises
establishments known as department stores primarily engaged in retailing
a wide range of the following new products with no one merchandise line
predominating: apparel, furniture, appliances and home furnishings; and
selected additional items, such as paint, hardware, toiletries, cosmetics,
photographic equipment, jewelry, toys, and sporting goods. merchandise lines
are normally arranged in separate departments.

5-YEAR TREND – ESTIMATED INDUSTRY SALES ($MILLIONS)

Year	Employee Size of Establishment									Total
	1-4 Emps.	5-9 Emps.	10-19 Emps.	20-49 Emps.	50-99 Emps.	100-249 Emps.	250-499 Emps.	500-999 Emps.	Unknown Emps.	Industry Sales
2016	0.1	0.1	0.3	25.7	466.1	1,496.7	619.5	89.6	3.8	2,702.0
2017	0.1	0.1	0.3	25.8	467.9	1,502.5	622.0	90.0	3.8	2,712.6
2018	0.1	0.1	0.3	26.0	472.5	1,517.4	628.1	90.9	3.9	2,739.3
2019	0.1	0.1	0.3	26.0	472.6	1,517.6	628.2	91.1	3.9	2,739.9
2019	0.1	0.1	0.3	26.3	477.3	1,532.6	634.4	92.2	3.9	2,767.2

INDUSTRY: WAREHOUSE CLUBS & SUPERCENTERS (NAICS 45291)
PRODUCT LINE: SPORTING & RECREATION GOODS (Main Category)

NAICS 45291: Warehouse Clubs and Superstores This industry comprises establishments known as warehouse clubs, superstores or supercenters primarily engaged in retailing a general line of groceries in combination with general lines of new merchandise, such as apparel, furniture, and appliances.

5-YEAR TREND — ESTIMATED INDUSTRY SALES ($MILLIONS)

Year	Employee Size of Establishment									Total
	1-4 Emps.	5-9 Emps.	10-19 Emps.	20-49 Emps.	50-99 Emps.	100-249 Emps.	250-499 Emps.	500-999 Emps.	Unknown Emps.	Industry Sales
2016	0.5	0.1	0.4	16.2	30.7	1,754.6	7,724.1	194.6	2.9	9,724.2
2017	0.5	0.1	0.5	16.6	31.6	1,802.9	7,936.9	200.0	3.0	9,992.3
2018	0.5	0.1	0.5	17.2	32.6	1,861.8	8,196.2	206.5	3.1	10,318.6
2019	0.6	0.2	0.5	18.5	35.1	2,003.7	8,820.9	222.3	3.4	11,105.2
2019	0.6	0.2	0.5	19.6	37.2	2,122.4	9,343.5	235.4	3.6	11,763.0

INDUSTRY: ELECTRONIC SHOPPING & MAIL-ORDER (NAICS 45411)
PRODUCT LINE: SPORTING & RECREATION GOODS (Main Category)

NAICS 45411: Electronic Shopping and Mail-Order Houses This industry comprises establishments primarily engaged in retailing all types of merchandise by means of mail or by electronic media, such as interactive television or computer. Included in this industry are establishments primarily engaged in retailing from catalogue showrooms of mail-order houses.

5-YEAR TREND — ESTIMATED INDUSTRY SALES ($MILLIONS)

Year	Employee Size of Establishment									Total
	1-4 Emps.	5-9 Emps.	10-19 Emps.	20-49 Emps.	50-99 Emps.	100-249 Emps.	250-499 Emps.	500-999 Emps.	Unknown Emps.	Industry Sales
2016	1,245.6	641.7	927.1	1,556.1	1,171.3	2,167.1	2,921.6	4,124.2	175.1	14,929.7
2017	1,317.5	678.7	980.6	1,645.9	1,238.9	2,292.1	3,090.2	4,362.2	185.2	15,791.5
2018	1,396.9	719.6	1,039.7	1,745.1	1,313.6	2,430.2	3,276.4	4,625.0	196.3	16,742.8
2019	1,565.5	806.4	1,165.1	1,955.7	1,472.1	2,723.6	3,671.8	5,089.3	220.0	18,669.7
2019	1,740.5	896.6	1,295.4	2,174.4	1,636.7	3,028.1	4,082.4	5,573.3	244.6	20,672.0

	INDUSTRY: DEPARTMENT STORES INDUSTRY (NAICS 45211)
	PRODUCT LINE: EXERCISE & FITNESS EQUIPMENT (Sub Category)

NAICS 45211: Department Stores Industry . this industry comprises establishments known as department stores primarily engaged in retailing a wide range of the following new products with no one merchandise line predominating: apparel, furniture, appliances and home furnishings; and selected additional items, such as paint, hardware, toiletries, cosmetics, photographic equipment, jewelry, toys, and sporting goods. merchandise lines are normally arranged in separate departments.

5-Year Trend – Estimated Industry Sales ($Millions)

Year	Employee Size of Establishment									Total
	1-4 Emps.	5-9 Emps.	10-19 Emps.	20-49 Emps.	50-99 Emps.	100-249 Emps.	250-499 Emps.	500-999 Emps.	Unknown Emps.	Industry Sales
2016	0.0	0.0	0.1	5.3	96.1	308.5	127.7	18.5	0.8	557.0
2017	0.0	0.0	0.1	5.3	96.5	309.7	128.2	18.5	0.8	559.2
2018	0.0	0.0	0.1	5.4	97.4	312.8	129.5	18.7	0.8	564.7
2019	0.0	0.0	0.1	5.4	97.4	312.8	129.5	18.8	0.8	564.8
2019	0.0	0.0	0.1	5.4	98.4	315.9	130.8	19.0	0.8	570.4

	INDUSTRY: WAREHOUSE CLUBS & SUPERCENTERS (NAICS 45291)
	PRODUCT LINE: EXERCISE & FITNESS EQUIPMENT (Sub Category)

NAICS 45291: Warehouse Clubs and Superstores This industry comprises establishments known as warehouse clubs, superstores or supercenters primarily engaged in retailing a general line of groceries in combination with general lines of new merchandise, such as apparel, furniture, and appliances.

5-Year Trend – Estimated Industry Sales ($Millions)

Year	Employee Size of Establishment									Total
	1-4 Emps.	5-9 Emps.	10-19 Emps.	20-49 Emps.	50-99 Emps.	100-249 Emps.	250-499 Emps.	500-999 Emps.	Unknown Emps.	Industry Sales
2016	0.1	0.0	0.1	3.2	6.0	344.0	1,514.4	38.2	0.6	1,906.6
2017	0.1	0.0	0.1	3.3	6.2	353.5	1,556.2	39.2	0.6	1,959.2
2018	0.1	0.0	0.1	3.4	6.4	365.0	1,607.0	40.5	0.6	2,023.2
2019	0.1	0.0	0.1	3.6	6.9	392.9	1,729.5	43.6	0.7	2,177.4
2019	0.1	0.0	0.1	3.8	7.3	416.1	1,832.0	46.2	0.7	2,306.4

	INDUSTRY: DEPARTMENT STORES INDUSTRY (NAICS 45211)
	PRODUCT LINE: FIREARMS & HUNTING EQUIPMENT (Sub Category)

NAICS 45211: Department Stores Industry . this industry comprises establishments known as department stores primarily engaged in retailing a wide range of the following new products with no one merchandise line predominating: apparel, furniture, appliances and home furnishings; and selected additional items, such as paint, hardware, toiletries, cosmetics, photographic equipment, jewelry, toys, and sporting goods. merchandise lines are normally arranged in separate departments.

5-YEAR TREND – ESTIMATED INDUSTRY SALES ($MILLIONS)

Year	Employee Size of Establishment									Total
	1-4 Emps.	5-9 Emps.	10-19 Emps.	20-49 Emps.	50-99 Emps.	100-249 Emps.	250-499 Emps.	500-999 Emps.	Unknown Emps.	Industry Sales
2016	0.0	0.0	0.0	4.0	73.1	234.8	97.2	14.1	0.6	423.9
2017	0.0	0.0	0.0	4.0	73.4	235.7	97.6	14.1	0.6	425.5
2018	0.0	0.0	0.0	4.1	74.1	238.0	98.5	14.3	0.6	429.7
2019	0.0	0.0	0.0	4.1	74.1	238.1	98.5	14.3	0.6	429.8
2019	0.0	0.0	0.0	4.1	74.9	240.4	99.5	14.5	0.6	434.1

	INDUSTRY: WAREHOUSE CLUBS & SUPERCENTERS (NAICS 45291)
	PRODUCT LINE: FIREARMS & HUNTING EQUIPMENT (Sub Category)

NAICS 45291: Warehouse Clubs and Superstores This industry comprises establishments known as warehouse clubs, superstores or supercenters primarily engaged in retailing a general line of groceries in combination with general lines of new merchandise, such as apparel, furniture, and appliances.

5-YEAR TREND – ESTIMATED INDUSTRY SALES ($MILLIONS)

Year	Employee Size of Establishment									Total
	1-4 Emps.	5-9 Emps.	10-19 Emps.	20-49 Emps.	50-99 Emps.	100-249 Emps.	250-499 Emps.	500-999 Emps.	Unknown Emps.	Industry Sales
2016	0.1	0.0	0.1	3.6	6.9	394.3	1,735.9	43.7	0.7	2,185.4
2017	0.1	0.0	0.1	3.7	7.1	405.2	1,783.7	44.9	0.7	2,245.6
2018	0.1	0.0	0.1	3.9	7.3	418.4	1,842.0	46.4	0.7	2,319.0
2019	0.1	0.0	0.1	4.2	7.9	450.3	1,982.4	50.0	0.8	2,495.8
2019	0.1	0.0	0.1	4.4	8.4	477.0	2,099.8	52.9	0.8	2,643.6

INDUSTRY: DEPARTMENT STORES INDUSTRY (NAICS 45211)
PRODUCT LINE: FISHING TACKLE EQUIPMENT (Sub Category)

NAICS 45211: Department Stores Industry . this industry comprises establishments known as department stores primarily engaged in retailing a wide range of the following new products with no one merchandise line predominating: apparel, furniture, appliances and home furnishings; and selected additional items, such as paint, hardware, toiletries, cosmetics, photographic equipment, jewelry, toys, and sporting goods. merchandise lines are normally arranged in separate departments.

5-YEAR TREND – ESTIMATED INDUSTRY SALES ($MILLIONS)

Year	Employee Size of Establishment									Total
	1-4 Emps.	5-9 Emps.	10-19 Emps.	20-49 Emps.	50-99 Emps.	100-249 Emps.	250-499 Emps.	500-999 Emps.	Unknown Emps.	Industry Sales
2016	0.0	0.0	0.0	2.2	40.3	129.3	53.5	7.7	0.3	233.4
2017	0.0	0.0	0.0	2.2	40.4	129.8	53.7	7.8	0.3	234.3
2018	0.0	0.0	0.0	2.2	40.8	131.1	54.3	7.8	0.3	236.6
2019	0.0	0.0	0.0	2.2	40.8	131.1	54.3	7.9	0.3	236.7
2019	0.0	0.0	0.0	2.3	41.2	132.4	54.8	8.0	0.3	239.0

INDUSTRY: WAREHOUSE CLUBS & SUPERCENTERS (NAICS 45291)
PRODUCT LINE: FISHING TACKLE EQUIPMENT (Sub Category)

NAICS 45291: Warehouse Clubs and Superstores This industry comprises establishments known as warehouse clubs, superstores or supercenters primarily engaged in retailing a general line of groceries in combination with general lines of new merchandise, such as apparel, furniture, and appliances.

5-YEAR TREND – ESTIMATED INDUSTRY SALES ($MILLIONS)

Year	Employee Size of Establishment									Total
	1-4 Emps.	5-9 Emps.	10-19 Emps.	20-49 Emps.	50-99 Emps.	100-249 Emps.	250-499 Emps.	500-999 Emps.	Unknown Emps.	Industry Sales
2016	0.1	0.0	0.1	2.1	3.9	223.3	982.9	24.8	0.4	1,237.4
2017	0.1	0.0	0.1	2.1	4.0	229.4	1,010.0	25.5	0.4	1,271.5
2018	0.1	0.0	0.1	2.2	4.1	236.9	1,043.0	26.3	0.4	1,313.0
2019	0.1	0.0	0.1	2.4	4.5	255.0	1,122.5	28.3	0.4	1,413.1
2019	0.1	0.0	0.1	2.5	4.7	270.1	1,189.0	30.0	0.5	1,496.8

INDUSTRY: DEPARTMENT STORES INDUSTRY (NAICS 45211)
PRODUCT LINE: CAMPING & BACKPACKING EQUIPMENT (Sub Category)

NAICS 45211: Department Stores Industry . this industry comprises establishments known as department stores primarily engaged in retailing a wide range of the following new products with no one merchandise line predominating: apparel, furniture, appliances and home furnishings; and selected additional items, such as paint, hardware, toiletries, cosmetics, photographic equipment, jewelry, toys, and sporting goods. merchandise lines are normally arranged in separate departments.

5-YEAR TREND – ESTIMATED INDUSTRY SALES ($MILLIONS)

Year	Employee Size of Establishment									Total
	1-4 Emps.	5-9 Emps.	10-19 Emps.	20-49 Emps.	50-99 Emps.	100-249 Emps.	250-499 Emps.	500-999 Emps.	Unknown Emps.	Industry Sales
2016	0.0	0.0	0.1	5.5	99.5	319.6	132.3	19.1	0.8	577.0
2017	0.0	0.0	0.1	5.5	99.9	320.9	132.8	19.2	0.8	579.3
2018	0.0	0.0	0.1	5.6	100.9	324.0	134.1	19.4	0.8	585.0
2019	0.0	0.0	0.1	5.6	100.9	324.1	134.2	19.5	0.8	585.1
2019	0.0	0.0	0.1	5.6	101.9	327.3	135.5	19.7	0.8	590.9

INDUSTRY: WAREHOUSE CLUBS & SUPERCENTERS (NAICS 45291)
PRODUCT LINE: CAMPING & BACKPACKING EQUIPMENT (Sub Category)

NAICS 45291: Warehouse Clubs and Superstores This industry comprises establishments known as warehouse clubs, superstores or supercenters primarily engaged in retailing a general line of groceries in combination with general lines of new merchandise, such as apparel, furniture, and appliances.

5-YEAR TREND – ESTIMATED INDUSTRY SALES ($MILLIONS)

Year	Employee Size of Establishment									Total
	1-4 Emps.	5-9 Emps.	10-19 Emps.	20-49 Emps.	50-99 Emps.	100-249 Emps.	250-499 Emps.	500-999 Emps.	Unknown Emps.	Industry Sales
2016	0.1	0.0	0.1	2.4	4.5	257.3	1,132.6	28.5	0.4	1,425.9
2017	0.1	0.0	0.1	2.4	4.6	264.4	1,163.8	29.3	0.4	1,465.2
2018	0.1	0.0	0.1	2.5	4.8	273.0	1,201.8	30.3	0.5	1,513.0
2019	0.1	0.0	0.1	2.7	5.1	293.8	1,293.4	32.6	0.5	1,628.4
2019	0.1	0.0	0.1	2.9	5.5	311.2	1,370.1	34.5	0.5	1,724.8

INDUSTRY: DEPARTMENT STORES INDUSTRY (NAICS 45211)
PRODUCT LINE: BICYCLES & ACCESSORIES EQUIPMENT (Sub Category)

NAICS 45211: Department Stores Industry . this industry comprises establishments known as department stores primarily engaged in retailing a wide range of the following new products with no one merchandise line predominating: apparel, furniture, appliances and home furnishings; and selected additional items, such as paint, hardware, toiletries, cosmetics, photographic equipment, jewelry, toys, and sporting goods. merchandise lines are normally arranged in separate departments.

5-YEAR TREND — ESTIMATED INDUSTRY SALES ($MILLIONS)

Year	Employee Size of Establishment									Total
	1-4 Emps.	5-9 Emps.	10-19 Emps.	20-49 Emps.	50-99 Emps.	100-249 Emps.	250-499 Emps.	500-999 Emps.	Unknown Emps.	Industry Sales
2016	0.0	0.0	0.0	3.5	62.9	202.0	83.6	12.1	0.5	364.7
2017	0.0	0.0	0.0	3.5	63.2	202.8	84.0	12.1	0.5	366.1
2018	0.0	0.0	0.0	3.5	63.8	204.8	84.8	12.3	0.5	369.8
2019	0.0	0.0	0.0	3.5	63.8	204.8	84.8	12.3	0.5	369.8
2019	0.0	0.0	0.0	3.5	64.4	206.9	85.6	12.4	0.5	373.5

INDUSTRY: WAREHOUSE CLUBS & SUPERCENTERS (NAICS 45291)
PRODUCT LINE: BICYCLES & ACCESSORIES EQUIPMENT (Sub Category)

NAICS 45291: Warehouse Clubs and Superstores This industry comprises establishments known as warehouse clubs, superstores or supercenters primarily engaged in retailing a general line of groceries in combination with general lines of new merchandise, such as apparel, furniture, and appliances.

5-YEAR TREND — ESTIMATED INDUSTRY SALES ($MILLIONS)

Year	Employee Size of Establishment									Total
	1-4 Emps.	5-9 Emps.	10-19 Emps.	20-49 Emps.	50-99 Emps.	100-249 Emps.	250-499 Emps.	500-999 Emps.	Unknown Emps.	Industry Sales
2016	0.1	0.0	0.1	2.1	4.1	232.5	1,023.5	25.8	0.4	1,288.5
2017	0.1	0.0	0.1	2.2	4.2	238.9	1,051.7	26.5	0.4	1,324.0
2018	0.1	0.0	0.1	2.3	4.3	246.7	1,086.0	27.4	0.4	1,367.3
2019	0.1	0.0	0.1	2.5	4.6	265.5	1,168.8	29.5	0.4	1,471.5
2019	0.1	0.0	0.1	2.6	4.9	281.2	1,238.1	31.2	0.5	1,558.7

INDUSTRY: DEPARTMENT STORES INDUSTRY (NAICS 45211)
PRODUCT LINE: BOATS & ACCESSORIES EQUIPMENT (Sub Category)

NAICS 45211: Department Stores Industry . this industry comprises establishments known as department stores primarily engaged in retailing a wide range of the following new products with no one merchandise line predominating: apparel, furniture, appliances and home furnishings; and selected additional items, such as paint, hardware, toiletries, cosmetics, photographic equipment, jewelry, toys, and sporting goods. merchandise lines are normally arranged in separate departments.

5-YEAR TREND – ESTIMATED INDUSTRY SALES ($MILLIONS)

| Year | Employee Size of Establishment | | | | | | | | | Total |
	1-4 Emps.	5-9 Emps.	10-19 Emps.	20-49 Emps.	50-99 Emps.	100-249 Emps.	250-499 Emps.	500-999 Emps.	Unknown Emps.	Industry Sales
2016	0.0	0.0	0.0	0.6	11.6	37.2	15.4	2.2	0.1	67.1
2017	0.0	0.0	0.0	0.6	11.6	37.3	15.4	2.2	0.1	67.4
2018	0.0	0.0	0.0	0.6	11.7	37.7	15.6	2.3	0.1	68.0
2019	0.0	0.0	0.0	0.6	11.7	37.7	15.6	2.3	0.1	68.1
2019	0.0	0.0	0.0	0.7	11.9	38.1	15.8	2.3	0.1	68.7

INDUSTRY: WAREHOUSE CLUBS & SUPERCENTERS (NAICS 45291)
PRODUCT LINE: BOATS & ACCESSORIES EQUIPMENT (Sub Category)

NAICS 45291: Warehouse Clubs and Superstores This industry comprises establishments known as warehouse clubs, superstores or supercenters primarily engaged in retailing a general line of groceries in combination with general lines of new merchandise, such as apparel, furniture, and appliances.

5-YEAR TREND – ESTIMATED INDUSTRY SALES ($MILLIONS)

| Year | Employee Size of Establishment | | | | | | | | | Total |
	1-4 Emps.	5-9 Emps.	10-19 Emps.	20-49 Emps.	50-99 Emps.	100-249 Emps.	250-499 Emps.	500-999 Emps.	Unknown Emps.	Industry Sales
2016	0.0	0.0	0.0	0.8	1.6	89.4	393.3	9.9	0.1	495.2
2017	0.0	0.0	0.0	0.8	1.6	91.8	404.2	10.2	0.2	508.9
2018	0.0	0.0	0.0	0.9	1.7	94.8	417.4	10.5	0.2	525.5
2019	0.0	0.0	0.0	0.9	1.8	102.0	449.2	11.3	0.2	565.5
2019	0.0	0.0	0.0	1.0	1.9	108.1	475.8	12.0	0.2	599.0

INDUSTRY: ELECTRONIC SHOPPING & MAIL-ORDER (NAICS 45411)
PRODUCT LINE: BOATS & ACCESSORIES EQUIPMENT (Sub Category)

NAICS 45411: Electronic Shopping and Mail-Order Houses This industry comprises establishments primarily engaged in retailing all types of merchandise by means of mail or by electronic media, such as interactive television or computer. Included in this industry are establishments primarily engaged in retailing from catalogue showrooms of mail-order houses.

5-YEAR TREND — ESTIMATED INDUSTRY SALES ($MILLIONS)

Year	Employee Size of Establishment									Total
	1-4 Emps.	5-9 Emps.	10-19 Emps.	20-49 Emps.	50-99 Emps.	100-249 Emps.	250-499 Emps.	500-999 Emps.	Unknown Emps.	Industry Sales
2016	97.9	50.4	72.9	122.3	92.0	170.3	229.6	324.1	13.8	1,173.2
2017	103.5	53.3	77.1	129.3	97.4	180.1	242.8	342.8	14.6	1,241.0
2018	109.8	56.5	81.7	137.1	103.2	191.0	257.5	363.5	15.4	1,315.7
2019	123.0	63.4	91.6	153.7	115.7	214.0	288.5	399.9	17.3	1,467.1
2019	136.8	70.5	101.8	170.9	128.6	238.0	320.8	438.0	19.2	1,624.5

INDUSTRY: ELECTRONIC SHOPPING & MAIL-ORDER (NAICS 45411)
PRODUCT LINE: OTHER SPORTING GOODS (Sub Category)

NAICS 45411: Electronic Shopping and Mail-Order Houses This industry comprises establishments primarily engaged in retailing all types of merchandise by means of mail or by electronic media, such as interactive television or computer. Included in this industry are establishments primarily engaged in retailing from catalogue showrooms of mail-order houses.

5-YEAR TREND — ESTIMATED INDUSTRY SALES ($MILLIONS)

Year	Employee Size of Establishment									Total
	1-4 Emps.	5-9 Emps.	10-19 Emps.	20-49 Emps.	50-99 Emps.	100-249 Emps.	250-499 Emps.	500-999 Emps.	Unknown Emps.	Industry Sales
2016	1,147.7	591.2	854.2	1,433.8	1,079.3	1,996.8	2,692.0	3,800.1	161.3	13,756.5
2017	1,214.0	625.4	903.5	1,516.6	1,141.6	2,112.0	2,847.4	4,019.4	170.6	14,550.5
2018	1,287.1	663.0	958.0	1,608.0	1,210.3	2,239.2	3,018.9	4,261.6	180.9	15,427.0
2019	1,442.5	743.1	1,073.6	1,802.0	1,356.4	2,509.5	3,383.3	4,689.4	202.7	17,202.6
2019	1,603.8	826.1	1,193.6	2,003.5	1,508.1	2,790.1	3,761.6	5,135.4	225.4	19,047.5

INDUSTRY: DEPARTMENT STORES INDUSTRY (NAICS 45211)
PRODUCT LINE: OTHER SPORTING GOODS (Sub Category)

NAICS 45211: Department Stores Industry . this industry comprises establishments known as department stores primarily engaged in retailing a wide range of the following new products with no one merchandise line predominating: apparel, furniture, appliances and home furnishings; and selected additional items, such as paint, hardware, toiletries, cosmetics, photographic equipment, jewelry, toys, and sporting goods. merchandise lines are normally arranged in separate departments.

5-Year Trend – Estimated Industry Sales ($Millions)

Year	Employee Size of Establishment									Total
	1-4 Emps.	5-9 Emps.	10-19 Emps.	20-49 Emps.	50-99 Emps.	100-249 Emps.	250-499 Emps.	500-999 Emps.	Unknown Emps.	Industry Sales
2016	0.0	0.0	0.1	4.6	82.6	265.3	109.8	15.9	0.7	478.9
2017	0.0	0.0	0.1	4.6	82.9	266.3	110.2	15.9	0.7	480.8
2018	0.0	0.0	0.1	4.6	83.7	268.9	111.3	16.1	0.7	485.5
2019	0.0	0.0	0.1	4.6	83.8	269.0	111.3	16.1	0.7	485.6
2019	0.0	0.0	0.1	4.7	84.6	271.6	112.4	16.3	0.7	490.4

INDUSTRY: WAREHOUSE CLUBS & SUPERCENTERS (NAICS 45291)
PRODUCT LINE: OTHER SPORTING GOODS (Sub Category)

NAICS 45291: Warehouse Clubs and Superstores This industry comprises establishments known as warehouse clubs, superstores or supercenters primarily engaged in retailing a general line of groceries in combination with general lines of new merchandise, such as apparel, furniture, and appliances.

5-Year Trend – Estimated Industry Sales ($Millions)

Year	Employee Size of Establishment									Total
	1-4 Emps.	5-9 Emps.	10-19 Emps.	20-49 Emps.	50-99 Emps.	100-249 Emps.	250-499 Emps.	500-999 Emps.	Unknown Emps.	Industry Sales
2016	0.1	0.0	0.1	2.0	3.7	213.9	941.4	23.7	0.4	1,185.2
2017	0.1	0.0	0.1	2.0	3.8	219.7	967.4	24.4	0.4	1,217.9
2018	0.1	0.0	0.1	2.1	4.0	226.9	999.0	25.2	0.4	1,257.7
2019	0.1	0.0	0.1	2.3	4.3	244.2	1,075.1	27.1	0.4	1,353.5
2019	0.1	0.0	0.1	2.4	4.5	258.7	1,138.8	28.7	0.4	1,433.7

	INDUSTRY: HOME CENTERS INDUSTRY (NAICS 44411)
	PRODUCT LINE: HARDWARE & BUILDING SUPPLIES (Main Category)

NAICS 44411: Home Centers. This industry comprises establishments
known as home centers primarily engaged in retailing a general line of
new home repair and improvement materials and supplies, such as
lumber, plumbing goods, electrical goods, tools, housewares, hardware,
and lawn and garden supplies, with no one merchandise line predominating.
The merchandise lines are normally arranged in separate departments.

5-YEAR TREND – ESTIMATED INDUSTRY SALES ($MILLIONS)

Year	Employee Size of Establishment									Total
	1-4 Emps.	5-9 Emps.	10-19 Emps.	20-49 Emps.	50-99 Emps.	100-249 Emps.	250-499 Emps.	500-999 Emps.	Unknown Emps.	Industry Sales
2016	73.6	143.2	363.2	742.7	563.3	37,145.5	2,900.9	60.4	25.7	42,018.7
2017	75.4	146.7	371.9	760.5	576.9	38,036.4	2,970.5	61.8	26.3	43,026.4
2018	77.6	150.9	382.8	782.8	593.7	39,150.1	3,057.5	63.7	27.1	44,286.2
2019	80.5	156.5	397.0	811.8	615.8	40,603.6	3,171.0	66.0	28.1	45,930.5
2019	84.2	163.8	415.4	849.3	644.2	42,478.7	3,317.4	69.0	29.4	48,051.5

	INDUSTRY: HARDWARE STORES (NAICS 44413)
	PRODUCT LINE: HARDWARE & BUILDING SUPPLIES (Main Category)

NAICS 44413: Hardware Stores. Establishments primarily engaged
in the retail sale of a number of basic hardware lines, such as tools,
builders' hardware, paint and glass, housewares and household appliances,
and cutlery.

5-YEAR TREND – ESTIMATED INDUSTRY SALES ($MILLIONS)

Year	Employee Size of Establishment									Total
	1-4 Emps.	5-9 Emps.	10-19 Emps.	20-49 Emps.	50-99 Emps.	100-249 Emps.	250-499 Emps.	500-999 Emps.	Unknown Emps.	Industry Sales
2016	943.5	1,599.5	3,218.7	4,601.5	914.3	298.2	52.9	2.7	82.5	11,713.9
2017	952.8	1,615.2	3,250.3	4,646.7	923.2	301.1	53.4	2.7	83.4	11,828.9
2018	967.7	1,640.6	3,301.3	4,719.5	937.7	305.9	54.3	2.7	84.7	12,014.3
2019	1,006.2	1,705.8	3,432.5	4,907.1	975.0	318.0	56.4	2.8	88.0	12,491.8
2019	1,056.1	1,790.5	3,602.9	5,150.8	1,023.4	333.8	59.2	2.9	92.4	13,112.0

INDUSTRY: SUPERMARKETS INDUSTRY (NAICS 44511)
PRODUCT LINE: HARDWARE & BUILDING SUPPLIES (Main Category)

NAICS 44511: Grocery Stores Industry. this industry comprises establishments generally known as supermarkets and grocery stores primarily engaged in retailing a general line of food, such as canned and frozen foods; fresh fruits and vegetables; and fresh and prepared meats, fish, and poultry. Included in this industry are delicatessen-type establishments primarily engaged in retailing a general line of food.

5-YEAR TREND – ESTIMATED INDUSTRY SALES ($MILLIONS)

Year	Employee Size of Establishment									Total
	1-4 Emps.	5-9 Emps.	10-19 Emps.	20-49 Emps.	50-99 Emps.	100-249 Emps.	250-499 Emps.	500-999 Emps.	Unknown Emps.	Industry Sales
2016	8.4	6.1	15.7	51.7	122.5	304.5	95.1	11.4	1.6	617.0
2017	8.4	6.0	15.6	51.4	121.7	302.6	94.5	11.3	1.6	613.1
2018	8.4	6.0	15.6	51.3	121.7	302.5	94.5	11.3	1.6	612.9
2019	8.5	6.2	15.9	52.4	124.2	308.7	96.4	11.5	1.6	625.5
2019	8.8	6.4	16.4	54.0	128.0	318.3	99.4	11.9	1.7	644.8

INDUSTRY: PHARMACIES & DRUG STORES (NAICS 44611)
PRODUCT LINE: HARDWARE & BUILDING SUPPLIES (Main Category)

NAICS 44611 Pharmacies and Drug Stores – this industry comprises establishments known as pharmacies and drug stores engaged in retailing prescription or nonprescription drugs and medicines.

5-YEAR TREND – ESTIMATED INDUSTRY SALES ($MILLIONS)

Year	Employee Size of Establishment									Total
	1-4 Emps.	5-9 Emps.	10-19 Emps.	20-49 Emps.	50-99 Emps.	100-249 Emps.	250-499 Emps.	500-999 Emps.	Unknown Emps.	Industry Sales
2016	6.1	15.1	60.9	178.9	18.1	7.2	2.8	0.9	0.5	290.5
2017	6.3	15.5	62.8	184.5	18.7	7.5	2.9	1.0	0.5	299.6
2018	6.5	16.1	65.1	191.2	19.3	7.7	3.0	1.0	0.5	310.4
2019	6.9	17.0	69.0	202.5	20.5	8.2	3.1	1.0	0.5	328.8
2019	7.3	18.2	73.6	216.3	21.9	8.8	3.3	1.1	0.6	351.1

INDUSTRY: GAS STATIONS W/CONVENIENCE STORES (NAICS 44711)
PRODUCT LINE: HARDWARE & BUILDING SUPPLIES (Main Category)

NAICS 44711: Gas Stations with Convenience Stores. this industry comprises establishments primarily engaged in selling gasoline and lubricating oils. These establishments frequently sell other merchandise, such as tires, batteries, and other automobile parts, or perform minor repair work. Gasoline stations combined with other activities, such as grocery stores, convenience stores, or carwashes, are classified according to the primary activity.

5-YEAR TREND – ESTIMATED INDUSTRY SALES ($MILLIONS)

Year	Employee Size of Establishment									Total
	1-4 Emps.	5-9 Emps.	10-19 Emps.	20-49 Emps.	50-99 Emps.	100-249 Emps.	250-499 Emps.	500-999 Emps.	Unknown Emps.	Industry Sales
2016	36.4	93.9	157.3	108.5	10.2	5.6	2.2	0.0	0.4	414.5
2017	37.9	97.9	163.8	113.1	10.6	5.8	2.3	0.0	0.4	431.8
2018	39.6	102.4	171.4	118.3	11.1	6.1	2.4	0.0	0.4	451.7
2019	42.2	109.1	182.6	126.0	11.8	6.5	2.6	0.0	0.5	481.3
2019	45.3	117.1	196.1	135.3	12.7	7.0	2.8	0.0	0.5	516.7

INDUSTRY: DEPARTMENT STORES INDUSTRY (NAICS 45211)
PRODUCT LINE: HARDWARE & BUILDING SUPPLIES (Main Category)

NAICS 45211: Department Stores Industry . this industry comprises establishments known as department stores primarily engaged in retailing a wide range of the following new products with no one merchandise line predominating: apparel, furniture, appliances and home furnishings; and selected additional items, such as paint, hardware, toiletries, cosmetics, photographic equipment, jewelry, toys, and sporting goods. merchandise lines are normally arranged in separate departments.

5-YEAR TREND – ESTIMATED INDUSTRY SALES ($MILLIONS)

Year	Employee Size of Establishment									Total
	1-4 Emps.	5-9 Emps.	10-19 Emps.	20-49 Emps.	50-99 Emps.	100-249 Emps.	250-499 Emps.	500-999 Emps.	Unknown Emps.	Industry Sales
2016	0.1	0.1	0.3	25.2	457.2	1,468.1	607.7	87.9	3.7	2,650.4
2017	0.1	0.1	0.3	25.3	459.0	1,473.9	610.1	88.3	3.7	2,660.8
2018	0.1	0.1	0.3	25.5	463.5	1,488.4	616.1	89.1	3.8	2,687.1
2019	0.1	0.1	0.3	25.5	463.6	1,488.6	616.2	89.4	3.8	2,687.6
2019	0.1	0.1	0.3	25.8	468.2	1,503.3	622.3	90.4	3.8	2,714.4

INDUSTRY: WAREHOUSE CLUBS & SUPERCENTERS (NAICS 45291)
PRODUCT LINE: HARDWARE & BUILDING SUPPLIES (Main Category)

NAICS 45291: Warehouse Clubs and Superstores This industry comprises establishments known as warehouse clubs, superstores or supercenters primarily engaged in retailing a general line of groceries in combination with general lines of new merchandise, such as apparel, furniture, and appliances.

5-YEAR TREND – ESTIMATED INDUSTRY SALES ($MILLIONS)

Year	Employee Size of Establishment									Total
	1-4 Emps.	5-9 Emps.	10-19 Emps.	20-49 Emps.	50-99 Emps.	100-249 Emps.	250-499 Emps.	500-999 Emps.	Unknown Emps.	Industry Sales
2016	0.4	0.1	0.3	12.6	23.9	1,365.2	6,010.0	151.4	2.3	7,566.3
2017	0.4	0.1	0.4	13.0	24.6	1,402.8	6,175.7	155.6	2.4	7,774.9
2018	0.4	0.1	0.4	13.4	25.4	1,448.7	6,377.4	160.7	2.4	8,028.8
2019	0.5	0.1	0.4	14.4	27.3	1,559.1	6,863.5	173.0	2.6	8,640.8
2019	0.5	0.1	0.4	15.2	28.9	1,651.4	7,270.1	183.2	2.8	9,152.7

INDUSTRY: ELECTRONIC SHOPPING & MAIL-ORDER (NAICS 45411)
PRODUCT LINE: HARDWARE & BUILDING SUPPLIES (Main Category)

NAICS 45411: Electronic Shopping and Mail-Order Houses This industry comprises establishments primarily engaged in retailing all types of merchandise by means of mail or by electronic media, such as interactive television or computer. Included in this industry are establishments primarily engaged in retailing from catalogue showrooms of mail-order houses.

5-YEAR TREND – ESTIMATED INDUSTRY SALES ($MILLIONS)

Year	Employee Size of Establishment									Total
	1-4 Emps.	5-9 Emps.	10-19 Emps.	20-49 Emps.	50-99 Emps.	100-249 Emps.	250-499 Emps.	500-999 Emps.	Unknown Emps.	Industry Sales
2016	276.7	142.6	206.0	345.7	260.2	481.4	649.1	916.3	38.9	3,316.9
2017	292.7	150.8	217.9	365.7	275.3	509.2	686.5	969.1	41.1	3,508.3
2018	310.3	159.9	231.0	387.7	291.8	539.9	727.9	1,027.5	43.6	3,719.7
2019	347.8	179.2	258.9	434.5	327.1	605.1	815.8	1,130.7	48.9	4,147.8
2019	386.7	199.2	287.8	483.1	363.6	672.7	907.0	1,238.2	54.4	4,592.6

INDUSTRY: HOME CENTERS INDUSTRY (NAICS 44411)
PRODUCT LINE: GENERAL HARDWARE (Sub Category)

NAICS 44411: Home Centers. This industry comprises establishments
known as home centers primarily engaged in retailing a general line of
new home repair and improvement materials and supplies, such as
lumber, plumbing goods, electrical goods, tools, housewares, hardware,
and lawn and garden supplies, with no one merchandise line predominating.
The merchandise lines are normally arranged in separate departments.

5-Year Trend – Estimated Industry Sales ($Millions)

| Year | Employee Size of Establishment | | | | | | | | | Total |
	1-4 Emps.	5-9 Emps.	10-19 Emps.	20-49 Emps.	50-99 Emps.	100-249 Emps.	250-499 Emps.	500-999 Emps.	Unknown Emps.	Industry Sales
2016	11.7	22.8	57.9	118.4	89.8	5,919.8	462.3	9.6	4.1	6,696.4
2017	12.0	23.4	59.3	121.2	91.9	6,061.7	473.4	9.9	4.2	6,857.0
2018	12.4	24.1	61.0	124.8	94.6	6,239.2	487.3	10.1	4.3	7,057.8
2019	12.8	24.9	63.3	129.4	98.1	6,470.9	505.4	10.5	4.5	7,319.8
2019	13.4	26.1	66.2	135.4	102.7	6,769.7	528.7	11.0	4.7	7,657.8

INDUSTRY: HARDWARE STORES INDUSTRY (NAICS 44413)
PRODUCT LINE: GENERAL HARDWARE (Sub Category)

NAICS 44413: Hardware Stores. Establishments primarily engaged
in the retail sale of a number of basic hardware lines, such as tools,
builders' hardware, paint and glass, housewares and household appliances,
and cutlery.

5-Year Trend – Estimated Industry Sales ($Millions)

| Year | Employee Size of Establishment | | | | | | | | | Total |
	1-4 Emps.	5-9 Emps.	10-19 Emps.	20-49 Emps.	50-99 Emps.	100-249 Emps.	250-499 Emps.	500-999 Emps.	Unknown Emps.	Industry Sales
2016	296.7	503.0	1,012.1	1,446.9	287.5	93.8	16.6	0.8	26.0	3,683.4
2017	299.6	507.9	1,022.1	1,461.2	290.3	94.7	16.8	0.8	26.2	3,719.6
2018	304.3	515.9	1,038.1	1,484.1	294.9	96.2	17.1	0.9	26.6	3,777.9
2019	316.4	536.4	1,079.3	1,543.0	306.6	100.0	17.7	0.9	27.7	3,928.0
2019	332.1	563.0	1,132.9	1,619.7	321.8	105.0	18.6	0.9	29.1	4,123.0

| INDUSTRY: HOME CENTERS INDUSTRY (NAICS 44411) |
| PRODUCT LINE: TOOLS & EQUIPMENT (Sub Category) |

NAICS 44411: Home Centers. This industry comprises establishments
known as home centers primarily engaged in retailing a general line of
new home repair and improvement materials and supplies, such as
lumber, plumbing goods, electrical goods, tools, housewares, hardware,
and lawn and garden supplies, with no one merchandise line predominating.
The merchandise lines are normally arranged in separate departments.

5-YEAR TREND — ESTIMATED INDUSTRY SALES ($MILLIONS)

| Year | Employee Size of Establishment | | | | | | | | | Total |
	1-4 Emps.	5-9 Emps.	10-19 Emps.	20-49 Emps.	50-99 Emps.	100-249 Emps.	250-499 Emps.	500-999 Emps.	Unknown Emps.	Industry Sales
2016	19.7	38.4	97.3	198.9	150.9	9,948.2	776.9	16.2	6.9	11,253.4
2017	20.2	39.3	99.6	203.7	154.5	10,186.8	795.6	16.6	7.1	11,523.2
2018	20.8	40.4	102.5	209.6	159.0	10,485.1	818.9	17.0	7.3	11,860.6
2019	21.6	41.9	106.3	217.4	164.9	10,874.4	849.3	17.7	7.5	12,301.0
2019	22.5	43.9	111.2	227.5	172.5	11,376.6	888.5	18.5	7.9	12,869.1

| INDUSTRY: HARDWARE STORES INDUSTRY (NAICS 44413) |
| PRODUCT LINE: TOOLS & EQUIPMENT (Sub Category) |

NAICS 44413: Hardware Stores. Establishments primarily engaged
in the retail sale of a number of basic hardware lines, such as tools,
builders' hardware, paint and glass, housewares and household appliances,
and cutlery.

5-YEAR TREND — ESTIMATED INDUSTRY SALES ($MILLIONS)

| Year | Employee Size of Establishment | | | | | | | | | Total |
	1-4 Emps.	5-9 Emps.	10-19 Emps.	20-49 Emps.	50-99 Emps.	100-249 Emps.	250-499 Emps.	500-999 Emps.	Unknown Emps.	Industry Sales
2016	329.9	559.3	1,125.4	1,608.9	319.7	104.3	18.5	0.9	28.9	4,095.6
2017	333.1	564.7	1,136.4	1,624.7	322.8	105.3	18.7	0.9	29.1	4,135.8
2018	338.3	573.6	1,154.2	1,650.1	327.9	106.9	19.0	1.0	29.6	4,200.6
2019	351.8	596.4	1,200.1	1,715.7	340.9	111.2	19.7	1.0	30.8	4,367.6
2019	369.3	626.0	1,259.7	1,800.9	357.8	116.7	20.7	1.0	32.3	4,584.4

INDUSTRY: HOME CENTERS INDUSTRY (NAICS 44411)
PRODUCT LINE: PLUMBING FIXTURES & SUPPLIES (Sub Category)

NAICS 44411: Home Centers. This industry comprises establishments
known as home centers primarily engaged in retailing a general line of
new home repair and improvement materials and supplies, such as
lumber, plumbing goods, electrical goods, tools, housewares, hardware,
and lawn and garden supplies, with no one merchandise line predominating.
The merchandise lines are normally arranged in separate departments.

5-YEAR TREND – ESTIMATED INDUSTRY SALES ($MILLIONS)

Year	Employee Size of Establishment									Total
	1-4 Emps.	5-9 Emps.	10-19 Emps.	20-49 Emps.	50-99 Emps.	100-249 Emps.	250-499 Emps.	500-999 Emps.	Unknown Emps.	Industry Sales
2016	20.6	40.0	101.4	207.3	157.3	10,369.5	809.8	16.9	7.2	11,729.9
2017	21.0	40.9	103.8	212.3	161.0	10,618.2	829.2	17.3	7.4	12,011.2
2018	21.7	42.1	106.9	218.5	165.7	10,929.1	853.5	17.8	7.6	12,362.9
2019	22.5	43.7	110.8	226.6	171.9	11,334.9	885.2	18.4	7.8	12,822.0
2019	23.5	45.7	116.0	237.1	179.8	11,858.4	926.1	19.3	8.2	13,414.1

INDUSTRY: HARDWARE STORES INDUSTRY (NAICS 44413)
PRODUCT LINE: PLUMBING FIXTURES & SUPPLIES (Sub Category)

NAICS 44413: Hardware Stores. Establishments primarily engaged
in the retail sale of a number of basic hardware lines, such as tools,
builders' hardware, paint and glass, housewares and household appliances,
and cutlery.

5-YEAR TREND – ESTIMATED INDUSTRY SALES ($MILLIONS)

Year	Employee Size of Establishment									Total
	1-4 Emps.	5-9 Emps.	10-19 Emps.	20-49 Emps.	50-99 Emps.	100-249 Emps.	250-499 Emps.	500-999 Emps.	Unknown Emps.	Industry Sales
2016	163.4	276.9	557.3	796.7	158.3	51.6	9.2	0.5	14.3	2,028.0
2017	165.0	279.7	562.7	804.5	159.8	52.1	9.2	0.5	14.4	2,048.0
2018	167.5	284.0	571.6	817.1	162.3	53.0	9.4	0.5	14.7	2,080.1
2019	174.2	295.3	594.3	849.6	168.8	55.1	9.8	0.5	15.2	2,162.7
2019	182.9	310.0	623.8	891.8	177.2	57.8	10.3	0.5	16.0	2,270.1

	INDUSTRY: HOME CENTERS INDUSTRY (NAICS 44411)
	PRODUCT LINE: WIRE & WIRING PRODUCTS (Sub Category)

NAICS 44411: Home Centers. This industry comprises establishments
known as home centers primarily engaged in retailing a general line of
new home repair and improvement materials and supplies, such as
lumber, plumbing goods, electrical goods, tools, housewares, hardware,
and lawn and garden supplies, with no one merchandise line predominating.
The merchandise lines are normally arranged in separate departments.

5-YEAR TREND – ESTIMATED INDUSTRY SALES ($MILLIONS)

Year	Employee Size of Establishment									Total
	1-4 Emps.	5-9 Emps.	10-19 Emps.	20-49 Emps.	50-99 Emps.	100-249 Emps.	250-499 Emps.	500-999 Emps.	Unknown Emps.	Industry Sales
2016	3.5	6.9	17.4	35.6	27.0	1,780.8	139.1	2.9	1.2	2,014.4
2017	3.6	7.0	17.8	36.5	27.7	1,823.5	142.4	3.0	1.3	2,062.7
2018	3.7	7.2	18.4	37.5	28.5	1,876.9	146.6	3.1	1.3	2,123.1
2019	3.9	7.5	19.0	38.9	29.5	1,946.5	152.0	3.2	1.3	2,201.9
2019	4.0	7.9	19.9	40.7	30.9	2,036.4	159.0	3.3	1.4	2,303.6

	INDUSTRY: HARDWARE STORES INDUSTRY (NAICS 44413)
	PRODUCT LINE: WIRE & WIRING PRODUCTS (Sub Category)

NAICS 44413: Hardware Stores. Establishments primarily engaged
in the retail sale of a number of basic hardware lines, such as tools,
builders' hardware, paint and glass, housewares and household appliances,
and cutlery.

5-YEAR TREND – ESTIMATED INDUSTRY SALES ($MILLIONS)

Year	Employee Size of Establishment									Total
	1-4 Emps.	5-9 Emps.	10-19 Emps.	20-49 Emps.	50-99 Emps.	100-249 Emps.	250-499 Emps.	500-999 Emps.	Unknown Emps.	Industry Sales
2016	42.0	71.1	143.1	204.6	40.7	13.3	2.4	0.1	3.7	520.9
2017	42.4	71.8	144.5	206.6	41.1	13.4	2.4	0.1	3.7	526.0
2018	43.0	73.0	146.8	209.9	41.7	13.6	2.4	0.1	3.8	534.3
2019	44.7	75.9	152.6	218.2	43.4	14.1	2.5	0.1	3.9	555.5
2019	47.0	79.6	160.2	229.1	45.5	14.8	2.6	0.1	4.1	583.1

INDUSTRY: HOME CENTERS INDUSTRY (NAICS 44411)
PRODUCT LINE: WELDING SUPPLIES (Sub Category)

NAICS 44411: Home Centers. This industry comprises establishments
known as home centers primarily engaged in retailing a general line of
new home repair and improvement materials and supplies, such as
lumber, plumbing goods, electrical goods, tools, housewares, hardware,
and lawn and garden supplies, with no one merchandise line predominating.
The merchandise lines are normally arranged in separate departments.

5-YEAR TREND – ESTIMATED INDUSTRY SALES ($MILLIONS)

| Year | Employee Size of Establishment | | | | | | | | | Total |
	1-4 Emps.	5-9 Emps.	10-19 Emps.	20-49 Emps.	50-99 Emps.	100-249 Emps.	250-499 Emps.	500-999 Emps.	Unknown Emps.	Industry Sales
2016	0.0	0.0	0.1	0.2	0.2	11.3	0.9	0.0	0.0	12.8
2017	0.0	0.0	0.1	0.2	0.2	11.6	0.9	0.0	0.0	13.1
2018	0.0	0.0	0.1	0.2	0.2	11.9	0.9	0.0	0.0	13.5
2019	0.0	0.0	0.1	0.2	0.2	12.4	1.0	0.0	0.0	14.0
2019	0.0	0.0	0.1	0.3	0.2	13.0	1.0	0.0	0.0	14.7

INDUSTRY: HARDWARE STORES INDUSTRY (NAICS 44413)
PRODUCT LINE: WELDING SUPPLIES (Sub Category)

NAICS 44413: Hardware Stores. Establishments primarily engaged
in the retail sale of a number of basic hardware lines, such as tools,
builders' hardware, paint and glass, housewares and household appliances,
and cutlery.

5-YEAR TREND – ESTIMATED INDUSTRY SALES ($MILLIONS)

| Year | Employee Size of Establishment | | | | | | | | | Total |
	1-4 Emps.	5-9 Emps.	10-19 Emps.	20-49 Emps.	50-99 Emps.	100-249 Emps.	250-499 Emps.	500-999 Emps.	Unknown Emps.	Industry Sales
2016	6.2	10.4	21.0	30.0	6.0	1.9	0.3	0.0	0.5	76.4
2017	6.2	10.5	21.2	30.3	6.0	2.0	0.3	0.0	0.5	77.1
2018	6.3	10.7	21.5	30.8	6.1	2.0	0.4	0.0	0.6	78.3
2019	6.6	11.1	22.4	32.0	6.4	2.1	0.4	0.0	0.6	81.5
2019	6.9	11.7	23.5	33.6	6.7	2.2	0.4	0.0	0.6	85.5

INDUSTRY: HOME CENTERS INDUSTRY (NAICS 44411)
PRODUCT LINE: ELECTRICAL SUPPLIES (Sub Category)

NAICS 44411: Home Centers. This industry comprises establishments known as home centers primarily engaged in retailing a general line of new home repair and improvement materials and supplies, such as lumber, plumbing goods, electrical goods, tools, housewares, hardware, and lawn and garden supplies, with no one merchandise line predominating. The merchandise lines are normally arranged in separate departments.

5-YEAR TREND — ESTIMATED INDUSTRY SALES ($MILLIONS)

Year	Employee Size of Establishment									Total
	1-4 Emps.	5-9 Emps.	10-19 Emps.	20-49 Emps.	50-99 Emps.	100-249 Emps.	250-499 Emps.	500-999 Emps.	Unknown Emps.	Industry Sales
2016	18.1	35.1	89.1	182.3	138.3	9,115.9	711.9	14.8	6.3	10,311.8
2017	18.5	36.0	91.3	186.6	141.6	9,334.5	729.0	15.2	6.5	10,559.1
2018	19.0	37.0	94.0	192.1	145.7	9,607.8	750.3	15.6	6.7	10,868.3
2019	19.7	38.4	97.4	199.2	151.1	9,964.5	778.2	16.2	6.9	11,271.8
2019	20.7	40.2	101.9	208.4	158.1	10,424.7	814.1	16.9	7.2	11,792.3

INDUSTRY: HARDWARE STORES INDUSTRY (NAICS 44413)
PRODUCT LINE: ELECTRICAL SUPPLIES (Sub Category)

NAICS 44413: Hardware Stores. Establishments primarily engaged in the retail sale of a number of basic hardware lines, such as tools, builders' hardware, paint and glass, housewares and household appliances, and cutlery.

5-YEAR TREND — ESTIMATED INDUSTRY SALES ($MILLIONS)

Year	Employee Size of Establishment									Total
	1-4 Emps.	5-9 Emps.	10-19 Emps.	20-49 Emps.	50-99 Emps.	100-249 Emps.	250-499 Emps.	500-999 Emps.	Unknown Emps.	Industry Sales
2016	105.5	178.8	359.8	514.4	102.2	33.3	5.9	0.3	9.2	1,309.5
2017	106.5	180.6	363.4	519.5	103.2	33.7	6.0	0.3	9.3	1,322.4
2018	108.2	183.4	369.1	527.6	104.8	34.2	6.1	0.3	9.5	1,343.1
2019	112.5	190.7	383.7	548.6	109.0	35.6	6.3	0.3	9.8	1,396.5
2019	118.1	200.2	402.8	575.8	114.4	37.3	6.6	0.3	10.3	1,465.8

INDUSTRY: HOME CENTERS INDUSTRY (NAICS 44411)
PRODUCT LINE: LAWN & GARDEN SUPPLIES (Main Category)

NAICS 44411: Home Centers. This industry comprises establishments known as home centers primarily engaged in retailing a general line of new home repair and improvement materials and supplies, such as lumber, plumbing goods, electrical goods, tools, housewares, hardware, and lawn and garden supplies, with no one merchandise line predominating. The merchandise lines are normally arranged in separate departments.

5-YEAR TREND — ESTIMATED INDUSTRY SALES ($MILLIONS)

| Year | Employee Size of Establishment | | | | | | | | | Total |
	1-4 Emps.	5-9 Emps.	10-19 Emps.	20-49 Emps.	50-99 Emps.	100-249 Emps.	250-499 Emps.	500-999 Emps.	Unknown Emps.	Industry Sales
2016	30.5	59.4	150.6	307.9	233.6	15,401.2	1,202.8	25.0	10.7	17,421.7
2017	31.3	60.8	154.2	315.3	239.2	15,770.6	1,231.6	25.6	10.9	17,839.5
2018	32.2	62.6	158.7	324.6	246.2	16,232.3	1,267.7	26.4	11.2	18,361.9
2019	33.4	64.9	164.6	336.6	255.3	16,835.0	1,314.8	27.4	11.7	19,043.6
2019	34.9	67.9	172.2	352.2	267.1	17,612.4	1,375.5	28.6	12.2	19,923.0

INDUSTRY: HARDWARE STORES (NAICS 44413)
PRODUCT LINE: LAWN & GARDEN SUPPLIES (Main Category)

NAICS 44413: Hardware Stores. Establishments primarily engaged in the retail sale of a number of basic hardware lines, such as tools, builders' hardware, paint and glass, housewares and household appliances, and cutlery.

5-YEAR TREND — ESTIMATED INDUSTRY SALES ($MILLIONS)

| Year | Employee Size of Establishment | | | | | | | | | Total |
	1-4 Emps.	5-9 Emps.	10-19 Emps.	20-49 Emps.	50-99 Emps.	100-249 Emps.	250-499 Emps.	500-999 Emps.	Unknown Emps.	Industry Sales
2016	252.7	428.4	862.1	1,232.5	244.9	79.9	14.2	0.7	22.1	3,137.4
2017	255.2	432.6	870.6	1,244.6	247.3	80.7	14.3	0.7	22.3	3,168.2
2018	259.2	439.4	884.2	1,264.1	251.2	81.9	14.5	0.7	22.7	3,217.9
2019	269.5	456.9	919.3	1,314.3	261.1	85.2	15.1	0.8	23.6	3,345.8
2019	282.9	479.5	965.0	1,379.6	274.1	89.4	15.9	0.8	24.7	3,511.9

INDUSTRY: SUPERMARKETS INDUSTRY (NAICS 44511)
PRODUCT LINE: LAWN & GARDEN SUPPLIES (Main Category)

NAICS 44511: Grocery Stores Industry. this industry comprises establishments generally known as supermarkets and grocery stores primarily engaged in retailing a general line of food, such as canned and frozen foods; fresh fruits and vegetables; and fresh and prepared meats, fish, and poultry. Included in this industry are delicatessen-type establishments primarily engaged in retailing a general line of food.

5-YEAR TREND – ESTIMATED INDUSTRY SALES ($MILLIONS)

Year	Employee Size of Establishment									Total
	1-4 Emps.	5-9 Emps.	10-19 Emps.	20-49 Emps.	50-99 Emps.	100-249 Emps.	250-499 Emps.	500-999 Emps.	Unknown Emps.	Industry Sales
2016	59.9	43.3	111.6	367.8	871.7	2,167.2	676.8	81.0	11.2	4,390.6
2017	59.5	43.0	110.9	365.5	866.2	2,153.4	672.5	80.5	11.2	4,362.7
2018	59.5	43.0	110.9	365.4	865.9	2,152.7	672.3	80.4	11.2	4,361.2
2019	60.7	43.9	113.2	372.9	883.8	2,197.1	686.2	82.0	11.4	4,451.1
2019	62.6	45.2	116.7	384.4	911.1	2,265.0	707.4	84.5	11.8	4,588.6

INDUSTRY: PHARMACIES & DRUG STORES (NAICS 44611)
PRODUCT LINE: LAWN & GARDEN SUPPLIES (Main Category)

NAICS 44611 Pharmacies and Drug Stores – this industry comprises establishments known as pharmacies and drug stores engaged in retailing prescription or nonprescription drugs and medicines.

5-YEAR TREND – ESTIMATED INDUSTRY SALES ($MILLIONS)

Year	Employee Size of Establishment									Total
	1-4 Emps.	5-9 Emps.	10-19 Emps.	20-49 Emps.	50-99 Emps.	100-249 Emps.	250-499 Emps.	500-999 Emps.	Unknown Emps.	Industry Sales
2016	5.4	13.4	54.0	158.7	16.0	6.4	2.5	0.8	0.4	257.6
2017	5.6	13.8	55.7	163.7	16.6	6.6	2.5	0.8	0.4	265.7
2018	5.8	14.3	57.7	169.6	17.2	6.9	2.6	0.9	0.4	275.3
2019	6.1	15.1	61.2	179.6	18.2	7.3	2.8	0.9	0.5	291.6
2019	6.5	16.1	65.3	191.8	19.4	7.8	3.0	1.0	0.5	311.4

<table>
<tr><td colspan="2">INDUSTRY: GAS STATIONS W/CONVENIENCE STORES (NAICS 44711)</td></tr>
<tr><td colspan="2">PRODUCT LINE: LAWN & GARDEN SUPPLIES (Main Category)</td></tr>
</table>

NAICS 44711: Gas Stations with Convenience Stores. this industry comprises establishments primarily engaged in selling gasoline and lubricating oils. These establishments frequently sell other merchandise, such as tires, batteries, and other automobile parts, or perform minor repair work. Gasoline stations combined with other activities, such as grocery stores, convenience stores, or carwashes, are classified according to the primary activity.

5-YEAR TREND — ESTIMATED INDUSTRY SALES ($MILLIONS)

Year	Employee Size of Establishment									Total
	1-4 Emps.	5-9 Emps.	10-19 Emps.	20-49 Emps.	50-99 Emps.	100-249 Emps.	250-499 Emps.	500-999 Emps.	Unknown Emps.	Industry Sales
2016	11.2	29.0	48.6	33.5	3.2	1.7	0.7	0.0	0.1	128.1
2017	11.7	30.2	50.6	34.9	3.3	1.8	0.7	0.0	0.1	133.5
2018	12.2	31.6	53.0	36.5	3.4	1.9	0.7	0.0	0.1	139.6
2019	13.1	33.7	56.4	38.9	3.7	2.0	0.8	0.0	0.1	148.7
2019	14.0	36.2	60.6	41.8	3.9	2.2	0.9	0.0	0.2	159.7

<table>
<tr><td colspan="2">INDUSTRY: DEPARTMENT STORES INDUSTRY (NAICS 45211)</td></tr>
<tr><td colspan="2">PRODUCT LINE: LAWN & GARDEN SUPPLIES (Main Category)</td></tr>
</table>

NAICS 45211: Department Stores Industry . this industry comprises establishments known as department stores primarily engaged in retailing a wide range of the following new products with no one merchandise line predominating: apparel, furniture, appliances and home furnishings; and selected additional items, such as paint, hardware, toiletries, cosmetics, photographic equipment, jewelry, toys, and sporting goods. merchandise lines are normally arranged in separate departments.

5-YEAR TREND — ESTIMATED INDUSTRY SALES ($MILLIONS)

Year	Employee Size of Establishment									Total
	1-4 Emps.	5-9 Emps.	10-19 Emps.	20-49 Emps.	50-99 Emps.	100-249 Emps.	250-499 Emps.	500-999 Emps.	Unknown Emps.	Industry Sales
2016	0.1	0.1	0.3	22.7	412.4	1,324.2	548.1	79.3	3.4	2,390.6
2017	0.1	0.1	0.3	22.8	414.0	1,329.4	550.3	79.6	3.4	2,399.9
2018	0.1	0.1	0.3	23.0	418.1	1,342.5	555.7	80.4	3.4	2,423.6
2019	0.1	0.1	0.3	23.0	418.1	1,342.7	555.8	80.6	3.4	2,424.1
2019	0.1	0.1	0.3	23.3	422.3	1,356.0	561.3	81.5	3.4	2,448.3

INDUSTRY: WAREHOUSE CLUBS & SUPERCENTERS (NAICS 45291)
PRODUCT LINE: LAWN & GARDEN SUPPLIES (Main Category)

NAICS 45291: Warehouse Clubs and Superstores This industry comprises establishments known as warehouse clubs, superstores or supercenters primarily engaged in retailing a general line of groceries in combination with general lines of new merchandise, such as apparel, furniture, and appliances.

5-YEAR TREND — ESTIMATED INDUSTRY SALES ($MILLIONS)

Year	Employee Size of Establishment									Total
	1-4 Emps.	5-9 Emps.	10-19 Emps.	20-49 Emps.	50-99 Emps.	100-249 Emps.	250-499 Emps.	500-999 Emps.	Unknown Emps.	Industry Sales
2016	0.6	0.1	0.5	17.3	32.8	1,875.1	8,254.7	208.0	3.1	10,392.3
2017	0.6	0.2	0.5	17.8	33.7	1,926.8	8,482.2	213.7	3.2	10,678.7
2018	0.6	0.2	0.5	18.4	34.8	1,989.7	8,759.2	220.7	3.3	11,027.5
2019	0.6	0.2	0.5	19.8	37.5	2,141.4	9,426.9	237.5	3.6	11,868.1
2019	0.7	0.2	0.6	20.9	39.7	2,268.2	9,985.4	251.6	3.8	12,571.1

INDUSTRY: ELECTRONIC SHOPPING & MAIL-ORDER (NAICS 45411)
PRODUCT LINE: LAWN & GARDEN SUPPLIES (Main Category)

NAICS 45411: Electronic Shopping and Mail-Order Houses This industry comprises establishments primarily engaged in retailing all types of merchandise by means of mail or by electronic media, such as interactive television or computer. Included in this industry are establishments primarily engaged in retailing from catalogue showrooms of mail-order houses.

5-YEAR TREND — ESTIMATED INDUSTRY SALES ($MILLIONS)

Year	Employee Size of Establishment									Total
	1-4 Emps.	5-9 Emps.	10-19 Emps.	20-49 Emps.	50-99 Emps.	100-249 Emps.	250-499 Emps.	500-999 Emps.	Unknown Emps.	Industry Sales
2016	405.6	208.9	301.8	506.6	381.4	705.6	951.2	1,342.7	57.0	4,860.8
2017	429.0	221.0	319.3	535.9	403.4	746.3	1,006.1	1,420.3	60.3	5,141.4
2018	454.8	234.3	338.5	568.2	427.7	791.2	1,066.7	1,505.8	63.9	5,451.1
2019	509.7	262.6	379.3	636.7	479.3	886.7	1,195.5	1,657.0	71.6	6,078.5
2019	566.7	291.9	421.8	707.9	532.9	985.9	1,329.1	1,814.6	79.7	6,730.4

INDUSTRY: HARDWARE STORES INDUSTRY (NAICS 44413)
PRODUCT LINE: CUT FLOWERS (Sub Category)

NAICS 44413: Hardware Stores. Establishments primarily engaged
in the retail sale of a number of basic hardware lines, such as tools,
builders' hardware, paint and glass, housewares and household appliances,
and cutlery.

5-YEAR TREND – ESTIMATED INDUSTRY SALES ($MILLIONS)

| Year | Employee Size of Establishment | | | | | | | | | Total |
	1-4 Emps.	5-9 Emps.	10-19 Emps.	20-49 Emps.	50-99 Emps.	100-249 Emps.	250-499 Emps.	500-999 Emps.	Unknown Emps.	Industry Sales
2016	1.6	2.8	5.6	8.0	1.6	0.5	0.1	0.0	0.1	20.4
2017	1.7	2.8	5.7	8.1	1.6	0.5	0.1	0.0	0.1	20.6
2018	1.7	2.9	5.8	8.2	1.6	0.5	0.1	0.0	0.1	21.0
2019	1.8	3.0	6.0	8.6	1.7	0.6	0.1	0.0	0.2	21.8
2019	1.8	3.1	6.3	9.0	1.8	0.6	0.1	0.0	0.2	22.9

INDUSTRY: DEPARTMENT STORES INDUSTRY (NAICS 45211)
PRODUCT LINE: CUT FLOWERS (Sub Category)

NAICS 45211: Department Stores Industry . this industry comprises
establishments known as department stores primarily engaged in retailing
a wide range of the following new products with no one merchandise line
predominating: apparel, furniture, appliances and home furnishings; and
selected additional items, such as paint, hardware, toiletries, cosmetics,
photographic equipment, jewelry, toys, and sporting goods. merchandise lines
are normally arranged in separate departments.

5-YEAR TREND – ESTIMATED INDUSTRY SALES ($MILLIONS)

| Year | Employee Size of Establishment | | | | | | | | | Total |
	1-4 Emps.	5-9 Emps.	10-19 Emps.	20-49 Emps.	50-99 Emps.	100-249 Emps.	250-499 Emps.	500-999 Emps.	Unknown Emps.	Industry Sales
2016	0.0	0.0	0.0	0.1	2.4	7.8	3.2	0.5	0.0	14.1
2017	0.0	0.0	0.0	0.1	2.4	7.9	3.3	0.5	0.0	14.2
2018	0.0	0.0	0.0	0.1	2.5	7.9	3.3	0.5	0.0	14.3
2019	0.0	0.0	0.0	0.1	2.5	7.9	3.3	0.5	0.0	14.3
2019	0.0	0.0	0.0	0.1	2.5	8.0	3.3	0.5	0.0	14.5

INDUSTRY: WAREHOUSE CLUBS & SUPERCENTERS (NAICS 45291)
PRODUCT LINE: CUT FLOWERS (Sub Category)

NAICS 45291: Warehouse Clubs and Superstores This industry comprises establishments known as warehouse clubs, superstores or supercenters primarily engaged in retailing a general line of groceries in combination with general lines of new merchandise, such as apparel, furniture, and appliances.

5-YEAR TREND – ESTIMATED INDUSTRY SALES ($MILLIONS)

Year	Employee Size of Establishment									Total
	1-4 Emps.	5-9 Emps.	10-19 Emps.	20-49 Emps.	50-99 Emps.	100-249 Emps.	250-499 Emps.	500-999 Emps.	Unknown Emps.	Industry Sales
2016	0.1	0.0	0.1	2.9	5.6	317.7	1,398.5	35.2	0.5	1,760.6
2017	0.1	0.0	0.1	3.0	5.7	326.4	1,437.0	36.2	0.5	1,809.1
2018	0.1	0.0	0.1	3.1	5.9	337.1	1,483.9	37.4	0.6	1,868.2
2019	0.1	0.0	0.1	3.3	6.4	362.8	1,597.1	40.2	0.6	2,010.6
2019	0.1	0.0	0.1	3.5	6.7	384.3	1,691.7	42.6	0.6	2,129.7

INDUSTRY: HOME CENTERS INDUSTRY (NAICS 44411)
PRODUCT LINE: INDOOR POTTED PLANTS (Sub Category)

NAICS 44411: Home Centers. This industry comprises establishments known as home centers primarily engaged in retailing a general line of new home repair and improvement materials and supplies, such as lumber, plumbing goods, electrical goods, tools, housewares, hardware, and lawn and garden supplies, with no one merchandise line predominating. The merchandise lines are normally arranged in separate departments.

5-YEAR TREND – ESTIMATED INDUSTRY SALES ($MILLIONS)

Year	Employee Size of Establishment									Total
	1-4 Emps.	5-9 Emps.	10-19 Emps.	20-49 Emps.	50-99 Emps.	100-249 Emps.	250-499 Emps.	500-999 Emps.	Unknown Emps.	Industry Sales
2016	1.6	3.2	8.1	16.5	12.5	824.0	64.4	1.3	0.6	932.1
2017	1.7	3.3	8.3	16.9	12.8	843.8	65.9	1.4	0.6	954.5
2018	1.7	3.3	8.5	17.4	13.2	868.5	67.8	1.4	0.6	982.4
2019	1.8	3.5	8.8	18.0	13.7	900.7	70.3	1.5	0.6	1,018.9
2019	1.9	3.6	9.2	18.8	14.3	942.3	73.6	1.5	0.7	1,065.9

INDUSTRY: HARDWARE STORES INDUSTRY (NAICS 44413)
PRODUCT LINE: INDOOR POTTED PLANTS (Sub Category)

NAICS 44413: Hardware Stores. Establishments primarily engaged
in the retail sale of a number of basic hardware lines, such as tools,
builders' hardware, paint and glass, housewares and household appliances,
and cutlery.

5-YEAR TREND – ESTIMATED INDUSTRY SALES ($MILLIONS)

Year	Employee Size of Establishment									Total
	1-4 Emps.	5-9 Emps.	10-19 Emps.	20-49 Emps.	50-99 Emps.	100-249 Emps.	250-499 Emps.	500-999 Emps.	Unknown Emps.	Industry Sales
2016	3.5	6.0	12.1	17.2	3.4	1.1	0.2	0.0	0.3	43.9
2017	3.6	6.1	12.2	17.4	3.5	1.1	0.2	0.0	0.3	44.3
2018	3.6	6.1	12.4	17.7	3.5	1.1	0.2	0.0	0.3	45.0
2019	3.8	6.4	12.9	18.4	3.7	1.2	0.2	0.0	0.3	46.8
2019	4.0	6.7	13.5	19.3	3.8	1.3	0.2	0.0	0.3	49.1

INDUSTRY: DEPARTMENT STORES INDUSTRY (NAICS 45211)
PRODUCT LINE: INDOOR POTTED PLANTS (Sub Category)

NAICS 45211: Department Stores Industry . this industry comprises
establishments known as department stores primarily engaged in retailing
a wide range of the following new products with no one merchandise line
predominating: apparel, furniture, appliances and home furnishings; and
selected additional items, such as paint, hardware, toiletries, cosmetics,
photographic equipment, jewelry, toys, and sporting goods. merchandise lines
are normally arranged in separate departments.

5-YEAR TREND – ESTIMATED INDUSTRY SALES ($MILLIONS)

Year	Employee Size of Establishment									Total
	1-4 Emps.	5-9 Emps.	10-19 Emps.	20-49 Emps.	50-99 Emps.	100-249 Emps.	250-499 Emps.	500-999 Emps.	Unknown Emps.	Industry Sales
2016	0.0	0.0	0.0	0.8	14.4	46.4	19.2	2.8	0.1	83.7
2017	0.0	0.0	0.0	0.8	14.5	46.6	19.3	2.8	0.1	84.1
2018	0.0	0.0	0.0	0.8	14.6	47.0	19.5	2.8	0.1	84.9
2019	0.0	0.0	0.0	0.8	14.6	47.0	19.5	2.8	0.1	84.9
2019	0.0	0.0	0.0	0.8	14.8	47.5	19.7	2.9	0.1	85.7

INDUSTRY: WAREHOUSE CLUBS & SUPERCENTERS (NAICS 45291)
PRODUCT LINE: INDOOR POTTED PLANTS (Sub Category)

NAICS 45291: Warehouse Clubs and Superstores This industry
comprises establishments known as warehouse clubs, superstores or
supercenters primarily engaged in retailing a general line of groceries
in combination with general lines of new merchandise, such as apparel,
furniture, and appliances.

5-YEAR TREND – ESTIMATED INDUSTRY SALES ($MILLIONS)

| Year | Employee Size of Establishment | | | | | | | | | Total |
	1-4 Emps.	5-9 Emps.	10-19 Emps.	20-49 Emps.	50-99 Emps.	100-249 Emps.	250-499 Emps.	500-999 Emps.	Unknown Emps.	Industry Sales
2016	0.0	0.0	0.0	0.8	1.5	87.3	384.1	9.7	0.1	483.6
2017	0.0	0.0	0.0	0.8	1.6	89.7	394.7	9.9	0.2	496.9
2018	0.0	0.0	0.0	0.9	1.6	92.6	407.6	10.3	0.2	513.2
2019	0.0	0.0	0.0	0.9	1.7	99.6	438.7	11.1	0.2	552.3
2019	0.0	0.0	0.0	1.0	1.8	105.6	464.7	11.7	0.2	585.0

INDUSTRY: HOME CENTERS INDUSTRY (NAICS 44411)
PRODUCT LINE: OUTDOOR NURSERY PLANTS (Sub Category)

NAICS 44411: Home Centers. This industry comprises establishments
known as home centers primarily engaged in retailing a general line of
new home repair and improvement materials and supplies, such as
lumber, plumbing goods, electrical goods, tools, housewares, hardware,
and lawn and garden supplies, with no one merchandise line predominating.
The merchandise lines are normally arranged in separate departments.

5-YEAR TREND – ESTIMATED INDUSTRY SALES ($MILLIONS)

| Year | Employee Size of Establishment | | | | | | | | | Total |
	1-4 Emps.	5-9 Emps.	10-19 Emps.	20-49 Emps.	50-99 Emps.	100-249 Emps.	250-499 Emps.	500-999 Emps.	Unknown Emps.	Industry Sales
2016	7.5	14.6	37.1	75.8	57.5	3,792.9	296.2	6.2	2.6	4,290.4
2017	7.7	15.0	38.0	77.7	58.9	3,883.8	303.3	6.3	2.7	4,393.3
2018	7.9	15.4	39.1	79.9	60.6	3,997.5	312.2	6.5	2.8	4,522.0
2019	8.2	16.0	40.5	82.9	62.9	4,146.0	323.8	6.7	2.9	4,689.9
2019	8.6	16.7	42.4	86.7	65.8	4,337.4	338.7	7.1	3.0	4,906.4

INDUSTRY: HARDWARE STORES INDUSTRY (NAICS 44413)
PRODUCT LINE: OUTDOOR NURSERY PLANTS (Sub Category)

NAICS 44413: Hardware Stores. Establishments primarily engaged
in the retail sale of a number of basic hardware lines, such as tools,
builders' hardware, paint and glass, housewares and household appliances,
and cutlery.

5-YEAR TREND — ESTIMATED INDUSTRY SALES ($MILLIONS)

| Year | Employee Size of Establishment | | | | | | | | | Total |
	1-4 Emps.	5-9 Emps.	10-19 Emps.	20-49 Emps.	50-99 Emps.	100-249 Emps.	250-499 Emps.	500-999 Emps.	Unknown Emps.	Industry Sales
2016	16.9	28.7	57.7	82.5	16.4	5.3	0.9	0.0	1.5	210.0
2017	17.1	29.0	58.3	83.3	16.6	5.4	1.0	0.0	1.5	212.1
2018	17.3	29.4	59.2	84.6	16.8	5.5	1.0	0.0	1.5	215.4
2019	18.0	30.6	61.5	88.0	17.5	5.7	1.0	0.1	1.6	224.0
2019	18.9	32.1	64.6	92.3	18.3	6.0	1.1	0.1	1.7	235.1

INDUSTRY: DEPARTMENT STORES INDUSTRY (NAICS 45211)
PRODUCT LINE: OUTDOOR NURSERY PLANTS (Sub Category)

NAICS 45211: Department Stores Industry . this industry comprises
establishments known as department stores primarily engaged in retailing
a wide range of the following new products with no one merchandise line
predominating: apparel, furniture, appliances and home furnishings; and
selected additional items, such as paint, hardware, toiletries, cosmetics,
photographic equipment, jewelry, toys, and sporting goods. merchandise lines
are normally arranged in separate departments.

5-YEAR TREND — ESTIMATED INDUSTRY SALES ($MILLIONS)

| Year | Employee Size of Establishment | | | | | | | | | Total |
	1-4 Emps.	5-9 Emps.	10-19 Emps.	20-49 Emps.	50-99 Emps.	100-249 Emps.	250-499 Emps.	500-999 Emps.	Unknown Emps.	Industry Sales
2016	0.0	0.0	0.0	4.2	76.7	246.3	102.0	14.8	0.6	444.7
2017	0.0	0.0	0.1	4.2	77.0	247.3	102.4	14.8	0.6	446.4
2018	0.0	0.0	0.1	4.3	77.8	249.7	103.4	15.0	0.6	450.8
2019	0.0	0.0	0.1	4.3	77.8	249.8	103.4	15.0	0.6	450.9
2019	0.0	0.0	0.1	4.3	78.5	252.2	104.4	15.2	0.6	455.4

INDUSTRY: WAREHOUSE CLUBS & SUPERCENTERS (NAICS 45291)
PRODUCT LINE: OUTDOOR NURSERY PLANTS (Sub Category)

NAICS 45291: Warehouse Clubs and Superstores This industry comprises establishments known as warehouse clubs, superstores or supercenters primarily engaged in retailing a general line of groceries in combination with general lines of new merchandise, such as apparel, furniture, and appliances.

5-YEAR TREND — ESTIMATED INDUSTRY SALES ($MILLIONS)

Year	Employee Size of Establishment									Total
	1-4 Emps.	5-9 Emps.	10-19 Emps.	20-49 Emps.	50-99 Emps.	100-249 Emps.	250-499 Emps.	500-999 Emps.	Unknown Emps.	Industry Sales
2016	0.1	0.0	0.1	2.6	4.9	279.1	1,228.5	31.0	0.5	1,546.6
2017	0.1	0.0	0.1	2.6	5.0	286.7	1,262.3	31.8	0.5	1,589.2
2018	0.1	0.0	0.1	2.7	5.2	296.1	1,303.6	32.8	0.5	1,641.1
2019	0.1	0.0	0.1	2.9	5.6	318.7	1,402.9	35.4	0.5	1,766.2
2019	0.1	0.0	0.1	3.1	5.9	337.6	1,486.0	37.4	0.6	1,870.9

INDUSTRY: HOME CENTERS INDUSTRY (NAICS 44411)
PRODUCT LINE: FERTILIZER & SOIL TREATMENTS (Sub Category)

NAICS 44411: Home Centers. This industry comprises establishments known as home centers primarily engaged in retailing a general line of new home repair and improvement materials and supplies, such as lumber, plumbing goods, electrical goods, tools, housewares, hardware, and lawn and garden supplies, with no one merchandise line predominating. The merchandise lines are normally arranged in separate departments.

5-YEAR TREND — ESTIMATED INDUSTRY SALES ($MILLIONS)

Year	Employee Size of Establishment									Total
	1-4 Emps.	5-9 Emps.	10-19 Emps.	20-49 Emps.	50-99 Emps.	100-249 Emps.	250-499 Emps.	500-999 Emps.	Unknown Emps.	Industry Sales
2016	5.9	11.4	29.0	59.2	44.9	2,962.9	231.4	4.8	2.1	3,351.6
2017	6.0	11.7	29.7	60.7	46.0	3,034.0	236.9	4.9	2.1	3,432.0
2018	6.2	12.0	30.5	62.4	47.4	3,122.8	243.9	5.1	2.2	3,532.5
2019	6.4	12.5	31.7	64.8	49.1	3,238.7	252.9	5.3	2.2	3,663.6
2019	6.7	13.1	33.1	67.7	51.4	3,388.3	264.6	5.5	2.3	3,832.8

INDUSTRY: HARDWARE STORES INDUSTRY (NAICS 44413)
PRODUCT LINE: FERTILIZER & SOIL TREATMENTS (Sub Category)

NAICS 44413: Hardware Stores. Establishments primarily engaged
in the retail sale of a number of basic hardware lines, such as tools,
builders' hardware, paint and glass, housewares and household appliances,
and cutlery.

5-YEAR TREND — ESTIMATED INDUSTRY SALES ($MILLIONS)

| Year | Employee Size of Establishment | | | | | | | | | Total |
	1-4 Emps.	5-9 Emps.	10-19 Emps.	20-49 Emps.	50-99 Emps.	100-249 Emps.	250-499 Emps.	500-999 Emps.	Unknown Emps.	Industry Sales
2016	40.4	68.5	137.8	196.9	39.1	12.8	2.3	0.1	3.5	501.3
2017	40.8	69.1	139.1	198.9	39.5	12.9	2.3	0.1	3.6	506.3
2018	41.4	70.2	141.3	202.0	40.1	13.1	2.3	0.1	3.6	514.2
2019	43.1	73.0	146.9	210.0	41.7	13.6	2.4	0.1	3.8	534.6
2019	45.2	76.6	154.2	220.4	43.8	14.3	2.5	0.1	4.0	561.2

INDUSTRY: DEPARTMENT STORES INDUSTRY (NAICS 45211)
PRODUCT LINE: FERTILIZER & SOIL TREATMENTS (Sub Category)

NAICS 45211: Department Stores Industry . this industry comprises
establishments known as department stores primarily engaged in retailing
a wide range of the following new products with no one merchandise line
predominating: apparel, furniture, appliances and home furnishings; and
selected additional items, such as paint, hardware, toiletries, cosmetics,
photographic equipment, jewelry, toys, and sporting goods. merchandise lines
are normally arranged in separate departments.

5-YEAR TREND — ESTIMATED INDUSTRY SALES ($MILLIONS)

| Year | Employee Size of Establishment | | | | | | | | | Total |
	1-4 Emps.	5-9 Emps.	10-19 Emps.	20-49 Emps.	50-99 Emps.	100-249 Emps.	250-499 Emps.	500-999 Emps.	Unknown Emps.	Industry Sales
2016	0.0	0.0	0.0	2.2	40.7	130.5	54.0	7.8	0.3	235.7
2017	0.0	0.0	0.0	2.2	40.8	131.1	54.2	7.8	0.3	236.6
2018	0.0	0.0	0.0	2.3	41.2	132.3	54.8	7.9	0.3	238.9
2019	0.0	0.0	0.0	2.3	41.2	132.4	54.8	7.9	0.3	239.0
2019	0.0	0.0	0.0	2.3	41.6	133.7	55.3	8.0	0.3	241.4

INDUSTRY: WAREHOUSE CLUBS & SUPERCENTERS (NAICS 45291)
PRODUCT LINE: FERTILIZER & SOIL TREATMENTS (Sub Category)

NAICS 45291: Warehouse Clubs and Superstores This industry comprises establishments known as warehouse clubs, superstores or supercenters primarily engaged in retailing a general line of groceries in combination with general lines of new merchandise, such as apparel, furniture, and appliances.

5-YEAR TREND – ESTIMATED INDUSTRY SALES ($MILLIONS)

Year	Employee Size of Establishment									Total
	1-4 Emps.	5-9 Emps.	10-19 Emps.	20-49 Emps.	50-99 Emps.	100-249 Emps.	250-499 Emps.	500-999 Emps.	Unknown Emps.	Industry Sales
2016	0.1	0.0	0.1	2.4	4.5	257.0	1,131.6	28.5	0.4	1,424.6
2017	0.1	0.0	0.1	2.4	4.6	264.1	1,162.8	29.3	0.4	1,463.9
2018	0.1	0.0	0.1	2.5	4.8	272.8	1,200.7	30.3	0.5	1,511.7
2019	0.1	0.0	0.1	2.7	5.1	293.5	1,292.3	32.6	0.5	1,626.9
2019	0.1	0.0	0.1	2.9	5.4	310.9	1,368.8	34.5	0.5	1,723.3

INDUSTRY: HOME CENTERS INDUSTRY (NAICS 44411)
PRODUCT LINE: LAWN & GARDEN TOOLS (Sub Category)

NAICS 44411: Home Centers. This industry comprises establishments known as home centers primarily engaged in retailing a general line of new home repair and improvement materials and supplies, such as lumber, plumbing goods, electrical goods, tools, housewares, hardware, and lawn and garden supplies, with no one merchandise line predominating. The merchandise lines are normally arranged in separate departments.

5-YEAR TREND – ESTIMATED INDUSTRY SALES ($MILLIONS)

Year	Employee Size of Establishment									Total
	1-4 Emps.	5-9 Emps.	10-19 Emps.	20-49 Emps.	50-99 Emps.	100-249 Emps.	250-499 Emps.	500-999 Emps.	Unknown Emps.	Industry Sales
2016	2.6	5.0	12.8	26.1	19.8	1,306.2	102.0	2.1	0.9	1,477.5
2017	2.7	5.2	13.1	26.7	20.3	1,337.5	104.5	2.2	0.9	1,513.0
2018	2.7	5.3	13.5	27.5	20.9	1,376.7	107.5	2.2	1.0	1,557.3
2019	2.8	5.5	14.0	28.5	21.7	1,427.8	111.5	2.3	1.0	1,615.1
2019	3.0	5.8	14.6	29.9	22.7	1,493.7	116.7	2.4	1.0	1,689.7

INDUSTRY: HARDWARE STORES INDUSTRY (NAICS 44413)
PRODUCT LINE: LAWN & GARDEN TOOLS (Sub Category)

NAICS 44413: Hardware Stores. Establishments primarily engaged
in the retail sale of a number of basic hardware lines, such as tools,
builders' hardware, paint and glass, housewares and household appliances,
and cutlery.

5-YEAR TREND – ESTIMATED INDUSTRY SALES ($MILLIONS)

Year	Employee Size of Establishment									Total Industry Sales
	1-4 Emps.	5-9 Emps.	10-19 Emps.	20-49 Emps.	50-99 Emps.	100-249 Emps.	250-499 Emps.	500-999 Emps.	Unknown Emps.	
2016	44.1	74.7	150.4	215.0	42.7	13.9	2.5	0.1	3.9	547.2
2017	44.5	75.5	151.8	217.1	43.1	14.1	2.5	0.1	3.9	552.6
2018	45.2	76.6	154.2	220.5	43.8	14.3	2.5	0.1	4.0	561.2
2019	47.0	79.7	160.3	229.2	45.5	14.9	2.6	0.1	4.1	583.5
2019	49.3	83.6	168.3	240.6	47.8	15.6	2.8	0.1	4.3	612.5

INDUSTRY: DEPARTMENT STORES INDUSTRY (NAICS 45211)
PRODUCT LINE: LAWN & GARDEN TOOLS (Sub Category)

NAICS 45211: Department Stores Industry . this industry comprises
establishments known as department stores primarily engaged in retailing
a wide range of the following new products with no one merchandise line
predominating: apparel, furniture, appliances and home furnishings; and
selected additional items, such as paint, hardware, toiletries, cosmetics,
photographic equipment, jewelry, toys, and sporting goods. merchandise lines
are normally arranged in separate departments.

5-YEAR TREND – ESTIMATED INDUSTRY SALES ($MILLIONS)

Year	Employee Size of Establishment									Total Industry Sales
	1-4 Emps.	5-9 Emps.	10-19 Emps.	20-49 Emps.	50-99 Emps.	100-249 Emps.	250-499 Emps.	500-999 Emps.	Unknown Emps.	
2016	0.0	0.0	0.0	0.5	8.5	27.4	11.4	1.6	0.1	49.6
2017	0.0	0.0	0.0	0.5	8.6	27.6	11.4	1.6	0.1	49.7
2018	0.0	0.0	0.0	0.5	8.7	27.8	11.5	1.7	0.1	50.2
2019	0.0	0.0	0.0	0.5	8.7	27.8	11.5	1.7	0.1	50.2
2019	0.0	0.0	0.0	0.5	8.8	28.1	11.6	1.7	0.1	50.7

NAICS 45291: Warehouse Clubs and Superstores This industry comprises establishments known as warehouse clubs, superstores or supercenters primarily engaged in retailing a general line of groceries in combination with general lines of new merchandise, such as apparel, furniture, and appliances.

5-YEAR TREND – ESTIMATED INDUSTRY SALES ($MILLIONS)

Year	Employee Size of Establishment									Total
	1-4 Emps.	5-9 Emps.	10-19 Emps.	20-49 Emps.	50-99 Emps.	100-249 Emps.	250-499 Emps.	500-999 Emps.	Unknown Emps.	Industry Sales
2016	0.0	0.0	0.0	0.5	1.0	58.2	256.1	6.5	0.1	322.4
2017	0.0	0.0	0.0	0.6	1.0	59.8	263.2	6.6	0.1	331.3
2018	0.0	0.0	0.0	0.6	1.1	61.7	271.7	6.8	0.1	342.1
2019	0.0	0.0	0.0	0.6	1.2	66.4	292.5	7.4	0.1	368.2
2019	0.0	0.0	0.0	0.6	1.2	70.4	309.8	7.8	0.1	390.0

NAICS 44411: Home Centers. This industry comprises establishments known as home centers primarily engaged in retailing a general line of new home repair and improvement materials and supplies, such as lumber, plumbing goods, electrical goods, tools, housewares, hardware, and lawn and garden supplies, with no one merchandise line predominating. The merchandise lines are normally arranged in separate departments.

5-YEAR TREND – ESTIMATED INDUSTRY SALES ($MILLIONS)

Year	Employee Size of Establishment									Total
	1-4 Emps.	5-9 Emps.	10-19 Emps.	20-49 Emps.	50-99 Emps.	100-249 Emps.	250-499 Emps.	500-999 Emps.	Unknown Emps.	Industry Sales
2016	6.9	13.4	34.1	69.7	52.9	3,488.3	272.4	5.7	2.4	3,945.9
2017	7.1	13.8	34.9	71.4	54.2	3,572.0	279.0	5.8	2.5	4,040.6
2018	7.3	14.2	36.0	73.5	55.8	3,676.5	287.1	6.0	2.5	4,158.9
2019	7.6	14.7	37.3	76.2	57.8	3,813.0	297.8	6.2	2.6	4,313.3
2019	7.9	15.4	39.0	79.8	60.5	3,989.1	311.5	6.5	2.8	4,512.5

INDUSTRY: HARDWARE STORES INDUSTRY (NAICS 44413)
PRODUCT LINE: LAWN & GARDEN MACHINERY (Sub Category)

NAICS 44413: Hardware Stores. Establishments primarily engaged
in the retail sale of a number of basic hardware lines, such as tools,
builders' hardware, paint and glass, housewares and household appliances,
and cutlery.

5-YEAR TREND — ESTIMATED INDUSTRY SALES ($MILLIONS)

Year	Employee Size of Establishment									Total
	1-4 Emps.	5-9 Emps.	10-19 Emps.	20-49 Emps.	50-99 Emps.	100-249 Emps.	250-499 Emps.	500-999 Emps.	Unknown Emps.	Industry Sales
2016	65.2	110.5	222.3	317.8	63.1	20.6	3.7	0.2	5.7	809.1
2017	65.8	111.6	224.5	320.9	63.8	20.8	3.7	0.2	5.8	817.0
2018	66.8	113.3	228.0	326.0	64.8	21.1	3.7	0.2	5.8	829.8
2019	69.5	117.8	237.1	338.9	67.3	22.0	3.9	0.2	6.1	862.8
2019	72.9	123.7	248.9	355.8	70.7	23.1	4.1	0.2	6.4	905.6

INDUSTRY: DEPARTMENT STORES INDUSTRY (NAICS 45211)
PRODUCT LINE: LAWN & GARDEN MACHINERY (Sub Category)

NAICS 45211: Department Stores Industry . this industry comprises
establishments known as department stores primarily engaged in retailing
a wide range of the following new products with no one merchandise line
predominating: apparel, furniture, appliances and home furnishings; and
selected additional items, such as paint, hardware, toiletries, cosmetics,
photographic equipment, jewelry, toys, and sporting goods. merchandise lines
are normally arranged in separate departments.

5-YEAR TREND — ESTIMATED INDUSTRY SALES ($MILLIONS)

Year	Employee Size of Establishment									Total
	1-4 Emps.	5-9 Emps.	10-19 Emps.	20-49 Emps.	50-99 Emps.	100-249 Emps.	250-499 Emps.	500-999 Emps.	Unknown Emps.	Industry Sales
2016	0.0	0.1	0.1	9.3	168.8	542.1	224.4	32.5	1.4	978.7
2017	0.0	0.1	0.1	9.3	169.5	544.2	225.3	32.6	1.4	982.5
2018	0.0	0.1	0.1	9.4	171.2	549.6	227.5	32.9	1.4	992.2
2019	0.0	0.1	0.1	9.4	171.2	549.7	227.5	33.0	1.4	992.4
2019	0.0	0.1	0.1	9.5	172.9	555.1	229.8	33.4	1.4	1,002.3

INDUSTRY: WAREHOUSE CLUBS & SUPERCENTERS (NAICS 45291)
PRODUCT LINE: LAWN & GARDEN MACHINERY (Sub Category)

NAICS 45291: Warehouse Clubs and Superstores This industry comprises establishments known as warehouse clubs, superstores or supercenters primarily engaged in retailing a general line of groceries in combination with general lines of new merchandise, such as apparel, furniture, and appliances.

5-Year Trend — Estimated Industry Sales ($Millions)

Year	Employee Size of Establishment									Total
	1-4 Emps.	5-9 Emps.	10-19 Emps.	20-49 Emps.	50-99 Emps.	100-249 Emps.	250-499 Emps.	500-999 Emps.	Unknown Emps.	Industry Sales
2016	0.2	0.0	0.2	5.7	10.7	612.9	2,698.1	68.0	1.0	3,396.8
2017	0.2	0.0	0.2	5.8	11.0	629.8	2,772.5	69.9	1.1	3,490.5
2018	0.2	0.1	0.2	6.0	11.4	650.4	2,863.1	72.1	1.1	3,604.5
2019	0.2	0.1	0.2	6.5	12.3	699.9	3,081.3	77.6	1.2	3,879.2
2019	0.2	0.1	0.2	6.8	13.0	741.4	3,263.8	82.2	1.2	4,109.0

INDUSTRY: HOME CENTERS INDUSTRY (NAICS 44411)
PRODUCT LINE: FARM MACHINERY (Sub Category)

NAICS 44411: Home Centers. This industry comprises establishments known as home centers primarily engaged in retailing a general line of new home repair and improvement materials and supplies, such as lumber, plumbing goods, electrical goods, tools, housewares, hardware, and lawn and garden supplies, with no one merchandise line predominating. The merchandise lines are normally arranged in separate departments.

5-Year Trend — Estimated Industry Sales ($Millions)

Year	Employee Size of Establishment									Total
	1-4 Emps.	5-9 Emps.	10-19 Emps.	20-49 Emps.	50-99 Emps.	100-249 Emps.	250-499 Emps.	500-999 Emps.	Unknown Emps.	Industry Sales
2016	0.1	0.3	0.7	1.3	1.0	66.5	5.2	0.1	0.0	75.2
2017	0.1	0.3	0.7	1.4	1.0	68.1	5.3	0.1	0.0	77.0
2018	0.1	0.3	0.7	1.4	1.1	70.1	5.5	0.1	0.0	79.3
2019	0.1	0.3	0.7	1.5	1.1	72.7	5.7	0.1	0.1	82.2
2019	0.2	0.3	0.7	1.5	1.2	76.0	5.9	0.1	0.1	86.0

INDUSTRY: HARDWARE STORES INDUSTRY (NAICS 44413)
PRODUCT LINE: FARM MACHINERY (Sub Category)

NAICS 44413: Hardware Stores. Establishments primarily engaged
in the retail sale of a number of basic hardware lines, such as tools,
builders' hardware, paint and glass, housewares and household appliances,
and cutlery.

5-YEAR TREND – ESTIMATED INDUSTRY SALES ($MILLIONS)

| Year | Employee Size of Establishment | | | | | | | | | Total |
	1-4 Emps.	5-9 Emps.	10-19 Emps.	20-49 Emps.	50-99 Emps.	100-249 Emps.	250-499 Emps.	500-999 Emps.	Unknown Emps.	Industry Sales
2016	10.5	17.8	35.7	51.1	10.1	3.3	0.6	0.0	0.9	130.0
2017	10.6	17.9	36.1	51.6	10.2	3.3	0.6	0.0	0.9	131.3
2018	10.7	18.2	36.6	52.4	10.4	3.4	0.6	0.0	0.9	133.4
2019	11.2	18.9	38.1	54.5	10.8	3.5	0.6	0.0	1.0	138.7
2019	11.7	19.9	40.0	57.2	11.4	3.7	0.7	0.0	1.0	145.6

INDUSTRY: HOME CENTERS INDUSTRY (NAICS 44411)
PRODUCT LINE: OTHER FARM SUPPLIES (Sub Category)

NAICS 44411: Home Centers. This industry comprises establishments
known as home centers primarily engaged in retailing a general line of
new home repair and improvement materials and supplies, such as
lumber, plumbing goods, electrical goods, tools, housewares, hardware,
and lawn and garden supplies, with no one merchandise line predominating.
The merchandise lines are normally arranged in separate departments.

5-YEAR TREND – ESTIMATED INDUSTRY SALES ($MILLIONS)

| Year | Employee Size of Establishment | | | | | | | | | Total |
	1-4 Emps.	5-9 Emps.	10-19 Emps.	20-49 Emps.	50-99 Emps.	100-249 Emps.	250-499 Emps.	500-999 Emps.	Unknown Emps.	Industry Sales
2016	0.1	0.1	0.3	0.6	0.4	28.5	2.2	0.0	0.0	32.2
2017	0.1	0.1	0.3	0.6	0.4	29.1	2.3	0.0	0.0	33.0
2018	0.1	0.1	0.3	0.6	0.5	30.0	2.3	0.0	0.0	33.9
2019	0.1	0.1	0.3	0.6	0.5	31.1	2.4	0.1	0.0	35.2
2019	0.1	0.1	0.3	0.7	0.5	32.5	2.5	0.1	0.0	36.8

INDUSTRY: HARDWARE STORES INDUSTRY (NAICS 44413)
PRODUCT LINE: OTHER FARM SUPPLIES (Sub Category)

NAICS 44413: Hardware Stores. Establishments primarily engaged
in the retail sale of a number of basic hardware lines, such as tools,
builders' hardware, paint and glass, housewares and household appliances,
and cutlery.

5-YEAR TREND – ESTIMATED INDUSTRY SALES ($MILLIONS)

| Year | Employee Size of Establishment | | | | | | | | | Total |
	1-4 Emps.	5-9 Emps.	10-19 Emps.	20-49 Emps.	50-99 Emps.	100-249 Emps.	250-499 Emps.	500-999 Emps.	Unknown Emps.	Industry Sales
2016	31.2	52.8	106.3	152.0	30.2	9.9	1.7	0.1	2.7	386.9
2017	31.5	53.4	107.4	153.5	30.5	9.9	1.8	0.1	2.8	390.7
2018	32.0	54.2	109.0	155.9	31.0	10.1	1.8	0.1	2.8	396.9
2019	33.2	56.3	113.4	162.1	32.2	10.5	1.9	0.1	2.9	412.6
2019	34.9	59.1	119.0	170.1	33.8	11.0	2.0	0.1	3.1	433.1

INDUSTRY: HOME CENTERS INDUSTRY (NAICS 44411)
PRODUCT LINE: OTHER LAWN & GARDEN SUPPLIES (Sub Category)

NAICS 44411: Home Centers. This industry comprises establishments
known as home centers primarily engaged in retailing a general line of
new home repair and improvement materials and supplies, such as
lumber, plumbing goods, electrical goods, tools, housewares, hardware,
and lawn and garden supplies, with no one merchandise line predominating.
The merchandise lines are normally arranged in separate departments.

5-YEAR TREND – ESTIMATED INDUSTRY SALES ($MILLIONS)

| Year | Employee Size of Establishment | | | | | | | | | Total |
	1-4 Emps.	5-9 Emps.	10-19 Emps.	20-49 Emps.	50-99 Emps.	100-249 Emps.	250-499 Emps.	500-999 Emps.	Unknown Emps.	Industry Sales
2016	5.8	11.3	28.7	58.6	44.4	2,930.3	228.8	4.8	2.0	3,314.7
2017	5.9	11.6	29.3	60.0	45.5	3,000.5	234.3	4.9	2.1	3,394.2
2018	6.1	11.9	30.2	61.8	46.8	3,088.4	241.2	5.0	2.1	3,493.6
2019	6.3	12.3	31.3	64.0	48.6	3,203.0	250.1	5.2	2.2	3,623.3
2019	6.6	12.9	32.8	67.0	50.8	3,351.0	261.7	5.4	2.3	3,790.6

INDUSTRY: HARDWARE STORES INDUSTRY (NAICS 44413)
PRODUCT LINE: OTHER LAWN & GARDEN SUPPLIES (Sub Category)

NAICS 44413: Hardware Stores. Establishments primarily engaged
in the retail sale of a number of basic hardware lines, such as tools,
builders' hardware, paint and glass, housewares and household appliances,
and cutlery.

5-YEAR TREND — ESTIMATED INDUSTRY SALES ($MILLIONS)

Year	Employee Size of Establishment									Total
	1-4 Emps.	5-9 Emps.	10-19 Emps.	20-49 Emps.	50-99 Emps.	100-249 Emps.	250-499 Emps.	500-999 Emps.	Unknown Emps.	Industry Sales
2016	39.3	66.7	134.2	191.9	38.1	12.4	2.2	0.1	3.4	488.5
2017	39.7	67.4	135.5	193.8	38.5	12.6	2.2	0.1	3.5	493.3
2018	40.4	68.4	137.7	196.8	39.1	12.8	2.3	0.1	3.5	501.0
2019	42.0	71.1	143.1	204.6	40.7	13.3	2.4	0.1	3.7	520.9
2019	44.0	74.7	150.2	214.8	42.7	13.9	2.5	0.1	3.9	546.8

INDUSTRY: DEPARTMENT STORES INDUSTRY (NAICS 45211)
PRODUCT LINE: OTHER LAWN & GARDEN SUPPLIES (Sub Category)

NAICS 45211: Department Stores Industry . this industry comprises
establishments known as department stores primarily engaged in retailing
a wide range of the following new products with no one merchandise line
predominating: apparel, furniture, appliances and home furnishings; and
selected additional items, such as paint, hardware, toiletries, cosmetics,
photographic equipment, jewelry, toys, and sporting goods. merchandise lines
are normally arranged in separate departments.

5-YEAR TREND — ESTIMATED INDUSTRY SALES ($MILLIONS)

Year	Employee Size of Establishment									Total
	1-4 Emps.	5-9 Emps.	10-19 Emps.	20-49 Emps.	50-99 Emps.	100-249 Emps.	250-499 Emps.	500-999 Emps.	Unknown Emps.	Industry Sales
2016	0.0	0.0	0.1	5.5	99.3	318.8	131.9	19.1	0.8	575.5
2017	0.0	0.0	0.1	5.5	99.7	320.0	132.5	19.2	0.8	577.7
2018	0.0	0.0	0.1	5.5	100.6	323.2	133.8	19.4	0.8	583.4
2019	0.0	0.0	0.1	5.5	100.7	323.2	133.8	19.4	0.8	583.5
2019	0.0	0.0	0.1	5.6	101.6	326.4	135.1	19.6	0.8	589.3

INDUSTRY: WAREHOUSE CLUBS & SUPERCENTERS (NAICS 45291)
PRODUCT LINE: OTHER LAWN & GARDEN SUPPLIES (Sub Category)

NAICS 45291: Warehouse Clubs and Superstores This industry comprises establishments known as warehouse clubs, superstores or supercenters primarily engaged in retailing a general line of groceries in combination with general lines of new merchandise, such as apparel, furniture, and appliances.

5-YEAR TREND — ESTIMATED INDUSTRY SALES ($MILLIONS)

Year	Employee Size of Establishment									Total
	1-4 Emps.	5-9 Emps.	10-19 Emps.	20-49 Emps.	50-99 Emps.	100-249 Emps.	250-499 Emps.	500-999 Emps.	Unknown Emps.	Industry Sales
2016	0.1	0.0	0.1	2.4	4.6	260.3	1,145.8	28.9	0.4	1,442.5
2017	0.1	0.0	0.1	2.5	4.7	267.5	1,177.4	29.7	0.4	1,482.3
2018	0.1	0.0	0.1	2.5	4.8	276.2	1,215.8	30.6	0.5	1,530.7
2019	0.1	0.0	0.1	2.7	5.2	297.2	1,308.5	33.0	0.5	1,647.4
2019	0.1	0.0	0.1	2.9	5.5	314.8	1,386.0	34.9	0.5	1,745.0

INDUSTRY: HOME CENTERS INDUSTRY (NAICS 44411)
PRODUCT LINE: LUMBER & BUILDING MATERIALS (Main Category)

NAICS 44411: Home Centers. This industry comprises establishments known as home centers primarily engaged in retailing a general line of new home repair and improvement materials and supplies, such as lumber, plumbing goods, electrical goods, tools, housewares, hardware, and lawn and garden supplies, with no one merchandise line predominating. The merchandise lines are normally arranged in separate departments.

5-YEAR TREND — ESTIMATED INDUSTRY SALES ($MILLIONS)

Year	Employee Size of Establishment									Total
	1-4 Emps.	5-9 Emps.	10-19 Emps.	20-49 Emps.	50-99 Emps.	100-249 Emps.	250-499 Emps.	500-999 Emps.	Unknown Emps.	Industry Sales
2016	87.3	169.9	430.9	881.0	668.3	44,064.6	3,441.3	71.6	30.5	49,845.5
2017	89.4	174.0	441.2	902.2	684.3	45,121.4	3,523.8	73.4	31.2	51,040.9
2018	92.0	179.1	454.1	928.6	704.3	46,442.5	3,627.0	75.5	32.2	52,535.4
2019	95.5	185.7	471.0	963.1	730.5	48,166.9	3,761.7	78.3	33.4	54,485.9
2019	99.9	194.3	492.8	1,007.5	764.2	50,391.2	3,935.4	81.9	34.9	57,002.1

INDUSTRY: HARDWARE STORES (NAICS 44413)
PRODUCT LINE: LUMBER & BUILDING MATERIALS (Main Category)

NAICS 44413: Hardware Stores. Establishments primarily engaged
in the retail sale of a number of basic hardware lines, such as tools,
builders' hardware, paint and glass, housewares and household appliances,
and cutlery.

5-Year Trend – Estimated Industry Sales ($Millions)

Year	Employee Size of Establishment									Total
	1-4 Emps.	5-9 Emps.	10-19 Emps.	20-49 Emps.	50-99 Emps.	100-249 Emps.	250-499 Emps.	500-999 Emps.	Unknown Emps.	Industry Sales
2016	113.6	192.6	387.6	554.2	110.1	35.9	6.4	0.3	9.9	1,410.7
2017	114.7	194.5	391.4	559.6	111.2	36.3	6.4	0.3	10.0	1,424.6
2018	116.5	197.6	397.6	568.4	112.9	36.8	6.5	0.3	10.2	1,446.9
2019	121.2	205.4	413.4	591.0	117.4	38.3	6.8	0.3	10.6	1,504.4
2019	127.2	215.6	433.9	620.3	123.2	40.2	7.1	0.3	11.1	1,579.1

INDUSTRY: WAREHOUSE CLUBS & SUPERCENTERS (NAICS 45291)
PRODUCT LINE: LUMBER & BUILDING MATERIALS (Main Category)

NAICS 45291: Warehouse Clubs and Superstores This industry
comprises establishments known as warehouse clubs, superstores or
supercenters primarily engaged in retailing a general line of groceries
in combination with general lines of new merchandise, such as apparel,
furniture, and appliances.

5-Year Trend – Estimated Industry Sales ($Millions)

Year	Employee Size of Establishment									Total
	1-4 Emps.	5-9 Emps.	10-19 Emps.	20-49 Emps.	50-99 Emps.	100-249 Emps.	250-499 Emps.	500-999 Emps.	Unknown Emps.	Industry Sales
2016	0.0	0.0	0.0	0.1	0.1	6.3	27.6	0.7	0.0	34.7
2017	0.0	0.0	0.0	0.1	0.1	6.4	28.3	0.7	0.0	35.6
2018	0.0	0.0	0.0	0.1	0.1	6.6	29.2	0.7	0.0	36.8
2019	0.0	0.0	0.0	0.1	0.1	7.1	31.5	0.8	0.0	39.6
2019	0.0	0.0	0.0	0.1	0.1	7.6	33.3	0.8	0.0	42.0

INDUSTRY: ELECTRONIC SHOPPING & MAIL-ORDER (NAICS 45411)
PRODUCT LINE: LUMBER & BUILDING MATERIALS (Main Category)

NAICS 45411: Electronic Shopping and Mail-Order Houses This industry comprises establishments primarily engaged in retailing all types of merchandise by means of mail or by electronic media, such as interactive television or computer. Included in this industry are establishments primarily engaged in retailing from catalogue showrooms of mail-order houses.

5-YEAR TREND — ESTIMATED INDUSTRY SALES ($MILLIONS)

Year	Employee Size of Establishment									Total
	1-4 Emps.	5-9 Emps.	10-19 Emps.	20-49 Emps.	50-99 Emps.	100-249 Emps.	250-499 Emps.	500-999 Emps.	Unknown Emps.	Industry Sales
2016	49.4	25.4	36.7	61.7	46.4	85.9	115.8	163.5	6.9	591.8
2017	52.2	26.9	38.9	65.2	49.1	90.9	122.5	172.9	7.3	625.9
2018	55.4	28.5	41.2	69.2	52.1	96.3	129.9	183.3	7.8	663.6
2019	62.1	32.0	46.2	77.5	58.4	108.0	145.5	201.7	8.7	740.0
2019	69.0	35.5	51.3	86.2	64.9	120.0	161.8	220.9	9.7	819.4

INDUSTRY: HOME CENTERS INDUSTRY (NAICS 44411)
PRODUCT LINE: NONTREATED LUMBER (Sub Category)

NAICS 44411: Home Centers. This industry comprises establishments known as home centers primarily engaged in retailing a general line of new home repair and improvement materials and supplies, such as lumber, plumbing goods, electrical goods, tools, housewares, hardware, and lawn and garden supplies, with no one merchandise line predominating. The merchandise lines are normally arranged in separate departments.

5-YEAR TREND — ESTIMATED INDUSTRY SALES ($MILLIONS)

Year	Employee Size of Establishment									Total
	1-4 Emps.	5-9 Emps.	10-19 Emps.	20-49 Emps.	50-99 Emps.	100-249 Emps.	250-499 Emps.	500-999 Emps.	Unknown Emps.	Industry Sales
2016	6.8	13.2	33.5	68.5	52.0	3,427.0	267.6	5.6	2.4	3,876.5
2017	7.0	13.5	34.3	70.2	53.2	3,509.1	274.1	5.7	2.4	3,969.5
2018	7.2	13.9	35.3	72.2	54.8	3,611.9	282.1	5.9	2.5	4,085.7
2019	7.4	14.4	36.6	74.9	56.8	3,746.0	292.5	6.1	2.6	4,237.4
2019	7.8	15.1	38.3	78.4	59.4	3,919.0	306.1	6.4	2.7	4,433.1

NAICS 44413: Hardware Stores. Establishments primarily engaged
in the retail sale of a number of basic hardware lines, such as tools,
builders' hardware, paint and glass, housewares and household appliances,
and cutlery.

5-YEAR TREND — ESTIMATED INDUSTRY SALES ($MILLIONS)

| Year | Employee Size of Establishment | | | | | | | | | Total |
	1-4 Emps.	5-9 Emps.	10-19 Emps.	20-49 Emps.	50-99 Emps.	100-249 Emps.	250-499 Emps.	500-999 Emps.	Unknown Emps.	Industry Sales
2016	10.6	18.0	36.2	51.7	10.3	3.4	0.6	0.0	0.9	131.7
2017	10.7	18.2	36.5	52.2	10.4	3.4	0.6	0.0	0.9	133.0
2018	10.9	18.4	37.1	53.0	10.5	3.4	0.6	0.0	1.0	135.0
2019	11.3	19.2	38.6	55.2	11.0	3.6	0.6	0.0	1.0	140.4
2019	11.9	20.1	40.5	57.9	11.5	3.8	0.7	0.0	1.0	147.4

NAICS 44411: Home Centers. This industry comprises establishments
known as home centers primarily engaged in retailing a general line of
new home repair and improvement materials and supplies, such as
lumber, plumbing goods, electrical goods, tools, housewares, hardware,
and lawn and garden supplies, with no one merchandise line predominating.
The merchandise lines are normally arranged in separate departments.

5-YEAR TREND — ESTIMATED INDUSTRY SALES ($MILLIONS)

| Year | Employee Size of Establishment | | | | | | | | | Total |
	1-4 Emps.	5-9 Emps.	10-19 Emps.	20-49 Emps.	50-99 Emps.	100-249 Emps.	250-499 Emps.	500-999 Emps.	Unknown Emps.	Industry Sales
2016	7.0	13.7	34.7	70.9	53.8	3,546.1	276.9	5.8	2.5	4,011.3
2017	7.2	14.0	35.5	72.6	55.1	3,631.1	283.6	5.9	2.5	4,107.5
2018	7.4	14.4	36.5	74.7	56.7	3,737.5	291.9	6.1	2.6	4,227.8
2019	7.7	14.9	37.9	77.5	58.8	3,876.2	302.7	6.3	2.7	4,384.8
2019	8.0	15.6	39.7	81.1	61.5	4,055.2	316.7	6.6	2.8	4,587.2

INDUSTRY: HARDWARE STORES INDUSTRY (NAICS 44413)
PRODUCT LINE: TREATED LUMBER (Sub Category)

NAICS 44413: Hardware Stores. Establishments primarily engaged
in the retail sale of a number of basic hardware lines, such as tools,
builders' hardware, paint and glass, housewares and household appliances,
and cutlery.

5-YEAR TREND – ESTIMATED INDUSTRY SALES ($MILLIONS)

Year	Employee Size of Establishment									Total
	1-4 Emps.	5-9 Emps.	10-19 Emps.	20-49 Emps.	50-99 Emps.	100-249 Emps.	250-499 Emps.	500-999 Emps.	Unknown Emps.	Industry Sales
2016	6.8	11.6	23.4	33.4	6.6	2.2	0.4	0.0	0.6	85.0
2017	6.9	11.7	23.6	33.7	6.7	2.2	0.4	0.0	0.6	85.8
2018	7.0	11.9	24.0	34.3	6.8	2.2	0.4	0.0	0.6	87.2
2019	7.3	12.4	24.9	35.6	7.1	2.3	0.4	0.0	0.6	90.7
2019	7.7	13.0	26.1	37.4	7.4	2.4	0.4	0.0	0.7	95.2

INDUSTRY: HOME CENTERS INDUSTRY (NAICS 44411)
PRODUCT LINE: BUILDING BOARDS (Sub Category)

NAICS 44411: Home Centers. This industry comprises establishments
known as home centers primarily engaged in retailing a general line of
new home repair and improvement materials and supplies, such as
lumber, plumbing goods, electrical goods, tools, housewares, hardware,
and lawn and garden supplies, with no one merchandise line predominating.
The merchandise lines are normally arranged in separate departments.

5-YEAR TREND – ESTIMATED INDUSTRY SALES ($MILLIONS)

Year	Employee Size of Establishment									Total
	1-4 Emps.	5-9 Emps.	10-19 Emps.	20-49 Emps.	50-99 Emps.	100-249 Emps.	250-499 Emps.	500-999 Emps.	Unknown Emps.	Industry Sales
2016	2.8	5.4	13.7	28.0	21.2	1,400.2	109.4	2.3	1.0	1,583.9
2017	2.8	5.5	14.0	28.7	21.7	1,433.8	112.0	2.3	1.0	1,621.9
2018	2.9	5.7	14.4	29.5	22.4	1,475.8	115.3	2.4	1.0	1,669.4
2019	3.0	5.9	15.0	30.6	23.2	1,530.6	119.5	2.5	1.1	1,731.4
2019	3.2	6.2	15.7	32.0	24.3	1,601.3	125.1	2.6	1.1	1,811.3

INDUSTRY: HARDWARE STORES INDUSTRY (NAICS 44413)
PRODUCT LINE: BUILDING BOARDS (Sub Category)

NAICS 44413: Hardware Stores. Establishments primarily engaged
in the retail sale of a number of basic hardware lines, such as tools,
builders' hardware, paint and glass, housewares and household appliances,
and cutlery.

5-YEAR TREND — ESTIMATED INDUSTRY SALES ($MILLIONS)

| Year | Employee Size of Establishment | | | | | | | | | Total |
	1-4 Emps.	5-9 Emps.	10-19 Emps.	20-49 Emps.	50-99 Emps.	100-249 Emps.	250-499 Emps.	500-999 Emps.	Unknown Emps.	Industry Sales
2016	4.3	7.3	14.7	21.0	4.2	1.4	0.2	0.0	0.4	53.6
2017	4.4	7.4	14.9	21.3	4.2	1.4	0.2	0.0	0.4	54.1
2018	4.4	7.5	15.1	21.6	4.3	1.4	0.2	0.0	0.4	54.9
2019	4.6	7.8	15.7	22.4	4.5	1.5	0.3	0.0	0.4	57.1
2019	4.8	8.2	16.5	23.6	4.7	1.5	0.3	0.0	0.4	60.0

INDUSTRY: HOME CENTERS INDUSTRY (NAICS 44411)
PRODUCT LINE: GYPSUM & SPECIALTY BOARDS (Sub Category)

NAICS 44411: Home Centers. This industry comprises establishments
known as home centers primarily engaged in retailing a general line of
new home repair and improvement materials and supplies, such as
lumber, plumbing goods, electrical goods, tools, housewares, hardware,
and lawn and garden supplies, with no one merchandise line predominating.
The merchandise lines are normally arranged in separate departments.

5-YEAR TREND — ESTIMATED INDUSTRY SALES ($MILLIONS)

| Year | Employee Size of Establishment | | | | | | | | | Total |
	1-4 Emps.	5-9 Emps.	10-19 Emps.	20-49 Emps.	50-99 Emps.	100-249 Emps.	250-499 Emps.	500-999 Emps.	Unknown Emps.	Industry Sales
2016	5.1	9.9	25.1	51.3	38.9	2,566.1	200.4	4.2	1.8	2,902.7
2017	5.2	10.1	25.7	52.5	39.8	2,627.6	205.2	4.3	1.8	2,972.3
2018	5.4	10.4	26.4	54.1	41.0	2,704.5	211.2	4.4	1.9	3,059.4
2019	5.6	10.8	27.4	56.1	42.5	2,805.0	219.1	4.6	1.9	3,172.9
2019	5.8	11.3	28.7	58.7	44.5	2,934.5	229.2	4.8	2.0	3,319.5

INDUSTRY: HARDWARE STORES INDUSTRY (NAICS 44413)
PRODUCT LINE: GYPSUM & SPECIALTY BOARDS (Sub Category)

NAICS 44413: Hardware Stores. Establishments primarily engaged
in the retail sale of a number of basic hardware lines, such as tools,
builders' hardware, paint and glass, housewares and household appliances,
and cutlery.

5-YEAR TREND – ESTIMATED INDUSTRY SALES ($MILLIONS)

Year	Employee Size of Establishment									Total
	1-4 Emps.	5-9 Emps.	10-19 Emps.	20-49 Emps.	50-99 Emps.	100-249 Emps.	250-499 Emps.	500-999 Emps.	Unknown Emps.	Industry Sales
2016	3.8	6.4	12.9	18.4	3.7	1.2	0.2	0.0	0.3	46.8
2017	3.8	6.4	13.0	18.6	3.7	1.2	0.2	0.0	0.3	47.2
2018	3.9	6.5	13.2	18.8	3.7	1.2	0.2	0.0	0.3	48.0
2019	4.0	6.8	13.7	19.6	3.9	1.3	0.2	0.0	0.4	49.9
2019	4.2	7.1	14.4	20.6	4.1	1.3	0.2	0.0	0.4	52.3

INDUSTRY: HOME CENTERS INDUSTRY (NAICS 44411)
PRODUCT LINE: ENGINEERED WOOD PRODUCTS (Sub Category)

NAICS 44411: Home Centers. This industry comprises establishments
known as home centers primarily engaged in retailing a general line of
new home repair and improvement materials and supplies, such as
lumber, plumbing goods, electrical goods, tools, housewares, hardware,
and lawn and garden supplies, with no one merchandise line predominating.
The merchandise lines are normally arranged in separate departments.

5-YEAR TREND – ESTIMATED INDUSTRY SALES ($MILLIONS)

Year	Employee Size of Establishment									Total
	1-4 Emps.	5-9 Emps.	10-19 Emps.	20-49 Emps.	50-99 Emps.	100-249 Emps.	250-499 Emps.	500-999 Emps.	Unknown Emps.	Industry Sales
2016	0.6	1.1	2.9	5.9	4.5	294.3	23.0	0.5	0.2	332.9
2017	0.6	1.2	2.9	6.0	4.6	301.3	23.5	0.5	0.2	340.9
2018	0.6	1.2	3.0	6.2	4.7	310.2	24.2	0.5	0.2	350.8
2019	0.6	1.2	3.1	6.4	4.9	321.7	25.1	0.5	0.2	363.9
2019	0.7	1.3	3.3	6.7	5.1	336.5	26.3	0.5	0.2	380.7

INDUSTRY: HOME CENTERS INDUSTRY (NAICS 44411)
PRODUCT LINE: STRUCTURAL PANELS (Sub Category)

NAICS 44411: Home Centers. This industry comprises establishments
known as home centers primarily engaged in retailing a general line of
new home repair and improvement materials and supplies, such as
lumber, plumbing goods, electrical goods, tools, housewares, hardware,
and lawn and garden supplies, with no one merchandise line predominating.
The merchandise lines are normally arranged in separate departments.

5-YEAR TREND – ESTIMATED INDUSTRY SALES ($MILLIONS)

| Year | Employee Size of Establishment | | | | | | | | | Total |
	1-4 Emps.	5-9 Emps.	10-19 Emps.	20-49 Emps.	50-99 Emps.	100-249 Emps.	250-499 Emps.	500-999 Emps.	Unknown Emps.	Industry Sales
2016	5.1	10.0	25.3	51.7	39.2	2,585.7	201.9	4.2	1.8	2,924.9
2017	5.2	10.2	25.9	52.9	40.2	2,647.7	206.8	4.3	1.8	2,995.1
2018	5.4	10.5	26.6	54.5	41.3	2,725.2	212.8	4.4	1.9	3,082.8
2019	5.6	10.9	27.6	56.5	42.9	2,826.4	220.7	4.6	2.0	3,197.2
2019	5.9	11.4	28.9	59.1	44.8	2,956.9	230.9	4.8	2.0	3,344.9

INDUSTRY: HARDWARE STORES INDUSTRY (NAICS 44413)
PRODUCT LINE: STRUCTURAL PANELS (Sub Category)

NAICS 44413: Hardware Stores. Establishments primarily engaged
in the retail sale of a number of basic hardware lines, such as tools,
builders' hardware, paint and glass, housewares and household appliances,
and cutlery.

5-YEAR TREND – ESTIMATED INDUSTRY SALES ($MILLIONS)

| Year | Employee Size of Establishment | | | | | | | | | Total |
	1-4 Emps.	5-9 Emps.	10-19 Emps.	20-49 Emps.	50-99 Emps.	100-249 Emps.	250-499 Emps.	500-999 Emps.	Unknown Emps.	Industry Sales
2016	3.4	5.7	11.5	16.5	3.3	1.1	0.2	0.0	0.3	42.0
2017	3.4	5.8	11.7	16.7	3.3	1.1	0.2	0.0	0.3	42.4
2018	3.5	5.9	11.8	16.9	3.4	1.1	0.2	0.0	0.3	43.1
2019	3.6	6.1	12.3	17.6	3.5	1.1	0.2	0.0	0.3	44.8
2019	3.8	6.4	12.9	18.5	3.7	1.2	0.2	0.0	0.3	47.0

INDUSTRY: HOME CENTERS INDUSTRY (NAICS 44411)
PRODUCT LINE: OTHER PANEL PRODUCTS (Sub Category)

NAICS 44411: Home Centers. This industry comprises establishments
known as home centers primarily engaged in retailing a general line of
new home repair and improvement materials and supplies, such as
lumber, plumbing goods, electrical goods, tools, housewares, hardware,
and lawn and garden supplies, with no one merchandise line predominating.
The merchandise lines are normally arranged in separate departments.

5-YEAR TREND – ESTIMATED INDUSTRY SALES ($MILLIONS)

| Year | Employee Size of Establishment | | | | | | | | | Total |
	1-4 Emps.	5-9 Emps.	10-19 Emps.	20-49 Emps.	50-99 Emps.	100-249 Emps.	250-499 Emps.	500-999 Emps.	Unknown Emps.	Industry Sales
2016	5.0	9.6	24.4	50.0	37.9	2,498.5	195.1	4.1	1.7	2,826.2
2017	5.1	9.9	25.0	51.2	38.8	2,558.4	199.8	4.2	1.8	2,894.0
2018	5.2	10.2	25.8	52.7	39.9	2,633.3	205.7	4.3	1.8	2,978.8
2019	5.4	10.5	26.7	54.6	41.4	2,731.1	213.3	4.4	1.9	3,089.4
2019	5.7	11.0	27.9	57.1	43.3	2,857.2	223.1	4.6	2.0	3,232.0

INDUSTRY: HARDWARE STORES INDUSTRY (NAICS 44413)
PRODUCT LINE: OTHER PANEL PRODUCTS (Sub Category)

NAICS 44413: Hardware Stores. Establishments primarily engaged
in the retail sale of a number of basic hardware lines, such as tools,
builders' hardware, paint and glass, housewares and household appliances,
and cutlery.

5-YEAR TREND – ESTIMATED INDUSTRY SALES ($MILLIONS)

| Year | Employee Size of Establishment | | | | | | | | | Total |
	1-4 Emps.	5-9 Emps.	10-19 Emps.	20-49 Emps.	50-99 Emps.	100-249 Emps.	250-499 Emps.	500-999 Emps.	Unknown Emps.	Industry Sales
2016	3.8	6.5	13.0	18.6	3.7	1.2	0.2	0.0	0.3	47.4
2017	3.9	6.5	13.1	18.8	3.7	1.2	0.2	0.0	0.3	47.8
2018	3.9	6.6	13.3	19.1	3.8	1.2	0.2	0.0	0.3	48.6
2019	4.1	6.9	13.9	19.8	3.9	1.3	0.2	0.0	0.4	50.5
2019	4.3	7.2	14.6	20.8	4.1	1.3	0.2	0.0	0.4	53.0

INDUSTRY: HOME CENTERS INDUSTRY (NAICS 44411)
PRODUCT LINE: BUILDING COMPONENTS (Sub Category)

NAICS 44411: Home Centers. This industry comprises establishments known as home centers primarily engaged in retailing a general line of new home repair and improvement materials and supplies, such as lumber, plumbing goods, electrical goods, tools, housewares, hardware, and lawn and garden supplies, with no one merchandise line predominating. The merchandise lines are normally arranged in separate departments.

5-YEAR TREND – ESTIMATED INDUSTRY SALES ($MILLIONS)

Year	Employee Size of Establishment									Total
	1-4 Emps.	5-9 Emps.	10-19 Emps.	20-49 Emps.	50-99 Emps.	100-249 Emps.	250-499 Emps.	500-999 Emps.	Unknown Emps.	Industry Sales
2016	0.5	0.9	2.2	4.6	3.5	228.0	17.8	0.4	0.2	257.9
2017	0.5	0.9	2.3	4.7	3.5	233.5	18.2	0.4	0.2	264.1
2018	0.5	0.9	2.3	4.8	3.6	240.3	18.8	0.4	0.2	271.8
2019	0.5	1.0	2.4	5.0	3.8	249.2	19.5	0.4	0.2	281.9
2019	0.5	1.0	2.5	5.2	4.0	260.7	20.4	0.4	0.2	294.9

INDUSTRY: HOME CENTERS INDUSTRY (NAICS 44411)
PRODUCT LINE: CONNECTORS (Sub Category)

NAICS 44411: Home Centers. This industry comprises establishments known as home centers primarily engaged in retailing a general line of new home repair and improvement materials and supplies, such as lumber, plumbing goods, electrical goods, tools, housewares, hardware, and lawn and garden supplies, with no one merchandise line predominating. The merchandise lines are normally arranged in separate departments.

5-YEAR TREND – ESTIMATED INDUSTRY SALES ($MILLIONS)

Year	Employee Size of Establishment									Total
	1-4 Emps.	5-9 Emps.	10-19 Emps.	20-49 Emps.	50-99 Emps.	100-249 Emps.	250-499 Emps.	500-999 Emps.	Unknown Emps.	Industry Sales
2016	0.6	1.1	2.8	5.8	4.4	289.5	22.6	0.5	0.2	327.5
2017	0.6	1.1	2.9	5.9	4.5	296.5	23.2	0.5	0.2	335.4
2018	0.6	1.2	3.0	6.1	4.6	305.1	23.8	0.5	0.2	345.2
2019	0.6	1.2	3.1	6.3	4.8	316.5	24.7	0.5	0.2	358.0
2019	0.7	1.3	3.2	6.6	5.0	331.1	25.9	0.5	0.2	374.5

INDUSTRY: HARDWARE STORES INDUSTRY (NAICS 44413)
PRODUCT LINE: CONNECTORS (Sub Category)

NAICS 44413: Hardware Stores. Establishments primarily engaged
in the retail sale of a number of basic hardware lines, such as tools,
builders' hardware, paint and glass, housewares and household appliances,
and cutlery.

5-YEAR TREND – ESTIMATED INDUSTRY SALES ($MILLIONS)

Year	Employee Size of Establishment									Total
	1-4 Emps.	5-9 Emps.	10-19 Emps.	20-49 Emps.	50-99 Emps.	100-249 Emps.	250-499 Emps.	500-999 Emps.	Unknown Emps.	Industry Sales
2016	2.6	4.4	8.9	12.7	2.5	0.8	0.1	0.0	0.2	32.3
2017	2.6	4.5	9.0	12.8	2.5	0.8	0.1	0.0	0.2	32.6
2018	2.7	4.5	9.1	13.0	2.6	0.8	0.1	0.0	0.2	33.1
2019	2.8	4.7	9.5	13.5	2.7	0.9	0.2	0.0	0.2	34.5
2019	2.9	4.9	9.9	14.2	2.8	0.9	0.2	0.0	0.3	36.2

INDUSTRY: HOME CENTERS INDUSTRY (NAICS 44411)
PRODUCT LINE: STEEL STUDS (Sub Category)

NAICS 44411: Home Centers. This industry comprises establishments
known as home centers primarily engaged in retailing a general line of
new home repair and improvement materials and supplies, such as
lumber, plumbing goods, electrical goods, tools, housewares, hardware,
and lawn and garden supplies, with no one merchandise line predominating.
The merchandise lines are normally arranged in separate departments.

5-YEAR TREND – ESTIMATED INDUSTRY SALES ($MILLIONS)

Year	Employee Size of Establishment									Total
	1-4 Emps.	5-9 Emps.	10-19 Emps.	20-49 Emps.	50-99 Emps.	100-249 Emps.	250-499 Emps.	500-999 Emps.	Unknown Emps.	Industry Sales
2016	0.2	0.4	1.1	2.2	1.7	109.3	8.5	0.2	0.1	123.6
2017	0.2	0.4	1.1	2.2	1.7	111.9	8.7	0.2	0.1	126.6
2018	0.2	0.4	1.1	2.3	1.7	115.2	9.0	0.2	0.1	130.3
2019	0.2	0.5	1.2	2.4	1.8	119.4	9.3	0.2	0.1	135.1
2019	0.2	0.5	1.2	2.5	1.9	124.9	9.8	0.2	0.1	141.3

INDUSTRY: HOME CENTERS INDUSTRY (NAICS 44411)
PRODUCT LINE: DOORS & MOULDING (Sub Category)

NAICS 44411: Home Centers. This industry comprises establishments known as home centers primarily engaged in retailing a general line of new home repair and improvement materials and supplies, such as lumber, plumbing goods, electrical goods, tools, housewares, hardware, and lawn and garden supplies, with no one merchandise line predominating. The merchandise lines are normally arranged in separate departments.

5-YEAR TREND — ESTIMATED INDUSTRY SALES ($MILLIONS)

Year	Employee Size of Establishment									Total Industry Sales
	1-4 Emps.	5-9 Emps.	10-19 Emps.	20-49 Emps.	50-99 Emps.	100-249 Emps.	250-499 Emps.	500-999 Emps.	Unknown Emps.	
2016	12.6	24.6	62.4	127.6	96.8	6,380.2	498.3	10.4	4.4	7,217.2
2017	12.9	25.2	63.9	130.6	99.1	6,533.2	510.2	10.6	4.5	7,390.3
2018	13.3	25.9	65.8	134.5	102.0	6,724.5	525.2	10.9	4.7	7,606.7
2019	13.8	26.9	68.2	139.4	105.8	6,974.2	544.7	11.3	4.8	7,889.1
2019	14.5	28.1	71.3	145.9	110.7	7,296.3	569.8	11.9	5.1	8,253.5

INDUSTRY: HARDWARE STORES INDUSTRY (NAICS 44413)
PRODUCT LINE: DOORS & MOULDING (Sub Category)

NAICS 44413: Hardware Stores. Establishments primarily engaged in the retail sale of a number of basic hardware lines, such as tools, builders' hardware, paint and glass, housewares and household appliances, and cutlery.

5-YEAR TREND — ESTIMATED INDUSTRY SALES ($MILLIONS)

Year	Employee Size of Establishment									Total Industry Sales
	1-4 Emps.	5-9 Emps.	10-19 Emps.	20-49 Emps.	50-99 Emps.	100-249 Emps.	250-499 Emps.	500-999 Emps.	Unknown Emps.	
2016	8.0	13.6	27.4	39.1	7.8	2.5	0.4	0.0	0.7	99.6
2017	8.1	13.7	27.6	39.5	7.9	2.6	0.5	0.0	0.7	100.6
2018	8.2	14.0	28.1	40.1	8.0	2.6	0.5	0.0	0.7	102.2
2019	8.6	14.5	29.2	41.7	8.3	2.7	0.5	0.0	0.7	106.2
2019	9.0	15.2	30.6	43.8	8.7	2.8	0.5	0.0	0.8	111.5

	INDUSTRY: HOME CENTERS INDUSTRY (NAICS 44411)
	PRODUCT LINE: WINDOWS & SKYLIGHTS (Sub Category)

NAICS 44411: Home Centers. This industry comprises establishments
known as home centers primarily engaged in retailing a general line of
new home repair and improvement materials and supplies, such as
lumber, plumbing goods, electrical goods, tools, housewares, hardware,
and lawn and garden supplies, with no one merchandise line predominating.
The merchandise lines are normally arranged in separate departments.

5-YEAR TREND – ESTIMATED INDUSTRY SALES ($MILLIONS)

Year	Employee Size of Establishment									Total
	1-4 Emps.	5-9 Emps.	10-19 Emps.	20-49 Emps.	50-99 Emps.	100-249 Emps.	250-499 Emps.	500-999 Emps.	Unknown Emps.	Industry Sales
2016	7.4	14.4	36.5	74.7	56.7	3,737.5	291.9	6.1	2.6	4,227.9
2017	7.6	14.8	37.4	76.5	58.0	3,827.2	298.9	6.2	2.6	4,329.3
2018	7.8	15.2	38.5	78.8	59.7	3,939.3	307.6	6.4	2.7	4,456.0
2019	8.1	15.8	40.0	81.7	62.0	4,085.5	319.1	6.6	2.8	4,621.5
2019	8.5	16.5	41.8	85.5	64.8	4,274.2	333.8	6.9	3.0	4,834.9

	INDUSTRY: HARDWARE STORES INDUSTRY (NAICS 44413)
	PRODUCT LINE: WINDOWS & SKYLIGHTS (Sub Category)

NAICS 44413: Hardware Stores. Establishments primarily engaged
in the retail sale of a number of basic hardware lines, such as tools,
builders' hardware, paint and glass, housewares and household appliances,
and cutlery.

5-YEAR TREND – ESTIMATED INDUSTRY SALES ($MILLIONS)

Year	Employee Size of Establishment									Total
	1-4 Emps.	5-9 Emps.	10-19 Emps.	20-49 Emps.	50-99 Emps.	100-249 Emps.	250-499 Emps.	500-999 Emps.	Unknown Emps.	Industry Sales
2016	3.7	6.3	12.7	18.2	3.6	1.2	0.2	0.0	0.3	46.4
2017	3.8	6.4	12.9	18.4	3.7	1.2	0.2	0.0	0.3	46.8
2018	3.8	6.5	13.1	18.7	3.7	1.2	0.2	0.0	0.3	47.6
2019	4.0	6.8	13.6	19.4	3.9	1.3	0.2	0.0	0.3	49.5
2019	4.2	7.1	14.3	20.4	4.1	1.3	0.2	0.0	0.4	51.9

INDUSTRY: HOME CENTERS INDUSTRY (NAICS 44411)
PRODUCT LINE: WINDOWS & SKYLIGHTS (Sub Category)

NAICS 44411: Home Centers. This industry comprises establishments known as home centers primarily engaged in retailing a general line of new home repair and improvement materials and supplies, such as lumber, plumbing goods, electrical goods, tools, housewares, hardware, and lawn and garden supplies, with no one merchandise line predominating. The merchandise lines are normally arranged in separate departments.

5-YEAR TREND – ESTIMATED INDUSTRY SALES ($MILLIONS)

Year	Employee Size of Establishment									Total
	1-4 Emps.	5-9 Emps.	10-19 Emps.	20-49 Emps.	50-99 Emps.	100-249 Emps.	250-499 Emps.	500-999 Emps.	Unknown Emps.	Industry Sales
2016	0.4	0.8	2.0	4.0	3.1	201.9	15.8	0.3	0.1	228.4
2017	0.4	0.8	2.0	4.1	3.1	206.8	16.1	0.3	0.1	233.9
2018	0.4	0.8	2.1	4.3	3.2	212.8	16.6	0.3	0.1	240.8
2019	0.4	0.9	2.2	4.4	3.3	220.7	17.2	0.4	0.2	249.7
2019	0.5	0.9	2.3	4.6	3.5	230.9	18.0	0.4	0.2	261.2

INDUSTRY: HARDWARE STORES INDUSTRY (NAICS 44413)
PRODUCT LINE: WINDOWS & SKYLIGHTS (Sub Category)

NAICS 44413: Hardware Stores. Establishments primarily engaged in the retail sale of a number of basic hardware lines, such as tools, builders' hardware, paint and glass, housewares and household appliances, and cutlery.

5-YEAR TREND – ESTIMATED INDUSTRY SALES ($MILLIONS)

Year	Employee Size of Establishment									Total
	1-4 Emps.	5-9 Emps.	10-19 Emps.	20-49 Emps.	50-99 Emps.	100-249 Emps.	250-499 Emps.	500-999 Emps.	Unknown Emps.	Industry Sales
2016	7.1	12.0	24.1	34.4	6.8	2.2	0.4	0.0	0.6	87.6
2017	7.1	12.1	24.3	34.7	6.9	2.3	0.4	0.0	0.6	88.4
2018	7.2	12.3	24.7	35.3	7.0	2.3	0.4	0.0	0.6	89.8
2019	7.5	12.8	25.7	36.7	7.3	2.4	0.4	0.0	0.7	93.4
2019	7.9	13.4	26.9	38.5	7.7	2.5	0.4	0.0	0.7	98.0

	INDUSTRY: HOME CENTERS INDUSTRY (NAICS 44411)
	PRODUCT LINE: MASONRY SUPPLIES (Sub Category)

NAICS 44411: Home Centers. This industry comprises establishments
known as home centers primarily engaged in retailing a general line of
new home repair and improvement materials and supplies, such as
lumber, plumbing goods, electrical goods, tools, housewares, hardware,
and lawn and garden supplies, with no one merchandise line predominating.
The merchandise lines are normally arranged in separate departments.

5-YEAR TREND – ESTIMATED INDUSTRY SALES ($MILLIONS)

Year	Employee Size of Establishment									Total
	1-4 Emps.	5-9 Emps.	10-19 Emps.	20-49 Emps.	50-99 Emps.	100-249 Emps.	250-499 Emps.	500-999 Emps.	Unknown Emps.	Industry Sales
2016	3.9	7.6	19.2	39.4	29.9	1,968.6	153.7	3.2	1.4	2,226.8
2017	4.0	7.8	19.7	40.3	30.6	2,015.8	157.4	3.3	1.4	2,280.2
2018	4.1	8.0	20.3	41.5	31.5	2,074.8	162.0	3.4	1.4	2,347.0
2019	4.3	8.3	21.0	43.0	32.6	2,151.8	168.1	3.5	1.5	2,434.1
2019	4.5	8.7	22.0	45.0	34.1	2,251.2	175.8	3.7	1.6	2,546.5

	INDUSTRY: HARDWARE STORES INDUSTRY (NAICS 44413)
	PRODUCT LINE: MASONRY SUPPLIES (Sub Category)

NAICS 44413: Hardware Stores. Establishments primarily engaged
in the retail sale of a number of basic hardware lines, such as tools,
builders' hardware, paint and glass, housewares and household appliances,
and cutlery.

5-YEAR TREND – ESTIMATED INDUSTRY SALES ($MILLIONS)

Year	Employee Size of Establishment									Total
	1-4 Emps.	5-9 Emps.	10-19 Emps.	20-49 Emps.	50-99 Emps.	100-249 Emps.	250-499 Emps.	500-999 Emps.	Unknown Emps.	Industry Sales
2016	13.7	23.2	46.7	66.7	13.3	4.3	0.8	0.0	1.2	169.9
2017	13.8	23.4	47.1	67.4	13.4	4.4	0.8	0.0	1.2	171.6
2018	14.0	23.8	47.9	68.5	13.6	4.4	0.8	0.0	1.2	174.3
2019	14.6	24.7	49.8	71.2	14.1	4.6	0.8	0.0	1.3	181.2
2019	15.3	26.0	52.3	74.7	14.8	4.8	0.9	0.0	1.3	190.2

NAICS 44411: Home Centers. This industry comprises establishments known as home centers primarily engaged in retailing a general line of new home repair and improvement materials and supplies, such as lumber, plumbing goods, electrical goods, tools, housewares, hardware, and lawn and garden supplies, with no one merchandise line predominating. The merchandise lines are normally arranged in separate departments.

5-YEAR TREND – ESTIMATED INDUSTRY SALES ($MILLIONS)

Year	Employee Size of Establishment									Total
	1-4 Emps.	5-9 Emps.	10-19 Emps.	20-49 Emps.	50-99 Emps.	100-249 Emps.	250-499 Emps.	500-999 Emps.	Unknown Emps.	Industry Sales
2016	2.0	3.9	9.8	20.0	15.2	999.8	78.1	1.6	0.7	1,131.0
2017	2.0	3.9	10.0	20.5	15.5	1,023.8	80.0	1.7	0.7	1,158.1
2018	2.1	4.1	10.3	21.1	16.0	1,053.8	82.3	1.7	0.7	1,192.0
2019	2.2	4.2	10.7	21.9	16.6	1,092.9	85.4	1.8	0.8	1,236.3
2019	2.3	4.4	11.2	22.9	17.3	1,143.4	89.3	1.9	0.8	1,293.4

NAICS 44413: Hardware Stores. Establishments primarily engaged in the retail sale of a number of basic hardware lines, such as tools, builders' hardware, paint and glass, housewares and household appliances, and cutlery.

5-YEAR TREND – ESTIMATED INDUSTRY SALES ($MILLIONS)

Year	Employee Size of Establishment									Total
	1-4 Emps.	5-9 Emps.	10-19 Emps.	20-49 Emps.	50-99 Emps.	100-249 Emps.	250-499 Emps.	500-999 Emps.	Unknown Emps.	Industry Sales
2016	4.8	8.1	16.3	23.2	4.6	1.5	0.3	0.0	0.4	59.2
2017	4.8	8.2	16.4	23.5	4.7	1.5	0.3	0.0	0.4	59.7
2018	4.9	8.3	16.7	23.8	4.7	1.5	0.3	0.0	0.4	60.7
2019	5.1	8.6	17.3	24.8	4.9	1.6	0.3	0.0	0.4	63.1
2019	5.3	9.0	18.2	26.0	5.2	1.7	0.3	0.0	0.5	66.2

INDUSTRY: HOME CENTERS INDUSTRY (NAICS 44411)
PRODUCT LINE: SIDING & EXTERIOR TRIM (Sub Category)

NAICS 44411: Home Centers. This industry comprises establishments
known as home centers primarily engaged in retailing a general line of
new home repair and improvement materials and supplies, such as
lumber, plumbing goods, electrical goods, tools, housewares, hardware,
and lawn and garden supplies, with no one merchandise line predominating.
The merchandise lines are normally arranged in separate departments.

5-YEAR TREND – ESTIMATED INDUSTRY SALES ($MILLIONS)

| Year | Employee Size of Establishment | | | | | | | | | Total |
	1-4 Emps.	5-9 Emps.	10-19 Emps.	20-49 Emps.	50-99 Emps.	100-249 Emps.	250-499 Emps.	500-999 Emps.	Unknown Emps.	Industry Sales
2016	1.1	2.1	5.4	11.1	8.4	554.8	43.3	0.9	0.4	627.6
2017	1.1	2.2	5.6	11.4	8.6	568.1	44.4	0.9	0.4	642.7
2018	1.2	2.3	5.7	11.7	8.9	584.8	45.7	1.0	0.4	661.5
2019	1.2	2.3	5.9	12.1	9.2	606.5	47.4	1.0	0.4	686.0
2019	1.3	2.4	6.2	12.7	9.6	634.5	49.6	1.0	0.4	717.7

INDUSTRY: HARDWARE STORES INDUSTRY (NAICS 44413)
PRODUCT LINE: SIDING & EXTERIOR TRIM (Sub Category)

NAICS 44413: Hardware Stores. Establishments primarily engaged
in the retail sale of a number of basic hardware lines, such as tools,
builders' hardware, paint and glass, housewares and household appliances,
and cutlery.

5-YEAR TREND – ESTIMATED INDUSTRY SALES ($MILLIONS)

| Year | Employee Size of Establishment | | | | | | | | | Total |
	1-4 Emps.	5-9 Emps.	10-19 Emps.	20-49 Emps.	50-99 Emps.	100-249 Emps.	250-499 Emps.	500-999 Emps.	Unknown Emps.	Industry Sales
2016	1.2	2.1	4.2	6.0	1.2	0.4	0.1	0.0	0.1	15.3
2017	1.2	2.1	4.2	6.1	1.2	0.4	0.1	0.0	0.1	15.4
2018	1.3	2.1	4.3	6.2	1.2	0.4	0.1	0.0	0.1	15.7
2019	1.3	2.2	4.5	6.4	1.3	0.4	0.1	0.0	0.1	16.3
2019	1.4	2.3	4.7	6.7	1.3	0.4	0.1	0.0	0.1	17.1

INDUSTRY: HOME CENTERS INDUSTRY (NAICS 44411)
PRODUCT LINE: ROOFING (Sub Category)

NAICS 44411: Home Centers. This industry comprises establishments
known as home centers primarily engaged in retailing a general line of
new home repair and improvement materials and supplies, such as
lumber, plumbing goods, electrical goods, tools, housewares, hardware,
and lawn and garden supplies, with no one merchandise line predominating.
The merchandise lines are normally arranged in separate departments.

5-YEAR TREND – ESTIMATED INDUSTRY SALES ($MILLIONS)

Year	Employee Size of Establishment									Total
	1-4 Emps.	5-9 Emps.	10-19 Emps.	20-49 Emps.	50-99 Emps.	100-249 Emps.	250-499 Emps.	500-999 Emps.	Unknown Emps.	Industry Sales
2016	3.4	6.6	16.8	34.4	26.1	1,721.9	134.5	2.8	1.2	1,947.8
2017	3.5	6.8	17.2	35.3	26.7	1,763.2	137.7	2.9	1.2	1,994.5
2018	3.6	7.0	17.7	36.3	27.5	1,814.8	141.7	3.0	1.3	2,052.9
2019	3.7	7.3	18.4	37.6	28.5	1,882.2	147.0	3.1	1.3	2,129.1
2019	3.9	7.6	19.3	39.4	29.9	1,969.1	153.8	3.2	1.4	2,227.5

INDUSTRY: HARDWARE STORES INDUSTRY (NAICS 44413)
PRODUCT LINE: ROOFING (Sub Category)

NAICS 44413: Hardware Stores. Establishments primarily engaged
in the retail sale of a number of basic hardware lines, such as tools,
builders' hardware, paint and glass, housewares and household appliances,
and cutlery.

5-YEAR TREND – ESTIMATED INDUSTRY SALES ($MILLIONS)

Year	Employee Size of Establishment									Total
	1-4 Emps.	5-9 Emps.	10-19 Emps.	20-49 Emps.	50-99 Emps.	100-249 Emps.	250-499 Emps.	500-999 Emps.	Unknown Emps.	Industry Sales
2016	5.0	8.4	16.9	24.2	4.8	1.6	0.3	0.0	0.4	61.5
2017	5.0	8.5	17.1	24.4	4.8	1.6	0.3	0.0	0.4	62.1
2018	5.1	8.6	17.3	24.8	4.9	1.6	0.3	0.0	0.4	63.1
2019	5.3	9.0	18.0	25.8	5.1	1.7	0.3	0.0	0.5	65.6
2019	5.5	9.4	18.9	27.0	5.4	1.8	0.3	0.0	0.5	68.9

	INDUSTRY: HOME CENTERS INDUSTRY (NAICS 44411)
	PRODUCT LINE: CEILINGS (Sub Category)

NAICS 44411: Home Centers. This industry comprises establishments known as home centers primarily engaged in retailing a general line of new home repair and improvement materials and supplies, such as lumber, plumbing goods, electrical goods, tools, housewares, hardware, and lawn and garden supplies, with no one merchandise line predominating. The merchandise lines are normally arranged in separate departments.

5-YEAR TREND – ESTIMATED INDUSTRY SALES ($MILLIONS)

Year	Employee Size of Establishment									Total
	1-4 Emps.	5-9 Emps.	10-19 Emps.	20-49 Emps.	50-99 Emps.	100-249 Emps.	250-499 Emps.	500-999 Emps.	Unknown Emps.	Industry Sales
2016	0.7	1.3	3.4	7.0	5.3	347.8	27.2	0.6	0.2	393.5
2017	0.7	1.4	3.5	7.1	5.4	356.2	27.8	0.6	0.2	402.9
2018	0.7	1.4	3.6	7.3	5.6	366.6	28.6	0.6	0.3	414.7
2019	0.8	1.5	3.7	7.6	5.8	380.2	29.7	0.6	0.3	430.1
2019	0.8	1.5	3.9	8.0	6.0	397.8	31.1	0.6	0.3	450.0

	INDUSTRY: HARDWARE STORES INDUSTRY (NAICS 44413)
	PRODUCT LINE: CEILINGS (Sub Category)

NAICS 44413: Hardware Stores. Establishments primarily engaged in the retail sale of a number of basic hardware lines, such as tools, builders' hardware, paint and glass, housewares and household appliances, and cutlery.

5-YEAR TREND – ESTIMATED INDUSTRY SALES ($MILLIONS)

Year	Employee Size of Establishment									Total
	1-4 Emps.	5-9 Emps.	10-19 Emps.	20-49 Emps.	50-99 Emps.	100-249 Emps.	250-499 Emps.	500-999 Emps.	Unknown Emps.	Industry Sales
2016	0.8	1.3	2.7	3.9	0.8	0.3	0.0	0.0	0.1	9.9
2017	0.8	1.4	2.7	3.9	0.8	0.3	0.0	0.0	0.1	10.0
2018	0.8	1.4	2.8	4.0	0.8	0.3	0.0	0.0	0.1	10.1
2019	0.8	1.4	2.9	4.1	0.8	0.3	0.0	0.0	0.1	10.5
2019	0.9	1.5	3.0	4.3	0.9	0.3	0.0	0.0	0.1	11.1

INDUSTRY: HOME CENTERS INDUSTRY (NAICS 44411)
PRODUCT LINE: KITCHENS & CABINETS (Sub Category)

NAICS 44411: Home Centers. This industry comprises establishments
known as home centers primarily engaged in retailing a general line of
new home repair and improvement materials and supplies, such as
lumber, plumbing goods, electrical goods, tools, housewares, hardware,
and lawn and garden supplies, with no one merchandise line predominating.
The merchandise lines are normally arranged in separate departments.

5-YEAR TREND – ESTIMATED INDUSTRY SALES ($MILLIONS)

| Year | Employee Size of Establishment | | | | | | | | | Total |
	1-4 Emps.	5-9 Emps.	10-19 Emps.	20-49 Emps.	50-99 Emps.	100-249 Emps.	250-499 Emps.	500-999 Emps.	Unknown Emps.	Industr y Sales
2016	14.1	27.4	69.4	141.9	107.7	7,099.4	554.4	11.5	4.9	8,030.8
2017	14.4	28.0	71.1	145.4	110.3	7,269.7	567.7	11.8	5.0	8,223.4
2018	14.8	28.8	73.2	149.6	113.5	7,482.5	584.4	12.2	5.2	8,464.2
2019	15.4	29.9	75.9	155.2	117.7	7,760.3	606.1	12.6	5.4	8,778.4
2019	16.1	31.3	79.4	162.3	123.1	8,118.7	634.0	13.2	5.6	9,183.8

INDUSTRY: HARDWARE STORES INDUSTRY (NAICS 44413)
PRODUCT LINE: KITCHENS & CABINETS (Sub Category)

NAICS 44413: Hardware Stores. Establishments primarily engaged
in the retail sale of a number of basic hardware lines, such as tools,
builders' hardware, paint and glass, housewares and household appliances,
and cutlery.

5-YEAR TREND – ESTIMATED INDUSTRY SALES ($MILLIONS)

| Year | Employee Size of Establishment | | | | | | | | | Total |
	1-4 Emps.	5-9 Emps.	10-19 Emps.	20-49 Emps.	50-99 Emps.	100-249 Emps.	250-499 Emps.	500-999 Emps.	Unknown Emps.	Industr y Sales
2016	10.1	17.1	34.3	49.1	9.7	3.2	0.6	0.0	0.9	124.9
2017	10.2	17.2	34.7	49.5	9.8	3.2	0.6	0.0	0.9	126.1
2018	10.3	17.5	35.2	50.3	10.0	3.3	0.6	0.0	0.9	128.1
2019	10.7	18.2	36.6	52.3	10.4	3.4	0.6	0.0	0.9	133.2
2019	11.3	19.1	38.4	54.9	10.9	3.6	0.6	0.0	1.0	139.8

INDUSTRY: HOME CENTERS INDUSTRY (NAICS 44411)
PRODUCT LINE: HEATING & HVAC UNITS (Sub Category)

NAICS 44411: Home Centers. This industry comprises establishments
known as home centers primarily engaged in retailing a general line of
new home repair and improvement materials and supplies, such as
lumber, plumbing goods, electrical goods, tools, housewares, hardware,
and lawn and garden supplies, with no one merchandise line predominating.
The merchandise lines are normally arranged in separate departments.

5-YEAR TREND – ESTIMATED INDUSTRY SALES ($MILLIONS)

Year	Employee Size of Establishment									Total
	1-4 Emps.	5-9 Emps.	10-19 Emps.	20-49 Emps.	50-99 Emps.	100-249 Emps.	250-499 Emps.	500-999 Emps.	Unknown Emps.	Industry Sales
2016	3.5	6.8	17.3	35.4	26.8	1,768.0	138.1	2.9	1.2	1,999.9
2017	3.6	7.0	17.7	36.2	27.5	1,810.4	141.4	2.9	1.3	2,047.9
2018	3.7	7.2	18.2	37.3	28.3	1,863.4	145.5	3.0	1.3	2,107.9
2019	3.8	7.5	18.9	38.6	29.3	1,932.6	150.9	3.1	1.3	2,186.1
2019	4.0	7.8	19.8	40.4	30.7	2,021.8	157.9	3.3	1.4	2,287.1

INDUSTRY: HARDWARE STORES INDUSTRY (NAICS 44413)
PRODUCT LINE: HEATING & HVAC UNITS (Sub Category)

NAICS 44413: Hardware Stores. Establishments primarily engaged
in the retail sale of a number of basic hardware lines, such as tools,
builders' hardware, paint and glass, housewares and household appliances,
and cutlery.

5-YEAR TREND – ESTIMATED INDUSTRY SALES ($MILLIONS)

Year	Employee Size of Establishment									Total
	1-4 Emps.	5-9 Emps.	10-19 Emps.	20-49 Emps.	50-99 Emps.	100-249 Emps.	250-499 Emps.	500-999 Emps.	Unknown Emps.	Industry Sales
2016	10.7	18.2	36.7	52.4	10.4	3.4	0.6	0.0	0.9	133.4
2017	10.8	18.4	37.0	52.9	10.5	3.4	0.6	0.0	0.9	134.7
2018	11.0	18.7	37.6	53.7	10.7	3.5	0.6	0.0	1.0	136.8
2019	11.5	19.4	39.1	55.9	11.1	3.6	0.6	0.0	1.0	142.2
2019	12.0	20.4	41.0	58.7	11.7	3.8	0.7	0.0	1.1	149.3

INDUSTRY: HARDWARE STORES INDUSTRY (NAICS 44413)
PRODUCT LINE: REFRIGERATION EQUIPMENT (Sub Category)

NAICS 44413: Hardware Stores. Establishments primarily engaged
in the retail sale of a number of basic hardware lines, such as tools,
builders' hardware, paint and glass, housewares and household appliances,
and cutlery.

5-YEAR TREND – ESTIMATED INDUSTRY SALES ($MILLIONS)

| Year | Employee Size of Establishment | | | | | | | | | Total |
	1-4 Emps.	5-9 Emps.	10-19 Emps.	20-49 Emps.	50-99 Emps.	100-249 Emps.	250-499 Emps.	500-999 Emps.	Unknown Emps.	Industry Sales
2016	1.1	1.9	3.8	5.4	1.1	0.4	0.1	0.0	0.1	13.8
2017	1.1	1.9	3.8	5.5	1.1	0.4	0.1	0.0	0.1	14.0
2018	1.1	1.9	3.9	5.6	1.1	0.4	0.1	0.0	0.1	14.2
2019	1.2	2.0	4.1	5.8	1.2	0.4	0.1	0.0	0.1	14.8
2019	1.2	2.1	4.3	6.1	1.2	0.4	0.1	0.0	0.1	15.5

INDUSTRY: HOME CENTERS INDUSTRY (NAICS 44411)
PRODUCT LINE: OTHER BUILDING MATERIALS (Sub Category)

NAICS 44411: Home Centers. This industry comprises establishments
known as home centers primarily engaged in retailing a general line of
new home repair and improvement materials and supplies, such as
lumber, plumbing goods, electrical goods, tools, housewares, hardware,
and lawn and garden supplies, with no one merchandise line predominating.
The merchandise lines are normally arranged in separate departments.

5-YEAR TREND – ESTIMATED INDUSTRY SALES ($MILLIONS)

| Year | Employee Size of Establishment | | | | | | | | | Total |
	1-4 Emps.	5-9 Emps.	10-19 Emps.	20-49 Emps.	50-99 Emps.	100-249 Emps.	250-499 Emps.	500-999 Emps.	Unknown Emps.	Industry Sales
2016	4.6	9.0	22.8	46.7	35.4	2,335.0	182.4	3.8	1.6	2,641.3
2017	4.7	9.2	23.4	47.8	36.3	2,391.0	186.7	3.9	1.7	2,704.7
2018	4.9	9.5	24.1	49.2	37.3	2,461.0	192.2	4.0	1.7	2,783.8
2019	5.1	9.8	25.0	51.0	38.7	2,552.4	199.3	4.1	1.8	2,887.2
2019	5.3	10.3	26.1	53.4	40.5	2,670.2	208.5	4.3	1.8	3,020.5

INDUSTRY: HARDWARE STORES INDUSTRY (NAICS 44413)
PRODUCT LINE: OTHER BUILDING MATERIALS (Sub Category)

NAICS 44413: Hardware Stores. Establishments primarily engaged
in the retail sale of a number of basic hardware lines, such as tools,
builders' hardware, paint and glass, housewares and household appliances,
and cutlery.

5-YEAR TREND – ESTIMATED INDUSTRY SALES ($MILLIONS)

Year	Employee Size of Establishment									Total
	1-4 Emps.	5-9 Emps.	10-19 Emps.	20-49 Emps.	50-99 Emps.	100-249 Emps.	250-499 Emps.	500-999 Emps.	Unknown Emps.	Industry Sales
2016	10.6	17.9	36.1	51.6	10.2	3.3	0.6	0.0	0.9	131.3
2017	10.7	18.1	36.4	52.1	10.3	3.4	0.6	0.0	0.9	132.6
2018	10.8	18.4	37.0	52.9	10.5	3.4	0.6	0.0	0.9	134.7
2019	11.3	19.1	38.5	55.0	10.9	3.6	0.6	0.0	1.0	140.0
2019	11.8	20.1	40.4	57.7	11.5	3.7	0.7	0.0	1.0	147.0

INDUSTRY: HOME CENTERS INDUSTRY (NAICS 44411)
PRODUCT LINE: PAINT & PAINTING SUPPLIES (Main Category)

NAICS 44411: Home Centers. This industry comprises establishments
known as home centers primarily engaged in retailing a general line of
new home repair and improvement materials and supplies, such as
lumber, plumbing goods, electrical goods, tools, housewares, hardware,
and lawn and garden supplies, with no one merchandise line predominating.
The merchandise lines are normally arranged in separate departments.

5-YEAR TREND – ESTIMATED INDUSTRY SALES ($MILLIONS)

Year	Employee Size of Establishment									Total
	1-4 Emps.	5-9 Emps.	10-19 Emps.	20-49 Emps.	50-99 Emps.	100-249 Emps.	250-499 Emps.	500-999 Emps.	Unknown Emps.	Industry Sales
2016	18.9	36.8	93.3	190.9	144.8	9,545.4	745.5	15.5	6.6	10,797.7
2017	19.4	37.7	95.6	195.4	148.2	9,774.4	763.3	15.9	6.8	11,056.7
2018	19.9	38.8	98.4	201.2	152.6	10,060.6	785.7	16.4	7.0	11,380.4
2019	20.7	40.2	102.0	208.6	158.2	10,434.1	814.9	17.0	7.2	11,803.0
2019	21.6	42.1	106.7	218.3	165.5	10,915.9	852.5	17.7	7.6	12,348.0

INDUSTRY: HARDWARE STORES (NAICS 44413)
PRODUCT LINE: PAINT & PAINTING SUPPLIES (Main Category)

NAICS 44413: Hardware Stores. Establishments primarily engaged
in the retail sale of a number of basic hardware lines, such as tools,
builders' hardware, paint and glass, housewares and household appliances,
and cutlery.

5-Year Trend – Estimated Industry Sales ($Millions)

Year	Employee Size of Establishment									Total
	1-4 Emps.	5-9 Emps.	10-19 Emps.	20-49 Emps.	50-99 Emps.	100-249 Emps.	250-499 Emps.	500-999 Emps.	Unknown Emps.	Industry Sales
2016	198.4	336.3	676.7	967.5	192.2	62.7	11.1	0.6	17.4	2,462.8
2017	200.3	339.6	683.4	977.0	194.1	63.3	11.2	0.6	17.5	2,487.0
2018	203.5	344.9	694.1	992.3	197.2	64.3	11.4	0.6	17.8	2,526.0
2019	211.5	358.6	721.7	1,031.7	205.0	66.9	11.9	0.6	18.5	2,626.4
2019	222.1	376.4	757.5	1,082.9	215.2	70.2	12.4	0.6	19.4	2,756.8

INDUSTRY: DEPARTMENT STORES INDUSTRY (NAICS 45211)
PRODUCT LINE: PAINT & PAINTING SUPPLIES (Main Category)

NAICS 45211: Department Stores Industry . this industry comprises
establishments known as department stores primarily engaged in retailing
a wide range of the following new products with no one merchandise line
predominating: apparel, furniture, appliances and home furnishings; and
selected additional items, such as paint, hardware, toiletries, cosmetics,
photographic equipment, jewelry, toys, and sporting goods. merchandise lines
are normally arranged in separate departments.

5-Year Trend – Estimated Industry Sales ($Millions)

Year	Employee Size of Establishment									Total
	1-4 Emps.	5-9 Emps.	10-19 Emps.	20-49 Emps.	50-99 Emps.	100-249 Emps.	250-499 Emps.	500-999 Emps.	Unknown Emps.	Industry Sales
2016	0.0	0.0	0.1	4.5	81.2	260.8	107.9	15.6	0.7	470.8
2017	0.0	0.0	0.1	4.5	81.5	261.8	108.4	15.7	0.7	472.6
2018	0.0	0.0	0.1	4.5	82.3	264.4	109.4	15.8	0.7	477.3
2019	0.0	0.0	0.1	4.5	82.3	264.4	109.5	15.9	0.7	477.4
2019	0.0	0.0	0.1	4.6	83.2	267.0	110.5	16.1	0.7	482.1

INDUSTRY: WAREHOUSE CLUBS & SUPERCENTERS (NAICS 45291)
PRODUCT LINE: PAINT & PAINTING SUPPLIES (Main Category)

NAICS 45291: Warehouse Clubs and Superstores This industry comprises establishments known as warehouse clubs, superstores or supercenters primarily engaged in retailing a general line of groceries in combination with general lines of new merchandise, such as apparel, furniture, and appliances.

5-YEAR TREND – ESTIMATED INDUSTRY SALES ($MILLIONS)

Year	Employee Size of Establishment									Total
	1-4 Emps.	5-9 Emps.	10-19 Emps.	20-49 Emps.	50-99 Emps.	100-249 Emps.	250-499 Emps.	500-999 Emps.	Unknown Emps.	Industry Sales
2016	0.1	0.0	0.1	2.7	5.1	289.3	1,273.4	32.1	0.5	1,603.2
2017	0.1	0.0	0.1	2.7	5.2	297.2	1,308.5	33.0	0.5	1,647.3
2018	0.1	0.0	0.1	2.8	5.4	306.9	1,351.2	34.1	0.5	1,701.1
2019	0.1	0.0	0.1	3.0	5.8	330.3	1,454.2	36.6	0.6	1,830.8
2019	0.1	0.0	0.1	3.2	6.1	349.9	1,540.4	38.8	0.6	1,939.3

INDUSTRY: ELECTRONIC SHOPPING & MAIL-ORDER (NAICS 45411)
PRODUCT LINE: PAINT & PAINTING SUPPLIES (Main Category)

NAICS 45411: Electronic Shopping and Mail-Order Houses This industry comprises establishments primarily engaged in retailing all types of merchandise by means of mail or by electronic media, such as interactive television or computer. Included in this industry are establishments primarily engaged in retailing from catalogue showrooms of mail-order houses.

5-YEAR TREND – ESTIMATED INDUSTRY SALES ($MILLIONS)

Year	Employee Size of Establishment									Total
	1-4 Emps.	5-9 Emps.	10-19 Emps.	20-49 Emps.	50-99 Emps.	100-249 Emps.	250-499 Emps.	500-999 Emps.	Unknown Emps.	Industry Sales
2016	1.9	1.0	1.4	2.4	1.8	3.4	4.5	6.4	0.3	23.2
2017	2.1	1.1	1.5	2.6	1.9	3.6	4.8	6.8	0.3	24.6
2018	2.2	1.1	1.6	2.7	2.0	3.8	5.1	7.2	0.3	26.1
2019	2.4	1.3	1.8	3.0	2.3	4.2	5.7	7.9	0.3	29.1
2019	2.7	1.4	2.0	3.4	2.5	4.7	6.4	8.7	0.4	32.2

INDUSTRY: HOME CENTERS INDUSTRY (NAICS 44411)
PRODUCT LINE: INTERIOR PAINT (Sub Category)

NAICS 44411: Home Centers. This industry comprises establishments known as home centers primarily engaged in retailing a general line of new home repair and improvement materials and supplies, such as lumber, plumbing goods, electrical goods, tools, housewares, hardware, and lawn and garden supplies, with no one merchandise line predominating. The merchandise lines are normally arranged in separate departments.

5-YEAR TREND — ESTIMATED INDUSTRY SALES ($MILLIONS)

Year	Employee Size of Establishment									Total
	1-4 Emps.	5-9 Emps.	10-19 Emps.	20-49 Emps.	50-99 Emps.	100-249 Emps.	250-499 Emps.	500-999 Emps.	Unknown Emps.	Industry Sales
2016	7.1	13.8	34.9	71.3	54.1	3,567.1	278.6	5.8	2.5	4,035.0
2017	7.2	14.1	35.7	73.0	55.4	3,652.6	285.3	5.9	2.5	4,131.8
2018	7.5	14.5	36.8	75.2	57.0	3,759.6	293.6	6.1	2.6	4,252.8
2019	7.7	15.0	38.1	78.0	59.1	3,899.1	304.5	6.3	2.7	4,410.7
2019	8.1	15.7	39.9	81.6	61.9	4,079.2	318.6	6.6	2.8	4,614.4

INDUSTRY: HARDWARE STORES INDUSTRY (NAICS 44413)
PRODUCT LINE: INTERIOR PAINT (Sub Category)

NAICS 44413: Hardware Stores. Establishments primarily engaged in the retail sale of a number of basic hardware lines, such as tools, builders' hardware, paint and glass, housewares and household appliances, and cutlery.

5-YEAR TREND — ESTIMATED INDUSTRY SALES ($MILLIONS)

Year	Employee Size of Establishment									Total
	1-4 Emps.	5-9 Emps.	10-19 Emps.	20-49 Emps.	50-99 Emps.	100-249 Emps.	250-499 Emps.	500-999 Emps.	Unknown Emps.	Industry Sales
2016	65.3	110.8	222.9	318.7	63.3	20.7	3.7	0.2	5.7	811.3
2017	66.0	111.9	225.1	321.8	63.9	20.9	3.7	0.2	5.8	819.3
2018	67.0	113.6	228.6	326.9	64.9	21.2	3.8	0.2	5.9	832.1
2019	69.7	118.1	237.7	339.9	67.5	22.0	3.9	0.2	6.1	865.2
2019	73.1	124.0	249.5	356.7	70.9	23.1	4.1	0.2	6.4	908.1

| INDUSTRY: HOME CENTERS INDUSTRY (NAICS 44411) |
| PRODUCT LINE: EXTERIOR PAINT (Sub Category) |

NAICS 44411: Home Centers. This industry comprises establishments known as home centers primarily engaged in retailing a general line of new home repair and improvement materials and supplies, such as lumber, plumbing goods, electrical goods, tools, housewares, hardware, and lawn and garden supplies, with no one merchandise line predominating. The merchandise lines are normally arranged in separate departments.

5-YEAR TREND – ESTIMATED INDUSTRY SALES ($MILLIONS)

| Year | Employee Size of Establishment | | | | | | | | | Total |
	1-4 Emps.	5-9 Emps.	10-19 Emps.	20-49 Emps.	50-99 Emps.	100-249 Emps.	250-499 Emps.	500-999 Emps.	Unknown Emps.	Industry Sales
2016	2.1	4.2	10.6	21.7	16.4	1,084.1	84.7	1.8	0.8	1,226.3
2017	2.2	4.3	10.9	22.2	16.8	1,110.1	86.7	1.8	0.8	1,255.7
2018	2.3	4.4	11.2	22.8	17.3	1,142.6	89.2	1.9	0.8	1,292.5
2019	2.3	4.6	11.6	23.7	18.0	1,185.0	92.5	1.9	0.8	1,340.5
2019	2.5	4.8	12.1	24.8	18.8	1,239.7	96.8	2.0	0.9	1,402.4

| INDUSTRY: HARDWARE STORES INDUSTRY (NAICS 44413) |
| PRODUCT LINE: EXTERIOR PAINT (Sub Category) |

NAICS 44413: Hardware Stores. Establishments primarily engaged in the retail sale of a number of basic hardware lines, such as tools, builders' hardware, paint and glass, housewares and household appliances, and cutlery.

5-YEAR TREND – ESTIMATED INDUSTRY SALES ($MILLIONS)

| Year | Employee Size of Establishment | | | | | | | | | Total |
	1-4 Emps.	5-9 Emps.	10-19 Emps.	20-49 Emps.	50-99 Emps.	100-249 Emps.	250-499 Emps.	500-999 Emps.	Unknown Emps.	Industry Sales
2016	42.2	71.5	143.9	205.7	40.9	13.3	2.4	0.1	3.7	523.5
2017	42.6	72.2	145.3	207.7	41.3	13.5	2.4	0.1	3.7	528.7
2018	43.3	73.3	147.5	210.9	41.9	13.7	2.4	0.1	3.8	537.0
2019	45.0	76.2	153.4	219.3	43.6	14.2	2.5	0.1	3.9	558.3
2019	47.2	80.0	161.0	230.2	45.7	14.9	2.6	0.1	4.1	586.0

INDUSTRY: HOME CENTERS INDUSTRY (NAICS 44411)
PRODUCT LINE: STAINS & VARNISHES (Sub Category)

NAICS 44411: Home Centers. This industry comprises establishments
known as home centers primarily engaged in retailing a general line of
new home repair and improvement materials and supplies, such as
lumber, plumbing goods, electrical goods, tools, housewares, hardware,
and lawn and garden supplies, with no one merchandise line predominating.
The merchandise lines are normally arranged in separate departments.

5-Year Trend — Estimated Industry Sales ($Millions)

Year	Employee Size of Establishment									Total
	1-4 Emps.	5-9 Emps.	10-19 Emps.	20-49 Emps.	50-99 Emps.	100-249 Emps.	250-499 Emps.	500-999 Emps.	Unknown Emps.	Industry Sales
2016	1.8	3.5	8.9	18.2	13.8	909.3	71.0	1.5	0.6	1,028.6
2017	1.8	3.6	9.1	18.6	14.1	931.1	72.7	1.5	0.6	1,053.2
2018	1.9	3.7	9.4	19.2	14.5	958.3	74.8	1.6	0.7	1,084.1
2019	2.0	3.8	9.7	19.9	15.1	993.9	77.6	1.6	0.7	1,124.3
2019	2.1	4.0	10.2	20.8	15.8	1,039.8	81.2	1.7	0.7	1,176.2

INDUSTRY: HARDWARE STORES INDUSTRY (NAICS 44413)
PRODUCT LINE: STAINS & VARNISHES (Sub Category)

NAICS 44413: Hardware Stores. Establishments primarily engaged
in the retail sale of a number of basic hardware lines, such as tools,
builders' hardware, paint and glass, housewares and household appliances,
and cutlery.

5-Year Trend — Estimated Industry Sales ($Millions)

Year	Employee Size of Establishment									Total
	1-4 Emps.	5-9 Emps.	10-19 Emps.	20-49 Emps.	50-99 Emps.	100-249 Emps.	250-499 Emps.	500-999 Emps.	Unknown Emps.	Industry Sales
2016	21.6	36.6	73.7	105.4	20.9	6.8	1.2	0.1	1.9	268.4
2017	21.8	37.0	74.5	106.5	21.2	6.9	1.2	0.1	1.9	271.0
2018	22.2	37.6	75.6	108.1	21.5	7.0	1.2	0.1	1.9	275.3
2019	23.1	39.1	78.6	112.4	22.3	7.3	1.3	0.1	2.0	286.2
2019	24.2	41.0	82.5	118.0	23.4	7.6	1.4	0.1	2.1	300.4

INDUSTRY: HOME CENTERS INDUSTRY (NAICS 44411)
PRODUCT LINE: PAINTING EQUIPMENT (Sub Category)

NAICS 44411: Home Centers. This industry comprises establishments known as home centers primarily engaged in retailing a general line of new home repair and improvement materials and supplies, such as lumber, plumbing goods, electrical goods, tools, housewares, hardware, and lawn and garden supplies, with no one merchandise line predominating. The merchandise lines are normally arranged in separate departments.

5-YEAR TREND — ESTIMATED INDUSTRY SALES ($MILLIONS)

Year	Employee Size of Establishment									Total
	1-4 Emps.	5-9 Emps.	10-19 Emps.	20-49 Emps.	50-99 Emps.	100-249 Emps.	250-499 Emps.	500-999 Emps.	Unknown Emps.	Industry Sales
2016	3.4	6.5	16.6	33.9	25.7	1,694.5	132.3	2.8	1.2	1,916.9
2017	3.4	6.7	17.0	34.7	26.3	1,735.2	135.5	2.8	1.2	1,962.8
2018	3.5	6.9	17.5	35.7	27.1	1,786.0	139.5	2.9	1.2	2,020.3
2019	3.7	7.1	18.1	37.0	28.1	1,852.3	144.7	3.0	1.3	2,095.3
2019	3.8	7.5	18.9	38.7	29.4	1,937.8	151.3	3.1	1.3	2,192.1

INDUSTRY: HARDWARE STORES INDUSTRY (NAICS 44413)
PRODUCT LINE: PAINTING EQUIPMENT (Sub Category)

NAICS 44413: Hardware Stores. Establishments primarily engaged in the retail sale of a number of basic hardware lines, such as tools, builders' hardware, paint and glass, housewares and household appliances, and cutlery.

5-YEAR TREND — ESTIMATED INDUSTRY SALES ($MILLIONS)

Year	Employee Size of Establishment									Total
	1-4 Emps.	5-9 Emps.	10-19 Emps.	20-49 Emps.	50-99 Emps.	100-249 Emps.	250-499 Emps.	500-999 Emps.	Unknown Emps.	Industry Sales
2016	41.7	70.7	142.2	203.3	40.4	13.2	2.3	0.1	3.6	517.5
2017	42.1	71.4	143.6	205.3	40.8	13.3	2.4	0.1	3.7	522.5
2018	42.7	72.5	145.8	208.5	41.4	13.5	2.4	0.1	3.7	530.7
2019	44.4	75.4	151.6	216.8	43.1	14.0	2.5	0.1	3.9	551.8
2019	46.7	79.1	159.2	227.5	45.2	14.7	2.6	0.1	4.1	579.2

| INDUSTRY: HOME CENTERS INDUSTRY (NAICS 44411) |
| PRODUCT LINE: PAINTING SUPPLIES (Sub Category) |

NAICS 44411: Home Centers. This industry comprises establishments
known as home centers primarily engaged in retailing a general line of
new home repair and improvement materials and supplies, such as
lumber, plumbing goods, electrical goods, tools, housewares, hardware,
and lawn and garden supplies, with no one merchandise line predominating.
The merchandise lines are normally arranged in separate departments.

5-Year Trend – Estimated Industry Sales ($Millions)

| Year | Employee Size of Establishment | | | | | | | | | Total |
	1-4 Emps.	5-9 Emps.	10-19 Emps.	20-49 Emps.	50-99 Emps.	100-249 Emps.	250-499 Emps.	500-999 Emps.	Unknown Emps.	Industry Sales
2016	4.5	8.8	22.4	45.8	34.7	2,290.5	178.9	3.7	1.6	2,591.0
2017	4.6	9.0	22.9	46.9	35.6	2,345.4	183.2	3.8	1.6	2,653.1
2018	4.8	9.3	23.6	48.3	36.6	2,414.1	188.5	3.9	1.7	2,730.8
2019	5.0	9.7	24.5	50.1	38.0	2,503.7	195.5	4.1	1.7	2,832.2
2019	5.2	10.1	25.6	52.4	39.7	2,619.3	204.6	4.3	1.8	2,963.0

| INDUSTRY: HARDWARE STORES INDUSTRY (NAICS 44413) |
| PRODUCT LINE: PAINTING SUPPLIES (Sub Category) |

NAICS 44413: Hardware Stores. Establishments primarily engaged
in the retail sale of a number of basic hardware lines, such as tools,
builders' hardware, paint and glass, housewares and household appliances,
and cutlery.

5-Year Trend – Estimated Industry Sales ($Millions)

| Year | Employee Size of Establishment | | | | | | | | | Total |
	1-4 Emps.	5-9 Emps.	10-19 Emps.	20-49 Emps.	50-99 Emps.	100-249 Emps.	250-499 Emps.	500-999 Emps.	Unknown Emps.	Industry Sales
2016	27.6	46.7	94.0	134.4	26.7	8.7	1.5	0.1	2.4	342.2
2017	27.8	47.2	94.9	135.7	27.0	8.8	1.6	0.1	2.4	345.5
2018	28.3	47.9	96.4	137.9	27.4	8.9	1.6	0.1	2.5	351.0
2019	29.4	49.8	100.3	143.3	28.5	9.3	1.6	0.1	2.6	364.9
2019	30.9	52.3	105.2	150.5	29.9	9.8	1.7	0.1	2.7	383.0

INDUSTRY: HOME CENTERS INDUSTRY (NAICS 44411)
PRODUCT LINE: GASOLINE & AUTOMOTIVE FUELS (Main Category)

NAICS 44411: Home Centers. This industry comprises establishments
known as home centers primarily engaged in retailing a general line of
new home repair and improvement materials and supplies, such as
lumber, plumbing goods, electrical goods, tools, housewares, hardware,
and lawn and garden supplies, with no one merchandise line predominating.
The merchandise lines are normally arranged in separate departments.

5-YEAR TREND – ESTIMATED INDUSTRY SALES ($MILLIONS)

Year	Employee Size of Establishment									Total
	1-4 Emps.	5-9 Emps.	10-19 Emps.	20-49 Emps.	50-99 Emps.	100-249 Emps.	250-499 Emps.	500-999 Emps.	Unknown Emps.	Industry Sales
2016	0.0	0.0	0.0	0.0	0.0	1.7	0.1	0.0	0.0	1.9
2017	0.0	0.0	0.0	0.0	0.0	1.7	0.1	0.0	0.0	2.0
2018	0.0	0.0	0.0	0.0	0.0	1.8	0.1	0.0	0.0	2.0
2019	0.0	0.0	0.0	0.0	0.0	1.9	0.1	0.0	0.0	2.1
2019	0.0	0.0	0.0	0.0	0.0	2.0	0.2	0.0	0.0	2.2

INDUSTRY: HARDWARE STORES (NAICS 44413)
PRODUCT LINE: GASOLINE & AUTOMOTIVE FUELS (Main Category)

NAICS 44413: Hardware Stores. Establishments primarily engaged
in the retail sale of a number of basic hardware lines, such as tools,
builders' hardware, paint and glass, housewares and household appliances,
and cutlery.

5-YEAR TREND – ESTIMATED INDUSTRY SALES ($MILLIONS)

Year	Employee Size of Establishment									Total
	1-4 Emps.	5-9 Emps.	10-19 Emps.	20-49 Emps.	50-99 Emps.	100-249 Emps.	250-499 Emps.	500-999 Emps.	Unknown Emps.	Industry Sales
2016	2.3	3.9	7.8	11.2	2.2	0.7	0.1	0.0	0.2	28.4
2017	2.3	3.9	7.9	11.3	2.2	0.7	0.1	0.0	0.2	28.7
2018	2.3	4.0	8.0	11.5	2.3	0.7	0.1	0.0	0.2	29.2
2019	2.4	4.1	8.3	11.9	2.4	0.8	0.1	0.0	0.2	30.3
2019	2.6	4.3	8.7	12.5	2.5	0.8	0.1	0.0	0.2	31.8

INDUSTRY: SUPERMARKETS INDUSTRY (NAICS 44511)
PRODUCT LINE: GASOLINE & AUTOMOTIVE FUELS (Main Category)

NAICS 44511: Grocery Stores Industry. this industry comprises establishments generally known as supermarkets and grocery stores primarily engaged in retailing a general line of food, such as canned and frozen foods; fresh fruits and vegetables; and fresh and prepared meats, fish, and poultry. Included in this industry are delicatessen-type establishments primarily engaged in retailing a general line of food.

5-YEAR TREND — ESTIMATED INDUSTRY SALES ($MILLIONS)

Year	Employee Size of Establishment									Total
	1-4 Emps.	5-9 Emps.	10-19 Emps.	20-49 Emps.	50-99 Emps.	100-249 Emps.	250-499 Emps.	500-999 Emps.	Unknown Emps.	Industry Sales
2016	48.6	35.1	90.6	298.6	707.6	1,759.2	549.4	65.7	9.1	3,564.0
2017	48.3	34.9	90.0	296.7	703.1	1,748.0	545.9	65.3	9.1	3,541.4
2018	48.3	34.9	90.0	296.6	702.9	1,747.4	545.7	65.3	9.1	3,540.2
2019	49.3	35.6	91.9	302.7	717.4	1,783.5	557.0	66.6	9.3	3,613.1
2019	50.8	36.7	94.7	312.1	739.6	1,838.6	574.2	68.6	9.5	3,724.8

INDUSTRY: BEER, WINE & LIQUOR STORES (NAICS 44531)
PRODUCT LINE: GASOLINE & AUTOMOTIVE FUELS (Main Category)

NAICS 44531: Beer & Wine & Liquor Stores. Establishments primarily engaged in the retail sale of packaged alcoholic beverages, such as ale, beer, wine, and liquor, for consumption off the premises. Stores selling prepared drinks for consumption on the premises are classified in SIC 5813.

5-YEAR TREND — ESTIMATED INDUSTRY SALES ($MILLIONS)

Year	Employee Size of Establishment									Total
	1-4 Emps.	5-9 Emps.	10-19 Emps.	20-49 Emps.	50-99 Emps.	100-249 Emps.	250-499 Emps.	500-999 Emps.	Unknown Emps.	Industry Sales
2016	29.5	29.7	25.4	18.6	2.7	1.6	0.0	0.9	1.7	110.0
2017	30.2	30.4	26.0	19.1	2.7	1.6	0.0	0.9	1.7	112.6
2018	31.0	31.3	26.7	19.6	2.8	1.6	0.0	0.9	1.7	115.8
2019	32.8	33.1	28.3	20.7	3.0	1.7	0.0	1.0	1.8	122.5
2019	35.1	35.3	30.2	22.1	3.2	1.8	0.0	1.0	2.0	130.8

INDUSTRY: GAS STATIONS W/CONVENIENCE STORES (NAICS 44711)
PRODUCT LINE: GASOLINE & AUTOMOTIVE FUELS (Main Category)

NAICS 44711: Gas Stations with Convenience Stores. this industry comprises establishments primarily engaged in selling gasoline and lubricating oils. These establishments frequently sell other merchandise, such as tires, batteries, and other automobile parts, or perform minor repair work. Gasoline stations combined with other activities, such as grocery stores, convenience stores, or carwashes, are classified according to the primary activity.

5-Year Trend – Estimated Industry Sales ($Millions)

Year	Employee Size of Establishment									Total
	1-4 Emps.	5-9 Emps.	10-19 Emps.	20-49 Emps.	50-99 Emps.	100-249 Emps.	250-499 Emps.	500-999 Emps.	Unknown Emps.	Industry Sales
2016	23,501.4	60,714.8	101,628.4	70,127.8	6,589.4	3,608.5	1,430.9	12.2	258.4	267,871.8
2017	24,485.3	63,256.7	105,883.3	73,063.9	6,865.3	3,759.6	1,490.8	12.7	269.2	279,086.9
2018	25,610.3	66,163.0	110,748.0	76,420.7	7,180.7	3,932.3	1,559.3	13.3	281.6	291,909.2
2019	27,291.4	70,506.2	118,018.0	81,437.2	7,652.1	4,190.5	1,661.6	14.0	300.1	311,071.1
2019	29,299.2	75,693.1	126,700.2	87,428.3	8,215.0	4,498.8	1,783.9	14.8	322.2	333,955.3

INDUSTRY: DEPARTMENT STORES INDUSTRY (NAICS 45211)
PRODUCT LINE: GASOLINE & AUTOMOTIVE FUELS (Main Category)

NAICS 45211: Department Stores Industry . this industry comprises establishments known as department stores primarily engaged in retailing a wide range of the following new products with no one merchandise line predominating: apparel, furniture, appliances and home furnishings; and selected additional items, such as paint, hardware, toiletries, cosmetics, photographic equipment, jewelry, toys, and sporting goods. merchandise lines are normally arranged in separate departments.

5-Year Trend – Estimated Industry Sales ($Millions)

Year	Employee Size of Establishment									Total
	1-4 Emps.	5-9 Emps.	10-19 Emps.	20-49 Emps.	50-99 Emps.	100-249 Emps.	250-499 Emps.	500-999 Emps.	Unknown Emps.	Industry Sales
2016	0.0	0.0	0.0	0.1	1.6	5.1	2.1	0.3	0.0	9.2
2017	0.0	0.0	0.0	0.1	1.6	5.1	2.1	0.3	0.0	9.2
2018	0.0	0.0	0.0	0.1	1.6	5.2	2.1	0.3	0.0	9.3
2019	0.0	0.0	0.0	0.1	1.6	5.2	2.1	0.3	0.0	9.3
2019	0.0	0.0	0.0	0.1	1.6	5.2	2.2	0.3	0.0	9.4

	INDUSTRY: WAREHOUSE CLUBS & SUPERCENTERS (NAICS 45291)
	PRODUCT LINE: GASOLINE & AUTOMOTIVE FUELS (Main Category)

NAICS 45291: Warehouse Clubs and Superstores This industry comprises establishments known as warehouse clubs, superstores or supercenters primarily engaged in retailing a general line of groceries in combination with general lines of new merchandise, such as apparel, furniture, and appliances.

5-YEAR TREND – ESTIMATED INDUSTRY SALES ($MILLIONS)

Year	Employee Size of Establishment									Total
	1-4 Emps.	5-9 Emps.	10-19 Emps.	20-49 Emps.	50-99 Emps.	100-249 Emps.	250-499 Emps.	500-999 Emps.	Unknown Emps.	Industry Sales
2016	0.0	0.0	0.0	0.4	0.8	46.8	206.2	5.2	0.1	259.6
2017	0.0	0.0	0.0	0.4	0.8	48.1	211.9	5.3	0.1	266.7
2018	0.0	0.0	0.0	0.5	0.9	49.7	218.8	5.5	0.1	275.4
2019	0.0	0.0	0.0	0.5	0.9	53.5	235.4	5.9	0.1	296.4
2019	0.0	0.0	0.0	0.5	1.0	56.7	249.4	6.3	0.1	314.0

	INDUSTRY: GAS STATIONS W/CONVENIENCE STORES (NAICS 44711)
	PRODUCT LINE: UNLEADED REGULAR GASOLINE (Sub Category)

NAICS 44711: Gas Stations with Convenience Stores. this industry comprises establishments primarily engaged in selling gasoline and lubricating oils. These establishments frequently sell other merchandise, such as tires, batteries, and other automobile parts, or perform minor repair work. Gasoline stations combined with other activities, such as grocery stores, convenience stores, or carwashes, are classified according to the primary activity.

5-YEAR TREND – ESTIMATED INDUSTRY SALES ($MILLIONS)

Year	Employee Size of Establishment									Total
	1-4 Emps.	5-9 Emps.	10-19 Emps.	20-49 Emps.	50-99 Emps.	100-249 Emps.	250-499 Emps.	500-999 Emps.	Unknown Emps.	Industry Sales
2016	16,043.7	41,448.1	69,378.7	47,874.1	4,498.4	2,463.4	976.8	8.3	176.4	182,867.9
2017	16,715.4	43,183.5	72,283.4	49,878.5	4,686.7	2,566.6	1,017.7	8.7	183.8	190,524.1
2018	17,483.3	45,167.5	75,604.3	52,170.1	4,902.1	2,684.5	1,064.5	9.1	192.2	199,277.5
2019	18,631.0	48,132.4	80,567.3	55,594.7	5,223.8	2,860.7	1,134.3	9.5	204.9	212,358.8
2019	20,001.6	51,673.4	86,494.4	59,684.7	5,608.1	3,071.2	1,217.8	10.1	219.9	227,981.2

INDUSTRY: GAS STATIONS W/CONVENIENCE STORES (NAICS 44711)
PRODUCT LINE: UNLEADED MID-GRADE GASOLINE (Sub Category)

NAICS 44711: Gas Stations with Convenience Stores. this industry
comprises establishments primarily engaged in selling gasoline and
lubricating oils. These establishments frequently sell other merchandise,
such as tires, batteries, and other automobile parts, or perform minor repair
work. Gasoline stations combined with other activities, such as grocery stores,
convenience stores, or carwashes, are classified according to the primary activity.

5-YEAR TREND – ESTIMATED INDUSTRY SALES ($MILLIONS)

Year	Employee Size of Establishment									Total
	1-4 Emps.	5-9 Emps.	10-19 Emps.	20-49 Emps.	50-99 Emps.	100-249 Emps.	250-499 Emps.	500-999 Emps.	Unknown Emps.	Industry Sales
2016	3,375.2	8,719.8	14,595.7	10,071.7	946.4	518.3	205.5	1.7	37.1	38,471.4
2017	3,516.5	9,084.8	15,206.8	10,493.3	986.0	540.0	214.1	1.8	38.7	40,082.1
2018	3,678.1	9,502.2	15,905.5	10,975.4	1,031.3	564.8	223.9	1.9	40.4	41,923.6
2019	3,919.6	10,126.0	16,949.6	11,695.9	1,099.0	601.8	238.6	2.0	43.1	44,675.6
2019	4,207.9	10,870.9	18,196.5	12,556.3	1,179.8	646.1	256.2	2.1	46.3	47,962.2

INDUSTRY: GAS STATIONS W/CONVENIENCE STORES (NAICS 44711)
PRODUCT LINE: UNLEADED PREMIUM GASOLINE (Sub Category)

NAICS 44711: Gas Stations with Convenience Stores. this industry
comprises establishments primarily engaged in selling gasoline and
lubricating oils. These establishments frequently sell other merchandise,
such as tires, batteries, and other automobile parts, or perform minor repair
work. Gasoline stations combined with other activities, such as grocery stores,
convenience stores, or carwashes, are classified according to the primary activity.

5-YEAR TREND – ESTIMATED INDUSTRY SALES ($MILLIONS)

Year	Employee Size of Establishment									Total
	1-4 Emps.	5-9 Emps.	10-19 Emps.	20-49 Emps.	50-99 Emps.	100-249 Emps.	250-499 Emps.	500-999 Emps.	Unknown Emps.	Industry Sales
2016	2,598.7	6,713.7	11,237.9	7,754.6	728.6	399.0	158.2	1.3	28.6	29,620.9
2017	2,707.5	6,994.8	11,708.4	8,079.3	759.2	415.7	164.8	1.4	29.8	30,861.0
2018	2,831.9	7,316.2	12,246.3	8,450.5	794.0	434.8	172.4	1.5	31.1	32,278.9
2019	3,017.8	7,796.5	13,050.2	9,005.2	846.2	463.4	183.7	1.5	33.2	34,397.8
2019	3,239.9	8,370.0	14,010.3	9,667.7	908.4	497.5	197.3	1.6	35.6	36,928.3

INDUSTRY: GAS STATIONS W/CONVENIENCE STORES (NAICS 44711)
PRODUCT LINE: LEADED GASOLINE (Sub Category)

NAICS 44711: Gas Stations with Convenience Stores. this industry
comprises establishments primarily engaged in selling gasoline and
lubricating oils. These establishments frequently sell other merchandise,
such as tires, batteries, and other automobile parts, or perform minor repair
work. Gasoline stations combined with other activities, such as grocery stores,
convenience stores, or carwashes, are classified according to the primary activity.

5-YEAR TREND – ESTIMATED INDUSTRY SALES ($MILLIONS)

Year	Employee Size of Establishment									Total
	1-4 Emps.	5-9 Emps.	10-19 Emps.	20-49 Emps.	50-99 Emps.	100-249 Emps.	250-499 Emps.	500-999 Emps.	Unknown Emps.	Industry Sales
2016	50.3	130.0	217.5	150.1	14.1	7.7	3.1	0.0	0.6	573.4
2017	52.4	135.4	226.6	156.4	14.7	8.0	3.2	0.0	0.6	597.4
2018	54.8	141.6	237.0	163.6	15.4	8.4	3.3	0.0	0.6	624.8
2019	58.4	150.9	252.6	174.3	16.4	9.0	3.6	0.0	0.6	665.8
2019	62.7	162.0	271.2	187.1	17.6	9.6	3.8	0.0	0.7	714.8

INDUSTRY: GAS STATIONS W/CONVENIENCE STORES (NAICS 44711)
PRODUCT LINE: DIESEL FUEL (Sub Category)

NAICS 44711: Gas Stations with Convenience Stores. this industry
comprises establishments primarily engaged in selling gasoline and
lubricating oils. These establishments frequently sell other merchandise,
such as tires, batteries, and other automobile parts, or perform minor repair
work. Gasoline stations combined with other activities, such as grocery stores,
convenience stores, or carwashes, are classified according to the primary activity.

5-YEAR TREND – ESTIMATED INDUSTRY SALES ($MILLIONS)

Year	Employee Size of Establishment									Total
	1-4 Emps.	5-9 Emps.	10-19 Emps.	20-49 Emps.	50-99 Emps.	100-249 Emps.	250-499 Emps.	500-999 Emps.	Unknown Emps.	Industry Sales
2016	1,310.0	3,384.3	5,664.9	3,909.0	367.3	201.1	79.8	0.7	14.4	14,931.4
2017	1,364.8	3,526.0	5,902.0	4,072.7	382.7	209.6	83.1	0.7	15.0	15,556.6
2018	1,427.5	3,688.0	6,173.2	4,259.8	400.3	219.2	86.9	0.7	15.7	16,271.3
2019	1,521.3	3,930.1	6,578.4	4,539.4	426.5	233.6	92.6	0.8	16.7	17,339.4
2019	1,633.2	4,219.2	7,062.4	4,873.3	457.9	250.8	99.4	0.8	18.0	18,615.0

INDUSTRY: GAS STATIONS W/CONVENIENCE STORES (NAICS 44711)
PRODUCT LINE: OTHER AUTOMOTIVE FUELS (Sub Category)

NAICS 44711: Gas Stations with Convenience Stores. this industry
comprises establishments primarily engaged in selling gasoline and
lubricating oils. These establishments frequently sell other merchandise,
such as tires, batteries, and other automobile parts, or perform minor repair
work. Gasoline stations combined with other activities, such as grocery stores,
convenience stores, or carwashes, are classified according to the primary activity.

5-YEAR TREND – ESTIMATED INDUSTRY SALES ($MILLIONS)

Year	Employee Size of Establishment									Total
	1-4 Emps.	5-9 Emps.	10-19 Emps.	20-49 Emps.	50-99 Emps.	100-249 Emps.	250-499 Emps.	500-999 Emps.	Unknown Emps.	Industry Sales
2016	123.4	318.9	533.7	368.3	34.6	19.0	7.5	0.1	1.4	1,406.8
2017	128.6	332.2	556.1	383.7	36.1	19.7	7.8	0.1	1.4	1,465.7
2018	134.5	347.5	581.6	401.3	37.7	20.7	8.2	0.1	1.5	1,533.0
2019	143.3	370.3	619.8	427.7	40.2	22.0	8.7	0.1	1.6	1,633.7
2019	153.9	397.5	665.4	459.2	43.1	23.6	9.4	0.1	1.7	1,753.9

INDUSTRY: HOME CENTERS INDUSTRY (NAICS 44411)
PRODUCT LINE: AUTOMOTIVE TIRES & OTHER PARTS (Main Category)

NAICS 44411: Home Centers. This industry comprises establishments
known as home centers primarily engaged in retailing a general line of
new home repair and improvement materials and supplies, such as
lumber, plumbing goods, electrical goods, tools, housewares, hardware,
and lawn and garden supplies, with no one merchandise line predominating.
The merchandise lines are normally arranged in separate departments.

5-YEAR TREND – ESTIMATED INDUSTRY SALES ($MILLIONS)

Year	Employee Size of Establishment									Total
	1-4 Emps.	5-9 Emps.	10-19 Emps.	20-49 Emps.	50-99 Emps.	100-249 Emps.	250-499 Emps.	500-999 Emps.	Unknown Emps.	Industry Sales
2016	0.2	0.4	1.1	2.3	1.7	115.2	9.0	0.2	0.1	130.3
2017	0.2	0.5	1.2	2.4	1.8	117.9	9.2	0.2	0.1	133.4
2018	0.2	0.5	1.2	2.4	1.8	121.4	9.5	0.2	0.1	137.3
2019	0.2	0.5	1.2	2.5	1.9	125.9	9.8	0.2	0.1	142.4
2019	0.3	0.5	1.3	2.6	2.0	131.7	10.3	0.2	0.1	149.0

INDUSTRY: HARDWARE STORES (NAICS 44413)
PRODUCT LINE: AUTOMOTIVE TIRES & OTHER PARTS (Main Category)

NAICS 44413: Hardware Stores. Establishments primarily engaged
in the retail sale of a number of basic hardware lines, such as tools,
builders' hardware, paint and glass, housewares and household appliances,
and cutlery.

5-YEAR TREND — ESTIMATED INDUSTRY SALES ($MILLIONS)

Year	Employee Size of Establishment									Total
	1-4 Emps.	5-9 Emps.	10-19 Emps.	20-49 Emps.	50-99 Emps.	100-249 Emps.	250-499 Emps.	500-999 Emps.	Unknown Emps.	Industry Sales
2016	13.8	23.4	47.0	67.2	13.4	4.4	0.8	0.0	1.2	171.0
2017	13.9	23.6	47.5	67.9	13.5	4.4	0.8	0.0	1.2	172.7
2018	14.1	24.0	48.2	68.9	13.7	4.5	0.8	0.0	1.2	175.4
2019	14.7	24.9	50.1	71.7	14.2	4.6	0.8	0.0	1.3	182.4
2019	15.4	26.1	52.6	75.2	14.9	4.9	0.9	0.0	1.3	191.5

INDUSTRY: SUPERMARKETS INDUSTRY (NAICS 44511)
PRODUCT LINE: AUTOMOTIVE TIRES & OTHER PARTS (Main Category)

NAICS 44511: Grocery Stores Industry. this industry comprises
establishments generally known as supermarkets and grocery stores
primarily engaged in retailing a general line of food, such as canned and
frozen foods; fresh fruits and vegetables; and fresh and prepared meats,
fish, and poultry. Included in this industry are delicatessen-type
establishments primarily engaged in retailing a general line of food.

5-YEAR TREND — ESTIMATED INDUSTRY SALES ($MILLIONS)

Year	Employee Size of Establishment									Total
	1-4 Emps.	5-9 Emps.	10-19 Emps.	20-49 Emps.	50-99 Emps.	100-249 Emps.	250-499 Emps.	500-999 Emps.	Unknown Emps.	Industry Sales
2016	0.6	0.4	1.0	3.4	8.2	20.3	6.3	0.8	0.1	41.1
2017	0.6	0.4	1.0	3.4	8.1	20.2	6.3	0.8	0.1	40.8
2018	0.6	0.4	1.0	3.4	8.1	20.2	6.3	0.8	0.1	40.8
2019	0.6	0.4	1.1	3.5	8.3	20.6	6.4	0.8	0.1	41.7
2019	0.6	0.4	1.1	3.6	8.5	21.2	6.6	0.8	0.1	43.0

INDUSTRY: PHARMACIES & DRUG STORES (NAICS 44611)
PRODUCT LINE: AUTOMOTIVE TIRES & OTHER PARTS (Main Category)

NAICS 44611 Pharmacies and Drug Stores – this industry comprises establishments known as pharmacies and drug stores engaged in retailing prescription or nonprescription drugs and medicines.

5-YEAR TREND – ESTIMATED INDUSTRY SALES ($MILLIONS)

Year	Employee Size of Establishment									Total Industry Sales
	1-4 Emps.	5-9 Emps.	10-19 Emps.	20-49 Emps.	50-99 Emps.	100-249 Emps.	250-499 Emps.	500-999 Emps.	Unknown Emps.	
2016	0.5	1.2	4.9	14.3	1.4	0.6	0.2	0.1	0.0	23.1
2017	0.5	1.2	5.0	14.7	1.5	0.6	0.2	0.1	0.0	23.9
2018	0.5	1.3	5.2	15.2	1.5	0.6	0.2	0.1	0.0	24.7
2019	0.5	1.4	5.5	16.1	1.6	0.7	0.2	0.1	0.0	26.2
2019	0.6	1.4	5.9	17.2	1.7	0.7	0.3	0.1	0.0	28.0

INDUSTRY: GAS STATIONS W/CONVENIENCE STORES (NAICS 44711)
PRODUCT LINE: AUTOMOTIVE TIRES & OTHER PARTS (Main Category)

NAICS 44711: Gas Stations with Convenience Stores. this industry comprises establishments primarily engaged in selling gasoline and lubricating oils. These establishments frequently sell other merchandise, such as tires, batteries, and other automobile parts, or perform minor repair work. Gasoline stations combined with other activities, such as grocery stores, convenience stores, or carwashes, are classified according to the primary activity.

5-YEAR TREND – ESTIMATED INDUSTRY SALES ($MILLIONS)

Year	Employee Size of Establishment									Total Industry Sales
	1-4 Emps.	5-9 Emps.	10-19 Emps.	20-49 Emps.	50-99 Emps.	100-249 Emps.	250-499 Emps.	500-999 Emps.	Unknown Emps.	
2016	184.4	476.4	797.4	550.2	51.7	28.3	11.2	0.1	2.0	2,101.8
2017	192.1	496.3	830.8	573.3	53.9	29.5	11.7	0.1	2.1	2,189.8
2018	200.9	519.1	868.9	599.6	56.3	30.9	12.2	0.1	2.2	2,290.4
2019	214.1	553.2	926.0	639.0	60.0	32.9	13.0	0.1	2.4	2,440.7
2019	229.9	593.9	994.1	686.0	64.5	35.3	14.0	0.1	2.5	2,620.3

	INDUSTRY: DEPARTMENT STORES INDUSTRY (NAICS 45211)
	PRODUCT LINE: AUTOMOTIVE TIRES & OTHER PARTS (Main Category)

NAICS 45211: Department Stores Industry . this industry comprises establishments known as department stores primarily engaged in retailing a wide range of the following new products with no one merchandise line predominating: apparel, furniture, appliances and home furnishings; and selected additional items, such as paint, hardware, toiletries, cosmetics, photographic equipment, jewelry, toys, and sporting goods. merchandise lines are normally arranged in separate departments.

5-YEAR TREND — ESTIMATED INDUSTRY SALES ($MILLIONS)

Year	Employee Size of Establishment									Total
	1-4 Emps.	5-9 Emps.	10-19 Emps.	20-49 Emps.	50-99 Emps.	100-249 Emps.	250-499 Emps.	500-999 Emps.	Unknown Emps.	Industry Sales
2016	0.0	0.1	0.1	11.4	206.1	661.7	273.9	39.6	1.7	1,194.5
2017	0.0	0.1	0.1	11.4	206.9	664.2	275.0	39.8	1.7	1,199.2
2018	0.0	0.1	0.1	11.5	208.9	670.8	277.7	40.2	1.7	1,211.0
2019	0.0	0.1	0.1	11.5	208.9	670.9	277.7	40.3	1.7	1,211.3
2019	0.1	0.1	0.1	11.6	211.0	677.5	280.5	40.7	1.7	1,223.3

	INDUSTRY: WAREHOUSE CLUBS & SUPERCENTERS (NAICS 45291)
	PRODUCT LINE: AUTOMOTIVE TIRES & OTHER PARTS (Main Category)

NAICS 45291: Warehouse Clubs and Superstores This industry comprises establishments known as warehouse clubs, superstores or supercenters primarily engaged in retailing a general line of groceries in combination with general lines of new merchandise, such as apparel, furniture, and appliances.

5-YEAR TREND — ESTIMATED INDUSTRY SALES ($MILLIONS)

Year	Employee Size of Establishment									Total
	1-4 Emps.	5-9 Emps.	10-19 Emps.	20-49 Emps.	50-99 Emps.	100-249 Emps.	250-499 Emps.	500-999 Emps.	Unknown Emps.	Industry Sales
2016	0.4	0.1	0.4	13.3	25.2	1,438.5	6,332.5	159.6	2.4	7,972.4
2017	0.4	0.1	0.4	13.6	25.9	1,478.1	6,507.1	164.0	2.5	8,192.1
2018	0.4	0.1	0.4	14.1	26.7	1,526.4	6,719.6	169.3	2.6	8,459.6
2019	0.5	0.1	0.4	15.2	28.8	1,642.8	7,231.8	182.2	2.8	9,104.5
2019	0.5	0.1	0.4	16.1	30.5	1,740.1	7,660.2	193.0	2.9	9,643.8

INDUSTRY: ELECTRONIC SHOPPING & MAIL-ORDER (NAICS 45411)
PRODUCT LINE: AUTOMOTIVE TIRES & OTHER PARTS (Main Category)

NAICS 45411: Electronic Shopping and Mail-Order Houses This industry comprises establishments primarily engaged in retailing all types of merchandise by means of mail or by electronic media, such as interactive television or computer. Included in this industry are establishments primarily engaged in retailing from catalogue showrooms of mail-order houses.

5-YEAR TREND – ESTIMATED INDUSTRY SALES ($MILLIONS)

Year	Employee Size of Establishment									Total
	1-4 Emps.	5-9 Emps.	10-19 Emps.	20-49 Emps.	50-99 Emps.	100-249 Emps.	250-499 Emps.	500-999 Emps.	Unknown Emps.	Industry Sales
2016	816.1	420.4	607.4	1,019.5	767.4	1,419.8	1,914.2	2,702.1	114.7	9,781.7
2017	863.2	444.7	642.5	1,078.4	811.7	1,501.8	2,024.6	2,858.0	121.3	10,346.2
2018	915.2	471.5	681.2	1,143.4	860.6	1,592.2	2,146.6	3,030.2	128.6	10,969.5
2019	1,025.7	528.4	763.4	1,281.4	964.5	1,784.4	2,405.7	3,334.4	144.2	12,232.0
2019	1,140.4	587.4	848.7	1,424.6	1,072.3	1,983.9	2,674.7	3,651.5	160.3	13,543.9

INDUSTRY: GAS STATIONS W/CONVENIENCE STORES (NAICS 44711)
PRODUCT LINE: AUTOMOTIVE TIRES & TUBES (Sub Category)

NAICS 44711: Gas Stations with Convenience Stores. this industry comprises establishments primarily engaged in selling gasoline and lubricating oils. These establishments frequently sell other merchandise, such as tires, batteries, and other automobile parts, or perform minor repair work. Gasoline stations combined with other activities, such as grocery stores, convenience stores, or carwashes, are classified according to the primary activity.

5-YEAR TREND – ESTIMATED INDUSTRY SALES ($MILLIONS)

Year	Employee Size of Establishment									Total
	1-4 Emps.	5-9 Emps.	10-19 Emps.	20-49 Emps.	50-99 Emps.	100-249 Emps.	250-499 Emps.	500-999 Emps.	Unknown Emps.	Industry Sales
2016	36.9	95.4	159.6	110.2	10.4	5.7	2.2	0.0	0.4	420.8
2017	38.5	99.4	166.3	114.8	10.8	5.9	2.3	0.0	0.4	438.4
2018	40.2	103.9	174.0	120.0	11.3	6.2	2.4	0.0	0.4	458.5
2019	42.9	110.8	185.4	127.9	12.0	6.6	2.6	0.0	0.5	488.6
2019	46.0	118.9	199.0	137.3	12.9	7.1	2.8	0.0	0.5	524.6

INDUSTRY: DEPARTMENT STORES INDUSTRY (NAICS 45211)
PRODUCT LINE: AUTOMOTIVE TIRES & TUBES (Sub Category)

NAICS 45211: Department Stores Industry . this industry comprises establishments known as department stores primarily engaged in retailing a wide range of the following new products with no one merchandise line predominating: apparel, furniture, appliances and home furnishings; and selected additional items, such as paint, hardware, toiletries, cosmetics, photographic equipment, jewelry, toys, and sporting goods. merchandise lines are normally arranged in separate departments.

5-YEAR TREND — ESTIMATED INDUSTRY SALES ($MILLIONS)

Year	Employee Size of Establishment									Total
	1-4 Emps.	5-9 Emps.	10-19 Emps.	20-49 Emps.	50-99 Emps.	100-249 Emps.	250-499 Emps.	500-999 Emps.	Unknown Emps.	Industry Sales
2016	0.0	0.0	0.0	1.3	24.4	78.3	32.4	4.7	0.2	141.4
2017	0.0	0.0	0.0	1.3	24.5	78.7	32.6	4.7	0.2	142.0
2018	0.0	0.0	0.0	1.4	24.7	79.4	32.9	4.8	0.2	143.4
2019	0.0	0.0	0.0	1.4	24.7	79.4	32.9	4.8	0.2	143.4
2019	0.0	0.0	0.0	1.4	25.0	80.2	33.2	4.8	0.2	144.9

INDUSTRY: WAREHOUSE CLUBS & SUPERCENTERS (NAICS 45291)
PRODUCT LINE: AUTOMOTIVE TIRES & TUBES (Sub Category)

NAICS 45291: Warehouse Clubs and Superstores This industry comprises establishments known as warehouse clubs, superstores or supercenters primarily engaged in retailing a general line of groceries in combination with general lines of new merchandise, such as apparel, furniture, and appliances.

5-YEAR TREND — ESTIMATED INDUSTRY SALES ($MILLIONS)

Year	Employee Size of Establishment									Total
	1-4 Emps.	5-9 Emps.	10-19 Emps.	20-49 Emps.	50-99 Emps.	100-249 Emps.	250-499 Emps.	500-999 Emps.	Unknown Emps.	Industry Sales
2016	0.2	0.0	0.2	5.6	10.5	602.1	2,650.4	66.8	1.0	3,336.7
2017	0.2	0.0	0.2	5.7	10.8	618.7	2,723.5	68.6	1.0	3,428.7
2018	0.2	0.1	0.2	5.9	11.2	638.9	2,812.4	70.9	1.1	3,540.7
2019	0.2	0.1	0.2	6.3	12.0	687.6	3,026.8	76.3	1.2	3,810.6
2019	0.2	0.1	0.2	6.7	12.8	728.3	3,206.1	80.8	1.2	4,036.3

INDUSTRY: DEPARTMENT STORES INDUSTRY (NAICS 45211)
PRODUCT LINE: AUTO PARTS & ACCESSORIES (Sub Category)

NAICS 45211: Department Stores Industry . this industry comprises
establishments known as department stores primarily engaged in retailing
a wide range of the following new products with no one merchandise line
predominating: apparel, furniture, appliances and home furnishings; and
selected additional items, such as paint, hardware, toiletries, cosmetics,
photographic equipment, jewelry, toys, and sporting goods. merchandise lines
are normally arranged in separate departments.

5-YEAR TREND – ESTIMATED INDUSTRY SALES ($MILLIONS)

| Year | Employee Size of Establishment | | | | | | | | | Total |
	1-4 Emps.	5-9 Emps.	10-19 Emps.	20-49 Emps.	50-99 Emps.	100-249 Emps.	250-499 Emps.	500-999 Emps.	Unknown Emps.	Industry Sales
2016	0.0	0.0	0.1	8.6	155.4	499.1	206.6	29.9	1.3	901.0
2017	0.0	0.0	0.1	8.6	156.0	501.0	207.4	30.0	1.3	904.5
2018	0.0	0.0	0.1	8.7	157.6	506.0	209.4	30.3	1.3	913.4
2019	0.0	0.0	0.1	8.7	157.6	506.0	209.5	30.4	1.3	913.6
2019	0.0	0.0	0.1	8.8	159.2	511.0	211.5	30.7	1.3	922.7

INDUSTRY: WAREHOUSE CLUB & SUPERCENTERS (NAICS 45291)
PRODUCT LINE: AUTO PARTS & ACCESSORIES (Sub Category)

NAICS 45291: Warehouse Clubs and Superstores This industry
comprises establishments known as warehouse clubs, superstores or
supercenters primarily engaged in retailing a general line of groceries
in combination with general lines of new merchandise, such as apparel,
furniture, and appliances.

5-YEAR TREND – ESTIMATED INDUSTRY SALES ($MILLIONS)

| Year | Employee Size of Establishment | | | | | | | | | Total |
	1-4 Emps.	5-9 Emps.	10-19 Emps.	20-49 Emps.	50-99 Emps.	100-249 Emps.	250-499 Emps.	500-999 Emps.	Unknown Emps.	Industry Sales
2016	0.2	0.0	0.2	5.8	11.0	626.3	2,757.1	69.5	1.1	3,471.1
2017	0.2	0.1	0.2	5.9	11.3	643.6	2,833.1	71.4	1.1	3,566.8
2018	0.2	0.1	0.2	6.1	11.6	664.6	2,925.7	73.7	1.1	3,683.3
2019	0.2	0.1	0.2	6.6	12.5	715.2	3,148.7	79.3	1.2	3,964.0
2019	0.2	0.1	0.2	7.0	13.3	757.6	3,335.2	84.0	1.3	4,198.9

INDUSTRY: GAS STATIONS W/CONVENIENCE STORES (NAICS 44711)
PRODUCT LINE: AUTO PARTS & ACCESSORIES (Sub Category)

NAICS 44711: Gas Stations with Convenience Stores. this industry
comprises establishments primarily engaged in selling gasoline and
lubricating oils. These establishments frequently sell other merchandise,
such as tires, batteries, and other automobile parts, or perform minor repair
work. Gasoline stations combined with other activities, such as grocery stores,
convenience stores, or carwashes, are classified according to the primary activity.

5-Year Trend — Estimated Industry Sales ($Millions)

Year	Employee Size of Establishment									Total
	1-4 Emps.	5-9 Emps.	10-19 Emps.	20-49 Emps.	50-99 Emps.	100-249 Emps.	250-499 Emps.	500-999 Emps.	Unknown Emps.	Industry Sales
2016	77.0	198.9	332.9	229.7	21.6	11.8	4.7	0.0	0.8	877.4
2017	80.2	207.2	346.8	239.3	22.5	12.3	4.9	0.0	0.9	914.1
2018	83.9	216.7	362.7	250.3	23.5	12.9	5.1	0.0	0.9	956.1
2019	89.4	230.9	386.5	266.7	25.1	13.7	5.4	0.0	1.0	1,018.8
2019	96.0	247.9	415.0	286.4	26.9	14.7	5.8	0.0	1.1	1,093.8

INDUSTRY: GAS STATIONS W/CONVENIENCE STORES (NAICS 44711)
PRODUCT LINE: BATTERIES (Sub Category)

NAICS 44711: Gas Stations with Convenience Stores. this industry
comprises establishments primarily engaged in selling gasoline and
lubricating oils. These establishments frequently sell other merchandise,
such as tires, batteries, and other automobile parts, or perform minor repair
work. Gasoline stations combined with other activities, such as grocery stores,
convenience stores, or carwashes, are classified according to the primary activity.

5-Year Trend — Estimated Industry Sales ($Millions)

Year	Employee Size of Establishment									Total
	1-4 Emps.	5-9 Emps.	10-19 Emps.	20-49 Emps.	50-99 Emps.	100-249 Emps.	250-499 Emps.	500-999 Emps.	Unknown Emps.	Industry Sales
2016	8.1	20.9	35.0	24.2	2.3	1.2	0.5	0.0	0.1	92.4
2017	8.4	21.8	36.5	25.2	2.4	1.3	0.5	0.0	0.1	96.2
2018	8.8	22.8	38.2	26.3	2.5	1.4	0.5	0.0	0.1	100.6
2019	9.4	24.3	40.7	28.1	2.6	1.4	0.6	0.0	0.1	107.2
2019	10.1	26.1	43.7	30.1	2.8	1.6	0.6	0.0	0.1	115.1

INDUSTRY: DEPARTMENT STORES INDUSTRY (NAICS 45211)
PRODUCT LINE: BATTERIES (Sub Category)

NAICS 45211: Department Stores Industry . this industry comprises establishments known as department stores primarily engaged in retailing a wide range of the following new products with no one merchandise line predominating: apparel, furniture, appliances and home furnishings; and selected additional items, such as paint, hardware, toiletries, cosmetics, photographic equipment, jewelry, toys, and sporting goods. merchandise lines are normally arranged in separate departments.

5-YEAR TREND – ESTIMATED INDUSTRY SALES ($MILLIONS)

| Year | Employee Size of Establishment | | | | | | | | | Total |
	1-4 Emps.	5-9 Emps.	10-19 Emps.	20-49 Emps.	50-99 Emps.	100-249 Emps.	250-499 Emps.	500-999 Emps.	Unknown Emps.	Industry Sales
2016	0.0	0.0	0.0	1.4	26.2	84.2	34.9	5.0	0.2	152.1
2017	0.0	0.0	0.0	1.5	26.3	84.6	35.0	5.1	0.2	152.6
2018	0.0	0.0	0.0	1.5	26.6	85.4	35.3	5.1	0.2	154.2
2019	0.0	0.0	0.0	1.5	26.6	85.4	35.4	5.1	0.2	154.2
2019	0.0	0.0	0.0	1.5	26.9	86.2	35.7	5.2	0.2	155.7

INDUSTRY: WAREHOUSE CLUBS & SUPERCENTERS (NAICS 45291)
PRODUCT LINE: BATTERIES (Sub Category)

NAICS 45291: Warehouse Clubs and Superstores This industry comprises establishments known as warehouse clubs, superstores or supercenters primarily engaged in retailing a general line of groceries in combination with general lines of new merchandise, such as apparel, furniture, and appliances.

5-YEAR TREND – ESTIMATED INDUSTRY SALES ($MILLIONS)

| Year | Employee Size of Establishment | | | | | | | | | Total |
	1-4 Emps.	5-9 Emps.	10-19 Emps.	20-49 Emps.	50-99 Emps.	100-249 Emps.	250-499 Emps.	500-999 Emps.	Unknown Emps.	Industry Sales
2016	0.1	0.0	0.1	1.9	3.7	210.1	925.0	23.3	0.4	1,164.5
2017	0.1	0.0	0.1	2.0	3.8	215.9	950.5	24.0	0.4	1,196.6
2018	0.1	0.0	0.1	2.1	3.9	223.0	981.5	24.7	0.4	1,235.7
2019	0.1	0.0	0.1	2.2	4.2	240.0	1,056.3	26.6	0.4	1,329.9
2019	0.1	0.0	0.1	2.3	4.5	254.2	1,118.9	28.2	0.4	1,408.7

INDUSTRY: GAS STATIONS W/CONVENIENCE STORES (NAICS 44711)
PRODUCT LINE: AUTO ACCESSORIES (Sub Category)

NAICS 44711: Gas Stations with Convenience Stores. this industry
comprises establishments primarily engaged in selling gasoline and
lubricating oils. These establishments frequently sell other merchandise,
such as tires, batteries, and other automobile parts, or perform minor repair
work. Gasoline stations combined with other activities, such as grocery stores,
convenience stores, or carwashes, are classified according to the primary activity.

5-Year Trend — Estimated Industry Sales ($Millions)

Year	Employee Size of Establishment									Total
	1-4 Emps.	5-9 Emps.	10-19 Emps.	20-49 Emps.	50-99 Emps.	100-249 Emps.	250-499 Emps.	500-999 Emps.	Unknown Emps.	Industry Sales
2016	15.2	39.4	65.9	45.5	4.3	2.3	0.9	0.0	0.2	173.6
2017	15.9	41.0	68.6	47.4	4.5	2.4	1.0	0.0	0.2	180.9
2018	16.6	42.9	71.8	49.5	4.7	2.5	1.0	0.0	0.2	189.2
2019	17.7	45.7	76.5	52.8	5.0	2.7	1.1	0.0	0.2	201.6
2019	19.0	49.1	82.1	56.7	5.3	2.9	1.2	0.0	0.2	216.5

INDUSTRY: GAS STATIONS W/CONVENIENCE STORES (NAICS 44711)
PRODUCT LINE: OTHER AUTO SUPPLIES (Sub Category)

NAICS 44711: Gas Stations with Convenience Stores. this industry
comprises establishments primarily engaged in selling gasoline and
lubricating oils. These establishments frequently sell other merchandise,
such as tires, batteries, and other automobile parts, or perform minor repair
work. Gasoline stations combined with other activities, such as grocery stores,
convenience stores, or carwashes, are classified according to the primary activity.

5-Year Trend — Estimated Industry Sales ($Millions)

Year	Employee Size of Establishment									Total
	1-4 Emps.	5-9 Emps.	10-19 Emps.	20-49 Emps.	50-99 Emps.	100-249 Emps.	250-499 Emps.	500-999 Emps.	Unknown Emps.	Industry Sales
2016	47.2	121.9	204.0	140.7	13.2	7.2	2.9	0.0	0.5	537.6
2017	49.1	127.0	212.5	146.6	13.8	7.5	3.0	0.0	0.5	560.1
2018	51.4	132.8	222.3	153.4	14.4	7.9	3.1	0.0	0.6	585.9
2019	54.8	141.5	236.9	163.4	15.4	8.4	3.3	0.0	0.6	624.3
2019	58.8	151.9	254.3	175.5	16.5	9.0	3.6	0.0	0.6	670.3

INDUSTRY: HOME CENTERS INDUSTRY (NAICS 44411)
PRODUCT LINE: PETS & PET FOODS & SUPPLIES (Main Category)

NAICS 44411: Home Centers. This industry comprises establishments
known as home centers primarily engaged in retailing a general line of
new home repair and improvement materials and supplies, such as
lumber, plumbing goods, electrical goods, tools, housewares, hardware,
and lawn and garden supplies, with no one merchandise line predominating.
The merchandise lines are normally arranged in separate departments.

5-YEAR TREND – ESTIMATED INDUSTRY SALES ($MILLIONS)

Year	Employee Size of Establishment									Total
	1-4 Emps.	5-9 Emps.	10-19 Emps.	20-49 Emps.	50-99 Emps.	100-249 Emps.	250-499 Emps.	500-999 Emps.	Unknown Emps.	Industry Sales
2016	0.8	1.5	3.9	7.9	6.0	397.3	31.0	0.6	0.3	449.5
2017	0.8	1.6	4.0	8.1	6.2	406.9	31.8	0.7	0.3	460.3
2018	0.8	1.6	4.1	8.4	6.4	418.8	32.7	0.7	0.3	473.7
2019	0.9	1.7	4.2	8.7	6.6	434.3	33.9	0.7	0.3	491.3
2019	0.9	1.8	4.4	9.1	6.9	454.4	35.5	0.7	0.3	514.0

INDUSTRY: HARDWARE STORES (NAICS 44413)
PRODUCT LINE: PETS & PET FOODS & SUPPLIES (Main Category)

NAICS 44413: Hardware Stores. Establishments primarily engaged
in the retail sale of a number of basic hardware lines, such as tools,
builders' hardware, paint and glass, housewares and household appliances,
and cutlery.

5-YEAR TREND – ESTIMATED INDUSTRY SALES ($MILLIONS)

Year	Employee Size of Establishment									Total
	1-4 Emps.	5-9 Emps.	10-19 Emps.	20-49 Emps.	50-99 Emps.	100-249 Emps.	250-499 Emps.	500-999 Emps.	Unknown Emps.	Industry Sales
2016	9.6	16.2	32.6	46.7	9.3	3.0	0.5	0.0	0.8	118.8
2017	9.7	16.4	33.0	47.1	9.4	3.1	0.5	0.0	0.8	119.9
2018	9.8	16.6	33.5	47.9	9.5	3.1	0.6	0.0	0.9	121.8
2019	10.2	17.3	34.8	49.8	9.9	3.2	0.6	0.0	0.9	126.7
2019	10.7	18.2	36.5	52.2	10.4	3.4	0.6	0.0	0.9	132.9

	INDUSTRY: SUPERMARKETS INDUSTRY (NAICS 44511)
	PRODUCT LINE: PETS & PET FOODS & SUPPLIES (Main Category)

NAICS 44511: Grocery Stores Industry. this industry comprises establishments generally known as supermarkets and grocery stores primarily engaged in retailing a general line of food, such as canned and frozen foods; fresh fruits and vegetables; and fresh and prepared meats, fish, and poultry. Included in this industry are delicatessen-type establishments primarily engaged in retailing a general line of food.

5-Year Trend – Estimated Industry Sales ($Millions)

Year	Employee Size of Establishment									Total
	1-4 Emps.	5-9 Emps.	10-19 Emps.	20-49 Emps.	50-99 Emps.	100-249 Emps.	250-499 Emps.	500-999 Emps.	Unknown Emps.	Industry Sales
2016	75.4	54.4	140.5	462.9	1,097.0	2,727.1	851.7	101.9	14.2	5,525.0
2017	74.9	54.1	139.6	459.9	1,090.0	2,709.8	846.3	101.3	14.1	5,490.0
2018	74.9	54.1	139.5	459.8	1,089.6	2,708.9	846.0	101.2	14.1	5,488.1
2019	76.4	55.2	142.4	469.2	1,112.1	2,764.7	863.5	103.2	14.3	5,601.1
2019	78.8	56.9	146.8	483.7	1,146.5	2,850.2	890.1	106.4	14.8	5,774.2

	INDUSTRY: BEER, WINE & LIQUOR STORES (NAICS 44531)
	PRODUCT LINE: PETS & PET FOODS & SUPPLIES (Main Category)

NAICS 44531: Beer & Wine & Liquor Stores. Establishments primarily engaged in the retail sale of packaged alcoholic beverages, such as ale, beer, wine, and liquor, for consumption off the premises. Stores selling prepared drinks for consumption on the premises are classified in SIC 5813.

5-Year Trend – Estimated Industry Sales ($Millions)

Year	Employee Size of Establishment									Total
	1-4 Emps.	5-9 Emps.	10-19 Emps.	20-49 Emps.	50-99 Emps.	100-249 Emps.	250-499 Emps.	500-999 Emps.	Unknown Emps.	Industry Sales
2016	2.5	2.5	2.1	1.6	0.2	0.1	0.0	0.1	0.1	9.2
2017	2.5	2.6	2.2	1.6	0.2	0.1	0.0	0.1	0.1	9.5
2018	2.6	2.6	2.2	1.6	0.2	0.1	0.0	0.1	0.1	9.7
2019	2.8	2.8	2.4	1.7	0.2	0.1	0.0	0.1	0.2	10.3
2019	2.9	3.0	2.5	1.9	0.3	0.2	0.0	0.1	0.2	11.0

INDUSTRY: PHARMACIES & DRUG STORES (NAICS 44611)
PRODUCT LINE: PETS & PET FOODS & SUPPLIES (Main Category)

NAICS 44611 Pharmacies and Drug Stores – this industry comprises establishments known as pharmacies and drug stores engaged in retailing prescription or nonprescription drugs and medicines.

5-YEAR TREND – ESTIMATED INDUSTRY SALES ($MILLIONS)

Year	Employee Size of Establishment									Total Industry Sales
	1-4 Emps.	5-9 Emps.	10-19 Emps.	20-49 Emps.	50-99 Emps.	100-249 Emps.	250-499 Emps.	500-999 Emps.	Unknown Emps.	
2016	4.6	11.4	46.0	135.2	13.7	5.5	2.1	0.7	0.4	219.5
2017	4.7	11.7	47.5	139.4	14.1	5.6	2.2	0.7	0.4	226.4
2018	4.9	12.2	49.2	144.5	14.6	5.9	2.2	0.7	0.4	234.6
2019	5.2	12.9	52.1	153.0	15.5	6.2	2.4	0.8	0.4	248.4
2019	5.6	13.8	55.6	163.4	16.5	6.6	2.5	0.8	0.4	265.3

INDUSTRY: GAS STATIONS W/CONVENIENCE STORES (NAICS 44711)
PRODUCT LINE: PETS & PET FOODS & SUPPLIES (Main Category)

NAICS 44711: Gas Stations with Convenience Stores. this industry comprises establishments primarily engaged in selling gasoline and lubricating oils. These establishments frequently sell other merchandise, such as tires, batteries, and other automobile parts, or perform minor repair work. Gasoline stations combined with other activities, such as grocery stores, convenience stores, or carwashes, are classified according to the primary activity.

5-YEAR TREND – ESTIMATED INDUSTRY SALES ($MILLIONS)

Year	Employee Size of Establishment									Total Industry Sales
	1-4 Emps.	5-9 Emps.	10-19 Emps.	20-49 Emps.	50-99 Emps.	100-249 Emps.	250-499 Emps.	500-999 Emps.	Unknown Emps.	
2016	25.4	65.7	109.9	75.8	7.1	3.9	1.5	0.0	0.3	289.7
2017	26.5	68.4	114.5	79.0	7.4	4.1	1.6	0.0	0.3	301.9
2018	27.7	71.6	119.8	82.7	7.8	4.3	1.7	0.0	0.3	315.7
2019	29.5	76.3	127.6	88.1	8.3	4.5	1.8	0.0	0.3	336.5
2019	31.7	81.9	137.0	94.6	8.9	4.9	1.9	0.0	0.3	361.2

INDUSTRY: DEPARTMENT STORES INDUSTRY (NAICS 45211)
PRODUCT LINE: PETS & PET FOODS & SUPPLIES (Main Category)

NAICS 45211: Department Stores Industry . this industry comprises establishments known as department stores primarily engaged in retailing a wide range of the following new products with no one merchandise line predominating: apparel, furniture, appliances and home furnishings; and selected additional items, such as paint, hardware, toiletries, cosmetics, photographic equipment, jewelry, toys, and sporting goods. merchandise lines are normally arranged in separate departments.

5-YEAR TREND – ESTIMATED INDUSTRY SALES ($MILLIONS)

Year	Employee Size of Establishment									Total
	1-4 Emps.	5-9 Emps.	10-19 Emps.	20-49 Emps.	50-99 Emps.	100-249 Emps.	250-499 Emps.	500-999 Emps.	Unknown Emps.	Industry Sales
2016	0.1	0.1	0.2	12.8	231.9	744.7	308.3	44.6	1.9	1,344.4
2017	0.1	0.1	0.2	12.8	232.8	747.6	309.5	44.8	1.9	1,349.7
2018	0.1	0.1	0.2	13.0	235.1	755.0	312.5	45.2	1.9	1,363.0
2019	0.1	0.1	0.2	13.0	235.1	755.1	312.6	45.3	1.9	1,363.3
2019	0.1	0.1	0.2	13.1	237.5	762.6	315.7	45.9	1.9	1,376.8

INDUSTRY: WAREHOUSE CLUBS & SUPERCENTERS (NAICS 45291)
PRODUCT LINE: PETS & PET FOODS & SUPPLIES (Main Category)

NAICS 45291: Warehouse Clubs and Superstores This industry comprises establishments known as warehouse clubs, superstores or supercenters primarily engaged in retailing a general line of groceries in combination with general lines of new merchandise, such as apparel, furniture, and appliances.

5-YEAR TREND – ESTIMATED INDUSTRY SALES ($MILLIONS)

Year	Employee Size of Establishment									Total
	1-4 Emps.	5-9 Emps.	10-19 Emps.	20-49 Emps.	50-99 Emps.	100-249 Emps.	250-499 Emps.	500-999 Emps.	Unknown Emps.	Industry Sales
2016	0.4	0.1	0.4	13.4	25.5	1,454.6	6,403.4	161.4	2.4	8,061.6
2017	0.4	0.1	0.4	13.8	26.2	1,494.7	6,579.9	165.8	2.5	8,283.8
2018	0.5	0.1	0.4	14.3	27.0	1,543.5	6,794.8	171.2	2.6	8,554.3
2019	0.5	0.1	0.4	15.3	29.1	1,661.1	7,312.7	184.3	2.8	9,206.4
2019	0.5	0.1	0.4	16.2	30.8	1,759.5	7,745.9	195.2	3.0	9,751.8

INDUSTRY: ELECTRONIC SHOPPING & MAIL-ORDER (NAICS 45411)
PRODUCT LINE: PETS & PET FOODS & SUPPLIES (Main Category)

NAICS 45411: Electronic Shopping and Mail-Order Houses This industry comprises establishments primarily engaged in retailing all types of merchandise by means of mail or by electronic media, such as interactive television or computer. Included in this industry are establishments primarily engaged in retailing from catalogue showrooms of mail-order houses.

5-YEAR TREND – ESTIMATED INDUSTRY SALES ($MILLIONS)

Year	Employee Size of Establishment									Total
	1-4 Emps.	5-9 Emps.	10-19 Emps.	20-49 Emps.	50-99 Emps.	100-249 Emps.	250-499 Emps.	500-999 Emps.	Unknown Emps.	Industry Sales
2016	127.9	65.9	95.2	159.8	120.3	222.5	300.0	423.5	18.0	1,533.0
2017	135.3	69.7	100.7	169.0	127.2	235.4	317.3	447.9	19.0	1,621.4
2018	143.4	73.9	106.8	179.2	134.9	249.5	336.4	474.9	20.2	1,719.1
2019	160.7	82.8	119.6	200.8	151.2	279.7	377.0	522.6	22.6	1,917.0
2019	178.7	92.1	133.0	223.3	168.1	310.9	419.2	572.3	25.1	2,122.6

INDUSTRY: BOOK STORES INDUSTRY (NAICS 451211)
PRODUCT LINE: PETS & PET FOODS & SUPPLIES (Main Category)

NAICS 451211: Book Stores. this industry comprises establishments primarily engaged in the retail sale of new books and magazines. Establishments primarily engaged in the retail sale of used books are classified in 5932.

5-YEAR TREND – ESTIMATED INDUSTRY SALES ($MILLIONS)

Year	Employee Size of Establishment									Total
	1-4 Emps.	5-9 Emps.	10-19 Emps.	20-49 Emps.	50-99 Emps.	100-249 Emps.	250-499 Emps.	500-999 Emps.	Unknown Emps.	Industry Sales
2016	0.0	0.1	0.1	0.3	0.1	0.1	0.0	0.0	0.0	0.8
2017	0.0	0.1	0.1	0.3	0.1	0.1	0.0	0.0	0.0	0.8
2018	0.0	0.1	0.1	0.3	0.1	0.1	0.0	0.0	0.0	0.8
2019	0.0	0.1	0.1	0.3	0.1	0.1	0.0	0.0	0.0	0.9
2019	0.0	0.1	0.1	0.4	0.2	0.1	0.0	0.0	0.0	0.9

INDUSTRY: SUPERMARKETS INDUSTRY (NAICS 44511)
PRODUCT LINE: STATIONERY PRODUCTS (Sub Category)

NAICS 44511: Grocery Stores Industry. this industry comprises establishments generally known as supermarkets and grocery stores primarily engaged in retailing a general line of food, such as canned and frozen foods; fresh fruits and vegetables; and fresh and prepared meats, fish, and poultry. Included in this industry are delicatessen-type establishments primarily engaged in retailing a general line of food.

5-YEAR TREND – ESTIMATED INDUSTRY SALES ($MILLIONS)

Year	Employee Size of Establishment									Total
	1-4 Emps.	5-9 Emps.	10-19 Emps.	20-49 Emps.	50-99 Emps.	100-249 Emps.	250-499 Emps.	500-999 Emps.	Unknown Emps.	Industry Sales
2016	3.7	2.7	6.8	22.5	53.4	132.8	41.5	5.0	0.7	269.1
2017	3.6	2.6	6.8	22.4	53.1	132.0	41.2	4.9	0.7	267.4
2018	3.6	2.6	6.8	22.4	53.1	131.9	41.2	4.9	0.7	267.3
2019	3.7	2.7	6.9	22.9	54.2	134.6	42.1	5.0	0.7	272.8
2019	3.8	2.8	7.1	23.6	55.8	138.8	43.4	5.2	0.7	281.2

INDUSTRY: PHARMACIES & DRUG STORES (NAICS 44611)
PRODUCT LINE: STATIONERY PRODUCTS (Sub Category)

NAICS 44611 Pharmacies and Drug Stores – this industry comprises establishments known as pharmacies and drug stores engaged in retailing prescription or nonprescription drugs and medicines.

5-YEAR TREND – ESTIMATED INDUSTRY SALES ($MILLIONS)

Year	Employee Size of Establishment									Total
	1-4 Emps.	5-9 Emps.	10-19 Emps.	20-49 Emps.	50-99 Emps.	100-249 Emps.	250-499 Emps.	500-999 Emps.	Unknown Emps.	Industry Sales
2016	7.1	17.5	71.0	208.5	21.1	8.4	3.2	1.1	0.5	338.5
2017	7.3	18.1	73.2	215.0	21.7	8.7	3.3	1.1	0.6	349.1
2018	7.6	18.7	75.9	222.8	22.5	9.0	3.4	1.2	0.6	361.7
2019	8.0	19.9	80.4	236.0	23.9	9.6	3.7	1.2	0.6	383.1
2019	8.6	21.2	85.8	252.0	25.5	10.2	3.9	1.3	0.7	409.1

INDUSTRY: DEPARTMENT STORES INDUSTRY (NAICS 45211)
PRODUCT LINE: STATIONERY PRODUCTS (Sub Category)

NAICS 45211: Department Stores Industry . this industry comprises establishments known as department stores primarily engaged in retailing a wide range of the following new products with no one merchandise line predominating: apparel, furniture, appliances and home furnishings; and selected additional items, such as paint, hardware, toiletries, cosmetics, photographic equipment, jewelry, toys, and sporting goods. merchandise lines are normally arranged in separate departments.

5-YEAR TREND — ESTIMATED INDUSTRY SALES ($MILLIONS)

Year	Employee Size of Establishment									Total
	1-4 Emps.	5-9 Emps.	10-19 Emps.	20-49 Emps.	50-99 Emps.	100-249 Emps.	250-499 Emps.	500-999 Emps.	Unknown Emps.	Industry Sales
2016	0.0	0.0	0.0	3.5	63.2	203.1	84.1	12.2	0.5	366.6
2017	0.0	0.0	0.0	3.5	63.5	203.9	84.4	12.2	0.5	368.0
2018	0.0	0.0	0.0	3.5	64.1	205.9	85.2	12.3	0.5	371.7
2019	0.0	0.0	0.0	3.5	64.1	205.9	85.2	12.4	0.5	371.7
2019	0.0	0.0	0.0	3.6	64.8	207.9	86.1	12.5	0.5	375.4

INDUSTRY: WAREHOUSE CLUBS & SUPERCENTERS (NAICS 45291)
PRODUCT LINE: STATIONERY PRODUCTS (Sub Category)

NAICS 45291: Warehouse Clubs and Superstores This industry comprises establishments known as warehouse clubs, superstores or supercenters primarily engaged in retailing a general line of groceries in combination with general lines of new merchandise, such as apparel, furniture, and appliances.

5-YEAR TREND — ESTIMATED INDUSTRY SALES ($MILLIONS)

Year	Employee Size of Establishment									Total
	1-4 Emps.	5-9 Emps.	10-19 Emps.	20-49 Emps.	50-99 Emps.	100-249 Emps.	250-499 Emps.	500-999 Emps.	Unknown Emps.	Industry Sales
2016	0.1	0.0	0.1	3.0	5.8	328.6	1,446.7	36.5	0.6	1,821.3
2017	0.1	0.0	0.1	3.1	5.9	337.7	1,486.5	37.5	0.6	1,871.5
2018	0.1	0.0	0.1	3.2	6.1	348.7	1,535.1	38.7	0.6	1,932.6
2019	0.1	0.0	0.1	3.5	6.6	375.3	1,652.1	41.6	0.6	2,079.9
2019	0.1	0.0	0.1	3.7	7.0	397.5	1,750.0	44.1	0.7	2,203.1

INDUSTRY: OFFICE SUPPLIES & STATIONERY STORES (NAICS 45321)
PRODUCT LINE: STATIONERY PRODUCTS (Sub Category)

NAICS 45321: Office Supplies and Stationery Stores . this industry comprises establishments primarily engaged in one or more of the following: (1) retailing new stationery, school supplies, and office supplies; (2) selling a combination of new office equipment, furniture, and supplies; and (3) selling new office equipment, furniture, and supplies in combination with selling new computers.

5-YEAR TREND — ESTIMATED INDUSTRY SALES ($MILLIONS)

Year	Employee Size of Establishment									Total Industry Sales
	1-4 Emps.	5-9 Emps.	10-19 Emps.	20-49 Emps.	50-99 Emps.	100-249 Emps.	250-499 Emps.	500-999 Emps.	Unknown Emps.	
2016	70.5	56.6	362.9	908.2	19.0	12.8	0.1	0.6	17.4	1,447.9
2017	69.9	56.1	359.9	900.7	18.8	12.7	0.1	0.6	17.2	1,436.0
2018	69.8	56.0	359.0	898.6	18.8	12.6	0.1	0.6	17.2	1,432.6
2019	67.5	54.2	347.4	869.4	18.1	12.2	0.1	0.6	16.6	1,386.2
2019	66.0	53.0	339.5	849.7	17.7	12.0	0.1	0.6	16.2	1,354.8

INDUSTRY: ELECTRONIC SHOPPING & MAIL-ORDER (NAICS 45411)
PRODUCT LINE: STATIONERY PRODUCTS (Sub Category)

NAICS 45411: Electronic Shopping and Mail-Order Houses This industry comprises establishments primarily engaged in retailing all types of merchandise by means of mail or by electronic media, such as interactive television or computer. Included in this industry are establishments primarily engaged in retailing from catalogue showrooms of mail-order houses.

5-YEAR TREND — ESTIMATED INDUSTRY SALES ($MILLIONS)

Year	Employee Size of Establishment									Total Industry Sales
	1-4 Emps.	5-9 Emps.	10-19 Emps.	20-49 Emps.	50-99 Emps.	100-249 Emps.	250-499 Emps.	500-999 Emps.	Unknown Emps.	
2016	321.8	165.8	239.5	402.0	302.6	559.9	754.8	1,065.5	45.2	3,857.1
2017	340.4	175.3	253.3	425.2	320.1	592.2	798.4	1,127.0	47.8	4,079.7
2018	360.9	185.9	268.6	450.8	339.4	627.9	846.5	1,194.9	50.7	4,325.5
2019	404.4	208.3	301.0	505.3	380.3	703.6	948.6	1,314.8	56.8	4,823.3
2019	449.7	231.6	334.7	561.8	422.8	782.3	1,054.7	1,439.9	63.2	5,340.6

| INDUSTRY: BOOK STORES INDUSTRY (NAICS 451211) |
| PRODUCT LINE: STATIONERY PRODUCTS (Sub Category) |

NAICS 451211: Book Stores. this industry comprises establishments primarily engaged in the retail sale of new books and magazines. Establishments primarily engaged in the retail sale of used books are classified in 5932.

5-YEAR TREND – ESTIMATED INDUSTRY SALES ($MILLIONS)

| Year | Employee Size of Establishment | | | | | | | | | Total |
	1-4 Emps.	5-9 Emps.	10-19 Emps.	20-49 Emps.	50-99 Emps.	100-249 Emps.	250-499 Emps.	500-999 Emps.	Unknown Emps.	Industry Sales
2016	2.9	4.4	8.7	23.2	10.1	4.7	1.1	2.8	1.5	59.4
2017	3.0	4.6	9.1	24.3	10.6	4.9	1.2	2.9	1.5	62.1
2018	3.2	4.8	9.6	25.5	11.1	5.1	1.3	3.0	1.6	65.2
2019	3.3	5.0	10.0	26.5	11.5	5.3	1.3	3.2	1.7	67.7
2019	3.4	5.2	10.4	27.7	12.1	5.5	1.4	3.3	1.7	70.8

| INDUSTRY: SUPERMARKETS INDUSTRY (NAICS 44511) |
| PRODUCT LINE: OFFICE PAPER (Sub Category) |

NAICS 44511: Grocery Stores Industry. this industry comprises establishments generally known as supermarkets and grocery stores primarily engaged in retailing a general line of food, such as canned and frozen foods; fresh fruits and vegetables; and fresh and prepared meats, fish, and poultry. Included in this industry are delicatessen-type establishments primarily engaged in retailing a general line of food.

5-YEAR TREND – ESTIMATED INDUSTRY SALES ($MILLIONS)

| Year | Employee Size of Establishment | | | | | | | | | Total |
	1-4 Emps.	5-9 Emps.	10-19 Emps.	20-49 Emps.	50-99 Emps.	100-249 Emps.	250-499 Emps.	500-999 Emps.	Unknown Emps.	Industry Sales
2016	0.8	0.6	1.6	5.2	12.3	30.5	9.5	1.1	0.2	61.7
2017	0.8	0.6	1.6	5.1	12.2	30.3	9.5	1.1	0.2	61.3
2018	0.8	0.6	1.6	5.1	12.2	30.3	9.4	1.1	0.2	61.3
2019	0.9	0.6	1.6	5.2	12.4	30.9	9.6	1.2	0.2	62.6
2019	0.9	0.6	1.6	5.4	12.8	31.8	9.9	1.2	0.2	64.5

INDUSTRY: PHARMACIES & DRUG STORES (NAICS 44611)
PRODUCT LINE: OFFICE PAPER (Sub Category)

NAICS 44611 Pharmacies and Drug Stores – this industry comprises
establishments known as pharmacies and drug stores engaged in retailing
prescription or nonprescription drugs and medicines.

5-YEAR TREND – ESTIMATED INDUSTRY SALES ($MILLIONS)

Year	Employee Size of Establishment									Total Industry Sales
	1-4 Emps.	5-9 Emps.	10-19 Emps.	20-49 Emps.	50-99 Emps.	100-249 Emps.	250-499 Emps.	500-999 Emps.	Unknown Emps.	
2016	2.2	5.4	21.8	64.1	6.5	2.6	1.0	0.3	0.2	104.1
2017	2.2	5.6	22.5	66.1	6.7	2.7	1.0	0.3	0.2	107.4
2018	2.3	5.8	23.3	68.5	6.9	2.8	1.1	0.4	0.2	111.3
2019	2.5	6.1	24.7	72.6	7.3	2.9	1.1	0.4	0.2	117.8
2019	2.6	6.5	26.4	77.5	7.8	3.1	1.2	0.4	0.2	125.8

INDUSTRY: DEPARTMENT STORES INDUSTRY (NAICS 45211)
PRODUCT LINE: OFFICE PAPER (Sub Category)

NAICS 45211: Department Stores Industry . this industry comprises
establishments known as department stores primarily engaged in retailing
a wide range of the following new products with no one merchandise line
predominating: apparel, furniture, appliances and home furnishings; and
selected additional items, such as paint, hardware, toiletries, cosmetics,
photographic equipment, jewelry, toys, and sporting goods. merchandise lines
are normally arranged in separate departments.

5-YEAR TREND – ESTIMATED INDUSTRY SALES ($MILLIONS)

Year	Employee Size of Establishment									Total Industry Sales
	1-4 Emps.	5-9 Emps.	10-19 Emps.	20-49 Emps.	50-99 Emps.	100-249 Emps.	250-499 Emps.	500-999 Emps.	Unknown Emps.	
2016	0.0	0.0	0.0	3.1	55.6	178.6	73.9	10.7	0.5	322.4
2017	0.0	0.0	0.0	3.1	55.8	179.3	74.2	10.7	0.5	323.6
2018	0.0	0.0	0.0	3.1	56.4	181.0	74.9	10.8	0.5	326.8
2019	0.0	0.0	0.0	3.1	56.4	181.1	74.9	10.9	0.5	326.9
2019	0.0	0.0	0.0	3.1	56.9	182.8	75.7	11.0	0.5	330.1

INDUSTRY: WAREHOUSE CLUBS & SUPERCENTERS (NAICS 45291)
PRODUCT LINE: OFFICE PAPER (Sub Category)

NAICS 45291: Warehouse Clubs and Superstores This industry comprises establishments known as warehouse clubs, superstores or supercenters primarily engaged in retailing a general line of groceries in combination with general lines of new merchandise, such as apparel, furniture, and appliances.

5-YEAR TREND – ESTIMATED INDUSTRY SALES ($MILLIONS)

Year	Employee Size of Establishment									Total Industry Sales
	1-4 Emps.	5-9 Emps.	10-19 Emps.	20-49 Emps.	50-99 Emps.	100-249 Emps.	250-499 Emps.	500-999 Emps.	Unknown Emps.	
2016	0.1	0.0	0.1	2.9	5.5	316.0	1,391.3	35.1	0.5	1,751.6
2017	0.1	0.0	0.1	3.0	5.7	324.8	1,429.6	36.0	0.5	1,799.8
2018	0.1	0.0	0.1	3.1	5.9	335.4	1,476.3	37.2	0.6	1,858.6
2019	0.1	0.0	0.1	3.3	6.3	360.9	1,588.9	40.0	0.6	2,000.3
2019	0.1	0.0	0.1	3.5	6.7	382.3	1,683.0	42.4	0.6	2,118.8

INDUSTRY: OFFICE SUPPLIES & STATIONERY STORES (NAICS 45321)
PRODUCT LINE: OFFICE PAPER (Sub Category)

NAICS 45321: Office Supplies and Stationery Stores . this industry comprises establishments primarily engaged in one or more of the following: (1) retailing new stationery, school supplies, and office supplies; (2) selling a combination of new office equipment, furniture, and supplies; and (3) selling new office equipment, furniture, and supplies in combination with selling new computers.

5-YEAR TREND – ESTIMATED INDUSTRY SALES ($MILLIONS)

Year	Employee Size of Establishment									Total Industry Sales
	1-4 Emps.	5-9 Emps.	10-19 Emps.	20-49 Emps.	50-99 Emps.	100-249 Emps.	250-499 Emps.	500-999 Emps.	Unknown Emps.	
2016	136.9	109.9	704.6	1,763.5	36.8	24.8	0.2	1.1	33.7	2,811.6
2017	135.8	109.0	698.8	1,748.9	36.5	24.6	0.2	1.1	33.4	2,788.3
2018	135.5	108.7	697.2	1,744.8	36.4	24.5	0.2	1.1	33.4	2,781.9
2019	131.1	105.2	674.5	1,688.2	35.2	23.7	0.2	1.1	32.3	2,691.6
2019	128.1	102.8	659.3	1,650.0	34.4	23.2	0.2	1.1	31.6	2,630.7

INDUSTRY: ELECTRONIC SHOPPING & MAIL-ORDER (NAICS 45411)
PRODUCT LINE: OFFICE PAPER (Sub Category)

NAICS 45411: Electronic Shopping and Mail-Order Houses This
industry comprises establishments primarily engaged in retailing all
types of merchandise by means of mail or by electronic media, such
as interactive television or computer. Included in this industry are
establishments primarily engaged in retailing from catalogue showrooms
of mail-order houses.

5-YEAR TREND – ESTIMATED INDUSTRY SALES ($MILLIONS)

Year	Employee Size of Establishment									Total
	1-4 Emps.	5-9 Emps.	10-19 Emps.	20-49 Emps.	50-99 Emps.	100-249 Emps.	250-499 Emps.	500-999 Emps.	Unknown Emps.	Industry Sales
2016	282.5	145.5	210.3	352.9	265.7	491.5	662.6	935.4	39.7	3,386.2
2017	298.8	153.9	222.4	373.3	281.0	519.9	700.9	989.4	42.0	3,581.6
2018	316.8	163.2	235.8	395.8	297.9	551.2	743.1	1,049.0	44.5	3,797.4
2019	355.1	182.9	264.3	443.6	333.9	617.7	832.8	1,154.3	49.9	4,234.4
2019	394.8	203.4	293.8	493.2	371.2	686.8	925.9	1,264.1	55.5	4,688.5

INDUSTRY: BOOK STORES INDUSTRY (NAICS 451211)
PRODUCT LINE: OFFICE PAPER (Sub Category)

NAICS 451211: Book Stores. this industry comprises
establishments primarily engaged in the retail sale of new books and
magazines. Establishments primarily engaged in the retail sale of used
books are classified in 5932.

5-YEAR TREND – ESTIMATED INDUSTRY SALES ($MILLIONS)

Year	Employee Size of Establishment									Total
	1-4 Emps.	5-9 Emps.	10-19 Emps.	20-49 Emps.	50-99 Emps.	100-249 Emps.	250-499 Emps.	500-999 Emps.	Unknown Emps.	Industry Sales
2016	1.0	1.5	3.0	7.9	3.4	1.6	0.4	0.9	0.5	20.1
2017	1.0	1.6	3.1	8.2	3.6	1.6	0.4	1.0	0.5	21.0
2018	1.1	1.6	3.2	8.6	3.7	1.7	0.4	1.0	0.5	22.0
2019	1.1	1.7	3.4	8.9	3.9	1.8	0.4	1.1	0.6	22.9
2019	1.2	1.8	3.5	9.3	4.1	1.9	0.5	1.1	0.6	23.9

INDUSTRY: SUPERMARKETS INDUSTRY (NAICS 44511)
PRODUCT LINE: OFFICE & SCHOOL SUPPLIES (Sub Category)

NAICS 44511: Grocery Stores Industry. this industry comprises establishments generally known as supermarkets and grocery stores primarily engaged in retailing a general line of food, such as canned and frozen foods; fresh fruits and vegetables; and fresh and prepared meats, fish, and poultry. Included in this industry are delicatessen-type establishments primarily engaged in retailing a general line of food.

5-YEAR TREND – ESTIMATED INDUSTRY SALES ($MILLIONS)

Year	Employee Size of Establishment									Total
	1-4 Emps.	5-9 Emps.	10-19 Emps.	20-49 Emps.	50-99 Emps.	100-249 Emps.	250-499 Emps.	500-999 Emps.	Unknown Emps.	Industry Sales
2016	6.9	4.9	12.8	42.1	99.8	248.0	77.5	9.3	1.3	502.4
2017	6.8	4.9	12.7	41.8	99.1	246.4	77.0	9.2	1.3	499.2
2018	6.8	4.9	12.7	41.8	99.1	246.3	76.9	9.2	1.3	499.1
2019	7.0	5.0	12.9	42.7	101.1	251.4	78.5	9.4	1.3	509.4
2019	7.2	5.2	13.3	44.0	104.3	259.2	80.9	9.7	1.3	525.1

INDUSTRY: PHARMACIES & DRUG STORES (NAICS 44611)
PRODUCT LINE: OFFICE & SCHOOL SUPPLIES (Sub Category)

NAICS 44611 Pharmacies and Drug Stores – this industry comprises establishments known as pharmacies and drug stores engaged in retailing prescription or nonprescription drugs and medicines.

5-YEAR TREND – ESTIMATED INDUSTRY SALES ($MILLIONS)

Year	Employee Size of Establishment									Total
	1-4 Emps.	5-9 Emps.	10-19 Emps.	20-49 Emps.	50-99 Emps.	100-249 Emps.	250-499 Emps.	500-999 Emps.	Unknown Emps.	Industry Sales
2016	13.0	32.2	130.1	382.2	38.7	15.5	5.9	2.0	1.0	620.5
2017	13.4	33.2	134.2	394.2	39.9	16.0	6.1	2.0	1.0	639.9
2018	13.9	34.4	139.1	408.4	41.3	16.5	6.3	2.1	1.1	663.1
2019	14.7	36.4	147.3	432.6	43.8	17.5	6.7	2.2	1.1	702.3
2019	15.7	38.9	157.3	461.9	46.7	18.7	7.1	2.4	1.2	749.9

NAICS 45211: Department Stores Industry . this industry comprises establishments known as department stores primarily engaged in retailing a wide range of the following new products with no one merchandise line predominating: apparel, furniture, appliances and home furnishings; and selected additional items, such as paint, hardware, toiletries, cosmetics, photographic equipment, jewelry, toys, and sporting goods. merchandise lines are normally arranged in separate departments.

5-YEAR TREND – ESTIMATED INDUSTRY SALES ($MILLIONS)

| Year | Employee Size of Establishment | | | | | | | | | Total |
	1-4 Emps.	5-9 Emps.	10-19 Emps.	20-49 Emps.	50-99 Emps.	100-249 Emps.	250-499 Emps.	500-999 Emps.	Unknown Emps.	Industry Sales
2016	0.0	0.0	0.0	4.0	73.0	234.4	97.0	14.0	0.6	423.2
2017	0.0	0.0	0.0	4.0	73.3	235.3	97.4	14.1	0.6	424.9
2018	0.0	0.0	0.0	4.1	74.0	237.7	98.4	14.2	0.6	429.1
2019	0.0	0.0	0.0	4.1	74.0	237.7	98.4	14.3	0.6	429.1
2019	0.0	0.0	0.0	4.1	74.8	240.0	99.4	14.4	0.6	433.4

NAICS 45291: Warehouse Clubs and Superstores This industry comprises establishments known as warehouse clubs, superstores or supercenters primarily engaged in retailing a general line of groceries in combination with general lines of new merchandise, such as apparel, furniture, and appliances.

5-YEAR TREND – ESTIMATED INDUSTRY SALES ($MILLIONS)

| Year | Employee Size of Establishment | | | | | | | | | Total |
	1-4 Emps.	5-9 Emps.	10-19 Emps.	20-49 Emps.	50-99 Emps.	100-249 Emps.	250-499 Emps.	500-999 Emps.	Unknown Emps.	Industry Sales
2016	0.2	0.1	0.2	6.7	12.8	731.1	3,218.3	81.1	1.2	4,051.7
2017	0.2	0.1	0.2	6.9	13.2	751.2	3,307.0	83.3	1.3	4,163.4
2018	0.2	0.1	0.2	7.2	13.6	775.7	3,415.0	86.1	1.3	4,299.4
2019	0.2	0.1	0.2	7.7	14.6	834.9	3,675.4	92.6	1.4	4,627.1
2019	0.3	0.1	0.2	8.2	15.5	884.3	3,893.1	98.1	1.5	4,901.2

	INDUSTRY: OFFICE SUPPLIES & STATIONERY STORES (NAICS 45321)
	PRODUCT LINE: OFFICE & SCHOOL SUPPLIES (Sub Category)

NAICS 45321: Office Supplies and Stationery Stores . this industry comprises establishments primarily engaged in one or more of the following: (1) retailing new stationery, school supplies, and office supplies; (2) selling a combination of new office equipment, furniture, and supplies; and (3) selling new office equipment, furniture, and supplies in combination with selling new computers.

5-YEAR TREND – ESTIMATED INDUSTRY SALES ($MILLIONS)

Year	Employee Size of Establishment									Total
	1-4 Emps.	5-9 Emps.	10-19 Emps.	20-49 Emps.	50-99 Emps.	100-249 Emps.	250-499 Emps.	500-999 Emps.	Unknown Emps.	Industry Sales
2016	193.8	155.5	997.0	2,495.3	52.1	35.1	0.3	1.6	47.7	3,978.4
2017	192.2	154.2	988.8	2,474.7	51.7	34.8	0.3	1.6	47.3	3,945.5
2018	191.7	153.9	986.5	2,469.0	51.5	34.7	0.3	1.6	47.2	3,936.4
2019	185.5	148.9	954.5	2,388.8	49.9	33.6	0.3	1.6	45.7	3,808.7
2019	181.3	145.5	932.9	2,334.7	48.7	32.8	0.3	1.6	44.6	3,722.4

	INDUSTRY: ELECTRONIC SHOPPING & MAIL-ORDER (NAICS 45411)
	PRODUCT LINE: OFFICE & SCHOOL SUPPLIES (Sub Category)

NAICS 45411: Electronic Shopping and Mail-Order Houses This industry comprises establishments primarily engaged in retailing all types of merchandise by means of mail or by electronic media, such as interactive television or computer. Included in this industry are establishments primarily engaged in retailing from catalogue showrooms of mail-order houses.

5-YEAR TREND – ESTIMATED INDUSTRY SALES ($MILLIONS)

Year	Employee Size of Establishment									Total
	1-4 Emps.	5-9 Emps.	10-19 Emps.	20-49 Emps.	50-99 Emps.	100-249 Emps.	250-499 Emps.	500-999 Emps.	Unknown Emps.	Industry Sales
2016	1,088.8	560.9	810.4	1,360.3	1,023.9	1,894.3	2,553.8	3,605.1	153.0	13,050.5
2017	1,151.7	593.3	857.2	1,438.8	1,083.0	2,003.6	2,701.3	3,813.2	161.9	13,803.8
2018	1,221.1	629.0	908.8	1,525.4	1,148.2	2,124.3	2,864.0	4,042.9	171.6	14,635.4
2019	1,368.5	704.9	1,018.5	1,709.6	1,286.8	2,380.7	3,209.7	4,448.7	192.3	16,319.8
2019	1,521.5	783.7	1,132.4	1,900.7	1,430.7	2,646.9	3,568.5	4,871.8	213.8	18,070.1

<table>
<tr><td colspan="2">INDUSTRY: BOOK STORES INDUSTRY (NAICS 451211)</td></tr>
<tr><td colspan="2">PRODUCT LINE: OFFICE & SCHOOL SUPPLIES (Sub Category)</td></tr>
</table>

NAICS 451211: Book Stores. this industry comprises establishments primarily engaged in the retail sale of new books and magazines. Establishments primarily engaged in the retail sale of used books are classified in 5932.

5-Year Trend — Estimated Industry Sales ($Millions)

Year	\multicolumn{9}{Employee Size of Establishment}									Total
	1-4 Emps.	5-9 Emps.	10-19 Emps.	20-49 Emps.	50-99 Emps.	100-249 Emps.	250-499 Emps.	500-999 Emps.	Unknown Emps.	Industry Sales
2016	5.7	8.7	17.3	46.1	20.1	9.2	2.3	5.5	2.9	117.8
2017	6.0	9.1	18.1	48.2	21.0	9.7	2.4	5.7	3.0	123.2
2018	6.3	9.6	19.0	50.6	22.0	10.1	2.5	6.0	3.2	129.3
2019	6.5	9.9	19.7	52.5	22.9	10.5	2.6	6.3	3.3	134.3
2019	6.8	10.4	20.6	54.9	23.9	11.0	2.7	6.6	3.5	140.4

<table>
<tr><td colspan="2">INDUSTRY: DEPARTMENT STORES INDUSTRY (NAICS 45211)</td></tr>
<tr><td colspan="2">PRODUCT LINE: OFFICE EQUIPMENT (Sub Category)</td></tr>
</table>

NAICS 45211: Department Stores Industry . this industry comprises establishments known as department stores primarily engaged in retailing a wide range of the following new products with no one merchandise line predominating: apparel, furniture, appliances and home furnishings; and selected additional items, such as paint, hardware, toiletries, cosmetics, photographic equipment, jewelry, toys, and sporting goods. merchandise lines are normally arranged in separate departments.

5-Year Trend — Estimated Industry Sales ($Millions)

Year	Employee Size of Establishment									Total
	1-4 Emps.	5-9 Emps.	10-19 Emps.	20-49 Emps.	50-99 Emps.	100-249 Emps.	250-499 Emps.	500-999 Emps.	Unknown Emps.	Industry Sales
2016	0.0	0.0	0.0	1.5	27.5	88.4	36.6	5.3	0.2	159.6
2017	0.0	0.0	0.0	1.5	27.6	88.8	36.7	5.3	0.2	160.3
2018	0.0	0.0	0.0	1.5	27.9	89.6	37.1	5.4	0.2	161.8
2019	0.0	0.0	0.0	1.5	27.9	89.7	37.1	5.4	0.2	161.9
2019	0.0	0.0	0.0	1.6	28.2	90.5	37.5	5.4	0.2	163.5

INDUSTRY: WAREHOUSE CLUBS & SUPERCENTERS (NAICS 45291)
PRODUCT LINE: OFFICE EQUIPMENT (Sub Category)

NAICS 45291: Warehouse Clubs and Superstores This industry comprises establishments known as warehouse clubs, superstores or supercenters primarily engaged in retailing a general line of groceries in combination with general lines of new merchandise, such as apparel, furniture, and appliances.

5-YEAR TREND — ESTIMATED INDUSTRY SALES ($MILLIONS)

Year	Employee Size of Establishment									Total
	1-4 Emps.	5-9 Emps.	10-19 Emps.	20-49 Emps.	50-99 Emps.	100-249 Emps.	250-499 Emps.	500-999 Emps.	Unknown Emps.	Industry Sales
2016	0.0	0.0	0.0	1.1	2.0	115.0	506.3	12.8	0.2	637.4
2017	0.0	0.0	0.0	1.1	2.1	118.2	520.3	13.1	0.2	655.0
2018	0.0	0.0	0.0	1.1	2.1	122.0	537.3	13.5	0.2	676.4
2019	0.0	0.0	0.0	1.2	2.3	131.3	578.2	14.6	0.2	728.0
2019	0.0	0.0	0.0	1.3	2.4	139.1	612.5	15.4	0.2	771.1

INDUSTRY: OFFICE SUPPLIES & STATIONERY STORES (NAICS 45321)
PRODUCT LINE: OFFICE EQUIPMENT (Sub Category)

NAICS 45321: Office Supplies and Stationery Stores . this industry comprises establishments primarily engaged in one or more of the following: (1) retailing new stationery, school supplies, and office supplies; (2) selling a combination of new office equipment, furniture, and supplies; and (3) selling new office equipment, furniture, and supplies in combination with selling new computers.

5-YEAR TREND — ESTIMATED INDUSTRY SALES ($MILLIONS)

Year	Employee Size of Establishment									Total
	1-4 Emps.	5-9 Emps.	10-19 Emps.	20-49 Emps.	50-99 Emps.	100-249 Emps.	250-499 Emps.	500-999 Emps.	Unknown Emps.	Industry Sales
2016	89.6	71.9	461.1	1,154.0	24.1	16.2	0.1	0.7	22.1	1,839.8
2017	88.9	71.3	457.3	1,144.4	23.9	16.1	0.1	0.7	21.9	1,824.6
2018	88.7	71.2	456.2	1,141.8	23.8	16.1	0.1	0.7	21.8	1,820.4
2019	85.8	68.9	441.4	1,104.7	23.1	15.5	0.1	0.7	21.1	1,761.4
2019	83.8	67.3	431.4	1,079.7	22.5	15.2	0.1	0.7	20.6	1,721.5

INDUSTRY: ELECTRONIC SHOPPING & MAIL-ORDER (NAICS 45411)
PRODUCT LINE: OFFICE EQUIPMENT (Sub Category)

NAICS 45411: Electronic Shopping and Mail-Order Houses This industry comprises establishments primarily engaged in retailing all types of merchandise by means of mail or by electronic media, such as interactive television or computer. Included in this industry are establishments primarily engaged in retailing from catalogue showrooms of mail-order houses.

5-YEAR TREND – ESTIMATED INDUSTRY SALES ($MILLIONS)

Year	Employee Size of Establishment									Total
	1-4 Emps.	5-9 Emps.	10-19 Emps.	20-49 Emps.	50-99 Emps.	100-249 Emps.	250-499 Emps.	500-999 Emps.	Unknown Emps.	Industry Sales
2016	200.0	103.0	148.8	249.8	188.0	347.9	469.0	662.1	28.1	2,396.9
2017	211.5	109.0	157.4	264.2	198.9	368.0	496.1	700.3	29.7	2,535.2
2018	224.3	115.5	166.9	280.2	210.9	390.2	526.0	742.5	31.5	2,687.9
2019	251.3	129.5	187.1	314.0	236.3	437.2	589.5	817.1	35.3	2,997.3
2019	279.4	143.9	208.0	349.1	262.8	486.1	655.4	894.8	39.3	3,318.8

INDUSTRY: SUPERMARKETS INDUSTRY (NAICS 44511)
PRODUCT LINE: GREETING CARDS (Sub Category)

NAICS 44511: Grocery Stores Industry. this industry comprises establishments generally known as supermarkets and grocery stores primarily engaged in retailing a general line of food, such as canned and frozen foods; fresh fruits and vegetables; and fresh and prepared meats, fish, and poultry. Included in this industry are delicatessen-type establishments primarily engaged in retailing a general line of food.

5-YEAR TREND – ESTIMATED INDUSTRY SALES ($MILLIONS)

Year	Employee Size of Establishment									Total
	1-4 Emps.	5-9 Emps.	10-19 Emps.	20-49 Emps.	50-99 Emps.	100-249 Emps.	250-499 Emps.	500-999 Emps.	Unknown Emps.	Industry Sales
2016	22.2	16.0	41.3	136.2	322.8	802.5	250.6	30.0	4.2	1,625.9
2017	22.0	15.9	41.1	135.3	320.8	797.4	249.0	29.8	4.1	1,615.5
2018	22.0	15.9	41.1	135.3	320.6	797.1	249.0	29.8	4.1	1,615.0
2019	22.5	16.2	41.9	138.1	327.3	813.6	254.1	30.4	4.2	1,648.3
2019	23.2	16.7	43.2	142.4	337.4	838.7	261.9	31.3	4.4	1,699.2

INDUSTRY: PHARMACIES & DRUG STORES (NAICS 44611)
PRODUCT LINE: GREETING CARDS (Sub Category)

NAICS 44611 Pharmacies and Drug Stores – this industry comprises establishments known as pharmacies and drug stores engaged in retailing prescription or nonprescription drugs and medicines.

5-YEAR TREND – ESTIMATED INDUSTRY SALES ($MILLIONS)

| Year | Employee Size of Establishment | | | | | | | | | Total |
	1-4 Emps.	5-9 Emps.	10-19 Emps.	20-49 Emps.	50-99 Emps.	100-249 Emps.	250-499 Emps.	500-999 Emps.	Unknown Emps.	Industry Sales
2016	37.2	92.0	372.4	1,093.8	110.6	44.3	16.9	5.6	2.8	1,775.7
2017	38.3	94.9	384.1	1,128.0	114.1	45.7	17.5	5.8	2.9	1,831.3
2018	39.7	98.4	398.0	1,168.9	118.2	47.3	18.1	6.0	3.0	1,897.6
2019	42.1	104.2	421.5	1,238.0	125.2	50.1	19.2	6.4	3.2	2,009.8
2019	44.9	111.2	450.1	1,322.0	133.7	53.5	20.5	6.8	3.4	2,146.2

INDUSTRY: DEPARTMENT STORES INDUSTRY (NAICS 45211)
PRODUCT LINE: GREETING CARDS (Sub Category)

NAICS 45211: Department Stores Industry . this industry comprises establishments known as department stores primarily engaged in retailing a wide range of the following new products with no one merchandise line predominating: apparel, furniture, appliances and home furnishings; and selected additional items, such as paint, hardware, toiletries, cosmetics, photographic equipment, jewelry, toys, and sporting goods. merchandise lines are normally arranged in separate departments.

5-YEAR TREND – ESTIMATED INDUSTRY SALES ($MILLIONS)

| Year | Employee Size of Establishment | | | | | | | | | Total |
	1-4 Emps.	5-9 Emps.	10-19 Emps.	20-49 Emps.	50-99 Emps.	100-249 Emps.	250-499 Emps.	500-999 Emps.	Unknown Emps.	Industry Sales
2016	0.0	0.0	0.1	6.0	109.5	351.5	145.5	21.0	0.9	634.5
2017	0.0	0.0	0.1	6.1	109.9	352.9	146.1	21.1	0.9	637.0
2018	0.0	0.0	0.1	6.1	111.0	356.3	147.5	21.3	0.9	643.3
2019	0.0	0.0	0.1	6.1	111.0	356.4	147.5	21.4	0.9	643.4
2019	0.0	0.0	0.1	6.2	112.1	359.9	149.0	21.6	0.9	649.9

	INDUSTRY: WAREHOUSE CLUBS & SUPERCENTERS (NAICS 45291)
	PRODUCT LINE: GREETING CARDS (Sub Category)

NAICS 45291: Warehouse Clubs and Superstores This industry comprises establishments known as warehouse clubs, superstores or supercenters primarily engaged in retailing a general line of groceries in combination with general lines of new merchandise, such as apparel, furniture, and appliances.

5-YEAR TREND – ESTIMATED INDUSTRY SALES ($MILLIONS)

Year	Employee Size of Establishment									Total
	1-4 Emps.	5-9 Emps.	10-19 Emps.	20-49 Emps.	50-99 Emps.	100-249 Emps.	250-499 Emps.	500-999 Emps.	Unknown Emps.	Industry Sales
2016	0.1	0.0	0.1	2.7	5.1	293.2	1,290.9	32.5	0.5	1,625.2
2017	0.1	0.0	0.1	2.8	5.3	301.3	1,326.5	33.4	0.5	1,670.0
2018	0.1	0.0	0.1	2.9	5.4	311.2	1,369.8	34.5	0.5	1,724.5
2019	0.1	0.0	0.1	3.1	5.9	334.9	1,474.2	37.1	0.6	1,855.9
2019	0.1	0.0	0.1	3.3	6.2	354.7	1,561.5	39.3	0.6	1,965.9

	INDUSTRY: OFFICE SUPPLIES & STATIONERY STORES (NAICS 45321)
	PRODUCT LINE: GREETING CARDS (Sub Category)

NAICS 45321: Office Supplies and Stationery Stores . this industry comprises establishments primarily engaged in one or more of the following: (1) retailing new stationery, school supplies, and office supplies; (2) selling a combination of new office equipment, furniture, and supplies; and (3) selling new office equipment, furniture, and supplies in combination with selling new computers.

5-YEAR TREND – ESTIMATED INDUSTRY SALES ($MILLIONS)

Year	Employee Size of Establishment									Total
	1-4 Emps.	5-9 Emps.	10-19 Emps.	20-49 Emps.	50-99 Emps.	100-249 Emps.	250-499 Emps.	500-999 Emps.	Unknown Emps.	Industry Sales
2016	1.8	1.4	9.3	23.2	0.5	0.3	0.0	0.0	0.4	37.0
2017	1.8	1.4	9.2	23.0	0.5	0.3	0.0	0.0	0.4	36.7
2018	1.8	1.4	9.2	23.0	0.5	0.3	0.0	0.0	0.4	36.6
2019	1.7	1.4	8.9	22.2	0.5	0.3	0.0	0.0	0.4	35.4
2019	1.7	1.4	8.7	21.7	0.5	0.3	0.0	0.0	0.4	34.6

NAICS 45411: Electronic Shopping and Mail-Order Houses This industry comprises establishments primarily engaged in retailing all types of merchandise by means of mail or by electronic media, such as interactive television or computer. Included in this industry are establishments primarily engaged in retailing from catalogue showrooms of mail-order houses.

5-YEAR TREND – ESTIMATED INDUSTRY SALES ($MILLIONS)

Year	Employee Size of Establishment									Total
	1-4 Emps.	5-9 Emps.	10-19 Emps.	20-49 Emps.	50-99 Emps.	100-249 Emps.	250-499 Emps.	500-999 Emps.	Unknown Emps.	Industry Sales
2016	27.2	14.0	20.3	34.0	25.6	47.4	63.9	90.2	3.8	326.4
2017	28.8	14.8	21.4	36.0	27.1	50.1	67.6	95.4	4.0	345.3
2018	30.5	15.7	22.7	38.2	28.7	53.1	71.6	101.1	4.3	366.1
2019	34.2	17.6	25.5	42.8	32.2	59.6	80.3	111.3	4.8	408.2
2019	38.1	19.6	28.3	47.5	35.8	66.2	89.3	121.9	5.3	452.0

NAICS 451211: Book Stores. this industry comprises establishments primarily engaged in the retail sale of new books and magazines. Establishments primarily engaged in the retail sale of used books are classified in 5932.

5-YEAR TREND – ESTIMATED INDUSTRY SALES ($MILLIONS)

Year	Employee Size of Establishment									Total
	1-4 Emps.	5-9 Emps.	10-19 Emps.	20-49 Emps.	50-99 Emps.	100-249 Emps.	250-499 Emps.	500-999 Emps.	Unknown Emps.	Industry Sales
2016	7.5	11.4	22.6	60.2	26.2	12.1	3.0	7.2	3.8	153.8
2017	7.8	11.9	23.6	62.9	27.4	12.6	3.1	7.5	4.0	160.8
2018	8.2	12.5	24.8	66.0	28.7	13.2	3.3	7.8	4.2	168.7
2019	8.5	12.9	25.8	68.5	29.8	13.7	3.4	8.2	4.3	175.2
2019	8.9	13.5	26.9	71.6	31.2	14.4	3.5	8.6	4.5	183.2

INDUSTRY: SUPERMARKETS INDUSTRY (NAICS 44511)
PRODUCT LINE: MAGAZINES & NEWSPAPERS (Sub Category)

NAICS 44511: Grocery Stores Industry. this industry comprises establishments generally known as supermarkets and grocery stores primarily engaged in retailing a general line of food, such as canned and frozen foods; fresh fruits and vegetables; and fresh and prepared meats, fish, and poultry. Included in this industry are delicatessen-type establishments primarily engaged in retailing a general line of food.

5-YEAR TREND – ESTIMATED INDUSTRY SALES ($MILLIONS)

Year	Employee Size of Establishment									Total
	1-4 Emps.	5-9 Emps.	10-19 Emps.	20-49 Emps.	50-99 Emps.	100-249 Emps.	250-499 Emps.	500-999 Emps.	Unknown Emps.	Industry Sales
2016	31.8	22.9	59.2	195.1	462.4	1,149.5	359.0	43.0	6.0	2,328.9
2017	31.6	22.8	58.8	193.9	459.5	1,142.2	356.7	42.7	5.9	2,314.1
2018	31.6	22.8	58.8	193.8	459.3	1,141.8	356.6	42.7	5.9	2,313.3
2019	32.2	23.3	60.0	197.8	468.8	1,165.4	364.0	43.5	6.0	2,361.0
2019	33.2	24.0	61.9	203.9	483.3	1,201.4	375.2	44.8	6.2	2,433.9

INDUSTRY: BEER, WINE & LIQUOR STORES (NAICS 44531)
PRODUCT LINE: MAGAZINES & NEWSPAPERS (Sub Category)

NAICS 44531: Beer & Wine & Liquor Stores. Establishments primarily engaged in the retail sale of packaged alcoholic beverages, such as ale, beer, wine, and liquor, for consumption off the premises. Stores selling prepared drinks for consumption on the premises are classified in SIC 5813.

5-YEAR TREND – ESTIMATED INDUSTRY SALES ($MILLIONS)

Year	Employee Size of Establishment									Total
	1-4 Emps.	5-9 Emps.	10-19 Emps.	20-49 Emps.	50-99 Emps.	100-249 Emps.	250-499 Emps.	500-999 Emps.	Unknown Emps.	Industry Sales
2016	14.2	14.3	12.2	8.9	1.3	0.7	0.0	0.4	0.8	52.9
2017	14.5	14.6	12.5	9.2	1.3	0.8	0.0	0.4	0.8	54.1
2018	14.9	15.0	12.8	9.4	1.3	0.8	0.0	0.4	0.8	55.6
2019	15.8	15.9	13.6	10.0	1.4	0.8	0.0	0.5	0.9	58.8
2019	16.8	17.0	14.5	10.6	1.5	0.9	0.0	0.5	0.9	62.8

INDUSTRY: PHARMACIES & DRUG STORES (NAICS 44611)
PRODUCT LINE: MAGAZINES & NEWSPAPERS (Sub Category)

NAICS 44611 Pharmacies and Drug Stores – this industry comprises establishments known as pharmacies and drug stores engaged in retailing prescription or nonprescription drugs and medicines.

5-YEAR TREND – ESTIMATED INDUSTRY SALES ($MILLIONS)

Year	Employee Size of Establishment									Total
	1-4 Emps.	5-9 Emps.	10-19 Emps.	20-49 Emps.	50-99 Emps.	100-249 Emps.	250-499 Emps.	500-999 Emps.	Unknown Emps.	Industry Sales
2016	7.4	18.3	74.0	217.3	22.0	8.8	3.4	1.1	0.6	352.7
2017	7.6	18.9	76.3	224.1	22.7	9.1	3.5	1.2	0.6	363.8
2018	7.9	19.5	79.1	232.2	23.5	9.4	3.6	1.2	0.6	376.9
2019	8.4	20.7	83.7	245.9	24.9	10.0	3.8	1.3	0.6	399.2
2019	8.9	22.1	89.4	262.6	26.6	10.6	4.1	1.4	0.7	426.3

INDUSTRY: GAS STATIONS W/CONVENIENCE STORES (NAICS 44711)
PRODUCT LINE: MAGAZINES & NEWSPAPERS (Sub Category)

NAICS 44711: Gas Stations with Convenience Stores. this industry comprises establishments primarily engaged in selling gasoline and lubricating oils. These establishments frequently sell other merchandise, such as tires, batteries, and other automobile parts, or perform minor repair work. Gasoline stations combined with other activities, such as grocery stores, convenience stores, or carwashes, are classified according to the primary activity.

5-YEAR TREND – ESTIMATED INDUSTRY SALES ($MILLIONS)

Year	Employee Size of Establishment									Total
	1-4 Emps.	5-9 Emps.	10-19 Emps.	20-49 Emps.	50-99 Emps.	100-249 Emps.	250-499 Emps.	500-999 Emps.	Unknown Emps.	Industry Sales
2016	150.3	388.3	650.0	448.6	42.1	23.1	9.2	0.1	1.7	1,713.4
2017	156.6	404.6	677.3	467.3	43.9	24.0	9.5	0.1	1.7	1,785.1
2018	163.8	423.2	708.4	488.8	45.9	25.2	10.0	0.1	1.8	1,867.1
2019	174.6	451.0	754.9	520.9	48.9	26.8	10.6	0.1	1.9	1,989.7
2019	187.4	484.2	810.4	559.2	52.5	28.8	11.4	0.1	2.1	2,136.1

<table>
<tr><td colspan="2">INDUSTRY: PRERECORDED TAPES & CDs STORES (NAICS 45122)</td></tr>
<tr><td colspan="2">PRODUCT LINE: MAGAZINES & NEWSPAPERS (Sub Category)</td></tr>
</table>

NAICS 45122: Prerecorded Tape, Compact Disc, and Record Stores .
This industry comprises establishments primarily engaged in retailing new
prerecorded audio and video tapes, compact discs (CDs), and phonograph
records.

5-Year Trend – Estimated Industry Sales ($Millions)

Year	Employee Size of Establishment									Total
	1-4 Emps.	5-9 Emps.	10-19 Emps.	20-49 Emps.	50-99 Emps.	100-249 Emps.	250-499 Emps.	500-999 Emps.	Unknown Emps.	Industry Sales
2016	2.3	4.5	11.5	23.5	17.8	1,175.4	91.8	1.9	0.8	1,329.6
2017	2.4	4.6	11.8	24.1	18.3	1,203.6	94.0	2.0	0.8	1,361.5
2018	2.5	4.8	12.1	24.8	18.8	1,238.8	96.7	2.0	0.9	1,401.4
2019	2.5	5.0	12.6	25.7	19.5	1,284.8	100.3	2.1	0.9	1,453.4
2019	2.7	5.2	13.1	26.9	20.4	1,344.2	105.0	2.2	0.9	1,520.5

<table>
<tr><td colspan="2">INDUSTRY: DEPARTMENT STORES (NAICS 45211)</td></tr>
<tr><td colspan="2">PRODUCT LINE: MAGAZINES & NEWSPAPERS (Sub Category)</td></tr>
</table>

NAICS 45211: Department Stores Industry . this industry comprises
establishments known as department stores primarily engaged in retailing
a wide range of the following new products with no one merchandise line
predominating: apparel, furniture, appliances and home furnishings; and
selected additional items, such as paint, hardware, toiletries, cosmetics,
photographic equipment, jewelry, toys, and sporting goods. merchandise lines
are normally arranged in separate departments.

5-Year Trend – Estimated Industry Sales ($Millions)

Year	Employee Size of Establishment									Total
	1-4 Emps.	5-9 Emps.	10-19 Emps.	20-49 Emps.	50-99 Emps.	100-249 Emps.	250-499 Emps.	500-999 Emps.	Unknown Emps.	Industry Sales
2016	0.0	0.0	0.0	2.7	48.1	154.6	64.0	9.3	0.4	279.1
2017	0.0	0.0	0.0	2.7	48.3	155.2	64.2	9.3	0.4	280.2
2018	0.0	0.0	0.0	2.7	48.8	156.7	64.9	9.4	0.4	283.0
2019	0.0	0.0	0.0	2.7	48.8	156.8	64.9	9.4	0.4	283.0
2019	0.0	0.0	0.0	2.7	49.3	158.3	65.5	9.5	0.4	285.8

INDUSTRY: WAREHOUSE CLUBS & SUPERCENTERS (NAICS 45291)
PRODUCT LINE: MAGAZINES & NEWSPAPERS (Sub Category)

NAICS 45291: Warehouse Clubs and Superstores This industry comprises establishments known as warehouse clubs, superstores or supercenters primarily engaged in retailing a general line of groceries in combination with general lines of new merchandise, such as apparel, furniture, and appliances.

5-YEAR TREND – ESTIMATED INDUSTRY SALES ($MILLIONS)

Year	Employee Size of Establishment									Total
	1-4 Emps.	5-9 Emps.	10-19 Emps.	20-49 Emps.	50-99 Emps.	100-249 Emps.	250-499 Emps.	500-999 Emps.	Unknown Emps.	Industry Sales
2016	0.1	0.0	0.0	1.7	3.2	183.7	808.5	20.4	0.3	1,017.9
2017	0.1	0.0	0.0	1.7	3.3	188.7	830.8	20.9	0.3	1,046.0
2018	0.1	0.0	0.0	1.8	3.4	194.9	857.9	21.6	0.3	1,080.1
2019	0.1	0.0	0.1	1.9	3.7	209.7	923.3	23.3	0.4	1,162.4
2019	0.1	0.0	0.1	2.1	3.9	222.2	978.0	24.6	0.4	1,231.3

INDUSTRY: ELECTRONIC SHOPPING & MAIL-ORDER (NAICS 45411)
PRODUCT LINE: MAGAZINES & NEWSPAPERS (Sub Category)

NAICS 45411: Electronic Shopping and Mail-Order Houses This industry comprises establishments primarily engaged in retailing all types of merchandise by means of mail or by electronic media, such as interactive television or computer. Included in this industry are establishments primarily engaged in retailing from catalogue showrooms of mail-order houses.

5-YEAR TREND – ESTIMATED INDUSTRY SALES ($MILLIONS)

Year	Employee Size of Establishment									Total
	1-4 Emps.	5-9 Emps.	10-19 Emps.	20-49 Emps.	50-99 Emps.	100-249 Emps.	250-499 Emps.	500-999 Emps.	Unknown Emps.	Industry Sales
2016	210.4	108.4	156.6	262.8	197.8	366.0	493.5	696.6	29.6	2,521.7
2017	222.5	114.6	165.6	278.0	209.3	387.2	522.0	736.8	31.3	2,667.3
2018	235.9	121.5	175.6	294.8	221.9	410.5	553.4	781.2	33.2	2,828.0
2019	264.4	136.2	196.8	330.3	248.7	460.0	620.2	859.6	37.2	3,153.4
2019	294.0	151.4	218.8	367.3	276.5	511.5	689.5	941.4	41.3	3,491.6

INDUSTRY: BOOK STORES INDUSTRY (NAICS 451211)
PRODUCT LINE: MAGAZINES & NEWSPAPERS (Sub Category)

NAICS 451211: Book Stores. this industry comprises establishments primarily engaged in the retail sale of new books and magazines. Establishments primarily engaged in the retail sale of used books are classified in 5932.

5-YEAR TREND – ESTIMATED INDUSTRY SALES ($MILLIONS)

Year	Employee Size of Establishment									Total Industry Sales
	1-4 Emps.	5-9 Emps.	10-19 Emps.	20-49 Emps.	50-99 Emps.	100-249 Emps.	250-499 Emps.	500-999 Emps.	Unknown Emps.	
2016	17.7	26.8	53.3	141.9	61.8	28.4	7.0	16.9	8.9	362.7
2017	18.5	28.0	55.8	148.3	64.6	29.7	7.3	17.6	9.3	379.2
2018	19.4	29.4	58.5	155.6	67.7	31.2	7.7	18.5	9.8	397.9
2019	20.1	30.5	60.7	161.6	70.3	32.4	8.0	19.3	10.2	413.2
2019	21.0	31.9	63.5	169.0	73.5	33.9	8.4	20.3	10.6	432.1

INDUSTRY: SUPERMARKETS INDUSTRY (NAICS 44511)
PRODUCT LINE: SOUVENIR & NOVELTY ITEMS (Main Category)

NAICS 44511: Grocery Stores Industry. this industry comprises establishments generally known as supermarkets and grocery stores primarily engaged in retailing a general line of food, such as canned and frozen foods; fresh fruits and vegetables; and fresh and prepared meats, fish, and poultry. Included in this industry are delicatessen-type establishments primarily engaged in retailing a general line of food.

5-YEAR TREND – ESTIMATED INDUSTRY SALES ($MILLIONS)

Year	Employee Size of Establishment									Total Industry Sales
	1-4 Emps.	5-9 Emps.	10-19 Emps.	20-49 Emps.	50-99 Emps.	100-249 Emps.	250-499 Emps.	500-999 Emps.	Unknown Emps.	
2016	7.5	5.4	13.9	46.0	108.9	270.8	84.6	10.1	1.4	548.7
2017	7.4	5.4	13.9	45.7	108.2	269.1	84.0	10.1	1.4	545.2
2018	7.4	5.4	13.9	45.7	108.2	269.0	84.0	10.1	1.4	545.0
2019	7.6	5.5	14.1	46.6	110.4	274.6	85.7	10.3	1.4	556.2
2019	7.8	5.6	14.6	48.0	113.9	283.0	88.4	10.6	1.5	573.4

INDUSTRY: BEER, WINE & LIQUOR STORES (NAICS 44531)
PRODUCT LINE: SOUVENIR & NOVELTY ITEMS (Main Category)

NAICS 44531: Beer & Wine & Liquor Stores. Establishments primarily engaged in the retail sale of packaged alcoholic beverages, such as ale, beer, wine, and liquor, for consumption off the premises. Stores selling prepared drinks for consumption on the premises are classified in SIC 5813.

5-YEAR TREND — ESTIMATED INDUSTRY SALES ($MILLIONS)

Year	Employee Size of Establishment									Total
	1-4 Emps.	5-9 Emps.	10-19 Emps.	20-49 Emps.	50-99 Emps.	100-249 Emps.	250-499 Emps.	500-999 Emps.	Unknown Emps.	Industry Sales
2016	6.6	6.6	5.7	4.2	0.6	0.3	0.0	0.2	0.4	24.5
2017	6.7	6.8	5.8	4.2	0.6	0.4	0.0	0.2	0.4	25.1
2018	6.9	7.0	6.0	4.4	0.6	0.4	0.0	0.2	0.4	25.8
2019	7.3	7.4	6.3	4.6	0.7	0.4	0.0	0.2	0.4	27.3
2019	7.8	7.9	6.7	4.9	0.7	0.4	0.0	0.2	0.4	29.2

INDUSTRY: PHARMACIES & DRUG STORES (NAICS 44611)
PRODUCT LINE: SOUVENIR & NOVELTY ITEMS (Main Category)

NAICS 44611 Pharmacies and Drug Stores – this industry comprises establishments known as pharmacies and drug stores engaged in retailing prescription or nonprescription drugs and medicines.

5-YEAR TREND — ESTIMATED INDUSTRY SALES ($MILLIONS)

Year	Employee Size of Establishment									Total
	1-4 Emps.	5-9 Emps.	10-19 Emps.	20-49 Emps.	50-99 Emps.	100-249 Emps.	250-499 Emps.	500-999 Emps.	Unknown Emps.	Industry Sales
2016	7.1	17.7	71.6	210.4	21.3	8.5	3.3	1.1	0.5	341.5
2017	7.4	18.3	73.9	216.9	21.9	8.8	3.4	1.1	0.6	352.2
2018	7.6	18.9	76.5	224.8	22.7	9.1	3.5	1.2	0.6	365.0
2019	8.1	20.0	81.1	238.1	24.1	9.6	3.7	1.2	0.6	386.5
2019	8.6	21.4	86.6	254.2	25.7	10.3	3.9	1.3	0.7	412.8

INDUSTRY: MEN'S CLOTHING STORES INDUSTRY (NAICS 44811)
PRODUCT LINE: SOUVENIR & NOVELTY ITEMS (Main Category)

NAICS 44811: Men's Clothing Stores. this industry comprises establishments primarily engaged in retailing a general line of new men's and boys' clothing. These establishments may provide basic alterations, such as hemming, taking in or letting out seams, or lengthening or shortening sleeves.

5-Year Trend – Estimated Industry Sales ($Millions)

Year	Employee Size of Establishment									Total
	1-4 Emps.	5-9 Emps.	10-19 Emps.	20-49 Emps.	50-99 Emps.	100-249 Emps.	250-499 Emps.	500-999 Emps.	Unknown Emps.	Industry Sales
2016	1.3	2.3	4.2	2.2	0.5	0.4	0.1	0.0	0.2	11.2
2017	1.3	2.3	4.3	2.3	0.5	0.4	0.2	0.0	0.2	11.6
2018	1.4	2.4	4.5	2.4	0.5	0.5	0.2	0.0	0.2	12.1
2019	1.4	2.5	4.7	2.5	0.5	0.5	0.2	0.0	0.2	12.5
2019	1.5	2.6	4.9	2.6	0.6	0.5	0.2	0.0	0.3	13.0

INDUSTRY: WOMEN'S CLOTHING STORES INDUSTRY (NAICS 44812)
PRODUCT LINE: SOUVENIR & NOVELTY ITEMS (Main Category)

NAICS 44812: Women's Clothing Stores . this industry comprises establishments primarily engaged in retailing a general line of new women's, misses' and juniors' clothing, including maternity wear. These establishments may provide basic alterations, such as hemming, taking in or letting out seams, or lengthening or shortening sleeves.

5-Year Trend – Estimated Industry Sales ($Millions)

Year	Employee Size of Establishment									Total
	1-4 Emps.	5-9 Emps.	10-19 Emps.	20-49 Emps.	50-99 Emps.	100-249 Emps.	250-499 Emps.	500-999 Emps.	Unknown Emps.	Industry Sales
2016	1.8	4.1	8.7	6.1	2.2	2.0	0.8	0.8	0.4	26.9
2017	1.9	4.2	8.9	6.3	2.2	2.1	0.8	0.8	0.4	27.7
2018	1.9	4.3	9.3	6.5	2.3	2.1	0.9	0.8	0.4	28.6
2019	2.0	4.6	9.8	6.9	2.4	2.2	0.9	0.9	0.5	30.2
2019	2.2	4.9	10.4	7.3	2.6	2.4	1.0	0.9	0.5	32.1

	INDUSTRY: FAMILY CLOTHING STORES INDUSTRY (NAICS 44814)
	PRODUCT LINE: SOUVENIR & NOVELTY ITEMS (Main Category)

NAICS 44814: Family Clothing Stores . this industry comprises establishments primarily engaged in retailing a general line of new clothing for men, women, and children, without specializing in sales for an individual gender or age group. These establishments may provide basic alterations, such as hemming, taking in or letting out seams, or lengthening or shortening sleeves.

5-YEAR TREND — ESTIMATED INDUSTRY SALES ($MILLIONS)

Year	Employee Size of Establishment									Total
	1-4 Emps.	5-9 Emps.	10-19 Emps.	20-49 Emps.	50-99 Emps.	100-249 Emps.	250-499 Emps.	500-999 Emps.	Unknown Emps.	Industry Sales
2016	3.6	7.4	28.0	93.0	82.1	22.6	21.3	12.3	1.0	271.2
2017	3.7	7.6	28.7	95.4	84.3	23.2	21.9	12.7	1.0	278.5
2018	3.8	7.8	29.6	98.5	87.0	23.9	22.6	13.1	1.0	287.4
2019	4.0	8.3	31.2	103.8	91.7	25.2	23.8	13.7	1.1	302.9
2019	4.3	8.8	33.2	110.4	97.5	26.8	25.3	14.5	1.2	321.9

	INDUSTRY: DEPARTMENT STORES INDUSTRY (NAICS 45211)
	PRODUCT LINE: SOUVENIR & NOVELTY ITEMS (Main Category)

NAICS 45211: Department Stores Industry . this industry comprises establishments known as department stores primarily engaged in retailing a wide range of the following new products with no one merchandise line predominating: apparel, furniture, appliances and home furnishings; and selected additional items, such as paint, hardware, toiletries, cosmetics, photographic equipment, jewelry, toys, and sporting goods. merchandise lines are normally arranged in separate departments.

5-YEAR TREND — ESTIMATED INDUSTRY SALES ($MILLIONS)

Year	Employee Size of Establishment									Total
	1-4 Emps.	5-9 Emps.	10-19 Emps.	20-49 Emps.	50-99 Emps.	100-249 Emps.	250-499 Emps.	500-999 Emps.	Unknown Emps.	Industry Sales
2016	0.0	0.0	0.1	4.3	77.6	249.1	103.1	14.9	0.6	449.8
2017	0.0	0.0	0.1	4.3	77.9	250.1	103.5	15.0	0.6	451.5
2018	0.0	0.0	0.1	4.3	78.7	252.6	104.6	15.1	0.6	456.0
2019	0.0	0.0	0.1	4.3	78.7	252.6	104.6	15.2	0.6	456.1
2019	0.0	0.0	0.1	4.4	79.4	255.1	105.6	15.3	0.6	460.6

<table>
<tr><td colspan="2">INDUSTRY: WAREHOUSE CLUBS & SUPERCENTERS (NAICS 45291)</td></tr>
<tr><td colspan="2">PRODUCT LINE: SOUVENIR & NOVELTY ITEMS (Main Category)</td></tr>
</table>

NAICS 45291: Warehouse Clubs and Superstores This industry comprises establishments known as warehouse clubs, superstores or supercenters primarily engaged in retailing a general line of groceries in combination with general lines of new merchandise, such as apparel, furniture, and appliances.

5-YEAR TREND – ESTIMATED INDUSTRY SALES ($MILLIONS)

Year	1-4 Emps.	5-9 Emps.	10-19 Emps.	20-49 Emps.	50-99 Emps.	100-249 Emps.	250-499 Emps.	500-999 Emps.	Unknown Emps.	Total Industry Sales
2016	0.0	0.0	0.0	1.2	2.2	125.5	552.4	13.9	0.2	695.4
2017	0.0	0.0	0.0	1.2	2.3	128.9	567.6	14.3	0.2	714.6
2018	0.0	0.0	0.0	1.2	2.3	133.1	586.1	14.8	0.2	737.9
2019	0.0	0.0	0.0	1.3	2.5	143.3	630.8	15.9	0.2	794.2
2019	0.0	0.0	0.0	1.4	2.7	151.8	668.2	16.8	0.3	841.2

<table>
<tr><td colspan="2">INDUSTRY: OFFICE SUPPLIES & STATIONERY STORES (NAICS 45321)</td></tr>
<tr><td colspan="2">PRODUCT LINE: SOUVENIR & NOVELTY ITEMS (Main Category)</td></tr>
</table>

NAICS 45321: Office Supplies and Stationery Stores . this industry comprises establishments primarily engaged in one or more of the following: (1) retailing new stationery, school supplies, and office supplies; (2) selling a combination of new office equipment, furniture, and supplies; and (3) selling new office equipment, furniture, and supplies in combination with selling new computers.

5-YEAR TREND – ESTIMATED INDUSTRY SALES ($MILLIONS)

Year	1-4 Emps.	5-9 Emps.	10-19 Emps.	20-49 Emps.	50-99 Emps.	100-249 Emps.	250-499 Emps.	500-999 Emps.	Unknown Emps.	Total Industry Sales
2016	0.7	0.5	3.5	8.8	0.2	0.1	0.0	0.0	0.2	14.0
2017	0.7	0.5	3.5	8.7	0.2	0.1	0.0	0.0	0.2	13.9
2018	0.7	0.5	3.5	8.7	0.2	0.1	0.0	0.0	0.2	13.9
2019	0.7	0.5	3.4	8.4	0.2	0.1	0.0	0.0	0.2	13.4
2019	0.6	0.5	3.3	8.2	0.2	0.1	0.0	0.0	0.2	13.1

INDUSTRY: ELECTRONIC SHOPPING & MAIL-ORDER (NAICS 45411)
PRODUCT LINE: SOUVENIR & NOVELTY ITEMS (Main Category)

NAICS 45411: Electronic Shopping and Mail-Order Houses This industry comprises establishments primarily engaged in retailing all types of merchandise by means of mail or by electronic media, such as interactive television or computer. Included in this industry are establishments primarily engaged in retailing from catalogue showrooms of mail-order houses.

5-YEAR TREND – ESTIMATED INDUSTRY SALES ($MILLIONS)

Year	Employee Size of Establishment									Total
	1-4 Emps.	5-9 Emps.	10-19 Emps.	20-49 Emps.	50-99 Emps.	100-249 Emps.	250-499 Emps.	500-999 Emps.	Unknown Emps.	Industry Sales
2016	440.2	226.7	327.6	549.9	413.9	765.8	1,032.4	1,457.4	61.9	5,275.7
2017	465.6	239.8	346.5	581.6	437.8	810.0	1,092.0	1,541.5	65.4	5,580.3
2018	493.6	254.3	367.4	616.7	464.2	858.8	1,157.8	1,634.3	69.4	5,916.4
2019	553.2	285.0	411.7	691.1	520.2	962.4	1,297.5	1,798.4	77.8	6,597.3
2019	615.1	316.8	457.8	768.4	578.4	1,070.0	1,442.6	1,969.5	86.4	7,304.9

INDUSTRY: BOOK STORE INDUSTRY (NAICS 451211)
PRODUCT LINE: SOUVENIR & NOVELTY ITEMS (Main Category)

NAICS 451211: Book Stores. this industry comprises establishments primarily engaged in the retail sale of new books and magazines. Establishments primarily engaged in the retail sale of used books are classified in 5932.

5-YEAR TREND – ESTIMATED INDUSTRY SALES ($MILLIONS)

Year	Employee Size of Establishment									Total
	1-4 Emps.	5-9 Emps.	10-19 Emps.	20-49 Emps.	50-99 Emps.	100-249 Emps.	250-499 Emps.	500-999 Emps.	Unknown Emps.	Industry Sales
2016	14.0	21.2	42.1	112.1	48.8	22.5	5.5	13.3	7.1	286.5
2017	14.6	22.1	44.1	117.2	51.0	23.5	5.8	13.9	7.4	299.6
2018	15.3	23.2	46.2	123.0	53.5	24.6	6.1	14.6	7.7	314.3
2019	15.9	24.1	48.0	127.7	55.6	25.6	6.3	15.3	8.0	326.4
2019	16.6	25.2	50.2	133.5	58.1	26.8	6.6	16.0	8.4	341.4

Definitions, Methodology and Terms

Methodology

Barnes Reports' Product Lines reports provide estimates of the sales of product lines in the largest retail industries. These estimates are produced by a proprietary economic model that is based on a number of sources and factors:

-The size and characteristics of the largest U.S. industries (based on the U.S. Bureau of the Census statistics, inflation rates and industry trends).
-The sales of product lines by industry. Main category and sub category product lines weights are a proportion of the U.S. total product lines sales.
-U.S. States statistics are based on industry breakdown and product lines weights are applied by size of firm.

NAICS codes (North American Classification System codes) are used in each industry definition in order to aid report users in clarifying and standardizing the definitions of each industry.
Product lines codes are available through the U.S. Bureau of the Census.

Number of Establishments

General Definition

An establishment is a single physical location at which business is conducted and/or services are provided. It is not necessarily identical with a company or enterprise, which may consist of one establishment or more. Economic census figures represent a summary of reports for individual establishments rather than companies. For cases where a census report was received, separate information was obtained for each location where business was conducted. When administrative records of other Federal agencies were used instead of a census report, no information was available on the number of locations operated. Each economic census establishment was tabulated according to the physical location at which the business was conducted.

When two activities or more were carried on at a single location under a single ownership, all activities generally were grouped together as a single establishment. The entire establishment was classified on the basis of its major activity and all data for it were included in that classification. However, when distinct and separate economic activities (for which different industry classification codes were appropriate) were conducted at a single location under a single ownership, separate establishment reports for each of the different activities were obtained in the census.

Sector-Specific Information

Construction sector. Establishments are defined as a relatively permanent office or other place of business where the usual business activities related to construction are conducted. Establishments do not represent each project or construction site. Includes all establishments that were in business at any time during the year. It covers all full-year and part-year operations. Construction establishments which were inactive or idle for the entire year were not included. Establishments are based on a survey which included all large employers and a sample of the smaller ones.

Information; Professional, Scientific, and Technical Services; Administrative and Support and Waste Management and Remediation Services; Educational Services; Health Care and Social Assistance; Arts, Entertainment, and Recreation; and Other Services (Except Public Administration) sectors. An establishment is included in the census if it is an employer, the establishment has $1,000 in payroll, and was in operation at any time during 1997. Leased service departments (separately owned businesses operated as departments or concessions of other service establishments or of retail businesses, such as a separately owned shoeshine parlor in a barber shop, or a beauty shop in a department store) are treated as separate service establishments for census purposes. Leased retail departments located in service establishments (e.g., a gift shop located in a hotel) are considered separate retail establishments. Manufacturing sector. Includes all manufacturing establishments (plants) with one employee or more and establishments in operation at any time during the year.

Mining sector. Includes all mineral establishments with one employee or more and establishments in operation at any time during the year. Establishments in the crude petroleum and natural gas and support activities for mining represent statewide operations rather than those at a single physical location.

Real Estate and Rental and Leasing sector. Data for individual properties leased or managed by property lessors or property managers are not normally considered separate establishments, but rather the permanent offices from which the properties are leased or managed are considered establishments. Data for separate automotive rental offices or concessions (e.g., airport locations) in the same metropolitan area for which a common fleet of cars is maintained are merged together and not considered as separate establishments.

Retail Trade sector. Leased departments are treated as separate establishments and are classified according to the kind of business they conduct. For example, a leased department selling shoes within a department store would be considered a separate retail establishment under the "shoe stores" classification.

Accommodation and Foodservices sector. Leased departments are treated as separate establishments and are classified according to the kind of business they conduct. For example, a leased department selling gifts/souvenirs within a hotel would be considered a separate retail establishment under the "gift, novelty, and souvenir stores" classification.

Auxiliaries sector. In the Standard Industrial Classification (SIC) system, auxiliary establishments (i.e., those establishments primarily serving other establishments of the same enterprise) were classified in the industry of the establishments served. In the North American Industry Classification System (NAICS), auxiliary establishments are classified according to the services performed rather than the industry served.

Sales, Shipments, Receipts, Revenue, or Business Done

General Definition

Includes the total sales, shipments, receipts, revenue, or business done by establishments within the scope of the economic census. The definition of each of these items is included in the information provided below.

Sector-Specific Information

Construction sector - Includes the value of construction work and other business receipts for work done by establishments during the year. Included is new construction, additions and alterations or reconstruction, and maintenance and repair construction work. Also included is the value of any construction work done by the reporting establishments for themselves.

Speculative builders were instructed to include the value of buildings and other structures built or being built for sale in the current year but not sold. They were to include the costs of such construction plus normal profit. Also included is the cost of construction work done on buildings for rent or lease.

Establishments engaged in the sale and installation of such construction components as plumbing, heating, and central air-conditioning supplies and equipment; lumber and building materials; paint, glass, and wallpaper; electrical and wiring supplies; and elevators or escalators were instructed to include both the value for the installation and the receipts covering the price of the items installed.

Excluded was the cost of industrial and other specialized machinery and equipment, which are not an integral part of a structure.

Finance and Insurance sector - Includes revenue from all business activities whether or not payment was received in the census year, including commissions and fees from all sources, rents, net investment income, interest, dividends, royalties, and net insurance premiums earned. Revenue from leasing property marketed under operating leases is included, as well as interest earned from property marketed in the census year under capital, finance, or full payout leases. Revenue also includes the total value of service contracts and amounts received for work subcontracted to others.

Revenue does not include sales and other taxes collected from customers and remitted directly by the firm to a local, state, or Federal tax agency.

Information sector - Includes receipts from customers or clients for services rendered, from the use of facilities, and from merchandise sold, whether or not payment was received. Receipts include royalties, license fees, and other payments from the marketing of intangible products (e.g., licensing the use of or granting reproduction rights for software, musical compositions, and other intellectual property). Receipts also include the rental and leasing of vehicles, equipment, instruments, tools, etc.; total value of service contracts; market value of compensation received in lieu of cash; amounts received for work subcontracted to others; dues and assessments for members and affiliates; this establishment's share of receipts from departments, concessions, and vending and amusement machines operated by others. Receipts from services provided to foreign customers from U.S. locations, including services preformed for foreign parent firms, subsidiaries, and branches are included. For public broadcast stations and libraries, include receipts from contributions, gifts, grants, and income from interest, rental of real estate, and dividends.

Receipts DO NOT include sales and other taxes collected directly from customers or clients and paid directly to a local, state, or Federal tax agency. Also excluded are gross receipts collected on behalf of others; gross receipts or departments or concessions operated by others; sales of used equipment previously rented or leased to customers; proceeds from the sale of real estate (land and buildings), investments, or other assets (except inventory held for resale); contributions, gifts, grants, and income from interest, rental of real estate, and dividends EXCEPT for public broadcast stations and libraries; domestic intracompany transfers; receipts of foreign subsidiaries; and other nonoperating income.

Management of Companies and Enterprises sector- For holding companies, revenue includes revenue of only the holding company establishment, including net investment income, interest, and dividends.

Manufacturing sector - Covers the received or receivable net selling values, f.o.b. plant (exclusive of freight and taxes), of all products shipped, both primary and secondary, as well as all miscellaneous receipts, such as receipts for contract work performed for others, installation and repair, sales of scrap, and sales of products bought and resold without further processing. Included are all items made by or for the establishments from materials owned by it, whether sold, transferred to other plants of the same company, or shipped on consignment. The net selling value of products made in one plant on a contract basis from materials owned by another was reported by the plant providing the materials.

In the case of multiunit companies, the manufacturer was requested to report the value of products transferred to other establishments of the same company at full economic or commercial value, including not only the direct cost of production but also a reasonable proportion of "all other costs" (including company overhead) and profit.

Mining sector - Includes the net selling values, f.o.b. mine or plant after discounts and allowances, excluding freight charges and excise taxes. Shipments includes all products physically shipped from the establishment during the year, including material withdrawn from stockpiles and products shipped on consignment, whether or not sold in the current year. Prepared material or concentrates includes preparation from ores mined at the same establishment, purchased, received from other operations of the same company, or received for milling on a custom or toll basis. For products transferred to other establishments of the same company or prepared on a custom basis, companies were requested to report the estimated value, not merely the cost of producing the items. Multiestablishment companies were asked to report value information for each establishment as if it were a separate economic unit. They were instructed to report the value of all products transferred to other plants of the company at their full economic value; to include, in addition to direct cost of production, a reasonable proportion of company overhead and profits. For all establishments classified in an industry, value of shipments and receipts includes (1) the value of all primary products of the industry; (2) the value of secondary products which are primary to other industries; (3) the receipts for contract work done for others, except custom milling; and (4) the value of products purchased and resold without further processing. Receipts for custom milling are not included to avoid duplication with the value of custom milled ores included in an industry's primary and secondary products. Some duplication exists in industry and industry group totals because of the inclusion of materials transferred from one establishment to another for mineral preparation or resale.

Professional, Scientific, and Technical Services; Administrative and Support and Waste Management and Remediation Services; Educational Services; Health Care and Social Assistance; Arts, Entertainment, and Recreation; and Other Services (Except Public Administration) sectors - TAXABLE ESTABLISHMENTS: Includes receipts from customers or clients for services rendered, from the use of facilities, and from merchandise sold whether or not payment was received. For advertising agencies, travel industries, and other service establishments operating on a commission basis, receipts include commissions, fees, and other operating income, NOT gross billings and sales. Excise taxes on gasoline, liquor, tobacco, etc., which are paid by the manufacturer or wholesaler and passed on in the cost of goods purchased by the service establishment are also included. The establishments share of receipts from departments, concessions, and vending and amusement machines operated by others are included as part of receipts.

Receipts also include the total value of service contracts, market value of compensation received in lieu of cash, amounts received for work subcontracted to others, and dues and assessments from members and affiliates. Receipts from services provided to foreign customers from U.S. locations, including services preformed for foreign parent firms, subsidiaries, and branches are included.

Receipts are net after deductions for refunds and allowances for merchandise returned by customers. Receipts DO NOT include sales, occupancy, admissions, or other taxes collected from customers and remitted directly by the firm to a local, state, or Federal tax agency, nor do they include income from such sources as contributions, gifts, and grants; dividends, interest, and investments; or sale or rental of real estate. Also excluded are receipts (gross) of departments and concessions which are operated by others; sales of used equipment rented or leased to customers; domestic intracompany transfers; receipts of foreign subsidiaries; and other nonoperating income, such as royalties, franchise fees, etc. Receipts DO NOT include service receipts of manufacturers, wholesalers, retail establishments, or other businesses whose primary activity is other than service. They do, however, include receipts other than from services rendered (e.g., sale of merchandise to individuals or other businesses) by establishments primarily engaged in performing services and classified in the service industries.

TAX EXEMPT ESTABLISHMENTS: Includes revenue from customers or clients for services rendered and merchandise, whether or not payment was received, and gross sales of merchandise, minus returns and allowances. Also included are income from interest, dividends, gross rents (including display space rentals and share of receipts from departments operated by other companies), gross contributions, gifts, grants (whether or not restricted for use in operations), royalties, dues and assessments from members and affiliates, commissions earned from the sale of merchandise owned by others (including commissions from vending machine operators), and gross receipts from fundraising activities. Receipts from taxable business activities of firms exempt from Federal income tax (unrelated business income) are also included in revenue. Revenue DOES NOT include sales, admissions, or other taxes collected by the organization from customers or clients and paid directly to a local, state, or Federal tax agency; income from the sale of real estate, investments, or other assets (except inventory held for resale); gross receipts of departments, concessions, etc., that are operated by others; and amounts transferred to operating funds from capital or reserve funds.

Real Estate and Rental and Leasing sector - Includes revenue from all business activities whether or not payment was received in the census year, including commissions and fees from all sources, rents, net investment income, interest, dividends, and royalties. Revenue from leasing property marketed under operating leases is included. Revenue also includes the total value of service contracts, amounts received for work subcontracted to others, and rents from real property sublet to others.

Revenue does not include sales and other taxes collected from customers and remitted directly by the firm to a local, state, or Federal tax agency.

Retail Trade sector - Includes merchandise sold for cash or credit at retail and wholesale by establishments primarily engaged in retail trade; amounts received from customers for layaway purchases; receipts from rental of vehicles, equipment, instruments, tools, etc.; receipts for delivery, installation, maintenance, repair, alteration, storage, and other services; the total value of service contracts; and gasoline, liquor, tobacco, and other excise taxes which are paid by the manufacturer or wholesaler and passed on to the retailer. Sales are net after deductions for refunds and allowances for merchandise returned by customers. Trade-in allowances are not deducted from sales. Sales do not include carrying or other credit charges; sales (or other) taxes collected from customers and forwarded to taxing authorities; gross sales and receipts of departments or concessions operated by other companies; and commissions or receipts from the sale of government lottery tickets.

Sales do not include retail sales made by manufacturers, wholesalers, service establishments, or other businesses whose primary activity is other than retail trade. They do include receipts other than from the sale of merchandise at retail, e.g., service receipts, sales to industrial users, and sales to other retailers, by establishments primarily engaged in retail trade.

Transportation and Warehousing sector - Includes revenue from all business activities whether or not payment was received in the census year, including commissions and fees for arranging the transportation of freight. Revenue does not include sales and other taxes collected from customers and remitted directly by the firm to a local, state, or Federal tax agency.

Utilities sector - Includes revenue from all business activities whether or not payment was received in the census year.

Revenue does not include sales and other taxes collected from customers and remitted directly by the firm to a local, state, or Federal tax agency.

Accommodation and Foodservices sector - Includes sales from customers for services rendered, from the use of facilities, and from merchandise sold. Also includes dues and assessments from members and affiliates. Sales do not include carrying or other credit charges; sales (or other) taxes collected from customers and forwarded to taxing authorities; gross sales and receipts of departments or concessions operated by other companies; and commissions or receipts from the sale of government lottery tickets.

Excludes sales from civic and social organizations, amusement and recreation parks, theaters, and other recreation or entertainment facilities providing food and beverage services.

Number of Employees

General Definition

Paid employees consists of full-time and part-time employees, including salaried officers and executives of corporations. Included are employees on paid sick leave, paid holidays, and paid vacations; not included are proprietors and partners of unincorporated businesses. The definition of paid employees is the same as that used on IRS Form 941.

Sector-Specific Information

Construction and Manufacturing sectors. Comprises all full-time and part-time employees on the payrolls of establishments who worked or received pay for any part of the pay period including the 12th of March, May, August, and November, divided by 4.

Finance and Insurance sector. Includes all employees who were on the payroll during the pay period including March 12. Excludes independent (nonemployee) agents.

Information; Professional, Scientific, and Technical Services; Administrative and Support and Waste Management and Remediation Services; Educational Services; Health Care and Social Assistance; Arts, Entertainment, and Recreation; and Other Services (Except Public Administration) sectors - Includes all employees who were on the payroll during the pay period including March 12. Includes members of a professional service organization or association which operates under state professional corporation statutes and files a corporate Federal income tax return. Excludes employees of departments or concessions operated by other companies at the establishment.

Management of Companies and Enterprises sector. Includes all employees who were on the payroll during the pay period including March 12.

Mining sector. Also included are employees working for miners paid on a per ton, car, or yard basis. Excluded are employees at the mine but on the payroll of another employer (such as employees of contractors) and employees at company stores, boardinghouses, bunkhouses, and recreational centers. Also excluded are members of the Armed Forces and pensioners carried on the active rolls but not working during the period. Includes all employees who were on the payroll during the pay period including March 12.

Real Estate and Rental and Leasing sector. Includes all employees who were on the payroll during the pay period including March 12. Excludes independent (nonemployee) agents.

Retail Trade and Accommodation and Foodservices sectors. Includes all employees on the payroll during the pay period including March 12. Excludes employees of departments or concessions operated by other companies at the establishment.

Transportation and Warehousing sector. Includes all employees who were on the payroll during the pay period including March 12.

Utilities sector. Includes all employees who were on the payroll during the pay period including March 12.